Sarah Loring Bailey

Historical sketches of Andover (comprising the present towns of North Andover and Andover), Massachusetts

Sarah Loring Bailey

Historical sketches of Andover (comprising the present towns of North Andover and Andover), Massachusetts

ISBN/EAN: 9783742872166

Manufactured in Europe, USA, Canada, Australia, Japa

Cover: Foto ©ninafisch / pixelio.de

Manufactured and distributed by brebook publishing software (www.brebook.com)

Sarah Loring Bailey

Historical sketches of Andover (comprising the present towns of North Andover and Andover), Massachusetts

PREFACE.

WHEN this book was announced with the title "Sketches of Old Andover," the intention of the writer was simply to make a collection of sketches of the romance and poetry of Old Andover history. But, subsequently, by request of friends, the task was undertaken of arranging these in chronological order in the form of a continuous history. This necessitated changes, — in fact, an almost entire alteration of the original plan, — and was attended with unforeseen difficulties and delays. The great amount of material for history, the time and expense required for its collection, to say nothing of the labor of arranging it in a readable form and obtaining means for its publication, have been among the causes of delay. And even now only a portion of the history has been covered, although the size of the book exceeds the expectation of the writer. Yet, for many reasons it has been thought best not to make further change, either reduction or addition, but to present what has been accomplished. The work, therefore, is offered to the public not without a sense of its deficiencies and inadequacy, yet in the hope that it may be not wholly devoid of interest and value. If the histories written by antiquaries and scholars, with ample facilities and abundant means, are found to contain errors, it will hardly be a matter of surprise that my sketches should prove faulty. But as no one else for fifty years has undertaken to search the ancient records for a connected history of the town, I venture to make the contribution, in the hope that it will at least awaken interest and stimulate research. Public spirited citizens and the towns themselves (North Andover and Andover) could hardly make a better appropriation of money than to found and endow an Old Andover Historical and Genealogical Society, which would possess means and influence to prosecute the work of historical research and collection. That such work may be done in the future and a complete and accurate history made of the town in all its departments of activity, none would more cordially desire or gladly aid in accomplishing than the writer of these "Historical Sketches of Andover."

I desire to thank the various librarians of historical and genealogical societies and the custodians of records and archives, who have courteously rendered me assistance. To mention their names would be less to honor them than to adorn these pages.

To the scholars and literary critics who took pains to examine the manuscript and who gave the influence of their opinion in the prospectus, I am under great obligation, which to repeat their names here would be to heighten.

To the subscribers, whose generous gifts have secured the publication and illustration of the book, I am deeply indebted, especially to the gentlemen who in addition to their large subscription assumed the chief part of the pecuniary responsibility.

To the scientific scholar who kindly prepared the geological introduction, not only the writer but the readers of these Sketches owe gratitude. His name is so well known that it does not need mention to friends of Andover, who will readily recognize the initials at the close of the chapter.

It is unnecessary to rehearse here the names of authors and the works consulted in the preparation of the book, yet thanks are due to the families and individuals who have intrusted me with valuable private papers.

In regard to one or two points in the book a word may be added. Some repetitions of statement occur in regard to persons and events in the several chapters, for the reason that the subject-matter is arranged topically rather than in the form of annals, and each chapter is intended to be sufficiently comprehensive to be in a measure independent of the other chapters. Many eminent names of Andover do not appear in these pages because the Sketches do not cover the departments of enterprise in which they were active, or the events in which they bore a conspicuous part.

Some additional matter, and emendations and corrections, will be found in the Appendix. Following this are the names of the subscribers who secured the publication.

S. L. B.

NORTH ANDOVER, *November*, 1880.

CONTENTS.

INTRODUCTION.

Prehistoric Andover.

                                                                             PAGE

Topographical Notes. — Mutilation and Unintelligibility of the earliest Rock Records. — Places where the Oldest Rocks appear and their Character. — Andover during the Middle Periods of Geologic Time. — Abundance and Plainness of the later Geological Record. — Places where Marks of the Glacial Epoch appear in the Rocks. — Remarkable Elevations of the Glacial Period. — Character of the Series of Hills extending from Wood Hill to the Hills around Great Pond. — Origin of their Scientific Name " Lenticular " Hills. — Explanation of the Manner in which they were formed. — Remarkable Ridges of the Glacial Period. — Character and Extent of Ridges illustrated in the Plates. — Origin of the Scientific Name " Kames." — Characteristics, Height, Slope, and Composition of the Ridges. — Description of Indian Ridge by President Edward Hitchcock. — Explorations and Descriptions of the Ridges made by Rev. G. F. Wright. — Discoveries of Parallel Systems. — Difference of Opinion as to the Manner in which Kames were formed. — Most probable Theory. — Formation of the Ponds in Andover. — Possibility that Andover Ponds, Peat Bogs, and Kettle Holes may afford aid in determining the Antiquity of Man xxiv

CHAPTER I.

MEMORIALS OF THE EARLY SETTLERS.

Scantiness of Relics. — First Mention of the Vicinity of Andover. — First Action with Reference to Settlement. — Letters of Mr. Ward and Mr. Woodbridge. — First Record of a Resident, Richard Barker. — First recorded Deed of Land, Mr. Bradstreet to Richard Sutton. — First Description. — Incorporation. — Name. — Mother Town in England. — List of first Freeholders. — Memorials of first Freeholders. — Mr. Simon Bradstreet, and his Draft of a Deed from Richard Sutton to George Abbot. — John Osgood, the first Representative to the General Court. — His Will and Inventory, Descendants, Burial-place. — John Stevens. — The Inventory of his Estate, his Descendants. — The Early Plantation. — Purchase from the Indians. — Roger's Reservation. — Laying out of the Village. —

House-lot Rights. — Common Lands. — Dwelling-places of first Settlers. — Proprietors — Mode of Taxation. — Town Meeting. — Action respecting Land Grants, Places of Abode, Roving Animals, Flocks and Herds. — Lawsuits and Troubles from Trespass of Domestic Animals. — Herdsmen and their Assistants. — Depredations of Wild Beasts. — Hunting. — Den Rock, Wolf Pit Meadow, and other suggestive Local Names. — Negro Slavery. — Hired Servants. — Apprentices. — Day-laborers. — Facilities for Communication with other Towns. — Roads. — Boats on the Merrimack River. — Vessels built at Andover. — Ferries. — Town Boundaries. — Land of Nod. — Mason's Claim. — Town Grants of Land. — Highways and Taverns. — Social Life. — Weddings. — Dress. — Sumptuary Laws. — Account in "The Magnalia" of the first Murder, a Wife by her Husband. — Memorials of Freeholders, continued. — Edmond Faulkner. — George Abbot, Senr. — John Frye. — Benjamin Woodbridge. — Richard Barker. — Daniel Poor. — Nicholas Holt. — Thomas Chandler. — John Lovejoy. — Andrew Foster, and other Fosters, Early Settlers in Andover. — William Ballard. — Joseph Parker. — Nathan Parker. — Robert Barnard. — Andrew Allen. — Other Names. — List of Citizens who took Oath of Allegiance in 1678. — Memoranda of Early Settlers, continued. — George Abbot of Rowley. — Daniel Bixby. — William Blunt. — John Bridges. — John Carlton. — Francis Dane. — The Farnums. — Robert Gray. — John Gutterson. — Henry Ingalls. — Thomas Johnson. — Lawrence Lacey. — Samuel Marble. — Marston, Martin, Phelps, Preston. — Joseph Robinson. — Robert Russell. — Salter. — Sessions. — Stone. — Samuel Wardwell. — Joseph Wilson. — Edward Whittington. — Walter Wright. — List of Tax-payers, 1692. — Memoranda of Early Settlers, continued — John Aslebe. — Samuel Blanchard. — Henry Bodwell. — Pascoe Chubb. — Thomas Carrier. — Joseph Emery. — Edward Farrington. — Abraham Graves. — Moses Hagget. — Abraham Mooar. — Andrew Peters. — Robert Swan. — Allen Toothaker. — Moses Tyler. — Robert Eames. — The Bradstreet House. — The Citizens in Town Meeting. — Conduct in Town Meeting — Times of Town Meetings. — Tax Collection. — Action in Respect to the Revolution of 1689. — List of Civil Officers in the First Fifty Years. — List of Town Officers and Description of some Offices and their Duties. — Reception of Newcomers. — Emigration. — Occupations of Citizens. — Mills. — Fisheries. — Distillery. — Stores and Trade. — Agriculture. — Lists of Names of Principal Families settled in the Second Fifty Years. — Memorials of Noted Families. — Phillips. — Kittredge. — Adams. — Peabody . . 1–162

CHAPTER II.

THE PART OF ANDOVER IN THE EARLY INDIAN WARS.

Aboriginal Inhabitants. — Treatment of the Natives. — Village of "Praying Indians" on the Merrimack. — Subjection of the Indians. — Military Organization at Andover. — List of Officers of Militia in the First Century. — Military Resources of the Colony described by E. R., 1676. — First Alarms of Hostile Indians at Andover. — Narraganset Soldiers from Andover. — Rumors and Alarms in the Spring of 1675. — Measures for Defence. — Garrisons, Stockades, etc. — Attack on Andover in April, 1676.

CONTENTS.

— Panic in the Town. — Garrisons. — Soldiers Killed in the Kennebec Expedition. — Capt. Dudley Bradstreet's Measures for Defence. — A Lull in Hostilities. — Renewal of Fighting. — Change in the Militia of Essex County. — Measures for Defence of Frontier Towns. — Travellers Slain. — Second Attack on Andover, and Murder of Captain Chubb. — Contemporary Accounts. — Peace by the Treaty of Ryswick. — Queen Anne's War. — Military Defences at Andover. — Scouting. — Stock of Ammunition. — Snow-shoe Men. — Capt. Benjamin Stevens's Expedition to Winnipiseogee. — The Romantic Story of Chaplain Frye . . 163–193

CHAPTER III.

WITCHCRAFT AT ANDOVER.

Nature and Effects of the Delusion. — Witchcraft at Andover in 1658. — Beginning of the "Salem Witchcraft." — The Origin of the Delusion at Andover. — Spread of the Epidemic. — List of Persons Accused. — Trial and Execution of Martha Carrier. — Condemnation and Execution of Mary Parker. — Trial and Execution of Samuel Wardwell. — Trial, Condemnation, and Death of Ann Foster. — Trial, Condemnation, and Reprieve of Abigail Faulkner. — Trial and Condemnation of Elizabeth Johnson, Jr., and Mary Lacey, Jr. — Condemnation of Sarah Wardwell. — Sufferings of the Prisoner's Children. — Accusation of Elizabeth Johnson's Children. — Confessions of Mary Marston, William Barker, Mercy Wardwell, and Others. — Confession of Mrs. Mary Osgood. — Mode of extorting Confessions. — Colonel Bradstreet's Examinations of Witches. — Sufferings of Prisoners in the Jail. — Protests of the Rev. Francis Dane and Others. — Mr. Brattle's "Full and Candid Account." — Petition for Release of the Prisoners on Bail. — Court of Assizes and Jail Delivery, and Letters of Mr. Dane. — Petition of Andover Citizens. — Petition of the Accused Women. — Reaction of Public Feeling. — Penitence of the Accusers. — Remorse and Confession of Judge Sewall. — The Grave of Timothy Swan, killed by Witchcraft. — End of the Delusion 194–237

CHAPTER IV.

THE PART OF ANDOVER IN THE FRENCH AND INDIAN WAR.

King George's War. — Deaths of Soldiers in the King's Service. — Petition of Capt. James Stevens for a Township. — Beginning of the Old French War. — Officers of the Fourth Essex Regiment of Militia. — Capt. John Abbot's Commission. — Kennebec River Expedition. — Petition of Daniel Mooar. — Cape Breton Expedition. — Colonel Frye's Men. — Petition of Jonathan Parker. — Petition of John Granger and Enoch Poor. — Destruction of Acadian Villages. — Acadians at Andover. — Andover Soldiers in Acadia. — Crown Point Expedition, 1755. — Deaths of Soldiers. — Petitions of Jacob Tyler, Sarah Stevens, John Barker, Israel Adams. — Oswego Expedition. — Petition of James Frye. — Letter of Rev. Samuel Chandler. — Crown Point Expedition, 1756. — Petitions of Stephen Lovejoy, Phineas Tyler, Hannah Johnson, James Parker for Margaret Furbush, Nicholas Holt. — Petition of Surgeon Ward Noyes. — Commission. — Petitions for Isaac Foster, John Foster, Joseph Abbot. — Campaign of 1757. — Service of Col. Joseph Frye. — Form of Enlistments. — Sufferings of Colonel Frye. — Memorial of Moody Bridges. — Sufferings of Soldiers. — Action of Colonel Frye for a Township. — Efforts in Behalf of Prisoners. — Jesse Parker. — Military Movements, 1758. — Attack on Ticonderoga. — Expedition against Canada. — Petitions of Capt. Asa Foster, John Farnum. — De Drucour at Andover. — Relics of Service, 1759. — Lieut. Jacob Farrington. — Moses Bailey. — Surgeon Abiel Abbot. — Mutiny of Colonel Frye's Men in Nova Scotia. — Expedition against Montreal. — Petitions of Oliver Holt, Capt. Peter Parker, John Beverly. — Diary of Isaac Noyes. — Expenses of the War. — Names of Officers. — Captain Farrington. — Militia. — Representatives to the General Court. — Sergeant Jonathan French. — Close of the War. — Manners and Customs of the Period. — Petition of James Kittredge. — Petition of John Kittredge. — Effects of the War. — Petition of Selectmen. — Every-day Life of the Time. — Will of John Peabody. — The Pre-Revolutionary Period a Pleasant Picture 238–285

CHAPTER V.

THE PART OF ANDOVER IN THE REVOLUTIONARY WAR.

Discontent at Unjust Taxation. — Opposition to the Stamp Act. — Adherence to Law and Order. — Non-importation Act Approved. — Action respecting the Boston Massacre. — Persons refusing to Sign the Non-importation Act. — Conservatism of Representative Samuel Phillips. — Ardor of Representative Moody Bridges. — Feeling against Governor Gage. — Declaration in Support of the Provincial Congress. — Dignified Bearing of Andover during the Crisis before Hostilities. — Distinguished Patriots. — Committees of Circumspection and Safety. — Town Taxes paid to the Receiver-general instead of Governor Gage's Treasurer. — Military Preparation at the beginning of 1775. — Muster of Town Foot-companies. — Enlistment of Two Companies of Minute Men for One Year. — Choice of Officers. — Muster-roll of Capt. Thomas Poor's Company. — Muster-roll of Capt. Benjamin Ames's Company. — Patriotic Zeal of Col. Samuel Johnson in Enlisting Men for Service. — Address to his Regiment. — Invasion of Essex County by Royal Troops. — Encounter with Provincial Militia. — Mediation of Rev. Thomas Barnard. — Suspense of waiting for Military Action. — Lexington Alarm. — March of Companies from Andover. — Muster-rolls. — Lieut. Peter Poor (acting Captain). — Capt. Henry Abbot, Capt. Nathaniel Lovejoy, Capt. Joshua Holt. — Service of Adjutant-general Bimsley Stevens. — Major Samuel Osgood. — Major Dunbar of the Royal Army. — Visit to Mrs. Osgood at Andover. — Sketch of the Life of Mrs. Osgood by her Husband. — Andover Soldiers on the March to Lexington and Cambridge. — Extract from the Diary of Lieut. Benjamin Farnum. — Reminiscences of Captain Furbush. — Extract from Thomas Boynton's Diary. — Camp Life at Cambridge in the Spring of 1775, described in James Stevens's Diary. — Taking a Schooner. — Major Poor. — Patriotic Song. — Scenes after the Battle. — Letter of Mrs. Winthrop, her Flight and Refuge in Andover.

CONTENTS.

— Vigilance against Enemies without and within the Town. — Action of the Provincial Congress to withdraw Allegiance from Governor Gage. — Town of Andover endorses it, chooses Samuel Phillips, Jr., Esq., Representative to the Congress. — His Important Service. — Col. Joseph Frye at Andover and Cambridge. — Battle of Bunker Hill. — Notes and Incidents of Andover Men's Service. — Captain Ames's Company. — Captain Furbush's Company. — Captain Farnum's Company. — Sergeant Boynton's Description of the Battle. — Col. James Frye's Courage. — Private John Barker. — Salem Poor's Bravery. — Samuel Bailey's Death on the Field. — Losses of Companies. — Captain Farnum Wounded. — Anxiety at Andover. — Departure of Rev. Mr. French to Camp on Sunday. — Eminent Men of Andover at Cambridge. — Rev. David Osgood, his Feelings in regard to the War. — Dr. Thomas Kittredge and other Surgeons and Physicians of the Time. — Col. Joseph Frye's Commission as General. — Refugees from Boston. — Nathaniel Appleton. — Joseph Hall. — Mrs. Lydia Smith. — Removal of Harvard College Library to Andover. — Extracts from the Diary of James Stevens describing Camp Life at Cambridge in the Summer of 1775. — Captain Furbush's Invitation to Dine with General Washington. — Col. James Frye's choleric Speech to General Washington. — Reënforcements to the Army about Boston. — Roll of Capt. John Abbot's Company. — Captain Farnum's Company. — Capt. John Peabody's Company. — Scarcity of Gunpowder. — Order of the General Court to put in Operation a Mill for its Manufacture at Stoughton. — Offer of Judge Phillips to build a Mill at Andover at his own Expense on certain Conditions. — Vote to grant him a Supply of Saltpetre, and to Purchase his Powder at Eight Pence per Pound. — Builder and Master-workman from the Mill at Stoughton secured. — Aid of Citizens Enlisted. — Mill put in Operation March, 1776. — Manufacture of One Thousand Pounds of Gunpowder per Week. — Guard about the Mill. — Scarcity of Saltpetre. — Practical Help of the Schoolmaster, Mr. Pearson, in Chemical Operations. — Workmen Exempted from Military Duty. — Meeting-house Stoves put in Requisition for the Powder-mill. — Interest felt in the Enterprise. — Gunpowder not a complete Success. — Complaints of Military Officers. — Order of the General Court for Re-manufacture of Defective Powder. — Inspector Burbeck to Visit Andover. — Explosion, 1778. — Mr. Phillips exonerated from Blame and requested to resume the Manufacture. — The State agrees to bear Expense in case of future Explosion. — Aid of Experts from France. — Letter of Mr. Phillips describing their Work. — Gradual Discontinuance of the Manufacture. — Explosion, 1796. — Relic of the Powder Manufacture, a Gravestone in the Old South Burying Ground. — Distress during the Winter of 1775. — Provision for Soldiers. — Coats for Eight Months' Men given by the State. — Receipt for Coats. — Death of Col. James Frye. — Graves of Colonels Frye and Johnson in the Old North Burying-ground. — Military Service in Distant Places. — Scanty Records. — Roll of Colonel Johnson's Regiment. — March of Andover Men to Reënforce Northwestern Army. — Roll of Capt. Samuel Johnson's Company. — Extract from Capt. Samuel Johnson's Note-book. — Declaration of Independence. — Measures for the Formation of a State Constitution. — Andover's Opposition to Immediate Action. — Colonel Johnson's Instructions. — Constitution drafted but not accepted. — Convention of Delegates. — Samuel Phillips, Jr., one of Committee to draft Constitution. — Vote of the Town to approve. — Discussion of Bill of Rights. — Andover in Favor of Religious Compulsion. — Notes of Military Service about Boston. — Rolls of Continental Service. — Principal Military Service of 1777 in the Northwest. — Roll of Capt. Benjamin Farnum's Company. — Extracts from Captain Farnum's Journal. — His Acquaintance with Miss Jane McRea. — Letter of Corporal Joseph Shattuck. — Surrender to the British, of Forts Ticonderoga and Independence. — Retreat of Colonel Francis. — His Death recorded by Captain Farnum. — Letter of Joseph Shattuck. — Battle of Bennington recorded by Captain Farnum. — Battle of Stillwater. — Journey down the Hudson. — March to Valley Forge. — Camp at Valley Forge. — Muster-roll of Captain Farnum's Company. — Letter of Colonel Tupper. — Colonel Johnson marches to Reënforce General Lincoln's Army in the Northwest. — Rolls of the Regiment. — Roll of Capt. John Adams's Company. — Roll of Capt. John Abbot's Company. — Roll of Capt. Samuel Johnson's Company. — Private Expedition of Colonels Brown and Johnson to Fort Ticonderoga. — Their Plan of Attack, its Partial Execution and Success. — Embarkation of Prisoners and Stores. — Attack from Enemy's Batteries on Diamond Island. — Retreat to Skenesborough and Pawlet. — Letters of Jonathan Stevens, a Soldier in the Expedition. — This Expedition a Check to General Burgoyne. — Colonel Johnson's Indefatigable Labors — Petition of a Soldier. — Tribute to the Memory of Colonel Johnson. — Town Petitions for a Representative in Place of Colonel Johnson while he was in Military Service. — Gen. Enoch Poor at Stillwater. — Some Particulars of his Life. — Service of Andover Men in Rhode Island. — Muster-roll of Capt. Samuel Johnson's Company. — Various Service of Men. — Relic of Service at Peekskill. — Petition of William Adams at West Point. — Discontent at the prolonged Military Service. — Captain Lovejoy's Statement of Grievances. — Action of the Town to prevent Treason. — Distressing and Demoralizing Effects of the War. — Extortioners rebuked by Mr. French. — Depreciation of Currency. — Provision for Soldiers' Families, and General Relief. — Town Bounties. — Memoranda of Military Service, 1779-80. — Capt. Stephen Abbot, and Capt. John Abbot, at West Point. — Muster-rolls of Captain Abbot's Company. — Commissions. — The Dark Day a Portent of Gloom. — Joy at the Victory of Yorktown. — Slaves in Military Service. — Proclamation of Peace as described by Prof. John Abbot, then a Student at Harvard College. — Death of the Patriot James Otis at Andover. — Lists of Military and Civil Officers during the Revolution. — Discontent at Taxation. — Disapproval of Paper Currency. — Committee to consider Grievances, their Report. — Shays's Insurrection. — Instructions to the Representative, Peter Osgood, Esq. — Samuel Phillips, Esq., in Favor of Good Order and Suppression of Rebellion. — Convention for Framing the Federal Constitution. — Important Part of the Andover Delegate, William Symmes, Esq., in favor of Adoption. — Hon. Samuel Osgood, First Postmaster-general. — Letter of Thomas Houghton, respecting the Military Service of Englishmen. — Adopted Citizens. — General Washington's Visit to Andover. — Visit of the Marquis de Chastellux. — Thomas Houghton's Description of the

Town, 1789. — Manners and Customs. — Travelling Facilities. — Stages. — Taverns. — Post-riders. — A Relic of Travelling. — Stores. — General Condition of Things in Andover at the Close of the Century. — Death of General Washington. — Commemorative Services, February 22, 1800. — Death and Funeral of Lieutenant-governor Phillips . . . 286-409

CHAPTER VI.

CHURCHES AND MINISTERS. — CHURCH-YARDS, OR BURYING GROUNDS.

Regard of our Forefathers for the Church. — First Meeting-house. — First Sexton. — Seating the Meeting-house. — Tything-men. — Sabbath Breakers. — Heretics. — Rhymed Address to the Church of Andover. — Organization of the Church. — First Minister, Rev. John Woodbridge. — Biography by Cotton Mather. — Rev. Francis Dane. — Creed. — Controversy with the Parish. — Colleague, Mr. Thomas Barnard. — Remainder of Mr. Dane's Ministry. — His Death. — Descendants. — Lines from his Note Book. — Students of Divinity: John Woodbridge, Simon Bradstreet, Joseph Stevens, Benjamin Stevens, Dudley Bradstreet, John Barnard. — Pastorate of Mr. Thomas Barnard. — Controversy about the Meeting-house. — Destruction of the Parsonage House by Fire, and Mr. Barnard's Removal to the Bradstreet House. — Division of Andover into Two Precincts. — Parishes. — Building of South Meeting-house. — Mr. Barnard requested to choose between the Parishes. — Letter of Mr. Barnard to the Governor. — Final Settlement of Parish Lines. — New North Meeting-house. — Mr. Barnard's Salary. — Mr. Barnard's Relations with the Minister of the South Parish. — His Death. — Burial Place. — Gravestone. — Descendants. — Rev. John Barnard. — Ordination. — Mr. Barnard's Action in Regard to the Evangelist Whitefield. — New Meeting house, 1753. — Communion Silver. — Bell. — Discipline. — Parishioners set off to Boxford Parish. — Death of Mr. Barnard. — His Marriages and Children. — Character as described by Mr. Phillips. — Published Writings. — Students of Divinity. — First Minister of the South Church, Rev. Samuel Phillips. — First Meeting-house. — Second Meeting-house. — Description by Josiah Quincy. — Mr. Phillips's Life and Ministry. — Preaching. — Family. — His Death. — Descendants. — Fifth Minister of the North Church, Rev. William Symmes, D. D. — Pastorate. — Anecdote of a Wedding Fee. — Seats in the Meeting-house for Wives of Negroes and Mulattoes. — Women's Hats. — Church Music. — Old Meeting-house. — Second Minister of South Parish, Mr. Jonathan French. — Birth and Education. — Patriotism. — Divinity School in his House. — Domestic Life. — "Special Providence" of Marriage. — Anecdote of Salary. — Meeting-house, 1788. — Noon-house. — Reading. — Prominent Supporters of the Church: Judge Phillips, Samuel Abbot, Esq., Samuel Farrar, Esq. — Students of Divinity who were Eminent Ministers: Stephen Peabody, David Osgood, John Abbot, Jonathan French, Abiel Abbot, of Beverly, Abiel Abbot, of Coventry, Thomas Merrill, John Lovejoy Abbot. — Contemporary Ministers, 1810-1850. — Three Parishes: North, South, West. — Church of Theological Seminary. — Organization of the West Church. — Importance of Churches diminished with Increase of Number. — Transition Period — Sixth Minister of the North Parish, Rev. Bailey

Loring. — Previous Action of the Parish. — Call of Mr. Loring. — Settlement and Ministry. — Theological Creed. — Withdrawal of Members to form Evangelical Church of North Andover. — New Meeting-house of First Church. — The Old Clock. — First Church identified with the Unitarian Congregationalists. — Mr. Loring's Preaching. — Resignation. — Death. — Resolutions of Parish. — Published Writings. — Later Ministers of the First Church: Rev. Francis C. Williams, Rev. Charles C. Vinal. — Gift of Parsonage-house by Bequest of William Johnson, Esq. — Rev. John H. Clifford. — Deacons of the First Church. — Absence of Memorials of Earlier Members. — Recent Memorials. — Third Minister of the South Parish, Rev. Justin Edwards, D. D., his Life and Work. — West Church and Parish. — First Minister, Rev. Samuel C. Jackson, D. D. — Second Minister, Rev. Charles H. Peirce. — Third Minister, Rev. James H. Merrill. — Later Pastors of the South Church: Rev. Milton Badger, D. D. — Rev. Lorenzo L. Langstroth. — Rev. John L. Taylor, D. D. — Rev. Charles Smith. — Rev. George Mooar, D. D. — Rev. Charles Smith, Second Pastorate. — Rev. James H. Laird. — Deacons of the South Church. — Formation of Societies. — Methodist Episcopal Church (Andover). — Baptist Church. — Evangelical Church of North Andover. — Protestant Episcopal Church (Andover); Rectors and Prominent Supporters. — Universalist Church. — List of Churches since 1840. — Methodist Episcopal Church (North Andover). — Free Christian Church (Andover). — Ballardvale Churches: Protestant Episcopal, Methodist Episcopal, Union Congregational. — Roman Catholic Church (Andover), Roman Catholic Church (North Andover). — Students of Theology of the Present Century. — Chronological List of Divinity Students. — Tabular Statement of Pastors and Churches. — Burying-grounds and Cemeteries: First (North Parish) Burying-ground. — Second Burying-ground of North Andover. — Ridgewood Cemetery. — South Parish "Burying-yard." — West Parish Burying-ground. — Chapel Cemetery (Theological Seminary). — Christ Church-yard. — Roman Catholic Cemetery. — Spring Grove Cemetery. — Selection from Scripture respecting Burial Places 410–516

CHAPTER VII.

PUBLIC SCHOOLS AND PUBLIC LIBRARIES.

The First Settlers' Esteem of Learning. — First Action of the Town for a Grammar School. — First Masters: Mr. Dudley Bradstreet. — Mr. Rust. — Mr. John Barnard. — Temporary Masters. — Difficulty of keeping up the School. — Various Masters. — Second School-house. — School for both Parishes. — Masters: Mr. James Bailey. — Mr. Philemon Robbins. — Latin Scholars from out of Town. — List of Masters. — College Graduates. — District Schools. — Relics of Early Teachers. — School Fund. — Miscellaneous Schools. — High Schools. — Punchard Free School. — Benjamin H. Punchard. — Bequest. — School Buildings. — First Principal, Peter Smith Byers. — Other Principals. — Johnson High School. — Founders. — Principals. — Public Libraries. — Social Library in 1770. — Memorial Hall. — North Andover Library 517–532

CHAPTER VIII.

ACADEMIES.

Phillips Academy. — Projector and Founders. — Constitution. — Trustees. — Academy Buildings. — Donations and Foundations. — Opening of the School. — Some Students of Note. — Reminiscences by Josiah Quincy. — Principals: Eliphalet Pearson. — Ebenezer Pemberton. — Mark Newman. — John Adams. — Osgood Johnson. — Samuel H. Taylor. — Frederic W. Tilton. — Cecil F. P. Bancroft. — Other Well-known Instructors. — Master Foster's Boarding School. — Franklin Academy. — Founding. — Building. — Records — Early Preceptors: Mr. Nathaniel Peabody. — Samuel L. Knapp. — Good Times at School. — Mr. Burnside and other Early Preceptors. — Mr. Simeon Putnam. — Tribute of Professor Felton to Mr. Putnam's Teaching. — Later Preceptors. — Female Department. — Education of Girls. — Letters of Young Ladies. — First Preceptress of Franklin Academy, Elizabeth Palmer Peabody. — Other Preceptresses. — Abbot Academy. — Foundation. — Donations. — Course of Study. — Semi-centennial Celebration, 1879. — Principals. — Trustees . . . 533–557

CHAPTER IX.

THEOLOGICAL SEMINARY.

Plan for a School of Theology. — Founders: Madam Phebe Phillips. — Hon. John Phillips. — Samuel Abbot, Esq. — Plan at Newbury for a Seminary. — Compromise effected by Dr. Pearson. — Associate Founders: Hon. William Bartlet. — Moses Brown, Esq. — Hon. John Norris. — Founders of Brechin Hall: Mr. John Smith, Dea. Peter Smith, Mr. John Dove. — Founders of the Professorships: Abbot, Bartlet, Brown, Hitchcock, Jones, Stone. — Sketches of the Early Professors: Dr. Pearson, Dr. Leonard Woods, Dr. Griffin, Dr. Porter, Dr. Murdock, Professor Stuart. — List of Names of the Professors in the Order of their Election. — Faculty as now Constituted. — Trustees Residents of Andover. — Mr. John Aiken. — Mr. Peter Smith. — The Library. — The Printing Press. — Summary of Biographical Memoranda of Professors who were long in Office or who Died in Office 558–573

CHAPTER X.

MILLS AND MANUFACTURES.

The Mill the earliest Industrial Enterprise. — Ancient Mills — Saw-mills and Grist-mills. — Joseph Parker's "Corne Mill" on the Cochichawick. — Stephen Johnson's Saw-mill. — Saw-mill near the Lower Ford of the Cochichawick. — Saw-mill on Musketo Brook, 1685. — Saw-mill on Ladle Meadow Brook. — Henry Gray's Mill for Grinding Scythes on "Scoonk River," 1715. — Saw-mill on Shawshin River, near Preston's Plain, 1753. — James Kittredge's Grist-mill on the Shawshin, 1752. — Spinning and Weaving. — Amy Holt, Spinster. — Fulling-mills, 1673–1689. — Edward Whittington and Walter Wright, Weavers, encouraged to erect a Fulling-mill. — Grants for a Saw-mill, Fulling-mill, and Grist-mill on

xiv   CONTENTS.

Shawshin River, near Roger's Brook, 1682. — Joseph and John Ballard's Mill on Shawshin River, 1689. — Samuel Frye's Saw-mill and Grist-mill on Shawshin River, 1718. — Iron Works, 1689. — Thomas Chandler's and Henry Lovejoy's Iron Works. — Powder-mill, 1776. — Paper-mill, 1789. — Business Embarrassments of the Paper-maker, Thomas Houghton. — Account of the Paper Manufacture from Contemporary Records. — Inventory of the Paper-mill. — Scarcity of Paper Rags and Means for Saving Them. — Difficu'ties in Starting the Manufacture at Andover. — Later History of the Paper-mill. — Woollen Manufactures. — Scholfield's Improved Carding Machines. — Scholfield's Fulling-mill at North Andover — Stephen Poor's Clothing-mill. — Abel and Paschal Abbot's Mill at North Andover. — Samuel Ayer's Mill. — William Sutton and Eben Sutton's Mills at North Andover. — "North Andover Mill." — George Hodges & Sons, Manufacturers. — Gen. Eben Sutton, Proprietor of the Sutton and North Andover Mills. — Capt. Nathaniel Stevens, the First Woollen Manufacturer, Native of North Andover. — Stevens Mills. — Hon. Moses T. Stevens, Proprietor of the Stevens and the Marland Mills. — Abraham Marland, the Pioneer Woollen Manufacturer. — Marland Mills. — Marland Manufacturing Company. — Abraham Marland, First President, Nathan Frye, Second President. — Treasurers. — Purchase of the Marland Mills by Mr. Moses T. Stevens. — Ballardvale Manufacturing Company. — Experiments in Manufacturing Silk. — Mr. John Marland's Enterprises. — Mr. J. S. Young. — Mr. J. P. Bradlee. — Abbot Brothers' Mill. — Daniel Saunders. — Howarth & Chase. — Flax-mills. — Mr. John Smith. — His Emigration to America. — Manufacture of Cotton Machinery. — Mr. John Dove. — Employment in the Machine Shop. — Plan for Manufacturing Flax. — Visit to England for Drawings of Flax Machinery. — Success of the Enterprise and Formation of the Copartnership, Smith, Dove & Company. — Value to Andover of this Business. — Present Members of the Smith and Dove Manufacturing Company. — Iron Works : Thomas Chandler's, 1678. — James Frye's, 1770. — Foundries : Davis & Furber's Foundry. — Mr. Edmund Davis. — E. Davis & Son. — Davis & Furber's Manufacture of Machinery. — Origin. — Machine-shop in Marland Mill. — Sawyer and Phelps. — Machine-shop in the Paper-mill. — Barnes, Gilbert, and Richardson. — Removal of Machine Manufacture to North Andover. — Manufactory Built. — Copartnership of George L. Davis, George H. Gilbert, and Benjam n W. Gleason. — Changes in the Firm. — Mr. Charles Furber a Partner. — Present Firm. — Davis, Wiley & Stone. — Ballardvale. — Manufacture of Machinery. — Whipple File Company. — Rubber Factory and Ink Factory. — The Manufactures the Chief Element in the Town's Prosperity. — The City of Lawrence. — Mr. Daniel Saunders. — His early Manufacturing and his Connection with the Building of Lawrence. — The Order of Topics in these Sketches in accordance with the Growth of the Town. — Subjects remaining to cover the Full History of the Town. — The Long and Honorable Record of Old Andover. — The Present Towns of North Andover and Andover 574–605

APPENDIX.

Additions and Corrections 606–613

LIST OF ILLUSTRATIONS.

I. Portrait of Mr. Simon Bradstreet . . . . Frontispiece.
II. Geological Plates . . . . To face page xvii
III. Facsimile of Deed of Richard Sutton 14
IV. Early Home of Maj.-Gen. Isaac I. Stevens, the Ancient
    Mansion House of Mr. Moody Bridges 26
    Stevens Hall and Johnson High School 26
V. Early Home of Rev. David Osgood, D. D., where James
    Otis was killed by Lightning 86
    Ancient Homestead of the Abbots, — Divines and Scholars 86
VI. The Bradstreet House 132
    Chaplain Frye's Elm and the Home of Col. James Frye 132
VII. The Home of Dr. Thomas Kittredge 157
    The Phillips Manse at North Andover 157
VIII. The Home of Col. Samuel Johnson 293
    The Home of Maj. Samuel Osgood 293
IX. Mansion House of Judge Phillips 401
    Abbot's Tavern, where General Washington breakfasted 401
X. Old South Parsonage 443
    Abbot Academy 443
XI. Memorial Hall 528
    Punchard Free School 528
XII. Phillips Academy, the "Classic Hall." 535
    Phillips Academy, the Present Building 535
XIII. The Phillips Family, Founders of Institutions . 558
XIV. The Theological Seminary 568
    Brechin Hall 568

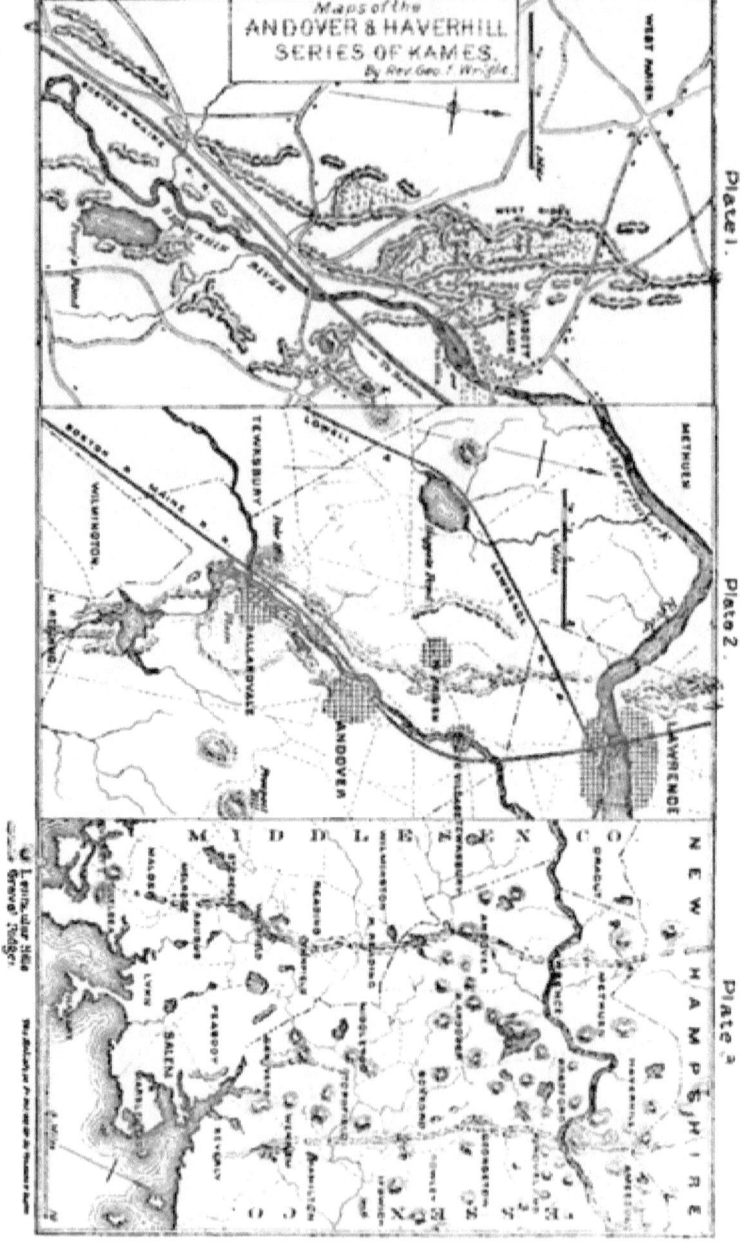

INTRODUCTION.

PREHISTORIC ANDOVER.

For the sake of chronological consistency, as well as for the intrinsic interest of the subject, this volume should begin with some account of prehistoric Andover. The accompanying plates,[1] prepared to illustrate a single geological feature, reveal at the same time both the topographical peculiarities of the town and its relation to surrounding political divisions. The territorial centre of "Old Andover," before the division of the town,[2] lies twenty-one miles north and four miles west of the State House, in Boston, in latitude 42° 40′, north, and longitude 5° 54′ east of Washington. The Merrimack River bounds it upon the north, while the Shawshin River, rising in Lincoln and Lexington, passes diagonally through the town from southwest to northeast. The southeast portion of the town is drained by tributaries to the Ipswich River. Hagget's Pond and Cochichawick, or Great Pond at North Andover, form distinct drainage basins, and empty into the Merrimack by separate outlets.

The "tablets of stone," containing the geological history

---

[1] These were drawn by Mr. G. W. W. Dove.

[2] Andover, before its division, contained about one sixth of the territory of Essex County. Its boundaries, before a portion was set off to Lawrence in 1847, were, the Merrimack River on the northwest (separating from Dracut and Methuen), Bradford and Boxford on the northeast, Middleton on the southeast, Reading and Wilmington on the south, and Tewksbury on the southwest. In 1709 the town was divided into two parishes, North and South, from the latter of which the West Parish was set off, and incorporated in March, 1827. In 1855 the town was divided nearly by the parish lines, the north division being incorporated as the town of North Andover. The name of Andover was relinquished to the south division, with whose institutions of learning it had become almost essentially identified. This transfer of the name makes it difficult to separate the history of the two towns, as the present North Andover was, for more than two hundred years, Andover.

of Andover, are so mutilated that we can read only the first chapter of the record and the last. The rocks are devoid of fossils, and belong to the Laurentian formation. This part of the story may well be styled sketches of "Old Andover," for the rocks are, according to Prof. C. H. Hitchcock, among the very oldest to be found in the world, antedating by a vast period the strata of the White Mountains of New Hampshire. The prevailing coarse gneiss rock, appearing near the depot in Andover, contains a large amount of iron, and upon exposure to the air rapidly disintegrates and becomes unsightly. Through the centre of the town, cropping out at Rattlesnake Ledge near Foster's Pond, at Sunset Rock, and upon the grounds of the Theological Seminary, there is an intercalation of granite about a half mile wide, remarkable for the size of its crystals of feldspar and for its freedom from iron. This terminates on the north at Carmel Hill, its eastern boundary being near Prospect Hill. To the southeast of this point there are extensive beds of an impure soapstone — a magnesian rock allied to the dark hornblendic rocks, which occur both in that vicinity and in several other portions of the town. The extreme southeastern portion of the town is crossed by the same uplift of ancient dioritic rocks (parallel to the general direction of the Appalachian chain), which contains the Newburyport silver mines. A belt of mica slate crosses the northeastern corner of the town.

But during the long period in which the Devonian and Carboniferous and Tertiary rocks of the central and western portions of our continent were being deposited, Andover was surmounted by an elevated plateau of land, which by its denudation was furnishing the gravel and sand and clay, out of which these later sedimentary deposits have been formed. The rocks which we here see exposed are but the stubs of mountains, which, during countless ages of exposure to denuding agencies, have been worn down to their present level.

While the geological record of Andover, during the earliest periods, is largely an untranslatable hieroglyphic, and the middle portion is absent, we are compensated by the abundance and intelligibility of the later record. The marks of the glacial epoch in Andover are open to inspection before every man's door. Glacial striæ can be seen, among other places, upon the rocks beside the road, a half mile out from Andover towards North Andover; on those back of the Punchard School-house; on the exposed quartz crystals of Sunset Rock, and in the vicinity of the school-house in Scotland district. Excellent exposures of glaciated rocks appear on the old turnpike from Lawrence to Salem, just beyond the North Andover line in Middleton, also on the Salem road from Andover. Scratched stones also abound everywhere in the "hard pan" at various depths.

Prospect Hill, rising four hundred and twenty-three feet above the sea, is one of the highest points of land in the county, and belongs to a very remarkable class of elevations, connected with the glacial period. Wood Hill, Pole Hill, Claypit Hill, Boston Hill, Woodchuck Hill, and the whole series of hills extending through to Great Pond, and surrounding it, are not, as might be expected, rocky elevations, but are vast heaps of unstratified compact clay containing scratched pebbles and gravel, and littered over with angular boulders.[1] The distribution of this class of hills over so much territory, as is represented in the plates, is shown on No. III. These elevations have been named by Prof. C. H. Hitchcock "lenticular hills," from their peculiar lens-shaped outline, as seen upon the distant horizon. This series of hills continues to the northeast as far as Portsmouth, N. H., and in an irregular course may be traced westward to the Connecticut River. A remarkable cluster of them appears also in the vicinity of Boston, upon one of which the State House stands. The hills in Charlestown and Chelsea, and in Boston harbor, are also conspicuous examples. So also is Asylum Hill in Danvers, and numerous others, extending to Ipswich Neck. A belt of land, four or five miles wide, from which they are absent, separates this series of lenticular hills from that passing through Andover.

[1] These boulders and pebbles have all been transported from the north. A well known belt of porphyritic gneiss cropping out in the neighborhood of Weirs, N. H., about eighty miles to the northwest, has furnished Andover with numerous unmistakable specimens. The pebbles of mica slate are perhaps from localities nearer by.

The best explanation which can be given of these unique and to the geologist perplexing hills, is that they are the remnants of an old terminal moraine, roughly marking what was for a long period of time the southern border of an earlier glacier in New England. Subsequently, upon the extension of this ice border to the south shore, this earlier moraine was first covered up beneath the ice sheet, and then by the movement of the ice over it was partially broken up and sculptured into its present forms. The *general* trend of this series of hills is northeast and southwest, but the longer axis of the *individual* hills is usually from northwest to southeast, which is the direction of the ice movement, as shown by the scratches upon the rocks. The extreme terminal moraine of the continental ice-sheet, composed of similar material to these hills, but continuous, forms the backbone of Cape Cod, of the Elizabeth Islands, of Long Island, and Staten Island, appearing at Perth Amboy, in New Jersey, and crossing that State to Belvidere, in Pennsylvania.

A later glacial deposit (now known in scientific circles as *Kames*) is represented in Andover by such formations as "Indian Ridge,"[1] a portion of which is shown in detail upon Plate I. Kame is a Scotch word, meaning sharp ridge. The extension of the system through the town is seen in Plate II., and of this and another series, through the county, in Plate III.

By reference to Plate I. the characteristics of this formation may easily be apprehended. At Smith & Dove's Flax Mill, near Andover Depot, a dam raises the Shawshin River fourteen feet. Measuring[2] from the river bed below the dam, the ascent to the peat bog, *o*, at the base of the east ridge is, in round numbers, forty-one feet. Taking this bog as a level, the height of the successive ridges, East Ridge, Indian, and West, at the points *a*, *b*, and *c*, is forty-one feet, forty-nine feet, and ninety-one feet, making West Ridge one hundred and thirty-two feet above the river, and one hundred and eighty-two feet above the sea. Until long after the set-

---

[1] "The Great Ridg" is the term used in deeds one hundred and fifty years ago.

[2] The measurements were made under superintendence of the writer by the class of 1875, Phillips Academy.

tlement of the town the enclosure between *b* and *c* was a shallow lake or bog. During the past century this has been drained partly by a channel of its own formation, and partly by artificial means. The peat or muck in this old lake basin is from twenty to thirty feet deep. A trigonometrical section of the West Ridge, at the point *c*, shows the height of the summit above the surface of the swamp to be sixty-one feet, with a breadth at its base of two hundred and fifty feet; that is, the slope upon each side is at the rate of one foot vertically, to two feet horizontally.

These ridges are composed of clay, sand, gravel, and pebbles of all sizes, up to those which are four or five feet in diameter. In most places there are some signs of irregular stratification. But frequently for a depth of twenty feet or more, signs of stratification are entirely absent. The stones in this formation are never scratched as in the hard-pan; but they are all more or less subangular, showing abrasion of some kind. These too are largely from the north.

In the "Transactions of the Association of American Geologists and Naturalists," for 1841 and 1842, Pres. Edward Hitchcock, of Amherst College, gave a detailed account of Indian Ridge, so far as then observed.[1] He there characterizes it as "decidedly the most interesting and instructive case [of the kind] which he had met with." A map of a mile and a half of it, then supposed to be its limit, was given by President Hitchcock in the same paper, prepared by Prof. Alonzo Gray, of Phillips Academy. This map, on a reduced scale, reappears in "Hitchcock's Elementary Geology,"[2] and covers nearly the ground of our first plate. Some other ridges of a similar nature were noticed by him, and the suggestion was made that further researches might show a system where now only a confused group was observed.

We could not improve upon the description of the main features of this formation given by Dr. Hitchcock in 1842.

"Our moraines form ridges and hills of almost every possible shape. It is not common to find straight ridges for a considerable distance. But the most common and most remarkable aspect assumed by these elevations is that of a col-

[1] See page 198.
[2] See page 260 (30th edition).

lection of tortuous ridges, and rounded, and even conical, hills with corresponding depressions between them. These depressions are not valleys, which might have been produced by running water, but mere holes, not unfrequently occupied by a pond."[1]

In 1874, the writer ascertained that this belt of ridges extended through the whole length of the town of Andover, as shown in Plate II., striking the Merrimack at the upper end of Lawrence, passing a little west of Frye village, crossing the Shawshin at Ballardvale, and forming the shores of Foster's Pond. Subsequently, in 1875, the details, as then ascertained, were published in a Bulletin of the Essex County Institute, at Salem, showing the extension of the system south as far as Wakefield, and north, to the New Hampshire line. The direction of the belt of ridges is northwest by southeast, conforming nearly to that of the glacial striæ. Kames frequently pass over the lenticular hills where their height is less than two hundred feet, and descend into shallow depressions, crossing river valleys without ceremony. Still later investigations brought to light a parallel belt of gravel ridges, reaching the sea at Beverly, and continuing north through Topsfield, Boxford, and Haverhill far into New Hampshire. These two series of kames are shown in Plate III.

When once the clew was discovered, numerous parallel systems of kames were found, stretching back in many instances from near the sea to the base of the mountains. In passing from Andover to New Brunswick by inland routes the traveller crosses more than thirty kames, each of which is as imposing as the series with which we are familiar in Andover, and some of which are continuous for one hundred and twenty miles; making the map of the kames and moraines of New England look like a gridiron.[2] Besides those marked upon our map, six or seven other kames cross the Merrimack Valley between Newburyport and the angle of the river, in Tyngsborough. These are all, however, less clearly defined and more subject to interruptions than the Andover or Haver-

---

[1] *Transactions of American Association of Geologists and Naturalists*, for 1841 and 1842, p. 191.
[2] Prof. Geo. H. Stone, of Kent's Hill, Maine, is the authority upon this subject in that State.

hill series. A kame system comes down from Hudson, N. H., through Tyng's Pond in Tyngsborough, Mass., and passes through Chelmsford. Another crosses about three miles above Lowell. Another just above the Pawtucket Bridge in Lowell, and on the other side of the river appears at the Poor Farm. Three miles below Lowell is still another very clear instance of a kame's crossing the river valley, where it is for some distance covered with alluvium. This kame appears south, in Tewksbury, towards Long Pond. Another is seen west of Hagget's Pond, appearing also one half mile east of the State Almshouse and again in North Woburn. The kames east of Hagget's Pond and those which match them north of the river, appear to be merged farther south in the main Andover series. A mile below Lawrence again, upon the north side of the river, is a small kame in line with the gravel deposits running through North Andover, and appearing as a kame near Marble Ridge Station, and farther south in Middleton. A well-marked kame, also, comes down from Amesbury to West Newbury.

The manner in which kames (called in Sweden Åsar) were formed, has long been a source of contention among geologists. It is possible that the early settlers supposed kames to be, like many mounds at the west, the work of Indians, and hence their name, "Indian ridge," not only in Andover, but in other places. More probably the name arose from Indians' choosing the kames for camping grounds, or burial places, as the whites now frequently do. No one who has studied them carefully, and is aware of their extent, could suppose the kames to be artificial. The most probable theory of the origin of these remarkable ridges is that they are somewhat of the character of *medial moraines*, and mark the courses of the surface flow of water during the last stages of the melting ice sheet. The ice had doubtless been thousands of feet in depth, and when the material forming the kames was deposited, still filled most of the depressions, and lingered in such transverse valleys as that which the Merrimack follows in the lower part of its course. Superficial streams, swollen by the action of the summer sun, would at that period flow with great violence during the hot season, and their course would be marked by vast accumulations of coarse gravel, which would in some places be lodged in ice channels, in others spread out over masses of ice. Finally, as the last masses and the lowest stratum of ice melted, the gravels thereon would settle down from the ice (as dirt does from snow-drifts in the spring) into the irregular forms in which we find these ridges.

Hagget's Pond doubtless marks a depression where the ice lingered while a kame-stream deposited in a temporary lake the sand plains to the south towards Tewksbury. Pomp's Pond was preserved from filling up by a similar mass of ice. The "kettle holes" near Pomp's Pond, and in the plain at Ballardvale, mark places where smaller masses of ice were covered up by the sand and gravel. When the ice melted, a hole would be formed without any outlet. The basin of Great Pond in North Andover was formed in a different manner. In this case the lake is hemmed in by lenticular hills, one of which partially dams its natural outlet. Lenticular hills have also in many places below North Andover determined the course of the Merrimack River.

Thus it appears that the citizen of Andover does not need to go to Switzerland, nor to Greenland, to study glacial phenomena. But he may enjoy that privilege to his heart's content among his own hills and gravel deposits. A most instructive portion of the skeleton of a continental ice sheet is spread out before his own doors. It is in gravels contemporary, in the period of their deposition, with the formation of Indian Ridge, that the palæolithic implements of northwestern Europe and eastern North America, especially in Trenton, N. J., are found. It is not improbable that the peat bogs, and "kettle holes," and ponds of Andover may furnish material aid in determining the antiquity of the glacial age, and so, of man, in America.[1] G. F. W.

[1] For fuller accounts of this class of formations, see *Proceedings of the Boston Society of Natural History*, vol. xix., pp. 47-63, also, vol. xx., pp. 210-220. The third volume of the Geological Report of New Hampshire, 1878, by Professor Hitchcock; and on this subject Mr. Warren Upham. The Geological Report of Wisconsin, by Professors Chamberlin and Irving, vol. ii., pp. 199-218, also 608-635. Report on New Jersey, by Geo. H. Cook, for 1877, pp. 9-22, and *Smithsonian Contributions to Knowledge*, by Col. C. Whittlesy, 1866. Also Geikie's *Great Ice Age*, 2d ed., pp. 239, 240, 242, 247, 469, and 478. And generally under titles of Kames and Eskers.

HISTORICAL SKETCHES OF ANDOVER.

CHAPTER I.

MEMORIALS OF THE EARLY SETTLERS.

WHOEVER tries to restore a picture of the life of past centuries in any locality, cannot fail to be impressed with the scantiness of ancient relics, — the meagreness of the actual material at command, in comparison with what has perished. Only here and there has a fragment been saved from the general destruction, and these relics are not for the most part the monuments that men have reared for the continuance of their name, but rather mere chance waifs preserved without thought or purpose. Especially is astonishment awakened at the wonderful duration of the seemingly most fragile and perishable of materials, while works designed to be strong and enduring have disappeared from off the face of the earth. Inscriptions graven in stone are obliterated; the stone itself crumbles to dust; buildings, raised in the pride of their owners and cherished with the affection of those owners' posterity, drop to ruin, while a scrap of paper, which the zephyr might blow away, or water soak to pulp, or a candle's flame consume, endures, and that not in careful keeping, but tossed hither and thither as waste or worthless, till, at last, somebody recognizing the jewel, it is picked out of the rubbish and thenceforth kept locked up and guarded in archive of brick and iron, destined again, perhaps, to outlast these strongholds of its security. Thus it is that in groping back for something tangible of the olden times, relics of ancient Andover, we find scarcely a trace or thread of continuity, by which hand can clasp hand with the men and women of the former generations, whose names are in our town and parish records and books of genealogy, perpetuated in their posterity and familiar to us as household words, and yet who themselves are almost as shadowy and unreal to us their descendants as though they had never walked the roads we walk, planted the trees we sit under, founded with toil and pain, and blood even, the institutions whose beneficence we enjoy. Hardly a relic now remains in the town — except on paper — of the first twenty-five years' labors of those hard-working pioneer settlers who cleared the forest, broke the ground, made their homes, reared their families, and found their graves during the first half century of Andover's incorporated existence. It seems fitting now, however, when the sentiment of the day tends to reminiscence, that the heirs of so rich a legacy of local history and tradition should make some effort to revive the ancestral associations, and quicken that feeling of obligation to former generations out of which grow all noble endeavors for the present generation and all generous solicitude for generations to come. The first glimpse through the vista of the centuries, which brings to view persons and places actually and directly influential and instrumental, in the founding of Andover, takes us back to the year 1639 and the ancient town of Agawam, or Ipswich. All along from the year 1604, and the exploring expedition of Sieur de Monts and Champlain (when a map of the Merrimack River was traced for them on a piece of bark by an Indian sachem), down to the date of the settlement of the town, the neighborhood of Andover receives frequent mention, either as the Valley of Merrimack [1] and Shawshin,[2] or as the territory near Cochichawick[3] River or the great pond of Cochichawicke. Several times action had been taken by the General Court relative to

---

[1] *Merrimack* is an Indian name, said to mean "the place of swift water."

[2] *Shawshin* (the spelling most common in the old records, although Shawshine, Shashin, Shashine, Shashene, Shawshene, and later, Shawsheen, are found) is said to mean "Great Spring."

[3] *Cochichawicke* (the most common and seemingly authorized ancient spelling) means the place of the Great Cascade. (See *N. H. Hist. Coll.*, vol. viii., p. 451.) Mr. Nathaniel Ward spelled the name Qui-chech'-acke and Qui-chich'-wick. Also Queacheck, Quyacheck, and various other spellings are found, but, in all, the guttural *chich* are found, evidently sounded as in wh*ich*. The Colonial officials adopt the spelling Cochichawicke, or without the final *e*.

"vieweing" it, with reference to a settlement; and committees had been appointed to license "any that may think meet to inhabit there," but at the close of the year 1639, when Salem, Lynn, Wenham, Newbury, Ipswich, Rowley, were thriving villages, or considerable towns, the forests of Andover remained uncleared by the white man's axe; only the Indian in rude agriculture tilled its fields, or hunted and fished along its streams. There seemed a probability, however, that it would eventually be occupied by "certain residents of Newton," who had petitioned the General Court and received favorable answer therefrom, but on the twenty-second of December, 1639, which begins this narrative of the town's history, a letter was written which decided the disposal of this valuable tract of territory. The writer was the Rev. Nathaniel Ward, ex-minister of Ipswich, and afterward author of the sagacious State paper, "The Body of Liberties," and the witty satire, "The Simple Cobbler of Agawam." The records of the time present a pleasant picture of the cheerful parson and his hospitable fire-side, with its Latin motto on the mantel, "*sobrie, juste, pie,*" to which the good man characteristically added "*laete,*" his somewhat heterodox supplement to the approved summary of Puritan virtues. The letter before mentioned, he wrote with earnestness, and, doubtless, also with despatch, for there was need of expedition, lest the action which it was designed to forestall should take place in the time that would of necessity intervene between its completion and its arrival at its destination, the distant city of Boston. Through the snows of the scarcely travelled roads, in woods whose trackless wilds bewildered wayfarers to and from settlements scarcely a dozen miles apart; among encampments of savages, of at least suspected friendliness, letter-carrying, done as it was by private messengers, and those often on foot, was precarious and uncertain. Therefore we may believe the writer's quill flew fast, and was mended without delay, as, in his sharp-pointed chirography, he jotted down sententiously the bits of advice on public affairs, which served as an excuse for a letter at this time " To our Honorable Governor at Boston."

Governor Winthrop had lived at Ipswich, and was connected by marriage with Mr. Ward. Moreover, the preacher was a prized counsellor to the Governor in State affairs, adding, to the qualifications for that service which his ministerial ordination was believed to confer, that of having been bred to the bar in the old country. Too worldly wise, some of the good folk of Ipswich parish thought Mr. Ward; and in truth he seems to have had considerable practical sagacity, as the sequel of his enterprise in connection with the new plantation shows; for these few strokes of his pen secured to himself, his townsmen and friends, a large part of the territory embraced in the ancient towns of Haverhill and Andover, with the privileges conferred by the Court on pioneer settlers, namely, "three years immunity from taxes, levies, and public charges and services whatsoever except military discipline."

Mr. Ward had a son, Mr. John Ward, who had studied divinity, and a son-in-law, Mr. Gyles Fyrmin, a physician, to whom the town of Ipswich did not afford a living practice, and who had even thought of giving up medicine for theology, or of combining the two, as it was the custom of the time to do, in circumstances of necessity. Mr. Nathaniel Ward was therefore desirous to find or to make places where the talents of his family might have scope. Accordingly, he wrote to Governor Winthrop:[1] —

"One more request, that you would not pass your promise, nor give any encouragement concerning any plantation att Quichichacke or Penticutt,[2] till myself and some others either speake or write to you about it, which shall be done so soone as our counsells and contrivalls are ripened. In too much hast, I commit you and your affaires to the guidance of God, on whom I rest, etc."

Four days after Mr. Ward's letter, Dr. Fyrmin himself sent one[3] seconding his father-in-law's request, and explaining fully his motives as already stated. "Considering that the gain of physicke will not find me with bread," he says, in giving his reasons for studying divinity; and, speaking of change of residence, he adds that he "thinks well of Pentuck-

---

[1] *Mass. Hist. Soc Coll.*, Fourth Series, vol. vii.
[2] The site of Haverhill, on the River Merrimack.
[3] *Hutchinson Papers*, p. 108.

ett" or of "Quichichwick by Shawshin." Mr. Ward soon after wrote again, pressing the matter: —

"We are led to continue our suite concerning the plantation, I have lately menčioned to you; our company increases apace from divers towns of very desirable men, whereof we desire to be very choise. This next week if God hinder us not, wee purpose to view the places & forthwith to resort to you; in the mean time we crave your secresy & rest. We have already more than 20 families of very good Christians purposed to goe with us."

These appeals accomplished the end desired. The Colony Records, May 13, 1640, have the following: —

"The desires of Mr. Ward and Newbury men is comited to the Governor [Thomas Dudley] Deputy Governor and Mr. Winthrop senior [not elected Governor 1640] to grant it to them p'vided they return answer within three weeks from the 27th p'snt & that they build there before the next Courte."

A year went by, and no village had yet been begun at the place granted, and it seemed doubtful whether there ever would be by the persons who had petitioned; for the neighboring plantation of Rowley had succeeded in getting its territory so enlarged that the men who had thought of settling at Cochichawick feared their prospect of a profitable enterprise was spoiled. Mr. John Woodbridge, of Newbury, who subsequently was the first minister of Andover, thus details his discouragements in a letter to Mr. Winthrop:[1] —

"To THE RIGHT HONL. JOHN WINTHROP SEN. ESQ. at his house in Boston, these present:

"*Right worthy sir:*— After my service promised &c I am bold to write a few lines to you, with desire that you would advise us to the best you can and as speedily as your occasions will permit. Some of us have desired to plant at Quichichwick & accordingly notwithstanding all the oppositions and discouragements that wee have had, having viewed the place since y'e court, were intended this spring to have built there; but there are two things that yet stand in the way to hinder us, the proceeding of either of which may be so great an annoyance that will quite cut off any hopes of being to a plantation there. The first is the intended taking of a farm by Rowley men which the Court allowed them to

[1] *Mass. Hist. Soc. Coll.*, Fifth Series, vol. i.

doe in lieu of a farme which Mr. Vane had within their bounds, adjoining to their bounds, which though it be not plainly expressed, yett we are credibly informed they intend to take neere Quichichwick so to take away 100 acres of meadow from that place which at best will entertain but a small company by reason of the little quantity of meadow. The second is, that notwithstanding all the agitations of the last court, Mr. Rogers being demanded whether he yett expected any more, answers that the contention, the last Court, was only about the neck & whereas he afterward expressed to the court that his first grant was eight miles into the country, he says, nobody speaking against it, he tooke for granted that he should have eight entire miles into the country, besides what was given, and they purchased from Ipswich & Newbury. These only are the impediments & reason of o' not proceeding. Now that wch wee would desire of your wo'p by way of advice is an answer to these three questions. 1. Whether you apprehend that the Court will allow of their so taking the farme aforesaid in such a place as will be so much praeiudiciall to a Plantation. 2. Whether the court will make good the grant of eight miles, to them or compell them to stand to those bounds only which were specified the last court. 3. Whether you would advise me nevertheless to proceed & trust to the Court more or to desist & leave it either all together. I have desired to propose these things first to yourselfe rather than the Governor[1] because I know that he hath allways heretofore bin opposite to my going thither. And the reason why I desire your speedy advice is because some of o' company have sold themselves out of house and home & so desire to bee settled as soone as may be. Divers others would gladly know what to trust to & some with some resolution affect Long Island intending speedily to be gone thither, if they settle not here, & for my owne part I have strong solicitations thither, by some not of the meaner sort & (being resolved that I cannot comfortably carry things along as I am) though not there yet elsewhere, I think I must resolve to labour to better myselfe. Thus leaving to your serious consideracion what I have written desiring your speedy advice, I humbly take my leave and rest   Your worp's to command
                                                        JNO WOODBRIDGE

"NEWBERRY this 22th of 1 mo 1640"
[MAR 22 1640–41]

[1] Governor Dudley, Mr. Woodbridge's father-in-law.

The "Mr. Rogers" referred to was the minister of Rowley, who was highly offended, and used some pretty sharp words, because the court at first refused to extend Rowley bounds for fear of injury to Cochichawick. Ten years afterward this neck of land was taken from Rowley and joined to Andover.[1] The line then drawn is presumed to be the same that now divides Bradford and Boxford from Andover.

It seems probable that soon after the above letter, sometime during 1641-1642, a settlement was begun at Andover, or steps taken to secure the grant to Newbury and Ipswich men. They would be likely to make a speedy decision; having, as Mr. Woodbridge's letter states, "sold themselves out of house and home," where they had been living. From an Act of the General Court, June 14, 1642, it would also appear that a settlement had been made, although the words may possibly refer to a prospective rather than an accomplished "village." Lands were granted along the Shawshin, Concord, and Merrimack rivers, to Cambridge men, on condition that they should build a village; but, "so as it shall not extend to *prejudice Charlestown village, or the village of Cochitawit.*"

On the 10th of May, 1643, the General Court ordered that "the whole plantation within this jurisdiction be divided into four shires." Essex was to contain the towns: "Salem, Linn, Enon [Wenham], Ipswich, Rowley, Newbury, Glocester, *Cochichawicke.*"

Neither Mr. John Ward nor Mr. Gyles Fyrmin was among the first settlers in the new plantations, though Mr. Ward ultimately went to Pentucket (Haverhill), and was the first minister of that town. Mr. Nathaniel Ward received a large grant of land on the Merrimack River, some six hundred acres, which he afterward made over in payment of a debt to Harvard College.

The first business transaction found of any resident of the town of Andover (the earliest evidence of any resident's being here), is dated August 13, 1643. It is a deed of land and stock in Ipswich to Richard Barker, "*of Cochichawicke.*"

[1] Gage's *History of Rowley.*

"Know all men by these presents,[1] that I, William Hughes of New Meadowe[2] have devised and granted bargained and sould for divers good causes & considerations me thereunto moving but more especially for ye sum of thirty-eight pounds in hand p'd, ye receipt whereof I acknowledge as alsoe for ye assurance of ye som of forty-one pounds more to bee p^d to me ye s^d William my heires, executors, administrators or assignes at or before ye fourteenth day of October next ensuinge ye date hereof, have devised granted assigned set over and sould unto *Richard Barker* of Cojichichicke 3 yearling heifers, 2 yearling bulles at twelve pounds ten shillings, twoe kine at tenne pounds, 4 calves at 3 pounds, one house & house-lot of 7 acres broken up and unbroken-up with all the corne . . . thereunto belonging, as also twelve loads of hay, with all the strawe of ye corne, at the farme of Mr. Paine where the said William now lives [the last clause is inserted between the original lines] at tenne pounds all whose above sd pticulars it may be lawful for the s^d Richard his heires or assignes to sell assign or dispose of, as his owne by right in witness whereof I have hereunto set my hand. WILLIAM HUGHES.

"Test ss ——— AVERY (?)
JOHN HUGHES."

In 1650, a house and land and three cows, in Andover, are mortgaged[3] by Job Tyler to John Godfrey, of Newbury.

The first sale of lands at Andover, of which a deed has been found recorded, was by Mr. Simon Bradstreet to Richard Sutton: a house-lot and dwelling-house and some fifty acres of meadow land. Richard Sutton came from Roxbury to Andover; he remained here only a few years, removing to Reading, and afterward to Roxbury again. He was active in the military service in the Indian wars, and, for his honorable service and sufferings, was, in advanced age, by order of the General Court, exempted from further duty. He left no descendants in Andover, but, as late as 1728 [ancient deed], a tract of land "in the township of Andover was known as Sutton's Plaine, the pine plaine "on ye borders joyning upon Billerica line."

Richard Sutton's descendants gained honorable distinction

---

[1] *Essex County Court Papers*, vol. i., p. 15.
[2] Afterward Topsfield. Here Mr. Bradstreet owned 500 acres.
[3] *Registry of Deeds*, "Ipswich," Book I.

in other towns, and by a curious coincidence, and without knowledge of an ancestral title of two hundred years' date, the family has now become one of the most influential in North Andover. Scarcely a half mile from where the early settler bought his " house lot, kort yard, and dwelling-house " of Mr. Simon Bradstreet, and where he lived, with his neighbors " George Abbot senr. on the north and George Abbot jr. on the south." (Mr. Bradstreet's house not far distant,) all of them probably in small and primitive houses of logs or unhewn timber, now rises, crowning the hill-top, the elegant mansion of General Eben Sutton, the owner of the large woolen mills [1] in the village which bears his name.

Following is the deed from Mr. Bradstreet to Richard Sutton, 1658 : [2] —

"Know all men by these presents, that we Simon Bradstreet of Andover and Ann his wife for and in consideration of several summes of money and other payments to be made to the said Symon & his heires or assignes more particularly mentioned and specified in another wrighting bearing date with these presents have sould and by these presents do give and grant, bargain, sell, assigne and sett over unto Richard Sutton of Roxbury husbandman all that our dwelling-house, situate and being in Andover aforesaid with the kort-yard and house lott thereunto belonging or therewithall now used conteining by estimation eight acres, be ye same more or less, having the house lott [3] of George Abbot sen^r on the north and a house lott of George Abbot jr on the south and abutting upon the street on the west with forty and eight acres of upland belonging to the sayd house lott lying on the farr side of Shawshin river, granted by the town of Andover for six acres, be the same more or less, together with the hovill, fences, proffits, privileges and appurtenances to the said house & premises belonging or appertaining (except a small parcell of meaddow contayning by estimation three acres ; be the same more or less, lying on the southeast side of Shawshin river aforesaid) together with such other divisions or allotments of meddow that belong to the sayd house or lott and may be hereafter granted and assigned

---

[1] See Chapter X.
[2] *Essex Registry of Deeds*, "Ipswich," Book II., p. 372.
[3] This indicates the truth of what is elsewhere suggested, that the villagers at first all lived in the north part of the town, and not till later removed to their outlying farm lands.

thereunto by the inhabitants of Andover aforesaid which are hereby reserved to the said Symon his heires and assignes. To have and to hould the aforesaid house and lott, meadow and upland with the profits and priviledges thereunto belonging (excepting before excepted) unto the s^d Richard Sutton, his heires and assignes forever; and we the sayd Simon Bradstreet and Ann his wife doe hereby covenant & promise to and with the said Richard Sutton that it shall and may be lawful for him the sayd Richard his heires, executors administrators & assignes from time to time and at all times forever, lawfully, quietly and peaceably to have hold, possess and injoye the said house and premises with the privileges and appurtenances thereunto belonging (except what is excepted) without any lett, trouble claim or molestation by or from us or either of us our heires, executors administrators or assignes or by or from any other person or persons whatsoever claiming in through by or from us or either of us, them or either of them, their heires or assignes. In witness whereof we have hereunto set our hands and seales this tenth of March one thousand six hundred & fifty-eight.

SIMON BRADSTREET (& seall).
ANN BRADSTREET.

"Signed, sealed and delivered in the presence of   GEORGE ABBOT
                         WILLIAM CHANDLER.

"Mr. Simon Bradstreet did acknowledge this wrighting to be his act and deed in Court held at Ipswich the 29th of March 1664."

The settlements of Andover and Haverhill are thus mentioned in " Good News from New England : " —

> "To raising Townes and Churches new in wilderness they wander
> First Plymouth and then Salem next were placed far asunder
> Woburn, Wenham, Redding, built with little Silver Mettle
> Andover, Haverhill, Berris-banks[1] their habitation settle."

The first formal description of the town of Andover is found in "The Wonder Working Providence of Zion's Saviour in New England," written by Captain Edward Johnson, of Woburn, published in London, 1654: —

"About this time [the date is approximately given 1648] there was a Town founded about one or two miles distant from the place where the goodly river of Merrimack receives her branches into her own body, hard upon the river of Shawshin, which is one of

---

[1] Portsmouth — Strawberry-banks.

her chief heads; the honored Mr. Simon Bradstreet taking up his last sitting there hath been a great means to further the work, it being a place well-fitted for the husbandman's hand, were it not that remoteness of the place from towns of trade bringeth forth some inconveniences upon the planters who are inforced to carry their corn far to market. This town is called Andover, and hath good store of land improved for the bigness of it."

Andover was incorporated May 6, 1646. It was named for the town of Andover, in Hants County, England, which had been the home of some of its principal settlers. The following extract from a letter written by a resident of Andover, England, to a gentleman of our town a few years ago, gives an idea of the mother town as compared with the daughter: —

"I find that Andover, in America, is of more importance than the same place in England. We have no institutions that can be named that in any way approach those in America, nothing of more note than an old endowed Grammar School. . . . ."

Speaking of the "South Church Manual," which he had received, he says: —

"I have been much interested in the minute particulars of the customs of the Congregational church. . . . . They differ but little from the old Congregational churches in England. . . . . The name of Abbot is not common here, but rare; Holt is often heard, but not common; Osgood is not known in our locality; Faulkner, Barnard, Ballard, Lovejoy but seldom; *Stevens, Poor,* and *Chandler*, are those oftenest occurring."

In the earliest book of the town records now existing is a list of names, which purports to be "*the names of all the freeholders* [householders is written above, as if by another hand, in explanation] *in order as they came to town*": —

MR. BRADSTREET, JOHN OSGOOD, JOSEPH PARKER, RICHARD BARKER, JOHN STEVENS, NICHOLAS HOLT, BENJAMIN WOODBRIDGE, JOHN FRYE, EDMOND FAULKNER, ROBERT BARNARD, DANIEL POOR, NATHAN PARKER, HENRY JACQUES, JOHN ASLETT, RICHARD BLAKE, WILLIAM BALLARD, JOHN LOVEJOY, THOMAS POOR, GEORGE ABBOT, JOHN RUSS, ANDREW ALLEN, ANDREW FOSTER, THOMAS CHANDLER.

Respecting these, information is scanty. Following are some notes and memoranda, — "memorials" of their life and times; such records of their individual history and the family lines of which they were progenitors, as have come to notice in tracing the general history, and also such incidental items as serve to illustrate the manners and customs of this early period of the town. The arrangement of the facts is, for the sake of graphic description and more vivid illustration, somewhat informal, and such as grows out of the connection of thought in the narrative, rather than the more methodical and logical arrangement which would be required were there fuller material to be disposed of under the several heads. The names are taken up in the order of their respective prominence in the town history.

SIMON BRADSTREET. It is doubtful if Mr. Bradstreet removed his residence to Cochichawick at the very first planting, as his name occurs in connection with Ipswich, in 1645. But he is said to have built a mill on the Cochichawick, 1644. He was the most influential citizen. The "worshipful Mr. Simon Bradstreet," he is most often styled. He held office in the colony as one of the Executive "Assistants," during most of the time of his residence in Andover, and afterward was Governor many years. A sketch of his life, and also a brief biography of his wife, Mrs. Anne Dudley Bradstreet, who is eminent as the first woman poet of America, are given in the history of the Bradstreet house, in another part of this chapter. The earliest relic found in Andover, of Mr. Bradstreet's life and work, is a deed, drawn and witnessed by him in 1663. This conveyed the land formerly sold by him to Richard Sutton. George Abbot bought the land, and the deed has been handed down to his descendants of the seventh generation. It is a document imposing and unique in style of execution. A fac-simile, is given herewith, of which the following is a translation, which the ancient writing makes necessary: —

"Know all men by these presents that I Richard Sutton of Andover in the county of Essex weaver and Rachel my wife for divers good causes & considerations mee thereunto moving & for recaived payment in Howse & Land wch I have resaived & had of George Abbot sen' of Andover afores⁴ husbandman every ryte & tytell whereof I do acknowledge myselfe satisfyed & payd. Have Bargained & sold & by this presents doe give, grant bargaine, sell, infeoff, assigne, & make over unto the said George Abbot senr All those my two pc'lls of ox-land or ploughing ground on the westerly side of y⁴ Shawshin river, the one lying & being By Little-hope brooke conteyning by estimation thirty acres, Be the same more or lesse & the other lyinge & being on the west syde of a lyttle peice of meadow belonging to the s⁴ George Abbot containing by estimation eighteen acres be the same more or less, both wch peeces I lately purchased of Mr. Simon Bradstreet & are within the bounds of the towne of Andover To have & to hold the afores⁴ two peices of Land with the wood & timber thereon growing or to be growing to the said George Abbot his heirs & assigns forever. And wee the said Richard Sutton & Rachel his wife doe hereby covenant & promise to & with the s⁴ George Abbot that hee the said George, his heirs, executors administrators & assignes shall or may from tyme to tyme & att all tymes forever lawfully quietly & peaceably have, hold, possesse occupye & enjoy the aforesaid two peeces of Land & every ryt & privilege thereof hereby granted or intended to be granted without any lett, troubles, hinderances, interruption or molestation by the aforesaid Richard or Rachel or either of them our heirs, executors, administrators or assignes, or by or from any person or psons whatsoever claiming in by through or under us or either of us our heirs or assignes, hee the sayd George paying or causing to be payd all rates, Levies, or assessments from tyme to tyme that shall be due or lawefully imposed for the above Land either by the Lawe of the Country or custome of the towne of Andover or otherwise, shall save harmless the said Richard & Rachel their heires & assignes forever from any damages for default thereof. In witness whereof we the said Richard & Rachel have hereunto sett o' hand and seales this eighteenth day of the first month commonly called March, in the yeare of our Lord one thousand six hundred sixty & three & in the fifteenth year of the raigne of y⁴ Soveragne Lord, King Charles the Second.

" Signed, Sealed & Delivered
  in the presence of   RICHARD SUTTON.
    SIMON BRADSTREET   her mk
    THOMAS CHANDLER   RACHEL (⌣ SUTTON." [1]
    JOHN BRADSTREET

[1] For women (except those of remarkable advantages of wealth and culture) to write was unusual in the earliest years of the town history. See Chapter VIII.

"This writing was acknowledged by Richard Sutton to be his act and deede & Rachel his wife did give her free consent thereto, this 6th of ffebruary 1664 before mee

SIMON BRADSTREET.

"ESSEX. ss. This Instrument is Recorded with the Records of s^d County Lib 31, fol. 209.   STEPH. SEWALL *Record*."

Mr. Simon Bradstreet, after the death of his wife (1672), removing to Salem, his house was occupied and his place filled in the town by his son,[1] Col. Dudley Bradstreet. The latter lived in Andover till his death, 1706. His wife was Ann Wood, widow of Theodore Price. His only son, the Rev. Dudley Bradstreet, first master of the Andover Grammar School, removed to Groton 1708, and was for some years pastor of the church there, but subsequently went over to England and took orders in the Established Church. The other sons of Mr. Simon Bradstreet having settled elsewhere, with the departure of Mr. Dudley Bradstreet the name became extinct in Andover. Of the other sons a word may be added : —

Samuel Bradstreet was a physician, graduated at Harvard College, 1653. He was representative for Andover to the General Court, 1670, although probably then a resident of Boston. He died in the West Indies.

Simon Bradstreet, graduate of Harvard College, 1660, was minister of New London, Connecticut.

John Bradstreet was the only son born in Andover. He was born July 22, 1652. He settled in Topsfield, on the grant of land made to his father.

Of the daughters : Dorothy was married to the Rev. Seaborn Cotton. Sarah was married to Richard Hubbard (H. U. 1653); also to Maj. Samuel Ward. Hannah or Anne, to Mr. Andrew Wiggin, of Exeter, N. H. Mercy, to Maj. Nathaniel Wade, of Medford.

Dr. Samuel Bradstreet's daughter Mercy was married to Dr. James Oliver, from whom are descended Dr. Oliver Wendell Holmes and Mr. Wendell Phillips.

[1] A sketch of his life and character and his influence in the town will be given in the history of the Bradstreet house.

Know all men by these presents that I [...]
Rachel my wife for divers good causes [...]
how see and with [...] appurtenances had of [...]
every [...] whereof I do acknowledge [...]
by these presents do give, grant, bargain [...]
Abbott son [...] those my two parcels of [...]
Shawshin Ryver, the one lying & being [...]
acres be the same more or less & the other [...]
belonging to the s[ai]d George Abbott, [...]
both with [...] lately purchased of m[...]
of Andover. To have & to hold the aforesaid [...]
growing or to be growing to the said [...]
the said Richard Sutton & [...] his [...]
Abbott, that he the said George, his heirs [...]
to give & at all tymes forever, lawfully qu[...]
aforesaid two parcels of Land, & every [...]
without any [...] trouble, hinderance, [...]
or either of us, our heires & [...]
Claiming, in, by, from, through, or under [...]
[...]
[...] for the aforesaid Land, either by the [...]
otherwise shall save harmless the s[ai]d [...]
for default thereof. In witness whereof [...]
and Seales the eighteenth day of the [...]
One thousand six hundred sixty & [...]
Lord King Charles the second [...]
Signed Sealed & Delivered
in the presence of
   Simon Bradstreete
Thomas Chandler
   John [...] Hoyt   [...] This Instru[ment]
                         Recorded with the [...]
                         County Lib 31 fol[...]

...d Sutton of Andover in the County of Essex weaver and
...rious me thereunto moueing & for a certaine payment...
George Abbott sen: of Andover aforesaid husband...
...ly satisfyed & payd, haue bargained, sold, gra...
...scott, assigne & make over vnto the said Georg...
...and or ploughing ground on the pightle? ly...
Little hope brooke contayneing by estimation thirty
...uy being on the west syde of a litle peece of meadow
...ny bye meadow eighteene acres be the same more or lesse
...mon Bradstreete, Esq: within the bounds of the Towne
...two poolls of land with the wood & tim̄ber thereon
...rge Abbott his heires & assignes for ever. And I...
... doe hereby Covenant & promise to & with the said Georg...
... operate administrate or assignes, shall or may from tyme
... etly & peaceably haue hold possesse occupy & enioy the
... thereof hereby granted or intended to be granted
... iction, or molestation, by me the said Richard or Rachel
... or assignes, or by or from any person or persons whatsoever
... le of me or our heires or assignes, hee the said Georg...
... from tyme to tyme, that shall be due or lawfully
... ... of the Country or custome of the Towne of Ando...
... hard & Rachel their heires & assignes for ever from any damage
... the said Richard & Rachel haue hereunto sett o' hand...
... mouth com̄only called March in the yeare of o' Lord
... in the fifteenth yeare of the raigne of o' Sou'raygn...

Rich: Sutton
her marke
Rachel ⋀ Sutton

This writing was acknowledged by Richard Sutton
to be his act and deede & Rachel his wife did giue
her free consent thereto this 3th of February 1664
... ... Before mee Simon Bradstreete
209
Steph'n Sewall Record

Rev. Simon Bradstreet's daughter Lucy was married to Hon. Jonathan Remington, of Cambridge. From them were descended Dr. William E. Channing and Mr. Richard H. Dana.

MR. JOHN OSGOOD, whose name stands second on the list of householders, and also next after that of the minister on the list of the ten members who formed the nucleus of the first church (a list of ten freeholders was necessary before a church could be organized), was probably the most influential citizen, after the Bradstreets and the ministers. He came from a town near Andover in England, and it is said that it was he who named the new plantation, but of this there does not appear any certain evidence.

Mr. Osgood was the town's first representative to the General Court, 1651. It is interesting to compare the affairs of town and commonwealth now with what they were then when the member from Andover wended his way on foot [1] or on horseback through the woods to the halls of legislation, all undreaming of the coming eras of railway, telegraph, telephone, etc., and without a suspicion that the debates, discussions, and declarations which he and the men of his time were indulging in at town meeting and General Court were the seeds destined to ripen into American independence. The great problem of the General Assembly just at that time was how to keep a safe neutrality in regard to the civil wars of the mother country, or rather how to seem submissive subjects to the powers that were and yet practically to manage the colonial affairs in their own way. The Massachusetts Colony was Puritan in sentiment, but had no mind to embroil itself in the quarrels across the water. The fact that the colonists thought possible to maintain neutrality is evidence that they had to some extent, even then, severed themselves from the parent government. Indeed, whether England was ruled by king or protector, Massachusetts contrived for the most part, for more than fifty years, to govern herself, and, while professing allegiance, to ignore or evade the laws

[1] Mr. Simon Bradstreet walked from Salem to Dover in 1641, on official business, as one of the Commissioners of the Colonies.

which she had no mind to know and obey. The General Court, to which Mr. Osgood was the deputy from Andover, voted, in reference to some of the demands of the beloved and honored Protector of England, to the effect that it would be inconsistent with the colonial conscience to submit its affairs to any laws except those made by the freemen of the colony; and especially they remonstrated against the appointment of any governor, by the Protector, for the colony; demonstrating that their charter entitled them to elect their chief executive in the colony. Cromwell, therefore, left the colonial magistrates undisturbed, — Endicott, Governor; Thomas Dudley, father-in-law of Mr. Bradstreet, Deputy Governor. Mr. Bradstreet was one of the Assistants at this time, Andover being honored in having two of her citizens at this early day influential in the colonial legislature and government. The acts of legislation which engaged the attention of Andover's first deputy did not concern especially the town of his residence, and are of no particular local interest, being in the main in regard to lands or boundaries, or the regulation of colonial trade and commerce. One or two characteristic acts are the following in 1651: —

"Whereas it is observable that there are many abuses and disorders by dancing in ordinaries [taverns] whether mixt or unmixt upon marriage of some persons this Court doth order that henceforward there shall be no dancing upon such occasion or at other times in ordinaries uppon the paine or penaltie of five shillings for every person that shall so daunce in ordinaries."

The author of a new book, Mr. Pincheon, was reprimanded by the Court for failing "to speak so fully as he ought of the price and merit of Christ's sufferings," but afterward he was pardoned, "since the Court conceive he is in a hopefull way of improvement." A citizen of Lynn was fined fifty pounds for having "defamed the management of the town and contrary to the lawe of God and the lawes here established reproached and slandered the courts, magistrates and government." Such were some of the (as they seem to us) frivolous or irrelevant subjects introduced among matters of practical and vital interest to the colony. Whether to men who looked upon life and civil government, as our ancestors looked upon them, they were questions frivolous and irrelevant to political legislation, and whether larger experience has given to the legislators of the nineteenth century wisdom to come to better and more just decisions respecting the questions which our forefathers disposed of so summarily, future centuries will give verdict.

Mr. Osgood's term of office was short. In October, 1651, he died, aged fifty-six years. During an illness some time before, he had made his will, the first, so far as has been found, of the many testaments of Andover citizens, by which hands reaching forth from beyond the tomb have held strong grip on the treasures which they had laid up on earth, and dead men's "wills" have been, considering the fluctuations of human motives, more potent than those of the living to control the transmission of their estates. The will was witnessed by two of Mr. Osgood's townsmen, both of whom outlived him by more than a quarter of a century. The reader will not grudge the space taken to transcribe this interesting memorial, one of the few relics [1] of these olden times: —

"The twelfth of April 1650, in the age of the testator fifty-four [born in 1595 June 23d] I John Osgood of Andover in the County of Essex in New England, Being Sick of Body but in perfect memory do institut and mak my last will & testament in manner and form as foloweth:

Imprimis, I do give unto my Sonn John Osgood my hous and hous-lot with all the accommodations thereunto belonging. Broaken-up and Unbroken-up land, with all the meadow thereunto belonging fforever, with the proviso that my wife Sarah Osgood shall have the moyety or the one half of the hous and lands and meadows during her natural life.

It. I do give & Bequeath to my Sonn Stephen Osgood 25 pounds to be payd at 18 years off age in Country pay.

It. I do give to my dater Elizabeth Osgood 25 pounds to be payd at 18 years off age in Country pay.

It. I do give to my daughter Sarah Clements 20 shillings to be payd when she is 7 years of age, but if she dy before that time to be null.

It. I do give to my servant Caleb Johnson one cow-calf to be payd

[1] *Essex County Court Papers*, vol. ii., p. 22.

3 yeares Before his time is out and to be kept at the cost of my executor till his time is out.

I do give to the meeting-hous off Newbury 18 shillings to Buie a cushion for the minister to lay his Book upon : all the rest of my Goods and Chattels unbequeathed I do give unto my son John Osgood and to Sarah my wife whom I do make joynt executors of my last will and testament & in witness hereof set my hand and seale. I do intreat John Clement of Haverhill and Nicholas Hoult of Andover to be overseers of this my last will and testament.

  By me   JOHN OSGOOD
  In presence off
    JOSEPH PARKER
    RICHARD BARKER."

The scene of this ancient will-making in Andover was very different from that of such occasions now. The house of the primitive settler was built of logs, or, if of hewn timber and more pretentious as that of the representative may have been, still plain and rude, and devoid of the elegancies or comforts of modern time, or of older settlements in the early time. For it does not appear from the few records left that any of the "first" families of Andover, except the Bradstreets (and, perhaps, the Woodbridges), had brought hither anything except the absolute necessarys of life, in the way of household furniture and appointments. Any ideas of there being here at the earliest day, choice china, delft, etc., or silver plate, such as are seen in old collections handed down as heirlooms (except, perhaps, in the families before named), are dispelled by a perusal of the inventory of the furniture and household goods of the next most prominent citizen, after Mr. Bradstreet. No family portrait, silver plate, china, or porcelain ware, mahogany, or oak, or damask-covered chair, were in the little humble abode, where this the town's first deputy to the General Court made his last will and testament; and in his pious regard for the Church of Christ he was more ready to expend his money for "cushions for the pulpit Bible," than he was to provide luxurious adornings for his own dwelling. A rude cottage, and plain furniture were all the worldly goods, except his broad acres, that the sick man had to dispose of, and take leave of, and his eye looked out on a landscape far different from the present aspect of old Andover. Through the narrow windows of the house, set in heavy leaden sashes (if glass windows were afforded, instead of oiled paper, often used to admit light), he looks off not on cultivated farm and smiling landscape stretching everywhere, but to the dense wood beyond the village clearing. He may, perhaps, descry stealthily creeping thence an Indian, intent on barter or plunder, or with friendly purpose, to bring a gift to the sick pale-face, — fish, or game, or powow-charm, and healing herb, to drive away the spell of disease.

When the twilight shadows fall, and the early-to-bed household sink to sleep and silence, except the drowsy watcher at the sick bed, the quick ear of the restless patient may catch the sound among the crackling brushwood of the deer's light tread, venturing near the dwelling, or by the moonlight may discern its graceful form and soft eyes peering out from copse or corn-field, or perchance he may, roused from dreams of Old England, and merry-making with rout of huntsman and bugle-horn, start to the dreadful reality of the wilderness, hear the howling of wolves, and see the glaring pack rush past, bearing down on some estray of flock or herd, or benighted traveller. It may be, the latch-string of the door left loose, a bear snuffing around thrusts his nose over the threshold, and draws back growling at sight of the embers burning on the hearth, while Reynard, the fox, interrupted thereby in his depredations on the chicken-coop, drops the fat cock from his back, and arouses up all the cackling brood. So drag on the weary hours; howls of wolves, baying of hounds, hoot of owl, cry of whip-poor-will, or of loon, startled from its reedy covert by the pond, disturbing the night, till in the glimmering dawn the chorus of morning bird-song begins, and the beat of drum summons the villagers to their daily rounds, and brings the solace of human society to the sick man. Thus wild and primitive is the scene, which fact dictates for fancy's sketch of the night-watches in the homes of ancient Andover. To make the picture true to life, we should set it in a frame-work of Scripture texts and pious ejaculations, and put into it numberless conflicts and wrestlings, fastings and prayers, witnessed only by the All-seeing. For, firm as was the faith of our fathers in the presence of the invisible God, as firm also was their belief in the presence, if not the omnipresence, of the invisible devil. As they held communion with their divine friend, so did they likewise hold conflict with their demoniac enemy. Prayer was the panoply in which the Puritan was ever clad, and as he kept his loaded musket at hand at all times, in health or in sickness, by day and by night, for defence against sudden attack of savage, so he kept his quivers of Scripture texts, and his magazine of petitions ever ready to quench all the fiery darts of the adversary. When the last enemy had gained the last victory over the militant saint, and, conflict, prayer, will and testament all ended, earth was to be returned to earth again, the funeral rites were simple and characteristic of the Puritan creed. Prayer at the grave of the dead was not allowed, lest it should seem to countenance the Romish masses for the repose of the soul. Whatever was allowed in the way of ceremony and funeral pomp, was no doubt done by the citizens of Andover, to render impressive the burial and honor the memory of their first deputy.

The Inventory [1] of Mr. Osgood's estate is as follows: —

"*An Inventorie of the Estate of John Osgood sen. of Andover lately deceased.*

	£	s	d
Foure oxen	30	0	0
Two steeres	10	0	0
Six cowes	29	0	0
Seven young cattel	24	0	0
Eight swine	25	0	0
120 Bushels of wheat	24	0	0
30 Bushels of Ry	5	0	0
120 Bushels of Indian	15	0	0
House Lands & Meadows	80	0	0
For Rie sowed	12	0	0
Due upon bond	20	0	0
Sixty Bushels of Barly	13	0	0

[1] *Essex County Court Records*, vol. ii.

	£	s	d
Fifty Bushels of Pease	8	15	0
A feather-bed & furniture	4	10	0
A flock bed (being half feathers) & furniture . . .	3	10	0
A flock bed & furniture	2	0	0
Five payre of sheets & an odd one	2	8	0
Table linen	1	0	0
Fower payre of pillow-beers	0	18	0
Nineteen yards of Carsamere	5	0	0
Sixe yards of Serge	1	4	0
Ten yards of Canvace	0	9	0
A remnant of Serge	0	9	0
Penistone (?) ten yards	1	10	0
Ten payre of stockings	0	18	0
Three yards of Stuffe	0	10	0
Twenty-two pieces of pewter	2	0	0
For ye copper & brasse	4	14	0
For Iron pott, tongs, cottrell & pot hooks . . .	1	0	0
Two muskets & a fowling-piece	2	10	0
Sword, cutlass & bandaleeres	1	5	0
Yarne & cotton-wool	0	15	0
Barrels, tubbs, trays, cheese-moates and pailes . .	1	10	0
A stand	0	5	0
Bedsteads, cords & chayers	0	14	0
Chests and wheeles	0	16	0
A hayre cloth	0	5	0
Bridle & Saddle	0	5	0
For sawes	0	10	0
Mault	1	16	0
A firkin of Butter	1	8	0
Bacon	2	0	0
A yard of holland	0	3	0
A yard & a half of calico	0	2	6
Household implements	1	0	0
The Sum of all	373	7	6

JOHN CLEMENTS
NICHOLAS HOULT
His H marke

Sarah Osgood
Her O marke

This was recorded 25th, 9th month, 1651.

From the first settler, whose home was, as appears from the inventory, devoid of the luxuries and even of many of the comforts of life, have descended generations reared in affluence. The pioneer settlers grew rich rapidly. Their estates became valuable. Lands which were "granted" to the fathers were sold by the children and grandchildren for large sums of money. The town of Andover did not long lack the refinements which come with wealth, when, as in the case of our townsmen, pains are taken to add to it intellectual culture.

The Osgood name has been remarkably influential in the town, connected both with civil and with military office. For a hundred and fifty years there was scarcely a time when there were not several military officers, captains, or colonels, in service, and in the list of representatives to the General Court, the name occurs thirty times before the year 1800. During the Revolutionary period, the Hon. Samuel Osgood, of Andover (North Parish), was State Senator, Representative to the National Congress, first Commissioner of the Treasury, and, after his removal from Andover to New York, Postmaster General. Among the representatives of the name in this period were the eminent divine of Medford, Rev. David Osgood, D. D., native of the South Parish, and the physicians at North Andover, Dr. Joseph Osgood, who died 1797, and his son Dr. George Osgood, who died 1823.

Isaac Osgood, Esq. (resident some time in Salem), Peter Osgood, Esq., Captain Timothy Osgood, were respectively heads of families influential at North Andover in the last fifty years.

Hon. Gayton P. Osgood, representative to Congress 1833 (died 1861), was a gentleman of rare culture. He lived at North Andover, in the fine mansion [1] (on the Haverhill road) built by his father, Isaac Osgood, Esq.

Captain Isaac Osgood, Rev. Peter Osgood (H. U. 1814), Mr. Henry Osgood, were among the later prominent representatives of the name. There are now very few [2] members

---

[1] Now the residence of Mr. James Davis.

[2] Miss Hannah Osgood, daughter of Peter Osgood, Esq, and sister of Rev. Peter Osgood, is living in her eighty-sixth year.

of this once large family left in the Andovers. The principal of these is Mr. Isaac Osgood, postmaster of North Andover.

Emigrants from old Andover have carried the name to many different places, and among their descendants are numbered many names of distinction. But to collect and record even a part of these would require time and space beyond our limits. The ancient estates on the Cochichawick are still owned by descendants [1] of the Osgood line.

No trace of memorial tablet, or grave-stone, remains, which marked the spot where was laid the body of John Osgood, the first settler, in the old burying-ground, nor any relic of the men, his neighbors, whose names are signed as witnesses of his will and stand next to his on the list of householders. This burying-ground is at North Andover Centre — at the southeast of the Bradstreet House, — on the hill near where was the first meeting-house, and is, besides the house, the only memorial left of the works of the first settlers.

Of all the tombstones erected in memory of the first householders, one alone remains, that in memory of JOHN STEVENS. Its broken stone has been re-set in a granite tablet: —

>Here lyes buried
>The Body of Mr.
>JOHN STEVENS
>Who deceased y^e
>11 Day of April
>1662 in ye 57
>year of his age.

The stone is quaintly carved and ornamented, but bears no eulogy or text. "He lived — he died," — this is indeed the sum and "abstract of the historian's page" in regard to the life of this, as of many another first settler of Andover, to whose memorial monument time and decay have given a longer reprieve than to most of those of his contemporaries. His name appears occasionally in the records of the County Court, and once in the records of the General Court, 1654: "John Stevens of Andover, Henry Short of Newbury, Jo-

---

[1] Mr. T. Osgood Wardwell, Mrs. S. Osgood Russell, and Mrs. C. Osgood Stevens.

seph Jewett of Rowley, a committee chosen to examine into the grounds of a dispute between Haverhill and Salisbury in regard to lands, and to return their apprehentions thereof to this Court." On the 19th of October, they made an elaborate and minute report of their action in the matter, detailing their surveying, etc., in its full particulars, and stating their conclusion that former surveyors had made a mistake by which land was cut off from Haverhill "to their great pjdice." Their report was accepted.

An idea of the house, estate, and style of living of John Stevens may be obtained from the following :—

"*An Inventory[1] of the goods and Chattels of John Stevens of Andover Deceased emprized by George Abbot, Richard Barker, Nathan Parker, Nicholas Noyes, the 28th of Aprill Anno 1662.*

"*Imp.* His wearing Apparell.

"*It.* In the hall, two beds with their furniture. *It.* One chest and foure boxes. *It.* Eight payre of sheetes, foure Bolster cases and three payre of pillow-beeres. *It.* Three table cloaths, 1 dozen of Napkins with other sleight Things.

"*It.* One brasse Pott, foure small Kettels one Skillett, a Scummer & warming pan. *It.* One Iron Pott, an iron posnett, two payre of pott hookes, two trammels, a spitt, a payre of tonges & fire-pan, a payre of Cob-irons with a smoothing iron & a trevett.

"*It.* Six pewter platters, two brazers, two porrengers, foure drinken cuppes, a salt-seller a chamber-pott, a dozen & half of spoones a latten-pan. *It.* A table board & foure chayres, two cushens two dozen of trenchers, half a dozen of dishes.

"*It.* A muskett, corslett & head piece a sword, cutlass and halberd. *It.* A bible with other books. *It.* In the Leaneto — Barrels, wheeles, with other lumber. *It.* In the Chamber — bedding. *It.* Wheate, twenty Bushells, Indian corn ten bushels. *It.* A bridle & saddle & pommel. *It.* Two flitches of Bacon. *It.* Baggs. *It.* Flax & yarne. *It.* Old tubbs with other lumber. *It.* Sawes, Axes, ploughes, with other working tooles. *It.* Eight oxen. *It.* Six cows. *It.* A heifer & two yearlings. *It.* Three calves. *It.* Swine. *It.* A colt & an asse. *It.* A horse. *It.* One stocke of bees. *It.* One carte, sleads, yoakes, chaines plowes & plow-irons, ropes, &c.

"*It.* House, barnes, upland, & meadow and corne upon ye grounde. Sum total £463. 4. 0."

[1] *Essex County Court Papers*, vol. viii., p. 18.

The inventories of the two citizens, John Osgood and John Stevens, are interesting to study, not only for the idea which they give of the amount of property owned by the rich citizens of ancient Andover, but also for the picture they present of the style of living of that time, the household furniture and farm implements. Some of the names of utensils are now unfamiliar in New England households, but they were those in use in the old country, and often occur in the English classics of that period. An "iron possnet" was a sort of porringer; "cob-irons" were andirons, with a round ball at the top; a "trevett" was a "three-footed stand," probably to accompany the smoothing-iron — a flat-iron stand, in modern parlance; a "latten-pan" was a pan made of latten, a sort of tin; "trenchers" were wooden plates, which were in common use for the table. Wooden plates and pewter platters, or dishes, pewter drinking cups and spoons, no knives and forks, are what constituted the table furniture of the two well-to-do farmers of North Andover in 1650–1660. The quantity of military outfit is noticeable: "Sword, cutlass, halberd, head-piece, corslet (an outfit for a knight of the middle ages), also a musket, but all only costing two pounds.

The Stevens name was prominent in the early military record. Sergeant John Stevens, 1661; Lieutenant John Stevens, 1689; Captain Benjamin Stevens, about 1725, was one of the most active officers in the frontier service, ranging in quest of Indians. He was representative to the General Court and justice of the peace.

The name of Stevens was widely known in the colonial time by the brilliant reputation of Rev. Joseph Stevens, grandson of John Stevens, the first settler; also of his son Rev. Benjamin Stevens, D. D., of Kittery, Me., once candidate for the presidency of Harvard College. Rev. Phineas Stevens, D. D., was a graduate of Harvard College, 1734; ordained at North Andover, 1740; settled at Boscawen. Capt. James Stevens, during the French and Indian war, did honorable duty in the King's service. He was also one of the deputies to the General Court. During the Revolution, Adjutant Bimsley Stevens was on the staff of General Ward.

Among the prominent names of the family are, in recent times, Capt. Nathaniel Stevens, one of the early manufacturers of North Andover (his five sons manufacturers — among them Mr. Charles Stevens, of Ware, and Hon. Moses T. Stevens, of North Andover); the late Justice William Stevens, of Lawrence; his son, Colonel William O. Stevens (attorney, of Dunkirk, N. Y.), killed in the battle of Chancellorsville, May 3, 1863; Major-general Isaac I. Stevens, Governor of Washington Territory, killed in the battle of Chantilly, Va., September 1, 1862; Oliver Stevens, Esq., now District Attorney of Suffolk County; Henry J. Stevens, Esq., counsellor at law, Boston; Mr. Phineas Stevens (deceased, 1864), builder of first mills at Lawrence, civil engineer; Mr. Augustus G. Stevens, now city engineer of Manchester. Mr. Warren Stevens and Mr. Enoch Stevens, traders fifty years ago, at North Andover, — also James Stevens, Esq., — were widely known in this vicinity, and many others of the family, especially in the West Parish, had a local name; but enough have been mentioned to indicate the descent and perpetuity of the family through the centuries.

Before tracing farther the early settlers we may here pause to take a survey of the every-day life in the new plantation, and gain a more vivid idea of the manners and customs of ancient Andover. First, as to their gaining a legal and moral right to the goodly territory on which they settled. We have already seen what the action of the General Court was in reference to the Cochichawick plantation, and that Mr. John Woodbridge was a prime mover in the matter of collecting a colony. He and Mr. Edmond Faulkner are said to have purchased the land from the Indian sachem, Cutshamache, or Cutshamakin, who lived near Dorchester, and who was a kinsman of Passaconaway, the sachem living in the region about the Merrimack River, "Old Will," as he was sometimes called.

For the paltry sum of six pounds, currency, and a coat, the township of Andover was bought, a tract of land included between Merrimack River, Rowley, Salem, Woburn, and Cambridge. This sale the Indian sachem acknowledged about the time of the town's incorporation, and confirmed before the General Court, as appears from the Colony records : —

BIRTHPLACE OF MAJOR GENERAL ISAAC I. STEVENS, GOVERNOR OF WASHINGTON TERRITORY
(Ancient "Mansion house" (remodelled) of Mr. Moody Bridges, officer of the Old French War and representative to the First Provincial Congress.)

JOHNSON HIGH SCHOOL AND STEVENS HALL

"At a General Court at Boston 6th 3d mo. 1646 Cutshamache, Sagamore of yͤ Massachusetts came into yͤ Corte & acknowledged yͭ for the sum of £6 & a Coat which he had already received, he had sold to Mr. John Woodbridge in behalfe of yͤ inhabitants of Cochichawicke now called Andover all his right interest & privilege in yͤ land 6 miles southward from yͤ towne, two miles eastward to Rowley bounds be ye same more or lesse, northward to Merrimack river, pvided yͭ yͤ Indian called Roger and his company may have liberty to take alewives in Cochichawicke River, for their owne eating; but if they either spoyle or steale any corne or other fruite to any considerable value of yͤ inhabitants there, this liberty of taking fish shall forever cease, and yͤ said Roger is still to enjoy four acres of ground where he now plants."

The name of Roger is still perpetuated in Roger's brook and Roger's rock,[1] the well-known landmark, near the present site of the South Meeting-house. "Roger and his company" taking alewives in the rivers, or even, in spite of their promises, "spoyling or stealing corn" in the white man's planting grounds, were no doubt familiar sights to the settlers of old Andover, for it is to be observed that the clause in the agreement does not imply the possibility of their abstaining wholly from plunder. "To any considerable value," left a wide leeway and margin, as a concession to the Indian's natural propensity. Roger's "reservation," of "four acres where he now plants," seems never to have occasioned any controversy; but he and "his company" (like all his race destined to fade away before the invader) have long ago ceased to be, — no descendant of an Indian is now[2] known to live on the soil sold by Cutshamache.

The "village of Cochichawicke" was laid out in house lots, chiefly of four acres and eight acres. To many persons who have not given special thought to the matter, and are not familiar with colonial life, it is a matter of wonder that the early settlers of the New England towns had not larger homesteads. When the country was all before them, why did not our forefathers each surround his house with an estate of hundreds of acres, instead of crowding as closely together in living as

[1] Now removed.
[2] Some persons now living remember a woman named Nancy Parker, who is said to have been the last Indian.

though land were scarce, and why are the estates, which have been held by families from the time of these first settlers, not contiguous territory, but scattered all over the town in patches here and there, a wood-lot in one place and a meadow two to five miles away?

A little reflection on the state of things, in which the pioneer settlers found themselves, and a study of the records of the town and of the proprietors, explain all this.

It was necessary that the population should be compact together, not only because of the danger of attack from Indians and of the ravages of wild beasts, and the guard to be kept against these, but, also, because the facilities of communication were few for transacting the business of the community. With no good roads, and few horses, it was desirable that a community mutually dependent should not be scattered over a wide territory. Some ancient rules [1] or directions, for laying out a "towne," are the following, which are likely to have been in general the plan followed at Andover: —

"Suppose y* towne square 6 miles every waye. The houses orderly placed about y* midst especially y* meeting-house, the which we will suppose to be y* center of y* wholl circumference. The greatest difficulty is for the employment of y* parts most remote, which (if better direction doe not arise) may be this; the whole being 6 miles, the extent from y* meeting-house in y* center will be unto every side 3 miles; the one half whereof being 2500 paces round about & next unto y* said center, in what condition soever it lyeth may well be distributed & employed unto y* houses within the compass of y* same orderly placed to enjoye comfortable convaniance. Then for y' ground lying without, y* neerest circumferance may be thought fittest to be imployed in farmes into which may be placed skillful bred husbandmen, many or fewe as they may be attayned unto to become farmers, unto such portions as each of them may well & in convenient time improve according to the portion of stocke each of them may be intrusted with."

The township was owned by the Proprietors. Some twenty-three names are found, but the original lists were lost, and after some years persons were counted as proprietors who were not among the original ones. The house-lots having been assigned, the farm lands (meadow lands, ox-ground,

[1] *Mass. His. Soc. Coll.*, Fifth Series, vol. i.

ploughing ground, mowing land, they were variously named) were distributed in proportion to each man's house-lot; that is, to a four-acre house-lot belonged a certain amount of meadow or farm land; to an eight-acre house-lot belonged double this amount of farm land, etc. These were called "house-lot rights" or "acre-rights," and thus when a man bought a house-lot of eight acres, he had also with it, and at first (as it would seem) inseparable from it in transfer, these farm lands. But the whole township was by no means used up and divided out. A large, perhaps the larger, part was kept in reserve by the proprietors, and called the "common or undivided lands." From these, grants and sales were made from time to time, up to the year 1800, when the whole was sold and the money divided for the support of free schools.[1]

The first house-lots were grouped around the meeting-house in the north part of the town. The old burying-ground marks the site (nearly) of the meeting-house. The estates remote from this centre, which are often said to have been the "homesteads" of the first settlers, from the fact that the land can be proved to have been held by them, it is not probable were in many instances the places of their first abode, although, in the progress of the settlement, many of the first owners of house-lots undoubtedly removed from their original residence, further from the centre, to their own farm lands, where, in time, residence became safer and more convenient. So, as was said, estates and homesteads have been handed down from first settlers which were not their first residence, or even perhaps their residence at all. This will appear more clearly in the course of the narrative.

It is apparent, from what has been said, that the "common" lands were not for any ornamental or decorative, or even sanitary purposes, such as the "common" of a city or village now serves, although in some instances the land now beautified and adorned as a public park is a remnant of the former common lands of the town — as Boston "Common," which was used for a pasture. The "common or undivided" lands served for the pasturage of the flocks and herds. Those common lands conveniently situated were often used as places

---

[1] See Chapter VIII., "District Schools;" also "Franklin Academy."

for military drill, which was rigidly enforced during the Indian wars. These were called "training fields":—

"1718. — Voted & passed That the three training-fields, that which is called Benjamin's Lott,[1] the old training field; and that between Capt. John Chandler's and Samuel Peters's and Ensign Henry Chandler's, and that by the South Meeting house, all three places shall lye common forever."

There were also common wood-lands, and for various purposes, as appears from the following in the Proprietors' records:—

"*Andover's Common Clay ground Laid out and Recorded for to Lye Common forever for the Use of all the Town.*

We the subscribers hereof who were chosen and appointed a Committee by the proprietors of Andover at their meeting that was on the 22: day January: 172½ for to lay out such Pieces of Clay Ground as was then common: whereupon on the seventh day of June 1722: was Laid out these three severall pieces of clay ground That is to Ly open to the Common and that the Clay in each place is to be free: and common for any of the inhabitance of the said Town of Andover forever: for their own use in Andover: To wit: the first piece of said clay-ground we Laid out for the End aforesaid. Lieth a Littell below Lieut John fries Dam just below his home meadow, that is about Thirty-five pole of Land be it more or Less. Bounded att the North West Corner with a Stake and Stons, then Run eastward four pole and a half to a great stump, then southward. . . . . The second piece of said clay-ground lieth att a place called the miller's meadow clay-pitts, containing about one hundred pole of land . . . . the north end of it the said hundred pole of Clay ground and the east side of it Joyneth to Robert Swan's Land and the West side to the way that Leadeth from Joseph Ingales to Edward faringtons. The third piece of said clay Ground lyeth att Rose meadow Broock by the South Side of the way that Leads from Jacob Mastons to Quarter master John barkers."

As late as 1794 there was a tract of land on Preston's Plain, lying west of Boston road and south of the road to Ballard's mill, which, "although divided by metes and bounds

[1] This is believed to have been the land north of or near the present house of Dr. Kittredge, on the hill — a lot owned by Benjamin Stevens at one time.

is yet improved by the owners in one common field," as says the ancient document[1] recording the action. A meeting of the proprietors was called at Mr. Isaac Blunt's tavern, September 21, and adjourned to meet at an Oak Tree, on the road to Ballard's mill, for the purpose of dividing this "commonage" for separate improvement by the owners, and the division was effected.

It is difficult to ascertain with certainty anything definite about the first house-lots and their occupants, who seem to have removed from place to place in the town. In 1658, Richard Sutton bought a house, which had belonged to Mr. Bradstreet. The deed gives a clew to the residence of some of the other settlers. George Abbot, senior, had his house-lot on the north, and George Abbot, junior (not the son, but a younger man, "George Abbot tailor," or, "of Rowley," as the "Genealogical Register" designates him), had the lot south. Robert Barnard's lot adjoined Mr. Bradstreet's; Mr. Dane lived near; John Stevens seems to have lived near the burying-ground, to the east. Joseph Parker had his lot "toward the mill river, southeast of the meeting-house, bounded by the house lot of Nicholas Holt, and by Mr. Francis Faulkner's on ye common."[2] This was probably as late as 1670. Henry Ingals lived near the meeting-house, 1687. The Osgood and Johnson lots were toward the Cochichawick, and north of it. Richard Barker's was contiguous. It is a tradition that John Frye lived south of the Bradstreet House, and the Poors near the Shawshin. Thus we learn that the first settlers, whose estates are now in the south and west parishes of Andover, lived in the beginning at the north part of the town. As is stated hereafter, the town at first forbade any to go to live on their farm lands without express permission.

The names of the proprietors, who had been also householders before 1681, are given in a list (which, it is stated in the record, was copied from the town books), in the proprietors' books. These, as has been said, were not all proprietors

---

[1] MSS. of Mr. Asa A. Abbot.
[2] That he had a lot would not necessarily imply that he lived on it, but more than once in allusions to transactions the families are spoken of as contiguous.

originally, but from time to time were voted into the number: —

Abbot, George, senior.	Farnum, Thomas.	Osgood, Capt. John.
Abbot, George, junior.	Faulkner, Edmond.	Parker, Joseph.
Abbot, John.	Foster, Andrew, Senr.	Parker, Nathan.
Allen, Andrew.	Foster, Andrew, Junr.	Poor, Daniel.
Ballard, William.	Frie, John, senr.	Rowell, Thomas.
Barker, Richard.	Frie, John, junr.	Russell, Robart.
Barnard, Robert.	Graves, Mark.	Russ, John, senr.
Blanchard,[1] Samuel.	Holt, Nicholas.	Stevens, John, senr.
Bradstreet, Simon.	Ingolls, Henry.	Stevens, John, junr.
Chandler, Thomas.	Johnson, Thomas.	Stevens, Nathan.
Chandler, William, senr.	Johnson, John.	Stevens, Timothy
Dane, Mr. Francis.	Lovejoy, John, senr.	Tyler, Job.
Farnum, Ralph.	Martin, Solomon.	Woodbridge,[2] Benjamin.

The Proprietors in 1714 bought new books, and began a careful record of their transactions and the grants made. The two volumes of their records are now in the Memorial Hall Library, Andover, and are of interest to the curious in local history. In looking through them we find frequent mention of houses and land-marks, helpful in identifying family estates and abodes.

The Proprietors' Records contain an account of what has already been said was the manner of dividing the lands, also of the mode of taxation, and when it underwent a change: —

"The Proprietors in Andover raised their Town Rate By their Lots, so that he which hath an eight acre lot paid double to him that had a four-acre Lott and had also double division of Land and meadow, until the year 1681. Then the proprietors came to a new agreement with themselves and also with all that were then householders: To raise our Town charges by Heads and their Ratable estate and then every man was to be priviledged in all town privileges according to what taxe he Bore and also to have an Interest in the Common Lands in Andover according to the Tax they Bore from the year 1681 to the year 1713."

The first town-meeting, of which there is any record,[3] was holden at the house of John Osgood, 9th inst., 1st, 1656, and was, as the record states, "chiefly warned and intended for the entering & recording of Town orders now in force and

[1] *Alias* Henry Jacques.   [2] *Alias* Thomas Chandler.
[3] The earliest books are lost.

particular men's grants of Land in a New Town Book ; the old being rent and in many places defective and some graunts lost."

In 1660 action was taken by the town in respect to persons' removing their residence, and all citizens were forbidden to go out of the village to live, which at that time of comparative security from Indian attacks many were inclined to do. The disadvantage of such residence to the general welfare is thus set forth and guarded against : —

"Att a generall Towne meeting March 1660, the Towne taking into consideration the great damage that may come to the Town by persons living remote from the Towne upon such lands as were given them for ploughing or planting and soe, by their hoggs & cattle destroy the meadows adjoyning thereunto have therefore ordered & doe hereby order that whosoever, inhabitant or other shall build any dwelling-house in any part of the towne but upon such house lott or other place granted for that end without express leave from the Towne shall forfeit twenty shillings a month for the time he shall soe live in any such p'hibited place p'vided it is not intended to restrain any p'son from building any shede for himself or cattle that shall be necessary for the ploughing of his ground or hoeing of his corne, but to restraine only from their constant abode there, the towne having given house lotts to build on to all such as they regard as inhabitants of the towne."

An instance of the damage done and the trouble caused by roving animals is found in a record,[1] 1665, of a lawsuit : "Simon Bradstreet *vs.* Daniel Gage" for damages done to the plaintiff's fields by swine owned by the defendant. The fence-viewers, Thomas Johnson and Richard Sutton, testified in regard to the condition of the fence, that they had viewed it, and found it "very sufficient against all orderly cattle." It was not expected that fences could be made so as to keep out swine, and therefore persons, except innholders, were forbidden by law to keep more than ten of these animals. The year before, Mr. Bradstreet, whose suits against his neighbors and others were many (the law seems to have been resorted to on the most trifling causes in those times), had had a case[2] in court against Richard Sutton, which arose

[1] *County Court Papers*, vol. xiv.   [2] *Court Papers*, vol. xiv.

primarily from the trespass of Mr. Bradstreet's horses on his neighbors' premises. The charge brought against Richard Sutton was that he intentionally struck and killed one of the horses. He claimed that he did not, — that the horses had been in his yard again and again (as he brought witnesses to prove) "eating up his cattle's fodder." One night, when they came, he called Mr. Bradstreet's dog and Mr. Dane's dog, and set them on the horses, and then was unable to call them off, and the dogs had killed a mare. "The doggs pulled her downe once in my yard & I beate them off & they fell upon her again & almost pulled her downe in Mr. Dane's cort yard & I did what I could to save her & I doe believe I can prove y^t Mr. Dane's dog & Mr. Bradstreet's killed her." This was what Richard Sutton said to a neighbor, Thomas Abbot, the next day after the affair, as Abbot testified in court. The defendant was fined ten pounds; but as his townsmen chose him for one of the fence-viewers the next year, it would seem that his reputation did not suffer seriously from the charge. It is noticeable that in his official capacity his evidence in the suit of "Bradstreet *vs.* Gage" was in favor of the plaintiff. He did not, however, long remain in Andover; Mr. Bradstreet was a man who would not brook contradiction by his neighbors of less commanding influence, and it would not be surprising if Richard Sutton was glad to sell the house which he had bought from him, and go out of the neighborhood. At any rate, he seems to have removed to where there would be no more danger of trouble from Mr. Bradstreet's horses.

The trespass of horses some years later caused yet more serious trouble between neighbors, — a hand-to-hand fight which came near ending fatally, between William Chandler, Jr., and Walter Wright. These instances, and many others, go to show that it is an error to infer from the strict rules and severe penalties for Sabbath-breaking, religious heresy, and extravagant dress, that the community was a model of good order and sobriety. Persons unfamiliar with the facts would be astonished to find how many offences there were against the moral and the civil law, and how common they were in the families of prominent citizens. Both the parties in the fray now alluded to were of respectable family connections. The young man was the son of William Chandler, and nephew of Thomas Chandler, the deputy to the General Court, that same year, 1678. Walter Wright was in 1689 the constable, and in 1673 had been granted encouragement by the town to erect a fulling-mill. The story is told simply to show the actual state of the town and of society, as it was here and elsewhere, and to correct an erroneous idea that the first century of our colonial history was in every respect superior to the present century, which, if it be true, is a sad commentary on all the labor expended to educate and cultivate and refine the masses. Our ancestors were good men, but their age had its faults, which were those of a primitive society, rude and not glossed over with any fine semblance, which makes right and wrong indistinguishable.

The trouble between our townsmen in August, 1678, was as follows (an extract from the evidence in court,[1] September, 1678) : —

"The Testimony of William Chandler aged about 19 years, who saith that a month ago last past, Goodman[2] Right early in the morning came by to my father's house and I being in the yard he s^d to me: Well, I will shoot your horse; I asked him why: because s^d he, he hath been in my lot tonight. I replyed I am sorry for that; for I did forget to fasten him tonight; but I hope I shall doe soe no more, but Goodman Right replyed : And so you will always forget it; but I will goe home & charge my gun & shoote him, for he hath done me forty shillings worth of hurt this summer."

The youth retorted, and being exasperated by some further offensive words, sprang upon Goodman Wright, and seized him by the collar. They grappled in a fierce tussle, in which Wright, being strangled by Chandler, drew a knife and gashed the face of the youth, " cut a long deepe gash on my cheeke which came very near my throat — his knife was in the in-

[1] *County Court Papers*, vol. xxix., p. 93.
[2] Only a few of the more wealthy and influential men were spoken of as Mr. All others were called Goodman. Only four of the first settlers have the title Mr.: Bradstreet, Osgood, Faulkner, Woodbridge.

deavour as I thought to *cut my throat*," — was the testimony of Chandler in court. This trial, like the former one, seems not to have been any great injury to the reputation of the parties, or to have interfered with their standing in the town.

But the many difficulties growing out of the trespassings of domestic animals made the watching of them important. They were also in danger of straying off and being lost in the woods, or in the boggy grounds. Officers to look after them were, therefore, appointed by the town, "reeves" and "branding men," — the latter to see that all cattle had the town-mark, and the former to superintend the driving of them to the common lands for pasture. Herdsmen were also employed to watch and drive the cattle and sheep. In the morning many of these were driven out, and back at evening, by the herdsmen, while some were out for the greater part of the season. In 1686 the town voted "that a parcel of land lying between ye land of William Ballard senior and ye pond called Ballards pond and soe to ye end of ye pine plaine and soe betweene ye land of Joseph Ballard, Hugh Stone, & William Blunt & soe to John Abbot shall forever lye for a sheep pasture."

The herdsmen were assisted in watching the flocks by boys and girls, who were obliged also to have some other employment meanwhile, so that their time might not be wasted, or habits of idleness formed.

"1642. The Court doe hereupon order and decree that in every towne the chosen men are to take care of such as are sett to keep cattle that they be sett to some other employment withall as spinning upon the rock, knitting & weaving tape &c that boyes & girls be not suffered to converse together."

A scene for the painter, if there had been one to appreciate it, would have been the wild, rocky pasture, with its flocks and herds browsing, tended by boys and girls with knitting-work in hand, or spinning-wheel on the rock, themselves watched by the sharp-eyed herdsman, lest they transgress the rule of silence, while from behind bush or tree the whole party is eyed by lurking Indian or savage beast, waiting an unguarded moment to spring upon a victim.

To clear the forests of wild beasts was no small part of the labor of the primitive settler. It was also in its way a pleasure, as well as a duty, — one of the few recreations permitted to the Puritan. That the settlers sometimes undertook the chase in another spirit than the motive of self-preservation, appears from "Josselyn's Account of Two Voyages to New England," 1675: —

"Foxes and wolves are usually hunted in England from Holy Rood to Annunciation. In New England they make best sport in the depth of winter. They lay a sledg-load of cods-heads on the other side of a paled fence when the moon shines, and about nine or ten of the clock, the foxes come to it; sometimes two or three or half a dozen and more, these they shoot and by that time they have cased them there will be as many more; so they continue, shooting and killing of foxes as long as the moon shineth. I have known half a score killed in a night."

He describes the sport in killing wolves, and narrates with gusto some acts which would point a moral for the advocate of prevention of cruelty to animals: —

"A great mastiff held the wolf. . . . . Tying him to a stake we bated him with smaller doggs, and had excellent sport; but his hinder leg being broken, they knocked out his brains. . . . . Their eyes shine by night as a Lanthorne. . . . . The fangs of a wolf hung about children's necks keep them from frightning and are very good to rub their gums with when they are breeding of Teeth."

Josselyn, in his "New England Rarities," also describes another method of catching wolves, which was perhaps used at Andover, and may offer some clew to the meaning of the term "Wolf-hook," of so frequent occurrence in the colonial records.

"Four mackerel hooks are bound with brown thread and wool wrapped around them and they are dipped into melted tallow, till they be as big and round as an egg. This thing thus prepared is laid by some dead carcase which toles the wolves. It is swallowed by them and is the means of their being taken."

Mr. Bradstreet, in one of his accounts, has an entry or order for "25 Wolf-hooks."

In 1686 it was voted in the town meeting "that those that catch wolves in yᵉ towne of Andover shall have ten shillings for each wolfe to be paid by yᵉ towne."

A valiant hunting feat of an Andover youth is recorded by Judge Sewall in his diary, 1680–81, February 3 :—

"Newes is brought of Mr. Dean's[1] [Dane] Son Robinson his killing a Lion with his axe at Andover."

The "lion" was probably a bear, it being common then to use the word lion for any great wild beast of which the settlers stood in terror. Bear-hunting is described by Josselyn. As this was no small part of the work and "sport" of the Andover settlers, we are not turning aside from our main path to note it :—

"Hunting with doggs they take a tree where they shoot them; when he is fat he is excellent venison, which is in Acorn time and in Winter, but then there is none dares to attempt to kill him, but the Indian; he makes his Den amongst thick bushes."

Den Rock no doubt received its name from being one of the haunts of the bear (although in later times the place has gained, perhaps named by divinity students, a theological significance, and been called "Devil's Den"). Bear Hill, Bruin Hill, Wolfe-pit Meadow, Wild-catt Swamp, Deer Jump, Crane Meadow, Rattle-snake Hill, Woodchuck Hill, Scoonk Hole, — suggest the denizens of the woods and meadows, most of which have long ago disappeared; and here a plea may be pardoned in behalf of the old significant and commemorative names. Plain and homely as they are, those already quoted, and others found on the ancient records, — Musquito Brook, Five-mile Pond, Great Pond, Dew Meadow, Heather Meadow, Rose Meadow, Flaggy Meadow, Rubbish Meadow, Half-moon Meadow, Rough Meadow, Ladle Meadow, Pudden-bridge Swamp, Falls Woods, Rockey Hill, Barn Plain, Rail Swamp, Cedar Swamp, Little-hope Brook, Roger's Brook, Rowell's Folly Brook, Job's Folly, Needless Bridge, Holt's Hill, Foster's Pond, Hagget's Pond, Aslebe Hill, Marble Ridge, and many others, — shall they be supplanted by the trite and flavorless commonplaces which can be found in nearly every

[1] Dean Robinson (?).

suburban town from Maine to Oregon? Let us hold to our local names, those which are time-honored and have a meaning; and in selecting new ones, almost anything, however devoid of elegance, which preserves a fact, is, we may venture to say, preferable to a merely pretty or fine-sounding title. In selecting names for streets, would it not be well to bear this in mind, and draw from our rich repository of local history, or have reference to some actual fact of natural history, or something distinctive and characteristic, even though it be humble? " Pomp's Pond,"[1] for instance, — who would make it romantic with a mellifluous name, and obliterate the memory of the old colored man, " Pompey Lovejoy" (servant of Capt. William Lovejoy), who had his cabin near it, and made 'lection cake and beer for the delectation of voters' palates on town-meeting days! This name is almost the only local reminder that negro slavery was one of our early institutions, and that for more than a hundred years men and women were bought and sold in Andover. Almost in the earliest days of the town history (that is to say in its first quarter-century), negro slavery existed. In 1683, Jack, negro servant of Capt. Dudley Bradstreet, died. In 1696, " Stacy, ye servant of Maj. Dudley Bradstreet, a mullatoe born in his house," was drowned. In 1690, Lieut. John Osgood complained to the court at Salem, that he had been taxed for a servant boy ("small as to his growth and strength, and in understanding almost a foole"),[2] as much as though the boy were an able-bodied man.

In 1730, the negro girl Candace was sold by her master, the Rev. John Barnard, to Mr. Benjamin Stevens, who seems to have owned several slaves. The following is the bill of sale:[3] —

"Know all men by these presents that I John Barnard of Andover in the County of Essex and Province of the Massachusetts Bay in New England Clerk, for and in Consideration of the sum of sixty pounds to me in hand paid or by bond secured by Ben-

[1] Formerly Ballard's Pond.
[2] *Essex County Court Papers*, vol. i., p. 14.
[3] The original, among the papers of Mr. Barnard's son, Rev. Thomas Barnard, of Salem, was preserved by his friend Col. Benjamin Pickman, among whose papers it was found by the Hon George B. Loring, and by him contributed to the *Essex Institute Collection*, 1865.

jamin Stevens junior of Andover aforesaid, husbandman, Have given, granted, sold, conveyed and by these Presents do for myself and Heirs, give, grant, sell, convey and confirm unto Him the said Benjamin Stevens, his Heirs and Assignes forever a certain Negro-Girl named Candace, to Have and to Hold the said Negro-girl, to him the said Benjamin Stevens His Heirs and Assignees forever.

Further. I the said John Barnard for myself, my Heirs, Executors and Administrators do Covenant and Promise to and with the said Benjamin Stevens his Heirs, Executors, Administrators and Assignes that he the said Benjamin Stevens, his Heirs, Executors, Administrators and Assignes shall legally and peacefully hold the s⁴ Negro Girl forever and that He the s⁴ Barnard his Heirs, Executors & Administrators will warrant and Defend the sale of said Girl to s⁴ Benjamin Stevens, his Heires and assignes against the lawful claims of all and every person whatsoever. In witness whereof I the said John Barnard have hereunto set my Hand and Seal this 14th day of December Anno Domini 1730 and in the fourth year of his Majesty King George the Second.

JOHN BARNARD (Seal)
SARAH BARNARD (Seal)"

The original bill of sale, or receipt for money paid for a negro girl, 1756, is among the papers preserved on the homestead of George Abbot, Senior, now owned by Mr. John Abbot : —

"DUNSTABLE, *September* 10, 1756.

"Received of Mr. John Abbot of Andover Fourteen pounds thirteen shillings, and seven pence, it being the full value of a negrow Garl named Dinah about five years of age of a Healthy, Sound Constitution, free from any Disease of Body and do hereby Deliver the same Girl to the said Abbot and promise to Defend him in the Improvement of her as his servant forever.

ROBERT BLOOD.

" Witness my hand — JOHN KIMBALL.
TEMPLE KIMBALL.

"This day Oct. 25 (the new style) the within named Girl was five years old."

Among the records of marriage is " Abraham & Dido servants to Mr. James Bridges Oct. 31, 1744."

Among the records of intentions of marriage is the following : —

"Oct. 4, 1755. The Intentions of Marige between Primas and Nan negrow servants to John Osgood Esqr. and Mr. Joseph Osgood were entered on record. Published and Certeficet Given."

Although not strictly within the scope of this chapter, the sketch of slavery may here be brought down to the time when it ceased to be legal in Massachusetts. It is not attempted to gather all the facts and details in regard to individual slaves (concerning the sales and transfers of some of whom accounts differ), but merely to present enough to show how prominent a feature of the town history slavery was.

Some families kept several servants, and (as in the case of Mr. Bradstreet's household and James Bridges's, and as in the Southern States recently) their affairs, and the domestic events and concerns of their households, were of almost as much interest among their masters' families as in their own. But, tender as were the attachments sometimes formed between the servant and the master, and kindly as many servants were treated through life, we have seen that even the minister sold Candace, and that the little five-year old Dinah changed masters, and was carried from her home in Dunstable to a stranger's at Andover. So, too, when masters had ceased to need the services of their slaves they advertised them to the highest bidder. Witness the following from the "Essex Gazette," 1770: —

"To be sold by the subscriber cheap for cash or Good Security, a Healthy, Strong, Negro Boy, 20 years old last month, very ingenious in the farming business and can work in iron-work both at blowing and refining and as I am done with the Iron works I have more help than I need on my farm.   JAMES FRYE.

"ANDOVER *Apr.* 9, 1770."

Not young men alone, but girls were offered for sale: —

"To be Sold a Likely, Healthy Negro girl about 14 years old, Enquire of Mr. Thomas Bragg, Deputy Sheriff in Andover."

"*September* 8, 1770."

Fugitive servants also were not unknown: —

"Ran away from the subscriber on the 24th day of September a Man Servant about 19 years of age, named Isaac Mott. He had on when he went away a blue serge coat and a flowered flannel jacket and leather breeches. Whosover will take up the said runaway and bring him to me shall be well rewarded.

JONATHAN ABBOT.

"ANDOVER *Oct* 10, 1770."

The Rev. Samuel Phillips had several slaves. One of these, Cato, lived to the age of eighty-five (dying 1851), and saw seven generations of his master's family. He was freed by the law in 1780, but stayed for some years in the service of his friends. He was a member of the North Church, uniting during the pastorate of Mr. Symmes. When he left his former master he wrote an address of farewell, which is creditable alike to his ability and to the labors of his protectors for his education. Many a white man in Andover could not compose so fair an epistle : —

"Being about to remove from the family where I have for some time resided, would with the greatest respect I am capable of to the heads of each family respectively take my leave. I desire therefore to return my hearty & unfeigned thanks for your care over me, your kindness to me, also for your timely checks, your faithful reproofs, necessary correction, your wise counsel, seasonable advice, for your endeavors being yet (or when) yet young & my mind tender to frame it in such a manner as to lay a foundation for my Present & future happiness ; and also by the blessing of Heaven I hope your endeavors have : nor will not be fruitless. Being unable to make a compensation either to the author (god) or instrument (yourself) of the advantages I have been favored with equal to them, I hope while in Life to Do all I can to promote the glory of the former and the welfare of the latter. I hope : you not only having the name but the Disposition of Christians and wishing to have your own imperfections over looked will I trust do the same by me. Some of the family being now in the Decline of Life and according to the course of nature have but a few days to spend here will ere Long I trust be in the enjoyment of that felicity which will be a full compensation for your kindness to me & to others whose Departure hence by many that survived will be greatly missed ; but while you tabernacle in the flesh I would Beg you for a remembrance of me in your addresses to the throne of grace.

"My present wish is that the Blessings of heaven may attend each family and all there Lawful undertakings also there children to the Latest generation. And I hope that I myself shall be with the rest enabled to Live in such a manner that I being made meet may be admitted with you into that haven of rest *where is no Distinctions* yours with respect.

       CATO. *May 24th* 1789."

A specimen of the correspondence of Pompey Lovejoy,[1] and his friends, is the following letter (a copy from the original) : —

         " BOSTON *September 16th* 1779

"DEAR POMPEY — I am in a very poor state of health at present by a fall. I hurt myself very much I should take it as a grate favor if you would come down nex Weak and carry me to Andover and by so doing you will oblidge me very much. My kind Love to all Inquiring Friends. No more at present but I remain your   Sincere Friend   PRINCE PROCTOR.

"Please to embrace an opportunity Next weeke at the Furthest If you can Donte let Jenney know that I send you a letter."

In 1795 a negro slave of Andover, Pomp (not the one of the pond), was hanged on the road between Ipswich and Rowley, Pingree's Plain, for murdering his master, Capt. Charles Furbush. This man had been subject to fits of insanity, and kept at times under guard ; but the community was shocked at the act and its circumstances of horror, and the negro was sentenced to the extreme penalty of the law.

A tribute to the virtues of a faithful servant is among the epitaphs in the Old Burying Ground : —

     In Memory of
      PRIMUS
    Who was a faithful
     Servant of Mr.
    Benjamin Stevens jr.
   Who died July 25, 1792
  Aged 72 years, 5 months, 16 days.

In the Old South Burying Ground is the grave of the last slave born in Andover, Rose Coburn, wife of Titus Coburn. She was daughter of Benjamin, a slave brought from the West Indies, and Phillis, brought from Africa at the age of ten years, a servant of Mr. Joshua Frye. The inscription on the gravestone is as follows : —

[1] "Pompey Lovejoy" had been a servant of Capt. William Lovejoy. He was the same for whom Pomp's Pond was named.

Here lies buried the body of
ROSE COBURN
Who died Mar. 19 1859 aet 92 years

She was born a slave in Andover and was the last survivor of all born here in that condition.

A pension was paid to her as the widow of a soldier of the Revolution.

She was a person of great honesty, veracity and intelligence and retained all her faculties in a singular degree to the last.

Also her daughter Colley Hooper died aged 58, who died first, neither of them leaving any descendants.

The difficulty of obtaining good hired servants in the colony was great; the golden age of servicedom, even in 1656, lying behind. The Rev. Ezekiel Rogers, of Rowley, wrote to his brother pastor, the Rev. Zechariah Symmes, of Charlestown, the following lament over the indocility of American domestics : —

"Much ado I have with my own family, hard to get a servant glad of catechising or family duties. I had a rare blessing of servants in Yorkshire and those I brought over were a blessing but the young brood doth much afflict me."

A specimen of some of the Andover hired servants, and the " trials," of which they were literally a cause, is the following : —

"TO THE CONSTABLE OF ANDOVER. You are hereby required to attach the body of John —— to answer such compt as shall be brought against him for stealing severall things as pigges, capons, mault, bacon, butter, eggs &c & for breaking open a seller doore in the night — several times &c. 7th 3d month 1661." [1]

This man was a servant of Mr. Bradstreet. It seems from the evidence that he was in the habit of taking chickens, "capons," from his master, and making a fire in the lot behind the barn, roasting the fowls, and eating a part himself and carrying some to the house of Goodman Russ, who shared the plunder. But Goodwife Russ, for fear of detection and punishment, seems to have betrayed them. She testified that once after John had brought victuals to her

---

[1] *County Court Papers*, vol. vi., p. 132.

house, — chickens, butter, malt, and other things, — she was up at Mr. Bradstreet's house, and learned that "the mayde had missed the things," and said her mistress would blame her and be very angry. So Goodwife Russ brought them back, and informed her husband and John what she had done.

This John at one time killed and roasted a "great fatt pigg" in the lot, and he and a comrade, who confessed this in the court, ate most of the pig, and gave the rest of it " to the dogges." John proposed that they should steal also some flitches of bacon, and put one of the dogs in the room where the bacon was hung, and let him "knaw" some, to give the idea that the dog was the thief. He boasted of his exploits in theft with a former master, how " 2 or 3 fellowes " used to let him down the chimney with a rope into a room where he could get " strong beare," and how he "stole a great fatt Turkey from his master Jackson ; that was fatted against his daughter's marriage & roasted it in the wood and ate it."

In regard to his doings, Hannah Barnard "did testifye that being in my father's lott near Mr. Bradstreet's Barn did see John run after Mr. Bradstreet's fowls & throughing sticks & stones at them & into the barne."

She said after a while peeping through a crack in the barn, she saw him throw out a capon which he had killed, and heard him call to Sam Martin to come ; but when he saw that John Bradstreet was with Martin, he ran and picked up the capon and hid it under a pear tree.[1]

The only extenuating evidence adduced was that of two persons who testified that they had heard Mr. Bradstreet say that John was one of the best servants to work that he ever had ; and of one witness who had worked in the same field with John when they carried their dinners. He gave as an excuse for and explanation of John's voracious appetite and craving for "capons, pigs, malt, cheese, butter, bacon," etc., that the food which was given him " was not fit for any man to eate," the bread was " black & heavy & soure."

---

[1] Within the memory of the writer a very large and evidently very old pear tree (the only one on the place) stood at the east of the present Bradstreet house. It died many years ago.

But this servant's offences did not consist in stealing alone. He was malicious or mischievous in doing injury to his master's property, aiding and abetting the youth of the village in the pranks of foolish sport. Stephen Osgood confessed that one morning, about half an hour after daybreak, he and Timothy Stevens and John were passing Mr. Bradstreet's house, and made a movement to run Mr. Bradstreet's wheels down hill into the swamp, which they did; and also John "took a wheele off Mr. Bradstreet's tumbril and ran it down hill and got an old wheel from Goodman Barnards land & sett it on the tumbrill."

Elizabeth Dane, the minister's daughter, deposed (her deposition taken by her father), that she "was milking[1] late in ye evening June 1661," and heard the voices of men and the sound of wheels; these same rogues being at other capers.

John was brought before the Court again for stealing, after he left Andover.

Besides slaves and hired servants there were, under "masters," "apprentices." Note that in the colonial days "servant," not "help," was the term, the ideas of fraternity coming in with the Revolution. Their relations were scarcely less independent toward their employers than were the relations of the slave owned by him. They were not only bound for a term of years, but they were often practically sold, the indentures being transferred, although this was probably not without the consent of the parties making the indenture. Often, however, these were the selectmen of the town, apprenticing paupers, and caring comparatively little what became of them, so the town were relieved of their support. But often apprentices were of good connections, put to learn a trade, in which they might rise to competence or to affluence. One of the earliest apprentices found on record was Hopestill Tyler. There is a tradition that his father, Job Tyler, was living at Andover when the settlers came here, as Blackstone lived at Boston, "monarch of all he surveyed," until the advent of the "lords brethren," as he said, put him to flight, as the rule of the "lords bishops" had driven him from the

[1] An accomplishment rare, it is safe to say, among the ministers' daughters of Andover now.

old country. Job Tyler had apprenticed his son Hopestill to Thomas Chandler, the blacksmith, 1658. But after the papers were drawn up, he broke the bargain, got possession of the instrument of indenture, entering the house of Nathan Parker, (who wrote the paper, and had it hid in, as he supposed, a safe place,) and stealing it in the absence of the owner of the house. The matter was a cause of long controversy and several trials, — "Chandler *vs.* Tyler" and "Tyler *vs.* Chandler," extending over a period of more than ten years, and carried from court to court. One paper of interest, in connection with this, is a deposition of a witness in regard to the terms of the indenture, which it was said "Mr. Bradstreet" saw, had perused, and judged "to be good and firme." In this the mutual obligations of master and apprentice are set forth : —

"That the s^d apprentice Hope Tiler should serve the said Thomas Chandler faithfully for nine years and a half after the manner of an apprentice, that the master, the said Chandler should teach him the trade of a blacksmith so farr as he was capable to learne, and to teach him to read the Bible & to write so as to be able to keepe a book, so as to serve his turne for his trade and to allow unto the s^d apprentice convenient meat & drinke, washing, lodging and clothes."

Job Tyler paid dear for his hard words against a man of so great influence as Thomas Chandler, who afterward became one of the town's deputies to the General Court, and who was one of the principal citizens in point of wealth, in the little community of husbandmen and artisans : —

"1665 A case in difference between Thomas Chandler of Andevour & Job Tiler having formerly been entered in Salem Court in an action of defamation being withdrawne & reference made as appears by their bond to that purpose to Colonel Browne, Edward Denison & Captain Johnson of Roxbury . . . . they not agreeing, wee the aforesaid Captain Johnson & Edward Denison doe give in our award as followeth : [Job Tyler, being poor, they judge he should not be fined above six pounds.] 'We doe order that Job Tiler shall nayle up or fasten upon the posts of Andivour & Roxbury[1] meeting-houses in a plaine leadgable hand, the acknowl-

[1] He seems to have removed to Roxbury about 1661.

edgment to remain so fastened to the posts aforementioned for the space of fourteen days, it to be fastened within the fourteen days at Andevour & tomorrow being the twenty-seventh of January '65 at Roxbury. .... The Confession and acknowledgment ordered by us for Job Tiler to make & poste as is above expressed is as followeth. —— *Whereas it doth apeare by sufficient testimony that I Job Tiler have shamefully reproached Thomas Chandler of Andevour by saying he is a base lying, cozening, cheating knave & that he hath got his estate by cozening in a base reviling manner & that he was recorded for a lyer & that he was a cheating, lying whoring knave fit for all manner of bawdery, wishing the devill had him, Therefore I Job Tiler doe acknowledge that I have in these expressions most wickedly slandered the said Thomas Chandler & that without any just ground, being noe way able to make good these or any of these my slanderous accusations of him & therefore can doe noe lesse but expresse myselfe to be sorry for them & for my cursing of him desiring God & the said Thomas to forgive me & that noe person would think the worse of the said Thomas Chandler for any of these my sinfull expressions And engaging myself for the future to be more carefull of my expressions both concerning him & otherwise desiring the lord to help me so to doe.*

ISAAC JOHNSON.
EDWARD DENISON."

Job Tyler brought suit against Chandler, and was allowed to sue in "*forma pauperis*," he having no means of paying charges; but although the suit was one of special interest, and is quoted in the judicial histories, it is not further pertinent to this narrative.

The apprentice, Hopestill, learned the trade of a blacksmith, and in 1687 the town granted him "liberty to" set up a "shop in ye streete near his house."

A case [1] of the sale of indentured apprentices occurs between Thomas Chandler and William Curtis, of Salem. The apprentice refused to stay with his new master: —

"The Complaint of William Curtis to the honered Cort .... humbly sheweth. .... May it please your honors to take notice that about 22 months since, I bought a sarvant of Thomas Chandler of Andover, Jacob Presson by name. .... My sarvant continued with me about eleven months, my family at that time being

[1] *County Court Papers*, vol. xxv.

very sick and Jacob not being well I gave him leave and lent him a horse to go to Andover to be a while amongst his friends, but being taken sick by the way at his Brothers there he lay for some time; after he recovered he went to Andover to his father Holt's where I was willing he should be awhile but in the beginning of the last winter I sent for my man to com home and he came hom." . . . .

He made an excuse to go for some corn again, and, instead of returning, he sent back the horse and stayed away himself. He seems to have had a rather unhappy apprenticeship; for after his transfer of masters, and his being compelled, as he was, by order of the Court, to serve out his time with William Curtis, he presents a petition to the court for the clothes promised him, saying that the said Curtis, of Salem, whom he was appointed by the Court, 1670, to serve, refused at the end of the time to fulfil the terms of the indenture, "in the matter of dubble apparel," . . . . and that the "poor petitioner prays for redress, ... for he is indeed come out of his tyme very poore & hath not wherewithall to goe to Law to recover his right."

This petition is made "*fforma pauperis.*"

The following is a copy of the indenture:[1] —

"This Indenture made and concluded this twenty day of May in the yeare of y⁶ Lord God one thousand six hundred seventy and one & in the three & twentieth year of the reign of y⁶ soveraigne Lord Charles the Second by the Grace of God of England, Scotland, France & Ireland, king, Defender of the Faith &c, Between Ensigne Thomas Chandler of the towne of Merrimack in the County of Essex in New England Blacksmith on y⁶ one part and Jacob Preston of Andover[2] with the full and free consent of Nicolas Holt of Andover[2] aforesaid, his Father-in-law by the marriage of his Mother and also with the full consent of his said Naturall mother hath and doth by these presents bind himselfe an apprentice to y⁶ said Thomas seven years to be compleated and ended accounting from the twenty-sixth day of March last past untill the said seven years next & immediately ensuing the said 26th of March 1671 shall be fully expired. During which time of seven yeares the said Jacob shall behave & demeane himself dur-

[1] *County Court Papers*, vol. xxx., p. 43.
[2] There was evidently a misplacement of the names of the towns in the writing.

ing his s⁴ apprenticeship as an apprentice or servant ought for to doe according to the usuall & lawdable customs of England in the like cases. During wh time also of seven yeares, the above named Thomas, Master unto yᵉ s⁴ Jacob, is hereby obliged & stands bound at his owne costs & charges to provide & procure for his said servant, meat, drink, cloathing, washing, and lodging with all other things convenient, necessary & sufficient for an apprentice as is usuall in England. And the said Chandler is also to learne or cause his s⁴ Apprentice to be learnt to read yᵉ English tongue perfectly to write & cypher or cast & keepe accounts sufficiently for his owne employment of a Blacksmith, if his capacities will attaine thereunto. And the s⁴ Thomas is also hereby obliged according to his owne best skill & abilitie to learne and instruct the s⁴ Jacob in the trade & art of a Blacksmith, if the s⁴ Jacob be capable of learning the same, and he shall keepe his said servant Jacob at worke upon the s⁴ trade as much as may be without damage to other necessary occasions that may fall out unavoidably to be done in a family; that so for want of time & use & instruction, yᵉ said Jacob may have no just ground to complaine of his owne want of experience or profitting under his s⁴ Master in yᵉ s⁴ Trade of a Blacksmith. Alsoe yᵉ s⁴ Thomas when the s⁴ seaven yeares are expired shall give the s⁴ Jacob two suits of Apparell from head to foot, suitable for a person of his degree, one good & hansom and suitable to weare on yᵉ Sabbath dayes, & the other convenient for yᵉ week days. The said Thomas doth bind himselfe, heires, executors, & administrators to the s⁴ Jacob his heires, & assignes to fulfill the articles herein conteined belonging to him to doe for the s⁴ servant. In witnesse whereunto yᵉ s⁴ parties Thomas & Jacob as they are severally concerned in this instrument & the articles of the same have hereunto interchangeably sett their hands & seales.

"Signed sealed & interchange-
ably delivered before
   GEORGE ABBOT JR
   ALEXANDER SESSIONS.

THOMAS CHANDLER
The Mark of
JACOB + PRESTON "

Edmond Bridges was another apprentice in Andover, at an early date. In 1656 he was presented before the Court for sundry offences. Among his misdemeanors was "lying, — saying he had got an hundred railes for Shawshin Bridge whereas it proved but 23 or thereabouts;" also the chief charge was his procuring money on pretence that it was by order of his father.

Another relic of an apprentice's service is the following, found among the papers handed down from the master, Mr. Ephraim Abbot. The original documents are now before the writer of this narrative; the painful autograph attesting the truth of the servant's statement in regard to his lack of learning: —

(Paper N? 1) — "This Indenture witnesseth that Arthur Cary of Boxford in the County of Essex in New England hath put & doth Bind his Son John Cary apprentice to Jeremiah Hunt of Billerica in the County of Midd^x husbandman and with him, his heirs, executors, administrators or assigns, after the manner of an apprentice to serve from the day of the date hereof during the term of eleven years & nine months to be compleated & ended next ensuing. During all which time the said apprentice, his said Master shall faithfully serve, his secrets keep, his lawful commands gladly every where obey; he shall not wast his master's goods nor lend them unlawfully to any; he shall not commit fornication nor contract matrimony within said term; at cards or dice he shall not play or any other unlawful game whereby his said master may be damaged, he shal not absent himself by day or by night from his master's service without leave, but in all things behave himself as a faithful apprentice ought to do toward his said master & during all his said term; and the said Jeremiah Hunt the said master for himself his heirs, executors, administrators or assignes doth hereby covenant promise to teach & Instruct the said apprentice to Read & write and cipher, well by the best way or means he or they can, Finding to the said apprentice good & sufficient meat, drink, apparel, washing, Lodging and all other necessaries both in sickness & health during the said term, and at the expiration thereof to give unto the said apprentice ten pounds currant money of the aforesaid Province and two good suits of apparel for all parts of his body; both lining & woolen sutable for such an apprentice. In witness whereof the parties to these presents have hereunto Interchangeably set their hands & the thirteenth day of December 1714 and in the first year of the Reign of our Sovereign Lord George King of England, Signed, Sealed & delivered" [There is no signature, but the paper is labelled "Arthur Cary's Indenture."]

Filed with the above is a paper written after the apprentice had served his time, he having meanwhile been transferred to Mr. Ephraim Abbot, of Andover, whom he seems to have been well pleased with as a master, if the formal paper to which his signature is affixed is any indication of his actual sentiment.

(Paper 2.) · " These may certifye all Persons whomsoever it may concern that I John Cary son of After [sic] Cary formerly living in ye Town of Boxford being Bound by my father unto Jeremiah Hunt of ye Town of Billerica in ye County of Middlesex in New England to him, his heirs, executors, administrators and assignes to serve eleven years and nine months by an Indenture bearing Date December ye thirteenth 1714 and Continuing with him some part of the Term of time it pleased my Master Hunt at my Request to assign my Indenture to Ephraim Abbot of ye Towne of Andover in County of Essex in New England oblidging him to fullfil my Indenture to me and I having continued with my master Abbot ye terme of time and being now free by my Indenture, my said Master Abbot has accordingly fulfilled my Indenture to me and every article thereof to my content and satisfaction although through my backwardness and incapacity I have not Larned to Read Wright and cypher as might be desired, though great pains has been taken with me by my abovesaid masters yet my above^{sd} master Ephraim Abbot has been so kind to me as to make it up to me in other things to my content and satisfaction, and I doe by these Presents fully, clearly, and freely acquit and discharge my above^{sd} masters Jeremiah Hunt and Ephraim Abbot of all that they were obliged to do for me by my above^{sd} Indenture and every article herein contained. In witness and Testimony hereof I have hereunto set my hand, This fifteenth day of September Anno Dom 1726. JOHN CARY.

" Witness JONATHAN ABBOT
DANIEL MOOAR.

" I John Cary above signing being informed that I was not Twenty one years old when I signed this above acquittance it being Scrupled by some whether it be sufficient to acquit my above^{sd} master Jeremiah Hunt I do now being of full age acquit and discharge my above^{sd} master Jeremiah Hunt from and of my above^{sd} Indenture having Rec^d the full of my Indenture of my above^{sd} master Ephraim Abbot as in the above written acquittance. In wittness hereof I have set my hand this 24 day of December 1726
JOHN CARY.

" WILLIAM CHANDLER }
JOHN DUNLAP } *witness* "

The same formal "indentures" were made to bind girls to service. An indenture is now at hand, dated 1771, between Samuel Pettengill, of Wilton, N. H., and Job Foster, of Andover, and Hannah his wife, whereby a child named Hannah Silver, daughter of Samuel Silver, was bound by the said Pettengill, who had taken the girl from the overseers of the poor of Andover. She was to be bound till she was eighteen, and to be provided when she should leave with two suits of apparel. She was also to "be learned to read" (nothing said about writing or ciphering, as in case of the boy).

A day-laborer or hired man of considerable notoriety in Andover and vicinity was one John Godfrey. He worked at odd jobs of various sorts, as herdsman, and at "carpentering," etc., and ultimately acquired considerable property. He is mentioned as living in various places, — Haverhill, Newbury, Andover; but about 1648 he became identified with Andover, so that the town may claim the *dis*honor of his name. It occurs more times on the county records, as plaintiff or defendant (it is perhaps safe to say), than the name of any other resident. Indeed, he is said[1] to have had more lawsuits than any other man in the colony. He is famous as the hero of the first important trial for witchcraft in Essex County, thirty-four years before the Salem delusion. He was noted for feats of strength, sleight of hand, and tricks of all sorts, and his boastfulness exceeded his power and cunning, while his quarrelsomeness was proverbial. Getting into a dispute with persons at Haverhill who owed him money, he threatened them, and threw out dark hints of judgments to fall upon their heads. They and their friends, either in vengeance or in terror, petitioned the court for his arrest on charge of witchcraft, representing that they had suffered losses in their persons and estates "which came not from any natural causes, but from some il disposed person; they afirme that this person is John Godfrey resident at Andover or elsewhere at his pleasure."[2]

The most extraordinary things were told which persons

---

[1] Upham's *Salem Witchcraft*.
[2] *Essex County Court Papers*, vol. iv. Also, Upham's *Salem Witchcraft*; Drake's *Annals*.

afflicted by Godfrey had seen and heard and suffered. The devil in various shapes had appeared; grinning devils, in the shape of bears, had terrified them; a bird had come to suck the wife of Job Tyler, of Andover, and she and others had fallen into strange fits and sickness.

The Rev. Mr. Dane used his influence in favor of the accused, and expressed his disbelief in such spiritual manifestations and witchcraft. Godfrey was acquitted, and soon he had a suit (for slander and defamation) before the court against his accusers. But to follow him from court to court would be tedious and profitless.

If the importance of the subject justified the outlay of time and pains, it would doubtless be possible to ascertain with certainty whether this John Godfrey was the same named in the following paper. That he was seems probable, as there is no record of any other person of the name in Andover:—

"This Indenture [1] made the third day of July anno Domini 1670 witnesseth y' John Godfrey of Andover in the county of Essex, planter,[2] in New England, being of good & perfect mynd & without fraud or deceit, divers valuable considerations him moving thereunto, wherewith the s⁴ Godfrey doth acknowledge himselfe fully satisfied hath given granted . . . . unto Benjamin Thomson of Boston in the county of Suffolke in New England School master all and singular my goods, chattels, implements, debts, bonds, bills, speshalties, sums of money lands, houses, clothings, whatsoever as well as moveables or immoveables of what kind . . . . soever they be . . . . my estate as well this side as beyond seas . . . . to have and to hold . . . . to enter into possession thereof immediately after the s⁴ Godfrey's decease, without any reckoning to be made or answer to any in his name

JOHN GODFREY, his marke"

After the settlers, or "planters," had laid out the town and established their homes, and provided the means for religious culture and education (which are elsewhere spoken of in full), their first care was the making and improving of roads for access to the older towns; this being essential to the comfort and safety of the new plantation. In 1647, persons were

[1] *Essex Registry of Deeds*, "Ipswich," Book IV., p. 8.
[2] Planter was the word used by the colonists, equivalent to settler.

appointed by the General Court to lay out the "way from Reading to Andover;" among them Nicholas Hoult, of Andover; John Osgood and Thomas Hale were to lay out "the road from Andivir to Haverhill," also to "viewe y⁰ river (Ipswich River) & make returne to y⁰ Corte of y⁰ necessity &. charge of a bridge." Some persons had offered to make a bridge and keep it in repair, provided that the General Court would grant them lands in the neighborhood of the river. Action was taken by the Court the next year in regard to this matter of the road and bridge. "For want of a bridge," [1] it was said, "over Ipswich river about 4 miles from Rowley especially in winter and at the springe when the waters are high, some travellers have been in great danger of drowninge, it being the common road to Andivver and Haverhill, the nearest way from the Bay by many miles to the Eastward." It was granted to Captain Keane [2] and others, to lay out the lands asked for in the place "whereabouts the bridge is to be built."

It is not to be inferred that there were bridges over the large rivers, or even over most of the smaller ones. Fording was the custom at the large rivers and at the smaller ones, except where bridges could be readily constructed.

At a later day ferries were established.

In 1653 the laying out of roads again came up before the General Court, and a committee presented the following report: —

"Whereas, by order from the Generall Court these fower towns, Ipswich, Newbury, Rowley & Andover should chose men to lay out the common highwayes for the county, from town to town, we whose names are hereunto subscribed being thereunto appoynted have accordingly done it, beginninge at the South end of Andover continuing it in the cartway neere half a mile unto a hill at the foot of the Hill called Bare hill as it is marked with trees, then cominge into the beaten way which leadeth over a playne belonging to Rowley, so leading on the South west of a pond called Five mile pond & then continuing the cartway unto a pond called Mr. Baker's pond, leaving the pond on the South & so passing a little

[1] *Mass. Colony Records.*
[2] First Captain of the Ancient and Honorable Artillery Company of Boston. He married a sister of Mrs. Anne Dudley Bradstreet.

strip of meddow & so on the cart way to Mr. Winthrop's playne & so still following the cartway on the South Side of Capt. Turner's hill & from thence the beaten way to Ipswich.

"Now half a mile short of the Five mile pond from Andover begines the way to Rowley & Newbury goinge on the beaten way of the south Side of the Bald Hills & continuinge the beaten way until it come to the uppermost Falls River then by marked trees leadinge into the cart path leadinge from Haverhill to Rowley & so on to a new field of Roweleys & from Andevour to Newbury goes on the old cart-way leaving Rowley-way at the beginning of a playne by a little swamp called Berberry Swampe & so on the old way to the Falls River & from thence straight upon the north side of Mr. Shewells high field as still doth appeare by marked trees, from thence keeping the old cart-way on the head of Cart Creeke & so running on the north side of Richard Hodges field as it is now fenced & so to John Halls bridge & so over the end of John Halls playne unto Mr. Woodman's bridge neere the mill at Newbury. Witness o' hands

    RICHARD BARKER JAMES HOW
    THOMAS HOLT   JOHN PICKARD."

There were frequent changes and laying out of better and shorter ways, the roads not being much more than rough wood paths. They are often called by this name, the "path to Newbury," the "path to Oburne."

The following is "a petition," in 1671, of the town of Salem,[1] complaining of the road to Andover: —

"*To the Honored Generall Court now Assembled at Boston, the humble petition of the Selectmen of Salem.*

"These may inform your Honers that their hath been for som years A Country Highway Laying out between Salem and Andovar the which of late is Layd out And we cannot but Judge very unequall with Respect to the Towne of Salem and prejudiciall to the Country, and we have long thought and spok with our neighbors of Andevour about finding A better way, but by Reason of Unseasonable Rains this two last Summers have been prevented of what we Intended and since by the Court of Salem, the town has been fined five pounds and is like to be fined five or ten pounds more Although we have now found a way by much shorter and so much better that will not cost a fourth part of the charge to mak it passable, as the way that was first layd out, having as

[1] *County Court Papers*, vol. xiv.

we Consider about a hundred rodd of meadow & Swamp in not much more than two myles & some of it very deep — &c" (petitioning to be allowed to lay out the "new way" which they had found)."

Imagination pictures those ancient road-makers in their lonely journeys through the forests, exposed to perils of wild beasts and of hostile Indians, who lurked about to steal, if not to kill. In these modern days a "ride through the woods" suggests something pleasant and refreshing, but when great unbroken forests extended all around, hemming in and cutting off from friendly neighbor the little communities, the woods were viewed with feelings of quite a different sort; to clear the timber and make roads were then of prime importance.

The people of Andover did not like "the newe waye" to Salem, and in turn presented[1] their grievances to the Court : —

"To ye Hon^d Court now sitting att Salem this 26th of June 1688, the petition of ye Selectmen of Andover in behalf of s^d Town humbly sheweth : That whereas ye law of ye Country allows us ye nearest and best way to every town and we being att present destitute of a way to Salem which is ye nearest Market Towne, there having been a way formerly lay^d out by Wills Hill[2] but again altered by a Committee to ye great damage and inconvenience of us ye inhabitants of Andover: it being almost impossible with a cart (which instrument inland Towns must make use of for Transportation) and ye former way being both nearer (as we have proved by measure) & far better and little charge in making of it good : Each ptickler of which Capt. Osgood, (whome we have appointed to attend this Honered Court in ye prosecution of s^d way) will further make appear our humble request to this Hon^d Court is that ye s^d old way may be settled & started that y^r Honors' humble petitioners may not be burthened any longer with such rocky impassable ways as indanger ye lives & limbs of o'selves & beasts."

The river Merrimack furnished facilities for Andover's communication with the towns along its course, and was made use of as early as 1674, between Bradford and New-

---

[1] *County Court Papers*, vol. xxxix., p. 144.
[2] In Middleton.

bury. At that time the bark *Adventure* ran up river, and Mr. Dudley Bradstreet, of Andover, sent for goods, to be delivered at Griffin's Tavern, Bradford. Failing to receive them, he served an attachment [1] on the boatman : —

. . . . "You are required in his majesty's name to attach y° body and goods of Edward Richardson jun. y° boatman & take bond of him to y° value of two hundred pounds with sufficient suretie or sureties for his appearance at y° next County Court to be holden at Salem upon y° last Tuesday in June next, then and there to answer to the complaint of Dudley Bradstreet of Andover in an action of the case for not delivering of severall goods received on board y° barke Adventure according to receipt under y° s⁴ Richardsons hand, bearing date Nov. y° 21 1673, which goods were received upon freight & to be delivered at y° house of John Griffin at Bradford as by y° said receipt will appear & for all just damage and soe make a true returne Under y° hand.

"By the Cort. DUDLEY BRADSTREET.
"Dated ye 14 *Aprill* 1674."

There were also vessels built and launched on the Merrimack at Andover. Major John March, of Newbury, an enterprising capitalist, and also prominent in military service, undertook the experiment at first : —

(Andover, town-meeting — 1697.) "Granted libertie to Maj. John March of Newbury to take what timber is convenient for y° building of two vessels not exceeding fifty tons apiece, provided he build such vessels in Andover and to use noe timber that is fitt for y° building of houses or making of posts . . . . what timber is to be felled and carted for s⁴ vessels, Andover men shall have y° benefit of, provided they will work with themselves & teems as reasonably as in other places they doe."

In 1711 Major, then Colonel, March is again granted "encouragement."

"Voted & passed that Coll. John March shall have libertie of trying the experiment of building a sloop in some convenient place for launching into Merrimack River and to have the benefit of what timber can be found already felled, and also if need be to supply him with the liberty of cutting half a dozen sticks for some choyse use for the vessel if Timber for such use cannot be found already felled."

[1] *Essex County Court Papers*, vol. xxii, p. 30.

Colonel March was called into active service in the Indian wars, and did not carry out his plan of ship-building, and the management of it was intrusted to an Andover man.

"Voted Liberty to Lieut John Aslebe to make use of the Timber which was voted for Coll. John March to build a sloop in Andover of about 40 Tons and to cutt off from the common what is still wanted to make it fitt for launching. This former vote not rightly understood in the entry and rectifyed as follows:

"Granted liberty to Lieut J^{no} Aslebe to cutt what timber is necessary for the Building of a vessel of about 40 tons."

In 1715 (perhaps earlier), there was a ferry between Andover and Haverhill.[1]

"March 1715 — Robert Swan of Haverhill[2] moving to this Court for liberty to keepe a ferry over Merrimack river having procured ye approbation of ye Selectmen of Haverhill & Andover in favour thereof Ordered that ye Said Robert Swan hath liberty & is hereby licensed to keep a ferry over Merrimack river nigh his house & from this time till further order of the Court to keep a good Classe boat for ye Transporting ye king's subjects & their horses as need may require safely. he observing therein ye Lawes of this province referring to Ferries.

Y^e fare allowed by this court is as followeth.

for man, or woman or children 2d
for horse 4d
for other creatures in proportion"

In 1735, Daniel Bodwell, of Methuen, had a ferry across the Merrimack, and made the following agreement with the selectmen of Andover to carry passengers: —

"*Articles of Agreement between Lieut Daniell Bodwell of Methuen, In His Majestys Province of the Massachusetts Bay in New England Gentleman on ye one part & Capt. Timothy Johnson, Capt. John Chandler, & Lieut. William Lovejoy. Selectmen for the Town of Andover on the other part.*

"Whereas the s^d Lieut. Bodwell hath a Ferry over Merrimack River against the Land of Mr. John Poor; I the said Lieut. Bodwell Do hereby oblige myself my Heires and assignes to carry over s^d Ferry any of the Inhabitants of Andover as Followeth

---

[1] Now Methuen, or Lawrence.
[2] The Swans attended church at Andover North Parish, and were assessed there.

(viz.) one person for a penny, a man and his horse for four pence & for other creatures as I carry them for our town."

Swan's ferry was also running at the same time, a committee being chosen by the town of Andover, in 1734, to discourse the ferry men, namely Swans ferrymen and Bodwells ferrymen to see whie Andover people may not pass s^d ferrys over to Methuen at the same price as Methuen people doth pass the ferries & Bring the terms of the s^d Ferrymen to Andover."

"The terms" were explained as in the agreement.

Not only were the travelling facilities, roads, paths, ferries, etc., a subject of frequent town action, but boundaries between towns were a fruitful source of discussion and of litigation. The amount of perambulating, or "pre-ambulating" (as the vernacular phrases it) on record is fatiguing even to read of. The lines run by "marked trees, stakes and stones," by each set of surveyors, seem to have been different from those run by their predecessors in office:—

"2nd March 1670. Whereas there is now a *difference between* our *towne and the towne* of *Woburn*, conserning the bounds between them and us, the towne hath given full power to the Selectmen to order and prosecute all measures whether by Law or otherwise to the ending all such differences and all charges to be borne by the Towne."

The following pathetic appeal indicates the distress and perplexity of the perambulators:—

"To ye Selectmen of Billerica: Loving friends and neighbors we have bine of late under such surcomstances that we could not tell whether wee had any bounds or no between our towne, but now we begine to think we have — this therefore are to desier you to send some men to meet with ours upon the third munday of ye next month by nine a'clock in ye morning, if it be a faire day, if not the next drie day and so to run one both side of the river and to meet at the vesil place and the west side of ye river.

"Andover, *March the* 21: 1688.

THOMAS CHANDLER *in ye name and by the order of ye Selectmen.*"

But one of the earliest and also one of the most interesting records of a contention about the bounds of the adjacent towns, is a petition [1] of the town of Andover, in 1658, in regard to the encroachments of the towns of Billerica and Reading. The incidental allusions to the founders of the plantation, their aims and motives, and their discouragements, also the autograph signatures of the proprietors at that early period, make this manuscript one of special interest among those of the archives: —

"TO THE HONERD GENERAL COURT NOW ASSEMBLED AT BOSTON,

"The humble petition of the Towne of Andover Humbly sheweth that the Inhabitants of this place ware incouraged to set downe here in a remote upland plantation farre from Neighbores and destitute of other conveniences that many other townes enjoy, not only out of general persuasion and assurance to obtayne such priviledges and accommodations as the Court doth ordinarily grant to ye like plantations and as the place would permit, but especially by a particular provision this honored Court was pleased to make that the great and large graunt to the Towne of Cambridge extending more than Twenty miles in length should not prejudice this plantation, yet so it falls out Much Honoured that the Inhabitants of Bilricay who through the favour and large grant of lands by this Court hath obtained the interest belonging to Cambridge doe notwithstanding presse so hard (and as we conceive) unreasonably upon us as not only to deprive us of that which we have purchased of the Indians, wth the consent and approbation of this Honored Court but also to take away part of our Meddow wh we have mowed these several yeares (of which they have little need) to the great prejudice, if not utter undoing, of some of our Inhabitants who know not whither to remove nor can this poor place (straightened for want of meadow more than most plantations) supply them wth more. We are therefore necessitated (though otherwise most unwilling to interrupt your more weighty occasions) to implore your just favour for reliefe, that by yourselves, or such as you shall please to appoint, our case may be heard & determined; and whereas the Inhabitants of Redding hath runne their Northerly lynes and marked trees for their bounds a mile or more within the limits granted to us by this Court our humble desire is that this honoured Court will be pleased likewise to Issue that differ-

[1] *Mass. Archives*, vol. cxii., p. 99.

ence also according to equity and the trew interest of the several respective graunts, and we shall humbly pray: —

"FRANCIS DANE   EDMOND FFAULKNER
GEORGE ABBOT   THOMAS JOHNSON
THOMAS CHANDLER   HENRY INGALS
DANIEL PORE   RICHARD BARKER
JOHN ASLET   JOHN STEVENS
WILLIAM BALLARD   JOSEPH PARKER
JOHN LOVEJOY   NIKLES HOULT
JOHN OSGOOD   JOHN FFRIE
                                           GEORGE ABBOT

"20th *May* 1658."

The Court granted this petition of Andover men so far as to confirm their right to thirty acres of meadow on the Shawshin River, which was claimed by Billerica. But the disputes, as we see, after more than twenty years, had not come to an end, — the Billerica people pressing their claims and making encroachments so often that, between the resistants and the claimants, pro and con, the puzzled perambulators might well say they "could not tell whether wee have any bounds or not."

When the town of Wilmington was laid out, the original bounds of Andover, Woburn, and Billerica again became a subject of dispute, and a controversy ensued between Wilmington and Andover which lasted above ten years, perambulation after perambulation being made, and the committees of the towns being unable to agree; Wilmington perambulators and Andover perambulators proceeding for a certain distance amicably and then separating in contention, — as for example: —

"Oct. 7th 1734. Then the Commity of Andover and Wilmington meet in order to preambulate the Line between Andover and Wilmington and Andover, and wee meet at Reading corner so called, whare according to the General Court Grant, Wilmington Begun with Andover; and the Commity of Andover Refused to preambulate with Wilmington Comitty unless thay would preambulate with them to a pine called Sutten's pine, which pine stands as we judg half a mile Downe upone Bildrica Line; and upone Andover Commitys Refusing to preambulate the Line, wee the Comitty of

Wilmington offered to preambulate the Line with them so far as wee Joyned upone them untill wee come to Bildrica Line."

[Signed by Wilmington perambulators.]

A tract of land long in dispute, not only by Andover claimants, but by the town of Charlestown and by Woburn citizens, was called the Land of Nod. It lay remote from villages, in a sort of wilderness region, which probably suggested to our Scripture-reading forefathers the place described as the refuge of the outcast Cain, and therefore gained its name of "Nod." A parcel of meadow in it was owned by John, Joseph, and Ephraim Abbot, of Andover, "Beaver-dam Meadow," but was claimed by Thomas Rich, of Reading, as being included in a purchase made by him from the town of Charlestown, of some two hundred and thirty acres of land in Woburn, it being the interest [1] of the town of Charlestown in the "Land of Nod." The Abbot brothers made a compromise and agreement with the purchaser, and relinquished their claim to him, but some citizens of Woburn were not so easily satisfied that the town of Charlestown had a right to dispose of this territory, and the "Land of Nod" became famous in the annals of that period's litigation.

The colonial boundaries and claims engaged the attention of Andover citizens in town meeting assembled, — the great dispute about the Mason and Gorges claims to the settlements in Maine and New Hampshire : —

"March 5th 1682 Capt. Bradstreet was chosen to goe to Ipswich ye first day of Ipswich Court, there to consult with & hear what ye Gentlemen of ye severall townes betwixt Naumkeake & Merrimack that are to meet there about Mr. Masons claims have to make report to ye same."

The claim of Mason extended to Salem, but, as appeared, without valid title.

The grants of land within the town were also a subject of discussion and difficulty, the indiscriminate giving out of lands being opposed by the more prudent. In 1674 the town took the following action on the subject : —

"Whereas there is a greate controversie in ye towne about giving

[1] The original deed is at hand.

out of land, the town therefore have chosen a committee to consider of y⁵ same to se if it be convenient to give away any more land or how & to whome ; they have therefore chosen Mr. Dudley Bradstreet, Left. Osgood, Ensigne Chandler, Goodman Barker, Goodman frie sen. Jono frie jun. George Abbot sen, Daniel Poore, Thomas Johnsin, John Lovejoy, Sergt. Steevens, to consider about y⁵ same and bring in y⁵ result against y⁵ next meeting-day."

Also the highways in the town, as well as the roads from the town, were a subject of much voting.

17th Oct. 1661. It is ordered "that every male person of sixteen years shall upon three or four days warning by the surveyor attend the mending of the highways upon forfeit of double damage for every day's neglect by any person and soe likewise everie teame, that is, every man fower shillings a day so neglecting."

In the course of time, if not at first, in order to accommodate the town, it became necessary to run roads through private lands. These were used as highways, but kept closed by gates or bars ; as, for example, in the proprietors' grant to John Aslebe : " Reserved a good and convenyant drift cartway through said land, and said Aslebee to make and maintaine good and handy gates or bares to pass & repass through forever." The following is a paper relating to the repairs of the highways in the west part of Andover, which has been kept among the papers of the citizen who received it, from the time of its date : —

"ESSEX SS. ANDOVER, *March* 25, 1746.

" To MR. EBENEZER LOVEJOY JR. *Surveyor of Highways* Greeting : —

"These are in His Majesty's Name to will & Requir you to see that each man named in this List work out the sums underneath his name on the Highways on the Months of May & June Next. On the Road that you ware ordered by the Selectmen to work on the year past, allowing each man 9*s* per day for a yoke of oxen ; 2*s* for a cart.

Eben' Lovejoy	.	.	.	.	.	.	.	1	2	0
Timothy More	.	.	.	.	.	.	.	1	7	3
John Lovejoy	.	.	.	.	.	.	.	0	15	7
Saml Blanchard	.	.	.	.	.	.	.	0	15	0
Jonathan Blanchard	.	.	.	.	.	.	0	7	2
Thomas Blanchard jr	.	.	.	.	.	.	0	5	3

Moses Hagget	0	6	9
Doc' Nehemiah Abbot	0	9	9
Stephen Blanchard	0	16	4
Benjamin Smith	0	5	0
Charles Furbush	0	5	0
Samuel Bayle	0	12	11
David Osgood	0	3	5

George Abbot
Nathl Frie
Timothy Ballard
} Selectmen of Andovir"

In granting land to Hamboro Blunt in 1718, it was excepted that there should be a "drift way through Bars for John Marston to pass and repass to his meadows and his heirs and sucksessors forever, *they always putting up the bars safe after them.*" There are many other stipulations in the records in which parties agree to maintain "good gates" across the highways that pass through their land. A deal of dismounting from horse or cart or tumbril there must have been in those days, to open and shut gates and put up bars. A journey two hundred years ago from one end of the town to the other, or from Andover to the neighboring towns, was made slowly and with many liabilities of delay, from the various causes before mentioned, the dangers of Indians and wild beasts, the bad roads, the often impassable streams, the perils of being lost in the woods in blinding storms, or of going far out of the way, misled by the imperfect landmarks of trees, stakes, and stones.

These journeys, slow and sometimes painful, necessitated many places of rest and refreshment, "entertainment for man and beast." A man in a town who had a large house often took in travellers as a matter of courtesy, and thus it happened that in some cases, especially in the early history of the towns, the innkeeper or "innholder" was one of the principal citizens. The public house was called an "inn," "tavern," or "ordinary." The owner, "innholder," or "taverner," was often a "vintnor," licensed to sell wines and strong liquors. The first on record to whom this license was granted [1] was Mr. Edmond Faulkner, in 1648, "he paying to the treas-

---

[1] *Colony Records.*

ury for what he draws, as others do." There were also, in the larger towns, persons licensed to sell liquors "out of doors," that is, to those persons who were not guests in their house as in an inn. These were called "Retailers."[1] The "taverners" kept a house of refreshment, as is supposed, without lodgings, a sort of restaurant. In Boston, in 1680, there were licensed six wine taverners, ten innholders, eight retailers for wine and strong liquors out of doors. Andover was allowed one "retailer for wine and liquors out of doors," and two public houses. The sale of liquors to Indians made much trouble, many of them, " by excessive and abusive drinking," as was stated in the act of the General Court regulating the sale of liquors, " being overcome with swinish drunkenness." The Court therefore ordered that only the most trustworthy citizens should be allowed to sell liquors to Indians, and that they should only sell what in their judgment " seems meete & necessary for their reliefe."

Deacon John Frye, of Andover, was in 1654 appointed retailer of strong liquors.

In 1689, Lieut. John Osgood was innholder. The following is a petition[2] made by him to the County Court, to renew his license for keeping a public house : — ·

" To the Honored County Corte now sitting at Salem : —

" I move to your Honers to renewing license ffor keeping a Publick house, & I would have waited upon the corte personally but a bizness of a publick nature hinders me : that is the comitee off molitiah are this day to make up the account about our soldiers & I have sent here-with my sone to pay the ffees : the granting of which will serve him who is yours to serve in whatsoever he may   John Osgood.

" Andover 27 : 9. 89 "   [Granted]

A rival innkeeper was William Chandler. Capt. John Osgood made complaint to the Court against him, that he " did retail & sell sider or strong drinke without License at his owne dwelling." Chandler produced evidence that he had a license and was acceptable to many of his townsmen, if not to all. The proof[3] of his license was as follows : —

[1] A name used afterwards for the seller of all kinds of merchandise.
[2] *Court Papers*, vol. xlviii., p. 74.
[3] *County Court Papers*, vol. xlvii.

"William Chandler Senior is recommended to yᵉ next County Court at Ipswich as a ffit man to keep a publick house of entertainment in the town of Andover and until the foresaid Court is licensed to sel Sider, bear, wine and strong liquor by me one of his Majesty's Council of his territory for New England ffebruary yᵉ 2, 1686.   JONA TYNG."

The proof[1] of his townsmen's good-will, and their wish for the success of his inn, is as follows : —

"*The humble petition of William Chandler to his Majesty's honoured Court of Sessions for the County of Essex now Sitting in Ipswich this 14 day of September 1687 humbly sheweth :* —

"That whereas your petitioner some time since obtained liberty from one of the Councill to keep a publick house of entertainment and that falling short I mayd my address to his Excellence by some friends who understanding my case induced these gentlemen to wright to the honoured Mr. Gedney and frome him to be communicated to the honered justices of Salem wherein he did expect they should grant me my License which accordingly they did while this Sessions; for the which I Render them hearty thanks and now I having in some measure fited myself for that worke and agreed with Captain Radford what customs to pay for the yeare, and it being the desier of many of my neighbors I should keep a publick house of entertainment as will appear by their subscriptions under their hands and the great complaynt of strangers that there is no house of entertainment upon that rode leading from Ipswich to Balrica and also my own necessity arising in regard of that money I was fined at Salem which I borrowed and have not payᵈ, all which considerations move to renew my License for this yeare : which will oblige your petitioner for ever as in duty bound to pray.   WILLIAM CHANDLER.

"Wee whose names are hereunder Righten : doe testifye : that we live upon the Rode at Andover that leadeth from Ipswich and the Townes that way to Baliraca and have often heard strangers much complain that there was no publick house of entertainment upon that Rode, but they must goe a mile and a elfe out of there way or goe without refreshing or else intrude upon privit houses which that neighborhood have found very burdensome. And we doe

[1] *County Court Papers*, vol. xlvii., p. 56.

humbly pray that William Chandler Senr. whose house stands convenient may be allowed for that worke

       JOHN + LOVEJOY, his marke.
       JOSEPH WILSON
       THOMAS JOHNSON
       THOMAS CHANDLER
       WILLIAM JOHNSON."

Another petition for Chandler has the signatures of thirty-five citizens of Andover; but in 1690 some of his opponents sent in the following petition,[1] rather discreditable to their townsman: —

"FROM ANDOVER ye 28: 1, 1690.
"*To the honered Court now sitting at Ipswich 31 off this instant March 1690.*

"Wee your most humble petitioners in the name of many more, if not of most of the town do make our address to your honors to exert so much of your power and authority as may release us of the matter of our greivance wch is grown so much an epidemicall evill that overspreads and is like to corrupt the greater part of our towne if not speedily prevented by your help: viz to put a stopp to William Chandler's license of selling of drink, that had been licensed formerly by authority: he had indeed ye approbation of the selectmen that were *pickt out for that end* in his first setting up: y^t were men spirited to give him their approbation to such a thing, and indeed at his first setting up he seemed to have some tendernesse upon his conscience not to admit of excess nor disorder in his house; but custom in his way of dealing and the earnest desire of money hath proved an evil root to him actively and effectively to others, for through his over forwardness to promote his own gaine he hath been apt to animate and to entice persons to spend their money & time to ye great wrong of themselves and family they belong to; and to that end will encourage all sorts of persons both old and young to spend upon trust, if they have not money, & to some he will proffer to lend them money to spend rather than that they should be discouraged from such a notion; servants & children are allowed by him in his house at all times [2] unseasonable by night and day, sometimes till midnight and past & till break of day, till they know not their way to their

[1] *County Court Papers*, vol. 1, 74.
[2] William Chandler was not alone in being complained of for this offence. Thomas Johnson, a constable, was charged with "allowing a barrel of cider to be drunke in his house at unseasonable hours by young people." One of the

habitations, and gaming is freely allowed in his house by which means the looser must call for drink wch is one thing y^t will uphold his calling : Many such pertiklers might be instanced and easily proved, but we be willing for brevity's sake to omitt much of what might be said of the like nater, but be sure if he be not restrained from the selling of drink our town will be for the greatest part of our young generation so corrupted thereby that wee can expect little else but a cours of drunkenness of them ; and what comfort will that be to parents to see such a posterity coming on upon the stage after them ? To this wee whose names are underwritten as your humble petitioners doe attest by our hands hereto.

        CHRISTOPHER OSGOOD   JAMES FRIE
        JOHN FRIE SEN   JOSEPH LOVEJOY
        JOHN FRIE JUN   SAMUEL FRIE
        SAMUEL BLANCHARD   BENJAMIN FRYE
        EPHRAIM FOSTER   SAMUEL ROWELL
        JOSEPH ROBINSON   THOS OSGOOD "

But the friends of William Chandler had got the start in the matter of petitioning, as appears from a record appended to this petition : "*This petition came not to the viewe of the Court untill after another was approved of.*"

The "other" referred to was doubtless the following certificate to the good order of Chandler's house : —

" William Chandler senr of Andover hath kept a house of publick entertainment for some considerable time past & hath kept good order in s^d house (soe far as wee are informed) & being an infirm man & not capable of hard Labour & deserving of approbation for his continuance in that employment we cannot but judge him a meet p'son for it & his house convenient for travellers.

" Dated ANDOVER ye 21st March 1689–90

                              DUDLEY BRADSTREET
         Selectmen   THOMAS CHANDLER
             of   HENRY HOULT
         Andover   JOSEPH BALLARD
                              JOHN ABBOT "

town treasurers was before the court for drunkenness and disorderly behavior. A prominent citizen was presented on a charge of being under the too great influence of liquor, although Mr. Bradstreet, the magistrate, termed it "some weaknesse that overtooke him." So we see that strong liquors were not so much " better " than they are now, or the community more temperate.

He was granted a license, and in 1692 was permitted by the selectmen to continue his house until such time as he might be regularly licensed by the Court: —

"These may certifye any that may be concerned that whereas the Towne of Andover (by reason of ye change[1] of Government) are destitute of an ordinarie for ye reliefe of strangers &c wee ye subscribers being ye selectmen of Andover aforesaid doe judge William Chandler Senr of s^d towne to be a meet person for ye aboves^d imployment he having been some years allready imployed in that service & gave good content soe far as we know.

"Dated Andover ye 29. Aug 1692 att a meeting of ye Selectmen then and wee doe alsoe order him to entertain strangers &c till ye Court or such as are appointed doe otherways determine." [Signed by the Selectmen.]

William Chandler's license is an interesting document, and curiously illustrative of the customs of the time and of the aspect of things in Andover. It will be noticed that the sign of his house was the *horse-shoe*, chosen, doubtless, from the occupation of the Chandlers — blacksmiths. It was the custom then to designate shops, public houses, and places of resort, not by numbers, but by hanging out a sign. A large town had a great variety of signs (as was the custom in England), the "anchor," the "bell," the "horse-shoe," etc. The only mention found of any such sign at Andover is this of the horse-shoe:[2] —

"Know all men by these presents, That we William Chandler as principle & Andrew Peters & George Herrick Suretyes do acknowledge ourselves to owe & be justly Indebted unto our Sovereign Lord and Lady KING WILLIAM AND QUEEN MARY, their Heirs and Successors, for the Support of their Majesties Government here, the sum of Fifty pounds for the true performance of which payment well and truly to be made we bind ourselves and each of us our and each of our Heirs Executors and Administrators firmly by these Presents, Sealed with our Seals, Dated in Salem, this 17 Day of Jan^ry 1692.

"The condition of this Obligation is such, That whereas the abovesaid William Chandler is admitted and allowed by their Maj-

[1] There being in the colony no authority for granting a formal license.
[2] Files of Court Papers.

esties Justices at a General Sessions of the Peace to keep a common house of entertainment and to use common selling of ale, beer, syder &c till the General Session of the Peace in .... next in the now-Dwelling-house of said Chandler in Andover commonly known by the sign of the horse-shoe and no other, If therefore the said William Chandler during the time of keeping a Publick House shall not permit, suffer or have any playing at *Dice, Cards, Tables Quoits, Loggets, Bowles, Ninepins, Billiards* or any other *unlawful Game* or *Games* in his house, yard, Garden, or Backside; nor shall suffer to be or remain in his House any person or persons not being of his own family *upon Saturday nights after it is Dark*, nor at any time on the *Sabbath* Day or Evening after the Sabbath, nor shall suffer any person to *lodge* or *stay* in his House above one day and one night; but such whose Name and Surname he shall deliver to some one of the Selectmen or Constables or some one of the officers of the Town unless they be such as he very well knoweth and will answer for his or their forthcoming: nor shall sell any Wine or Liquors, to any *Indians* or *Negroes* nor suffer any servants or apprentices or any other persons to remain in his house Tippling or drinking after nine of the clock in the night time; nor buy or take to Pawn any stolen goods, nor willingly harbor in his said House, Barn, Stable or otherwhere any Rogues, Vagabonds, Thieves, nor other notorious offenders whatsoever nor shall suffer any person or persons to sell or utter any *ale, beer, cyder* &c by Deputation or by colour of this License and also keep the true assize and measure in his Pots, Bread and otherwise, in uttering of *ale, beer, cyder, wine, rum* &c, and the same sell by sealed measure. And in his said House shall and do use and maintain good order and Rule: Then this present obligation to be void or else to stand in full Force Power and Virtue.

" Signed, sealed and delivered WILLIAM CHANDLER
 in the presence of   GEORGE HERRICK
  JONATHAN PUTNAM ANDREW PEETERS "
  STEPHEN SEWAL.

Andrew Peters, the bondsman of William Chandler, afterward became innholder on the death of Chandler. He came to Andover from Ipswich (as seems probable) between 1686 and 1692, and had a still-house, and was a "retailer." The following record [1] shows these facts: —

[1] Files of Court Papers.

"This may certifye any that may be concerned y^t Mr. Andrew Peeters (now an inhabitant in Andover)[1] being lately burnt out by ye Indians & put by his husbandry & being a stiller of strong liquors by his calling & having sett up his still-house in ye towne of Andover we the subscribers being ye selectmen of Andover doe desire & judge it a benefit to ye towne y^t he may have liberty to retaile his liquor by ye quart out of his owne house to the house-holders of ye Towne or others which he may think have need of it. We judging him a man carefull of observing law & good order in those matters.   DUDLEY BRADSTREETE
                  JOHN ABBOT   } Selectmen
                  JOHN ASLEBE   } of
                  SAMUEL FRIE   } Andover.
                  JOHN CHANDLER

"ANDOVER ye 21 December 1692"

There is also, later, a petition to the Court for Mr. Peters to be innholder, he "being one of the selectmen and our town-treasurer."

The following names are found among the innholders licensed: —

Edmond Faulkner		1648 a vintnor
John Frye		1654 vintnor
Lieut John Osgood innholder		1689
William Chandler "		1687–1699
Andrew Peters "		1700–1713
Joseph Parker "		1714
Joseph Parker 2nd		1715–1723
John Frye senr		1723
Joseph Parker 3d		1735
Capt James Frye		1745

Timothy Poor was an early innholder also.

These inns were not like those with which the last generation was familiar in the days of stage-coaches, and the bustle of the arrivals and departures of the regular coaches, the relays of horses, and all the commotion of the hostlers and the servants, and the important and obsequious host. These most ancient inns had no regular arrivals of vehicles or

---

[1] "Andrew Peters of Ipswich." — *Registry of Deeds*, "Ipswich," Book I., p. 681.

guests. The chance-travellers going to and from Salem, Ipswich, Boston, either on horseback or on foot, to attend Court, to go to market, to visit,— in short, the whole community who went on any errand whatever, must make use of the inn for a greater or less period of time, so that a thriving business was done. The deputies to the General Court, and the other various officers of the Colonial Government, made no small part of the patronage of the inns and taverns. Some of the innholders suffered from the delinquency of their guests in paying their bills. Joseph Armitage, of the Anchor Inn, Lynn, makes a petition concerning "Sum expences at my hous by the Honered Magistrates and deputies of this County which I never received." The "honored magistrate" from Andover had a small account with Armitage, and also had some law-suits against the innholder for indebtedness to himself for goods ; for Mr. Bradstreet did a considerable trading business in shipping lumber to the Barbadoes and exchanging it for West India goods, which he sold to parties throughout the county. His memorandum of his debts to the Anchor Inn landlord is as follows : —

"Due to Goodman Armitage for beare or wyne att severall times as I came by in the space of about three years . . . . 4s. 3d"

"MAY 15, 1649.

"More for my man and horse as hee returned home the last year when I was a commissioner, hee having been delayed on Sabbath day . . . . . 6s. 3d"

There were unwelcome guests, travellers at this early time from town to town, — vagrants, the prototype of the modern tramp. One of these, in 1665, paid a visit to Andover, was arrested, and sent to jail ; also one John Upton, at whose house he spent a night, was tried for harboring him and receiving stolen goods. Thomas Johnson, constable of Andover deposed [1] as follows : —

"Henry Spencer coming to the house of John Upton the said Upton told this deponent that he brought a pack with him to his house, in which was a coate, a rapier, two bibles, a payre of French

[1] *County Court Papers*, vol. x.

fall (?) shoes & other things "—that "he lay at his house one night & the next day he sett him on the way to Andover & carried his things from his house with him & further this deponent saith that Edward Hutchinson told me that he came to his house the same day in the afternoon without any pack."

The movements of military companies, or of soldiers going to join the companies to march against the "Indian enemy," or of scouts and rangers, was also a considerable feature of the travelling of the colonial period, and there was no small stir and flutter in the domestic inns when the young officers, with cutlass and halberd and head-piece, musket and pike, and the various paraphernalia of the military outfit, arrived and tarried for entertainment, and told the tale of their own heroism or their comrades' exploits. One such company stopping at the inn of Joseph Parker, of Andover, were, as tradition says, "sumptuously entertained," and a soldier, John Varnum, of Dracut, afterward took to himself Miss Phebe Parker, the innkeeper's daughter, for his wife; from which marriage was descended General Varnum of Revolutionary fame.

It was a not uncommon thing to have marriage ceremonies performed at the inn, it being the largest house and most convenient for a wedding-party or merrymaking; the relish for which festivities the colonists had not all laid aside when they quitted the shores of Old England.

It was against the too great hilarity that sometimes arose, when the "strong liquors" of the inn, or ordinary, had circulated freely on such bridal occasions among the rustic guests, that the Great and General Court fulminated its edicts, before quoted, prohibiting "dancing in ordinaries on occasions of marriage."

Apropos of the ancient weddings, the first recorded marriage of an Andover citizen is that of the first settler, Edmond Faulkner : —

"Edmond Faulkner and Dorothy Robinson married at Salem by Mr. John Winthrop. 4 Feb. 1647."

George Abbot married Hannah Chandler, sister of Thomas Chandler, "at Andover, 1647," says Abbot's "Genealogical

Register;" but this is not on the town records, and Ellis's "History of Roxbury" says that George Abbot married in that town Mary or Hannah Chandler. (The Chandlers came from Roxbury to Andover.) The first record of a marriage ceremony in Andover is in 1653.

"Henry Ingolls & Mary Osgood were married at Andover 6 July 1653 by Mr. Simon Bradstreet."

It is to be noted that these marriages were made by the magistrate, according to the Puritan doctrine that marriage is a civil compact, and not a church sacrament. In 1678 Captain Dudley Bradstreet was appointed by the General Court, "to joyne persons together in marriage at Andover one or both of whom being settled inhabitants there & being published according to law" (that is, in the house of God on a day of service). This Puritan custom of "publishing did much to throw around the ordinance of marriage the sanctity of a religious rite; and moreover, in those times the magistrates were expected to be among the most religious men of the community, so that the institution of marriage was by no means reduced to that merely secular plane and bare civil contract which it is sometimes represented to have been. In the most public and solemn manner, before the whole congregation, on the Sabbath day, the announcement must be made of the intention of marriage, and in a modified form this custom of publishing in the house of God continued in the town for two hundred years; after the custom of reading the names from the pulpit was discontinued, the names of the persons intending marriage being posted in the vestibule of the meeting-house in a small closet with a glass door, called the "publishing-box."

The following are the first ten records of marriage in the town register: —

1647. Feby 4. Edmond Faulkner & Dorothy Robinson married at Salem by Mr. John Winthrop.

1650. Oct. 20. Daniel Pore & Mary Farnum married at Boston by Mr. Wiggins.

1651. Jan. 1. John Lovejoy & Mary Osgood[1] married at Ipswich by Mr. Simons.

[1] The Osgood family had a branch in Ipswich.

1653. July 6. Henry Ingolls & Mary Osgood married at Andover by Mr. Simon Bradstreet.
1653. Nov. 15. John Osgood & Mary Clemants married at Haverhill by Mr. Robert Clemants.
1654. June 14. Mr. Seaborn Cotton & Mrs. Dorothy Bradstreet by Mr. Bradstreet.
1657. Thomas Johnson & Mary Holt married by Mr. Bradstreet.
1658. Jan. 6. Thomas Eaton & Unity Singletary married by Mr. Bradstreet.
1658. Apr. 26. George Abbot & Sarah Farnum married by Mr. Bradstreet.
1658. June 12. Nicholas Holt & Hannah Pope widdow.

"Mrs." Dorothy Bradstreet, whose name is here given, was the daughter of Mr. Simon Bradstreet. The title "Mrs." was simply a term of respect, and had no reference to the marriage relation, — a lady of high social standing, whether married or single, being addressed as Mistress, or with the abbreviated form Mrs.

How proposals of marriage were made and preliminaries settled in good society, we learn from a statement [1] of Mr. Simon Bradstreet, in reference to the marriage of his daughter Mercy to Major Nathaniel Wade, of Medford, which took place 31st October, 1672: —

"When Mr. Jonathan Wade of Ipswich came first to my house att Andover in y⁐ yeare '72 to make a motion of marriage betwixt his sonne Nathaniell and my daughter Mercy he freely of himself told me what he would give to his sone. . . . . After he came home hee told several of my Friends & others that hee had offered to give his son better than one thousand pounds and I would not accept of it."

Notwithstanding these disagreements of the fathers at first, they finally came to a mutually satisfactory arrangement of terms, and "soe agreed that the young p'sons might p'cede in marriage, with both our consents, which they accordingly did."

Another relic [2] is found of the prudence of the elders in regard to the worldly prospects of the young persons: —

[1] *Essex County Court Papers*, vol. xliii., p. 66.
[2] *Ibid.*, vol. lii., p. 116.

"The testimony of Thomas Chandler aged about 64 and William Chandler aged about 56 (1692) who say: that about tenn years since Andrew Allen of Andover junior who was a sutor to Elizabeth Richisson an shee being related to Major Thomas Hinchman and Cap. Josiah Richisson both of Chalmsford they came to Andover to the hous of William Chandler abovesaid and Andrew Allen Senier being present: the foresd hinchman and Richison asked the foresd Andrew Allen Sanier what he would give his sonn for incorridgment for a livelihood and that which he then promised upon the contrict of marriage was: That he would give his hous and land lying about three miles from the town and the meadow belonging to it, and halfe his orchard at hom, and after his and his mothers decease he should have all his house & land at Town and the home meadow that belong to it."

The wedding festivities in the great families of colonial time were not unattended with display; and the extravagance of the ladies and the varieties of the toilet on these and other social occasions were the subject of comment of writers of the time. The Rev. Nathaniel Ward gave his views of some of the styles of fashionable dress, in plain language:—

"If I see any of them accidentally I cannot cleanse my phansie of them for at least a month after."

As to the folly of women whose great desire is to "find out the latest fashion, and to inquire what dress the queen is in this week," he says:—

"I look upon her as the very gizard of a trifle, the product of a quarter of a cipher, the *epitome of nothing*, fitter to be kickt if she were of a kickable substance, than either honored or humored."

Undoubtedly new fashions and fine clothes found their way to Andover as soon as to any of the inland plantations; for the Bradstreet family maintained correspondence with the nobility of England, and Mr. Bradstreet, often sending, had every facility for obtaining as elegant dress as the taste, good sense, and religious principle of his household would permit them to wear. Mrs. Bradstreet was a lady whose literary tastes kept her from inordinate love of dress; and moreover she was in feeble health, and from principle also indisposed to great display. Still, the relics handed down in this family show that they had rich furniture and apparel. Nor was this in disagreement with the sumptuary laws of the Puritans. These were directed mainly against the wearing of expensive clothes by unsuitable persons at improper times. An act of the General Court, 1651, is as follows (admitting the suitability of fine clothing in some cases) : —

"Although we acknowledge it to be a matter of much difficultie to sett down exact rules to confine all sorts of persons, we declare our utter detestation and dislike that men or women of *meane condition educations & callings* should take uppon them the *garbe* of *gentlemen*, by the wearing of gold or silver lace, or buttons or poynt at their knees, to walk in great bootes [leather was very costly] or women of the same rank to weare *silk* or tiffany hoods, or scarfs, which though allowable to persons of greater estates or more liberal education, yet wee cannot but judge it intolerable in p'sons of such like condition. . . . .

"It is ordered that the selectmen of every towne . . . . are hereby enabled & required to assesse such persons so offendynge in any of the particulars above-mentioned, but any magistrate or officer their wives and children are left to their discretion in wearynge of apparel."

Mrs. Bradstreet's neighbors thought her too little interested in dress. They criticised her writing so much, and said it would be more becoming in her to use the needle than to have her pen always in hand; but doubtless her daughters, on social occasions of importance, when visitors from out of town — their connections the Dudleys, and their friends the Winthrops, and the President of the College, and other dignitaries — were guests, made no little display of elegant attire. Brocade and ruff, and lace, velvet, gold lace, point, buttons, were not wanting when the Puritan aristocracy were gathered to do honor to the wisdom of the magistrate, the genius of his poet-wife (the "tenth Muse sprung up in America," as one of the scholars called her), and the beauty and virtues of the daughters. Mr. Simon Bradstreet, when he went over to England in 1661, on his mission to the court of King Charles II., we may be sure, appeared in the presence of royalty in no homespun garb, and it is more than likely that he did not return without many a purchase or present of the fabrics of the old country for his family.

But, as has been before said, there were great distinctions in dress in the different classes of society. The wardrobe of a well-to-do yeoman, a century after Andover settlement, was the following : —

"*A True Inventoree of y*ᵉ *personal estate of Capt. Samuel Osgood late of Andover His wearing apparel :* —

 A Red coat & Breeches
 A Blue coat & Breeches
 A Dark green coat & Jacket
 An Old white Coat
 A Camlet Coat & Jacket
 2 Fustian Jackets
 1 Blue great coat
 1 Old pr plush Breeches
 1 Fine Linnen Shirt
 3 Cotton do
 3 old Cotton do
 3 pr worsted stockings
 2 pr yarn
 2 old Hats
 3 pr old shoes
 5 neck bands
 1 Silke Handkerchief
 2 Walking Staffs
 1 pair shoe buckles."

The termination of one wedding contract of old Andover was tragic. "In 1689, died Hannah wife of Hugh ——,[1] *murdered* by her husband April 20, 1689." In respect to this, Savage's "Genealogy" says : —

"Hugh —— Andover m. 15 Oct. 1667 Hannah Foster perhaps d. of Andrew. had John born 1668 and others . . . . from the records we find the death of his wife 2d Apr. 1689 murdered by her husband, whence it is safe to conclude that he was insane."

Cotton Mather, in the "Magnalia," gives a detailed account of the execution of one of this name, undoubtedly the same man, for murdering his wife, and says that the particulars were told him by a minister, who attended the prisoner on

[1] It is not known that there are any descendants in the town, yet to avoid an erroneous connection with names now existing, but not related, the name is suppressed.

the scaffold. Although such details are not, ordinarily, pleasant or profitable reading, still, forming as this does a part of the famous "Magnalia" of Mather, it cannot properly be passed by. The account here presented is much abbreviated: —

"One Hugh —— upon a Quarrel between himself and his wife about selling a Piece of Land having some Words, as they were walking together on a certain Evening very barbarously reached a stroke at her Throat with a sharp knife and by that one stroke fetched away the Soul of her who had made him a Father of several children and would have brought yet another to him if she had lived a few weeks longer in the world. The wretched man was too soon surprised by his Neighbors to be capable of denying that Fact and so he pleaded Guilty upon his Tryal. There was a Minister that walked with him to his execution; and I shall repeat the Principall Passages of the Discourse between them in which the Reader may find or make something useful to himself, whatever it were to the Poor man who was more immediately concerned in it."

The conversation of the minister with him on the scaffold is repeated, in which he inquires if the prisoner is now prepared to stand before the tribunal of God, and on receiving an answer that he having repented of his sin, hopes that he is, the clergyman examined him still further to ascertain whether he had repented of the sin *of Adam*, for which said he you "deserved to be destroyed as soon as you first came into this world." The prisoner seeming to have doubts, or not to be quite clear on this point, the minister instructed him and demonstrated that he had broken every commandment of the Decalogue. Going on to inquire what led to this commission of murder, the prisoner made answer: —

"It was Contention in my Family. I had been used to something of Religion, and I was once careful about the Worship of God, not only with my Family but in Secret also, But upon Contention between me and my wife I left off the ways of God and you see what I am come to."

The prisoner from the scaffold made an address to the company: —

"Young men and maids. Observe the Rule of Obedience to

your Parents; and Servants to your Masters, according to the Will of God and to do the will of your Masters: If you take up wicked ways, you set open a Gate to sins to lead in bigger afterwards. Thou canst not do anything but GOD WILL SEE thee, though thou thinkest thou shalt not be catched. . . . .

"O *young woman* that is married and *young man*, look on me here! Be sure in that solemn engagement you are obliged to one another. Marriage is an ordinance of God: have a care of breaking that bond of Marriage Union. If the Husband provoke his wife and cause a Difference, he sins against God and so does she in such carriage; for she is bound to be an obedient wife.

"O you Parents that give your children in Marriage remember what I have to say. You must take notice when you give them in marriage you give them freely to the Lord. . . . . Here is this murderer; look upon him, and see how many are come with their eyes to behold this man that abhors himself before God. . . . . There are here a great many young People and O Lord that they may be thy servants. . . . . I will tell you that I wish I never had had the opportunity to do such a murder. If you say when a Person has provoked you 'I will kill him,' tis a thousand to one but the next time you will do it. . . . ."

He then intimates that it was under the effect of strong drink that he gave way to his passion:—

"When thou hast thy head full of drink, remembrance of God is out of thy heart. I have cause to cry out and be ashamed of it, that I am guilty of it because I gave way to that sin more than any other and then God did leave me to practice wickedness and to murder that dear woman whom I should have taken a great deal of contentment in; which if I had done, I should not have been here to suffer this Death."

The author of the "Magnalia" adds this brief description of the melancholy end of the life of this first murderer in Andover:—

"After this he was by the prayers of a minister then present recommended unto the divine mercy, which being done, the poor man poured out a few broken ejaculations, in the midst of which he was turned over into the Eternity which we leave him in."

Having now gained a general idea of the mode of life in primitive Andover, and an acquaintance with some of its principal citizens, we resume the review of such few memorials as are found of the other first settlers.

Mr. EDMOND FAULKNER was one of the few honored with the title "Mr." He, with Mr. Woodbridge, negotiated the purchase of the plantation from the Indians. He was, as has been already stated, the first whose name is recorded as a licensed vintner.

One of his daughters was married to Capt. Pasco Chubb, and with her husband was murdered by the Indians.

His son, Lieut. Francis Faulkner, married Abigail Dane (daughter of Rev. Francis Dane), who was accused of witchcraft and condemned, but reprieved, and finally saved from hanging by the influence of friends, who interposed to check the delusion.

A grandson of Francis Faulkner removed, when a boy, with his parents to the town of Acton. He was Col. Francis Faulkner, of Revolutionary fame, who led the company to the fight at Concord Bridge in 1775, and commanded the regiment that guarded General Burgoyne's army when prisoners of war.

One branch of the Faulkner family settled in the South Parish. A recent representative of the name was Joseph Faulkner, who, in 1825, engaged with Mr. John Smith (Smith, Dove & Co.) in the manufacture of machinery at Andover. His son, Joseph W. Faulkner, studied divinity in the Theological Seminary, 1838. Abiel Faulkner was a soldier of the Revolution and of the War of 1812. There is an ancient house on one of the early Faulkner homesteads at North Andover, which is said to be more than one hundred and seventy years old. It is at Marble Ridge, southeast of the homestead of Gen. William J. Dale. It is of quaint construction, and has been apparently but little changed from its original style. The sloping roof in the rear, the exact southern front, the heavy beams in the ceilings, the huge chimney in the middle of the house, the staircase going up in the front entry to the garret, the little cupboards nicked in at odd corners over the mantel-piece, the small windows high above the floor, and other peculiarities of construction indicate that it belonged to the colonial period. It was last owned by Joseph Faulkner. In 1789 his daughter, Dorcas Faulkner, was "married by Rev. Mr. Symmes to Mr. John Adams Jr." (as the town records note); "Major" Adams, the bridegroom was afterward commissioned. The Faulkner estate subsequently was sold to Benjamin Fish, and is now owned by an aged couple from Marblehead. With their stores of goodies, apples, hickory-nuts, cranberries, etc., gathered about them in kitchen and pantry, their flower-pots of chrysanthemums, and "jelly"-flowers in the window, their bird-cage on the floor, and their china and glass-ware set up for show in the parlor cupboard, the shelves nicely covered with newspapers, the pictured looking-glass, with its battle scene of the *Constitution* and "*Guirèar*," as described by the hostess, the ancient house and its occupants seem a relic of the old times, veritable *genii loci*.

Another Faulkner house is near by, whence emigrated Daniel Faulkner to Bluehill, Maine, and Dr. Joseph Faulkner to Hamilton.

GEORGE ABBOT, Senior, married Hannah Chandler, at an early period in the town history. She was sister of Thomas Chandler, and daughter of William Chandler, of Roxbury. The descendants of George Abbot, Sen., have been very numerous and influential. They include, among others, John Abbot, deputy to the General Court, 1701; Dea. Isaac Abbot, graduate of Harvard College, 1723; Abiel Abbot, graduate of Harvard College, 1737, who died while fitting for the ministry; Dr. Abiel Abbot, surgeon in the French and Indian wars; Capt. John Abbot, of the French and Indian War, and of the Revolutionary War; Capt. Henry Abbot and Capt. Stephen Abbot, in the Revolutionary service; George Abbot, Esq.; the three sons of Capt. John Abbot (all eminent graduates of Harvard College), namely, Prof. John Abbot, of Bowdoin College; Benjamin Abbot, LL. D., Principal of Exeter Academy, and Rev. Abiel Abbot, D. D., minister of Haverhill and Beverly; also, Rev. Abiel Abbot, D. D. (native of Wilton, N. H.), author of the "History of Andover," 1829; Mr. Henry Abbot, graduate of Harvard

College, 1796, trader of Andover, father of the late Henry W. Abbot, trader; Rev. John Lovejoy Abbot, graduate, 1805, and Librarian of Harvard College, and minister of the First Church, Boston; Samuel Abbot, Esq., one of the founders of the Theological Seminary, and many others of honorable name. The manufacturers, Messrs. Abel and Paschal Abbot, were well known at Andover, 1815–1837.

The descendants of George Abbot, Sen., on the two hundredth anniversary of the settlement of the town, erected a monument to his memory in the South Church Burying Ground.[1]

> GEORGE ABBOT.
> Born in England,
> Was one of the first settlers
> of Andover A. D. 1643
> Where in 1647 he married
> HANNAH CHANDLER.
> He died Dec 1681 æt 66
> She died June 1711 æt 82
> Their descendants
> in reverence for their moral
> worth and Christian virtues
> Erected this monument
> A. D. 1843.

The will of George Abbot[2] is noticeable for its tribute to the fidelity and virtues of his wife.

"Considering the great love & affection I beare unto my loving wife Hannah Abbot and also considering her tender love and respect she hath had to me and also considering her care and diligence in helping to gett and save what God hath blessed us withall, and also her prudence in management of the same, I doe therefore leave my whole estate to her & for her use during the time of her naturall life and at her death my will is that with the advice of my overseers . . . . shall dispose of my estate that her necessity doth not enforce to spend amongst my children." . . . .

It was also the will of the father that if "any of the sons

---

[1] He was buried, doubtless, at North Andover, as there was no other burial-place when he died.
[2] *Essex Registry of Deeds*, vol. iv., p. 44.

should be guilty of disobedient carriage " toward their mother, they should be "cutt short " in their portion.

The "overseers" alluded to were "my loving brothers Thomas Chandler & William Chandler & my loving friend John Barker."

The will was signed 12th December, 1681. The inventory of the estate was £587 12s. 5d.

Some facts, culled from the "Genealogical Register," are of general interest, showing the marriage connections made by the children [1] of George and Hannah Abbot, with the sons and daughters of the other first settlers, from which unions sprang at least seventy-three grandchildren : —

John, b. 1648, m. 1673 Sarah, dr. of Richard Barker.
George, b. 1655, m. 1678 Dorcas, dr. of Mark Graves.
William, b. 1657, m. 1682 Elizabeth Gray, dr. of Robert (?)
Benjamin, b. 1661, m. 1685 Elizabeth, dr. of Ralph Farnum.
Timothy, b. 1663, m. 1717 Mary Foster . . . .
Thomas, b. 1666, m. 1697 Hannah Gray.
Nathaniel, b. 1671, m. 1695 Dorcas Hibbert.
Hannah, b. 1650, m. 1676 John Chandler, son of Thomas.
Sarah, b. 1659, m. 1680 Ephraim Stevens, son of John.
Elizabeth, b. 1673, m. 1692 Nathan Stevens, son of John.

The mother of this family, the widow Hannah Abbot, became the third wife of the Rev. Francis Dane. She was, at the death of her first husband, fifty-two years of age. There is before the writer an original deed of " HANNAH ABBOT *alias* DANE." It is the only deed found in which a woman alone conveys real estate. It was made, of course, after the death of both her husbands. The paper is as follows : —

"Know all men by These presents that I Hannah Abbott: *alias* Dane Relick to gorg Abbott late of Andover deceased for the natural afectean I bare to my sons : Timothy : Thomas : and Nathaniel Abbott : doe give to my sons : above named : all my rights in the common and undivided land in the Township of Andover aforesaid : which doth or may heareafter belong to the lott of my former husband : gorg Abbott late of Andover deceased : To have and to hold the abovesaid . . . . [and so forth in legal tautology]

[1] Other children died, — one infant, Joseph ; one son, Joseph, slain by Indians, 1676.

"Whereto I have hereunto set my hand and seal: this: 10: of February: 1706–7.

JOHN CHANDLER
ABIALL CHANDLER
HANNAH CHANDLER

The mark of
HANNAH (H) ABBOT
Alias DANE

"ESSEX
"Mrs Hannah Dane the relict of Mr francis Dane personally appeared in andeure this 2d of December 1707: and owned this above written Instrument to be Hir voluntary act and deed before me.
THOMAS NOYES
Justice of the peace."

John Abbot, the eldest son of the first settler, George Abbot, was the first deacon of the South Church. He died 1721. He made his will 1716. It and the wills of John Abbots, third, fourth, and fifth generation, are in possession of Mr. John Abbot, seventh generation, who lives on the homestead, and is the seventh John Abbot who has lived there. This homestead is in Andover South Parish, on Central Street, west of the South Church. Doubtless George Abbot, Sen., removed thither from his first residence at the north part of the town (some time before 1676, if the family tradition be correct, that this was the scene of the Indian attack in April, 1676).

The will of John Abbot gives some particulars respecting the mode of life of the wife and mother in early time at Andover, — the "relict," as she is styled : —

"I order my executors to take the whole care to provide for their honoured mother, after my decease. first, she shall have the liberty of which roome she pleases for to live in, and my executors to provide for her sutable clothing of all sorts, for Lining and wooling, and meat, drinke and washing and firewood and candels; the wood to be cut and brought into the house, and phisicke and tendance in case of sickness, and whatever she wants for her comfort so long as she remains my widow if it be to the day of her death, and at her death, I order my executors to give there honored mother a decent and Christian Burial, If she dyes my widow, but if she shall se Reason to marry again then my executors to be free from what I have ordered them to do for her."

One of the daughters, Priscilla, received a portion of the

THE EARLY HOME OF REV. DAVID OSGOOD, D.D.
[*Where James Otis was killed by lightning.*]

ANCIENT HOMESTEAD OF THE ABBOTS, D. VINES AND SCHOOLS
["The old Red House," built in 1705, taken down in 1858.]

property, for which her receipt (with *autograph* signature) remains : —

"*May* 5, 1722 Received of my brothers John Abbot & Joseph Abbot executors, tow cows and six sheep which was given to me by the will of my honered father John Abbot late deceased
                                        PRISCILA ABBOT "

Priscilla Abbot was never married. She is the first of whom any special record remains of the great company of "old maids" of Andover. In point of age she stands first. At her death, she lacked only a few weeks of being one hundred years old. She was born 1691, 7th July; died 1791, 24th May. She was of great service as a nurse in Andover families. She is described as "mild and meek, kind and cheerful, industrious, pious, and contented."

A grand-niece of this estimable woman, Sarah Abbot, daughter of Ephraim Abbot, was another remarkable single woman. She was "help" in the family of the Hon. Samuel Phillips, North Andover. After his death, she took care of the farm, — raised a nursery of a thousand trees, which she grafted and sold profitably. She lived to the age of ninety-four (1737-1831). She was a large, strong woman, as able for out-door work as housework. She was blind before she died, and being unable to give up her out-door exercise, used to walk by a rope.

The names of these women are not selected as representative of the women of the Abbot family, or of Andover, or as models, but simply given as the few which, from their being out of the ordinary course of woman's life, have become traditional. Those who from choice or necessity stepped aside out of the beaten path of woman's dependence are, as a consequence, conspicuous, while the names of others, many of whom were equal in merit, and superior in mental and social culture, are lost in oblivion, or are kept only in the unwritten memory of family affection and reverence. The only printed memorial of the mother of Prof. John Abbot, Dr. Benjamin Abbot, and Rev. Abiel Abbot, D. D., is a sentence that she was a woman of " good understanding, sound discretion, active benevolence, and unfeigned piety." It is high praise;

and yet it might, no doubt, truly be said of hundreds of women of this name and of other names who are unknown, because the unobtrusiveness of their lives and the custom of the time have kept them from finding a record.

Besides the ancient homestead of George Abbot, Sen., that of his son, Timothy Abbot, is of special interest. It is now owned by Mr. Asa A. Abbot, and Mr. Sylvester Abbot, who hold the original deeds of its transmission from the first occupant. Timothy Abbot was, when a lad of thirteen, carried into captivity by the Indians. [See Chapter II.]. Mr. Asa A. Abbot, now eighty years old, remembers hearing his great-grandmother (who had seen Timothy Abbot) tell the legends of his captivity and of his suffering from hunger.

A volume would hardly suffice to trace the descent and the topics of historic interest in connection with the Abbot name in the line of George Abbot, Senior.

JOHN FRYE was one of the settlers who was of great note in his day, and had a posterity of distinguished reputation. An ancient manuscript pedigree makes the following summary : —

"Mr. Fry was one of the first settlers in this Towne and his offspring men of Grate Note ; there was Copprils, Sergeants, Clarks, Ensignes, Lieuts, Twelve Captains, Magrs, Cornels and Mager Generals, Two Judges of the Corts Superer and Court of Common Pleas and two that had the titel of the Honoral Counsellors and severall justices of the Peace and some of the Rest Excelen Good Citizens."

Among the eminent names were Chaplain Jonathan Frye, mortally wounded in Lovewell's fight, 1725 ; Capt. Nathaniel Frye, representative, 1743 ; Col. James Frye and Gen. Joseph Frye, of the French War and Revolutionary service ; Col. Peter Frye, resident in Salem, a Tory and refugee ; Hon. Simon Frye, who settled in Fryeburg, Me. Mr. Frederick Frye was a prominent citizen of North Andover about 1800 and thereafter. Mr. Enoch Frye now lives on one of the ancient homesteads ; the house was built about 1730 by "Great John Frye," who weighed three hundred pounds. "Frye Village" was named from Samuel Frye (and his descendants), owner of a mill there about 1720. Mr. Theophilus C. Frye, one of the descendants of Samuel Frye, and son of Theophilus Frye (owner of the estate now the residence of Mr. John Smith), has written a pedigree of the Frye family. Other representatives of the name are Mr. Nathan Frye, lately treasurer of the Marland Manufacturing Company; Newton Frye, Esq., representative to the Legislature for North Andover, 1879.

BENJAMIN WOODBRIDGE. It has been conjectured by some persons that this name on the list of first freeholders was an error, and should have been John Woodbridge, the minister. But ministers had no house-lot rights, and, moreover, the name of Benjamin Woodbridge occurs on the lists of persons assessed for ministers' rates again and again, but with his rights or estates credited to another man, "*alias* Thomas Chandler." This shows that he had left the town. He was undoubtedly the distinguished brother of Rev. John Woodbridge, the first graduate of Harvard College, whom President Dunster called the "most honorable of his class," and whom Cotton Mather named "Leader of the Whole Company, A Star of the first magnitude," and of whom Calamy says: "He was a great man every way, the lasting glory, as well as the First Fruits of that Academy."

When he graduated from the college there was probably no special opening for him that promised better than the new plantation which his brother had an interest in, and he, it is not unlikely, at once secured house-lot or acre rights, which he might do by a brief residence. In 1647 he went back to England and resumed his studies at Oxford, where he took his second degree. He entered the ministry, and became minister of a church in Newbury, England, but he was for a time silenced for his non-conformity. He, however, afterward was allowed to continue his office, and he gained a great reputation for learning and eloquence.

His house-lot rights at Andover remained in the possession of Thomas Chandler. In 1724, some descendants of the Rev. John Woodbridge laid claim to house-lot rights, but their claim was disputed by the proprietors, and there is no evidence that it was allowed.

About 1750 there were Woodbridges living in Andover, and it is supposed they were descendants of the Rev. John Woodbridge. This I have not verified. A private of Andover in the Revolutionary service bore the illustrious combination of names, Dudley Woodbridge. This family is still in the town, but, since the departure of the two eminent brothers and ministers, the name has been inconspicuous in the town history.

RICHARD BARKER is the only citizen *known* from the records to have been in the town in 1643. His name is connected with the first[1] recorded business transaction, and hardly any town affair of importance for fifty years is on record which does not bear his name as party or witness, petitioner, etc. He was prominent in church matters, chosen in ecclesiastical committees, was selectman again and again, and was entrusted with the administration of many estates. He lived near the house-lot of John Osgood, on the north side of Cochichawicke. His descendants ultimately settled on their farm lands; the several families of Barkers circling almost the entire shore of the Great Pond, on the north, east, and south.

The son of Richard Barker, John Barker, was one of the first deacons of the North Church. Lieut. John Barker was quartermaster during the Indian wars. The title is given him in the epitaph on his gravestone, 1751.

Private John Barker, in the battle of Bunker Hill, was the hero of his company, and displayed a coolness and bravery which have given him a name more honorable than titles.

A brother of the soldier, John Barker, was the Hon. Stephen Barker. He was born 1771, died 1849; was representative to the General Court seven years between 1812 and 1824; was a member of the Convention for revising the Constitution, 1820; and member of the Council, 1825. Others of the name, native or resident of Andover, have been Dr. Charles Otis Barker, graduate of Harvard College, 1822, a physician in Nashua, N. H., and Lynn, Mass.; Mr. John Barker, of Michigan City and Chicago (died 1878), who made a large fortune in the manufacture of railway cars and in the

[1] See page 7.

grain trade; Jonathan Tyler Barker, an eccentric man of saving habits, a peddler and trader, who left a large bequest of money to found a free school in Boxford; Mr. Stephen Barker, a graduate of Cambridge Divinity School, 1856, pastor of Leominster, and chaplain in the United States service in the War of the Rebellion. Other members of the Barker family, in several branches, have been rich and respected farmers in North Andover, and their descendants are among the young men of influence in the town.

"DANIEL POORE and Mary Farnum were married at Boston, Oct. 20, 1650." The estates of the Poor family lay along the Shawshin River, at North Andover, on the old road to Lawrence. The house still stands on the right bank of the river, which was occupied by the third generation, from Daniel Poor, and it is said that not far from here was one of the block houses, built in "Shawshin Fields" by order of the Colonial Government in 1704.

The will [1] and inventory of Daniel Poor were on record 1689: —

"In the name off God Amen : I Daniel Poor senr. of Andover in the County of Essex in New England Husbandman, being at ppsent of a sound mind & memory though very sick of body, & considering ye dangerousness of my disease & not knowing how soone my great change may be, have thought it meet & doe accordingly make this my last will and testament in manner & form following : ffirst I bequeath & resign my soul unto ye hands of god that gave it & my body to be decently interred in the earth from whence it was taken, in hope & firm assurance of ye pardon of all my sins & of a blessed and happy resurrection through the alone meritt & mediation of my Lord & Saviour Jesus Christ. And as for my worldly goods and outward estate, whether real, personal or mixt, (my just debts & funeral expenses being discharged) I give & bequeathe in manner following.

Imp. I give and bequeath unto my dear wife Mary my dwelling house with all my household stuff & ye one half of my Land on this side Shawshin River both arable land, pasture land & mowing ground, together with my whole stock of neat cattle, sheep, swine & horses. (and alsoe above two thirds of my kort

[1] *Essex County Court Papers*, vol. xlix., p. 32.

yard) Barn and corne upon ye ground & what provision I have in ye house & what money I shall leave out of this aboves'd estate I would have my aboves'd wife as soon as conveniently she can pay to my daughter Ruth twenty pounds & to my daughter Lucy twenty pounds. Confiding in my s^d wife that she will deal by them as well as she hath by her other daughters; and after that she will pay all my honest and just debts and receive what is due to me after, I give my sd wife all my husbandrie tackling of what kind or nature soever & after my Dear wife's decease ye abovesaid Land shall goe to my eldest son Daniell.

Imp. I give to my son Daniell ye other half of my land on this side of Shawshin river (excepting three acres I have given to my daughter Martha which her husband has built upon & mostly improved) alsoe a parcell of lowe ground on ye west side of Shawshin river being bounded with the highway & land of John Granger, ye River & ye Common: my sayd son Daniell paying within two years after my Decease ten pounds apiece to my Daughters, Ruth & Lucy in good merchantable pay att ye current price.

Itt. To my son John all my upland . . . . with the meadow-ground.[1]

. . . .

As for my daughters Mary, Sarah, Hannah, Deborah, they have already received their full portions according to intent & ability.

Itt. I give to my daughter Martha twenty acres of land . . . .

Itt. I give to my daughter Elizabeth all the meadow I have in Wade's meadow . . . .

Itt. I give to my daughter Priscilla my meadow on the west side of Shawshin River commonly called the Pond meadow.

Itt. To my daughters Ruth & Lucy who are yet unmarried, I give forty pounds to each of them to be paid as is before exprest.

Itt. I give to my brother in law Jno ffarnum a Parcell of meadow — two acres . . . . on furthest side of Woodchuck meadow . . .

Itt. I constitute and appoint my two sons Daniell & John Poor to be my executors, Desiring and commending them according to their ability to be help full unto their mother as her necessity shall require, Hereby making void all former wills or writings of this nature.

As witness my hand & seal this 1st day of June in the year of our Lord sixteen hundred eighty nine.

His mark
DANIEL + POOR

[1] The will is here abridged, only an outline given to indicate noticeable points.

"Signed & sealed DUDLEY BRADSTREET
in presence of   THOMAS BARNARD
                 CHRISTOPHER OSGOOD.

"Mr. Dudley Bradstreet, Mr. Tho. Barnard & Christopher Osgood made oath in Court att Salem 24th June 1690 that they were present & Saw Daniell Poore signe seall & declare ye above written to bee his last will & testament & y^t he was of disposing mind to ye best intent and understanding.

Attest BENJ. GERRISH, Clerk."

It is interesting and instructive to compare the inventory of this estate of a first settler, who had lived nearly fifty years in the town, with the inventories of the two other first settlers who died, the former within ten, the latter within twenty years of the first planting of Cochichawick. The third, and latest, is noticeably larger than the two earlier ones, and indicates a much greater degree of luxury in household furniture : —

Imp. To apparell & purse,
Itt. To bedding & furniture with bedsteads cords & malts,
Itt. To a pair of curtains & Vallons,
Itt. To bed linen, sheets & pillow beers,
Itt. To table-linen clothes & napkins & towels,
Itt. To 20 yds of new cloth unmade with bed linen,
Itt. To Iron pots, brass kettles, trammels tongs &c.,
Itt. To chests, boxes, wooden ware, tables chaires &c,
Itt. To arms & ammunition,
Itt. To flax, hemp, wool, feathers, & other things overlooked,
Itt. To books,
Itt. To provision, wheat, rye, Indian corn &c,
Itt. To mowing grass,
Itt. To husbandry, tackling, old iron, boards &c,
Itt. To stock of cattle, horses, sheep & swine,
Itt. To Housing, barns & kort yard,
Itt. To about 100 acres of upland, mowing ground and pasture (£250),
Itt. To about an hundred acres of wilderness Land,
Itt. To meadowe at Woodchuck meadowe,
Itt. To meadowe over Shawshin river,
Itt. To meadow part of his last Division,

Sum Total £756. 14s. 8d.

Among the principal names of this family were the distinguished officers of the Revolution, Col. Thomas Poor, of Andover (North) and Methuen, and Gen. Enoch Poor, of Exeter, N. H., a native of North Andover. Others of considerable local influence were Dea. Daniel Poor, a wealthy farmer of Andover (South Parish), owner of the "Captain Perry House,"[1] Andover, which he built for his residence; Dea. Joseph Poor, who lived at Danvers, father of the Rev. Daniel Poor, D. D., one of the early missionaries to India; the late Mr. Henry Poor, merchant, of New York, some time resident of North Andover. George H. Poor, Esq., trial justice, Andover, attorney and counsellor at law, Boston; Mr. Albert Poor, graduate of Harvard College, 1879, and many others of the name are well-known and respected citizens. In the present city of South Lawrence, the "Shawshin Fields," during the Revolutionary time, Mr. John Poor was a large landholder and a man of influence. In that region, in the pre-revolutionary time, lived Timothy Poor, innholder, and after the Revolution, down to 1800 or thereabouts, Ebenezer Poor and Benjamin Poor kept the inn known subsequently as the "Shawsheen House." Capt. Stephen Poor had a fulling mill about 1800, at the mouth of the Shawshin River.

NICHOLAS HOLT was a town officer of some note, and a man of considerable estate, yet he oftener made his mark than wrote his name, although there is one instance found when he with difficulty signed his autograph to a petition. An original deed is before me by which, in 1680, he conveyed about twenty acres of upland to his son-in-law, in consideration of the

"Naturall Love and affection I bear unto my daughter Sarah not long since married unto Roger Marks." &c.

his
NICHOLAS H HOLT.
mark

This settler was, however, the progenitor of a line of descendants noticeable for their attention to learning. The

[1] Central Street, now owned by Mr. Lyman A. Belknap.

Holt family includes four college graduates prior to 1800: Joseph Holt, son of Timothy, graduate H. U. 1739, teacher of the Andover Grammar School; Rev. Nathan Holt, graduate H. U. 1757, minister of Danvers; Moses Holt, graduate H. U. 1767, trader at Portland; Rev. Peter Holt, son of Joshua Holt, Esq., graduate H. U. 1790, minister, Epping, N. H.; also, in 1813, Jacob Holt, son of Dane Holt, graduated at Dartmouth College, and ordained at Brookline, N. H.

During the Revolution, Joshua Holt, Esq., commanded a company of minute-men, April 19, 1775; was representative to the General Court fifteen times between 1776 and 1800, and several times thereafter, was justice of the peace and deacon of the South Church thirty-four years. His homestead is south of the West Parish Meeting-house. His son, Solomon Holt, was among the first deacons of the West Church, and was succeeded in office by his son, Dea. Solomon Holt, now in the fiftieth year of his office, and in the eighty-first of his age.

The Holt family, in all its branches, is very large, and includes many names of considerable influence in town affairs. The most ancient dwelling-house, now disused, was the residence of the late Mr. Dean Holt (owned by Mr. Ballard Holt), on Holt's Hill, sometimes called Prospect Hill, Andover. There is a tradition that it was the dwelling-house of Nicholas Holt, the first settler, or that it was built more than two hundred years ago. Its style of construction does not correspond with that of the houses known to have been of that age in the town; but there is little doubt that Nicholas Holt lived, if not in this house, on this homestead at some period. In the beginning he, like all the first householders, dwelt on one of the house-lots at North Andover; but from a paper found among the manuscripts of the Abbot family (with which the Holts intermarried), it appears that in March, 1675, the land around the house of Nicholas Holt had not been laid out, and that it was not one of the original four- or eight-acre lots bounded by the house-lots of other settlers. The presumption is that he had then built a house out of the village on his farm lands; and it is not unlikely that he and George Abbot, Sen., and other settlers, took up their abode about the same time in the south part of the town. The clause in the paper in regard to the highway "going *up*" to his house is an unusual form of expression in the ancient descriptions, and seems to imply a *height* of land, and to point to this ancient homestead as the one referred to. The following is the paper: —

"We whose Names are under-written being desired and deputed by y* Town of Andover To state or New Marke Nicholas holts senr his Land about his house, we have agreed and stated the Bounds as under-written (viz) The Southwest corner in the fence there is a walnut tree marked; from Thence we Run upon a straight Line to a white Oak Tree upon a straight Line To a white oak marked with H: which we judge to be near an Easterly Line from y* white Oak marked with H. To a Black Oak marked which Line is southerly: from that Black oak we Ran westerly To a black oak standing in y* fence Near the highway going up to his house and from Thence to the First named Walnutt: as the fence Now standeth and To these our agreement we have sett To our hands y* 8 off 1st month 167¾

"Vera Copia out of Andover Book of Records for Land.

CHRISTOPHER OSGOOD *Clerk*."

At the ancient dwelling-house now standing on the estate, Mr. Bache, of the Coast Survey, spent some weeks to obtain outlines of the coast, the view from the hill being one of the most extensive in the vicinity. This hill is said to have been, on the 17th of June, 1775, thronged with citizens, anxiously watching the flames of Charlestown.

THOMAS CHANDLER and WILLIAM CHANDLER stood among the most influential of the first settlers. They were brothers, sons of William Chandler, of Roxbury. Their sister Hannah was the wife of George Abbot, Sen., and of the Rev. Francis Dane. There were four different representatives to the General Court of the Chandler name in the first century of the town history, — Ensign Thomas Chandler, 1678; Captain Thomas Chandler, 1690; Captain John Chandler, 1704; Mr. Thomas Chandler, Jr., 1735. The descendants [1] of the Chand-

---

[1] A *Genealogy*, written by Dr. Chandler of Worcester, is a work of great research, and in many parts of graphic interest.

ler name, in Andover and in other towns of the State, have been numerous and honorable.

Thomas Chandler — the representative, 1678 — was a blacksmith, ultimately a rich man, carrying on considerable iron works, of which he makes mention in his will, giving to each of his sons a fourth part of his share in the iron works. It is traditional, though not authenticated, that these works were on the Shawshin, at or near the present site of Marland village.

There is before the writer an original deed of the first settler, Thomas Chandler, which has been kept in the family of the "party" to whom it was given. Thomas Chandler wrote a quite handsome hand, but his wife made "her marke." This deed classes him as yeoman. It conveys to John Abbot, "for nine pounds currant money, one end of a meadow commonly called Beaver dam meadow lying in the bounds of Andover about six miles southward from the Towne of Andover and contayneth about six Akers be the same more or less bounded south west with the meadow of Joseph Balard and a beaver dame, east with Oburne lyen" (and so on, the other bounds being marked trees). This deed is dated November 25, 1684.

William Chandler, brother of Thomas Chandler, kept an inn on the Ipswich road to Billerica. His troubles with some of his townsmen have been previously related. Thomas Chandler's son Thomas was likewise representative to the General Court. The Chandlers were military men of considerable local fame in the Indian wars, Captain Thomas Chandler doing some service in scouting.

Ensign John Chandler was famous for his athletic prowess and strength. He was a great wrestler, and loved to challenge to the contest any one who boasted of skill in this art, formerly so fashionable. But he met his match in the Rev. Mr. Wise, of Ipswich, who, at first declining the contest as improper for his profession, at last yielded, and, taking his opponent off his guard, with a "trip and a twitch," threw him high over the garden wall, which was built against an embankment.

Another story, which has some elements of improbability,

is that, having been impressed for military duty in the king's service in the French and Indian wars, he was walking beside the officers on his way to the place of rendezvous, when, coming to a cellar of a house which had been burnt, and where the ashes were still smoking, he seized and threw into the hole the two officers of guard and went his way. This [1] Ensign or Captain (afterward) John Chandler settled at Concord, N. H.

One of the ancient homesteads of the Chandlers, connected with names of note, is in the West Parish, northeast of the Meeting-house, owned by Mr. Joshua Chandler. It is now of large extent, and was anciently larger, including the estate of the late Mr. Joseph Chandler. The Chandlers were regardful of education, some of them in their will making provision for the liberal education of their sons at "the college." In the first century of the town history there were three graduates of Harvard College, ministers, of the Chandler name, all of whom were of some considerable note in their time : Rev. James Chandler graduated 1728, settled at Rowley ; Rev. Samuel Chandler graduated 1735, settled at York, Me. ; Rev. John Chandler graduated 1743, settled at Billerica.

Other names of more or less note are Philemon Chandler, conspicuous in town affairs during the Revolutionary war ; Capt. Joshua Chandler, representative to the Legislature, 1817 (whose homestead was the one mentioned in the West Parish, north of the Meeting-house). Among his sons were Mr. John Chandler, of the firm of Chandler & Co., dry goods merchants, Boston, and Mr. Nathan Chandler, of the firm of Monroe & Chandler, bankers, New York. Mr. Joseph Chandler, Jr., son of Joseph Chandler (the owner of a part of the ancient West Parish homestead), died in the United States service, at Ship Island, 1861, a young man of great promise. The family is large, and has many other locally influential names, besides a wide connection of distinction in other towns.

[1] Such seems to be the statement of the genealogist. Possibly it was a son of Ensign John Chandler.

JOHN LOVEJOY and Mary Osgood, of Ipswich, were married 1651. Their son, William Lovejoy, settled in the South Precinct, and was one of the first deacons of the South Church, 1711. There are sixty members of this name on the lists of the South Church before the West Parish was set off. The name has been perpetuated chiefly in the South and West Parishes. The families there have been among the good yeomanry, upholders of order, sobriety, and religion. In the west part of the town, the homesteads of Deacon John Lovejoy, Deacon Ballard Lovejoy, and the late Deacon Ebenezer Lovejoy, are within a short distance of each other, about a mile west of the Meeting-house. Among the conspicuous names of this family were Capt. Nathaniel Lovejoy, in the Revolutionary period, and his son, Gen. Nathaniel Lovejoy, a graduate of Harvard College 1766, a trader at North Andover; also Capt. William Lovejoy, of Andover (South). Among the emigrants from the town were the late Deacon William R. Lovejoy, East Boston, and the late Mr. Joseph Lovejoy, founder of the firm of Lovejoy & Sons, carpet merchants, Boston. The ancient homestead of Deacon Ebenezer Lovejoy is now owned and occupied by Mr. Isaac Carruth. Some of the family papers show the transmission of estates from the year 1692. In 1876 the widow of James Lovejoy, mother of Dea. Ballard Lovejoy, died, in her one hundredth year, in remarkable possession of her faculties of mind and body.

ANDREW FOSTER, the first, as it seems, of the many of this name in Andover, died 1685, aged 106, or thereabouts. His will leaves to his "deare and loving wife Ann Foster the use & sole liberty of living in that end of my house I now live in." This aged woman ended her days in Salem jail, under condemnation for witchcraft. Abraham Foster, son of the above, had estates in the southwest part of the town, and, either from him or from his father, Foster's Pond probably received its name. A deed dated 1721, signed Abraham Foster, Junior, conveys land on the southerly side of Foster's Pond, from the "great Ridg and Reeding medow and to Nod line to a littel Brook that Runs into foster pond."

The name of Foster in the Andovers has sprung from several sources, and to trace their origin and descent would be a work of much genealogical research.

One of the prominent names in the early town history was Ephraim Foster. He was a grandson of Reginald Foster, a citizen of Ipswich of some consideration, and who is said by genealogists to have been descended from an ancient family of Forster mentioned by Walter Scott in his tales and ballads of Scottish border warfare. Ephraim Foster was a man conspicuous in the town matters of Andover, although not connected prominently with the military or the civil history. He seems, judging from the numerous documents in his handwriting, to have excelled as a scribe, and to have been versed in the art of punctuation, then little known to the majority of our town officials. His favorite point was the colon, with which his papers are plentifully besprinkled, without regard to the grammatical or rhetorical construction. This characteristic appears in the "Proprietors' Records," where his handwriting occurs.[1]

Some of the family estates were in the east part of North Andover. On one of the ancient homesteads (that afterward occupied by J. M. Hubbard, Esq., and noted for the large and beautiful elm tree, still vigorous) was born one of the most eminent of the natives of North Andover, the Hon. Jedediah Foster, son of Ephraim Foster. After graduating at Harvard College, 1744, he studied law and settled in Brookfield, was prominent as a statesman before the Revolution, and a distinguished patriot in the Revolutionary struggle. He was justice of the Court of Common Pleas and of the Superior Court. He died 1779. The names of his descendants have been among the most honored, and of national reputation. His son was the Hon. Dwight Foster, of Brookfield, United

---

[1] The following record in his handwriting, which is remarkably clear and legible, illustrates this peculiarity: —

"At a Lawfull metting of the proprietors of the town of Andover: on the: 21: day of desember: 1714: By virtue of a warrant from Collonal Samuell Appleton: Esquier one of his majesties: justises of the peece for the county of Essex . . . . Ephraim floster was chosen the proprietors clerke: for ye year ensuinge: or untell Another: is chosen and sworne in his Rome And was then sworne: Before: Joseph: Woodbridge Esquire:" etc. — *Prop. Rec.*, i., p. 8.

States Senator, who died 1823. His grandson is the Hon. Dwight Foster, of Boston, Of the Ephraim Foster line of connection are Moses Foster, Esq., cashier of Andover Bank, and Mr. David Foster, sometime mayor of Beloit, Wisconsin, sons of Mr. Moses Foster, the well-known innkeeper of North Andover fifty years ago.

Other representatives of the Foster name in North Andover were Rev. Stephen Foster, son of John Foster, a graduate of Dartmouth College, 1821, a home-missionary and teacher in the Southern States, and afterward resident in North Andover; and Isaac Foster, graduate of Dartmouth College, 1828. Mr. Daniel Foster and Mr. John Foster were traders of North Andover many years. The latter, now living, was also postmaster. The name is now represented by some of the most enterprising farmers in the town, among them, especially, Mr. John Plummer Foster has an excellent farm, formerly owned by his father, Dea. Charles Foster, near the Great Pond, and is well known in local affairs.

The homestead of Daniel Foster, Dr. Simon Foster, and their three sisters (on the north side of the Great Pond) was, at the death of the last sister, about sixteen years since, by mutual bequest left to be sold for the benefit of the Andover Theological Seminary and Missionary Societies. It is now owned by the Hon. William A. Russell, of Lawrence, who has enlarged and improved it at a great outlay of money and labor, so that it is now one of the finest and most noted farms in the county.

William Foster, of Rowley village (Boxford), also a descendant of Reginald Foster, in 1678 removed to North Andover, and subsequently to the west part of the town. Among his descendants were the brothers, Capt. Asa Foster, of the French War service, and Ensign John Foster, active patriots of the Revolution. A son of Capt. Asa Foster was Rev. Abiel Foster, minister of Canterbury, N. H., 1761, who entered into politics and became celebrated in his adopted State, was appointed Justice of the Court of Common Pleas, and elected member of the United States Congress. One of the homesteads of this family was not far from the West Meeting-house, — near the present residence of Mr. Charles Shattuck, — where an inn or public house was kept. Of this line of descent — grandson of Capt. John Foster — was Mr. William Foster, who kept a boarding-school for boys in Andover, South Parish, about 1794–1817, and who was father of the late William P. Foster. Other well-known citizens of the name were Capt. Thomas C. Foster, proprietor of the Eagle Hotel, and representative to the Legislature, 1838, and his son, Rev. Thomas E. Foster, a teacher in Phillips Academy. Among others of the name now prominent in Andover are Hon. George Foster, editor of the "Andover Advertiser" department of the "Lawrence American," and his son, George W. Foster, Esq.; town clerk; Mr. William H. Foster, connected with the Boston Public Library, and Mr. Joseph W. Foster, son of Capt. Thomas C. Foster, merchant of Boston.

WILLIAM BALLARD was a considerable land-owner, though not so much in public offices as some of the first settlers. His son, Joseph Ballard, was constable in 1688, and has the fame of bringing the first charge of witchcraft against Andover citizens. Joseph and John Ballard were the first who started a fulling-mill in Andover. The Ballard mill is often mentioned in the ancient records. Timothy Ballard was a large land-owner about 1790, in the district afterward named the Ballardvale.

Hezekiah Ballard was an innkeeper of Revolutionary time. Some of the Ballard descendants, emigrants from Andover, have engaged successfully in manufactures.

JOSEPH PARKER and NATHAN PARKER were citizens of much consideration. Joseph Parker owned a tannery and had a corn-mill. His property was apprized at "546 pounds sterling, the dwelling-house 68 pounds, the corn mill on the Cochichawick 20 pounds." In 1678 he made his will [1] ("considering my great age and infirmity"), appointing as overseers of it "my loving brother Nathan Parker, my loving friend Left. John Abbot, my loving friend Henry Ingalls, and loving friend Ensigne Thomas Chandler." After bequests to his sons, Stephen, Samuel, and Thomas, he makes bequests

---

[1] *County Court Papers*, vol. xxx., p. 24.

to Mary, Sarah, and Ruth, his daughters, and "to my deare wife (Mary) I give all my estate in old England, that of Rumsey and any legacies left me by friends." Afterward the son petitions that he may be allowed to take charge of money come from England to his mother, as she was incapable "of managing it by reason of distemper of mind." The name of Mary Parker is that of one of the Andover women hanged for witchcraft in 1692, and there is a probability that she was the same person here alluded to, and that her mental disorder tended to heighten the public belief in her complicity with evil spirits — in practising witchcraft.

Joseph Parker, 2d, to whom the corn-mill was left, made his will[1] in 1684. He was a carpenter. His property was apprized at 402 pounds sterling; the mill at 100 pounds. He bequeathed it absolutely, with every part, "to my deare and loveing wife Elizabeth till my only child Joseph shall come to the age of twenty-one years." He was an innholder, as was also his son, Joseph Parker, 3d. The latter was representative to the General Court.

Capt. James Parker and Capt. Peter Parker, sons of Joseph Parker, 3d, were prominent citizens and officers in the French and Indian War.

Mr. Isaac Parker kept a public house at North Andover, about 1800.

Nathan Parker, first settler, had not a large estate, yet he seems to have been a man of some consequence. He drew up a great many papers, as, for instance, that of the apprentice Job Tyler before alluded to. He may have been a professional scrivener; there were men of this trade or profession in the colonies, and although their learning, or technical skill, might give them some advantage, they would not be likely to get riches in a small country town. Whether or no Nathan Parker was a writer, he was not a reader, or owner of many books. His inventory[2] has the following items: "Bridle, sadle, and pillion, pewter, glass bottles *and bookes*," — all valued at two pounds. The entire inventory amounted to 148 pounds sterling.

[1] *Court Papers*, vol. xlii., p. 56.
[2] *Court Papers*, vol. xxxi., p. 95.

Two sons of Nathan and Mary Parker were killed by the Indians at Scarborough. Nathan Parker left his whole estate to his wife, "for the education and bringing up of Mary ye daughter of ye deceased til she come of age & then she is to have half the estate." The unusual circumstance of mentioning the education of a daughter would imply, on the part of the father, a special interest in learning.

The name of Parker has been connected prominently with Boxford Parish, members of which were residents of North Andover. Among these, Capt. Asa Parker, deacon of the Second Church, was a prominent citizen during the Revolutionary period.

ROBERT BARNARD, the first settler, had a house-lot and dwelling near Mr. Simon Bradstreet's. Stephen Barnard was a weaver. The descendants removed to the west part of the town, and the ancient Barnard estates lay along the Merrimack River.

Robert Barnard, a grandson of the first settler, had a lawsuit with the Proprietors of Andover for some years, 1715–1720. The following is the first mention made of it in the "Proprietors' Records":—

"At a lawful meeting of the Proprietors of ye common and undivided Lands in Andover on the 27: day of June 1715 Capt. George Abbot was chosen moderator for said meeting.

"Voatted and passed to chuse agents or attornies to defend our wrights against Robert Barnard Administrator to the estate of his grandfather Robert Barnard formerly of Andover desest at the next Inferer Court of Common pleas to be holden at Salem the Last Tuesday of June Currant for the County of Essex.

"Capt. James Frie, Mr. John Ames and Mr. William Foster was chosen agents and attornies for the proprietors of Andover for the Service abovesaid to defend their Rights from Cort to Cort."

The Barnard name has not in this line of descent ever been prominent in the town history, though the citizens have been men of some local note in their places of abode. The oldest representative of the name now living in Andover is Mr. Osgood Barnard, of the West Parish, aged eighty. He is an old-fashioned shoemaker, and in his neat little shop in the front yard of his comfortable dwelling-house, seated on his bench, surrounded by the various implements of his craft, all in perfect order, he receives with simple dignity his visitors, and talks with more good sense on current topics and past events than some men talk who wear broadcloth and sit with dignitaries in seats of honor. On the shelf above his bench is a small but well-read pile of books, ancient school-readers, old memoirs, hymn-book, and the Bible. The village mail has sometimes been sent here for distribution, so that the shoemaker is also a sort of postmaster. If Andover had a Mr. Longfellow the little shop and its owner might have found an immortality like that of the village smithy under the spreading chestnut tree.

The name of Barnard is among those locally well known in several parts of Andover. The name is in some of the branches continued, probably by descendants of the Rev. Thomas Barnard; but in none of the lines of descent has it attained eminence in the town history since the colonial period.

ANDREW ALLEN was constable at an early day in Andover. He had a son, Andrew Allen, whose suit to Elizabeth Richardson and his father's "incorridgement for a livelihood" have been already described.[1] There is before me an original deed, given by this Elizabeth Allen after her husband's death, — one of the few in which a woman is the principal. In this deed the widow, jointly with the children, gives the quitclaim.

". . . . Elizabeth Allen Relect of Andrew Allen, and Elizabeth, Andrew and Sarah Allen . . . . all of us Relect and cheldren of Andrew Allen . . . . know yee that wee ye said Elizabeth and my three children Elizabeth Andrew and Sarah Allen &c" [after this and other repetition supposed to be needful to legal dignity, the main fact is arrived at] "for eighty nine pounds we the abovesaid . . . . granted, Remised, Released and quit claimed to Ephraim Abbot their part share and dividend of that Mescuage or Tennament where ye abovenamed Andrew Allin formerly lived, containing about twenty two acres in the homestead . . . . and . . . . (other land) near Flaggy Meadow."

[1] Page 77.

Four red wax seals, with an elaborate stamp, — an S and a star, and other emblems, are appended to the document, and the marks of the widow and the daughters, and the autograph of the son: —

       her
  Elizabeth X Allen. [Seal.]
       marke

       her
  Elizabeth E A Allan. [Seal.]
       marke

  Andrew Allin. [Seal.]

     her
  Sarah S A Allin. [Seal.]
     mark

The daughter of Andrew Allen, Sen. (first settler), was married to Thomas Carrier, and was hanged for witchcraft. Another daughter, married to Roger Toothaker of Billerica, was murdered by the Indians.

Of the other first settlers on the list, the following are said [1] to have had no descendants in the town fifty years ago: Henry Jacques, Richard Blake, Thomas Poor, John Russ, John Aslet.

The will of John Aslet is preserved in the "County Court Papers" (vol. xvii., p. 105).

"The last wil & Testament of me, John Aslet upon the 15th day of the third month 1671, being in perfect memory blessed be the Lord.

 Francis Dane.   }   John A Aslet."
 Alexander Sessions.} witnesses. his marke

The family names in the first list of freeholders, which have now all been referred to, are as follows: *Abbot, Allen, Aslet, Ballard, Barker, Barnard, Blake, Bradstreet, Chandler, Faulkner, Foster, Frye, Holt, Jacques, Lovejoy, Osgood, Parker, Poor, Russ, Stevens, Woodbridge.*

In the year 1678 all the male citizens [2] in each town were

---

[1] *Abbot's History*, 1829.

[2] Not alphabetically arranged in the original. *Registry of Deeds*, "Ipswich," Book IV. Those surnames marked * are not in the first list of freeholders. It will be noticed that the name *Sutton* does not appear on either this list or the foregoing, — the arrival and removal of Richard Sutton being between the two dates. Mr. *Woodbridge* was also removed before 1678.

ordered to take the oath of allegiance to the king. The following is the list of names recorded for the town of Andover:—

"*A List of all the Male Persons in Andover from sixteen years old that took oath of Alegance ffebruary* 11, 1678."

Abbot, George, Senr.
Abbot, George, Junr.
Abbot, George, tailor.
Abbot, John.
Abbot, John, Junr.
Abbot, Thomas.
Abbot, William.
Abbot, Benjamin.
Allen, Andrew, Senr.
Allen, Andrew, Junr.
Allen, John.
Aslett, John.
*Balden, Titus.
Ballard, William, Senr.
Ballard, William, Junr.
Ballard, Joseph,
Ballard, John.
Barker, Richard, Senr.
Barker, Richard, Junr.
Barker, Ebenezer.
Barker, John.
Barker, Stephen.
Barker, William.
Barnard, Stephen.
*Bigsbie, Daniel.
*Blunt, William.
Bradstreet, Mr. Dudley.
*Brewer, Thomas.
*Bridges, John.
*Carlton, John.
Chandler, John.
Chandler, Ens. Thomas.
Chandler, William, Senr.
Chandler, William, Junr.
Chandler, Wm., son of Tho.
*Dane, Francis.
Dane, Francis, Junr.
Dane, Nathaniel.

*Eirres, Zecharias.
*Farnum, John.
Farnum, Ralph, Senr.
Farnum, Ralph, Junr.
Farnum, Thomas.
Faulkner, Mr. Edmond.
Faulkner, John.
Foster, Andrew, 101 yrs. old.
Foster, Ephraim.
Frie, John.
Frie, John, Junr.
Frie, Samuel.
Frie, James.
*Gray, Robert.
*Gutterson, John.
Holt, Nicholas, Senr.
Holt, Nicholas, Junr.
Holt, James.
Holt, Samuel.
Holt, Henry.
Holt, Daniel.
*Hutchinson, Samuel.
*Ingalls, Henry, Senr.
Ingalls, Henry, Junr.
Ingalls, John.
Ingalls, Samuel.
*Johnson, Thomas.
Johnson, John.
Johnson, Stephen.
Johnson, Returne.
Johnson, William.
*Kempe, Samuel.
*Lacey, Lawrence.
Lovejoy, John, Senr.
Lovejoy, John, Junr.
Lovejoy, William.
Lovejoy, Christopher.
*Marble, Samuel.

Marble, Jacob.
Marble, Joseph.
*Marston, John, Senr.
Marston, John, Junr.
Marston, Jacob.
Marston, Joseph.
*Martin, Samuel.
*Nichols, Nicholas.
Osgood, Left. John.
Osgood, Christopher.
Osgood, John, Junr.
Osgood, Stephen.
Osgood, Thomas.
Osgood, Timothy.
Parker, Joseph.
Parker, Nathan.
Parker, John.
*Phelps, Edward, Junr.
Poore, Daniel, Senr.
Poore, Daniel, Junr.
Poore, John, Junr.
*Preston, John.
Preston, Samuel.
*Robinson, Joseph.
*Russell, Robert.
Rust, John, Senr.
Rust, John, Junr.
*Salter, Henry.
*Sessions, Alexander.
Stevens, John.
Stevens, Nathan.
Stevens, Ephraim.
Stevens, Benjamin.
*Stone, Hugh.
*Wardwell, Samuel.
*Wilson, Joseph, Senr.
Wilson, Joseph, Junr.
*Whittington, Edward.
*Wright, Walter.

Following are some brief memoranda respecting the family names on the above list which did not appear on the list of first freeholders. These, however, are merely outlines, neither biographies of individuals nor genealogies of families, but merely collections of such scattered relics and records as have been found of these early settlers, with some notes to indicate the comparative perpetuity and influence of the several families.

The Abbot line had other founders than George Abbot, Sen., already named, — there being two or three settlers at an early day of this name. The principal one of these was "*George Abbot, tailor,*" as he is often designated. He was from Rowley in 1655. He died 1689, leaving a large family of children and a widow. The latter was subsequently married to Henry Ingalls. The estate was settled as described in the following paper:[1] —

"Know all men by these presents that whereas George Abbot of Andover in y^e County of Essex taylor deceased y^e 22^d of March 168$\frac{8}{9}$ and left noe written will behind him, that could be found & about that time y^e Government of y^e Country being in an unsettled posture, we y^e subscribers, being his wife & children (except such as are under age) thought it our best way to take an inventory of his estate and to agree upon y^e division of it which is as followeth : The widdowe of s^d Abbot hath accepted of about 25 pounds which she hath received already as her full satisfaction for her part or share reserving an interest in one end of the house, if she see cause to make use thereof at any time during her life.

"George Abbot, eldest son of the s^d George Abbot deceased hath accepted of 16 acres of upland on which he had built a house during his fathers life & was given to s^d George by his late father, tho there was noe legall conveyance and alsoe a parcell of meadowe commonly called Woodchuck meadowe with some part of stock now in his hands of about (?) pounds value and about one Sixth pt of ye household stuff which he is now possessed of and alsoe half of ye meadowe in ye farther side of s^d Woodchuck valued at five pounds." . . . .

The other sons were assigned portions, and the daughters were to have such parts as they had accepted already. The instrument is signed by the second husband of the widow Abbot : —

"I Henry Ingalls sen^r having married ye widowe of ye aboves^d George Abbot deceased before ye Signing of this agreement have consented unto & signed with them.

[1] *Essex County Court Papers,* vol. xlvii., p. 12.

"Alsoe we John Faulkner & Stephen Barker having married Sarah & Mary Abbot have consented .... &c

> HENRY INGALLS
>   Her mark
> SARAH + INGALS *alias* ABBOT
> GEORGE ABBOT
> JNO ABBOT
> NEHEMIAH ABBOT
> JOHN FAULKNER
>   Her mark
> SARAH + FAULKNER *alias* ABBOT
> STEPHEN BARKER
>   Her mark
> MARY + BARKER *alias* ABBOT
>   Her mark
> HANNAH + ABBOT
>   Her mark
> LYDIA + ABBOT"

Among the descendants of this George Abbot were in early time Mr. Nehemiah Abbot, deputy to the General Court, 1717, and Dr. Nehemiah Abbot, settled as a physician in Andover, 1748. A sister of the latter was married to Amos Lawrence, of Groton. From this marriage sprung the illustrious union of families and names represented by the Hon. Abbot Lawrence, and Hon. Amos A. Lawrence. Hon. Amos Abbot, of Andover, member of the United States Congress, father of the Hon. Alfred A. Abbot, of Peabody, was of this line of descent. Also Dea. Albert Abbot, trader of Andover, is of this branch of the Abbot line.

Thomas Abbot, another early settler, also founded a line of posterity at Andover. The name is probably more numerously represented than any other.

Baldwin, Bixby, and Brewer have not been conspicuous names in Andover. A relic of the deeds of DANIEL BIXBY, 1697. is at hand, whereby he conveyed to John Abbot for five pounds, thirteen shillings and eight pence " in currant money," a parcel of swamp land lying " within ye Township of Andover, ' and " formerly in ye possession of Capt. Thomas Chandler on ye East Side of ye Ridge near Little Hope " . . . . containing " . . . . about five acres and one half & twenty-nine rods." . . . .

" In witness whereof I have hereunto sett my hand and seall

this twentieth daye of May Anno Dom one thousand six hundred ninety & seaven & in ye ninth year of ye Reyne of our Sovereigne Lord William by ye Grace of God. King of England, Scotland, France & Ireland Defender of ye faith.

"Signed sealed and Delivered
in ye presence of :
us: SAMUEL HUNT
       his mark
  WALTER + WRIGHT
  ANDREW PEETERS .... Befor me DANIEL BAXBEE
                        Her marke
                        HANNAH ∽ BIGSBIE
                        DUDLEY BRADSTREET,
                                Just of Peace.

WILLIAM BLUNT was progenitor of a line of descendants who have owned considerable estates especially on the Hill at Andover. Some of these estates form a part of the grounds of the Theological Seminary. Mr. Isaac Blunt made a donation of land to the Institutions of learning. He was an innkeeper during and after the Revolutionary War, and was also a hat or "felt"-maker. He lived on the present Salem Street, east of the Seminary buildings. His descendants, Mr. Charles K. Blunt and Mr. Samuel Blunt, live not far from the ancestral estates. One branch of the family lives at North Andover. In the colonial times the Rev. John Blunt, son of William Blunt, graduated at Harvard College, 1727, and was ordained minister of Newcastle, where he preached till his death, 1746, at the age of forty-two years. He was much esteemed, and a man of ability.

JOHN BRIDGES was constable in 1678. In 1723, Mr. James Bridges was representative to the General Court, and was a man of great influence and considerable wealth, the owner of several slaves. His "mault-house" is referred to in some of the records. His death is curiously described in the epitaph on his grave-stone : —

      Erected in Memory
    of Mr. JAMES BRIDGES
    who departed this life
    July 17th 1747 in y^e
    51st year of his age
    Being melted to death
      by extreme heat.

James Bridges, 2d, in 1750, seems to have had much difficulty and controversy with Moody Bridges. From the Proprietors' Books it appears that in 1750 they laid out a grant of land to Moody Bridges in "ye new field." This was in possession of and claimed by James Bridges, who refused to give it up: —

"He with Holds ye same from me ye s^d Moody Bridges. Put to vote to see if ye proprietors would put Moody Bridges in possession. *Negative.*

"To see if they w^d warrant the premises to Moody Bridges, by a lawful deed of sale. *Neg.*

"To see if they would enable him to draw money from ye proprietors' treasury to carry on a Law suite against ye said James Bridges to recover ye privileges out of His hands by a writ of ejectment. *Neg.*

"To see if the proprietors would take it into their own hands & ejecte ye s^d James Bridges outt of said premises. *Neg.*

"To see if ye Proprietors will give up to Moody Bridges the note of sixteen pounds he gave for the grant. *Affirm.*"

Col. Moody Bridges was Adjutant to Colonel Fry in the French and Indian War, and performed arduous service (elsewhere referred to). He was an ardent patriot and made stirring Revolutionary speeches. He was delegate to the Provincial Congress, 1774–75. He died 1801, aged seventy-eight.

The epitaph on his grave-stone says: —

> "He was a man eminently useful in his day
> He lived, beloved, revered, and died greatly
> lamented by all his family & acquaintances."

Col. Moody Bridges, who died at North Andover, 1865, was for nearly fifty years deputy sheriff of the county. He was a man of genial hospitality and hearty good fellowship, and conspicuous in all the trainings and musters and county cattle shows, where his portly figure and ruddy face, beaming with good nature, his flowing gray locks under his cocked hat, and his stentorian voice, made him a prince of marshals, — the observed of all observers.

Of Colonel Bridges's large family, all have either died or removed from their former residence at North Andover.

JOHN CARLTON, whose name appears on the list of 1678, died at the age of eighty-seven. Neither he nor his descendants for a hundred years, appear in any prominent public connection, but the family in all its branches of descent has been of marked excellence and probity. The traces of them are few in the public records, they having, as appears, lived remarkably free from the litigation and complaints which have made some names conspicuous, and have served (if no other good) to preserve interesting facts of manners and customs.

An epitaph on the gravestone of one of the family, perhaps sums up the character of the majority of the Carlton name : —

"He was benevolent, just and
peaceable with all."

Dr. John Ingalls Carlton, son of Mr. Dean Carlton, was a graduate of Harvard College 1814, and settled as a physician in North Andover.

Among those who have entered into business successfully, is Mr. Jacob F. Carlton, who kept the United States Hotel in New York, and is now resident at Andover. Mr. Henry Carlton was a teacher in San Francisco.

The name is represented at North Andover, by several excellent citizens of local influence.

MR. FRANCIS DANE was the second minister of Andover. A history of his ministry is given in the chapter on the churches. His influence in the town was greater than that of any other man, except, perhaps, Captain Bradstreet, during the time of the witchcraft delusion, to stay the frenzy. His descendants have been numerous in Andover, the west part of the town, but none have been eminent as was the founder of the line. Dea. John Dane was a prominent member of the South Church. Rev. John Dane, son of Daniel Dane, a graduate of Dartmouth College, 1800, was minister of Newfield, Maine.

No tombstone or relic of the Dane family is found in the Old North Burying Ground, near the site of the meeting-house, where Mr. Francis Dane ministered. . . . .

The name of EIRRES has never been conspicuous in the town.

RALPH FARNUM married Elizabeth Holt, 1658.
Thomas Farnum married Elizabeth Sibborn, 1660.
John Farnum married Rebekah Kent, 1667.

Among the noteworthy names of this large family, or families, are, Capt. John Farnum, during the French War; Mr. John Farnum, graduate of Harvard College, 1761, member of the Convention for forming the State Constitution; Capt. Benjamin Farnum, an officer of long service in the Revolution, and deacon of the North Church till his death, 1833, at the age of eighty-seven; Dea. Jedediah Farnham, of the First Church and the "Evangelical" Church; his sons, Timothy Farnum, Esq., graduate of Harvard College, 1808, counsellor-at-law, Monmouth, Me.; Rev. Enoch Farnham,[1] minister at Wayne, Me.; Mr. Edwin Farnham, trader, and conductor on the Boston and Maine Railroad (killed in an accident on the road, 1841), and Mr. Armstrong Farnham. merchant at Philadelphia and Boston. The latter was the original owner of the present residence of Gen. Eben Sutton at North Andover, built 1857.

Other citizens, Capt. Levi Farnham, Dea. Joseph Farnham, have been influential locally, and the descendants of the ancient settlers are very numerous in the Andovers.

ROBERT GRAY was a mariner, the only one of whom record has been found in Andover among the early settlers. In 1699 he bought some hundred acres of land, more or less, from Henry Holt, Sen., and Mr. Dudley Bradstreet. These estates lie in the Holt district of the South Parish; one parcel is described as between Colonel Bradstreet's "Upper Falls Meadow" and Lieutenant Osgood's "Gibbet Plaine Meadow." The deeds have been handed down in the families which have continued to occupy the homestead to the present owner, Mr. Henry Gray. In February, 1718, Robert Gray made his will, giving lands and house and stock and "all [his] wareing cloaths and [his] cane with a silver head" to his son Henry Gray. This son bought the rights of other members of the family to their lands, and owned large estates. He bargained in 1748 with Robert Gray (probably his brother)

[1] This family adopted the more correct orthography of the old country.

to rent to the latter a mill privilege on the "westerly side of Salem road on the southerly side of the brook in my Paster by the Bridg" for the latter to grind scythes, he agreeing to pay therefor two good new scythes ready ground." In course of time, " Anno Dom. 1740," Henry Gray made his will, and bequeathed to his beloved son Henry Gray, 2d, his "lands and stock of Bruit creatures and Husbandry — tools and tackling, and wearing apparel, and weaving loom and tackling, and best Gun and Stelyars." and to other sons lands and money, and to his six daughters pewter plates, and dishes, and all his books. In 1754, Henry Gray, 2d, made his will, a total inventory of £810 2s. 9d. His widow, subsequently married to Jonathan Peabody of Boxford, in 1766 made her will, giving to her daughter Alice, besides her household utensils, as "Box iron, heaters, spinning wheel," etc., her "best riding-hood," and to other daughters, her "camblet gound and amber beads, black quilted coat and silk crape gound and worsted gound and white apron."

A son of Robert Gray was the Rev. Robert Gray, graduate of Harvard College, 1786, minister of Dover, N. H. A descendant of this family is Samuel Gray, Esq., of Andover, now President of the Merrimack Insurance Company, and for forty years treasurer of the company. Among other descendants have been Mr. David Gray, and his son, Mr. Samuel Gray, city engineer of Providence, also Mr. Braviter Gray, of Tewksbury.

The name of GUTTERSON has continued to the present time, but no special relics or memorials of its continuous generations have been found in the records of the town's history. The Rev. George H. Gutterson graduated at the Punchard School, and the Andover Theological Seminary, and was ordained Missionary to India of the American Board, 1878.

The name of HUTCHINSON has not, so far as has been ascertained, been at any point conspicuous in the town history.

HENRY INGALLS, son of Edmond Ingalls of Lynn, in 1653 married Mary Osgood, and, in 1689, married again the widow of George Abbot, tailor. A descendant thus records the genealogy: —

"Mr. Edmond Ingalls from whom all these sprung was born in the year 1627 and died in the year 1719 who lived ninety-two years, and two months after his death I Henry Ingalls was born who have lived 83 years. So that we two Henry Ingalls both lived on this earth one hundred and seventy-five years."

Capt. Henry Ingalls, writer of the above, died 1803, aged eighty-four years. He was an officer in service in the French and Indian War. The Ingalls descendants owned large farms in North Andover, chiefly in the Centre district, near the borders of the Farnham district. In the early history of the town, Henry Ingalls had his house-lot near the meeting-house at the Centre, which he exchanged for land more remote, in order to accommodate the town in respect to the location of the new meeting-house, as appears from a petition to the General Court: —

"We have found out a place in the towne neere the meeting-house very convenient which is the lott of Henry Ingalls which we have procured by way of exchanging for seventy acres of the above-said hundred" (the hundred "being a mile from our meeting-house").

Among the representatives of the Ingalls name of considerable repute, have been Col. John Ingalls of North Andover, a large farmer and a schoolmaster; Dr. Jedediah Ingalls, a graduate of Harvard College, 1792, physician at Durham, N. H.; his son, Dr. Charles Ingalls, born at Durham, N. H., 1807, graduate of Dartmouth College, 1829, resident of North Andover, and some time in practice of his profession; Rev. Wilson Ingalls of Andover (South), graduate of Union College, 1836, pastor in Glenville, New York.

This family is not, perhaps, so largely represented in the town now as some others of ancient origin, but there are several families of estimable citizens.

The name of JOHNSON has been one of the most continuously influential in the history of the Andovers. The Johnsons who settled here, and at Charlestown and Woburn, were emigrants from Hern Hill, in Kent County, England. THOMAS JOHNSON and TIMOTHY JOHNSON were among those earliest in office at Andover. The former, a son of John Johnson, was constable in 1665, and was in town as early as 1658, when he married a daughter of Nicholas Holt. Stephen Johnson, carpenter, owned one of the first saw-mills. He married Elizabeth Dane, accused of witchcraft. His son, Francis, married Sarah Hawkes, who had been accused of witchcraft. Timothy Johnson was constable about 1676. His daughter,[1] Penelope, was murdered by Indians, 1698, March 4th. The homestead was the estate on the Haverhill road, in North Andover, at the corner of the street to Stevens's mills. The ancient house, where the young lady was murdered, stood east of the one now on the place. Capt. Timothy Johnson built the present house, and in 1771 gave it in his will to his son, Col. Samuel Johnson, whose home it afterward was. Colonel Johnson's distinguished part in the Revolutionary War is elsewhere noted. His son, Capt. Samuel Johnson, was also a gallant officer. He lived in the house which also had been for a time the residence of his father, and which was lately owned by Mr. Samuel K. Johnson. This homestead is now owned and occupied in summer by Mr. J. D. W. French, of Boston, an amateur and scientific farmer, author of valuable works on agriculture and stock raising.

The ancient Timothy Johnson homestead, after being the residence of Col. Samuel Johnson, was the home of his son, Capt. Joshua Johnson, and the birth-place of Dr. Samuel Johnson, graduate of Harvard College, 1814, and physician in Salem. It is now the residence of a son of Dr. Johnson, Rev. Samuel Johnson, formerly minister of an Independent Religious Society in Lynn, now engaged in writing an extended work on Comparative Religion, two volumes of which have been published, "India" and "China."

Lieutenant (afterward Captain of the Militia) William Johnson was in the Revolutionary service. Three of his sons have been prominent citizens of North Andover: William John-

---

[1] Genealogists differ as to whether she was daughter of Thomas or of Timothy Johnson.

son, Esq., seven years representative, ten years senator, died 1857, in his eightieth year, unmarried, bequeathing six thousand dollars for the North Parish parsonage. His homestead is now the residence of his nephew, Gen. William Johnson Dale, Surgeon-general of Massachusetts. Mr. James Johnson, merchant, of Boston, died 1855, leaving a large fortune, the fruit of his own enterprise and success. He was one of the trustees of the North Andover Cemetery, where, by his request, he was buried. Col. Theron Johnson is now living in his eighty-seventh year. He helped to found the Johnson High School.

Other names of eminence are Samuel Johnson, M. D., of Andover (South Parish), died 1864; Mr. Osgood Johnson, Principal of Phillips Academy, 1833; Mr. Osgood Johnson, Principal of Cambridge High School, died 1857.

Many names are locally well known, as Mr. Samuel K. Johnson, Andover Express, and Mr. Charles F. Johnson, eighteen successive years selectman of North Andover.

A descendant of a kindred line of Johnsons, of Charlestown, is Rev. Francis Johnson, Andover.

KEMPE is a name not entering into the general history.

LACEY is a respected name of North Andover, not prominent in the history, except in the period of the witchcraft.

SAMUEL MARBLE was the eldest son of Samuel Marble, of Salem. He was a bricklayer, and he and his son acquired considerable estates. His brother was Noah Marble, a yeoman, living near his house. From them and their descendants comes the name "Marble Ridge," at North Andover. Lieut. Cyrus Marble was in the Revolutionary service. Mary Marble, wife of Capt. William Johnson, was mother of the eminent citizens before named.

MARSTON has acquired local permanence as a name in Marston's Ferry, across the Merrimack River, at North Andover, and it is still represented among the citizens of the town.

MARTIN has never been a prominent name in the town history. It was of very early establishing. In 1662 a record says, that "Samuel Martin, late of Andover, had been gone out of the country six or seven years and his house and lands going to ruine and decay," his wife resigned them to the care of Nathan Parker, for the use of her son, Solomon Martin.

NICHOLS is not among the names which enter into the general history.

SAMUEL PHELPS and EDWARD PHELPS were weavers. An ancient deed signed by them and their wives, respectively, "Sarah S Phelps" and "Ruth Y Phelps" conveys, 1697, land near "rattlesnake rode" to Timothy Abbot. The name is honorably represented in the three parishes.

SAMUEL PRESTON'S surname survives in the local name "Preston's Plain" near Ballardvale.

JOSEPH ROBINSON lived near Boxford, and was in 1740 set off to Boxford North Parish. A serious disaster befell the family in 1741, chronicled in the "Boston News-Letter:—

"ANDOVER, *July* 28 — Last Friday in the afternoon, a serious and awful accident occurred by Lightning at the House of Mr. Joseph Robinson of this Town. A stream of Lightning coming down the chimney of the Back room and in its passage breaking out Sundry Bricks and tearing up and breaking a Board of the Floor, bent its course into the Front Room, filled that part of the House with Fire and Smoke of a sulphurous smell, struck two young women who were sitting by the window, forced them back against the wall, one of which was found actually dead with her Hair and Back much burnt; the others Life for a time was despaired of, she being almost breathless but thro the goodness of God she after a while revived tho' with great bodily distress, and is now in comfortable circumstances."

The Robinson family in one branch settled on the homestead of Gen. Nathaniel Lovejoy, now the North Parish parsonage. From this branch is descended the well known naturalist Dr. John Robinson of Salem.

ROBERT RUSSELL is said to have been from Scotland, and from this fact the district of his residence received the name "Scotland District." The ancient homestead is now owned by Dea. Ammon Russell of the Free Christian Church. His brother, Mr. Abiel Russell, ninety-one years old, is the oldest man now living in Andover. He is one of the few pensioners of the War of 1812.

In West Andover are branches of the Russell family, which is, though not so numerous as some, a large and respectable element of the citizenship.

The names of SALTER, SESSIONS, and STONE,[1] are not prominent.

SAMUEL WARDWELL was hanged for witchcraft in 1692, a martyr to his firmness in refusing to confess. Solomon Wardwell's estate was a part of the property bought for Phillips Academy, his cabinet or joiner's shop the first Academy. Among the names of this family of prominence are Dr. Daniel Wardwell, physician, of Andover, 1822–1850; Mr. William H. Wardwell, formerly printer and publisher at Andover, now of Boston, agent for S. D. Warren & Co., Paper Manufacturers; Mr. T. Osgood Wardwell, owner of the old Osgood farm, North Andover, and Mr. B. F. Wardwell, Andover.

JOSEPH WILSON was a cooper by trade. The statement is made [2] that he was probably a son of Rev. John Wilson, of Boston. Among the representatives of the family name have been Dea. Joshua Wilson, 1813–1823, of the North Church, and Mr. Isaac Wilson. The ancient estates lay on the borders of the two parishes. The first Grammar School, 1701, was near Joseph Wilson's.

EDWARD WHITTINGTON and WALTER WRIGHT were weavers, who were granted liberty to set up a fulling mill in 1673, but seem not to have done it. Lieut. Joseph Wright, and Capt. John Wright in the French War, are the chief names of prominence.

[1] The manufacturers of machinery of that name did not originate in Andover.
[2] Abbot's *History of Andover*.

The foregoing list may not include all who were residents at the time, as some doubtless failed to take the oath of allegiance. The following is a list of the taxpayers in the town at the end of fifty years after the settlement: —

"*A Rate*[1] *made for the minister in the year 1692 for the North End of the towne of Andover.*

Abbot, George, senior.
Abbot, George, junr.
Abbot, Thomas, senr.
* Andrew, Joseph.
* Aslebe, John.
* Austin, Samuel.
Barker, Richard, senr.
Barker, Left. John.
Barker, Stephen.
Barker, Benjamin.
* Bodwell, Henry.
Bradstreet, Capt. Dudley.
Bridges, John.
Bridges, James.
Carlton, John.
Carlton, Joseph.
Chandler, William.
* Chub, Pasco.
* Cromwell, Job.
Dane, Nathl.
Eires, Nathan.[2]
Eimes, Robert.[2]
* Emery, Joseph.
ffarnum, Ralph, senr.
ffarnum, John, junr.
ffarnum, Thomas.
* ffarrington, Edward.

ffaulkner, ffrancis.
ffaulkner, John.
ffoster, Ephraim.
ffoster, Abraham.
ffrye, Benjamin.
ffrye, Samuel.
* Granger, John.
* Graves, Mark, sen.
Gray, Robert.
Hoult, Nicholas.
Hoult, Hannah, widdowe.
Hutchinson, Samuel.
Ingalls, Henry.
Ingalls, Henry, jr.
Ingalls, Saml.
Ingalls, John.
Johnson, ffrancis.
Lacey, Lawrence.
Lovejoy, Joseph.
Marble, Samuel.
Marston, John, senr.
Marston, John, junr.
Marston, Jacob.
Marston, Joseph.
Martin, Ensign Samuel.
Nichols, Nich.
Osgood, Capt. John.

Osgood, John, junr.
Osgood, Timothy.
Parker, Joseph.
Parker, Stephen.
Parker, John.
Poor, Daniel.
Poor, Widdow.
* Post, John.[2]
Preston, John.
Robinson, Joseph.
Stevens, Cornet Nathan.
Stevens, Joseph.
Stevens, Benjamin.
Stevens, Nathan, junr.
Stevens, Widdow.
Stevens, Joshua.
Stone, Simon.
* Swan, Samuel.
. Tiler, John. ,
Toothaker, Allen.
* White, John.[2]
* Singletary, Benjamin.[2]
Tiler, Moses, senr.[2]
Tiler, Moses, junr.[2]
Swan, Robert.[2]
Swan, Timothy.[2]

South End of the Towne.

Abbot, John, senr.
Abbot, George, senr.
Abbot, Nehemiah.
Abbot, Timothy.
Abbot, Benjamin.
Abbot, William.
Abbot, Thomas.
Abbot, Nathaniel.
Allen, Widdow.

Asten, Thomas.
Ballard, Joseph, senr.
Ballard, William.
Barnard, Stephen.
Barker, Hananiah.(?)
Bixby, Daniel.
* Blanchard, Jonathan.
Blanchard, Samuel.
Blunt, William.

* Bussell, Samuel.
Chandler, Capt.
Chandler, William, senr.
Chandler, William, junr.
Chandler, Henry.
Chandler, Joseph.
Chandler, Thomas.
* Carrier, Thomas.
Dane, Francis.

[1] *Assessors' Records.* The names marked * are not in the former list.
[2] These seem to have been Haverhill and Boxford men who belonged to the religious parish of Andover. Some, perhaps, lived within the bounds of Andover.

Dane, William.	Johnson, John, jr.	Preston, Samuel.
ffarnum, Ralph, junr.	Lovejoy, William.	Phelps, Samuel.
ffoster, Andrew.	Lovejoy, Christopher.	Phelps, Edward.
ffrye, Deacon.	Lovejoy, Nath.	Phelps, Widow.
ffrye, James.	Lovejoy, Eben.	Russell, Robert.
* Graves, Abraham.	Marble, Joseph.	Stevens, John.
Gutterson, John.	* More, Abraham.	Stone, John.
* Haggit, Moses.	Osgood, Christopher.	· Tyler, Hopestill. *
Hoult, Samuel.	Osgood, Hooker.	* Wardwell, Saml's estate.
Hoult, Henry.	Osgood, Widow.	Wilson, Joseph.
* Hooper, Thomas.	* Peters, Andrew.	Wright, Walter.
Johnson, William.		

Following are brief notes regarding such of the family names on this list (not found on the two preceding lists) as have been conspicuous in the course of the centuries.

JOHN ASLEBE was a man of wealth and influence, representative to the General Court, 1701, and afterward. He lived probably on the hill, near the old burying-ground at North Andover. A record speaks of the "way over the hill from the meeting-house to Timothy Osgood's by Mr. John Aslebe's." His farm lands were in the south part of the town, in the present Holt and Farnham districts. Aslebe Hill and Aslebe Pond preserve his memory. He died 1728, aged seventy-two. Mrs. Mary Aslebe, "relict of Lieut. John Aslebe, died Feb. 13th, Anno Dom. 1739, in ye 84th year of her age," as the epitaph on her gravestone records. She made a bequest of a silver tankard to the North Church.

SAMUEL BLANCHARD was Selectman in 1687. It has been stated [1] that he removed to Andover from Charlestown in 1686, but the name had become established in the town as early as 1679. In that year, land near " Blanchard's Pond " was bought by Moses Haggit. Also the list of proprietors states that he was a householder before 1681. There are more than forty of the name Blanchard on the list of members of the South Church, and eight assessors of the parish. Among the more recent representatives of the name were Mr. Abel Blanchard, who carried on the paper mill before it was bought by the Marland Manufacturing Company ; Dea. Amos Blanchard,

[1] Abbot's *History of Andover.*

the first cashier of the Andover Bank, a man of strict integrity and great executive ability ; Rev. Amos Blanchard, D. D., graduate of Yale College, 1826, minister at Lowell for nearly a half century. The name has also been represented honorably by other citizens.

HENRY BODWELL lived on the Merrimack River, probably on the Haverhill side, and in the present limits of Methuen. In 1735, the Bodwells' Ferry was in operation. The tradition is that the Bodwell family were much exposed to the Indians who crossed the river at the fords, and making raids for cattle into the common lands or pastures, along the Shawshin, escaped easily across the river to their hiding-places. There is a story that one of the Bodwells, an old man, but with keen sight, for he was a great hunter and marksman, seeing an Indian on the opposite bank of the Merrimack River, somewhere between the mouth of the Shawshin and the Falls (named from him ' Bodwell's Falls), took aim and fired, killing the savage while, thinking himself out of range of shot, he was making taunting gestures. Bodwell, taking a boat and rowing across, found the Indian dead, and secured his scalp and his fine wolf-skin blanket.

PASCOE CHUBB had an unenviable reputation in his day. He was, as is related in the chapter on the Indian wars, cashiered for treasonable or inefficient conduct at Fort Pemaquid, imprisoned in Boston jail, and finally set at liberty and allowed to live in seclusion at Andover. He had married in this town a daughter of Mr. Edmond Faulkner, and previous to his military misdemeanors had been presented before the court of the county for offences. He seems to have been an unprincipled man, whose connection with Andover families brought chiefly disgrace and sorrow. He and his wife were murdered by the Indians, 1698. With their death the name perished from Andover annals.

THOMAS CARRIER removed to Andover from Billerica. He is said to have been a native of Wales. He is noteworthy principally as having been the husband of Martha (Allen)

Carrier, who was hanged for witchcraft. He seems to have been not greatly disturbed by any of the events of life. He lived to a good old age, as is said, attaining one hundred and nine years. His name is given on the list of the South Church members removed by death, but he had then become a resident of the town of Colchester, Conn. He was of remarkable physical strength, and walked six miles shortly before his death.

JOSEPH EMERY was not in any prominent civil or military office connected with the town. In 1719, he had three grants of land laid out to him by the proprietors: One in Merrimack Woods, one on the Shawshin near his dwelling-house, bounded at the west by his former land on Shawshin River, and near Paul Faulkner's house, "just below the place commonly called the 'Marchants ford.'"

Jacob Emery was a graduate of Harvard College, 1761, and ordained minister of Pembroke, N. H., 1768.

In 1831, Rev. Joshua Emery, and in 1834, Rev. Samuel H. Emery, graduated from Amherst College. They were sons of Joshua Emery, formerly resident of Boxford and sometime resident of North Andover, afterward of Andover.

EDWARD FARRINGTON. The family name was conspicuous, especially during the French and Indian War, and in the Revolution.

Lieut. Jacob Farrington, in the military company known as Rogers' Rangers, on the borders of Canada, performed some valiant exploits. Several privates were in the Revolutionary service. Capt. Thomas Farrington, an officer of Andover, in the French and Indian War, removed to Groton, and there became famous.

Capt. Philip Farrington was a well-known citizen of North Andover fifty years ago. He lived on the estate now owned by Mr. Edward Frothingham of Boston.

Abraham Graves, son of Mark Graves, was a weaver. The name has not entered conspicuously into the town history.

MOSES HAGGIT of Ipswich, in 1679, bought of Stephen Johnson fourteen acres of upland and seven acres of meadow on the southwest side of a pond called Blanchard's Pond, agreeing to pay twelve shillings a year to all charges of church and town. From him and his descendants the pond received its present name, Hagget's [1] Pond. The land thereabouts keeps the name Blanchard's Plain.

It is stated, in a historical discourse of Mr. Symmes, that in 1676 Mr. Hagget and his two sons were "captivated" by Indians; but I cannot find that they were then residents.

They may have been visiting and viewing the land where they ultimately settled. The change in the name of the pond seems to have come about gradually. In 1720 it was still called Blanchard's: —

"On the 20th of January 1720, then laid out to Moses Haggot and Timothy More all the great Island in *Blanchards Pond* so called. .... Said Moses Haggot is to have the one half of s^d Island for allowance for a way over his upper dam."

ABRAHAM MOAR died 1706. Timothy More (the name is variously spelled) his son born 1688, was a member of the South Church 1728. Anne (Blanchard) Mooar, wife of Timothy, became a member of this church, 1716. Twenty-one of this family name were members of the South Church before the division of the parish. The families lived chiefly in the west part of the town. Dea. Nathan Mooar has been an officer of the West Church many years.

The Rev. George Moor, D. D., President of the Pacific Theological Seminary, formerly minister of the South Church, was the second minister native of the town, who was pastor of a church in its limits.

ANDREW PETERS came to North Andover between 1686 and 1692, from Ipswich.[2] He was a man of means, a distiller and licensed retailer, and his arrival in the town was regarded as of advantage to the settlement. He took a prominent part in affairs, and was the first town treasurer of whom record has been found. He also kept a public-house. He died 1713, aged ninety-six. His gravestone still remains. His grand-

---

[1] Now generally spelled Haggett.
[2] Unless there was another Andrew Peters of Ipswich.

son was Rev. Andrew Peters, a graduate of Harvard College, and master of the Andover Grammar School, 1723, the first minister of Middleton. Others of this family of prominence have been, Henry Adams Peters, a graduate of Harvard College, 1818, a teacher; John Peters, Esq., who settled at Bluehill, Me. Mr. Andrew Peters was a patriotic citizen of some prominence in the Revolutionary time. He lived in the house now standing on the Salem turnpike near the Andover road. The ancestral estates extended along northwest toward Den Rock. Mr. John Peters, son of Andrew Peters, purchased the estates of Col. Joseph Frye and Col. James Frye, living for a time in the house of the former and ultimately removing to the homestead of the latter now owned by Mr. Nathaniel Peters.

Mr. Willard Peters was a teacher in Tennessee. Andrew Peters, son of Mr. John Peters, studying for the ministry, died while a student in Harvard College, 1831.

Mr. Nathaniel Peters and Mr. William Peters, among the influential citizens of North Andover, are the last male representatives of the name in the town.

ROBERT SWAN was a resident of Haverhill, or Methuen (as it was later), but the Swans living near the river were not distant from the North Andover meeting-house, and became members of the parish, some of the family ultimately settling in the town where their descendants are living.

ALLEN TOOTHAKER was a nephew of Martha Carrier, and testified against her in the witchcraft trials. He came from Billerica. The name of Toothaker has disappeared.

MOSES TYLER and HOPESTIL TYLER were sons of Job Tyler, who removed to Roxbury. His troubles with Thomas Chandler have been alluded to already. His son, Hopestil Tyler, seems to have established himself as a blacksmith, in the south end of the town. Moses Tyler lived in Boxford. He had, as is supposed, a son Job. In 1701 "Job Tyler and John Chadwick of Boxford with Ephraim Foster of Andover petition for liberty to hang up two gates in ye road in y^e

bounds of Boxford that leadeth from Ipswich to Andover." Moses Tyler died 1727, "Oct. ye 2^d in the 86th year of his age," and was buried at North Andover. The descendants of this family, in some of its branches, scattered throughout New England, are eminent, but in Andover history the name is only locally known.

Another resident of Boxford, who attended meeting at North Andover, was ROBERT EIMES, or AMES. After a time he, or another of the same name, lived in North Andover, near Mr. James Frye's. Mr. John Ames, in 1715, was one of the town's attorneys, or agents, to prosecute a lawsuit against Robert Barnard, in regard to a claim for land During the Revolutionary War, the name became one of the most conspicuous, Capt. Benjamin Ames commanding one of the companies at Bunker Hill. He lived in the west part of Andover, "The South Parish" at that time. His son, Benjamin Ames, Jr., built the tavern (the present Elm House) at Andover, and was landlord. In conformity with the wishes and provision of his grandfather, Mr. Timothy Chandler, his son, Benjamin Ames (the third), was "brought up to learning and the college." He graduated at Harvard College, 1803, studied law at Groton, the residence of his uncle, Nathan Ames, settled in Bath, Maine, and became distinguished as a lawyer and politician, President of the Senate, Justice of the Court of Common Pleas. He died 1835. His brother, Nathan Ames, was deputy sheriff of Lincoln County, Maine. Another brother, Ezra C. Ames, was clerk in the tavern, schoolmaster, trader of Haverhill, deacon of the Congregational Church, a man much respected. He was the father of Judge Isaac Ames.

Of all the works of the settlers in the first fifty years no relics remain besides their written papers and deeds, the few gravestones in the burying ground, and one or two dwelling-houses. Of the latter there is only one, in regard to which satisfactory evidence is found of its having been the residence of one of the original settlers. This one is the Bradstreet house. The tradition has always been that this was the residence of Mr. Simon Bradstreet. That it was the home of his son, Col. Dudley Bradstreet, is authenticated. The latter died 1702. He was married 1673. His mother died the year before. His father, Mr. Simon Bradstreet, removed to Salem about the time of the marriage, doubtless relinquishing the house to his son. It is stated in the Journal of Mrs. Anne Bradstreet, that their house was burned to the ground July, 1666. Undoubtedly they built another immediately. The tradition has been that the frame of the house was brought from England; but, however this may be, it is not likely that Mr. Simon Bradstreet was houseless for seven years, or, that if he had within so recent a period built a house, his son would immediately build a new one.

Some years ago the writer, whose birth-place the house was, took some pains to trace its history through the centuries. The sketch then printed[1] is here by request inserted (somewhat abbreviated), although it repeats and anticipates to some extent other parts of this history: —

THE BRADSTREET HOUSE — HOME OF THE FIRST WOMAN-POET IN AMERICA.

In the original North Parish of Andover, on the Haverhill and Boston road, stands an ancient house, around which cluster the associations of two centuries, and which is especially interesting and memorable as having been the home of the first woman-poet of America, Anne Dudley Bradstreet. It was built probably about the year 1667 by the Hon. (afterwards Deputy-governor and Governor) Simon Bradstreet, and was his family residence and that of his son Col. Dudley Bradstreet, until the death of the latter in 1702. Old as it is, it had been preceded by another built many years earlier and destroyed by fire July, 1666. The present house seems likely, with care, to last another half-century at least. Its frame is massive, of heavy timbers; its walls lined with brick, and its enormous chimney, heavily buttressed, running up through the centre, shows in the garret like a fortification. On the lawn in front are two venerable elm trees, supposed to be as old as the house itself. They are of remarkable size, vigor, and beauty, though latterly[2] marred by the ravages of the canker-worm.

Simon Bradstreet was one of the first settlers of Andover, as he had been one of the first settlers of Charlestown, Boston, Cam-

[1] Boston *Daily Advertiser*.
[2] The branches of one are now nearly all dead.

bridge, and Ipswich. When there were only eight towns in E sex County, before Andover was incorporated, and soon after the land had been bought of the Sagamore Cutshamache for £6 and a coat, this enterprising and far-seeing Puritan' man of affairs brought hither his family, and in 1644 built the first mill on the Cochechevicke, near its junction with the Merrimack, in the district now crowded with the manufacturing industries of the city of Lawrence and the villages of Sutton's and Stevens's mills, North Andover.

Anne Dudley, reared amid the refinements and elegancies of an English castle (her father, Governor Thomas Dudley, had been steward to the Earl of Lincoln), at the age of eighteen, having been then two years married, came with her husband, Simon Bradstreet, to seek a home in the "wilderness of North America." They were of the party consisting of Governor Winthrop, Mr. Johnson and his wife, the lady Arbella, sister of the Earl of Lincoln, and other eminent colonists, who in June, 1630, landed at Salem. Messrs. Dudley and Bradstreet, after several removals, first from Salem to Charlestown, thence to Boston, settled at Cambridge, where Bradstreet built a house near the present site of the University bookstore. In 1635 Bradstreet had again moved to Ipswich. The hardships and privations of pioneer life told severely upon the delicate constitution of Anne Bradstreet, and though she did not, like the gentle lady Arbella, droop and die, she soon became a confirmed invalid, as she says : " I fell into a lingering sicknesse like a consumption, together with a lamenesse, which correction I saw the Lord sent to humble and try me and doe me good." At the time of her husband's removal to Andover, she was about thirty years of age, the mother of five children, to whom three more were afterward added. Of the little brood, she thus quaintly writes : —

"I had eight birds hatcht in one nest,
Four cocks there were, and hens the rest.
I nurst them up with pain and care,
Nor cost nor labor did I spare,
Till at the last they felt their wing,
Mounted the trees and learned to sing."

She chronicles her devotion to her husband as follows : —

"If ever two were one, then surely we;
If ever man were loved by wife, then thee ;
If ever wife was happy in a man,
Compare with me ye women, if you can."

The neighbors of Mistress Bradstreet looked with a jealous eye upon her talent for verse-making and her ability to put her feelings into fine phrases: —

> "I am obnoxious to each carping tongue,
> Who say my hand a needle better fits."

But the *literati* of her time regarded her as a prodigy. President Rogers, of Harvard College, said that "twice drinking of the nectar of her lines" left him "weltering in delight." Edward Phillips, the nephew of Milton, speaks of her as "the tenth muse sprung up in America;" and John Norton says: —

> "Could Maro's muse but hear her lively strain,
> He would condemn his works to fire again."

Her poems were first published without her knowledge through the agency of her brother-in-law, the Rev. John Woodbridge, first minister of the church at Andover. She seems to have written as a diversion from bodily suffering and a solace for the lack of society; also with a desire to leave something which would be of interest and value to her children after her death: —

> "That being gone, you here may find
> What was your loveing mother's mind,
> Make use of what I leave in Love
> And God shall blesse you from above."

The burning of her house in Andover was a great blow to Mrs. Bradstreet. For, after her many movings and breakings up, she had hoped to spend here the remnant of her days in peace and quiet. With the house perished treasures that money could not replace — a library of eight hundred volumes, rare and costly books; family portraits and heirlooms; furniture of rich pattern brought from England; and, what was beyond price to the gentle poet, store of tender and sacred associations. She thus describes her feelings at the time of the fire: —

> "I, starting up, the light did spye,
> And to my God my heart did cry,
> To strengthen me in my distresse,
> And not to leave me succourlesse,
> Then coming out beheld a space,
> The flames consume my dwelling place."

She never quite liked the "newe house," although it was undoubtedly finer than the old one, and furnished with an elegance befitting the wealth and rank of its owner.

Simon Bradstreet, honored citizen, exemplary Christian, kind husband, provided for his family an abundant home; took pride in his wife's poetical talent, and satisfaction in her lines concerning the various occasions of his life, — such, for instance, as his mission to England to propitiate Charles II. toward the colonies; cherished her tenderly; and when, after forty years of faithful devotion, she died, mourned her sincerely. Four years after her death, he, hale and hopeful at the age of seventy-three, married again; lived twenty-one years thereafter; served as deputy governor six months, and as governor thirteen years — with two years' interruption by the loss of the charter — and died in 1697 at the age of ninety-four.

His tomb still stands in Salem, to which city he removed soon after the death of his wife. On the tomb, but now obliterated, was the following tribute, copied and preserved in the records of the last century: —

"SIMON BRADSTREET, armiger ex ordine Senatoris in Colonia Massachosettensi ab anno 1630 usqe ad annom 1673. Deinde ad annum 1679 Vice-Gubernator; deinde ad annum 1686 ejusdem coloniæ communi & constanti Populi Suffragio GUBERNATOR. Vir judicio Lynceato præditus quem nec Minæ nec Honos allexit, Regis authoritatem & Populi libertatem æqua Lance libravit. Religione Cordatus vita innocuus, mundum et vicit et deseruit Die XXVII Marcij. Anno Dom: M. D. C. X. CVII, Annoque Regis Gullielmi tertii IX. et ætatis suæ XCIV."

No trace of Anne Bradstreet's grave is to be found. She was probably laid in the parish burying-ground, whose moss-grown stones on the hillside can be seen from the windows of the Bradstreet house. All the monuments of her time have crumbled to dust, save only one broken tablet, which serves to prove that this was the burial-place of the first settlers. But though the gentlewoman lacks the memorial of "storied urn or animated bust," her "poems," as Cotton Mather remarks in the Magnalia, "divers times printed, have afforded a monument for her memory beyond the stateliest marbles." Among her descendants, besides those bearing the family name, may be mentioned William Ellery Channing, Oliver Wendell Holmes, Wendell Phillips, Richard H. Dana.

Dudley Bradstreet took his father's house and filled his father's place as a citizen of Andover, being selectman, colonel of militia and magistrate. Well it was for his town and for the colonies that the magistrate's office fell to a man inheriting the united qualities of Simon Bradstreet and Anne Dudley; for largely to the compassion and courage of Dudley Bradstreet was due the first check upon the fury of the witchcraft frenzy. He drew up and headed a testimonial and plea for some wretched women of

Andover who had made confession of witchcraft "by reason," as they afterward declared, "of sudden surprisal, when exceedingly astonished and amazed and consternated and affrighted even out of reason." He asserted — and with personal risk — his belief in their innocence.

Then the cloud darkened over the Bradstreet house. The magistrate was accused of having himself practised witchcraft, and thereby killed nine persons, and the man who for twenty years had gone in and out before the people, trusted and loved of all, was now forced by their clamors to flee from his home and hide himself from their fury. If the voices of the centuries could become audible in the old house, what agonized prayers and anguished partings would come borne on the night-wind of that dreadful past of the witchcraft delusion!

Even more startling and terrifying would be the lifting of the veil on the scenes of the memorable March day of 1698, when the snow-bound house was suddenly invaded by forty savages and its inmates dragged out into the wintry air, to see their neighbors' homes in flames and the snow stained with the blood of their townspeople. Here again the gentle humanities of Anne Bradstreet living in her son brought salvation; for an act of kindness, conferred by the magistrate some years before upon an Indian of the party, he and his family were spared a cruel death. They were carried about fifty rods from the house and released unharmed. During the half-century which includes the French and Indian war, the Revolution, and the adoption of the Federal Constitution, the Bradstreet house was occupied by the Rev. William Symmes, D. D.

There was reared the first lawyer of Andover, William Symmes, Esq., son of the minister, who left his native town because of the censure of his townsmen for his conscientious change of convictions and action in advocating the adoption of the Federal Constitution.

The Bradstreet house, after the death of Dr. Symmes, was purchased for a summer residence by Hon. John Norris, one of the associate founders of the Theological Seminary. A manuscript diary kept by Mrs. Norris, now in possession of one of her descendants living in Salem, gives some pleasant glimpses of the household ways of the manse those three-score summers ago: "A deal of papering and painting, and making of currant-jelly, and bottling of 'cyder,' and going to Haverhill, eight miles away, for a barrel of flour, and picking raspberries 'on the South Parish

Road,' and tea-drinkings, with such guests as Dr. Worcester, Dr. Pearson, Dr. Griffin, Dr. Woods; also 'Mr. Spring, a student' of the Seminary, spends the night often and writes his sermons 'sitting by the keeping-room fire, the weather being cool.'"

A few years later there were sermons of another school of theology than that of Gardiner Spring written in the keeping-room, when it was occupied by the young Unitarian minister, the Rev. Bailey Loring (father of Dr. George B. Loring), who lived for a time with the family then owning the Bradstreet house, that of Mrs. Elizabeth Parks, the widow of General Parks and mother of Gorham Parks, Esq., counsellor-at-law, Waldoborough, Me.

The next scene that rises to view in the tableaux of the centuries is the boarding-school, the principal figure the school-master. "A man severe he was and stern to view — Master Simeon Putnam, the pedagogue of fifty years ago." The neighbors say that the grass was worn smooth by the roadside, where he kept the idlers and dunces sitting to con their tasks, a spectacle to passers-by. The windows of the school-room bear marks of the youthful propensity for rhyming as follows: —

> "Stranger, these tainted walls depart,
> Within are fetters to a freeman's heart!"

Two of "the boys" have left their autographs cut on the glass: Amos A. Lawrence, Chandler Robbins. One of the sons of Master Putnam was Professor Putnam, of Dartmouth College, at the time of his death professor-elect of Andover Theological Seminary.

Thus the Bradstreet house has gathered to itself store of history and tradition; and its rooms are shadowy with the forms of by-gone centuries. A veritable ghost is said once to have haunted it and made a frightful clattering in the chamber of a young negro-servant; but we do not need its help to fill up our collection of portraits, or to start the question of spiritual manifestations; for, as Mr. Longfellow, with the truth of poetry, assures us, —

> "All houses wherein men have lived and died
> Are haunted houses. Through the open doors
> The harmless phantoms on their errands glide
> With feet that make no sound upon the floors;
> We have no title-deeds to house or lands.
> Owners and occupants of earlier dates
> From graves forgotten stretch their dusty hands,
> And hold in mortmain still their old estates."

To this summary of the lives and posterity of the early

THE BRADSTREET HOUSE.

[House of Mr. Simon and Mrs. Anne Bradstreet, Col. Dudley Bradstreet, Rev. Thomas and Rev. John Barnard, and Rev. William Symmes, D. D.]

HOME OF COLONEL JAMES FRYE

[Elm Tree planted 1725 by Chaplain Frye, recently cut down, being dead.]

settlers may be added a brief notice of them in their united capacity, as in town-meeting assembled.

The town-meetings were regarded as hardly less important than the church-meetings, and were held generally in the meeting-house. All the freeholders not present at meetings were fined. It was agreed, in 1664, that "any seven" of the voters should have power to act, and "their action should be as authoritive and vallid as if the whol Town were assembled." Decorum was enforced by penalties.

"Feb. 10. 1673. It is ordered and voted that if any man shall speake in the town meeting whilst anything of towne affaires is either in voting or in agitation after ye moderator hath commanded silence twice, he shall forfeit twelve pence for each time ; the twelve pence shall be levied by the constable. This order to stand good, *forever*."

It was customary in the beginning to hold town-meetings whenever they seemed necessary. It was thought a great grievance when Sir Edmund Andros prohibited them from being held oftener than once a year. In 1675 the regular yearly meeting was voted to be holden in March, although this was not always done. For twenty years after the settlement of Andover, only church-members could vote for Governor and Assistants ; but after the restoration of Charles Second to the throne, he insisted on the admission to the number of freemen or voters of all men of honest and moral deportment. A perceptible difference in the warrants and town documents appears after the Restoration. There is more precise and formal recognition of the royal authority. All the papers are in the name of the "Sovereign Lord the King," etc. In 1678, as has been said, an oath of allegiance to the king was exacted from every male resident over sixteen years of age.

The supervision of the towns, in their corporate capacity, as well as of the action of the colony, was more systematic, and the power exercised arbitrary, until, by the royal mandate, the colonial charter was declared forfeited.

In 1683 Andover and Bradford were fined for not collecting the due amount of taxes ; not rating their waste lands : —

"The Court being informed that the Selectmen of Andover &

Bradford did wholly neglect the observance of the late order relating to the rating of wast lands, the Secretary was ordered to send a warrant for their or one of their appearance before this Court to give an account for ye same. Warrant issued out accordingly & Left. John Osgood & Capt. Shuball Walker appeared & gave in their answers. The Court ordered the selectmen of Andover and Bradford to bring in a just & true account of all the wast lands in their respective towns," &c.

The following town action was taken in 1686 in regard to collection of taxes : —

"168$\frac{5}{6}$ Mar. 1. Voted & passed that y^e Constable from year to year shall y^e last Monday in August at nine of y^e clock in y^e morning call all y^e inhabitants of y^e towne by name (by inhabitants is meant all house holders & persons that have y^e management of any estate & hired servants) and if any such persons shall not then appear at ye meeting-house and bring the bills of their ratable estates they shall pay five shillings to ye use of ye towns, ye selectmen making ye constable a reasonable allowance for his care & pains."

In May, 1686, the Colonial charter, so highly prized, was abrogated. Governor Bradstreet was superseded by a President appointed by the Crown (Joseph Dudley, his wife's step-brother) and a Council. Although appointed members of the President's Council, Mr. Bradstreet and Colonel Dudley Bradstreet declined to serve, the President being neither in age or temper a congenial associate. But Joseph Dudley's term as President was short. In December he was set aside, and Sir Edmund Andros appointed Governor of New England. The town of Andover was not likely to cherish any warm regard for the usurper of the office so long held by their distinguished townsman, the former Governor. Indeed, Mr. Dudley Bradstreet declined to collect the extortionate taxes assessed by order of the royal Governor, and was, therefore, imprisoned at Fort Hill. A glimpse of this first Andover rebel against royal tyranny, in his imprisonment, is given in the diary of Judge Sewall. He probably had not anticipated such summary measures, and he was of the temperament and disposition, sensitive to wrong, to feel keenly the injury.

"1687. *Wednesday Sept.* 28. This day went with Mr. Mather and visited Capt. Bradstreet, who was much distracted last night; but now pretty well; said he had not slept in several nights, being confined at Fort Hill."

It was useless to hold out, and perhaps Mr. Bradstreet acted in the beginning not so much from an unwillingness to collect the taxes, as with a view to serve the wishes of his townsmen. They could hardly expect him individually to suffer to the extent of remaining in prison. He acknowledged (as, indeed, he might truthfully without sacrifice of principle) "*great imprudence* and *folly,*" and, giving bonds for one thousand pounds, was released.[1] The town, in March, 1687, had taken action in regard to the laws of the royal Governor.

"*Voted* that Deacon John Frie shall goe downe to Boston and inquire of ye authority [note the avoidance of the titles of officers or recognition of rights] how they understand ye meaning of their proclamation about ye Selectman and Constable continuing in place till further orders; informing them of ye actions herein and to make report to Capt. Osgood whoe shall inform ye town thereof."

When the Revolution came, that brought Andros low, Andover was prompt to testify its sympathy with the movement.

"Att a gen^{ll} towne meeting ye 20th day of May 1689, Capt. John Osgood was chosen moderator. It was voted & declared that it is their mind and desire that the Governor, Deputy Governor, and Assistants chosen in the year 1686 (with the addition of such Gentlemen as shall be chosen by the major vote of the inhabitants of this colony to make up the number according to charter) and the Deputyes then sent by the freemen of ye sevll towns of ye said Colony [shall be the authority] according to Charter Rights until ye Government be more orderly settled by the Crown of England. Capt. John Osgood was chosen as representative of ye Towne to carry ye abovesaid vote of ye Town to Boston and alsoe ye votes for such magistrates & others as are wanting in the former choice in ye yeare ('86)."

A tract, "An Account of the Late Revolution in New England, &c., April 18, 1689," published soon after the events

---

[1] Palfrey's *History of New England*, vol. iii.

occurred, describes the sufferings of the towns from the tyranny of Andros, and alludes to Andover. After stating that Andros imposed heavy duties and excise, and prohibited town-meetings, it says: —

"When the inhabitants of Ipswich were required to choose a Commission to tax that town, some principal persons there, that could not comply with what was demanded of them did modestly give their reasons, for which they were committed to goal as guilty of high misdemeanors and denied an *habeas corpus* and were obliged to answer at the Court of Oyer and Terminer at Boston. These were severely handled . . . . Mr. Appleton was fined fifty pounds and to give a thousand pounds bond for good behavior and moreover declared incapable to bear office &c . . . . Likewise the townsmen of Rowley, Salisbury, Andover, etc. had the same measures. John and Christopher Osgood complain of being sent to prison nine or ten days without a *mittimus* or anything laid to their charge, and that afterward they were obliged to pay excessive charges. Thus was major Appleton dealt with; thus Captain Bradstreet."

That was a day of rejoicing at Andover, which brought news of the revolution in England, consigned Andros to the prison, where he had incarcerated their townsmen, and restored to the gubernatorial chair the venerable Simon Bradstreet, and made his son, Col. Dudley Bradstreet, a member of the new Council.

Following is a list of the civil officers from Andover. It will be noticed that the towns sometimes elected deputies non-residents, as Mr. Samuel Bradstreet, living in Boston (as is supposed) at the time of his election, and Mr. Thomas Savage, also of Boston: —

REPRESENTATIVES TO THE GENERAL COURT.
1646-1746.
First Century from the Incorporation of the Town.

1651	Mr. John Osgood (died Oct. 1651).	1680–83	Capt. Dudley Bradstreet.
1669	Lieut. John Osgood.	1686	Capt. Dudley Bradstreet.
1670	Mr. Samuel Bradstreet.	1689	Capt. John Osgood.
1672	Capt. Thomas Savage.	1690	Capt. John Osgood, Feb. Capt. Thomas Chandler, May. Capt. Christopher Osgood Oct., Dec.
1677	Lieut. Dudley Bradstreet.		
1678–80	Ensign Thomas Chandler.		

1691	Capt. Dudley Bradstreet.	1716	Mr. John Osgood.
1692	{ Capt. Dudley Bradstreet. { Mr. John Frye.	1717–21	Mr. Nehemiah Abbot.
		1721	Benjamin Stevens, Esq.
1693	Mr. Christopher Osgood.	1722	Mr. James Bridges.
1694	Capt. Thomas Chandler.	1723	Mr James Frye.
1695	Major Dudley Bradstreet.	1724	Mr. James Bridges.
1696	Capt. Christopher Osgood.	1725	Mr. Benjamin Barker.
1697	Lieut. John Osgood.	1726	Mr. Nehemiah Abbot.
1698	Col. Dudley Bradstreet.	1727	Mr. Timothy Osgood.
1699	Col. Dudley Bradstreet.	1728–30	Benjamin Stevens, Esq.
1700	Mr. John Abbot.	1730–35	Mr. Joseph Parker.
1701	Mr. John Aslebe.	1737–39	Capt. Timothy Johnson.
1702	{ Mr. John Osgood. { Capt. James Frye.	1739	Mr. Joseph Parker.
		1740–41	Mr. Timothy Johnson.
1703	Mr. John Aslebe.	1741	{ Capt. Timothy Johnson. { John Osgood, Esq.
1704	Mr. John Chandler.		
1705–09	Capt. Christopher Osgood.	1742	John Osgood, Esq.
1709–11	Mr. John Aslebe.	1743–5	Capt. Nathaniel Frye.
1711	Capt. John Chandler.	1745	{ Capt. Timothy Johnson. { Capt. Nathaniel Frye.
1712–16	Mr. Benjamin Stevens		

Mr. Simon Bradstreet was one of the Assistants or Council during most of the time of his residence in Andover. He was one of the United Commissioners in 1644, and Agent to the Court of Charles II., 1662.

Mr. Dudley Bradstreet was appointed Councillor in 1686, but declined to serve.

DUDLEY BRADSTREET,
BENJAMIN STEVENS, } *Justices of the Peace.*
JOHN OSGOOD,

A List[1] of the Principal Town Officers in the First Fifty Years from the Incorporation.

1665. Thomas Johnson, *constable;* Richard Sutton, *fence-viewer.*

1669. Sergt. Henry Ingalls, *constable;* John Lovejoy, William Chandler, *fence-viewers* ffor the southerly parte of the towne ; Samuel Martin and Nathan Stevens ffor the northerly parte of the towne ; Nathan Parker & John Abbot for the new-field ; Daniel Poor & John ffarnum ffor the ffields over Shawshin. Thomas Chandler is chosen to *cary the votes* to Salem. Daniel Poor, *grand juryman.*

[1] The records are scattered and immethodical, and the alphabetical index lost, so that it is possible some names have been overlooked. The quaint method of recording has been in a measure copied. The mode of dating 1670–71 (and sometimes either date indiscriminately from January to March), adds to the uncertainty of the dates.

1670. Mr. Bradstreet, John ffry, senior, Richard Barker, Lieutenant Osgood, *selectmen;* William Chandler, *constable;* Stephen Osgood, *grand juryman.*

1671. Mr. Bradstreet, Lieutenant Osgood, Richard Barker, John Stevens, John ffry, *selectmen;* Sergeant Ingalls is impowered by the towne to raise to be brought to Mr. Dane all his rates and wood and to sue or distrain upon any that shall neglect or lie behind. Richard Barker, John ffry, junior, Henry Ingolls, and Thomas ffarnum, *surveyors.*

1672. Mr. Bradstreet, Lieut. Osgood, Richard Barker, John Stevens. Ensign Chandler, *selectmen;* Stephen Johnson, *constable;* Henry Abbot, senr., *grand juryman;*[1] John Stevens to view all such things as cutting down trees; Ensign Chandler, John Stevens, Richard Barker, *survaires* for mending the high roads; William Chandler, *grand juryman.*[1]

1673. Mr. Dudley Bradstreet, Lieut. Osgood, Nathan Barker, Ensign Chandler, *selectmen;* Samuel Martin, *constable;* Stephen Johnson, *grand juryman;* Dudley Bradstreet, *clerk of ye writts and of the towne* and likewise to record all Grants laid out in the Towne booke. Feb. 2. John Stevens, Stephen Johnson, George Abbot, senr., Daniel Poor, *surveiors.*

1674. Richard Barker, sen., Mr. Edmond Faulkner, Daniell Poore, Sergt. Thomas ffarnum, John frie, junr., *selectmen;* John Lovejoy, Nathan Parker, *constables;* John Barker, *grand juryman;* William Ballard & William Chandler, *surveyors* for ye south end of ye towne, Sergeant ffarnum & Dudley Bradstreet for ye north end of ye towne.

1675. Richard Barker, Daniel Poor, Edmond ffaulkner, *selectmen;* Nathaniel Dane, Steven Osgood, *constables;* John ffry, junr., *grand juryman;* Edmond ffaulkner, *town clerk.*

1676. George Abbot, senr., *branding man;* Left. John Osgood, Ensign Thomas Chandler, John ffrie, jr., Stephen Johnson, Dudley Bradstreet, *selectmen;* Christopher Osgood, *constable* (south part of the towne); Timothy Johnson, *constable* (north part of the towne); Sergt. John Stevens and Thomas Johnson, *surveiors;* Dudley Bradstreet, *town clerke,* to enter all graunts in ye great towne booke, for which he is to have two pence a graunt in money or else he is not obliged. . . . .

1677. Left. John Osgood, Ensign Thomas Chandler, Daniel Poor, John ffrie, Stephen Johnson, Dudley Bradstreet, *selectmen;* Corp^l. Samuel Martin, *constable* (north end); Thomas Osgood (south end); John Marston, senr., *grand juryman.*

[1] Two town meetings, January 6, February 3.

1678. John ffrie, junior, Richard Barker, senr., William Chandler, John Barker, Christopher Osgood, *selectmen;* John Bridges, *constable* (north end); Samuel Hoult, *constable* (south end); Samuel Martin, *grand juryman.*

1679. Richard Barker, senr., Deacon ffrie, John Barker, William Chandler, Christopher Osgood, *selectmen;* Joseph Robinson, *constable* (north end); Joseph Wilson, *constable* (south end); Ralph Farnum, *grand juryman.*

1680. Capt. Dudley Bradstreet, Left. John Osgood, Ensign Thomas Chandler, Sergt. John Stevens, Sergt. John Barker, *selectmen;* George Abbot, *constable* (north end); Joseph Ballard, *constable* (south end); Richard Barker, senr., *grand juryman.*

1681. Capt. Bradstreet, Left. Osgood, Ensign Thomas Chandler, Richard Barker, senr., Deacon ffrie, *selectmen;* Samuel ffrie, *constable* (south end); Joseph Stevens, *constable* (north end); Daniel Poor, sen., *grand juryman.*

1682. Capt. Bradstreet, Left. Osgood, Ensigne Chandler, Richard Barker, senr., Sergt. John Stevens, *selectmen;* John Abbot, *constable* (north end); Joseph Ballard, *constable* (south end); John Abbot, senr., *grand jury.*

1683. Christopher Osgood, Steven Osgood, Sergt. Barker, John Marston, senr., Daniel Poor, senr., *selectmen;* William Barker, *constable* (north end); Left. Chandler, *constible* (south end); John Farnum, *grand juryman.*

1684. Capt. Bradstreet, Sergt. Barker, Christopher Osgood, Daniel Poor, senr., John Marston, *selectmen;* John Osgood, *constable* (for north end); George Abbot, *constable* (for south end). April 25th: Abraham Foster, *constable* (for south end); Capt. John Abbot, *grand juryman.*

1685. Capt. Dudley Bradstreet, Capt. John Osgood, Left. Chandler, Ensign John Stevens, Corporal Samuel Marston, *selectmen;* Corporal Nathan Stevens, *constable* (north end); James Frie, *constable* (south end); Corp¹ Samuel Holt, *grand juryman;* Left. Chandler, *lot-layer.*

1686. Capt. John Osgood, Richard Barker, senr., Daniel Poor, senr., Stephen Osgood, Christopher Osgood, *selectmen;* Francis Faulkner, *constable* (north end); John Chandler, *constable* (south end).

1687. Capt. John Osgood, Daniel Poor, senr., Christopher Osgood, John Aslebe, Joseph Ballard, *selectmen;* Stephen Parker, *constable* (north end); Samuel Blanchard, *constable* (south end).

1688. Capt. Bradstreet, Capt. Osgood, Left. John Stevens,

Christopher Osgood, Capt. John Aslebe, Corp¹ Joseph Ballard, *selectmen;* Capt. Thomas Chandler, *commissioner;* Stephen Parker, *constable* (north end) ; Samuel Blanchard (south end).

1689. There was "no choice" or election till [1] July ; "whereas ye time was lapsed" the election then made was only till January following : Captain Bradstreet, Capt. John Osgood, Capts. John Aslebe, John Osgood, junr., Richard Barker, senr., *selectmen;* Daniel Poor, *constable* (north end) ; ffrancis Dane, *constable* (south end).

1690. Capt. Bradstreet, Capt. Chandler, Sergt. Joseph Ballard, John Abbot, senr., Henry Holt, *selectmen;* Walter Wright, Ephraim Foster, *constables.*

1691. [January 5, 1690, for the year 1691, which was not reckoned to begin till March.] Capt. Thomas Chandler, Left. Jno. Barker, Sergt. Jno. Chandler, John Abbot, senr., *selectmen;* George Abbot, William Johnson, *constables;* William Lovejoy, *grand juryman;* Sergt. Henry Ingalls, *jury of trials.*

1692. Capt. Dudley Bradstreet, Sergt. John Chandler, Sergt. John Aslebe, John Abbot, jr., Corp¹ Sam¹ ffrie, *selectmen;* Timothy Osgood, Joseph Ballard, *constables;* Quartermaster James Frie, *grand juryman.*

1693. Capt. Dudley Bradstreet, Capt. Osgood, Andrew Peters, John Chandler, Christopher Osgood, *selectmen;* Benjamin Stevens, William Abbot, *constables;* Ephraim Stevens, *clerk of yᵉ market;* Left. John Barker, *commissioner for assessments;* Corp¹ George Abbot, *sealer of leather;* Henry Hoult, senr, ffrancis Dane, *surveiors* (south end) ; Ephraim Stevens, John Osgood, *surveiors* (north end) ; Ensign Samuel Martin, Corp¹ Nathan Stevens, Hopestill Tyler, Walter Wright, *tything-*men ; Stephen Parker, Timothy Osgood, Abraham Foster, Joseph Wilson, Samuel Phelps, Joseph Marble, senr., *fence viewers.*

1694. Capt. Dudley Bradstreet, *town clerk;* Mr. Andrew Peters, John Abbot, senr., Mr. James ffrie, Sam¹ Blanchard, senr., John Osgood, *selectmen & overseers of poor;* John Barker, *commissioner;* Richard Barker, Henry Holt, senr., *constables;* Sergt. Ephraim Stevens, Joseph Stevens, Capt. George Abbot, William Lovejoy, *surveyors;* Sergt. Jno. Aslebe, Sergt. Jno. Bridges, Francis Dane, Nehemiah Abbot, *tithing men;* Corp¹ Samuel Osgood, Benj. Barker, *fence-viewers* (for north end) ; William Johnson, William Chandler, jun., *fence viewers* (for south end) ; Sergt. Ephraim Stevens, *clerk of yᵉ market;* Corp¹ George Abbot, *leather sealer;* Benjamin Barker, *pound-keeper* (north end) ; William Johnson,

[1] On account of the disturbances caused by the Revolution of '89.

pound-keeper (south end); Benjamin Stevens, Sam¹ Marble, John Marston, jr., Jno. Ballard, Benjamin Abbot, Jno. Stevens, *Hawards*[1] or *field-drivers*.

1695. Mr. Andrew Peters, *treasurer;* Capt. Thomas Chandler, Deacon John ffrie, Jno. Abbot, *assessors;* Dudley Bradstreet, *town clerk;* Majr. Dudley Bradstreet, Left. John Osgood, Quartermaster James ffric, John Abbot senr., Sergt. Ephraim Stevens, *selectmen;* John Carlton, William Lovejoy, *constables;* Sergt. Ephraim Stevens, Joseph Stevens, Sergt. George Abbot, William Lovejoy, Henry Holt, Stephen Parker, *surveiors;* Ensign Martin, Nathaniel Dane, Benjamin Abbot, William Chandler, *Tything men;* Francis Dane, Joseph Marble, Nathan Stevens, Samuel Marble, *fence viewers;* Sergt. Ephraim Stevens, *clerk of y² market;* Sergt. George Abbot, *leather-sealer;* haywards same as last year; Benjamin Barker & William Johnson, *pound-keepers;* Andrew Peters, *treasurer;* Left. John Barker, John Chandler, Joseph Stevens, *a standing committee*, to take care to keep y² meetinghouse in good repair & to hire suitable workmen for that end & to give their accounts yearly to y² selectmen whoe shall order y² treasurer to pay them, they putting money or moneys worth into y² treasurer's hand to enable him thereto; Samuel Ingalls, *grand juryman*, for y² *quarter* sessions att Ipswich; Andrew ffoster & William Chandler, *tertius*, chosen upon y² jury of trials at y² inferior Court of pleas.

1696. Maj. Dudley Bradstreet, *clerk;* Maj. Dudley Bradstreet, Left. John Osgood, Capt. Christopher Osgood, Left. Chandler, Mr. Andrew Peters, *selectmen;* Sergt. William Chandler, Sergt. Samuel Osgood, *constables;* Sergt. Ephraim Stevens, Dea. Joseph Stevens, Corp¹ Stephen Parker, Sergt. George Abbot, Sergt. William Lovejoy, Henry Holt, *surveyors;* Qr. Mr. James Frie, Corp¹. Benjamin Barker, Thomas Chandler, jr., Henry Holt, jr., *tything men;* Timothy Osgood, Samuel Hutchinson, Corp¹. Benj. Abbot, Nehemiah Abbot, *fence viewers;* Sergt. Ephraim Stevens, *clerk of the market;* Sergt. George Abbot, *leather sealer;* Benjamin Barker, William Johnson, *pound-keeper;* Mr. Andrew Peters, *town treasurer*.

[There were town meetings in March, May, and August, this year.] May elections as follows : —

[1] "Hayward" [Fr. *haie, hedge,* and *ward* = hedgeward.] A person appointed to keep cattle from doing injury to hedges. In New England the hayward's duty is to impound cattle and swine, which are running at large contrary to law. — *Webster.*

Dea. Joseph Stevens, Sergt. Saml. ffrie, grand jurymen to serve at y⁕ superiour court att Ipswich ; Corpl. Hooker Osgood, Jno. Ballard, jury of tryalls at y⁕ above⁕ᵈ court ; Capt. Christopher Osgood, representative for y⁕ town.

A List of the Selectmen Second Half Century from the Incorporation, 1696-1746.

1696. (August elections.) Sergt. John Aslebe, Qr. Mr. John Frie, John Abbot sr., assessors for y⁕ tax of seventy-six pounds granted at y⁕ Genl. Cort 27 May 1696, ye assessors refused to serve for y¹ y⁕ selectmen this year are to be the assessors as y⁕ law directs & took their oath as y⁕ law directs Aug. 2, 1696.

Maj. Dudley Bradstreet, Capt. Christopher Osgood [2], Left. John Osgood [2], Mr. Andrew Peters, Left. John Chandler (1697).[1] [Sergt. John Aslebe is chosen a lott layer in y⁕ roome of Left. Thomas Johnson, his age calling for a writt of ease], Left. Samuel Frye (1698), Capt. James ffrie, Ensign John Aslebe (1699), Samuel Osgood [2], Samuel Ingalls, Ephraim Stevens (1703), John Osgood [6], George Abbot [9], John Frie [8] (1710), John Chandler [16], Richard Barker [2] (1714), Nathanel Abbot, William Lovejoy [2] (1715), Ephraim Foster [2], John Abbot [6] (1719), Francis Dane [2], Timothy Johnson [9] (1720), Joseph Osgood, Benjamin Barker [4] (1722), Nehemiah Abbot, William Foster (1723), Joseph Robinson [2], John Johnson (1725), John Farnum [2] (1725), Ephraim Abbot [4] (1726), Henry Ingalls (1727), James Bridges, Thomas Chandler (1728), Ebenezer Abbot (1734), James Stevens, Joseph Sibson (1742), Nathaniel Frye (1743), James Ingalls [2] (1745).[2]

Town Treasurers.

Andrew Peters (1697-1704), Lieut. John Aslebe (1704-1706), Andrew Peters (1707-1713), William Foster (1714-1716), Timothy Osgood (1717-1721), James Stevens (1721-1729), James Ingalls (1729-1732), James Stevens (1733-1734) Henry Ingalls (1734-1737), Isaac Frie, 1738 . . . . Joshua Frye, 1745.

A word or two may not be amiss in regard to some of the offices above specified : that of tithing-man is described in the

---

[1] The date of year after the names denotes the time when first found recorded. The figure in brackets denotes the number of times recorded as in office.

[2] These are collected from memoranda scattered throughout the records, and possibly may be incomplete.

chapter on the churches; it referring principally to the conduct of persons in regard to public worship and observance of the Sabbath.

The haywards, as has been said, took care in regard to the injury to property by domestic animals.

The office of branding-man had to do with the safety of the cattle which ran loose, also horses and other animals. Each town had its brand-mark. The General Court in 1647, ordered that the brand-mark of Andover is A, ordered "for horses to be set upon one of y^e neare quarters."

Each individual owner also had his brand-mark. The following is from the Town Records: —

James Fries Ear-Mark Recorded.

"December the 25th 1734 the ear mark that James Frie Giveth his cattel and other Creatures is as followeth *viz*, a half crop cut out of the under side of the Left ear split or cut out about the middel of the Top of the ear, called by som a figger of seven."

From many records of stray animals taken up, the following are selected: —

"Thomas Abbot of Andover hath taken up a blak horse as a stray, no eare marke or brand but a few white haires in his forehead and a few in his neck, prysed by William Chandler & Samuel Martin at 4 £ 10 s, the 18th day of December 1671." [1]

"Benjamin Frye of Andover hath a darke bay mare, a blaze in her forehead, branded with the letter P on her neare shoulder, taken up as a stray the 26th of December '72, prized at 3£ 10s by John Lovejoy & William B———. Entered 13 March 1672."

"1686. Andrew Peeters of Ipswich hath a browne bay horse, a star in the forehead, mealy belly, browne nose, noe ear-marke, nor brand that is seen, doct: — alsoe a sorell mare, a white slip on the nose & white in the forehead, mealy under the belly, a little piece cut, a snip neare eare, doct & lame; prized both of them at 40s by Simon T[uttle?]."

[1] *Registry of Deeds*, "Ipswich," Book I.

Not the horses and cattle only, but the settlers themselves were liable to go astray and become bewildered and lost in the trackless wilds. Death in the woods was no uncommon occurrence. Witness the following, the first record of a coroner's jury: —

"The verdict of jury appyointed upon the body of Peter Allyn whoe going forth into the woods to worke in March last could not be found nor heard of notwithstanding the diligent search that was made for him several days till this 21 : 4th '64. An Indian informed there was an Englishman found in the River called Shawshin about a myle from the Towne of Andover, wee repared to the place & found the s^d Peter Allyn lying in the s^d river pt of his clothing on & girt about him, his breaches gone, stockings being rolled or torne off & p^t of his flesh consumed soe wee concluded according to our best apprehension that hee lost himself in the woods & going over the bridge accidentally fell in & was drowned; that our verdict witness our hands this 21 : 4th '64

                    JOHN FRIE
                    RICHARD BARKER
The mark of JOHN JOHNSON
                    HENRY INGALS
                    RALFE + FFARNUM (his mark)
                    JOHN + RUSSE (his mark)
                    GEORGE ABBOT
                    MARK + GRAVES (his mark)
                    ROBERT + RUSSEL (his mark)
                    TIMOTHY JOHNSON
                    WALTER WRIGHT (his mark)"

Among the above named officers of the town was the clerk of the market. He had the care of the standard weights and measures. In 1649 the "two Constables of Andover" (no names), were presented before the County Court "for want of settled weights and measures" Witnesse Nathaniel Parker of Andover.

The following record in regard to the clerk of the market is found in the selectmen's accounts: —

"21 April 1719: Received of Robart Swan executor to the estate of Ensign Ephraim Stevens clark of the market for the town of Andover deceased, the said Towne Stander for waits and mesures: *viz*, two half-bushels, one peck, one half-peck; one ale quartt-pott, one pint pott, one half pint. Waits; one half-hundred, one quarter of a hundred, one half quarter of a hundred, one seven pound wait, one four pound wait, one two-pound wait, one half-pound wait, one quarter of a pound wait, one two ounce wait, one melting-ladle, iron sealer, one yard-measure, and delivered unto Abiel Stevens clerke of the market."

In 1716, the town voted "that an iron melting-ladle be procured for the clerk of ye market to melt lead to make weights, as occasion may be for the inhabitants and to be paid for by ye town and kept for the town's use."

In 1717 there was an attempt made to keep the accounts more clearly and improve upon the method of arrangement, with the purchase of a "new booke." In this book was the following entry: —

"This Book was bought in the month of August, in the yeare of our Lord anno dom. 1717. For ye Town of Andover for their selectmens youse sucksessively f^r to keep their accounts for the s^d Town Reackonings. And they have begun the book with an alphabett[1] to the Ready finding their accounts and Reckonings and so have begun for to page this Book and Desir it may be paged out by those that shall suckseed in place."

The town of Andover was, as Mr. Woodbridge stated, made up at the beginning of "choice men" "very desirable" and "good Christians." These settlers took care to insure as far as possible the continuance of such a class of citizens. The selectmen were empowered to examine into the character and habits of all persons seeking residence and to admit none who were idle or immoral.

"ANDOVER, *the 30th of January*, 1719-20."
"To MR. EBENEZER LOVEJOY, *Constable*, Greeting:

"Whereas there is severall Persons com to Reside in our Towne and we feare a futer charge and as the Law directs to prevent such charge; you are Requested in his Majesty's name forthwith to warn the severall parsons under wrighten: to depart out of our Towne as the law directs to, least they prove a futer charge to the Towne." [Signed by the Selectmen.]

The town also encouraged desirable persons to settle by

[1] The alphabet being not now with the Book the "ready finding" is somewhat hindered.

making them grants of land, or furnishing facilities for the investment of capital as in mills, iron-works, ferries, etc. Ministers and masters of grammar schools were exempt from taxation.

The town grew with considerable rapidity, considering its inland situation and its exposure to attacks of Indians. Yet it was hardly a large or an old settlement before emigration from it began.

It would be natural to suppose that the children of the first settlers, who had heard from their fathers, or had themselves shared in the privations and hardships of pioneer life, would in their manhood have been thankful to be in a measure exempt from such a lot and to enjoy in peace and quiet the advantages of a comparatively old settlement. But there was a fascination in the wilderness and a temptation in town building which were irresistible. To hew a way to fortune, as his axe cleaved the path in the forest, was the pioneer's hope; to have lands which would be all his own in a place where acres could be got for the clearing, even though it were at the cost of ease and comfort, seemed better to the ambitious sons of the planters than to be content with the comparatively small portion of the paternal estates which fell to any one of the usually many children of the first settlers. Moreover, a new town offered opportunities for "advancement," and this was the object of all the settlers, from Governor Thomas Dudley, seeking it for his son-in-law, the first minister of Andover, down to the blacksmith's apprentice, who looked to the day when he should set up a shop like his master's, and perhaps become, like that master, a representative to the Great and General Court. Capitalists also sought investment for their money in building new towns, setting in operation corn-mill and saw-mill, and carrying on lumber trade with Barbadoes and other places, whither the colonists shipped their products and exchanged them for commodities of comfort and luxury.

Thus, as always, where land invites, emigration began. Indeed, the planters of Andover seem to have felt very much cramped for room from the outset. The territory which now seems ample for thousands was "too strait" for a hundred or two hundred. Witness the following petition. It is not dated, but must have been within the first fifty years:—

"To ye Hon^b Genl Court[1] .... Humbly Sheweth.—That ye wise and gracious providence of God having Disposed ye petitioners condicions and habitations soe y^t now by ye blessings y^t God hath given them in their estates and posterity they find themselves exceedingly straitened in their possessions and accommodations, many of your petitioners having for ye benefitt of gods ordinances and christian communion and neighborhood many years kept themselves and children under a narrow confinement, and whereas this Honble Court have always in order to ye promoting ye publick weale been willing and ready to incourage all reasonable requests with respect to ye orderly and sociable settlement of towns and plantations; and whereas many of y^r petitioners are much straitened in their p'sonall acommodations and most of their children grown up and many others of ye petitioners wholly destitute of land for settlement and soe under a necessity to look out for inlargment and places of habitation.

"And forasmuch as: This Honble Court have by sundry petitions granted, given and disposed sundry large and accomodable ffarms to sundry p'sons viz to ye worshipful ye deputy Govr Majr Denison and to ye Reverend Mr. Cobbett and Mr. Higginson and to Marshall Murcheson and others lying to ye northward of Merrimack river, as they are now laid out and to the north west of Haverhill bounds and southerly from Exeter and forasmuch as between and about ye s^d farms and bounds of s^d Town There is sundry pieces and Tracts of land which added and granted as a township to ye s^d farms may make a convenient township and forasmuch as your petitioners have consulted ye proprietors of ye farmes and find them ready and willing to give all Due incouragement for ye settling of a town or plantation y^r petitioners humbly pray that ye Lands adjacent to ye bounds and farmes aforesaid being not already appropriated and laid out may be granted to ye petitioners and ye proprietors of s^d farmes with such enlargement as may according to ye place and nature of ye Land be thought convenient; there being besides y^r petitioner forty persons at least in ye whole under one hundred, if accommodations be found ready to settle themselves, sons and servts upon, and y^t ye s^d Graunt may be with and upon tender and favourable considerations and conditions granted to y^m with respect to ye extent and

---

[1] *Mass. Archives*, vol. cxii., page 202.

tyme of settlement y^t soe such of ye petitioners as cannot comfortably make a suddayne remove may not be discouraged.

JOSEPH PARKER, SENR.	JOSHUA WOODMAN.
NATHAN PARKER.	EPHRAIM STEVENS.
WALTER WRIGHT.	SAMUEL FRYE.
SAMUEL PRESTON.	JAMES FFRY.
SAMUEL HOULT.	TIMOTHY JOHNSON.
EDWARD WHITTINGTON.	STEPHEN OSGOOD.
NATHAN STEVENS.	JOSEPH MARBLE.
ROBT. RUSSELL.	SAMUEL MARBLE.
THO. JOHNSON.	SAMUEL MARTYN.
STEPHEN JOHNSON.	JNO. RUSS.
STEPH. BARNATT.	JOSEPH PARKER, JUNR."
RICHARD BARKER.	

In 1723[1] Stephen Barker and others of Andover, Bradford, and Haverill, petitioned for the grant of a tract of land called Pennacook, the present site of Concord, N. H. Their petition, though granted by the House, did not find favor with the Council; but they obtained another tract, now the site of Methuen. A relic of their exploration at Pennacook is the following:[2] —

"PENNECOOK, *March* 22, 172¾.

"Marching, Capt. James Frie and Lieut. Stephen Barker with thirty men moved from Andover to go to Pennecook; ye 1st day was stormy, but we went to Nutfield and lodged there that night; the 2d day we came to Amiskeage and Lodged there; the 3d day we came to Suncook, in s^d Pennecook and built four camps and Lodgd there; the 4th day we came to Pennecook Plains att ye Intervale Lands about 11 of the clock. There we found five of those men who came from N. Ireland (?) Mr. Houston was one of them; they came to us and we choze Capt Frie to discourse them with 4 men. They say that they have a Graunt of this Pennecook on both sides of the River. They call us Rebbels and commande us to discharge the Place both in the Kings name and in the Provinces and if we dont in a fortnight they will gett us off.

---

[1] In 1719 some Scotch-Irish emigrants, who had landed in Boston, came to Andover and stayed here for some months, while waiting for their party to proceed to Londonderry to make a settlement. They introduced the *potato* into the town.

[2] *Mass. Archives*, vol. lii., 45.

We therefore desire you Justice Stevens, with the Committee to send us word whether we have any encouragement to stay or else to draw off. But Capt. Frie's courage is so that he will stay allone rather than Let them usurpers drive us off."

"A True coppy of ye Journal sent from Pennecook and of their Treatment When they got there."

The Pennacook tract was ultimately granted to Mr. Benjamin Stevens and others. Among them was the Rev. Samuel Phillips, who in the petition stated that, having no house-lot rights at Andover, and being the father of several sons, he desired to make provision for his family. Mr. Timothy Walker, of Woburn, who had been master of the Andover Grammar School, was also one of the party interested, and became the first minister. The beginning of active operations was in the spring of 1726. The place was then, as is said in an ancient description of it, "a perfect wilderness, having not the least sign that human foot ever trod there, and twenty miles up into the Indian country." Numerous meetings of the persons principally interested in the settlement were held at Andover, "at Mr. Stevens dwelling;" at Bradford, at Griffin's tavern; at Haverhill, at Eastman's tavern, and at Ipswich, for almost a year before things were brought to the point of setting out. In September, 1726, Ensign John Chandler, of Andover, John Ayer, of Haverhill, and Mr. William Barker, of Andover, were chosen "to clear a sufficient cart way to Pennecook the nighest and best way they can from Haverhill." Other still more important leaders of the enterprise were Lieutenant-governor William Tailer and J. N. Wainwright, Esq., Clerk of the Committee of the General Court. The latter two had been up in May to view the place, and Mr. Wainwright wrote an account of their journey. Ensign John Chandler went with them and helped survey the land. He was a man peculiarly fitted for a pioneer's adventures, — athletic and strong, and of great courage, a noted wrestler, and a man whom to lay violent hands on was dangerous. The travellers went by way of Londonderry, where was a tavern at which they refreshed themselves with "Small Beer." While they were prospecting, they were waited upon by a committee sent by Governor Wentworth of New Hampshire, who warned them that they would attempt to make a plantation there at their peril ; for the place belonged to the jurisdiction of New Hampshire. The settlers made bold answer that, as the committee were sent by the Governor of New Hampshire, so were they sent by the Governor of Massachusetts, and that they should proceed with their work, which they accordingly did. Their chief fear seems to have been of rattlesnakes. "We saw divers rattle-snakes but thanks to God, nobody was harmed." They voted to pay three pence per tail for every rattlesnake's tail (the snake killed in Pennacook), to be paid by the treasurer on sight of the tail. Capt. Benjamin Stevens was first treasurer of the company, succeeded by Dea. John Osgood. They voted to build a block-house, a saw-mill, and a ferry-boat, in 1726. In 1730, November 18, the minister was ordained. The two ministers from Andover, Mr. Phillips and Mr. Barnard, and Mr. Brown of Haverhill, officiated. Among the settlers were several of the Abbot family of Andover. One of these was the son of Timothy Abbot, who had been carried captive by the Indians into this very region, as is supposed.

The bard of the Merrimack has made the name of Pennacook immortal in his "Legend of the Bridal" of the Indian maiden Weetamoo, daughter of Passaconaway, whose haunts were the region along the river, and who often pitched his wigwam in Andover meadows and woods. As the men of Andover, stout Ensign Chandler, and Edward Abbot, and William Barker, and the others plunged into the thick woods, axe in hand, or chopped down trees, and cut off the tails of rattlesnakes, or loaded their guns to shoot a "redskin," and pulled out their hunting-knives to scalp him as coolly as they would have to take the hide from the red-deer, they did not think much about the poetry of the scene. They had seen the homes of old Andover too often fired, and the blood of their children stain the savage's tomahawk, to have any compunctions about killing him.

When Mr. Barnard preached the ordination sermon of the minister of Pennacook, he gave thanks that here God was now to be worshipped by Christians, where formerly there had been only heathen "salvages."

Beautiful as is the legend of Pennacook, and great as is our sympathy with the wrongs of the race that has been exterminated by the Christian "pale-face," we cannot agree that times were better when the Indian's wigwam was the only dwelling, or think that the poet means literal truth when he suggests that the river of swift waters would lament if it could find voice, over the changes which the centuries have brought, —

> "O stream of the mountains, if answer of thine
> Could rise from thy waters to question of mine,
> Methinks, through the din of thy thronged banks, a moan
> Of sorrow would swell for the days that are gone."

From the narrative thus far it is evident that the town, though projected by a few of the rich and influential men of the colony, was composed, for the most part, of the middle and humbler classes, yeomen and artisans. There were not at Andover in the beginning more than a half-dozen men, in fact, hardly so many, who could be called rich or learned. Good, honest, plain citizens, self-respecting and respected, were the first planters of old Andover, with one or two families among them of the highest social position and connections in the colony.

The following list, showing the occupations of the principal settlers, has been made up from incidental records in various documents: —

Minister. Rev. John Woodbridge, 1644; Rev. Francis Dane.

Gentleman. Mr. Simon Bradstreet, Col. Dudley Bradstreet.

Yeoman.[1] Mr. John Osgood, 1650; George Abbot, senr., John Stevens, Richard Barker.

Husbandman.[1] Daniel Poor, Richard Sutton, Henry Ingalls, Job Tyler, William Ballard, William Chandler, Samuel Martin, John Abbot, Francis Faulkner.

Carpenter. Thomas Johnson, Stephen Johnson, Stephen Osgood, Joseph Parker, 2d, Samuel Wardwell.

Tanner. Joseph Parker, John Osgood, Christopher Osgood.

Mason. John Marble.

Bricklayer. Samuel Marble.

Cooper. Joseph Wilson.

[1] Convertible terms.

Wheelwright. John Farnum, 1712.
Blacksmith. Thomas Chandler, John Bridges, 1692; Hopestil Tyler, 1692; Jacob Preston.
Weaver. Richard Sutton, 1658; Walter Wright, Mark Graves, Samuel Phelps, Edward Phelps, Samuel Frye, Stephen Barnard, John Abbot, William Abbot.
Tailor. Thomas Farnum, George Abbot.
Shoemaker. John Johnson.
Cordwainer. George Abbot, 1693.
Distiller. Andrew Peters.
Mariner. Robert Gray.

The history of the industrial enterprises and the educational and religious institutions founded by the first settlers, will be related in subsequent chapters. A few words may here be said to outline this period of the early history. The first industry which engaged general interest was the saw-mill and corn-mill. The town built a mill at its own expense. Mr. Bradstreet is said also to have owned a mill. Joseph Parker had also a mill (perhaps the same which the town helped to build) on the Cochichawick. Stephen Johnson owned a saw-mill in 1667. The town gave encouragement to Walter Wright and Edward Whittington to build a fulling-mill in 1673; but there seems to have been none built till 1689, and then the Ballard brothers were the owners. Mr. Bradstreet owned iron works in Boxford, and there were iron works set up at Andover, probably before 1700.

The fisheries were a great source of profit for a long time, and a monopoly of the fishing places was granted to individuals who carried on extensive operations. In 1681 a vote was passed granting a monopoly of fishing for twenty-one years : —

"Granted to Capt. Bradstreet, Left. Osgood & Ensign Chandler and such others as they shall associate to themselves, the libertie & privilege of fishing in Shawshin River from ye mouth of said river up to ye old bridge and upon Merrimack river twenty rods below ye mouth of s^d river of Shawshin and twenty rods up the said river of Merrimack from the mouth of said river of Shawshin and twenty rods into ye said river of Merrimack from ye upper end and lower end of ye aforesaid twenty rods & ye aboves^d persons with such as they shall joyne with them are to enjoy y⁰ aboves⁴ privileges the full and just terme of twenty-one years from y⁰ first day of May next. The first ten years they shall have it for nothing, ye other eleven years either to pay y⁰ towne 10 pounds per annum or resigne up their future interest in y⁰ s⁴ place, and alsoe they are to sell to any inhabitant basse at 5ᵈ per piece provided those yᵗ buy, buy two at one time, y⁰ parties buying to chose one, y⁰ parties selling to chose another ; and if y⁰ parties buying choose rather to pay 3 pence per piece for basse in money y⁰ owners of said privilege shall not refuse y⁰ same, provided as above said, they buy two at a time."

Another vote, 1696, provides for making a "ware for y⁰ catching of fish."

"4 *May* 1696. Voted and passed yᵗ these tenn men hereafter named shall have the libertie of making a ware for y⁰ catching of fish in Merrimack River att a place commonly called y⁰ fishing place against Maj. Bradstreets his Ground. According to these terms following; viz, to sell to y⁰ inhabitants of this town at any price not exceeding twelve pence y⁰ score & y⁰ inhabitants of this town to be supplied before strangers :

"Mr. Andrew Peeters, Left. John Chandler, Left. Thomas Johnson, Sergt John Aslebe, William Chandler senr, Andrew Foster, Walter Wright senr, Henry Holt sr. Thomas Osgood, Daniel Bigsbee are y⁰ s⁴ tenn men.

"This aboves⁴ ware to be erected & finished as soon as y⁰ streame will permit upon y⁰ forfiture of y⁰ grant."

The making of spirituous liquors was a profitable industry. Mr. Andrew Peters was a distiller, and Mr. James Bridges, 1721, and earlier, owned a malt-house.

There seem to have been no "stores" proper for about seventy-five years. Salem was "y⁰ nearest market towne" for many years. In 1693 there was a "market" at Andover. Doubtless it displayed country produce of various sorts, as the markets of England. The precise duties of "y⁰ clerke of y⁰ market" are not ascertained.

A bill of goods bought by an Andover citizen, 1677, and which he was sued for non-payment of, is on record. Paul White (of Haverhill ?), brought the suit. The amount claimed was ten pounds, ten shillings. Among the items were : —

3 y^ds of blew linen.
2 glass bottles & 2 qts of rum.
3½ lbs of sugar @ 7d.
5 y^ds of sarge @ 6d.
Silke & buttons & a combe & horne-book.
Tobacco, tongs, knife.
5 qts rum.
Gingerbread.

3 lbs of fruit.
A pt of wine and liquor.

Latting-ware.
1 gallon of molasses.

A large part of the trade was by barter, neighbors exchanging with each other their surplus products.

The first stores of which record has been found were that of Mr. Isaac Abbot, in the South Parish, and that kept by the son of Rev. Samuel Phillips, Deacon (the Hon.) Samuel Phillips, in North Andover. The advice given by the minister of the South Church to his son, in regard to carrying on his business, is not too old fashioned to be of use now : —

"*Sept 27th* 1738
"Andover, South Parish.

.... "As to your trading, keep fair and true accounts, and do wrong to no man ; but sell as cheap to a child as you would to one that is adult ; never take advantage of any, either because of their Ignorance or their Poverty ; for if you do it will not turn to your own advantage ; but ye contrary. And as you may not wrong any person, so neither wrong ye TRUTH in any case whatever, for ye Sake of gain or from any other motive. Either be silent or else speak ye Truth.

"And be prudent but yet not over timorous and over Scrupulous in ye article of Trusting, lest you stand in your own light. Some people are more honest p'haps than you think for, and it may be will pay sooner than you expect. Keep to your shop, if you expect that to keep you and be not out of ye way when customers come."

The agricultural industries, which were at the foundation of all the others, were at the outset of the simplest sort. The farming implements were few and rude. A great part of the country being covered with forests, it required much time and labor to fell the trees, and clear space for dwellings and house-lots, orchards and gardens. The largest farmers had not over four oxen, and six to eight cows. Horses were scarce. John Stevens had one horse, an ass, and colt, and two sheep (these were scarce), and a "stock of bees."

But the second fifty years made a great change. New settlers came in. Schools were established, and professional men were common in the town, and from numbering a score the town had increased to near a thousand.

Following is a list of the names not found on any of the former lists, but appearing among the tax-payers at the end of the first century from the incorporation: —

ADAMS, AVERY, BAILEY, BEARD, BERRY, BEVENS, BRAGG, BROWN, CHICKERING, CLARK, COLE, COLEBE, CUMMINS, DELAP, DILOWAY, DODGE, DOWNING, FAVER, FIELDS, FISH, FISKE, FURBUSH, GAGE, JACKSON, JENKINS, GOOLD, GORDON, HALL, HARDY, HOW, JONES, KIMBALL, KITTREDGE, LAHORS, LATHON, LEVALY, LEWES, MECARNEY, MERRILL, MORIAH, NOYES, PEABODY, PEARCE, PERSON, PEVY, PHILLIPS, SCALES, SETON, SHACKFORD, SHATTUCK, SIBSON, SMITH, STEEL, STEWARD, STILES, THURSTON, TOMSON, TOWNS, WALCOT, WARNER, WHISTON; WILEY, WOSSON.

Of the foregoing list of residents a very few of the more prominent will be now noticed.

PHILLIPS stands among the names most widely known. The Rev. Samuel Phillips (grandson of Rev. Samuel Phillips of Rowley, and great grandson of Rev. George Phillips, the first minister of Watertown) came to Andover, 1710, as pastor of the South Church. He was, as a minister, not entitled to house-lot rights, but, as his family grew, he obtained large grants of land in new townships, in Londonderry, Wenham, Chester, Hampshire, Freetown, etc. His sons, born in Andover, were the Hon. Samuel Phillips, who settled in North Andover, the Hon. John Phillips, of Exeter, the Hon. William Phillips, merchant, of Boston, father of Lieut.-governor William Phillips.

Hon. Samuel Phillips, a graduate of Harvard College, 1735, entered into trade and established himself at North Andover. He built for his residence, about 1752, the house still owned by the family, the gambrel-roofed manse on the

Boston road west of the burying-ground, and next south of the Bradstreet house, then the parsonage of the Rev. John Barnard. Mr. Phillips married Elizabeth Barnard, a cousin of the minister. His household was a model of a Christian family, his wife being a lady of rare virtues, and himself, deacon of the North Church, a man of inflexible principles and integrity. He was among the most distinguished men in the Revolutionary period, being representative, senator, and the friend of some of the most eminent statesmen of the time. He was conservative and cautious, though patriotic.

Of his family of seven children, only one survived the parents, Samuel Phillips, Jr., "Judge Phillips," also Lieutenant-governor. Through his influence Phillips Academy was founded by his father and uncle. He, after his marriage to Miss Phebe Foxcroft, of Cambridge. lived in the South Parish, and built the "mansion house" for his residence.

The Hon. Samuel Phillips, Sen., died 1790. Judge Phillips took charge of the estate until his son (born 1776), the Hon. John Phillips, entered into business and made it his residence.

Col. John Phillips, a graduate of Harvard College, 1795, studied law for a time, entered into trade in Charlestown, where he married Miss Lydia Gorham, daughter of the Hon. Nathaniel Gorham. Removing to North Andover, he lived here until his sudden death (1820), at the age of forty-four. His wife, only thirty-six years old, was left with thirteen children, three sons. Few ladies could have shown more wisdom and ability, and none in North Andover have commanded greater respect, or won more cordial regard, than Madam Lydia Gorham Phillips. She maintained a dignified family rule, bringing up her children all to adult years, and to occupy positions of honor and usefulness. Samuel Phillips, Esq., graduated at Harvard College, 1819, was attorney at law, Andover, 1829, and afterward in Newburyport. Mr. John Phillips was a merchant of Boston. Mr. Gorham Phillips is a merchant resident of the State of Georgia. One of the daughters (married to Mr. William Gray Brooks) was mother of the Rev. Phillips Brooks.

HOME OF DR THOMAS KITTREDGE SURGEON OF COLONEL FRYE'S REGIMENT 1775

THE PHILLIPS HOUSE AT NORTH ANDOVER

The latest representative of the family in the male line is Mr. Samuel Phillips, son of Samuel Phillips, Esq., lately cashier of the Maverick Bank, Boston.

The Phillips manse is probably the richest of any in the town in ancient relics of ancestral grandeur. The fine old family portraits, the portrait[1] of Washington, presented by his nephews, the antique silver tankards and porringers, the massive sideboard, the carved cabinet, in which used to be kept mysterious packets of ancient letters too private and sacred to be read by any outside the family, the tapestries wrought by hands long ago mouldered to dust, the samplers in frames over the mantel, and the profiles of the first master and mistress of the manse, in the hall, the library of quaint old books owned by generations of ministers, dating back to the settlement of the colony, — all these appeal powerfully to the imagination, and stir the feelings deeply, as one goes from room to room in this ancient house.

The Phillips name is also now represented at North Andover by a descendant from another branch of the ancient Watertown family, the Hon. Willard Phillips, of Salem. He, in 1867, purchased an estate and various adjoining lands on the Lawrence Road, remodelled and added to the buildings, and laid out extensive pleasure grounds, — landscape garden and woodland, — which make the place one of peculiar beauty and picturesqueness.

KITTREDGE is a name among the most eminent in the town history. Dr. John Kittredge came from Tewksbury to North Andover about 1741, and ever since there has been a physician[2] of this family in the town. Dr. Kittredge's father, a physician of Tewksbury, was often employed by Andover citizens in the west part of Andover, and this, doubtless,

[1] Formerly hanging here, now removed.
[2] Five names of physicians are on this list (at the end of the first fifty years there were none): Dr. Israel How came to Andover (South Parish) 1718, died 1740, succeeded by his son, Dr. Daniel How; Dr. Nehemiah Abbot came from Lexington to Andover (S. P.), removed to Chelmsford 1770; Dr. Nicholas Noyes came to North Andover 1725, died 1765; succeeded by his son, Dr. Ward Noyes. Dr. Parker Clark removed from Andover after about ten years' residence.

led to his son's establishing himself here. Dr. Kittredge lived near the present site of the machine-shop at North Andover, in the old house long disused and dilapidated and lately taken down. He owned land covering almost the whole of the present village. He was a surgeon of great repute. He had three sons physicians: Dr. Benjamin Kittredge, of Tewksbury, Dr. Jacob Kittredge, of Dover, Dr. Thomas Kittredge, of North Andover. He had also a daughter, Elizabeth, who assisted him in surgical operations, and after her marriage and removal to Londonderry, N. H., was frequently called on for medical advice. Once, in going to visit a patient in the evening, she made a misstep and fell, breaking her leg. She set the bone, and did it so well that she suffered no serious inconvenience. Dr. Thomas Kittredge succeeded his father (who died 1776) in practice at Andover. His valuable services in the Revolutionary period as surgeon of the First Massachusetts Regiment, and on the field at Bunker Hill, his fame as a physician in all the neighborhood round about Andover, his prominent part in the political history, when the party feeling between Federalists and Republicans, or Anti-Federalists, was strong (he being a fearless and staunch Republican), his honorable influence as a member of the Massachusetts Medical Society, make the name of Dr. Thomas Kittredge one of the most distinguished in the County of Essex.

Dr. Kittredge built, in 1784, the fine mansion, now the family residence. This, at the time of its erection, had no equal for elegance in the North Parish, and was only rivalled by the Mansion House of Judge Phillips in the South Parish. The Kittredge mansion remains nearly unaltered from its original construction. The lofty ceilings, the great hall and broad staircase (a contrast to the small entry and winding, narrow stairs of the great houses of the colonial period), the heavy door and ponderous brass knocker, the long avenue leading up from the front yard gate, mark it as one of the stately homes of a yet courtly period, when even the most "republican" and democratic in theory held, in respect to style of living and social customs, the aristocratic ideas of the Old Country traditions.

Dr. Kittredge had colored servants or slaves; and their affairs — weddings,[1] the birth of their children and domestic matters — were of no small interest in their master's household. When the "great house" was raised (the former house stood farther north), an old negro servant, Cæsar, carried the baby (Dr. Joseph Kittredge, 1st), then nine months old, in his arms, and held him up among the crowd, so that he might have it to say, when he should be a man, that "he was at the raisin'."

Dr. Thomas Kittredge married Miss Susanna Osgood, sister of the Hon. Samuel Osgood. They had two sons, physicians: Dr. John Kittredge, of Gloucester, and Dr. Joseph Kittredge, 1st, of North Andover. One of the four daughters, Martha Osgood Kittredge, was married to Lemuel Le Baron, M. D. Catherine and Maria were successively married to Judge David Cummins.

Dr. Joseph Kittredge, 1st, graduated at Dartmouth College 1806, studied medicine with his father, and succeeded him in practice at his death, 1818. Dr. Kittredge was one of the most successful practitioners in the town, and rode far and near on his professional calls, his cheerful voice and cordial greeting everywhere welcome. Dr. Kittredge married Miss Hannah Hodges, of Salem, a lady of remarkable strength and beauty of character. Of their three sons, two were educated for the medical profession: Dr. Joseph Kittredge, 2d, of North Andover, Dr. John Kittredge, of Taunton. One daughter was married to a physician, Dr. George C. S. Choate, formerly Superintendent of Taunton Insane Asylum, now of Pleasantville, New York.

Dr. Joseph Kittredge, 2d, took his father's practice, and was an esteemed physician of North Andover until his death, 1878. Two of his sons have studied the medical profession: Dr. Thomas Kittredge, City Physician of Salem, and Joseph Kittredge, 3d, graduate of Harvard Medical School, 1880.

ADAMS has also been one of the influential names of North Andover. Israel Adams, whose name is on the list, was father of Capt. John Adams. He came to Andover from

[1] See Chapter VI., the marriage of Cato by Dr. Symmes.

Newbury. He was a soldier in the French and Indian war. His son, Capt. John Adams (also in the French war), was an able officer in the Revolutionary service, and afterward settled down quietly, and was an honored deacon of the North Church, of exemplary character and influence. He married Miss Hannah Osgood, daughter of Peter Osgood, Esq. They had two sons who lived to manhood, Dr. Isaac Adams and Maj. John Adams. He married twice again, but had no other children that lived to adult years. He bought of his father-in-law the Adams homestead, on the southeast end of the Great Pond.

Dr. Isaac Adams studied at Harvard College, with the class of 1789, but did not graduate; he practised medicine in Newburyport, and entering into trade made several foreign voyages as master of a vessel, and finally removed his home to the State of Michigan.

Maj. John Adams lived on the homestead. He was in active military service against the insurgents in Shays' Rebellion, and was subsequently commissioned Adjutant to General Lovejoy, with the rank of major. His eldest son, Col. Joseph Adams, was President of the Mutual Marine Insurance Company, Boston. Mr. Joseph H. Adams, the eldest son of Col. Adams, occupies the homestead as a summer residence. Major Adams's eldest daughter was married to Mr. Daniel Appleton, of Haverhill (Appleton's Publishing House, New York), another was married to Prof. Asa Smith, D. D., of Dartmouth College. A daughter of Col. Joseph Adams is the wife of Gen. William J. Dale, of North Andover.

PEABODY is another name formerly of note in town. John Peabody, whose name is on the list, was father of Lieut. Oliver Peabody, Capt. John Peabody, and Rev. Stephen Peabody. The homestead was in the extreme northeast part of the town, on the Boxford line, and near the Bradford line. It is one of the most beautiful locations in that part of the town. The ground is high, commanding a near view of the farms and woodlands of the adjoining towns, and a more distant outlook to the heights of Haverhill and Lawrence and other towns, while on the horizon Mts. Monadnock and Wachusett and other hills rise among the clouds. The estate was sold in 1791 by the heirs of John Peabody, Sen., to Mr. Nathaniel Gage. The house and buildings were in excellent condition, and the place was one having a good deal of style and rural elegance. This homestead is one of exceptional interest among those of the outskirts, as having been the birth-place of three men, all eminent in the town history, and having a line of eminent descendants in other towns.

Lieut. Oliver Peabody was an active patriot, on the Committee of Correspondence in the Revolution, and respected for his prudence and discretion. His son, the Hon. Oliver Peabody, born at North Andover, 1752, graduated at Harvard College, 1773, settled in practice of law at Exeter, N.H., was Judge of the Court of Common Pleas, President of the Senate, and in other important offices. The twin sons of Judge Peabody were Oliver William Bourne Peabody, Esq., and Rev. William Bourne Oliver Peabody.

Capt. John Peabody commanded a company in the Revolution, and was also adjutant to the colonel of a regiment near Boston, 1776.

His son, Augustus Peabody, Esq., born at North Andover, was a graduate of Dartmouth, 1803, and counsellor at law, Boston.

Rev. Stephen Peabody,[1] the third son of John Peabody, Sen., was the first minister of Atkinson, N. H., a man of eminence among the clergy of New Hampshire at that time. His life and character are sketched in subsequent chapters of this history.

The Peabody homestead was also the home of another minister, the Rev. Nathaniel Gage, settled at Nashua, N. H., 1822. His brother, Mr. Daniel K. Gage, lived on the farm. It is now owned by his son, Mr. Nathaniel Gage, and other heirs. A beautiful house has recently been built on a part

---

[1] Some writers speak of him as a native of Boxford, some of North Andover. The homestead is on the North Andover side of the line. In 1746 John Peabody petitioned to be set off to Andover, which seems to have been done. The Rev. Stephen Peabody was born 1741.

of the estate by Mr. George Edmund Davis, who married a daughter of Mr. D. K. Gage.

The Peabody family in several branches has been resident in the town, or connected with the North Parish. A son of David Peabody, Thomas Peabody, baptized soon after his birth, 1762, in the North Meeting-house, by Dr. Symmes, was the father of the banker and philanthropist, George Peabody.

Samuel Peabody, Esq., a native of Boxford, was a much respected citizen of Andover from 1842 till his death, in 1859. He was a graduate of Dartmouth College, 1803, and practised law at Sandwich, Epsom, and Tamworth, N. H. Of his sons, still identified with Andover interests, is Judge Charles A. Peabody, counsellor at law, New York.

In respect to the foregoing memorials and relics, the remark may here be repeated that they claim neither to be biographical nor genealogical in any strict sense of the word, but simply to collect such scattered memoranda as have been found of the first settlers and early residents, and to indicate the comparative influence of the several families. This has been a work of some difficulty, and its imperfections will, it is hoped, be charitably received.

CHAPTER II.

THE PART OF ANDOVER IN THE EARLY INDIAN WARS.

IN regard to the Indians who occupied the territory of Andover either for camping or for hunting ground, no record has been found. The sachem who acknowledged before the General Court in 1646 that he had made sale of the Cochichawick territory to Mr. Woodbridge and Mr. Edmond Faulkner, was Cutshamache or Cutshamakin, a dweller near Dorchester. What special claim he had to, or right to dispose of, the lands about Andover, does not appear. The following statement, taken from the "History of Dorchester," may be the explanation: "This chief appears to have been a mere tool in the hands of the colonial government, used for the purpose of deeding away Indian lands and acting as a spy upon the movements of neighboring Indians." He is said to have been a kinsman of Passaconaway, of the Agawam tribe, who made their camping places along the Merrimack from the mouth to Pentucket, or to Cochichawick. There are remains of an Indian burial-ground at West Andover, on the bank of the Merrimack, a mile or more above Lawrence. Skeletons of men, women, and children have been exhumed.[1] They were wrapped in hemlock bark. One was of a man of great size and powerful build. He had been buried with especial care, and, it is not unlikely, was a sachem or chief. Allusion is made in some of the ancient records of land sales and surveys, to a tract in this vicinity, originally laid out as "near Haverhill," and again "near Andover" and in the neighborhood of "Old Will's wigwam." Old Will was a name sometimes applied to Passaconaway. "Will's Hill" was between [2]

[1] The graves were explored by Mr. Francis G. Sanborn, of Andover.
[2] In the present limits of Middleton.

Andover and Rowley. It may be that this Indian burying place marks one of the places of Passaconaway's abode, and that these are the bones of his tribe. In regard to him, Governor Thomas Dudley wrote in 1631, to the Countess of Lincoln: "Upon the river Merrimack is seated Sagamore Passaconaway, having under his command four or five hundred men, being esteemed by his countrymen a false fellow and by us a wich."

The one sole local name of an aboriginal resident is that of the Indian Roger. Standing on the spot known as Roger's Rock [the rock has been taken away], near the South Meetinghouse, or watching the course of Roger's Brook, it is not difficult with fancy's eye to see at our side, also viewing the landscape o'er, this ancient lord of the soil, clad in blanket and with belt of wampum, and bow and arrow, or arrayed in one of the "coates" of Indian admiration, and proud in the possession of a musket and powder and shot. It was no doubt the intention of our ancestors to deal fairly with the natives of the country, so far as they could consistently with their policy of getting the better part of that country for themselves. They bought the lands at such a price as the Indians valued them, and though, as in the purchase of Andover, many square miles of territory were got for a paltry sum, the buyers could hardly blame themselves for a transaction which, at the time, the sellers professed to be satisfied with. As a Christian commonwealth, also, the colony took measures for promoting the welfare of the Indians. Philanthropists especially, devoted zealous labors to the conversion of the Indians from heathenism, and instructing them in the knowledge of the true God. Indians were taught the catechism and also classic lore, and were even admitted to Harvard College and ordained ministers of the gospel. But, put beside these the facts also that the masses of the tribes still kept to their traditions of tomahawk and war-whoop, that for the few who were converted and civilized, there were the many who learned all the vices and none of the virtues of the white man, and furthermore, that of the white men there were many whose vices exceeded their virtues, and it is easy to see how the problem of Indian treatment soon became one of the most difficult with which our forefathers had to deal. The missionaries to the Indians were enthusiasts, as Eliot the great apostle, whose indefatigable zeal translated the Bible into the Indian language, but all whose efforts have failed to transmit to the present age a human being able to read the translation. These missionaries hoped all things and were ready to endure all things in their faith in ultimate results. Through their labors, thousands of the natives were induced to adopt the Christian religion. Many of these forsook their forest-life and wigwam abodes and were gathered in small villages or settlements called " towns of the praying Indians." There they lived, in some measure like the whites, having a town government (their officers, magistrates, and teachers being Indians), and practising the useful arts. One of these towns, called Wamesit, was so near to the borders of Andover, that the Indians from it often had dealings with the Andover inhabitants. The Indian town is thus described by a writer [1] in 1674: —

"Wamesit is the fifth praying town, and this place is situate upon Merrimack river, being a neck of land where Concord river falleth into Merrimack river. It is about 20 miles from Boston, North, north west and within 5 miles of Billerica, and as much from Chelmsford, so that it hath Concord river upon the west, north west and Merrimack river upon the north, north east. It hath about fifteen families, above 75 souls, 2500 acres, variety of fish, salmon, shads, lamprey eels, sturgeon, bass. There is a great confluence of Indians that usually resort to this place in the fishing seasons. Of these strange Indians, divers are vitious and wicked men and women, which Satan makes use of to obstruct the prosperity of religion here. The ruler of this people is called Numphow.[2] He is one of the blood of their chief sachems."

From this village (the present site of Lowell and suburbs) and from other places the Indians used to go up and down the Merrimack, and ascend its tributaries to fish or hunt. They used also to meet the English, while friendly relations existed, at certain places of conference for the purpose of

---

[1] Gookin's *Historical Collections*.
[2] In a trial of Indians accused of stirring up strife sometime after the attack on Andover, Timothy Abbott bore witness against this Indian Numphow.

trade or barter, exchanging skins, venison, game, for coats, powder and shot, trinkets, and bright colored beads, or wampum. A sail on the river to-day, from Lawrence (Old Andover, West Parish), to Lowell or to Haverhill, cannot fail to bring to vivid imagination pictures of those most ancient days, when the stream which now turns the wheels of great manufactories and keeps millions of spindles in motion, and which has all along its course thriving villages and populous cities, had its tranquil surface only now and then broken by the birch canoe or log raft, and the echoes of its hills disturbed only by the shout or war-whoop of the Indian, and the cries of wild bird or beast.

Besides the villages of friendly or praying Indians, there were many individual instances of "converted Indians." These Indians were often taken into the settlers' families, and did house-work, or labored in the fields. In fact, all the more prudent of the natives at first submitted to the superior strength and wisdom of the English, making a virtue of necessity. At a meeting of the General Court, January, 1643, five Indian sachems, Cutshamache among the number, signed a paper promising "to be true and faithful to the said government to bee willing from time to time to be instructed in the knowledge of God." Yet under this submission was often a deep hatred of the invaders and a jealous fear of their powerful God. The English did much to increase this hatred, for not all were philanthropists, and in place of faith and prayer, the Indian often met fraud and force. He was quick to retaliate and resort to tomahawk and firebrand. To discuss the causes which led to the long series of Indian hostilities would lead us aside from our main path. We can only glance at the effect of these hostilities on the community whose history we are studying. The period of Indian hostilities began about the time of Andover's settlement ; but the Indians in this immediate neighborhood were not at first drawn into the conspiracies. The colonists prepared for defence by organizing the militia, in which all able-bodied and "not timorous" males over sixteen years of age were enrolled. This organization was made in 1644. The colony was divided into four counties: Suffolk, Norfolk,

Essex, Middlesex. There was one regiment in each county. The commanding officer of a regiment was called Sergeant-major. The commanding officer of all the forces was Sergeant-major-general. The first Major-general was Thomas Dudley. He was father of Mrs. Anne Bradstreet, of Andover. The Sergeant-major of the Essex regiment was Daniel Dennison, of Ipswich. He was brother-in-law to Mrs. Anne Bradstreet, and also to Mrs. Mercy Woodbridge, wife of the Rev. Mr. Woodbridge, of Andover [his wife was Patience Dudley, daughter of Governor Thomas Dudley]. He is described [1] as the "proper and valiant Major Daniel Denison, a good souldier and of a quick capacity his company are well instructed in feats of warlike activity." When the Indian depredations in the neighborhood of Andover, in the year 1675, became formidable, Major Dennison used every effort for the protection of the town, having not only his honor as a soldier at stake, but also the lives and property of his near and dear kindred. It was, doubtless, owing to his vigorous measures in coöperating with the local officers that the town of Andover suffered so little, in comparison with other frontier settlements.

The following is one of the first Records found of military organization at Andover. It bears no date, but is placed in the books of the County Court Records, with papers from 1658 to 1659: [2] —

"To THE HONORED COURT AT SALEM, You may be pleased hereby to take notice that the inhabitants of Andover have made choyse of John Osgood to be their Sergeant and chief commander in the roome of Sergeant Stevens who is willing and desirous to be dismissed. It is therefore our desire that the cort would bee pleased to allow and confirme our choyse of John Osgood for our Sergeant.

FRANCIS DANE.	GEORGE ABBOTT.
JOHN STEVENS.	THOMAS CHANDLER.
HENRY INGOLLS.	JOHN LOVEJOY.
THOMAS JOHNSON.	ANDREW GRAVES.
ROBART RUSSELL.	DANIEL POOR.
RICHARD BARKER.	WILLIAM BALLARD.
THOMAS FARNUM.	EDMOND FAULKNER.
GEORGE ABBOTT, JR.	ROBERT BARNARD."
WILLIAM CHANDLER.	

[1] *Wonder-working Providence of Zion's Saviour.*   [2] Vol. iv., p. 121.

There are records which show that John Osgood was Sergeant in 1661. In 1666 [1] the officers at Andover were Lieutenant John Osgood, Ensign Thomas Chandler, Sergeant Henry Ingalls, also the same in 1675. In 1677 Dudley Bradstreet was Captain, and John Osgood Lieutenant. In 1680 the Essex militia was divided into two regiments. One of these (including Newbury, Rowley, Bradford, Andover, Topsfield, Salisbury, Amesbury, Haverhill) was put under command of Maj. Nathaniel Saltonstall, of Haverhill, who had been captain of a company. The officers at Andover, 1680, were Captain Dudley Bradstreet, Lieutenant John Osgood, Ensign Thomas Chandler, Sergeant John Stevens, Sergeant John Barker. In 1683 several of the inhabitants of Andover petitioned the General Court for permission to raise another company to "compleat their troope to the number of forty eight men." This was granted, and the command was given to Capt. John Osgood. In 1689 the militia of Essex County was divided into three regiments, — Newbury, Salisbury, Haverhill, Andover, Amesbury, and Bradford forming one. The following is a list of Andover officers, covering, as regards those of the rank of captain, a period of one hundred years. The dates indicate the first record found : —

Colonel. Dudley Bradstreet (1698).
Major. Dudley Bradstreet (1695).
Captain. Dudley Bradstreet (1677) ; John Osgood (1683) ; Thomas Chandler (1688) ; Christopher Osgood (1690) ; James Frye (1702) ; Benjamin Stevens (1706) ; John Chandler (1711) ; Timothy Johnson (1737) ; Joseph Sibson (1744) ; Nathaniel Frye (1745).
Lieutenant. John Osgood (1666) ; Thomas Chandler (1685) ; John Barker (1696) ; John Chandler (1696) ; Thomas Johnson (1697) ; Samuel Frye (1698) ; John Aslebe (1704) ; William Lovejoy (1714) ; Francis Dane (1717) ; George Abbott (1742) ; John Chandler (1724).
Ensign. Thomas Chandler (1661) ; John Aslebe (1700) ; Francis Dane (1713).
Sergeant. John Stevens (1660) ; John Osgood (1661) ; Henry Ingalls (1666) ; Thomas Farnum (1674) ; John Aslebe (1692) ; Ephraim Stevens (1695) ; William Chandler (1696) ; William Lovejoy (1696).

[1] *Essex County Court Papers*, vol. xii., p. 24.

Corporal. Samuel Martin (1677); Nathan Stevens (1685); Samuel Holt (1685); Joseph Ballard (1688); Hooker Osgood (1689); Samuel Frye (1692); George Abbot (1693); Samuel Osgood (1694); Benjamin Barker (1690): Nehemiah Abbot (1707).[1]

In 1676 a letter, written by E. R.[2] [Edward Rawson or Edmund Randolph (?)], describes, for the information of the British Government, the condition of the colonial military force: —

"They have no standing army, but their trained bands are twelve troops of horse and six thousand foot; each troop consisting of sixty horse besides officers are all well mounted and completely armed with back, breast, head-piece, buffe coat, sword, carbine, and pistols, each troop distinguished by their coats. The foot also are very well furnished with swords, muskets, and bandaleers. There are no pikmen, they being of no use in the wars with the Indians. . . . . There is only one 'old soldier' in the colony, the Governor, Mr. Leverett. He served in the late rebellion under the usurper Oliver Cromwell as a captain of horse. The governor of the colony is always generall, and out of the rest of the magistrates is chosen the major generall. They are places of good profit and no danger; they may stay at home and share the spoyle while younger men command the army in the field against the enemy."

The first record of alarms of hostile Indians at Andover is in the year 1675, the month of October. Then the whole colony was in a state of excitement, on account of the league made by Philip (sachem of the Wampanoags) of all the New England tribes against the English. No town felt secure against a sudden outbreak of the heretofore friendly Indians, or an onslaught of hostile tribes marching swiftly from remote encampments. Major Dennison writes,[3] from Ipswich, to the Council in Boston, October 28, 1675: —

"I am now advancing to Major Pike. I think I shall be able to afford him no more than the comfort of our presence for a

---

[1] This list is perhaps not complete; but it contains the names which have been found after such search as the importance of the subject warrants.
[2] *Mass. His. Soc. Coll.*, Fourth Series, vol. iv.
[3] *Mass. Archives*, vol. lxviii., p. 30.

while, our posts at Topsfield & Andover being affrighted with the sight, as they say, of Indians which I have not time to examine till my return. It is hardly imaginable the panick fears that is upon our upland plantations & scattered places. . . . . The almighty and merciful God pity & helpe us. In much haste I brake off ——"

In the month of November, impressments of men from the militia were made in all the towns, to fill up the quota of Massachusetts for an expedition into the country of the Narragansetts, who had joined with Philip. Twelve men were taken from Andover to complete the company commanded by Captain Gardiner. These were the following : [1] —

Joseph Abbot.	John Faulkner.	John Preston.
Ebenezer Barker.	John Lovejoy.	Samuel Phillpes [Phelps].
John Ballard.	John Marston.	Nathan Stevens.
James Frie.	John Parker.	Edward Whittington.

Lieutenant Osgood, the commander of the Andover militia, in his return of their names describes the state of the company : —

"They are most of them now well fixed with armes and ammunition & cloathing. Edward Whittington wants a better musquete which wee know not well how to supply, except we take from another man which these times seems harde ; we air now sending to Salem for sum . . . . for shoes and cloth for a coate for one or two."

These soldiers were marched in the dead of winter into the country of the Narragansetts and, December 19th, met the savages in the famous swamp-fight, where they defeated and completely destroyed their foe. In this fight Ebenezer Barker was wounded.[2]

In subsequent years, large grants of land were made to the soldiers of the Narraganset fight. Seven different townships being laid out, " Narraganset, number three," Amherst, N. H., was granted to inhabitants of Salem, Marblehead,

---

[1] *Mass. Archives*, vol. lxviii., p. 68.

[2] In the list of Major Appleton's men killed is named one of Andover, Robert Mackey (?) Drake's *Annals and Antiquities of Boston* names Joseph Abbot and Roger Marks, of Andover, as wounded. I do not find record of these names in the returns in the *Archives*.

Lynn, Gloucester, Andover, and other towns. Andover was allowed for nine soldiers.

The defeat of his allies did not daunt King Philip, but rather served to exasperate him for more desperate revenge. As soon as the spring opened, town after town was surprised and destroyed, and the most dreadful atrocities were committed. February 10 occurred the attack on Lancaster, so graphically described by Mrs. Rowlandson, and familiar to every reader of New England history. Flying rumors came to Andover of the shocking fate of the inhabitants of this town, the mangled bodies of infants, and the painful captivity of mothers, the burning of houses, and the bloody fight of soldiers and savages.

The Indians were on the march, so the rumor went, toward Chelmsford, and would soon attempt to cross the Merrimack and descend on Andover. Lieutenant Osgood sent despatches post haste to the Council at Boston, imploring help, and begging to be relieved from the order for soldiers to march out of town to Woburn,[1] since all were needed at home: —

"HONOURED GOVERNOR AND COUNCILL, these few lines are to let your Honours understand that the Indians have taken and destroyed the coburrg (?) which is a great threatening of near approaching danger unto us. It brings but ten or twelve miles from us, and this day seaven of our men are to march to Oburn according to your honours orders: we humbly crave this favour, if it may stand with your honours wisdom & favour to release our men that are to goe forth, as wee being an outside town & in as greate danger in our apprehension as any and may stand in as great need as any other town of help, this makes us bould to request this favour att your hands & shall acknowledge ourselves your obedient servants to serve to extent of our abilities with all readiness, thus desiring God to direct & guide your councills in all the greate & weighty difficulties & distress that are now on our hands, we Rest your humble servant,   JOHN OSGOOD, *Left.*
   In the name & behalf of our towne.
"ANDOVER, 16 *Feb.* 1675."

[1] *Mass. Archives*, vol. lxviii., p. 138.

Measures were taken as soon as possible to put the town in a state of defence; garrison[1] houses were built, and men appointed to defend them. A committee chosen to visit the town reported[2] it to be in a state of good defence:—

"In pursuance of your Honourable Councills orders dated March ye 15, 167¾ appointing us ye subscribers as a committy for Essex to view & consider ye severall townes & to propose ye thoughts of what may bee advisable: In order for ye securing of ye people & their planting in this time of trouble: Wee met at Andover, where wee found twelve substantial Garrisons well fitted: which wee hope through God's blessing may bee sufficient to secure them from any sudden surprisal of the enemy to which Garrisons ye inhabitants of ye town are respectively appointed.

"By your humble servants

JOHN APPLETON.
JOHN PUTNAM.
THOMAS CHANDLER.

"29th March 167¾."[3]

It was also ordered by the Court that a fence of stockades, or stones, be built eight feet high from Charles River to Concord River, in Billerica, thence connecting by way of the large ponds with Merrimack River, which river, down "to the bay" with the bay would complete the circuit of some twenty towns, including Andover. These would be "environed round for the security and safety under God of the people, their houses goods & catell from the rage and fury of the heathen enemy."

The Andover people did not approve this means of defence, or feel willing to contribute men to guard the line of forts. They thought a more effectual protection would be to strengthen the garrisons and to send out, with parties of

---

[1] "These were built of hewn logs which lay flat upon each other; the ends being fitted for the purpose, were inserted in grooves cut in large posts erected at each corner. They inclosed an area of several square rods, were raised to the height of the roof of a common dwelling-house, and at two or more of the corners were placed boxes where sentinels kept watch. In some cases, several small buildings raised for the temporary accommodation of families were within the inclosure." — Bouton's *History of Concord*.

[2] *Mass. Archives*, vol. lxviii, p. 184.

[3] Ibid., p. 174.

workmen in the fields, guards of soldiers. They say that their planting grounds are mostly " environed by swampy and boughie ground," and are therefore comparatively easy to defend. They pray the Council to order the men to " work in such companies as they shall judge meete for their safety and defence."

On the 18th of March [28th, N. S.], the Indians crossed the Merrimack and sent two scouts to Andover. What depredation they committed is not recorded, but the people in great alarm despatched post riders to Ipswich, one by night and one by day, to beg for help. Major Dennison, not slow to protect his kindred and friends, hastened forward sixty men and at once apprised the Council in Boston of the condition of things. He writes that " if he had received orders he might have brought off from Andover some of his brother Bradstreet's best things." He commits the result to Heaven exclaiming, " Let God arise and our enemies be scattered."

But, in spite of all the vigilance and precautions, the Indians surprised the town at last. This was on the 8th [or 18th, N. S.] of April, 1676. In this attack, one of the soldiers, who had passed safely through the bloody Narragansett fight in the winter, was slain within sight of his own dwelling.[1] It is not impossible that the savages knew who were the men in town that had helped to murder their brethren in the swamp fight; at any rate, they, on this day, whether by accident or design, took revenge on two of these. They directed their course to the house of George Abbot, one of the garrisons. Tradition says that they were seen crossing the river, and that Ephraim Stevens, a scout, gave the alarm. The villagers fled to the garrisons; but the Abbot brothers were at work in the fields, and did not reach the shelter before the savages were upon them. Joseph Abbot, the soldier, a strong, athletic young man about twenty-four years of age, made a brave resistance, and killed one or more of the Indians, but was finally set upon by the whole band and cut down, — the first, and perhaps the only, Andover soldier

[1] Site of the garrison-house on the estate of the present residence of Mr. John Abbot, Central Street, west of the South Meeting-house.

ever slain in the town. His brother Timothy, a lad of thirteen years, was taken captive. The savages then hurried off, leaving the smitten household to its desolation. That such desolation ever came to the now peaceful spot it is difficult to realize. In the calm of a summer afternoon, the writer of this sketch stood upon the ground once trodden by the hurrying feet of the fleeing citizens and red with the blood of the slain. Now the scene is tranquil, and bears no token that any deed of violence was ever done here. Broad fields stretch away, just greened after the mower's scythe; elm, ash, and maple, with the friendly apple tree, make a pleasant shade, and through their foliage the sun streaming in, tessellates the grass with a shifting carpet of light and shade. Birds nest and sing undisturbed; from distant fields come sounds of labor; the cattle are driven into the farm-yard; the lengthening shadows and the striking of the meeting-house clock remind of the evening hour. In vain we try to call back to this serenity the struggle, the blood, the groans of the battle, the tears and the lament for the youthful dead. May they never come again to any home of Old Andover!

Besides their bloody work at George Abbot's, the savages also attacked the house of Edmond Faulkner, and wreaked their vengeance on dumb brutes. Their attack is described by the Rev. Increase Mather, in his "History of King Philip's War":—

"In the beginning of April they did some mischief at Chelmsford and Andover, where a small party of them put the town into a great fright, caused the people to fly into garrison houses, killed one man and burnt one house, and to show what barbarous creatures they are, they exercised cruelty towards dumb creatures. They took a cow, knocked off one of her horns, cut out her tongue, and so left the poor creature in great misery. They put an horse, ox, and cow into a hovel and then set it on fire only to show how they are delighted in exercising cruelty."

The most interesting account, however, is from the pen of one of Andover's own citizens. It is a letter to the Council, describing the situation of the town, — its anxiety and distress, and praying to be aided to maintain a sufficient guard. The letter bears marks of haste and trepidation, and is, even more than most of the old records, difficult to decipher. Possibly some words have not been exactly made out in the following copy: —

"TO THE HONOURED COUNCILL. The malitiah of our towne do humbly request your Honours to consider our condition the enemy has twice assaulted us; the last was Saturday last, who slew a lusty (?) younge mane & took his brother a youth & carried him away: we have had sum fforces to helpe us bute the enemy cannot be found when we goe after them; and wee ffind that wee are not abell to goe to worke about Improveing oure lands but are liable to bee cutt off nor are we able to raise . . . . men at our charge to defend ourselves wee fear greatly that wee shall not bee able to live in the towne to Improve our lands to raise a subsistence without som force be kept above us upon the river of merrimack & to Concord river, which being speedily & well defended with a competent quantity of soldiers all the Townes within might be in sum reasonable safty to follow theyre Imployes to raise corne & persue theyre catell . . . . [we] thought if one third off the men of each towne did attend that service so the other might bee in sum reasonable safty about their work, for now we are so distressed to thinke that our men are liable to bee shot whenever we stirr from our houses & our children taken by the cruell enemy, itt doe so distress us that wee know not what to doe, iff sum defence bee not made by ye forces above us wee must remove off iff we can tell where, before we have lost all lives & catell & horses by the enemy; we are compleatly able to fende ourselves in our garison iff we have warning to rest in, but otherwise out off oure house we are in continuall danger."[1]

The letter goes on to say that the town of Andover, being a guard to the towns below, ought not in its distress to bear the whole burden of keeping a guard sufficient, but should receive help. It concludes: —

"Praying God to directe & counsel you we rest.

"Your humbell servantes

JOHN OSGOOD, Left.

"ANDOVER II: 10, 76."

The captive carried away from Andover — the boy Timothy Abbot — was brought back in August by a squaw who took pity on his mother. His return is mentioned in Cobbet's

[1] *Mass. Archives*, vol. lxviii., p. 202.

"New England Deliverances": "And Good-wife Abbot's boy of Andover was brought home, almost starved, by a poor squaw that had always been tender to him whilst in captivity."

Hubbard says: "He was much pined with hunger."[1]

In this attack, the Indians also wounded[2] Roger Marks, another soldier of the Narragansett fight (son-in-law of Nicholas Holt). "About two months after this," says "Abbot's History," quoting from Mr. Symmes's Thanksgiving sermon, "the Indians surprised and captivated Mr. Haggit and two of his sons." But, although this may be correct and the persons named made captive in Andover, there is no evidence of their being then residents of the town. No such name is found in the list of residents, 1678, and it is not till 1679 that Moses Haggit of Ipswich bought land southwest of Blanchard's [since Hagget's] Pond, and agreed to pay church and town rates as a citizen. It is not unlikely, however, that in the summer of 1676, the Haggits, father and sons, came from Ipswich to Andover to look at the land and arrange for the purchase, which may have been delayed on account of their captivity. The remoteness of the region from the town, and its proximity to the Indian resorts about Wamesit, especially its nearness to the pond, which would attract the Indians for fishing, rendered them liable to attack. A garrison house was built in this section at an early period. On account of the losses sustained by the town this year, the General Court abated their county rates. The attacks threatened to greatly injure the plantations. Many families were about to remove from Andover, there being a scarcity of corn and no security in planting. Lieutenant Osgood wrote at this time to the Council, praying them to take measures to prevent the desertion of the town. There were, consequently, garrisons and guards stationed across the country. The following is an extract from a report of them: —

[1] Timothy Abbot, when master of a family, never allowed a child to say he was hungry, saying that they did not know the meaning of the word hunger. He lived on the present homestead of Mr. Asa A. Abbot and Mr. Sylvester Abbot.

[2] Mr. Symmes's *Thanksgiving Sermon*, 1768. Drake's *Annals and Antiquities of Boston*.

"Between Exeter & Haverhill a Garrison and 70 men.
"Near Andover a garrison and 40 men.
"At Pawtucket near Wamesit 'already settled.'
"Between Chelmsford & Concord a garrison & 40 men.
"Between Concord & Sudbury a garrison & 40 men.
"Between Sudbury & Medfield a garrison & 40 men.
"South side of Medfield a garrison & 40 men."[1]

There was ordered also a "flying or moving army of three hundred men," one hundred of them to be friendly Indians.

There was from time to time more or less call for soldiers to serve out of town; some were impressed, or volunteered for an expedition in the summer of 1677, to the region of the Kennebec River. The company, under the command of Capt. Benjamin Swett, fell into an ambush[2] at Black Point, Scarborough, and were cut off. Their leader and many men were slain.

The following list of the slain is found in the Andover records:—

"Killed by Indians June 29 1677 John, son of Joseph & Mary Parker.
"John, son of Edward & Elizabeth Phelps.
"James, son of Nathan & Mary Parker.
"Daniel Blackhead, servant of Christopher Osgood."

In the year 1677, Mr. Dudley Bradstreet was made Captain of the foot company in Andover. He took vigorous measures for defending the town, petitioning the General Court to increase the penalty for not working "in companies" and to compel all the "towns to keep out a small party to range y⁰ outskirts whereby y⁰ inhabitants may in their spirits be more settled and goe about their work for[3] their English and Hay harvest."

After the defeat and death of King Philip, the hostile spirit subsided, and for a series of years there was a time of rest and comparative security. But the Revolution in England,

---

[1] *Mass. Archives*, vol. lxviii., page 251.
[2] Southgate's *History of Scarborough*.
[3] *Mass. Archives*, vol. lxix., page 152.

1689, and the wars [1] of England and France embroiled the colonies, and the Indians were drawn into the contest, mainly acting with the French.

In 1689, the General Court made a change in the militia of Essex County which was objected to by the Andover inhabitants as prejudicial to their interests. They petitioned for a different organization of the troops:—

"To the honoured Generall Court *now sitting in Charles Towne this ninth day of March 1689–90*, the petition of ye townes of Andover & Boxford, Humbly Sheweth.—

"That whereas yᵉ Humble petitioners have been informed that this Honᵈ Court hath taken off yᵉ Towne of Boxford with other townes from yᵉ upper Regiment in Essex & joyned them to another Regiment which wee Humbly conceive is greatly prejudicial to yᵉ Country & to or Sd Townes in pticlar, by reason we lyinge soe neare to each other & ready upon all occasions of yᵉ enemy's approach to relieve each other, which if disjoyned wee cannot doe, & for many other Reasons we humbly pray that this Honoured Court would please to take into their farther & serious consideration, this our petition. viz, that Boxford might still continue as part of yᵉ upper Regiment in Essex, & farther yᵗ our Souldiers may bee free from any press that may happen till yᵉ Indian enemy be subdued or quieted, in Granting of which yʳ Honrᵉ humble petitioners shall as in Duty bound for ever pray &c.

"*for Andover* { Dudley Bradstreet.
John Osgood.
John Barker.
Stephen Johnson. }

"Moses Tyler by order & in yᵉ name of yᵉ Town of Boxford."

During the year 1689, the following deaths are recorded in the town books as having occurred either in the wars abroad, or by savage violence at home:—

---

[1] The following classification of the wars may be convenient for reference:—
1688–1698. Governor Phipps. King William's War.
1703–1713. Governor Dudley. Queen Anne's War.
1722–1725. Lieutenant-governor Dummer. Ralle's War.
1744–1749. Governor Shirley. King George's War.
1749–1761. Governor Shirley.
" Pownal.
" Bernard. } French and Indian War.
Lieutenant-governor Hutchinson.

"Lieut. John Stevens at Casko March 5 1689.

"Eleazar Streaton a servant & kinsman of Dea. John Frie died at y⁴ eastward at Fort Ann Mch 15 1688-9.

"John Peters killed by the Indians Aug. 14, 1689.

"Andrew Peters killed by the Indians Aug. 14, 1689."

Early in 1690, active measures were taken by the Government for the defence of the frontier towns. By order [1] of the Governor and Council, May 14th, eighty troopers were to be detached from the several companies of the Essex Regiment, which was in command of Maj. Robert Pike. These troopers were to rendezvous at Andover on the 16th, and forty of them, under command of Captain Davis, to go to the defence of Concord; forty to be under Capt. Thomas Chandler, of Andover. On the 28th of May, it was further ordered, that two hundred soldiers well appointed with arms and ammunition be raised "for security of Bradford, Andover, Dunstable, Chelmsford, Groton, Lancaster, and Marlborough." These, it was ordered, "should constantly be kept together and improved moving up and down in their respective stations on the outside of the towns whereto they shall be assigned for defence of such towns, and the frontier towns shall send out one or two of the inhabitants who are acquainted with the woods for daily scouting." The following action was also taken in regard to the raising of more men in Andover, in answer to the petition of Captain Osgood: —

"It is granted that in case the captain of the foot company see it beneficial to them to make up said troop to the number of forty out of the foot company, of persons sufficient to attend such service otherwise the troops there to be serted into the Foot company and that to be divided, the new company to nominate their own officers and to send down their names to the Council to be allowed and commissionated before the last day of this inst."

On the 28th of May, Capt. Thomas Chandler was appointed "to command the company that are to be impressed for the defence of the frontier towns from Dunstable eastward as far as Bradford, downwards, which company is to consist of forty troopers and thirty foot-soldiers." Notwithstanding all this scouting and ranging of troopers and foot-soldiers who by day

[1] *General Court Records*, May, 1690.

and by night were active and alert, travelling from town was unsafe. There were twenty fordable places in the Merrimack River between Wamesit and Haverhill, and, at any moment, the Indians were liable to cross and make an attack.

In 1696 (records the Rev. John Pike in his journal [1]), "old John Hoyt of Amesbury and young Peters of Andover were slain upon the road between Andover and Haverhill." This Hoyt had before suffered from the Indians who had "plundered and despoiled him and burnt his house."[2] These deaths are registered in Andover records: —

"John Hoyt of Alms-bury was killed here by Indians, Aug. 13, 1696.

"William Peters killed by Indians Aug. 13, 1696."

On the twenty-second of February, 169¾ (O. S.), the fourth of March, 1698 (N. S.), occurred the most considerable attack ever made on the town of Andover. In this attack, retribution followed and (it would seem), deliberate vengeance was taken for the crimes of one man whose wickedness was thus the means of bringing suffering on his innocent townsmen. Capt. Pascoe Chubb, the son-in-law of Mr. Edmond Faulkner, two years before this attack in the same month, had committed an act of treachery toward the Indians. He was in command of Fort Pemaquid (which in 1693, had been built by Capt. John March),[3] and held a conference with a delegation of Penobscot Indians in regard to the exchange of prisoners. While the council, about a dozen Indians, and as many of the English, were in session, Chubb having previously made the plot, and had the Indians supplied with strong liquor to the verge of drunkenness, gave orders for a massacre. The English soldiers fell upon the unsuspecting victims and slew several, two chiefs among them. Subsequently a force of French and Indians attacked the fort and threatened death with torture to the captain, if he should not surrender. In his terror and remorse, he forgot his honor as commander, and in the most cowardly manner, gave up the fort, stip-

---

[1] *Mass. Historical Society's Proceedings*, 1875, "Journal of Mr. Pike."
[2] *Mass. Col. Records*, 1695, June 15.
[3] Of Newbury, — the same who began to build the vessel at Andover.

ulating only for personal safety. For this act of treason, as it was almost thought to be, he was cashiered, and put in Boston jail, whence he was released and allowed to live in seclusion at Andover, owing to the petitions and influence of friends.

Following is a petition made by him from the jail [1]: —

"To the Great and Genll Court of his Majestys Province of the Massachusetts Bay in New England *Assembled att Boston by adjournment November 18th 1696.*

"The Petition of Pasco Chubb late Commander of his Majestys ffort William Henry at Pemaquid, Humbly sheweth.

"That y' Petitioner stands committed a Prisoner in Boston Goale for his Late surrendering & delivering up the aforesd Fort and Stores thereto belonging unto his Majestys enemies. . . . .

"And whereas y' Petitioner is a very poore man, having a wife and children to Looke after wch by reason of his confinement & poverty are reduced to a meane and necessitous condition having not wherewithall either to defray his present necessary charges or to relieve his Indigent family. . . . .

"Your Petitioner therefore humbly prays that this high and hon¹ Court will please to consider the premises soe as that he may now either be Brought to his Tryall or else upon giving sufficient Bayle be delivered from his present confinement, whereby he may be enabled to take some care of his poore family for their subsistence in this hard & deare winter season."

The Indians, doubtless in revenge for his cruelties (although Hutchinson thinks it was by "mear accident"), attacked the house where he was, and killed him and his wife. "It is not probable they had any knowledge of the place [2] of his abode," says Hutchinson; "but it caused them greater joy than the taking of many towns." "Rapin," he goes on to say, "would have pronounced such an event the immediate judgment of Heaven. Voltaire, that in the place of supposed safety, the man could not avoid his destiny."

All the facts, however, go to indicate that it was the deliberate act of Indian revenge. The attack was led by the fierce and implacable foe of the whites, Assacumbuit. At this time

---

[1] *Mass. Archives*, vol. lxx., 307.
[2] In North Andover.

was made the attack on Captain Bradstreet's house, which is elsewhere [1] narrated. The tradition goes that the leader of the Indians had given his promise to an Indian, a friend of the Bradstreet family, that if he would guide them to the house, none of the family should be hurt. But he, it seems, could not, or did not, wholly control his company, for they killed the guest and relative of the family, " Major Wade's son of Mystick," and were about to carry off some of the household as prisoners. But, the leader interposing, these were released unharmed. This attack is mentioned (with a different reason for the Indians' mercy) by Cotton Mather, in the " Magnalia : " —

"The Winter was the severest that ever was in the memory of Man. And yet February must not pass without a stroke upon Pemaquid Chub,[2] whom the Government had mercifully permitted after his examination to retire unto his habitation in Andover. As much out of the way as to Andover there came above Thirty Indians about the middle of February as if their errand had been for vengeance upon Chub whom (with his wife) they now massacred there. They took two or three horses and slew three or four persons ; and Mr. Thomas Barnard the worthy minister of the Place very narrowly escaped their fury. But in the midst of their Fury there was one piece of mercy the like whereof had never been seen before : For they had got Colonel Dudley Bradstreet into their hands, but perceiving the town Mustering to follow them, their Hearts were so changed that they dismissed their captives without any further Damage unto their Persons. Returning back by Haverhill, they killed a couple," etc.

Judge Sewall[3] records the same attack : —

" *Feb.* 24, 8¾. — Feb. 22 at Break of day Andover is surprised. Lt. Col. Bradstreet's house rifled, his kinsman Wade slain, Capt. Chubb and his wife slain and three more. Some houses and Barns burnt and in one a considerable quantity of corn and twenty head of Cattel. Pulpit cushions taken away, fired but not quenched."

The Rev. John Pike,[4] in his journal, also chronicles the same attack : —

[1] Chapter I., p. 130.
[2] Mather's opinion concerning the cause here appears.
[3] *Mass. Hist. Soc. Coll*, Fifth Series, vol. v.
[4] *Mass. Hist. Soc. Proceedings*, 1875.

"Feb. 22, $\frac{2}{3}$, about 30 Indians came to Andover, took Col. Bradstreet's house and two more, killed Capt. Pasco Chub and his wife, Maj. Wade's son of Mystick and two others. Carried Col. Bradstreets family a little way & upon Cond : Released them. As they returned by Haverhill they met with Jonath : Hains and Sam. Ladd with ye elder sons. The two fathers were slain & the sons carried away, but young Hains soon after Returned which was his second escape from the enemy in less than two years time."

They also attacked the house of Mr. Timothy Johnson, and killed his daughter, Miss Penelope Johnson, a young lady of nineteen years. The explicit statements of contemporaries, noting the events in diary, agree in the date, February 22, and 1697, or March 4, 1698. Some town histories have made the statement that there were two attacks : one in February, and one in March, but this error must have arisen from a confusion of dates in some of the earlier histories, owing to the difference of writing in the "old style" and the "new style."

In this attack some of the town records were carried off or destroyed, as appears from the following vote : —

"1698. Voted that a committee be chosen to receive anew the records of the town lands, according to what papers may be found that have been upon record before ; *our town records being taken away by the enemy Indians.*"

The hostilities between the English and French were nominally put an end to by the Treaty of Ryswick, in 1697 ; but the towns were by no means relieved of their apprehensions of Indian attacks, since savages, once maddened with the fury of slaughter, could not be immediately quieted by treaties made thousands of miles away, and sometimes from that very cause they rallied for a final and retaliative blow. The interval of rest had, therefore, been brief, when the formal renewal of the wars of the European nations again brought fresh danger to the struggling colonies.

"Queen Anne's War" was under the control in America of her Majesty's Governor of the Province, Joseph Dudley. The military expeditions were mainly to the eastern frontiers. Col. John March was obliged to give up his shipbuilding operations in Andover to enter on active military service. For his valorous conduct he received a tribute from the government : —

"*Nov.* 30, 1703 : Resolved passed us the house of Representatives, — that there be allowed & paid out of y* publick treasury to Lieut. Coll. March the sum of Fifty pounds for the brave defence which by his conduct was made of her Majesty's Fort at Casco Bay when lately attacked by y* French & Indians & in consideration of his wounds & damage which he then received."

There are accounts in the town records of extra provision made for supplies of ammunition ; also, by order of the government, the soldiers were furnished with snow-shoes ; one hundred and twenty-five pairs were ordered for the North Regiment of Essex.[1] Four block-houses were built on the Merrimack River, two of which were in Andover. The following orders[2] were issued to the military officer at Andover, Capt. Christopher Osgood : —

"I am directed by his Excellency our Governor to build two[3] block houses in your town upon the brink of Merrimack river, one at the fording place called Deare's Jump and one at a fording place commonly called Mr. Petters wading place both Places I am informed is in the Precinct of your company therefore I order that you build them twelve foot wide & fifteen foot long with . . . . at one end & well covered that the men may be dry in wet weather, as to the charge I am not informed how it might be, but have desired Lieut. Barker to inform you how wee at Newbury have built ours," etc.

Captain Osgood impressed ten men from his company, and in six weeks had the buildings done.[4] While some worked, others guarded, and were on the scout along the river.

In July, 1706, Capt. Benjamin Stevens went in command of a company into the woods in "quest of the Indian enemy," and, while he was gone, his house was broken into, and some

[1] *General Court Records,* 1704, Nov. 18. *Mass. Archives,* vol. lxxi., pp. 67 and 152.
[2] *Mass. Archives,* vol. lxxi., p. 69.
[3] Two, three, and four houses are spoken of in different documents.
[4] See petition in *Records of General Court ;* also, *Mass. Archives,* vol. lxxi., p. 69.;

things stolen, among them five certificates of wages due him and his soldiers for service in January and February. He petitioned for five other certificates, to be delivered him by the treasurer. Three of the certificates were ordered to be paid by the constables of Boston, one by the constable of Bradford, another by the constable of Haverhill. The total amount was £84 3s. 9d.[1]

The following from the town records shows what stock of ammunition was in the town in 1713: —

"Feb. y^e 20th 17$\frac{12}{13}$. This may sertifye those selectmen that shall succeed us: that where as some time since our Town Stock of Ammunition was divided to Sundry persons, viz to Capt. John Chandler, Capt. Christopher Osgood, and some others we the subscribers have gathered it together all but some small parsels, the which we have given Ensign Ephraim Stevens for to gather and put to the Rest, as soon as he can: And we have left all the Town Stock of Ammunition of powder, bullets, and flints with Left. John Aslebe for one year and then to be taken care of by ye select men for the time being. And the powder we left at Left. John Aslebes is one hundred and sixty-six pounds 166; and of bullets four hundred, twenty and eight pounds 428, and of flints thirteen pounds: wanting one ounce, (13). And we have Left the keas of the Town Stock of Ammunition with Ensign Ephraim Stevens, to be at ye selectmen's service, when they shall have ocation for them, and there is two dry casks of the Towns left standing on ye chest that the Amonition is locked up in. One is a small powder cask headed up at both ends, the other open at one head.

"Signed the day and year abovesaid.

EPHRAIM STEVENS
GEORGE ABBOTT
JOHN OSGOOD
EPHRAIM FOSTER
NEHEMIAH ABBOTT
} *Selectmen of Andover.*"

The towns were never safe. In winter the Indians came on snow-shoes, and in summer by the rivers, plundering and killing, and then disappearing as suddenly as they had come, plunging into the depths of the forests. In the winter of 1705, Governor Dudley wrote to Col. Saltonstall in regard to being prepared to meet the enemy: —

[1] *Mass. Archives*, "Petitions," 1704.

"I pray you to give direction that your snow-shoe men from Newbury to Andover be ready at a moment's warning till the weather break up, then we may be quiet awhile."

In the autumn of 1724 (September 25th) a petition was sent to the General Court to commission Capt. Benjamin Stevens, of Andover, leader of an expedition to Winipeseog Pond, "to discover the Indians camping places & haply find their canoes & by what or what manner they come down upon us in summer."

Of all the tales of Indian warfare connected with old Andover history, the one which has the most melancholy and romantic interest is that of Chaplain Jonathan Frye, who was mortally wounded in the year 1725, in the famous Lovewell's fight at Pequauket. He wandered for some time in the woods, and, as is supposed, died fifty miles from any English settlement, and twenty miles from the fort whence his company had marched. The English were at prayers when they first discovered the approach of an enemy. The young chaplain (he was only twenty) was ready to fight as well as to pray. Says a record : "Mr. Frye and another scalped the first Indian who was slain." The scalps were kept, as a reward was paid for them. A history of the fight, taken from the testimony of an eye-witness, was written soon after by the Rev. Thomas Symmes, of Bradford. The quaint language is worth preserving : —

"About the middle of the Afternoon, the Ingenious Mr. Jonathan Frie only son of Capt. James Frie of Andover, a young Gentleman of a Liberal Education, and who was chaplain to the company and was greatly Beloved by them for his excellent Performances and good Behavior and who fought with Undaunted Courage till that time of Day was mortally wounded. But when he could fight no longer, he prayed audibly severall times for the Preservation and Success of the Residue of the Company."

Is there anything more pathetic in our annals of youthful heroism than this plain, unvarnished tale of the young chaplain of Andover? It shows not only how dominant over the spirit of the time was the moral and religious sentiment, which alone lifts the battle-field above the plane of brute force, and redeems its passions from utter fiendishness, but it pays an affectionate tribute to the rare qualities of the young man. He must have had a character remarkably uniting manly and Christian virtues, who could, at twenty, act as religious guide and at the same time comrade-in-arms of a company of frontier savage-hunters (of however excellent material it might be made), and secure the common respect and affection.

A week after the fight the Rev. Mr. Symmes pronounced "A SERMON OCCASIONED BY THE FALL OF THE BRAVE CAPT. JOHN LOVEWELL, AND SEVERAL OF HIS VALIANT COMPANY IN THE LATE HEROIC ACTION." This was printed and prefaced by the historical narrative before alluded to. There can be no doubt that to listen to this discourse, referring to their townsman's tragic death, the Andover people went in large numbers. In fact the discourse may be regarded as largely commemorative of that special loss, Mr. Symmes having intimate acquaintance with Andover; his sister being the wife[1] of Capt. Benjamin Stevens. The text of the sermon was, "How are the mighty fallen and the weapons of war perished." 2 Sam. i. 27.

This sermon repays perusal. It is thoughtful and forcible, full of odd turns of expression that rival some of old Fuller's "Good Thoughts in Bad Times," and withal it has a martial ring, characteristic of the preaching of these times; when the wars of the Israelites furnished more acceptable texts than the gospel of peace:—

"We must not be Disheartened & cast down because a crew of Salvages have killed a few Brave Men. No, verily, its beneath a Man, much more a Christian whose heart is fixed trusting in the Lord, to be thus affected. Such news should not daunt and terrify a soldier, but whet his Courage. Especially it should rouse 'em on such occasions to Rally forth and come to March with utmost expedition to Recover if possible our Dear Brethren that lie Wounded and without Relief in a Howling Wilderness, that they mayn't Perish with Famine or fall into the hands of a Barbarous Enemy, to be killed over again & Tortured with *Indian Cruelty*,

---

[1] "*Here lyes what was mortal of Mrs. Susannah Stevens widow of Benjamin Stevens, Esq. and Daughter of ye Revd. Mr. Zechariah Symmes of Bradford who died July 30 1753, in ye 83 year of Her Age.*"
                                                       Epitaph — Old Burying Ground.

and also to give Christian Burial to the Remains of our Departed Heroes. . . . . We that tarry at home must get into the Mount and Pray for em'. A *Good Woman* in her Closet (tho' she's afraid to take a Gun in her hand) may serve her Country to a very good purpose even in respect of the War as really as the Magistrate at the Council Board or the most daring and well advised commander in the open Field in a thro' engagement. *For Prayer and Faith always* were, are, and will be the *Church's Best Weapons*."[1]

The place of the fight was on the northeast end of Saco Pond, on the edge of a wood "where there were few trees and scarce any brush." There were about forty English engaged, and twice as many Indians, by whom the English had been ambushed. The fight lasted all day, when the savages retreated. Seventeen of the English made their way back through the woods to the fort at Ossipee Lake; twelve died in the woods, and their bodies were afterwards found and buried where they lay; three were "lost by the way and never found."

The English, retreating from the fight at the wood, fell back upon the pond, and to its waters the wounded crept, to slake their thirst and staunch their wounds; crimsoning the water with their blood. Some crawled off into the thick wood and died there, while a few, wounded but able to walk, started on their way toward the camp. Among the latter was Chaplain Frye. After journeying painfully for some miles with his friends, Eleazar Davis, of Concord, and Lieutenant Farwell, of Dunstable, he begged them to save themselves and leave him to his fate, "not to hinder themselves any longer for his sake; for that he found himself Dying." Then he lay down, "telling them he should never rise more." He gave a message to be delivered to his father, that he "expected in a few hours to be in eternity and that he was not afraid to die." "Whereupon," says the record, "they left him; and this Hopeful Gentleman Mr. Frie who had the Journal of the March in his pocket has not been heard of since."

This incident of the abandoning a dying comrade in the wilderness forms the ground-work of Hawthorne's tale of

[1] The Italics are in the original.

"Roger Malvin's Burial." No one who compares the facts with the romance can fail to see that in the psychological and ethical studies of this parting of Chaplain Frye with his comrades, the greatest of New England romance writers found the materials for his tale. He himself says it was an incident of Lovell's fight in 1725, and that the characters may be recognized notwithstanding the substitution of fictitious names. The only recorded instance of a comrade's being deliberately left is that of the chaplain from Andover. Therefore the probability amounts to certainty that with name and age changed, Jonathan Frye is Roger Malvin, and Eleazar Davis, who survived to reach home, his comrade, Reuben Bourne; the details, and the subsequent history of their lives being varied by the romancer's imagination to suit the purposes of his story.

The reluctance of Reuben to leave his dying friend; that friend's persuading him to do so, appealing to his affection for his betrothed, the daughter of Reuben, and holding out the hope that he may yet come back with a party and rescue the comrade whom he leaves (a hope which Roger, while holding it out as a motive to his friend to quit him for the present, knows to be vain); the final leave-taking; Reuben Bourne's life-long remorse for this act, his final unwitting expiation of the sin that haunted his imagination, by shooting his own son, by accident, on the very spot, — these are all evolved from the poet-philosopher's musing on the fate of Chaplain Frye, and the words of the ancient chronicler, " Whereupon, *they left him.*"

"*Roger.* 'There is not two days' life in me Reuben, and I will no longer burden you with my useless body, when you can scarcely support your own. Your wounds are deep and your strength is failing fast, yet, if you hasten onward alone you may be preserved. For me there is no hope, and I will await death here.'

"*Reuben.* 'Should I therefore leave you to perish and to lie unburied in the wilderness! No, if your end be in truth approaching, I will watch by you and receive your parting words. I will dig a grave here by the rock, in which if my weakness overcomes me, we will rest together; or if Heaven gives me strength, I will seek my way home.'

"*Roger.* 'In the cities and wherever men dwell they bury their dead in the earth: they hide them from the sight of the living; but here, where no step may pass perhaps for a hundred years, wherefore should I not rest beneath the open sky covered only by the oak leaves when the autumn winds shall strew them?'"

Thus it was that Jonathan Frye rested, the forest around him, the sky above. On the spot where tradition says he died, now surrounded by the homes and busy industries of the city which commemorates his name, a wild rose-tree sprang and flourished, and its annual flowers, plucked with a half superstitious feeling by the visitor, have been a more effectual memorial than "storied urn or animated bust."

A ballad written in 1725, called the "Most-beloved song in all New England" contains this stanza alluding to Mr. Frye:—

> "Our worthy Captain Lovewell among them there did die
> They killed Lieutenant Robbins and wounded good young Frye
> Who was our English chaplain he many indians slew
> And some of them he scalped when bullets round him flew."

The large elm tree which has stood in beauty and verdure until within a few years, and whose trunk now remains, on the roadside near the birthplace of Chaplain Frye, was set out by his hands,—(a sapling from the wood) the year of his death. Mr. Frye was engaged to be married to a young girl whom his parents did not regard with approval as suited to him in point of birth and fortune.

It is said by a writer,[1] whose residence in Andover seventy-five years ago made him familiar with the then current traditions, and who was an enthusiast in the search for the romance of history, that the enlistment of young Frye in military service arose from the conflict of duties and feelings which was caused by his parents' disapproval of his love. The story is thus told:—

"Among the number who fell was Mr. Jonathan Frye, a student in divinity, who was Lovewell's chaplain and who had joined this little band from some affair of the heart. He made himself conspicuous in the fight, and as described, acted with the reckless

[1] Samuel L. Knapp's *Lectures on American Literature*. He was Preceptor of Franklin Academy, 1805.

valour, which is often found to belong to such a state of mind. The fair one to whom he was thought by his friends to be imprudently attached was not content with the praises others were ready to bestow upon the lost object of her affections; and, although only fourteen years of age, struck her harp in mournful lays upon her Philander's fate and produced an elegy which has survived to this day; being lately found in an ancient manuscript of a gentleman of the native place of the lovers and lately transmitted to me. If it does not burn with a Sapphic blaze it gives more of the light of history than all the odes of the Lesbian dame on her lost Phaon. Miss Susannah Rogers calls on her muse to assist her in describing the youthful warrior, who afar off was resting without his shroud on the battle-field of glory. She says that his person was comely, his age just twenty-one — his genius of the highest excellence, and that he was the only son of his parents, beloved by all who knew him. His valor, his piety, his prayers amidst the fight, his wounds all bleeding, pass in review before her streaming eyes and she sees the howling wilderness where he fell. She notes the fortitude and resignation with which he died or rather his exhibition of it, when they left him to die, for he was not dead when his companions were under the necessity of leaving him to perish. The parental grief is not forgotten and her own loss is touched upon with truth and delicacy. . . . . This elegy of the bereaved fair is too long for my purpose."

Although too long for a lecture on American Literature, it is, however long and however devoid of poetic fire, properly to be preserved in any sketch of Andover history. And surely it is not to be regarded lightly, though its composition may provoke a smile. If a town wept the fate of this fallen brave, and spoke his praise, surely the grief of this poor girl whose love had been of so melancholy an ending, in whatever phrases it finds vent, should awaken sympathy and excite compassion. Her address to the parents of her lover is certainly evidence of a heart free from malice and moved to sympathy even with those who scarcely acknowledged her right to sympathy.

"THE MOURNFUL ELEGY ON MR. JONATHAN FRYE. 1725.

"Assist ye muses; help my quill
Whilst floods of tears do down distil

Not from mine eyes alone, but all
That hears the sad and doleful fall
Of that young student Mr. Frye
Who in his blooming youth did die.
Fighting for his dear country's good
He lost his life and precious blood.
His father's only son was he
His mother loved him tenderly
And all that knew him loved him well
For in bright parts he did excel
Most of his age: for he was young
Wounded and bleeding he was left
And of all sustenance bereft
Within the hunting desert great
None to lament his dismal fate
A sad reward, you 'll say, for those
For whom he did his life expose
He marched out with courage bold
And fought the Indians uncontrolled
And many of the rebels slew.
At last, a fatal bullet came
And wounded this young man of fame
And pierced him through and made him fall
But he upon the Lord did call
He prayed aloud; the standers-by
Heard him for grace and mercy cry
The Lord did hear and raised him so
That he enabled was to go.
For many days he homeward went
Till he for food was almost spent
Then to the standers-by declared
Death did not find him unprepared.
And there they left him in the wood
Some scores of miles from any food
Wandered and famished all alone
None to relieve or hear his moan
And there without all doubt did die —
   "And now I 'll speak to Mr. Frye,
Pray sir be patient; kiss the rod
Remember this the hand of God
Which has bereft you of your son.
Your dear and lovely Jonathan

"Although the Lord has taken now
Unto himself your son most dear
Resign your will to God and say
'Tis God that gives and takes away;
And blessed be his name; for he —
For he has caused this to be.
And now to you, his mother dear
Be pleased my childish lines to hear,
Mother refrain from flowing tears;
Your son is gone beyond your cares
And safe at rest in Heaven above
With Christ who was his joy and love,
And in due time I hope you 'll be
With him to all eternity.
Pray madam pardon this advice
Your grief is great, mine not much less,
And if these lines will comfort you
I have my will, Farewell, adieu."

A poem of much beauty and pathos has been written by Mr. Upham of New Hampshire, "On Visiting the Scene of Lovewell's Fight." The following stanzas selected from it are a not inappropriate requiem for all the soldiers of our own and other towns who perished in the early Indian[1] wars: —

"The bugle is silent, the war-whoop is dead,
There 's a murmur of waters and woods in their stead,
And the raven and owl chant a symphony drear
From the dark-waving pines o'er the combatants' bier.

"Sleep, soldiers of merit, sleep, gallant of yore,
The hatchet is fallen, the struggle is o'er;
While the fir-tree is green and the wind rolls a wave
The tear-drop shall brighten the turf of the brave!"

[1] The history of the later Indian wars, 1744-1761, is separated from that of the first century, because it seems to connect more properly with the Revolutionary period, the same men being in service in the Revolution who had been trained in the old French War.

CHAPTER III.

WITCHCRAFT AT ANDOVER.[1]

THE fiftieth anniversary of Andover's settlement (1692), was destined to be a year of peculiar trial and distress. At the opening of the year it seemed that the town might reasonably hope to enjoy a season of prosperity. There were no near alarms of hostile Indians; the church controversies, which had been a source of trouble, were settled; there was nothing, apparently, to hinder the growth or disturb the peace of the community. But a cloud was gathering which was to bring darkness and desolation, a convulsion heaving that threatened to break up the very foundations of society. Few persons, who have not made the subject a special study, have an adequate conception of the magnitude of this calamity of the witchcraft delusion. It is often said that too much stress has been laid upon it; the number who suffered death was small, the pains of their execution were as a drop in the ocean compared with the sufferings of thousands slain for conscience in other countries and other communions. It is not, however, by numerical computations that the magnitude of the crisis can be estimated and the peril to the community and to the Puritan church appreciated. What made the peculiar danger of this panic, was its creation of universal distrust. Every man doubted whether his neighbor, his minister, his friend, the wife of his bosom, the children of his household, were not of those given over to Satan, sold to the service of the enemy of souls. And in his very doubt, querying whether or no such terrible suspicion could have foundation in truth, the

---

[1] The principal authorities consulted for this account, are *The Essex County Court Papers, Mass. Archives,* Woodward's *Copies of Court Papers,* Drake's *Annals,* Upham's *Salem Witchcraft,* Calef's and Mather's *Accounts, Historical Collections, Assistants' Records, Suffolk County Court Papers.*

suspecter finds himself suspected, arrested, hurried to jail, brought to trial, sentenced to death; his protestations unheeded, his denials pronounced obstinacy, his prayers blasphemy and imprecation. The insecurity of all institutions, domestic and social, in such a state of things is apparent. If the examinations and trials had been conducted by any ordinary processes and according to any rules of evidence, there might have been a hope of arriving at truth. But the character of the witnesses, the nature of their testimony, the methods of their examination, — all tended to increase rather than allay the excitement. The examiners proceeded on the assumption that the accused were guilty; they invited evidence against them, in their zeal almost put words into the mouths of reluctant confessors and faltering witnesses, and they placed implicit faith in every statement corroborative of their preconceived opinions. Not that these men, some of the best and most conscientious of their time, delighted in the punishments inflicted or did not grieve for the necessity laid upon them. What made the situation most hopeless was that the magistrates were, as they believed, "verily doing God service," engaging for the sake of Christ's kingdom in a contest with the Prince of Evil, — a contest in which at every cost they must persist and conquer; though to do so they should be forced to sacrifice all which they held dearest. At least, such seems to the writer of this history the character and motives of the men who prosecuted the trials and advocated severity. But, whatever our estimate of the actors in the tragedy, the acts themselves are of thrilling interest, bringing to view in most prominent parts the men and women and even the children of our town.

A belief in witchcraft was everywhere prevalent at the period of the colonial settlements. That Satan often worked through human agency to perform wonders was almost an essential article of the theological dogmas of the time, and this doctrine was surrounded and overlaid with many vulgar traditions and superstitions. Now and then, in the course of controversies and litigations, especially among the illiterate classes of society, accusations would be brought against persons, of malicious connivings with the devil, to injure their opponents by Satanic arts. Such a charge was brought in 1658 against one John Godfrey of Andover. The principal sufferer from his wiles was the wife of Job Tyler of Boxford, who attended the church and was one of the tax-payers of Andover. The charge was brought in connection with a lawsuit of Haverhill men against Godfrey for non-payment of a debt, but seems not to have been satisfactorily established, and Godfrey subsequently brought suit for defamation. With John Godfrey's lawsuit the craft of witches seems to have ceased, and even at this time not to have much disturbed the community; the minister, Rev. Francis Dane, giving decided opinion against its probability.

The beginning of "the witchcraft" proper was in the winter of 1691, in Salem village (Danvers). Some young girls were in the habit of meeting together for entertainment, — games, amusements, such as were permitted to young people. They tried sleight-of-hand, tricks of fortune-telling, looking into the palm of the hand and reading the future of the person's life by the interlacing lines there visible, as has been a custom of the credulous from that day to the present. The old historians call this "practising palmistry." Filling their minds with thoughts of this sort, they became fascinated and wonder-stricken, in talking about the supernatural. Ghosts, hobgoblins, devils, were the theme of their story-telling, and the subjects of their imaginings by night and by day. Some of them soon began to see strange sights, hear voices, dream dreams. They consulted an old Indian fortune-teller, gifted in wonder-working; some of them began to be seized with convulsions, and to experience physical contortions of various sorts; the others caught the infection. They vied with each other in strange exhibitions; their conduct having become a subject of general notice and curiosity and of scientific or theological study. Stimulated and excited, they were wrought up to every species of hysterical manifestation; they barked and mewed; they wriggled themselves off into corners under tables; they did all frenzied acts which the human mind, left a prey to morbid and unbridled imaginations, can invent. Their bodies, too, showed strange and inexplicable marks of torture and violence. Purple spots, as of bruises or violence from human hands, marks of teeth, prickings of pins, were visible on them; they grew emaciated, and had the appearance of being the victims of a wasting disease. The physicians could not cure them, and, as was not uncommon, suggested that they were under the affliction of an evil spirit. The ministers then made their case a subject of special prayer. Eminent clergymen from Boston were summoned. Preeminent among them was the Rev. Cotton Mather, a zealous investigator and curious, "entertained," as he phrases it, in considering these morbid manifestations. The unanimous conclusion was, that the unhappy victims were afflicted of the devil. This view of their case was communicated to the girls, and did not tend to alleviate their sufferings. Whether these were real or feigned, due wholly to diseased fancies, or were, in the case of any, sheer hypocrisy and of malice contrived, opinions differ. The sufferers, either of their own accord or by suggestion, intimated that their sufferings were caused by some persons in the community through whose agency Satan worked to torture them. The persons whom they at first selected for accusation were two or three poor vagrant creatures, objects of common contempt or charity, — a terror to children, such forlorn souls as almost every village had when asylums and alms-houses were few. These half-crazed and outcast wretches were readily believed to be guilty of the sin charged upon them. They were tried with more or less satisfactory results. Others than they were soon accused; the wonder grew; whenever a person had any disease which baffled medical skill, these afflicted girls, who were supposed to have clairvoyant power, or " spectre-evidence," as to the cause of sickness, were consulted. They usually pronounced the cause of the sickness to be due to the affliction of some person, — " witchcraft."

It chanced, in the spring of 1692, that the wife of Joseph Ballard, of Andover, having long been ill, and having found no relief in medicine, her husband became anxious to try the spiritual method of ascertaining the cause of her ailment. Accordingly, he sent to Salem and brought two of the girls to Andover. One who came was Ann Putnam, of Salem. These girls were received with great solemnity, taken to the meeting-house, and, prayer having been made by the Rev. Mr. Barnard (Mr. Dane seems to have kept aloof from the proceedings, which was perhaps the reason of suspicion's falling on him and his family), they were adjured to tell the truth.

They named certain persons of Andover and other places as the tormentors of the sick woman. John Ballard, the constable, forthwith obtained a warrant for the arrest of the accused, and hurried them off to Salem jail. They, being plied with questions as to their accomplices and partners in guilt, named others, who also followed them to jail, till, in about three months, some forty or more were under arrest, and lying in irons, manacles, and fetters (all these instruments are mentioned in the records) in the crowded and miserable jail. The consternation and excitement of the community were beyond bounds. The belief gained ground that the devil had made a plot to destroy the Christian faith in the community and win over the people to himself. These men and women, fathers and mothers of Andover, — and their innocent children, — were thought to have sold themselves and their families to him. It was said he had made them sign their names in blood in his book, and bind themselves to do his bidding for a term of years : " Did wickedly, maliciously and feloniously covenant with the devil, did signe' the Devils Book with Blood, did give himself soul and body to the Devill, by which wicked and diabolical covenant he is bound a Detestable Witch," is the form of indictment found against the prisoners, from children of eight years old to men and women gray-headed, parents and grandparents. Many confessed the charge to be true ; said the devil had baptized them in the Shawshin River, or in Five-mile Pond, on whose borders they held midnight meetings, stealing out of their houses and riding through the air on sticks, going as far as Salem village, the gathering-ground of witches. These stories, creations of a diseased imagination, were implicitly believed by the friends and relatives of the accused, at least by many. Instead of directing their efforts to calm the frenzied mind and restore to right reason their unhappy friends, near and dear kindred joined their voices to those of the magistrates and ministers, begging the accused to make full confession.

One of the saddest features of the delusion was that it held for nothing the former high character of the accused. At first, it is true, only the friendless and the strange, eccentric persons in the community or the high-tempered, or those who for any bold stand had incurred spite or made enemies, were selected. But, an epidemic of audacity seemed at length to seize the afflicted. One of the "higher powers" accused, and the magic circle broken, which birth, social position, and religious character had at first put their barriers around, a rivalry seems to have begun who should "bring out" (as was said) the most improbable and unsuspected of guilt. The sort of vulgar satisfaction which rejoices in the degradation and humiliation of those above its own level, now revelled in reducing the pride of the lofty. Into the most honored households the tongue of accusation thrust itself, and fastened its venomous touch upon the purest and gentlest there. The ladies who had walked hitherto as examples in the community, the admired, but the envied of many, were brought low. Mistress Mary Osgood, and the wife of the deacon of the church, Mrs. Eunice Frye, a woman of all Christian virtues, and the Rev. Mr. Dane's daughter, Mrs. Abigail Faulkner, and her innocent children, Dorothy and Abigail Faulkner, and another of Mr. Dane's daughters, Elizabeth Johnson, and her daughter, "Elizabeth Johnson jr.," and Mr. Dane's daughter-in-law, Mrs. Deliverance [Hazeltine] Dane, were accused; and finally, Mr. Dane himself was hinted at, Mrs. Dudley Bradstreet named, and Mr. Dudley Bradstreet compelled to seek safety in flight. Such was the frenzy which seized the community and loosed its basest and most dangerous passions. The people clamored for trial and punishment of the accused, as they always clamor when superstition or suspicion of crime is rife, and each thinks to prove his own innocence by zeal for his fellows' conviction of guilt.

In the trials, eight citizens of Andover were condemned. Three of these were hanged: Martha Carrier, Samuel Wardwell, Mary Parker; one died in prison, Ann Foster; Abigail Faulkner was reprieved, and by the delay ultimately saved; Sarah Wardwell and Elizabeth Johnson and Mary Lacey were condemned at the very latest trial, January, 1693, and set free on the general jail delivery, when the frenzy was checked. The following is a list of those names of the accused which have been found,[1] and the various identifying notes in regard to them: —

Barker, Abigail, wife of Ebenezer Barker, not guilty.
Barker, Mary, single woman, daughter of John Barker, not guilty.
Barker, William, Sen., brother of John Barker, not guilty.
Bridges, Mary, single woman, not guilty.
Bridges, Mary, wife of John Bridges, not guilty.
Bridges, Mary, Jr., aged twelve years, daughter of John Bridges.
Bridges, Sarah, single woman, afterward wife of John Preston, not guilty.
Carrier, Martha [Allen], wife of Thomas Carrier, hanged.
Carrier, Andrew, son of Thomas Carrier.
Carrier, Richard,[2] son of Thomas Carrier.
Carrier, Thomas, son of Thomas Carrier.
Carrier, Sarah, age seven years, daughter of Thomas Carrier.
Dane, Deliverance, wife of Nathaniel.
Draper, John.
Farrington, Edward.
Faulkner, Abigail, wife of Francis Faulkner, sentenced.
Faulkner, Dorothy, ten years, daughter of Francis Faulkner.
Faulkner, Abigail, eight years, daughter of Francis Faulkner.
Foster, Ann, mother of Abraham Foster, condemned (died in prison).
Frye, Eunice, wife of Dea. John Frye, not guilty.
Fawkes, Sarah, single woman, afterward wife of Francis Johnson, not guilty.
Johnson, Elizabeth [Dane], wife of Stephen Johnson, mother of Francis Johnson.
Johnson, Elizabeth, Jr., sister of Francis Johnson, condemned.
Johnson, Abigail, eleven years, sister of Francis Johnson.
Johnson, Stephen, thirteen years, brother of Francis Johnson.
Johnson, Rebecca, widow, mother of John Johnson.
Lacey, Mary [Foster], wife of Lawrence Lacey, condemned.

[1] Nehemiah Abbot was of Topsfield — sometimes named of Andover.
[2] A Richard Carrier, son of Andrew Carrier, is mentioned.

Lacey, Mary, Jr., daughter of Lawrence Lacey.
Osgood, Mary, wife of Capt. John Osgood.
Parker, Mary, mother of Joseph Parker, hanged.
Parker, Sarah.
Post, Mary, of Boxford,[1] daughter of Rebecca Johnson, condemned.
Sawdey, John, apparently an apprentice.
Tyler, Mary, wife of Hopestil Tyler, not guilty.
Tyler, Johanna, daughter of Hopestil Tyler.
Tyler, Hannah, single woman, not guilty.
Wardwell, Samuel, hanged.
Wardwell, Sarah, wife of Samuel Wardwell, condemned.
Wardwell, Mercy, daughter of Samuel Wardwell, not guilty.
Wilson, Sarah, wife of Joseph Wilson.
Wilson, Sarah, daughter of Joseph Wilson.

The above marked "not guilty" were those on whom verdict was pronounced at the court which sat January, 1692 (1693). The others were perhaps not all formally tried. "Examinations," so-called, in which many confessed, preceded the trials and the evidence of the witnesses. Besides the above names, some others were reckoned with Andover. Rebecca Eames of Boxford, was one. The reason of this was that the Andover deputy to the General Court received the restitution money ultimately allowed to their legal representatives for losses. In the examinations of the accused which preceded the regular trial, most made confession and thus averted the extreme penalty. Martha Carrier was the only one of all, male or female, who did not at some time or other make an admission or confession. From the first moment to the last, under all the persuasions and exhortations of friends, under denunciations and threats of the magistrates and examiners, she held firm, denying all charges, and neither overborne in mind nor shaken in nerve, met death with heroic courage.

The charge of witchcraft was not the first of Martha Carrier's troubles ; indeed, the former may have been in a sense the cause of the later affliction. The Carrier family, who came to Andover from Billerica [they were living in the latter town about 1685], were not welcome residents. Thomas Carrier

[1] Often mentioned as of Andover.

was of Welsh birth, say the earlier historians. He seems to have been blessed with a comfortable temperament, for notwithstanding the misfortunes which befell him as a husband and father in the course of these witchcraft trials: his wife hanged, his sons imprisoned and cruelly handled, his daughter of tender years accused and made to confess against her mother,— sorrows enough to have brought some men to a premature grave, — he lived to the age of one hundred and nine years, his head not bald nor his hair gray, and of such bodily activity that he walked[1] six miles a few days before his death.

The wife, Martha Allen, was a resident of Andover before her marriage, the daughter of Andrew Allen, Sen. Her sister Mary was married to Roger Toothaker of Ipswich and Billerica, and her nephew, Allen Toothaker, was a resident of Andover. The family were obnoxious, and were warned out of the town, because they had the small-pox, as appears from the following extract from the town records : —

"To SAMUEL HOLT, ANDREW ALLEN AND JOHN ALLEN, *Neighbors and ffriends* — We the subscribers of Andover have been informed that your sister Carrier and some of her children are smitten with that contagious disease the small-pox and some have been soe inconsiderate as to think that the care of them belongs to the salact men of Andover which does not, for they took care when first they came to towne to warne them out again and have attended the law therein : and shall only take care that they doe not spread the distemper with wicked carelessness which we are afraid they have already done: you had best take what care you can about them, nature and Religion requiring of it. We hope we have done faithfully in this information and are your friends and servants.

"Dated 14*th Oct*. 1690."

Later the selectmen issue the following warrant to the constable to provide for their support and the safety of the town : —

To WALTER WRIGHT *Constable:* Whereas it has pleased God to visit those of the widdowe Allen's family which she hath taken into her house with that contagious disease the small-pox, it being as we think part of our duty to prevent the spreading of sd distemper

---

[1] Abbot's *History of Andover*, 1829.

we therefore requier you in their Majesties' names to warn sd family not to goe near any house soe as to endanger them by sd infection nor to come to the public meeting till they may come with safety to others: but what they want let them acquaint you with: which provide for them out of their own estates.

"Dated the 4: 9. 1690."

These intruders who made so much trouble would not be likely to suffer last or least when witchcraft was supposed to be abroad. Martha Carrier was, too, a woman of a disposition not unlikely to make enemies: plain and outspoken in speech, of remarkable strength of mind, a keen sense of justice, and a sharp tongue. She, doubtless (from all that appears), took largely upon herself the care of the household, and no small interest in the management of the out-of-door affairs, in which she sometimes came into collision with the neighboring farmers. If the stories of witnesses can be credited (they were, it is plain, in some instances, greatly exaggerated) she had more than once threatened vengeance upon persons who, as she thought, over-reached and cheated her husband in his bargains. Among her unguarded speeches was brought against her, that she had declared "she would stick as close as the bark of a tree" to Benjamin Abbot (who had a dispute with her and her husband about laying out land), and he "should repent his conduct afore seven years came to an end," and "she would hold his nose so close to the grindstone as ever it was held since his name was Benjamin Abbot." As this man soon after had a swelling on his foot, and "a paine in his side which bred a sore that discharged several gallons of corruption," he was convinced that Martha Carrier had bewitched him. She was also accused of witchcraft exercised upon some of the afflicted girls of Salem, and on complaint of Joseph Houlton and John Walcott, of Salem, a warrant was issued for her arrest May 28, 1692. She was the first arrested at Andover, so far as record is found. John Ballard, the constable, carried her off, and as soon as she was gone Benjamin Abbot "began to mend and grew better every day," as the witnesses in the trial averred, until he was quite well.

On the 31st of May the prisoner underwent an examination; being confronted with the persons who claimed to be suffering from her, five women and children of Salem and vicinity: —

"Abigail Williams, who hurts you? Goody Carrier of Andover.

"Elizabeth Hubbard who hurts you? Goody Carrier.

"Susan Sheldon who hurts you? Goody Carrier; she bites me, pinches me, and tells me she would cut my throat, if I did not signe her book."

These are specimens of the questioning, and the sort of answers which it elicited. The witnesses were seized with fits as soon as she looked at them, and "fell into the most intolerable outcries and agonies," as the chroniclers of the time relate. They said they saw a black man standing beside her. She denied that she knew anything of what they affirmed, and her manner was so defiant, as the magistrate thought, that it proved conclusively her guilt and impenitence. "I see the souls of thirteen persons whom she has murdered at Andover," cried one of the accusers. Goaded to desperation at this foul charge, the exasperated woman exclaimed, "*You lie; I am wronged!*" then turning to the magistrates she boldly made appeal and rebuke: "It is false; and it is a shame for you to mind what these say, that are out of their wits!" But the accusers persisted that they saw the black man, and that even then the prisoner was practising diabolical arts upon them, and their tortures seemed (and doubtless were) so great that, as the records say, "there was no enduring it." So she was "ordered away and to be bound hand and foot with all expedition, the afflicted in the meanwhile almost killed to the great trouble of all spectators, magistrates and others." Thus handcuffed and fettered she was put into jail, where also her sons and her little daughter were soon incarcerated, to await further trial. A summons for witnesses was issued July 30: —

"Wm & Mary by y⁰ Grace of God of England, Scotland, ffrance & Ireland King & Queen Defend⁰ of y⁰ faith &c. ss. To y⁰ Constable or Constables of Andover Greeting.

"Wee Comand you to Warn and give Notice unto Allen Toothaker, Ralph ffarnum junr, John ffarnum son of Ralph ffarnum senr,

Benjamin Abbot and his wife, Andrew Foster, Phebe Chandler daughter of William Chandler, Samuel Holt senr, Samuel Preston junr, that they and every one of them be and personally appear at ye Court of Oyer and Terminer to be held by adjournment on Tuesday next at Ten of ye Clock in ye Morning there to testifye ye truth to ye best of their knowledge on certain indictments to be exhibited against Martha Carrier of Andover; hereof fail not at your utmost perill and make return of your doings herein.

STEPHEN SEWALL, *Clerk*."

" Dated in Salem July 30th 1692."

Of the examination of Martha Carrier, Upham says: —

"The examination of Martha Carrier must have been one of the most striking scenes of the whole drama. The village meeting-house presented a truly wild and exciting spectacle; the fearful and horrible superstition which darkened the minds of the people was displayed in their aspect and movement. Their belief that then and there they were witnessing the great struggle between the kingdom of God and of the Evil One and that everything was at stake on the issue gave an awe-struck intensity to their expression. The blind unquestioning confidence of the magistrates, clergy and all concerned in the prosecutions, in the evidence of the accused, the loud outcries of their pretended sufferings, their contortions, swoonings, and tremblings excited the usual consternation in the assembly. In addition to this, there was the more than ordinarily bold and defiant bearing of the prisoner, stung to desperation by the outrage upon her poor children; her firm and unshrinking courage, facing the tempest that was raised to overwhelm her, sternly rebuking the magistrates: 'It is a shameful thing that you should mind these folks that are out of their wits,' her whole demeanor proclaiming her conscious innocence, and proving that she chose chains, the dungeon, and the scaffold rather than to belie herself. Seldom has a scene in real life, or a picture wrought by the inspiration of genius and the hand of art in its individual character or its general grouping surpassed that presented on this occasion."

After two months' imprisonment in the heat of midsummer, the unhappy woman was brought out on the first of August to face the neighbors and relations who were summoned to bear testimony. One and all they testified against her, — that she had afflicted them in their persons and estates, causing diseases to fall upon them and their cattle, and blight upon their crops. But, notwithstanding all the accumulation of evidence, she was undaunted and firm in maintaining her innocence. Others might confess to save themselves, or, because by so much evidence and argument they were driven to the belief that in some mysterious way they were actually, though unconsciously working with the devil, and drawn into his toils; but Martha Carrier's strong, clear mind no sophistry could bewilder, and her intrepid courage no threats terrify. The Rev. Cotton Mather was shocked at her impiety and her obduracy. An "arrant hag" he calls her, and says that as a reward of her adherence to Satan she had received the promise that she should be "queen of hell." He also says that even her own sons testified against her; but it appears from a letter written by one of their fellow prisoners that this confession was extorted from them by violence, which reminds us of the tortures of the Spanish Inquisition: "The sons of Martha Carrier would not confess anything till they had tied them neck and heel till the blood was ready to come out of their noses."

The little girl, Sarah Carrier, was brought into court August 11, 1692. There is something peculiarly touching in the scene, — this simple child, before the assembled magistrates and dignitaries, arraigned on a charge which she could not in the least comprehend, and confessing to the vagaries and overwrought fancies excited in her childish mind by fear, or prompted by the suggestions of her interrogators: —

"'How long hast thou been a witch?'
"'Ever since I was six years old.'
"'How old are you now?'
"'Near eight years old; brother Richard says I shall be eight years old in November.'
"'Who made you a witch?'
"'My mother. She made me set my hand to a book.'
"'How did you set your hand to it?'
"'I touched it with my fingers and the book was red and the paper of it was white.'
"'You said you saw a cat once. *What did the cat say to you?*'
"'It said it would tear me in pieces, if I did not set my hand to the book.'

"' How did you know *that the cat was your mother?*'
"' The cat told me that she was my mother.'"

With such absurd notions was the mind of the child filled by the grave and reverend magistrates and ministers, of whom it now seems impossible to conceive that they could have seriously put these questions about *cats' talking*, and a woman's assuming the form of a cat to delude her own child. Yet these were men who, in the ordinary affairs of life, were sensible and sagacious. If the facts teach anything it certainly is a lesson of human fallibility.

Several women of Andover who confessed, accused Martha Carrier as the cause of their being led into witchcraft. Three of these were, Ann Foster, her daughter Mary Lacey, and her granddaughter, Mary Lacey, Jr. Ann Foster said she rode on a stick with Martha Carrier to Salem village, that the stick broke and she saved herself by clinging around Martha Carrier's neck. She said they met three hundred witches at Salem village, among them the Rev. Mr. Burroughs, and *another minister with gray hair* (Mr. Dane, of Andover, was supposed to be hinted at). This story was confirmed by the daughter and the granddaughter. Besides these ridiculous charges there were others which had more foundation in truth. All the events of Martha Carrier's past life were gone over, and her rash speeches and revengeful words brought up, with some facts which looked greatly against her. Long ago, as one witness testified, she, angry with him, "gave forth several threatening words as she often used to doe," and, "soon after, the deponent found one of his large lusty sowes dead near Carrier's house, and one of his cowes which used to give a good Mess of milk would give little or none." Said the witness, John Roger: —

"I did in my conscience believe then in ye day of it and have so done ever since and doe yet believe that Martha Carrier was ye occasion of those Ill accidents by means of Witchcraft; she being a very malicious woman."

Her nephew, Allen Toothaker, testified that "he had lost a three year old heifer, next a yearlin and then a cow and he knew not of any naturall causes of ye death of the above s^d

creatures, but have always feared it hath been yᵉ effect of my aunt Carrier's her malice."

Samuel Preston had also lost a cow, after Martha Carrier had a difference with him. In all these cases the witnesses deposed that she had threatened these losses.

Phebe Chandler, eleven years old, testified: —

"About a fortnight before the prisoner was sent for to Salem, yᵗ upon yᵉ Sabbath day when yᵉ psalm was singing sᵈ Martha Carrier took me by yᵉ shoulder & shaked me in yᵉ meeting-house & asked me where I lived but I made her no answer, not doubting but that she knew me, having lived some time the next door to my father's house[1] on our side of the way."

She also said further, in relation to the prisoner's poisoning her: —

"That day that sᵈ Martha Carrier was accused my mother sent me to carry some beer to yᵉ folks yᵗ were att work in yᵉ lott & when I came within Carriers yᵉ fence, there was a noise in yᵉ bushes which I thought was Martha Carriers voice (which I knew well) but I saw nobody & yᵉ voice asked me what I did there & whither I was going which greatly frighted me."

She goes on to say that she heard a voice again telling her that she would be poisoned in two or three days. And so it was, her right hand swelled, and she had "a great weight on her breast and pain in her leges." When she got better, and went to meeting, Richard Carrier looked upon her "and the pains returned and she was struck deaf and heard none of yᵉ prayers."

"During the trial one of the afflicted," says Cotton Mather, "had her hands unaccountably tied together with a wheel-band, so fast that without cutting it could not be loosened." This was said to be done by the spectre or evil spirit working with and through Martha Carrier.

The prisoner was hanged August 19, 1692, along with four men, among them the Rev. George Burroughs. They were carried in a cart through the streets of Salem, crowds thronging to see the sight. Even from the scaffold, Martha

---

[1] In the south part of the town, on the road from Ipswich to Billerica, lived William Chandler, Sen. See petition for a public-house, Chapter I.

Carrier's voice was heard asseverating her innocence.[1] Her dead body was rudely treated, thrust into the ground in the same hole or grave with the bodies of Mr. Burroughs and John Willard. Calef describes the burial: —

"When he (Mr. Burroughs) was cut down, he was dragged by a halter to a hole or grave between the rocks about two feet deep; his shirt and breeches being pulled off and an old pair of trousers of one executed put on his lower parts; he was so put in together with Willard and Carrier that one of his hands and his chin and a foot of one of them was left uncovered."

Nothing more is found recorded of Martha Carrier, till, in the year 1711, her name occurs on a list of sufferers, whose legal representatives received money for losses sustained by the imprisonment and death of their relations. Seven pounds six shillings was allowed to the representatives of Martha Carrier. Some persons received fifty pounds. This has been commented on as an unjust and partial discrimination; but it appears to have been simply according to the claim presented for money expended or loss incurred. Some families, whose friends were long in prison and during the winter, were at great expense to provide them with comforts, and some had property seized as forfeited to the government, on the ground that it was the estate of a condemned criminal; some, also, were at expense in caring for the bodies of their friends and rescuing them from an ignominious burial.

To compensate friends for the greatest wrong done, the moral one, or to make reparation for the outrages inflicted on the innocent and defenceless prisoners, or the cruelty to their families of giving their bodies to the hangman, was not contemplated in the Acts of the General Court for "Reversal of Attainders and Restitution for Losses." For such wrongs and losses, the deepest and most real, done to individuals, governments offer no redress.

In regard to the other woman of Andover who was hanged, no particulars are found recorded. Several facts go to prove that she was the widow of Joseph Parker, who had been of a

---

[1] "All of them said they were innocent, Carrier and all." — Account of the Execution in the Diary of Judge Sewall. *Mass. Hist. Soc. Coll.*, Fifth Series, vol. v.

somewhat "distempered mind," and incapable of the care of her estate. The following petition tells her story in brief: —

"Whereas our honored mother was Imprisoned and upon her Tryal was condemned for supposed witchcraft upon such evidence as is now generally thought to be insufficient and suffered the Pains of Death at Salem in the year 1692 we being well satisfied not only of her innocency of that crime that she was condemned for, but of her piety humbly desire that the attainders may be taken off, that so her name that has suffered may be restored."

The sons of Mary Parker also show in their petition that after their mother's execution an officer sent by the sheriff came to Andover to seize her estate. The sons told him that she left no estate. Whereupon he seized their cattle, corn, and hay, and threatened that their estate should be sold, unless they could make a contrary agreement with the sheriff. They were therefore obliged to make a journey to Salem and expend much money to save their property from sale. They claimed eight pounds restitution.

In the trial of Mary Parker, she was accused by Mercy Wardwell and by William Barker (who both confessed to be witches), of joining with them to afflict one Timothy Swan of Andover. Several persons were also in the presence of the Court restored by the touch of her hand. On such evidence she was sentenced.

Samuel Wardwell was hanged September 22, 1692. He at his first examination had confessed, but in a short time recanted his confession. He did this in the spirit of martyrdom, saying that he had once "belyed himself," but that he begged forgiveness for it, and though he knew that to persist in his recantation would cost him his life he would hold to the truth. Two indictments were found against him. The first of these was as follows: —

" . . . . That Samuel Wardwell of Andover in the County of Essex, carpenter on or about the fifteenth day of August in the yeare aforesaid and divers other days and times as well before as after, certain detestable arts called witchcraft and sorceries wickedly mallitiously and felloniously hath used practised and exercised at and in the Towne of Boxford in the County of Essex in and upon and against one Martha Sprague of Boxford in the

County of Essex aforesaid single woman; by which said wicked Arts the said Martha Sprague of Boxford in the County of Essex aforesaid, the day and yeare aforesaide and divers other days and times both before and after was and is tortured, afflicted, Consumed, Pined, Wasted and Tormented and also for sundry other acts of witchcraft by the said Samuel Wardwell comited and done before and since that time against the peace of our Sovereign Lord and Lady the King and Queen their Crowne and dignity. And the form in the Statute in that case made and Provided."

In the second indictment it was presented that about "Twenty yeares agoe in the Town of Andover, he the said Samuel Wardwell with the evill speritt, the Devill a covenant did make, wherein he promised to honor, worship and believe the devil contrary to the statute of King James the First in that behalfe made and Provided, etc."

The witnesses against him were Martha Sprague [1] and several girls, also three prominent men of Andover, Joseph Ballard, Ephraim Foster, Thomas Chandler.

The last was a man sixty-five years old, of much experience in affairs, civil and military. His testimony shows how cautious the more practical and sensible men were in regard to their utterances about the witchcraft: —

"The testimony of Thomas Chandler aged about sixty-five, who saith that I have often heard Samuel Wardwell of Andover tell young persons their fortune and he was much adicted to that and mayd sport of it, and further saith not."

Here again in the accused we see one of those odd geniuses, or wonder-loving characters, of whom every community has some always, who deal in the marvellous, tell great stories, dupe the credulous to the amusement of the crowd, and who, in an age of superstition, were apt to claim a knowledge of future events, and who, perhaps, believed in a measure in their own supernatural gifts.

Ephraim Foster seemed to put some faith in his townsman's prophecies. He testified that Wardwell had made some predictions in regard to the birth of his (Foster's) children, that there would be five girls in the household before a son should be born. This had proved true. The

[1] "*Alias* Tyler."

witness had also often seen Wardwell "tell fortins," and he observed that in doing so the fortune-teller always "looked first into the hand of the person, and then cast his eyes down on the ground." This was proof of his being in league with Satan, though the connection is not obvious.

Wardwell himself confessed that he was guilty of covenanting with the devil. He said it was on this wise: Some years ago he had "fallen into a discontented state of mind because he was in love with a maid named Barker who slighted his love." While thus melancholy, one day, being behind Mr. Bradstreet's house, he saw "some catts together." One of these cats, as he related, "assuming the form of the black man," spoke to him, promising that "he should live comfortably and be a captain"[1] if he would sign the book. He was induced to make the signature, and was baptized in the Shawshin River, where "he was dipt all over, and renounced his former baptism."

In his recantation of this confession, the prisoner gave as his reason for ever making such a statement, that the examiners had insisted that he was a servant of the devil, and had urged him to name the time when he made the covenant; and being thus driven to specify the time, he had persuaded himself there must have been such a time, and he had gone back to this period of dejection as the only one in which he was likely to have done the deed. It would seem as though he and the others who confessed were unsettled in their own right reason and judgment by the many voices against them, the overwhelming evidence, and the importunities of the examiners that they would confess, and searching back over their past lives for some consciously or unconsciously-made covenant, found it in circumstances of mental depression or bodily suffering, the remembrance of which became clouded with phantoms conjured up by the fears of the hour. Nor would it be strange that a person, especially, who had so often exercised the pretended gift of fortune-telling, should half suspect himself of being under the power of supernatural beings. Even in the materialism of the nineteenth century, the mystery is

[1] Captains then were the chief men, — as Captain Bradstreet, owner of the house near the scene of temptation.

not all solved, of those at least almost preternatural powers which some persons seem to have in certain abnormal conditions. It cannot, therefore, be much wondered at that the simple-minded fortune-teller of the seventeenth century, in old Andover, when his minister and all the most devout magistrates told him he was a witch, should, temporarily at least, believe that he was.

But it shows that he had, in spite of all his odd ways, more strength of character and real principle than might at first be supposed, that he did not long remain thus obscured as to his estimate of himself. At the last, although he knew that his only hope of safety was in adhering to his confession, he wholly denied its truth. His mind, once cleared, became strong and steady, and his statements true and consistent.

On the gallows he protested his innocence. While he spoke, the wind blew a puff of smoke from the executioner's pipe into his face. The accusers exclaimed : " The devil doth hinder his words ! "

Seven other persons were hanged at the same time with Wardwell. The Rev. Mr. Noyes, pointing to the bodies, addressed the crowd with a moral : " What a sad thing it is to see eight *firebrands of hell* hanging there ! "

The account presented by the sons of Samuel Wardwell shows that there was taken by the government to pay the expenses of his trial and execution the following : —

Five cowes	£10	0 0
One heifer and a yearling	2	5 0
Nine hogs	7	0 0
Eight loads of hay	4	0 0
A set of carpenter's tools	1	10 0
Six acres of corn upon the ground . . .	9	0 0
	£36	15

Another who was condemned was Ann Foster. She, however, was not hanged, having died in the prison before the law could take its course. She was an aged woman, a widow, without friends of influence to give aid in her distress. She was evidently weak in mind and body, and was ready at the trial to confess almost anything, and believe everything which was suggested against herself. Indeed, some of these women had been so long used to contemplate their natural and acquired depravity, in its most aggravated forms, that some of the sensitive and self-accusing were ready, even in their ordinary religious meditations, to regard themselves as guilty of almost all sin, believing literally that "he that offendeth in one point is guilty of all." The piety of Ann Foster is especially spoken of by her sons, and there can be little doubt that she was led to charge herself with the sin of witchcraft in all sincerity and contrition. A broken-down old woman in her decrepitude and weakness, torn from her quiet home, brought on a long journey to a prison and a court-room, accused of blaspheming her God and forsaking her Saviour, — what wonder if she sank and died under such a weight of miseries. She was four times examined, — July 15th, 16th, 18th, 21st. It is pitiful to think of this poor, tottering, feeble creature, dragged again and again before her accusers, and finally dismissed to the sheriff to be "taken care of" as guilty.

She overdid in confession, or she would, like the others, have doubtless been saved. But the law must have victims, and here was one who *proved herself* to be deeply guilty. She confessed that she bewitched a hog of John Lovejoy's, caused the death of one of Andrew Allen's children, made another child sick, and "hurt" Timothy Swan. She said her manner of hurting was to make images of the persons with rags ("poppets" they are called in the records), and stick pins in these, or "tye knots in the rags," or burn them in the fire. The persons whom these images were supposed to represent would suffer whenever she pinched or burned, or pricked the "poppet."

The deluded woman also described extraordinary apparitions which she had seen, — birds, with great eyes, which first were white and became black when they flew away, by which she knew they were devils, also black men who were devils. She had been at the witch-meetings and seen the Rev. George Burroughs and another minister with gray hair. Again and again she repeated and owned this confession. But on one point she was obstinate. She would accuse herself to any extent, but she would not accuse her daughter. For this her examiners lost patience with her. "You have been already three times examined," they exclaim, "and yet you do not confess"—that is, she did not confess to making her daughter a witch; even though the daughter admitted that she was one and charged it upon her mother's influence and agency:—

"Your daughter was with you and Goody Carrier when you did ride upon the stick?

"I did not know it.

"How long have you known your daughter to be engaged?

"I cannot tell nor have I any knowledge of it at all.

"Do you not acknowledge that you did so?

"No and I know no more of my daughter's being a witch than what day I shall die upon.

"You cannot expect peace of conscience without a free confession.

"If I knew anything more, I would speak of it to the utmost."

But in spite of this denial the daughter alleged that it was true that they were both witches, and she cried out: "O mother, we have left Christ and the devil hath got hold of us!" The distressed mother moving her lips in prayer was asked what she was doing, and replied that she was "praying to the Lord." "What Lord?" said the examiners sternly. "What God do witches pray to?" Thus taunted and overborne, the harassed woman in confusion and distraction exclaimed: "I cannot tell; the Lord help me!"

The granddaughter confirmed her mother's statements that they were both witches, made so by the prisoner. The story of Ann Foster is graphically told in a petition presented by her son. It was written by some abler pen than his, for he only made his mark:—

"TO THE HONORABLE COMMITTEE NOW SITTING AT SALEM:—

"Whereas my mother Ann Foster of Andover suffered imprisonment twenty-one weeks and upon her Tryall was condemned for supposed witchcraft upon such evidence as now is Generally thought Insufficient and died in prison, I being well persuaded of my mother's innocency of the crime for which she was condemned I humbly desire that the attainder may be taken off. The charges and expenses for my mother during her imprisonment is as follows : — The money which I was forced to pay the keeper before I could have the dead body of my mother to bury her was £2. 10s.

    Money and provisions
   Expended while She was in prison . . £4
    Total expenses . . . . £6. 10s."

This sum of money the petitioner received, and also for his sister Mary Lacey £8 10s, on petition and by order of her husband Lawrence Lacey.[1]

Mrs. Abigail Faulkner was sentenced to death, but, by the intercession of friends, delay was obtained, and finally she was set free, when orders were given for a general release. Her trial is one of the most noteworthy. She was the daughter of the minister who for forty-five years had lived in Andover, and she was the first who had been condemned in the town of those in high social standing. Her conduct in the courts was worthy of her position, free alike from credulous weakness on the one hand and from scornful defiance on the other. Either from her own good sense, or upheld by the wise counsels of her father (who never yielded to the delusion), she showed the greatest discretion, paying due deference to the court, yet never losing her firmness and dignity. That she was not to be intimidated by superstitious terrors, the examiners knew, it is evident, for they forbore to argue with her about "peace and judgment to come," but they urged her to confess "*for ye credit of her Towne!*" This seems almost to have a spice of malice and meanness in it, at all events to be very shrewd to bring about the desired end, for to hint even that the fair name of the town was to suffer from the family of the minister was not to help him who had recently been involved in difficulties with his parishioners.

However, the daughter had her father's spirit, and even this innuendo, if it were one, did not move her. She merely made reply in the dignity of simple truth, that "God would not require her to confess that she was not guilty of." Still later, when witnesses were numerous and evidence overwhelming, she made admissions, guardedly, and as if with the design of conceding all that could be conceded with a view to appeasing the clamor for her confession. She admitted it was

[1] *Mass. Archives*, "Witchcraft Petitions."

possible that the devil might be working through her, but if so she was not conscious of it and did not consent to it. She explained some of the charges against her by saying, that when so many of her relations had been accused she had been "raised in her spirit" [that is, excited and indignant], and almost frantic, and she "had pinched her hands together" in her distress. The examiners had charged that by this "pinching of her hands" the afflicted were tortured. She admitted that possibly it was so, but yet it was not she who hurt them, but the devil working through her without her knowledge or consent. It was noted against her that she was unmoved by the sufferings of the afflicted ; though she said she was sorry for them "she did not shed a tear." Some seven or eight charged upon her their tortures. Added to the distress of so many accusers was the greatest of all, that of having her two little girls (eight and ten years old) confess themselves witches and charge their mother with being their teacher. Also, Martha Tyler, Johanna Tyler, Sarah Wilson, and Joseph Tyler, confessing themselves witches, "did all acknowledge that they were led into that dreadful sin of witchcraft by the means of the aforesd Abigail Faulkner."

She was kept in prison thirteen weeks, and when set free, by the general "jail delivery," was legally liable to penalty. In the year 1700 she presented a memorial to the General Court praying for the defacing of the record against her, by which she was under the attainder of a convicted criminal : —

"I am as yet suffered to live, but only as a malefactor convicted upon record of ye most heinous crimes that mankind can be supposed to be guilty of, which besides its utter ruining and defaming my Reputation will certainly expose myself to Imminent Danger by new accusations which will thereby be the more readily believed will remain a perpetual brand of infamy upon my family. I do humbly pray that the High and Honourable Court will please to take my case into serious consideration and order the Defacing of ye record against me, so that I may be freed from ye evil consequences thereof."

Not until after eleven years, and much petitioning, was the attainder taken off. The record remains to this day one of the most conspicuous on the pages of the "Book of Witchcraft," in the State Archives. Its clear and distinct writing, among many nearly illegible papers, make it one of the noticeable records ; so that even the casual turner of the leaves cannot fail to read it : —

> "THE JURY FIND ABIGAIL FAULKNER
> *wife of Francis Faulkner of Andover*
> GUILTY OF Y^e FELONY OF WITCHCRAFT
> *Comited on ye body of Martha*
> *Sprague also on ye body of Sarah Phelps*

SENTENCE OF DEATH PASSED ON ABIGAIL FAULKNER.
Copia vera."

The niece of Abigail Faulkner, granddaughter of Mr. Dane and daughter of Stephen and Elizabeth Dane Johnson, "Elizabeth Johnson Jr.," was also condemned and reprieved, and thereby saved (Mr. Dane and his friends using every effort to stop the tide of superstition, and finally succeeding). A petition of the brother of Elizabeth Johnson attests the fact of her condemnation : —

"TO THE HONOURABLE COMMITTEE SITTING AT SALEM *Sept* 3, 1710.

"Whereas my sister Elizabeth Johnson jr of Andover was imprisoned six months for ye supposed witchcraft and upon her Tryall was condemned by such evidence as is now generally thought to be Insufficient in the year 1692 She the said Elizabeth Johnson humbly prays that the attainder may be taken off.

"My expences for maintaining my sister with provisions during her imprisonment was £3. 0. 0. which I pray may be allowed.

by FRANCIS JOHNSON — in behalf of my sister."

Again, in 1712, the petitioner makes request, her name having by some mistake been omitted from the list of those named in the Reversal of Attainder, October 17, 1711 : —

"Whereas the Honble General Court hath lately made an act for taking off the attainder of those that were condemned for witchcraft in the year 1692, I thought meet to inform your Honors that I was condemned by the Court at Salem in January in the year 1692 as will appear by the Records of the Tryals at said Court, but my name is not inserted in said act. Being very desirous of the favour of that act am bold humbly to pray your

Honors to represent my case to the General Court at their next Session that my name may be inserted in that act; if it may be and that the Honourable Council would please to allow me something in consideration of my charges by reason of my long imprisonment which will be thankfully acknowledged as a great favor by your Honors most humble servant

ELIZABETH JOHNSON, JUNR.[1]

"ANDOVER *Feb* 19 1711-12."

Elizabeth Johnson's confession ought to have saved her from condemnation, if, as some persons argued, confession implied penitence, and penitence was salvation from the penalty of the law. She owned to everything charged. It would seem that the few verdicts of guilty rendered at the trials of January 1692-3, when the reaction of feeling had set in, were merely formal. The confession of Elizabeth Johnson was that Goodwife Carrier persuaded her, and she had been baptized in Goodwife Carrier's well by the devil. He "dipt her head over in water." She had been at witch-meeting, and seen bread and wine at the devil's sacrament. She had afflicted many persons by poppets. She had some poppets made of rags, and some of "birch Rhine" [bark?]. She afflicted Ann Putnam "with a speare of iron." She showed red spots on her body, where she said her "familiar," the evil spirit, sucked her.

Mary Lacey, daughter of Ann Foster, was condemned. She said the devil had carried her in his arms to Newbury falls, and there he had baptized some of the "higher powers." She also said (to use the words of the deposition) "if she doe but take a ragg, clout or any such thing and roll it up together and imagine it to represent such and such a person, then whatsoever she doth to that Rag or clout so rouled up the person represented thereby will be in lyke manner afflicted."

The trials and confessions are so similar that repetition is needless.

Sarah Wardwell, wife of Samuel Wardwell, was found guilty at the Court of Trials, January 2, 1693. The record[2] of the verdict is as follows: —

---

[1] Elizabeth Johnson, Jr., and Mary Lacey, Jr., were, it would seem, young persons under parental authority.

[2] *Suffolk County Records* — "Assistant's Records."

"A jury being called, Nathan Howard foreman and accordingly sworne, the jury went out to agree on their verdict, who returning did then and there in open court deliver their verdict that the said Sarah Wardwell was Guilty of covenanting with the Devill for which she stood Indicted in the first Indictment as also Guilty of the ffelony by witchcraft, for which she stood indicted in the second Indictment."

The sons of Samuel and Sarah Wardwell petitioned for restitution, and especially to have their mother's name inserted in the list of those whose attainder was taken off by the Act of Reversal: —

"Whereas my mother Sarah Wardel was condemned by the Court at Salem some time in January in the year 1692 (Jan. 169¾) as I suppose will appear by the Records of the Tryalls at that Court, but her name is not inserted in the late Act of the Generall Court for the taking of the attainder off those that were condemned in that year, my mother being since deceased I thought it my duty to endeavor that her name may have the Benefit of the Act. . . . .

"I mentioned only what was seized of my father's estate by the sheriffe, but gave no account of other charges which did arise from the imprisonment of my Father and Mother; they having provided for their own subsistence, while they were in Prison, and I suppose there was something considerable payd to the keeper of the Prison, though I am not able now to give a particular account how much it was. If your Honors please to allow me something upon that account it will be thankfully acknowledged by your honors most humble servant   SAMUEL WARDEL."

"*Feb* 19 1711-12

What was the condition of the young children of Samuel and Sarah Wardwell, their father hanged and their mother in prison, we learn from a record of the selectmen of Andover, part of which also is recorded in the " Essex County Court Papers " : —

"Wee y⁰ subscribers selectmen of Andover y⁰ abovesd year, having informed y⁰ Quarter Sessions at Ipswich y⁰ 27th of y⁰ abovesᵈ September that there was severall children of Samˡ Wardwels yᵗ was in a suffering condition begging their advice direction & order therein which they were pleased to Consider of & order as followes yᵗ y⁰ Selectmen for y⁰ time being should place out, or if

need require binde out s⁴ children in good & honest families, referring to a law in that case provided. Persuant to this order of yᵉ Court wee have placed them as follows; viz Samuel Wardwell we placed with John Ballard his uncle for one year, William we placed with Corpl Saml ffrie till he come to be of yᵉ age of one and twenty years; s⁴ ffrie to learne him yᵉ trade of a weaver. Eliakim we placed to Daniel Poor till he was twenty-one years of age & Elizabeth we placed with John Stevens till eighteen years of age, all yᵉ abovesd were to find them with suites of apparel att yᵉ end of s⁴ term of tyme.   SAMˡ FRIE
              JOHN ASLEBE } *Selectmen*"
              JOHN ABBOT

Of the prisoners tried and acquitted, one of those highest in standing was Elizabeth Dane, wife of Stephen Johnson. She suffered five months' imprisonment. Her daughter Elizabeth, as has been said, was condemned, and her daughter Abigail, and her son Stephen, were accused and imprisoned five weeks. Her son Francis Johnson, received restitution-money in her behalf.

The boy Stephen Johnson was thirteen years of age. He did (in the words of the indictment) "wickedly, malitiously & feloniously with the devil a covenant make, wherebye he gave himselfe soule and body to the Devil and signed the Devils Booke with his blood and by the devil was baptized and renounced his Christian baptism, by which wicked & Diabolical covenant with the Devil made the said Stephen Johnson is bound a detestable witch," etc.

Mary Marston, wife of John Marston, made a full confession, that one evening, when she was alone in the house, the black man came in and offered her a paper book to sign, which she did sign with a pen dipped in ink, "and therewith made a Strooke."

She accused William Barker of joining with her to afflict.

William Barker, examined August 29th, confessed that, being a poor man, and having a large family, and unable to pay his debts, he signed the devil's book, Satan agreeing to pay all his debts, and give him a comfortable life. He said that the world hitherto had "gone hard with him."

Mercy Wardwell, Richard Carrier, and others, also confessed. The most remarkable confession was that of Mrs. Mary Osgood, the wife of Mr. John Osgood. She was a woman of exemplary character, and had always been respected and beloved in the community. Yet, though of unblemished life and incapable of falsehood, as every one believed, she now confessed that for eleven years she had been devoted to the service of Satan; she had prayed to the devil instead of to God; she had been baptized by the devil in Five-mile Pond; she had taken many midnight journeys through the air, in company with Deacon Frye's wife, and Ebenezer Barker's wife, and Goody Tyler; she had expected to have great satisfaction in the devil's service, but he had never given it to her, and she was miserable. Her husband testified that he believed in the truth of her statements. The principal evidence, besides her own confession, against Mrs. Osgood, was that of Goody Tyler. But what that was worth, and how it was extorted, may be learned from a second confession, or recantation, made by this woman to the Rev. Increase Mather. This minister, less credulous than his son, and also probably enlisted in the cause of, and laboring with, the Rev. Francis Dane and others, to bring about a reaction of feeling and save the prisoners, the kinsfolk and parishioners of Mr. Dane, visited the Andover women in the prison, and obtained counter-confessions. The reasons for the first confessions he states, as given him by the women themselves: —

"Goodwife Tyler did say that when she was first apprehended she had no fears upon her and did think that nothing could have made her confess against herself. But, since she hath found to her great grief that she had wronged the truth and falsely accused herself."

The account goes on to say that, on the way from Andover to Salem, her brother Bridges rode with her, and told her that it must be that she was a witch, because the afflicted were raised out of their fits at her touch. She constantly denied and begged him not to urge her to confess. After she got to Salem, she was carried into a room where her "brother on one side and Mr. John Emerson on the other side" did tell her she was certainly a witch, and Mr. Emerson said he could see the devil before her eyes, and with his hands "*tried* to *beat him away from her eyes*." And they " so urged her to confess that she wished herself in any dungeon rather than be so treated. 'Well, I see you will not confess, well I will now leave you and then you are undone body and soul forever.'"

They told her that in confessing "she could *not lie*," to which she answered, "Good brother, do not say so, for I *shall* lie, if I confess, and then who shall answer unto God for my lie." They said she would surely be hanged if she did not confess; that God would not suffer so many good men to be in error, and that she surely was a witch. She told Mr. Mather "that they continued so long and so violently to urge and press her to confess, that she thought verily her life would have gone from her," and at last she said "almost everything that they propounded to her."

She told Mr. Mather, also, that "she wronged her conscience in so doing," was "guilty of a great sin in belying of herself and desired to mourn for it so long as she lived." This she said, and "a great deal more of the like nature" (as the clergyman relates), "and all with such affliction, sorrow, relenting, grief and mourning that it exceeds any pen to describe and express the same."

Mrs. Osgood likewise explained to Mr. Mather the way in which she was led to confess. She said that the examiners asked her at what time she became a witch. She told them she did not know. They said she *did* know and she *must* tell, and thus beset she considered, that "about twelve years before when she had her last child she had a fit of sickness and was melancholy and so thought that time might be as proper a time to mention as any and accordingly did prefix the said time."

She explained her saying that the devil appeared to her, by relating that the *examiners told* her the devil did appear, and pressed her to say in what shape, and remembering that just before her arrest she saw a cat, she "at length did say it was in the shape of a cat. Not as though she in any whit suspected the said cat to be the devil in the day of it, but because *some creature she must mention*, and this came into her mind at the time."

It will be noticed, in considering these examinations and confessions, that it was not the least conscientious, the least scrupulous in morals, who uttered the seeming falsehoods and perjuries. It was the religiously brought up, the shrinking women and children, accustomed to rely implicitly on the judgment and advice of their superiors in worldly wisdom, or in theological learning. Martha Carrier, having no importunate advisers begging her not to ruin herself and them, and being used to depend on her own judgment, stood firm, the sole one of forty or more who did not make an admission of complicity or agency in the devil's works, and who did not indeed even admit (what the wisest believed) that there was Satanic agency in the matter. Abigail Faulkner, who made only partial admissions, acted no doubt under the instructions of her father, who saw that only concession of some points would save her, and could advise it conscientiously, since neither he nor any one else could know for a certainty that the devil was not concerned in these extraordinary manifestations.

Some of the accused were examined by Mr. Dudley Bradstreet, Justice of the Peace, at Andover, August 10, 1692. He seems to deprecate the necessity laid upon him, and to disclaim any judgment in the matter. He evidently, though humane and not so credulous as many in regard to the wild stories current, had not the determination and strength that characterize the minister, Mr. Dane. His letter to the magistrates and examiners, relating what action he took, is as follows:[1] —

"GENTLEMEN: I thought it meet to give you this broken account hoping it may be of some service. I am wholly unacquainted with affairs of this nature neither have the benefit of books for forms &c.; but 'being unadvisedly entered upon service I am wholly unfit' for beg that my ignorance and failings may be as much covered as conveniently may be which will ever be acknowledged by your poor and unworthy servant.

[1] *Mass. Hist. Soc. Coll.*, Third Series, vol. i.

"I know not whether to make any returns. Bonds I have taken. The *custos rotulorum* I know not, ...

"To the Honored Bartholomew Gedney, John Hathorne, Esq., or any of their Majesties Justices of the Peace in Salem *these humbly present*."

The condition of the women and children of Andover, delicately reared as some of them had been, and used to the comforts of as luxurious homes as could be found in new inland plantations, now thrust with all sorts of prisoners into the common jail at Salem, was pitiable indeed. Many of them were six months in prison, and some even eight months.[1] Their sufferings were great in the heat of summer, and with the approach of winter it seemed probable that they would be extreme. To procure, if possible, some alleviation of their misery, their friends petitioned[2] for their release from jail, under bonds, before winter should set in : —

"To the Honoured Court now sitting in Boston this 12th of October 1692. *Right Honoured Gentlemen and Fathers*, We, your humble petitioners, whose names are underwritten, petition your honors as followeth: We would not trouble you with a tedious Diversion, but briefly spread open our distressed condition and beg your honour's favor and pity in affording what relief may be thought convenient. As for the matter of our Troubles it is the distressed condition of our wives and Relations in prison at Salem who are a company of poor distressed creatures as full of inward grief and trouble as they are able to bear up in life withall. And besides the agrivation of outward troubles and hardships they undergo and want of food; and the coldness of the winter season that is coming may soon despatch such out of the way that have not been used to such hardships.

"And besides this, the exceeding great charges and expences that we are at upon many accounts which will be Tedious to give a particular account of, which will fall heavy upon us, especially in a time of so great charge and expence upon a general account in the country, which is expected of us to bear a part as well as others, which if all put together our families and estates will be brought to Ruin, if it cannot in time be prevented. Having

[1] Rebekah Johnson, who was the sexton of the North Church (the only woman appointed by the town to take care of the Meeting-house), was in jail eight months.
[2] *Mass. Archives*, vol. cxxxv., page 59.

spread open our condition, we humbly make our address to your Honors, to Grant that our Wives and Relations (being such that have been approved as penitent Confessors), might be returned home to us upon what bond your honors may see good. We do not petition to take them out of the hand of Justice, but to remove them as Prisoners under bonds in their own families where they may be more tenderly cared for and be ready to appear to answer further when the Honored Court shall call for them. We humbly crave your Honors favor and pitty for us and ours. Having set down our Troubled State before you, we hereby pray your honors:

    JOHN OSGOOD in behalf of his wife.
    JOHN FFRY in behalf of his wife.
    JOHN MARSTON in behalf of his wife Mary Marston.
    CHRISTOPHER OSGOOD in behalf of his daughter Mary Marston.
    JOSEPH WILSON in behalf of his wife & children.
    JOHN BRIDGES in behalf of his wife & children.
    HOPE TYLER in behalf of his wife & daughter.
    EBENEZER BARKER for his wife.
    NATHANIEL DANE for his wife."

This petition was accompanied by another of about the same date, October 18th, from the ministers and other inhabitants of Andover. The name of Dudley Bradstreet is not among the signatures to it; the reason being that he was now under suspicion or accusation, had fled the town, and was living secreted in hope the storm would blow over. The allusion in the petition to "more of our neighbors of good reputation," doubtless points to Colonel Bradstreet, and the petitions were intended to operate in his favor by turning the tide of public feeling, so that he might venture to appear.[1] The following is the full text of the petition: —

"We being deeply sensible of the heavy judgment that the Righteous God hath brought upon this place thought it our duty (after our earnest prayers to the God of Heaven to give us help from our trouble) to lay before this Honourable Assembly our present distressed state and to crave a redress of our grievances. It is well known that many persons of this town have been accused of witchcraft, by some distempered persons in these parts[2] and upon

[1] *Mass. Archives*, vol. cxxxv., page 61.
[2] This, it will be noted, is strong language and high ground to take, — to charge the persons as being distempered, when in the popular and the theological judg-

complaint made have been apprehended and committed to prison. Now, though we would not appear as advocates for any who shall be found guilty of so horrid a crime, but we heartily desire that this place and the whole land may be purged from that great wickedness, yet if any of our friends and neighbors have been misrepresented, as is possible some of them have been, we would crave leave (if it might be without offence) to speak something in their behalf, having no other design therein than that the truth may appear. We can truly give this Testimony of the most of them belonging to this town that have been accused that they never gave the least occasion as we hear of to their nearest relations or most intimate acquaintances to suspect them of witchcraft. Several of the women that are accused were members of the church in full communion, and had obtained a good report for their blameless conversation and their walking as becometh women professing godliness ; but whereas it may be alledged that the most of our people that have been apprehended for witchcraft have upon examination confessed it. To which we answer that we have nothing to plead for those that freely and upon conviction own themselves guilty ; but we apprehend the case of some of them to be otherwise ; for from the information we have had and the discourse some of us have had with the Prisoners, we have reason to think that the *extream urgency* that was used with some of them by their friends and others who privately examined them, and the fear they were then under hath been an inducement to them to own such things as we cannot since find they are conscious of. And the truth of what we now declare we judge will in time more plainly appear. And some of them have exprest to their neighbors that it hath been their great trouble that they have wronged themselves and the truth in their confessions.

"We are also very sensible of the distressed condition of several poor families on whom this great trouble is fallen. Some of our neighbors are likely to be impoverished or ruined by the great charge they are at to maintain such of their families as are in Prison, and by the fees that are demanded of them, whose case we pray may be considered.

"Our troubles which have hitherto been great we foresee are likely to continue and increase ; if other methods be not taken than as yet have been ; for there are more of our neighbors of good reputation and integrity who are still accused and we know not who can think himself safe, if the accusation of children and

ment the afflicted were gifted with supernatural powers of seeing the cause of diseases and those who caused their own affliction.

others who are under *Diabolicall influence* shall be received against persons of good fame."[1]

The petition[2] is signed with twenty-six names: Francis Dane, Sen.; Thomas Barnard; John Osgood; Thomas Johnson, and others.

A letter,[3] written about the same time by Mr. Brattle of Boston, giving a "Full and Candid Account of the Delusion called Witchcraft," shows that this was the date of Mr. Bradstreet's seclusion and also rehearses in full the story of "poor Andover." It is perhaps the fullest contemporary account of the delusion in this town. It is not improbable that Mr. Dane's influence had something to do with its writing:—

"*Oct.* 8, 1692.

". . . . This consulting of these afflicted children about their sick was the unhappy beginning of the unhappy troubles at poor Andover. Horse and man were sent to Salem village from the said Andover for some of the said afflicted and more than one or two of them were carried down to see Ballard's wife and to tell who it was that did afflict her. I understood that the said B. took advice before he took this method but what pity was it that he should meet with and hearken to such bad counsellors. Poor Andover does now rue the day that ever the afflicted went among them; they lament their folly and are an object of great pity and commiseration. Capt. B. and Mr. St. [Stevens (?)] are complained of by the afflicted, have left the town and do abscond. Deacon Fry's wife, Capt. Osgood's wife and some others remarkably pious and good people in repute are apprehended and imprisoned and that which is more admirable the forementioned women are become a kind of confessors, being first brought thereto by the urgings and arguings of their good husbands, who having taken up that corrupt and highly pernicious opinion that whosoever were accused by the afflicted were guilty did break charity with their dear wives upon their being accused and urge them to confess their guilt, which so far prevailed with them as to make them say they were afraid of their being in the snare of the devil and which through the rude and barbarous methods (you may possibly think that my terms are too severe, but should I tell you what a kind of

[1] The charge of being under the influence of Satan, it will be noted, is here brought against the accusers, and it had the designed effect in reversing the popular sentiment.
[2] *Essex County Court Records.*
[3] *Mass. Hist. Soc. Collections.*

blade was employed in bringing these women to their confessions; what methods from damnation were taken; what violence used; how unseasonably they were kept up; what buzzings and chuckings of the head were used and the like, I am sure that you would call them as I do rude and barbarous methods) that were afterward used at Salem, issued in somewhat plainer degrees of confession and were attended with imprisonment: The good deacon and Captain are now sensible of the error they were in; do grieve and mourn bitterly that they should break their charity with their wives and urge them to confess themselves witches. They now see and acknowledge their rashness and uncharitableness and are very fit objects for the pity and prayers of every good Christian. Now I am writing concerning Andover I cannot omit the opportunity to send you this information, that whereas there is a report spread abroad the country how that they were much addicted to sorcery in the said town and that there were forty men in it that could raise the devil as well as any astrologer and the like; after the best search that I can make into it, it proves a mere slander and a very unrighteous imputation.

The Rev. Elders [1] of the said place were much surprised upon their hearing of the said report and faithfully made inquiry about it, but the whole of naughtiness that they could discover and find out was only this that two or three girls had foolishly made use of the sieve and scissors as children have done in other towns. This method of the girls I do not justify in any measure; but yet I think it very hard and unreasonable that a town should lie under the blemish and scandal of sorceries and conjuration merely for the inconsiderate practices of two or three girls in the said town. But although the chief judge and some of the other judges be very zealous in these proceedings yet this you may take for a truth that there are several about the Bay, men for understanding, judgment and piety inferior to few if any in New England that do utterly condemn the said proceedings and do deliver their judgment in the case to be this that these methods will utterly ruin and undo poor New England. I shall nominate some of these to you." . . . .

Among the magistrates whom he names as disapproving the action of the Court of Oyer and Terminer in the trials was the "Hon. Simon Bradstreet our Late Governor."

The petition made of the Andover people seems not to have had the desired effect to secure the removal of the prisoners to their homes.

[1] Mr. Dane and his colleague Mr. Barnard.

On the sixth of December, another petition was made by several inhabitants of Andover saying that their "wives have been exposed to great sufferings which daily increase by reason of the winter coming on and they are in *extream danger of perishing*, and the petitioners beg that their friends may be permitted to come home on such terms as your honors may judge meet." They offer to give bonds for the appearance of the prisoners whenever called for. This appeal and the sufferings of the prisoners could hardly fail to move compassion. Toward the last of December, the work of removing the prisoners home began. At that season of the year and with the scanty means of conveyance, even the journey to Salem and back to Andover was attended with no slight discomfort.

The following persons gave bonds for prisoners removed : —

December 20, Dea. John Frye and Mr. John Osgood, for the appearance of Mary Osgood and Eunice Frye.

In October John Osgood and Nathaniel Dane had taken into custody the bodies of the children Dorothy and Abigail Faulkner, and January 13th, Francis Faulkner and John Marble gave bonds for their appearance. January 13th, John Osgood and John Barker gave bonds for William Barker and Mary Barker.

Francis Johnson and Walter Wright gave bonds for Stephen Johnson, about thirteen years old ; Abigail Johnson about eleven years, Sarah Carrier about eight years. The same persons also gave bonds, five hundred pounds sterling, for John Sawdey, about thirteen years. This was a very large bond, two hundred pounds being the largest commonly paid. Hopestil Tyler and Jno. Bridges gave bonds for Martha Tyler and Joanna Tyler.

The efforts in behalf of those prisoners who were not allowed to be removed, had been so far successful that Governor Phipps ordered a session for the third of January of a "Court of Assizes and General Goal Delivery." The Court of Oyer and Terminer, before which the trials in the summer had been conducted, had then ceased to exist. The object of this court was to give verdict on the cases of those still in the jail and release the innocent from their confinement. Those in the foregoing list of names marked "not guilty" were the persons cleared at this court.

To attend this court as jurors four citizens of Andover were chosen.[1] The following is the warrant and return : —

"These are in their Majestys names to Require you forthwith to assemble the free-holders and others the Inhabitants of your Towne who are hereby also required to choose foure good and Lawfull men of the same towne, each whereof to have a real estate of forty shillings per annum or a personal estate of fifty pounds, to serve as Jurors. Two upon the Grand Jury and two upon the Jury of Tryalls at a Court of Assizes and General Goal Delivery to be held at Salem for the County of Essex on Tuesday the third day of January next ensuing the days of the date hereof, which psons so chosen you are to summons to Attend the said Court by nine of the clock in the morning of ye said Day, and make returne hereof with the names of said p'sons the day before the said Court and hereof not to faile.

"Dated in Boston the Twenty-third Day of December 1692.

"To the Constables of Andover or either of them. } JONA. ELARSON, *Clerk*."

"In obedience unto this Above Riten Warant I have assembled the ffreeholders & others the Inhabitants of our Town Togither & they have chosen Joseph Marble sener & henry holt senr, ffor the grand jury & Left Christopher Osgood & Saml Osgood senr for the jury of Tryalls for s^d above mentioned Cort & have sumoned them to Apeare according to Warenis.

EPHRAIM FOSTER, *Constable*."

The Rev. Mr. Dane addressed to this court a bold and firm but respectful letter, designed nominally to exculpate the town of Andover from blame, but really to condemn and discredit the "spectre-evidence" so largely relied on as ground of condemnation. It is a paper of special interest.[2]

"Whereas there have been divers reports raysed, how and by what hands I know not, of the Towne of Andover and the Inhabitants, I thought it my bounden duty to give an account to others so farr as I had the understanding of anything amongst us. Therefore doe declare that I believe the reports have been scandalous and unjust, neither will bear ye light. As for that of the sieve and scissors, I never heard of it till this last summer, and the Sabbath after I spake publickly concerning it, since which I believe it hath not been tryed. As for such things of charms and wayes to

[1] *Mass. Archives*, vol. cxxxv., p. 92.
[2] *Essex County Court Papers*, "Witchcraft," vol. i., p. 142.

find their cattle I never heard, nor doe I know any neighbors that ever did so, neither have I any grounds to believe it. I have lived above Fortie foure yeares in the Towne and have been frequent among y⁰ Inhabitants and in my healthfull yeares oft at their habitations and should certainly heard if so it had been. That there was a suspicion of Goodwife Carrier among some of us, before she was apprehended I know; as for any other persons I had no suspicion of them and had charity been put on, the Devil would not have had such advantage against us; and I believe many Innocent persons have been accused & Imprisoned; y⁰ conceit of spectre evidence as an infallible mark did too far prevaill with us. Hence we so easily parted with our neighbors of an honest & good report & members in full communion; hence we so easily parted with our children when we knew nothing in their lives nor any of our neighbors to suspect them, and thus things were hurried on; hence such strange breaches in families; severall that came before me that spake with much sobrietie, professing their innocency, though through the devil's subtilty they were too much urged to confesse and we thought we did doe well in so doing; yet they stood their ground, professing their innocency; . . . . that they knew nothing; never saw y⁰ devile, never made a covenant with him & y⁰ like & some children that we have cause to feare that dread has overcome them to accuse themselves in that they knew not. Stephen Johnson, Mary Barker y⁰ daughter of Leftenant Barker and some others by what we had from them with suitable assertions, we have come to believe they were in the truth and so held to it; if after many endeavors they had not been overcome to say what they never knew. This hath been a trouble to me, considering how oft it hath been sayd 'you are a witch,' 'you are guilty and who afflicts this maid,' or the like & more than this hath been said charging persons with witchcraft, and what flatteries have past from and threats and telling them they must goe to prison for it, &c., I feare have caused many to fall. Our sinne of Ignorance wherein we thought we did well will not excuse us, when we know we did amiss; but whatever might be a stumbling block to others must be removed, else we shall procure divine displeasure & evill will unavoidably brake in upon us.

"Your s⁰ who am a friend though unworthie to them y⁰ are friends to Sion.   FRANCIS DANE, SENR."

"ANDOVER,[1] *Jan.* 2, '92."

[1] This was 1693. The year did not begin till March, according to the old style of reckoning.

"Concerning my daughter Elizabeth Johnson I never had ground to suspect her, neither have I heard any other accuse her, till by *spectre evidence* she was brought forth; but this I must say, she was weake and incapacious, fearfull, and in that respect I feare she hath falsely accused herself & others. Not long before she was sent for, she spake as to her owne particular that she was sure she was no witch, and for her Daughter Elizabeth she is but simplish at ye best, and I feare the common speech that was frequently spread among us, of their liberty, if they would confesse and the like expression used by some have brought many into a snare. The Lord direct & guide those that are in place and give us all submissive wills & let the Lord doe with me and mine what seems good in his own eyes."

Mr. Dane also wrote to his brother ministers condemning in strong terms the belief in spectre-evidence, and all this, combined with the influence of Mr. Simon Bradstreet, now one of the Assistants to Governor Phipps, helped to effect a change in the public sentiment and embolden to further effort. When the Court of Assize was held, a petition signed by fifty inhabitants of Andover was presented. It bore the names of thirty-eight men and twelve women: —

"To THE HONOURED COURT OF ASSIZE *held at Salem, the Humble Address of Several of the Inhabitants of Andover:* May it please this Honored Court, we being sensible of the great sufferings our neighbors have been long under in prison and charitably judging that many of them are clear of that great transgression which hath been laid to their charge have thought it our duty to endeavor their vindication as far as our testimony for them will avail. The persons in whose behalf we are desired and concerned to speak something at present are Mrs. Mary Osgood, Eunice Frye, Deliverance Dane, Sarah Wilson, and Abigail Barker, who are women of whom we can truly give this character and commendation that they have not only lived among us so inoffensively as not to give the least occasion to any that know them to suspect them of witchcraft, but by their sober, godly and exemplary conversation have obtained a good report in the place where they have been well esteemed and approved in the church of which they are members.

"We were surprised to hear that persons of known integrity and piety were accused of so horrid a crime, not considering then that the most innocent were liable to be so misrepresented and abused. When these women were accused by some afflicted, persons of the neighborhood their relations and others, though they had so good grounds of charity that they should not have thought any evil of them; yet, through a misrepresentation of the truth of that evidence that was so much credited and improved against people, took great pains to persuade them to own what they were by the afflicted charged with and indeed did unreasonably urge them to confess themselves guilty, as some of us who were then present can testify. But these good women did very much assert their innocency; yet some of them said they were not without fear lest Satan had some way ensnared them because there was that evidence against them which then was by many thought to be a certain indication and discovery of witchcraft; yet they seriously professed they knew nothing by themselves of that nature. Nevertheless by the unwearied solicitations of those that privately discovered them both at home and at Salem they were at length persuaded publicly to own what they were charged with, and so submit to that guilt which we still hope and believe they are clear of. And it is probable that fear of what the event might be and the encouragement that it is said was suggested to them, that Confessing was the only way to obtain favor might be too powerful a temptation to timorous women to withstand in the hurry and distraction that we have heard they were then in. Had what they said against themselves proceeded from conviction of the fact we should have had nothing to have said for them; but we are induced to think that it did not, because they did soon privately retract what they had said, as we are informed, and while they were in prison they declared to such as they had confidence to speak freely and plainly to that they were not guilty of what they had owned and that what they had said against themselves was the greatest grief and burden they labored under.

"Now though we cannot but judge it a thing very sinful for innocent persons to own a crime they are not guilty of, yet considering the well-ordered conversation of those women while they lived among us, and what they now seriously and constantly affirm in a more composed frame, we cannot but in charity judge them innocent of the great transgression that hath been imputed to them. As for the rest of our neighbors who are under the like circumstances with these that have been named, we can truly say of them, that while they lived among us we have had no cause to judge them such persons as of late they have been represented to be, nor do we know that any of their neighbors had any just grounds to suspect them of that evil thing they are now charged with.

DUDLEY BRADSTREET.
FRANCIS DANE, SENR.
THOMAS BARNARD, and others."

A carefully prepared petition signed by the accused women was also presented. This related the history of their arrest and trial; explained why they were ever led to confess, etc. : —

".... Our nearest and dearest relations seeing us in that dreadful condition and knowing our great danger apprehended there was no other way to save our lives..... Indeed that confession that it is said we made was no other than what was suggested to us by some gentlemen, they telling us that we were witches and *they knew it* and *we knew it*, which made us think that it was so, and our understanding, our reason, our faculties almost gone, we were not capable of judging our condition. As also the hard measures they used with us rendered us incapable of making our defence, but said anything and everything which they desired, and with most of us what we said was but in effect a consenting to what they said."

The petition further says that, when the prisoners refused to confess, they were told to think of the fate of Wardwell who renounced his confession, and to remember that they would "goe after him."

The effect of these petitions on the court and the public, joined to the unwearied exertions of the Rev. Francis Dane, by private letters and solicitations to induce the clergy to discredit and condemn "spectre evidence," produced a strong reaction. Only a few persons were condemned in the trials of January, 1693, and these condemnations were, it is evident, simply for form's sake. The Andover prisoners released under bonds were not summoned to appear till May, just before the proclamation to open the prison doors and let the accused go free. Effectually to put an end to the delusion, and ensure the safety of the released, action for slander was brought against some of the accusers. These now doubly "afflicted" unfortunates, from having been objects of sensational curiosity and sympathy, became victims of public reproach and odium. It was believed by many that they had been actuated by malicious motives, or instigated by the devil, to make the false charges.

One of these afflicted girls, Ann Putnam, of Salem (who had been at Andover, and had accused several citizens of the town of tormenting her, and Elizabeth Johnson of afflicting her with a spear), repented long and bitterly of her "sin." She was only twelve years of age at the time of the witchcraft, and when at twenty she sought refuge and peace of mind in the consolations and shelter of the church, her conscience (and probably the church officers) would not permit her to become a member until she had endured the humiliation of a public confession of her sin in the witchcraft accusations. Before the great congregation, which crowded to see and hear, she stood and gave her assent to the statement read by the minister: —

"I desire to lie in the dust and to be humbled for it and earnestly beg forgiveness of God and from all those unto whom I have given just cause of offence whose relatives have been taken away or accused."

The indignation against the accusers, and the popular clamor for their punishment, seems in one of its aspects, almost as senseless as that had been against the accused; for it was really a renewal of the charge of witchcraft, now accusing the afflicted of having been influenced by the devil to make their first accusations. But the magistrates and ministers had no mind to re-open the question of Satanic agency, or possession of persons by evil spirits. Who was guilty and who was innocent, the wisest men in the colony thought best to leave to the judgments of Heaven and each man's own conscience.

How the good Judge Sewall viewed the part which he had taken in condemning the accused, and his yearly confession of the sin before the church, every reader of the colonial history knows. It is related by the poet who has immortalized so many New England names: —

> "Touching and sad a tale is told,
> Like a penitent hymn of the Psalmist old,

Of the fast which the good man life long kept
With a haunting sorrow that never slept,
As the circling year brought round the time
Of an error that left the sting of crime,
When he sat on the bench of the witchcraft Courts
With the laws of Moses and Hale's Reports,
And spake, in the name of both, the word,
That gave the witch's neck to the cord,
And piled the oaken planks that pressed
The feeble life from the warlock's breast."

One relic of the witchcraft delusion remains at North Andover, — the gravestone of a man who was said to have died by witchcraft : —

TIMOTHY SWAN,[1]
Died February ye 2 1692
And in ye 30 year of his Age.

Some ten or more persons confessed to having "tortured, afflicted, consumed, wasted," this man. Three or four at a time, their spectres stood at his bedside and tortured him with iron spindles, pins, tobacco pipe, etc.

Andover as a community (both North and South Parishes), from that time to this, has been remarkably free from delusions and slow to be carried away by excitements, or frightened into panics.

As late as 1742 the church at Salem began to be again disturbed by such agitations, and at a church-meeting it was voted "that for Christians to seek to and consult reputed witches or fortune tellers is highly impious and scandalous."

But no such disposition appeared at Andover. Whether the experience of 1692 has served as a warning, or whether the fortresses of theology frowning down from the Hill have intimidated spiritual foes, or whether spectres yet appear on occasion to belated students and others, — Ichabod Cranes, along the lonely paths of Pomp's Pond, and the by-ways of Den Rock, and the roads by the Shawshin, or whether aerial broomsticks ever are visible to the young folks in their rides at eventide around Five-mile Pond, we leave to those who are versed in " witchcraft "to discover.

[1] The Swan family were of Haverhill, but attended the North Church of Andover. Haverhill included a part of Methuen and a part of Lawrence.

CHAPTER IV.

THE PART OF ANDOVER IN THE FRENCH AND INDIAN WAR.

In the wars with the Indians during the first century of Andover's history, the colony had received little help from the mother country, but had planned and carried forward expeditions according to its own pleasure and largely at its own expense. But the series of wars which began with the second century, and continued till near the Revolutionary disturbances, were carried on by the joint operations of the British and the Provincial governments. The possession of the country called by the French, Acadie (Nova Scotia), which, they claimed, extended to the Kennebec River, was stoutly contested by the rival nations in the war which occupied the five years from 1744 to 1749. This war was conducted for the Province by Governor Shirley; Louisburg and Annapolis as the keys of Acadie, and Crown Point as the key of Canada, were the points aimed at. The two former were taken by the English, the latter attempted, but not taken, when the treaty of Aix-la-Chapelle put an end to the hostilities, and by its terms of mutual restoration of conquered territory, left the two nations in America just where they were before the waste of blood and treasure. During this war the captains in the militia,[1] at Andover, were Capt. Timothy Johnson, Capt. George Abbot, Capt. Joseph Sibson, Capt. Nathaniel Fry, Capt. James Stevens.

Capt. James Stevens commanded a company in the expedition to Cape Breton, in which Louisburg was captured. James Fry, afterward Lieutenant-colonel at Crown Point, 1756, and Colonel in the Revolution, was at the taking of Louisburg, and he at the battle of Bunker Hill rallied his men by reminiscences of that anniversary — the 17th of June, 1745:

[1] See town officers, also parish officers in town and parish records.

"This day thirty years I was at the taking of Louisburg when it was surrendered to us; it was a fortunate day for America, we shall certainly beat the enemy." Colonel, afterward General, Joseph Fry, also began [1] in this war his long and brilliant career of military service.

The town records present the following register of deaths "in the king's service:" —

"1745. *June* 14. Benj. son of John & Ruth Frie died at Lewisburg, in the king's service. He was shot with a gun and died.

"*Aug.* 27. Samuel Farnum Jr. in the king's service at Lewisburg.

"*Sept.* 12. Ephraim son of Joseph & Sarah Barker in the king's service at Lewisburg.

"*Oct.* 1. Andrew son of Andrew & Hannah Johnson at Lewisburg in the king's service.

"*Oct.* 25. Jonathan son of Joseph & Sarah Chandler at Lewisburg in the king's service with sickness in the place.

"*Oct.* 29. David son of Andrew & Hannah Johnson at Lewisburg in the king's service.

"*Nov.* 3. Isaac son of Thomas & Hannah Abbott with sickness in the king's service aged 28 yrs. 8 mo. & 21 days.

"*Nov.* 12. Francis son of John & Sarah Dane died with sickness in the king's service at Lewisburg in the 20th yr of his age.

"*Dec.* 15. Andrew Allen the son of Andrew & Mary Allen with sickness in the king's service at Lewisburg.

"1746. *Jan.* 4. Benj. son of Christopher & Martha Carlton died with sickness in the king's service at Lewisburg in the 20th year of his age.

"*Jan.* 29. Joseph son of Noah & Mary Marble died with sickness in the king's service at Lewisburg.[2]

"*Jan.* 31. Philip son of Ebenezer & Elizabeth Abbot died with sickness in the king's service at Lewisburg.

"*Feb.* 18. Isaac son of Philemon & Elizabeth Chandler died with sickness in the king's service at Lewisburg in the 19th year of his age.

"*Mar.* 21. Jonathan Darlin at Lewisburg with sickness."

---

[1] *Mass. Archives*, vol. lxxiii., p. 737.

[2] Rev. Samuel Chandler, of York, in his Journal, May 12, 1745, alluding to a visit to his native town, speaks of this death: "Went up to uncle Marble's. They are mourning for their son who died at Louisburg; tarried there half an hour and got to father's at 9 o'clock."

"*April* 26. Jacob Martin son of Joseph & Mary Martin who was in the kings service at Lewisburg came sick from thence to Boston & died April 26, 1746.

"*Dec.* 16. Timothy Johnson Jr. died with sickness in the king's service at Lewisburg."

For the "famous victory," which cost so much loss of life, great rejoicings were had. In the old South Church, in Boston, the Rev. Mr. Prince preached a sermon entitled: "*Extraordinary Events the Doings of God and Marvellous in Pious eyes.*"

Some of the Andover company who were in the expedition, and the relatives of those who died, subsequently petitioned the State for a reward of their services, in the form of a grant of land in the county of York : —

"To His Honor Spencer Phipps,[1] Esq., *Lieut. Governor and Commander in Chief in and over His Majesty's Province of the Massachusetts Bay in New England:* To the Honble His Majesty's Council and House of Representatives in General Court Assembled, *Nov. 22, 1751.*

"The Petition of us the subscribers Inhabitants of the Town of Andover & other towns in the County of Essex & Middlesex who were most of us in the expedition against Cape Breton and the Rest the Representatives of others who lost their lives in s'd. expedition.

"Most humbly sheweth that when the Legislature of the Province thought an expedition against said Place was of ye utmost Importance, and had Resolved therein, we with the utmost cheerfulness engaged to serve the Interest of our king and country, apprehending, if the expedition should fail, the enemy would gain upon us, they having (at the Commencement of the War) taken & burnt the habitations of the English at Canso which filled us with apprehension our frontiers were likely to share the same fate, for the prevention of which we engaged as aforesaid. And we humbly hope our doing so with the view we had will Recommend us to your Honorable regards. And as your Honour and Honours in your wisdom manifest that the cultivation of our unimproved lands is of the highest importance to the well-being of the country and with grief behold the neglect thereof by those to whom lands have been granted for that purpose we beg leave to sympathyze with you and to say we desire ever to be profitable members of the common-

---

[1] Governer Shirley was in England from 1749 to 1753.

wealth and in order we might further shew ourselves such, humbly pray your Hon'r and Honours in Consequence of our Service aforesaid and Desire to be still serviceable would grant us a Township of the unappropriated Lands of this Government somewhere in the County of York which if your Hon. & Hon'rs should see cause to do we expect to submit to such Injunctions as you think proper to Lay upon us.

JAMES STEVENS,
JAMES FRYE,
[and fifty-six other signers.]

"The Committee to whom was referred the Petition of Capt. James Stevens & others, officers and soldiers & the Representatives of soldiers who were in the expedition against Cape Breton Praying for a Township of Land in the County of York in consequence of their Service in said expedition Have taken the same under Consideration and agreed to Report that a Township of the Contents of Six miles square on the Northwestern side of the line from Sebago Pond to the head of Berwick Boundary North Easterly on Saco River as near opposite the Township Granted to Capt. Moses Peirson & Capt. Humphrey Hobbs & their company as the land will admit of. . . . . Granted to said James Stevens . . . . on conditions that they take associates of the Cape Breton Soldiers, not excluding representatives of those who are dead so as to make the whole number of grantees one hundred and twenty," etc.

The other conditions provided for a suitable Meeting-house "for the publick worship of God," to be built in the township, and a "learned Protestant Minister of Good Conversation to be settled," also for schools.

The renewal of European quarrels, and the mutual jealousies of the English and French colonies, in respect to the territory of the New World, after a brief respite of scarcely four years, again revived the desolating wars. Great numbers of troops were sent over from England, and from them the provincial officers gained knowledge of military tactics, which in later years they turned to account against their teachers.

Governor Shirley returned from England, 1753, and at once took measures for prosecuting the war. In June, 1754, Richard Saltonstall, John Osgood, Jr., Richard Saltonstall, Jr., were appointed to administer the oaths to the soldiers and officers enlisted for the Fourth Regiment of Militia, in

Essex County, September 12, 1754. They made returns[1] of the following names of officers: —

Captain James Frye.
Capt. Daniel Bodwell.
Capt. John Foster.
Capt. John Abbot, Jr.
Capt. Isaac Adams.
Lieut. Saml. Johnson, Jr.
Lieut. Francis Swan.
Lieut. Nathan Chandler.

Lieut. John Farnum, Jr.
Lieut. Joseph Hovey.
Ensign John Pearson.
Ensign Benj. Berry.
Ensign Nathan Messer.
Ensign Asa Stevens.
Ensign George Abbot, Jr.

The following is a copy of the commission of Capt. John Abbot, 1754: —

Province of the 𝔐𝔞𝔰𝔰𝔞𝔠𝔥𝔲𝔰𝔢𝔱𝔱𝔰-𝔅𝔞𝔶, } *WILLIAM SHIRLEY*, Efq; Captain-General and GOVERNOUR in Chief, in and over His MAJESTY's Province of the *Maſſachuſetts-Bay* in *New-England*, &c.

SEAL.

To JOHN ABBOTT, Jun.ʳ Gentⁿ *Greeting.*

Y Virtue of the Power and Authority, in and by His Majeſty's Royal Commiſſion to Me granted to be Captain-General, &c. over this His Majeſty's Province of the *Maſſachuſetts-Bay*, aforeſaid ; I do (by theſe Preſents) repoſing eſpecial Truſt and Confidence in your Loyalty, Courage and good Conduct, conſtitute and appoint You the ſaid John Abbott Captain of the second Foot-Company in the Town of Andover in the fourth Regiment of Militia in the County of Eſſex whereof Rich⁴. Saltonſtall Eſq.ʳ is Colonel

You are therefore carefully and diligently to diſcharge the Duty of a Captain in leading, ordering and exerciſing ſaid Company in Arms, both inferiour Officers and Soldiers, and to keep them in good

Maſſ. Archives, vol. "Military," 1754–1755.

Order and Difcipline; hereby commanding them to obey you as their Captain and your felf to obferve and follow fuch Orders and Inftructions, as you fhall from Time to Time receive from Me, or the Commander in Chief for the Time being, or other your fuperior Officers for His Majefty's Service, according to military Rules and Difcipline, purfuant to the Truft repofed in You.

Given under My Hand & Seal at Arms at Boston, *the second Day of July In the twenty eighth Year of the Reign of His Majefty King* GEORGE *the Second*, Annoq; Domini, 1754.

By *His* EXCELLENCY'S W. SHIRLEY.
  Command,
    J. WILLARD.

When he received this and took the oath of fidelity to the King, George II., he little thought that he should live to see filed with the commission, twenty years later, another constituting his son captain of a company to bear arms against King George III. But the two commissions are tied up together, as their owners probably left them.

During the summer of 1754, Governor Shirley, accompanied by General Winslow, in command of five hundred men, made an expedition to the Kennebec River, and inspected the forts and built new ones. An Andover soldier, who was in the company, has left a memorial of his services [1] : —

"The Petition of Daniel Mooar of Andover most humbly sheweth that his son Jacob Mooar went on the expedition to the eastern frontiers the summer past under the command of Major Genl. Winslow and came home sick which continued for thirty days after his arrival and then he Died. During which time your petitioner was put to expenses to Doctors and nursing, &c., as will appear by the accounts herewith exhibited which he humbly prays your excellency and Honors he may be allowed, and as in Duty bound will ever pray. DANIEL MOOAR."

The petitioner was allowed the amount which he asked

[1] *Mass. Archives*, vol. lxxiv., p. 321.

for, namely, four pounds four shillings. Indeed, it may here be said that almost all the many petitions and memorials presented in the course of this chapter received the favorable attention which they prayed for.

In the spring of 1755, four expeditions were planned: one, that of the ill-fated General Braddock against Fort Du Quesne, one to Lakes George and Champlain and Fort Crown Point, one to Oswego, and one to Nova Scotia. Of the latter, General Winslow took command, and was completely successful. He captured the enemy's strongholds, and reduced the Province of Acadie to subjection. Maj. Joseph Fry of Andover was in command of a part of the force under General Winslow. A considerable number of the privates in the expedition were from Andover, either natives or residents of the town.

Several petitions of soldiers who were sufferers from this expedition are found.

One is for Jonathan Parker,[1] in Capt. Edmund More's company in Colonel Bagley's regiment. He had been, with other invalids, sent back to Boston, and there taken sick with "a Feaver," and remained "in a very poor state of health."

Another petition was as follows (the summary of it made in the journals of the House of Representatives) : —

"1755, *June* 4. A petition of John Granger and Enoch Poor of Andover in the County of Essex, soldiers in the late expedition under the command of Major General Winslow, setting forth that they were employed in cutting Timber, &c., for the building Fort Halifax, for which they were promised one shilling and four pence per day, but that their account of Labour was never rendered by reason of the sickness and death of Capt. Fox: therefore praying that they may receive the wages due to them for their said service."

The sufferings undergone by the colonists in prosecuting these wars of the mother country were extreme, not only in their actual military service, but in their taxation and in the generally unsettled condition of the country, which was in a perpetual commotion of military musterings, impressments,

---

[1] *Mass. Archives*, vol. lxxix., p. 721.

etc., and with the burden of many sick and disabled soldiers. We are used to thinking of the Revolutionary period as one of stir in military matters, but perhaps we do not fully realize how largely war and its attendant evils interfered with the prosperity of the province and the towns in the thirty years before the Revolution. Nor were the colonies of English settlement the only sufferers in these quarrels of the rival nations of the old world. Some of the Acadians who took no part of the fighting, but professed to be neutral, met with a hard fate. Their neutrality was viewed with suspicion; it being at best compulsory, and they being bound by ties of blood and religion to the cause of the enemy. Therefore, to prevent all trouble from them, they were taken from their homes, put on board vessels, and sent off to all parts of the States to spend in exile a wretched existence; families sundered, children sent to one town, parents to another, according as they chanced to be separated on board the vessels to which they were driven at the point of the bayonet. The story of some of these Acadians is known to every reader through the poet's tale of "Evangeline," a story of Grand Pré.

After the villagers had been driven out, their houses were set on fire, and as they sailed away, they saw the flames of their beloved homes redden the skies. In the destruction of the Acadian villages, the force under Major Frye took an active part. From all that can be gathered in regard to him, it would seem that this officer was a humane and remarkably tender-hearted man, and this military duty which he was called upon to perform must have been exceedingly repugnant to his feelings. He was ordered[1] to burn buildings, over two hundred and fifty houses from which the owners had been removed, and to bring off the few women and children that remained. The wretched people had for the most part submitted with little resistance; but when they saw their houses of worship in flames, some three hundred French and Indians, who were concealed in the woods, came upon our forces and killed twenty or thirty before they realized that an enemy was near.

[1] See Haliburton's *History of Nova Scotia*

The dislike and distrust felt toward the poor Acadians in Massachusetts was very great, owing to the prejudice against their nation and their religion. This appears in an address presented to the Governor, deprecating their residence here, especially their being quartered in Boston : " The receiving among us so great a number of persons whose gross bigotry to the Roman Catholick religion is notorious and whose loyalty to his Majesty is suspected is a thing very disagreeable to us."

When the Acadians were sent to the various towns, the selectmen were ordered to bind out to service all children for whom places could be found. Thus, many were torn from their parents and put to serve hard task masters and to perform heavy toils. In the execution of these, perhaps, in the circumstances, inevitable orders, instances of great inhumanity occurred, actual violence being used to separate parents and children. One aged man (not, however, of Andover) petitioned the General Court, stating his sufferings at the hands of town officers, that his hands and feet were tied and he was nearly strangled to prevent his running after and calling out to his children who were carried away.

Some of these Acadians drew up a petition[1] to the General Court, praying for a redress of their grievances. It is signed by persons from Chelmsford, Waltham, Oxford, Concord, Worcester, and Andover. The signers from Andover were Jacques Esbert[2] and Joseph Vincent : —

---

[1] *Mass. Archives*, vol. xxiii., p. 49.

[2] The Andover officials, spelling according to the spoken pronunciation, wrote this name "Jockey Bear." Also, after a time the Acadians adopted the Anglicized name. A curious instance of this corruption and changing of names is related in the journal of Col. Joseph Adams. His uncle, Dr. Isaac Adams, had a serving boy whose name was Thomas Blumpy. His family name in England was Whitefoot. They removed to France and were called *Blancpied*. They came to America and in the Yankee tongue this French surname became Blumpy, which was written as pronounced, and finally adopted by the owners of the name as their orthography.

"A son Excellence Le Gouverneur General de la province de Massachusetts Bay de La Nouvelle Engleterre et au honorable Gentilhommes du Conseile.

"Nous avons pris la liberte de vous presenter cette Requeste, comme nous sommes en chagrin par Rapart a nos enfans. La perte que nous avons souffris de nos habitations et d'etre amené icy, et nos separations Les un des autres n'est Rien a Comparé a cell que nous trouvon a present, que de prendre nos enfants par force devant nos yeux. La nature mesme ne peut souffrir cela. S'il etait dans notre pouvoir d'avoir notre chois, nous choisirions plustot de prendre nos corps et nos ames que d'etre separé d'eux. C'est pourquoy nous vous prions en grace et a vos honours que vous ayé La bonté d'apaiser cette crueltey. Nous ne Reffusons au commencement de travailler pour l'entretienne de nos enfans, moyennant que si c'etait suffert pour nos familles. Vous priant en grace que d'avoir Le bonte d'avoir egart a notre Requeste; ainsy faisent; vous obligerai votre tres humble et tres obeissent serviteurs."

This in a literal translation reads as follows:—

"To his Excellency the Governor General of the province of Massachusetts Bay of New England and to the honorable Gentlemen of the Council.

"We have taken the liberty to present you this request, as we are in sorrow on account of our children. The loss which we have suffered at your hands [from you], of our houses, and being brought here and our separation from one another is nothing to compare with what we experience at present, that of losing our children by force before our eyes. Nature herself cannot endure that. If it were in our power to have our choice we should choose rather to lose our body and our soul than to be separated from them. Wherefore we pray your honors that you would have the goodness to mitigate this cruelty. We have not refused from the first to work for the support of our children, provided it were permitted for our own families. Praying you in mercy to have the goodness to have regard to our Petition, thus doing you will oblige your very humble and obedient servants."

This petition had the effect to procure the order that there should be no more binding out, but that houses should be provided for each family that they might "keep together."

In February, 1756, twenty-two of these Acadians were

sent to Andover: "Germain Laundry, his wife, seven sons and thirteen daughters," says the record[1] of the selectmen, "and one born since, making in all twenty-three who came to town."

Another record[2] thus gives the account:—

"There is twenty-six of the afores'd French which we keep in three Distinck places, that so they might be more constantly Imployed, the old man German Laundre is an Infirm man and not capable of any Labour, and in the winter time he was confined to his Bedd, and needed a Great deel of Tendance more than his wife could perform and his son Joseph is under such weekly Scorcomstances that we are oblidged to support him altogether.

"There is three families that have eleven children, the oldest of them is not above eight years of age, which there Fathers are not Able to support; there is two young men and four young women that for the most part support themselves."

There are several accounts rendered by the selectmen of their expense in providing for the support of the French neutrals,— provisions, "pork, beef, Indian meal, pease, beans, sider, &c." Also, there is an account, October, 1757, for medicine and attendances by Dr. Abiel Abbot, and for "sundries delivered to the French by Mr. Isaac Abbot, Retailer, and sundries delivered by Mr. Samuel Phillips." To this account is annexed a memorandum: "Germain Laundry & Joseph his son, Jockey Bear[3] and Charles Bear, have been sick & Indisposed ever since the date of the last account." (The last account was June, 1757, from November, 1756.)

After a time, houses were provided for the families, and most of the Acadians in Andover became self-supporting. The family of Jacques Esbert and Charles Esbert were placed in a house on the estate of Mr. Jonathan Abbot, now owned by his grandson, Mr. Stephen Abbot. The house was empty, Mr. Abbot having lately built a new one. It was, however, a great annoyance to the Puritan farmer to have these tenants,— foreigners and Roman Catholics, quartered near his own residence. But, as his descendants relate, the

---

[1] *Mass. Archives*, vol. xxiii., p. 44.
[2] *Ibid.*, vol. xxiv., p. 47.
[3] Jacques Esbert, Charles Esbert.

Acadians completely conquered the prejudices of this family and of the community and gained the good-will of all acquaintances. They were industrious and frugal. The women worked in the fields pulling flax and harvesting. They practised the rites of their religion in an inoffensive manner and commended it by their good conduct. When they went away from Andover, Mr. Abbot's family parted from them with sincere regret. Two of them sent a souvenir to Mr. Abbot, which the family still keep, a beautifully carved and polished powder-horn, made by their own hands. It is inscribed : —

> "JONATHAN ABBOT
> His horn made in Alenstown
> April y* 5 1770
> *I powder with my brother ball
> Most hero-like doth conquer all.*"

It is embellished with figures of animals, — a turtle, a deer, a fox, dolphins, etc., and also with representations of armies fighting, soldiers in uniform with muskets, sabre, bayonet, (all the soldiers with hair tied in queues hanging down behind), also artillery men and field pieces.

In the year 1760, some of the Acadians were removed from Andover and "sett off to the county of Hampshire." The names of those in town July 20, 1760, as given in the returns[1] were the following : —

Charles Bear, age 36.	Amon Dupee, age 30.
Margaret Bear, age 24.	Mary, his wife, age 29.
Molly Bear, age 4.	Mary Joseph, age 5.
Charles Bear, age 2.	Margaret Dupee, age 2.
Margaret Bear, age 1.	Hermon Dupee, age 3.

Jno Laundry, age 26 (weakly).
Mary Laundry, age 26.

While the French exiles from home were thus suffering, the provincial troops also, detained to garrison forts in the conquered country, were scarcely less unhappy. Their wretched condition is described in a letter of Col. Joseph Frye to the Council and House of Representatives,[2] in which he begs

---
[1] *Mass. Archives,* vol. xxiv.
[2] *Ibid.,* vol. lv., page 384.

for their discharge, their term of enlistment having expired. The soldiers were, for the most part, from Andover and vicinity, and therefore the letter is as pertinent to this history, as it is in itself interesting : —

"FORT LAWRENCE
IN CHEGNECTO, *July* 23^d, 1756.

"MAY IT PLEASE YOUR HONOURS: It is matter of great Grieff to me to be a spectator of the effects of a Raging sickness among the Remainder of the Troops sent here from New England last year for the removal of the French encroachments in this Province, and Daily to hear their just complaints of their being Detained here so long after the time is expired they Inlisted for, and not to have it in my power to extricate them out of their troubles and anxieties of mind. I am well assured in my own mind His Excellency Governor Shirley must be absent from his Government, otherwise he would certainly have taken such measures before this time as would have brought us to New England. Although I am sensible he was absent, yet I could not have thought we should have been kept so long, seeing this Government are no longer strangers to Governor Shirley's Promise that those soldiers should be discharged at the expiration of twelve months from the time of their Inlistment and especially as he has wrote to Governor Lawrence in the most pressing terms to have them sent home at a time they should have a right to demand a Discharge. But I find myself mistaken in judgment; for I see no signs of compliance with his directions, which has thrown the poor soldiers into such dejection of mind as is Grievous to behold.

"Therefore knowing the weight your Remonstrance on this head must have with this Government (if anything will) with my own Inclination and on the Desire of the other New-England officers most humbly beg your interposition in the case. And that you would speedily take such measures for the deliverence of the poor distressed soldiers as your Honor's wisdom shall direct.

"I am with the greatest regard

"Your Honor's most humble and most obedient servt.

JOSEPH FRYE."

The expedition to Lake Champlain and Crown Point was not so successful as that had been against Acadia.

Several Andover soldiers who died in the service are named in the town records : —

1755. Sept. 27. Ebenezer Frie died at the camp near Lake George.
Oct. 2. Jeremiah, son of Jacob and Abigail Tyler died with sickness at Lake George in the 23rd year of his age.
Nov. 17. Captain Jonathan Poor died at Albenoy[1] with sickness in the intended expedition against Crown Point in the 32d year of his age.
Nov. 28. Ensign James Stevens died at the Camp near Lake George, 35th year of his age.
Dec. 20. Capt. Asa Stevens at Albenoy on his return from Lake George, 38 years, 6 days.

Respecting two of the above named soldiers, are memorials in the State Archives.

The father of Jeremiah Tyler[2] (Jacob Tyler) shows that his son "was in Colonel Titcomb's regiment, in the expedition against Crown Point, and was very sick at the time of the Battel that was fought at Lake George and his Gun was stolen from him," and that "his wages were cut short by reason of this loss of his gun." He obtained two pounds in answer to his petition.

Another is a petition[3] of Sarah Stevens, "widow of James Stevens, late of Andover, deceased."

This "humbly sheweth:"—

"That whereas my late Husband who was an Ensine in the service of s'd Province in the expedition Towards Crown Point in the Company under the command of Capt. Abiel Frye was in the detachment under the command of Col. Williams in the morning of the Day the Battle was fought near Lake George and in sd morning Ingagement my sd Husband, closely pursued by the enemy, was in his Retreat obliged to leave his coat and blanket which undoubtedly fell into the Hands of the enemy; which coat of itself was of the vallue of one pound and twelve shillings, and my sd Husband was obliged immediately to purchase another coat and Blanket to fit himself to do his Duty in the camp. Further that my sd husband was sick in the camp at the time when the army marched from the camp for Albany of which sickness he died soon after, and for his nursing in his sickness I am charged

[1] Albany.
[2] *Mass. Archives*, vol. lxxv., page 332.
[3] *Ibid.*, vol. lxxv., page 364.

ten shillings, and there being no officer belonging to sd company in the camp at the time of his death to take care of his clothes and other effects in the camp I have never Recd any of sd effects except his Gun and Hanger, which effects exclusive of what I Rec'd was worth four pounds or more, of which effects I have no Reason to expect to receive any more.

"Wherefore your humble petitioner prays that y^r Excellency and Honors would take my case under your wise Consideration and grant me such allowance for sd articles and expences as you in your Great wisdom and goodness shall think proper which your humble petitioner as in duty bound shall ever pray.

SARAH STEVENS."

Another petitioner, John Barker,[1] shows that he was an enlisted soldier in Capt. Samuel Draper's company of Colonel Browne's regiment, in the expedition to Crown Point; was taken sick, and was thirteen weeks on the way from Fort Edward before he got home; was still "very poorly," and had "nothing but his hands to depend upon." He prays that he may receive allowance for his "expenses of travel." He was granted four pounds.[2]

Israel Adams also petitions, March 30, 1756, showing that he had a son, who on his return from Lake George, was taken sick of a fever by the way, ... and "that from the time of his dismission at Lake George to the Thirtieth day of March Instant his son hath been incapacitated for any Business & continued still in a weak state of health," etc.

He prayed for a full allowance of wages, and received two pounds eight shillings.

Of the expedition to Oswego and the western frontiers, a relic remains, — a petition[3] of Capt. James Frye, in behalf of his son : —

"That in the year of our Lord one thousand seven hundred & fifty (five?) James Frie jr. your petitioner's son was a soldier in His Majesty's service on the Western frontiers under the command of Capt. Thomas Farrington, that on the 27th of November in that year he was taken sick at Schenectady with the small-pox which detained him there near two months which sickness together with

---

[1] *Mass. Archives*, vol. lxxv., p. 403.
[2] *Ibid.*, vol. lxxv., p. 526.
[3] *Ibid.*, vol. lxxix., p. 720.

the expense in getting him home cost your petitioner the sum of twenty-four pounds six shillings as per account."

The full amount asked for was not granted. Only forty-four shillings was allowed, since, as was said, his son might have remained in the hospital, and the expense thus have been avoided.

Rev. Samuel Chandler, native of Andover, pastor of York, Me., and afterward of Gloucester, Mass., was chaplain of this expedition. He writes in his journal, September 29, 1755 : —

"I set out from home about 10 o'clock on the expedition against Crown Point as chaplain to Col. Ichabod Plaisted's Regiment. I dined at Coll. Plaisted's & set out with him to Andover where we arrived abt sunset. He lodged at Coll. Fryes, I at my mothers."

In 1756, General Shirley having been superseded by Lord Loudon, the plans for the campaign were somewhat changed, all energies and forces being concentrated for the capture of Crown Point. But the result was disastrous; jealousies occurred between the Provincial and the regular officers; the troops were delayed, sickness broke out in camp, and the contemplated attack on Crown Point was not consummated. In this expedition, James Frye was Lieutenant-colonel of Colonel Plaisted's regiment, and Ward Noyes was Surgeon's Mate. Capt. Henry Ingals and Capt. Joseph Holt were in service in this campaign.

The sufferings of a soldier who belonged originally to Andover, and was here under medical treatment, are described in a petition [1] : —

"Stephen Lovejoy late a soldier in the service of this Province under Capt. Joseph Holt in Col. Plaisted's regiment in the late expedition to Lake George Humbly sheweth that upon his being Disbanded there, fell sick and in about the space of nine days was carried in a cart & with much difficulty to a place called Glasco where he continued sick ten days reduced to great necessities so as even to sell his Gun and borrow two dollars, to purchase necessaries. From thence he was at the expense of Five pounds one shilling and four pence by His Father Henry Lovejoy in the space of about seven days carried in a slay to Andover where at great cost and expense of nursing, Tendance and necessaries he contin-

---

[1] Mass. Archives, vol. lxxvii., p. 457.

ued at his Fathers in a very weak and feable condition & for the most part not able to help himself for the space of twenty-eight days more and then with the help of a man & Hired Horse the cost of which amounted to twenty one shillings he got home to York."

A soldier of Capt. Henry Ingals's company, Phineas Tyler, of Boxford, petitions for allowance for his expenses, he having been "impressed and marched to Lake George, and being taken sick, been conveyed back to Albany and thence having sent to Boxford for a Hors and man to convey him home." He states that the man was twenty-one days on the journey from and to Boxford. He was granted fifty shillings. It is not improbable that some Andover men had similar experiences in the tedious march to Lake George, and some, perhaps, were not so fortunate as to have a horse and man at command to convey them home.

The following is a pathetic story, told by the widow of a soldier who died from his exposures and hardships : —

"The petition [1] of Hannah Johnson humbly sheweth That my leate Husband Andrew Johnson Leate of Andover Deceased was in the Country service in Coll. James Frye's Company in the expedition formed against Crown Point in the year 1756, and in his Return hom he was taken sick by the way and was oblidged to sell his Gun & Blanket for less than one half their worth for necessary to support him by the way, or he thought he must have perished, for he had no money and he was brought so weak and low that I was oblidged to send a man and hors to fetch him home, which cost me twelve shillings and he was brought hom the 25th day of November 1756 and so he remained in a Languishing Condition and at great expence for nurses, watchers and necessaries for nine weeks and then he Died.

"I pray your Excellency and Honors to make me such allowance for said Gun and for Nursing & Necessary for the said Deceased as in your wisdom you shall think proper, and your petitioner as in duty bound shall ever pray.   HANNAH JOHNSON."

The petitioner's request was granted.

Another widow of a deceased soldier is petitioned [2] for by one of the Andover officers : —

---

[1] *Mass. Archives*, vol. lxxvii., p. 300.
[2] *Ibid.*, vol. lxxvii., p. 453.

THE FRENCH AND INDIAN WAR.   255

"The Petition of James Parker in behalf of Margaret Furbush widow & Relict of Charles Furbush Deceased Humbly Sheweth.

"That the said Charles Furbush entered into the Province service about the 1st Day of July A. D. 1756 and proceeded with Captain John Wright as far as Fort Edward, where he was taken sick, by which means he was prevented joyning his Respective Regiment and company at Lake George (so was not made up in any muster rolls) and was brought back as far as Saratoga and there Dyed the 9th of September 1756.

"As the said Charles was not made up on any muster rolls, your Petitioner was not enabled to Receive any part of his wages. Your petitioner therefore humbly prays your Excellency and your Honours (in behalf of said widow) would take her case into your consideration and order a Derect Payment of the said Charles's Wages or otherwise make her such consideration as in your great goodness you shall think fit, and your petitioner as in duty bound shall ever pray.   JAMES PARKER."

Some further particulars and traditions are told by the great grandson of Charles Furbush: —

"Charles Furbush[1] had a son of the same name. Charles the son as soon as he was of age was called to serve in the French and Indian War at the forts on Lakes George and Champlain. He was so young that his father chose to enlist and go with him. Father and son camped and bivouacked together and they were sleeping under the same blanket upon the ground one night when Charles awoke and ascertained by the light of the moon shining in his father's face that he was dead."

The son was Capt. Charles Furbush, who commanded an Andover Company at Bunker Hill.

November[2] 23, 1757, Nicholas Holt, afterward a captain, then a second lieutenant, petitioned for pay for his services, a mistake having been made in omitting his name from the rolls.

Dr. Ward Noyes kept a journal of this expedition. It has unfortunately within a few years been destroyed. It is said by those who have read it to have been interesting, and curiously illustrative of the manners and customs of the time. A

---

[1] *Revolutionary Reminiscences* (Simeon Flint), *Lawrence American (Andover Advertiser)*, 1875.
[2] *Mass. Archives*, vol. lxxvii., p. 271.

petition from him in the State Archives[1] sets forth some of the annoyances experienced by army surgeons in old-time campaigning : —

"*May 25th* 1757. The Petition of Ward Noyes of Andover humbly sheweth that your petitioner was in his Majesty's service in the expedition against Crown Point in the year 1756 as mate to Dr. John Calef in Col. Plaisted's Regiment, and in that capacity was often called forth to visit the sick soldiers, and even so it was at a certain time, when your petitioner was called forth hastily for the Relief of such sick soldiers, he left his Gun in his tent supposing it to be safe & secure, but when he returned to his tent his Gun was stolen away and your Petitioner (by his utmost care and endeavor) could never discover or hear of the same again. Now, your petitioner begs leave to say that he thinks it could not be reasonably expected that he should carry his Gun with him at all Times when and where he was called from Tent to tent, to attend upon such sick, and humbly conceives, consequently, its being stolen away as aforesaid could not be charged as any misconduct in him, yet for want of said Gun's being returned there is withheld from the Petitioner of his wages the sum of four pounds. Your petitioner therefore Humbly supplicates the serious consideration and favor of your Honours, praying (with submission) that you would be pleased to grant him the whole of his wages notwithstanding the said Gun not being Returned or otherwise, as your Honours in your great wisdom and Goodness shall see mete to order, and your Petitioner as in duty bound shall ever pray.

"ESSEX, ANDOVER, *April* 30, 1757. . . . ."

The "great wisdom and goodness" of the Court granted the doctor's petition. About two weeks before this, he had received his commission as Surgeon's Mate. It is an impressive document, written on parchment of a fine quality, sealed with the royal seal. The following is the text : —

"Province of the
   Massachusetts Bay.
         His Majesty's Council for the
          Province of the Massachusetts Bay in New England
"To WARD NOYES, *Gentleman,* Greeting.
   By virtue of the Power and Authority by the Royal Charter

---

[1] *Mass. Archives,* vol. lxxvii., p. 271.

granted to the Council of this Province in Case of the death or Absence of the Governour and Lieutenant Governour; We do, by these Presents, confiding in your Loyalty, Skill, & Ability, Constitute and appoint you the said *Ward Noyes* to be the Surgeon's Mate to the Forces raised within this Province and put under the Command of His Excellency the Right Honourable John Earl of Loudon, General & Commander in Chief of all His Majesty's Forces in North America: Of which forces *Joseph Frye* Esqr. is Chief Officer.

"You are therefore carefully & dilligently to perform the Duty of Surgeon's Mate to the said Forces in all Things pertaining to the said office, and to observe and follow all such orders and Directions as you shall receive from your Superior officers for his Majesty's service, pursuant to the Trust reposed in you.

"Given under Our Hands and the publick Seal of the Province of the Massachusetts Bay aforesaid, at Boston, the fifth Day of April In the Thirtieth Year of the Reign of His Majesty King George the Second, Annoque Domini 1757.

JAMES MINOT.	JNO. OSBORNE.
ANDᵂ OLIVER.	JACOB WENDELL.
JOSEPH PYNCHON.	BENJ. LYNDE.
JOHN OTIS.	DAVE PASCH.(?)
THO. HUTCHINSON.	JOHN GREENLEAF.
STEPHEN SEWALL.	SAML. WALTS.
ISAAC ROYALL.	GEORGE LEONARD.
JOHN ERVING.	J. CHANDLER.
WM. BRATTLE.	

"By their Honours Command.
THOS. CLARKE, *Dpty. Secry.*"

The following petitions present a vivid picture of the wanderings and adventures of an Andover soldier, who was taken captive by the Indians. These were the tales which our great grandfathers used to tell to their children gathered around the fire of winter evenings, when the back-log blazed and the "mug of cider simmered slow," and, sipping it ever and anon, the hero of many fights waxed warm, and shouldering crutch, or seizing musket from over the chimney piece, showed how battles were fought in the "Old French War," kindling in young breasts the martial ardor that flamed up in Revolutionary fires.

"The Petition [1] of Isaac Foster of Andover Humbly Sheweth that whereas he was an Inlisted soldier in the service of this Province in the company [2] of Lieut. Col. James Frye in the year Seventeen Hundred & Fifty six & in sd company proceeded to Fort William Henry & on the Eighteenth Day of September following was by Detachment sent on a Scouting Party under the command of Capt. Hodges to the Westerly side of Lake George and, on the nineteenth, the Party being surprised by a Large Body of the enemy & mostly killed or taken, he had the unhappy Fate to fall into the Hands of a Number of those barbarous Indians called Ottawas inhabiting beyond Lake Superior; who after having riffled his Pockets of Four Dollars obliged him to proceed with them to a Lake called Almipagon lying Northerly of Lake Superior one hundred and fifty miles and (as the French say) eleven hundred miles from Montreal. With these savages he was detained two years. During which time he suffered inconceivable hardships, and at the expiration of it being permitted by his Indian owner to accompany him down the Lake to a French Place called Detroit he there interceded with a Frenchman to ransom him, which he accordingly effected for three Hundred Livers; which sum your Petitioner Discharged by Labour, And after being detained by the French at sd Detroit & Montreal near Fourteen Months Longer he was brought to Crown Point at the time of the late exchange of Prisoners and is since returned Home, having been absent (from the day he was taken) three years & two months. And whereas he has received pay no longer than till the Day of his Captivity, he humbly begs your Excellency & Honors would take His case under your wise Consideration & make him such further allowance for his time &c as in your great goodness & wisdom shall seem mete, which your humble petitioner as in Duty bound shall ever Pray. ISAAC FOSTER.

"ANDOVER, Jan. 7th, 1760."

This petition drawn up so carefully, and written in every respect so correctly, bears evidence of being the composition of a man more accustomed to the use of the pen than the captive was, who had been three years campaigning. Who wrote it may be surmised from the fact that it was ordered to pay to Samuel Phillips, Esq., for the use of the petitioner,

[1] Mass. Archives, vol. lxxviii., p. 681.
[2] The word company is used several times of "Colonel" Frye's troops.

in full remuneration for his services and sufferings within mentioned, the sum of eight pounds.

Three years before, the father of the petitioner, John Foster, had presented a petition [1] for his son's pay to be given to him. He then supposed his son to be dead, not having heard from him for so long. Thus did the youth of Andover early mature in life's experience, and such were the suspense and anxiety of kindred "in regard to soldiers in the king's service":—

"*The Petition of John Foster of Andover, April 2, 1757.*

"Humbly sheweth that Isaac Foster, a minor, the son of your petitioner, was a soldier in his Majesty's service in the expedition against Crown Point in the year 1756 in the company of Col. James Frye, and in the month of September the said Isaac (as he was scouting on his duty, was either killed by the enemy or taken captive, by reason whereof his Gun was not Returned. Yet there is kept back, out of his wages, from your petitioner for said Gun the sum of four pounds. So that without the Interposition of your Honr and Honrs your Petitioner might be a sufferer for omitting that which it was not in his power to perform; your petitioner therefore humbly supplicates the consideration and favor of this Great and wise Court, praying (with submission) that your Honr and Honrs would be pleased to allow him the said sum of four pounds retained as aforesaid or otherwise as in your wisdom & Goodness you shall think fit and judge mete, and your Petitioner as in duty bound shall ever pray, ...   JOHN FOSTER.

"Ordered to be paid the full wages due to his son without any deduction."

What a day of happy surprise that must have been when the long lost son returned to relate his manifold escapes and adventures!

The fate of another Andover captive was long a matter of doubt, as appears from comparing the two following records, one a petition [2] of his father before he knew whether his son were alive or dead, the other a record of the death in the town books. The latter is as follows:—

"Joseph, son of Thomas and Elizabeth Abbot, was taken captive

---

[1] *Mass. Archives*, vol. lxxvi., p. 519.
[2] *Ibid.*, vol. lxxvi., p. 526.

by the Indians at Lake George, Sept. 19, 1756, was carried to Canada and died in prison at Quebeck sometime in January, 1758, in the 24th year of his age."

The petition [1] is as follows: —

"*April* 4, 1757. The petition of Thomas Abbot of Andover humbly sheweth that Joseph Abbot the son of your Petitioner was a soldier in His Majesty's service against Crown Point in the year 1756 in the company of Col. James Frye, and in the month of September, as he was in his Duty Scouting, he was either killed or taken captive by the enemy, by reason whereof his Gun was not returned — and if part of his wages be retained and kept back for the said Gun your Petitioner must suffer loss. Your petitioner therefore humbly supplicates the favorable Interposition of your Honr and Honrs, praying that your sons wages notwithstanding the sd Gun not being returned or otherwise, as your Honor or Honors in your wisdom & Goodness shall think fit & judge mete, and your petitioner as in duty bound shall ever pray.

THOMAS ABBOT."

In January, 1757, a vigorous campaign was projected, Lord Loudon meeting in council at Boston all the Governors of New England, to arrange details. It was decided to raise 1,800 men in Massachusetts to reënforce the troops of General Webb, and attempt the capture of Crown Point. To Col. Joseph Frye, of Andover, was assigned the raising and the command of the troops, eighteen hundred in number. This officer had been in active service from the beginning of the war, was greatly beloved by the men under his command, and was in all respects an able man. His sufferings during the war were extreme, as will be seen in the sequel. From the soldiers under his command in the expedition to Acadia he received a silver tankard, as a testimonial of their regard. It is still in possession of his descendants. It bears the following inscription [2]: —

[1] *Mass. Archives*, vol. lxxvi., p. 526.
[2] See Centennial Address at Fryeburgh.

TO JOSEPH FRYE, ESQ.
COLONEL AND COMMANDER IN CHIEF OF THE FORCES
in the service of the Province of the Massachusetts Bay and late
MAJOR OF THE SECOND BATTALION OF
General Shirley's Provincial Regiment
THIS TANKARD
From a just sense of his care and conduct of the Troops while under his command at Nova Scotia and a proper Resentment of his Paternal Regard for them since their Return to New England Is Presented by His Most Humble Servants
THE OFFICERS OF S° BATTALION.

BOSTON, *Apr. 2d*, 1757.

A document signed by Lieutenant-colonel Osgood, relating to the enlistment of men for this service, has been found among the papers of Capt. John Abbott. It is a printed form, with the blanks for dates and names filled out in manuscript: —

"ESSEX *ss*. To JOHN ABBOT, *Gentleman, Captain of the Military Foot Company in Andover*, Greeting.

"A°reable to Law and pursuant to a Warrant from the Honourable Spencer Phips, Esq., Lieut. Governor and Commander in Chief in and over his Majesty's Province of the Massachusetts Bay in New England, to Me directed:

"In His Majesty's Name, you are hereby requested to raise, if in your Power, for his Majesty's Service by Inlistment ffive able-bodied effective men, to be employed for the Security of His Majesty's Dominions in North-America, on or before the Twenty-first of March next; but least said Number should not be inlisted by said Time, You are alike required forthwith to cause all the trained band soldiers in your company to be warned to appear on the Twenty-second Day of March next in Arms; and if the Quota assigned you to be raised shall not be obtained by Inlistment, as aforesaid, You are then to cause said Number to be completed by Impress out of said Company; And if any Person or Persons then impressed shall pay his or their Fines within Twenty-four hours from their Impressment You are to continue the Impress till the Number ordered you to be raised is completed: You are alike required to make Return to Me of the Names of the Persons raised, and who were raised by Inlistment and when, on or before y° 25th day of March Next. You are by no Means to return any man, inlisted that shall be impress:d, or was not inlisted as aforesaid; and you are to cause the Persons inlisted and impressed to appear before Me at my house on or before the Twenty-fifth of March next to be Mustered, on Pain of forfeiting and paying the Sum of Ten Pounds for each neglect ; and for not making a Return as aforesaid Twenty Pounds. Hereto fail not at your Peril. Given under my Hand and Seal at Andover the 25th Day of February 1757.

JOHN OSGOOD, JUN., Lieut. Col."

Moody Bridges was appointed to the command of the men detached from Lieutenant-colonel Osgood's regiment for the expedition, and, as he relates, did duty as a field officer.[1]

"*May 31, 1759. The Memorial*[2] *of Moody Bridges of Andover most humbly sheweth* —

"That Anno Domini 1757, your Memorialist, Pursuant to his order from Coll John Osgood of s^d Town, had the Honor of the command of the whole detachment of officers & soldiers raised in s^d Coll Osgood's regiment for the Relief of General Webb, & That he did the Duty of a field officer in Leading ordering & Marching s^d Detachment, which consisted of Two Hundred & Forty men," etc. [He prays for more than adjutant's pay.]

The troops were marched to Fort William Henry, on the southern shore of Lake George. In the garrison, here, was stationed Colonel Monro, in command of five hundred British regulars. Colonel Frye's militia intrenched themselves outside the fort. About fifteen miles distant, at Fort Edward, was General Webb, with a force five thousand strong.

Apprehending no enemy near, the little garrison at Fort William Henry awaited orders and reënforcements to march toward Crown Point. But suddenly, on the first day of August, the tranquil lake swarmed with Indian canoes, and following them came a French fleet, bearing down upon the fort. Montcalm, the active, swift, secret, was upon them with a force of from eight to nine thousand French and Indians. What followed, every reader of American history knows, — how the brave little garrison hurled back defiance to the summons to surrender, how they sent post haste to

---

[1] There were no regular field officers in the regiment under Colonel Frye, says that officer in a memorial.

[2] *Mass. Archives*, vol. lxxviii, p. 532.

General Webb for reënforcements, but got none, only in their stead a letter of advice to capitulate.

In spite of all, Colonel Monro held out till his guns were disabled and ammunition failed, and finally he only yielded on honorable terms, and upon promise from the French general of protection to the prisoners. This promise, however, Montcalm did not, or could not, keep. He was either indisposed or powerless to restrain the ferocity of the savages, and, while the English and Provincial troops were marching under nominal protection of a French escort to Fort Edward, the Indians fell upon them and massacred them with every species of cruelty.

Colonel Frye, it is said, never favored the capitulation. He offered in the outset to lead out his regiment to a hand-to-hand fight with the enemy, but was obliged to submit to the dictation of the British officer, Colonel Monro. In the massacre that followed the surrender, he was dragged into the woods, stripped of his clothes, except his shirt, and was about to be murdered when, in the sudden strength of desperation, he sprang upon his foe, and, all unarmed and naked as he was, beat down and dispatched the warrior who was already exulting in his anticipated scalping. Three days he ran through the forests in a state bordering on distraction, suffering in body and mind from the long protracted horrors of the fight, the terrible scenes of the massacre, and his perils and exposure. At last, he found his way back to Fort Edward in a most pitiable condition, half starved and nearly crazed, and in the same naked condition in which he had escaped from the savage. But, with tender nursing, he regained strength of body and mind, and lived to render more valiant service in this war, and in the Revolution he received the commission of Brigadier-general.[1] His extraordinary labors and hardships in the Crown Point expedition of 1757 are thus detailed by him in a memorial[2] to the government : —

"A Memorial of Joseph Frye of Andover in the County of Essex, Esq., setting forth that he was commissioned Colonel of the

[1] Major-general from the Provincial Congress.
[2] *Records of the General Court*, 1759.

Regiment consisting of eighteen hundred men, raised by the Government for His Majesty's Service under the command of his Excellency the Earl of Loudon in the year 1757, and faithfully performed the Duty of his office though attended with uncommon Labour, having no Field officers allowed him for his assistance (as was originally designed) whereby the Duty of the Field officers of more than three regiments as formed for the preceding expedition devolved upon him alone, and a great saving accrued to the Province; that, being the only Field officer, his expences in providing for his Table, &c., were increased beyond what was granted him for that purpose; that besides his personal suffering from the salvages he had the Misfortune to lose all his camp equipage, stores, arms and clothing through the Perfidy and Inhumanity of the enemy at the time of the surrender at *Fort William Henry;* that after his return he was employed for several months in assisting in making up the muster rolls in the best manner he could to prevent Injury to the Public, his papers being all lost, and praying that his faithful services, uncommon fatigues, sufferings, and losses may be taken into Consideration and such Recompense made him as shall be judged reasonable."

"*Read and ordered* that Col. Lawrence, Mr. Wilt, and Capt. Morey be a committee to take this memorial under consideration and Report what they judge proper for this Court to do thereon."

"In Council, *January* 9, 1759."

"30*th Feb.* 1759. The committee appointed on the Memorial of Joseph Fry, Esq., reported according to order.

"Read, and after a large debate thereon voted that Col. Frye have liberty to be heard on the Floor before the House on the subject matter of the said Memorial on the second Tuesday of the next sitting of this Court."

"16 *Mar.* 1759. The House being informed that Col. Frye was at the Door according to the order of the House the last session, he was admitted into the House; and having been fully heard upon the Subject matter of his memorial he withdrew and after a debate; *voted:* that the memorialist be allowed wages from the time of his entering into the service till the 4th of April 1758 at eighteen pounds per month, deducting what he has already received out of the treasury for said service."[1] [Concurred in.]

In another memorial (the petitions of Colonel Frye, during

[1] *Journals of the House of Representatives.*

this war and the Revolutionary War, would make quite a thick pamphlet), Colonel Frye describes the sufferings of his soldiers after the capitulation at Fort William Henry.[1] The object of his presenting the petition is to obtain pay for them from the day of the surrender to their arrival at home; their wages having been allowed only for the time in which they might have reached home by travelling every day, at the rate of fifteen miles per day, whereas they had not been able to come directly home, but had been detained in captivity or had wandered in the woods.

..... "A great part of the officers and soldiers were taken after the capitulation by the Enemy and Detained Prisoners with them till they had Demolished Fort William Henry, carried off the stores, and get ready to return to Canada, which took near a week, and then sent almost naked to Fort Edward where and at Albany they were under necessity to make some stay to get something to cover their Bodies before they could set out for their Respective Homes. Others of them were drove off naked into the woods where they wandered several days before they could get to Fort Edward, and when they came there they were under the same necessity and not only for the same reason to stop as those mentioned before, but being so emaciated by starving in the woods it took some time to recover nature before they were able to Travel." ....

Colonel Frye praises in the highest terms the bravery and fortitude of his men, and shows the most tender regard for their welfare.

In 1762 the same petitioner, Colonel Frye, asked for liberty to settle a township, in consideration of his services and sufferings. The petition contains a statement of the time of his military service, and is interesting as being his own record of this portion of his life : —

"*March*, 1762.[2] A Petition of Joseph Frye, Esq., Praying liberty to purchase a Tract of land sufficient for a township in some place between a River called great Osapee running into Saco River and the mountains above Pigwacket, and as there are sundry tracts of Land that would make good settlements and are not yet disposed

---

[1] *Mass. Archives*, vol. lxxvii., p. 448.
[2] *General Court Records.*

of by the Government, lying below on Saco river, which would be much advanced by the settlements which the Petitioner proposes to make, and as he has spent the prime of his Life in the defense of his country, viz: the last war from the beginning of the year 1745 till the settlement of a peace and the present war from the year 1754 till last December (saving a suspension of eighteen months occasioned by his falling into the hands of the enemy when Fort William Henry was taken and by which he sustained a very heavy loss), he humbly hopes he may be favored in the Purchase."

The petition was granted, and settlement made by emigrants from Andover and vicinity. About the year 1770 Colonel Frye took up his residence [1] there, although he was often subsequently in Andover, and during the Revolutionary War spent some time here and did much to promote the spirit of patriotism.

Some of the soldiers of Colonel Frye's company, at Fort William Henry, were carried into captivity, and spent weary months or years, or, perhaps, their life-time in the enemy's country.

Efforts were made by the government, in 1758, to ransom such captives, and lists were asked for, from all towns which had lost any soldiers. Capt. James Parker, in forwarding the name of his "dear son Jesse Parker," expresses his gratitude and joy for this movement on the part of the government:[2] —

"HONORED SIRS — In obedience to his Excellency the Governor, Directing all persons who have any relatives (Inhabitants of this Province) in captivity in Canada to send a list of y⁰ names into the Secretary's office, with pleasing hopes that some Kind Designs are Entertained and will shortly be put in execution for the redeeming of poor Captives, Do now (with utmost Gratitude to his Excellency and all concerned in so Gratious a design) Inform that my dear Son Jesse Parker of Andover and also Timothy Merick of Methuen in this province were taken captive by the Indians on

---

[1] His homestead, at North Andover, was a part of the estate owned by Mr. Nathaniel Peters, about a quarter of a mile south of his residence (the Col. James Frye house). The house occupied by Col. Joseph Fry was for a time occupied by Mr. John Peters. It has been since taken down.

[2] *Mass. Archives*, vol. lxxvii., p. 705.

or about the 10th of August and after capitulation & have been often heard of since in prison in Canada. . . . .

"Your most obedt humble servant
JAMES PARKER.

"P. S. Benjamin Pettengill of Methuen taken at ye same time but not since heard of."

In 1758 the attempts to take the forts on Lake Champlain and vicinity were again renewed, and also to take Louisburg, which by the treaty of 1748 was restored to France.

Of the military activities at Andover, the following relic is found among the papers of Capt. John Abbot : —

"TO SERGEANT TIMOTHY HOLT,
ANDOVER, *April* 30*th*, 1758.

"You are hereby ordered to Warn in His Majesty's Name all the Train.... Soldiers Belonging to your Precinct under my command to appear upon the Greene by the South Meeting House in Andover aforesaid on Tuesday the Second Day of May next at ten o'clock in the Forenoon with arms complete; all but those whose arms ware Taken for Bayonets, there to attend further orders.

"N. B. The fine for not appearing is £6 lawful Money. Hereof fail not & make Timely return to me of your Doing." [Not signed.]

There are also several printed forms of enlistment — the blanks not filled — among Captain Abbot's papers : —

"I ——— do acknowledge to have voluntarily enlisted myself as a private Soldier to serve His Majesty King George the Second in a company of Foot to be raised for a general Invasion of Canada.

"As witness my Hand this ——— Day of ——— In the year of our Lord 1758.

"County ——— ———

"These are to Certify that ——— Aged ——— years ——— born ——— came before Me, one of His Majesty's justices of the Peace for the said County; and acknowledged to have voluntarily enlisted himself to serve His Majesty King George the Second in the abovesaid service; and that he also acknowledged he had heard read unto him the Second and Sixth Sections of the Articles of War against Mutiny and Desertion and took the Oath of Fidelity mentioned in the articles of War."

On the 7th and 8th of July, 1758, occurred disastrous defeats of the English and Provincial troops, near Ticonderoga, by the French, under General Montcalm. Lord Howe was killed. A paper addressed, "To Mr. John Abbot the 4th, The Account of our Loss At Ticonderoga," gives the names of the killed and wounded. The names of their residence not being given, it is a matter of uncertainty who of them belonged to Andover. The town records register the following death in this year: —

"1758, *Sept.* 2. Jonathan son of Jonathan & Elizabeth Hutcheson died at Lake George in the 18th year of his age."

Capt. Asa Foster commanded a company in the expedition against Canada, in 1758. He presented a "Remonstrance,"[1] dated Andover, March 28, 1759, in regard to a mistake in his muster rolls, by which two of his men were deprived of their pay: —

"To THE HONOURABLE COMMITTEE OF COUNCIL *appointed to examine the muster Rolls of the several Captains in the last expedition towards Canada.*

"The Remonstrance of Asa Foster one of the captains in sd expedition humbly sheweth:

"That in making the muster Roll, there is a mistake in the following persons' wages, viz John Peirce, Simon Frye and Thomas Richardson, each of which persons are made up ten shillings short of their just due in the Collomb of the whole of wages due, as will appear by examining the coppy of sd muster roll; for they all Listed y'e 13th day of April and were all in the service until the 12th of November, which is sevene months and eighteen days, which amounts to £13, 15 and they are Cast £13. 5. 1; wherefore your Remonstrant prays that your Honrs would Rectifie sd mistakes, whereby justice may be done to the persons injured and you will much oblige your very Humble Servt.   ASA FOSTER."

Another relic of the expedition of 1758 to Canada, is the following petition[2] of a father whose son sickened and died on the way: —

"The Memorial of John Farnum of Andover most humbly sheweth that Nathan Farnum, son of your memorialist, in the year 1758

[1] *Mass. Archives*, vol. lxxviii., p. 365.
[2] *Ibid.*, p. 484.

was a soldier in Col. Prebble's regiment in Capt. Herrick's company for the expedition then formed against Canada, and having marched as far as Hadly was taken sick, and upon your memorialist's receiving intelligence that he was unable either to march forward or to Return Home, he made a journey to Hadly to take care of his son; his expence on said journey was one pound six shillings. But before your memorialist arrived at Hadly, his son, then very unable, was marched by the officers Left to bring up the Rear, and soon after his arrival at Lake George he was again taken sick and sent of in a waggon without any assistant to Albany, but was left by the way Near fort Edward unable to help himself, & Sending word of his Difficulties your memorialist was at the expense of a Journey to Albany, which Besides his Time cost him two pounds six shillings, where meeting with an officer of said Capt. Herrick's company he received the News of the death of his son & that nothing could be found of his cloathing, as by the account thereof herewith exhibited may more fully appear.

"Therefore your Memorialist Doth humbly Intreat his Excellency & your Honors to Grant him such a Consideration as in your Great Wisdom & Justice shall appear to be reasonable & Just to defray the charges of your memorialist's journey as aforesaid & make him a compensation for his time and loss of clothing as aforesaid & may it please his Excellency & your Honor your memorialist as in duty bound shall ever pray.

JOHN FARNUM, JUNR.

"ANDOVER, *May* 23, 1759."

The petitioner was granted forty shillings.

The expedition against Louisburg was successfully conducted by General Amherst, who after a few days' siege reduced the fortress to surrender. By the terms [1] of capitulation the garrison was to be sent to England, the merchants and other residents were to be permitted to go to France. In a collection of papers from the Archives of France printed in "Documents Relating to the Colonial History of New York," [2] is a letter written by the Governor of Louisburg who signed the terms of capitulation and was, at the time of writing, a prisoner of war. The letter is dated, "Andover, 23d September, 1758." It is indexed as from Andover, Mass.,

---

[1] See Haliburton's *History of Nova Scotia*, vol. i.
[2] Vol. x., p. 833. Letter of Chevalier de Drucour to M. De Massiac.

although there does not appear to a casual reader anything to determine where the Andover was, whether in America or England. There may have been reasons why it was important for the French Governor to remain in America to arrange the terms of surrender, etc., more fully, and if so there could not have been selected a more safe and at the same time comfortable residence for a paroled prisoner of rank than Andover. Here also was the home of two of the colonels in the service, and as Col. James Frye's house was a public house of entertainment it is not unlikely that the honorable Chevalier de Drucour may have enjoyed the hospitalities of the Andover hero of the siege of Louisburg, in 1745.[1]

An Andover officer, Lieut. Jacob Farrington, was connected with an exploit of the year 1759, which received the great praise of contemporaries, but which, says Bradford, "would be severely reprobated" now "as an act of cruelty." This was the surprisal and destruction of the defenceless Indian village of St. Francois by the celebrated Rogers' Rangers, to which band Lieutenant Farrington belonged. "Reminiscences of the French War," by Caleb Stark, thus describes the exploit alluded to: "The night before the surprise of St. Francis the Indians were engaged in a wedding frolick. Lieut. Jacob Farrington of Andover, Mass., and Benjamin Bradley of Concord, N. H., two of the stoutest men of their time, headed one of Rogers' parties. They came to the door of the house where the wedding had taken place and rushed against it so violently that the hinges gave way and Bradley fell in headlong among the Indians who were asleep upon the floor. They were all slain before they could make any resistance."

Another relic of the service of 1759,[2] is a petition of Moses Bailey, then of Methuen: —

"To His Excellency Thomas Pownal, Esq., *Captain General and Governor in Chief in and over His Majesty's Province of the*

---

[1] The English Lieutenant-governor of Nova Scotia in 1740 was Paul Mascarene. In 1775, Paul Mascarene at Andover advertised in the *Essex Gazette* that he had found some saddle-bags. Whether the two were in any way connected is not ascertained.

[2] *Mass. Archives*, vol. lxxix., page 536; vol. lxxviii., p. 577.

Massachusetts Bay in New England. TO THE HONOURABLE HIS MAJESTY'S COUNCIL AND HOUSE OF REPRESENTATIVES of said Province in General Court Assembled at Boston, January 30th, 1760.

"The Petition of Moses Bailey, of Methuen,[1] Humbly Sheweth that your Petitioner enlisted himself a soldier in his Majesty's service in the company of Capt. Francis Peabody in Col. Willard's Regiment in the year 1759, and at Tyconderoga on the twenty-fourth Day of July as I was in my duty carrying the Cannon I received a wound in one of my legs, by which means I was disabled for Duty and exercised with much pain until the sixth day of October, and then I was ordered by the General to return home and was carried in Boats & Carts to Albany flats in about six days and being then unable to travel I sent to my brother John Bayley to come and help me along home, and I tarried there till he came to me, being about eighteen days, and for my entertainment and attendance there, my brother paid four dollars and a half. My Brother then attended upon me with the utmost care & Diligence and brought me to my father's house in Methuen in ten days and he paid for the whole of my support while he was with me, and I received nothing at the cost of the Province as I returned home from said flats; my brother was eighteen days in his journey and his expenses for the support of himself for me and for his horse (including the four dollars and an half above mentioned) was four pounds fourteen shillings and ten pence. When I arrived at home I applied myself to Doctor Kittredge in Andover for help and cure and tarried at his house and am still under his care, the wound not being yet healed, neither am I as yet able to labour for my support. Your petitioner went forth with a design to exert himself to the utmost of his power and ability (if his life and health should be continued and occasion required) in his Majesty's righteous cause against his enemies in the years past and in that which is coming, but hath been prevented by that unhappy wound and also thereby hath suffered much pain and loss of time. He therefore begs leave to lay his case before your Excellency and your Honours praying for such allowance as in your Great wisdom and prudence you shall think fit and judge meet and your Petitioner (as in Duty bound shall ever pray).

MOSES BAYLEY."

During 1759 and 1760 Colonel Frye's regiment, or a part

[1] This petitioner subsequently removed to Andover West Parish, and settled on the banks of the Merrimack, in the North District. He received a lieutenant's commission, and served in the War of the Revolution.

of it, was in Nova Scotia. Dr. Abiel Abbot,[1] of Andover, was Surgeon's Mate in his regiment, and sent the following petition for pay for service rendered : —

"*June* 9, 1761. Abiel Abbot of Andover humbly shews that he was Surgeon's mate of Col. Frye's regiment & in that department of it which Garrisoned Annapolis Royal in 1759 & 1760, that he was not discharged till the tenth June last, when he was discharged by Gov. Hutchinson; and it seems he is only made up in the Pay Roll until the last of April & the intermediate time between that and said 10th of June is lost to your memorialist tho' he was then in actual service without your Excellency's & Honor's relief.

"Wherefore he humbly prays he may have an order upon the Treasurer for said pay. And as in Duty Bound shall ever pray.

ABIEL ABBOT."

Seven pounds were allowed him.

The government detained the troops in Nova Scotia beyond the time for which they were enlisted, which, though claimed to be a necessity, caused much ill-feeling and mutiny. A petition of a captain from Cambridge,[2] shows that, while Colonel Frye was at Fort Cumberland, Nova Scotia, November 2, 1759, his regiment mutinied and refused to do duty, because the time they enlisted for had expired the day before : " There being no troops at hand to relieve this regiment, if they had deserted the Fort, it would have fallen into the hands of the enemy. Colonel Frye therefore ordered the Captains to demand the arms from the men." The petitioner, Captain Angier, states that in obeying this order to demand the guns, he was in peril of his life ; one man refused to give up his gun, and, when the captain offered to take it, forcibly thrust one end of it violently against his breast, while many of the other men cocked their guns.

The courageous captain, knowing, as he says, that at all hazard "it was his duty to put his colonel's orders in execution, was obliged to draw his sword and strike at the soldier, in order to intimidate him and the company." Colonel Frye testified that, owing to Captain Angier's determination the regiment was subdued, and a general mutiny prevented,

[1] *Mass. Archives*, vol. lxxix., p. 767.
[2] Paige's *History of Cambridge*, quoted from *Mass. Archives*, vol. lxxx., p. 95.

and the Fort saved from the enemy. But the soldier, having had his fingers cut with the sword, sued the captain for striking him, and got a verdict from the jury against the defendant. The captain petitioned the General Court for reimbursement. He was granted fifteen pounds.

There have not been found any records to indicate that Andover men were at Quebec when that city fell before the English, and the famous battle was fought of September, 1759, in which Generals Wolfe and Montcalm were both slain.

The campaign of 1760 was directed against Montreal, which was finally taken. The following is a relic of this expedition : —

"The Petition [1] of Oliver Holt humbly sheweth that your petitioner was a private soldier in the expedition to Montreal in the year 1760 in Capt. Jenks's company, and being sent off as an Invalid was so much Indisposed that he was not able to Travil, when he arrived at Capt. Day's about tenn miles on this side Springfield, and was at the expence of a horse and man to assist him from there to Andover. Therefore, your petitioner prays that your excellency and Honors would take his case under your wise consideration and make me such allowance for s^d expences as in your Great wisdom you shall think proper, which your petitioner as in duty bound shall ever pray. OLIVER HOLT.

"ANDOVER, *April* 6, 1761."

Another petition [2] shows that Capt. Peter Parker, of Andover, was in an expedition to Cape Breton, 1760, in Colonel Bagley's regiment, and that the vessel in which the company set sail for home was blown by storms to the West Indies, and did not reach home till 1761.

Thus were our townspeople driven and tossed hither and thither, on sea and on land, a sacrifice to the ambition and the folly of princes and leaders, in " His Majesty's Service."

A humble sufferer from the campaign of 1760 was one John Beverly, who subsequently became a frequent petitioner and a source of annoyance to the town of Andover. This case affords a melancholy illustration of the sometimes de-

---

[1] *Mass. Archives*, vol. lxxix., p. 656.
[2] *Ibid.*, vol. lxxx., p. 717.

moralizing effects of extreme poverty. His first petition excites sympathy, but, after following him through the town treasurer's accounts for a series of years, and counting up the moneys expended for his maintenance, at least a thousand dollars, we hardly wonder at the impatience which is evinced in the action of the town officers.

"The Petition [1] of John Beverly Humbly Sheweth that your Petitioner, in the year 1760, Inlisted as a Private soldier into Col. Abijah Willard's Regiment, under Capt. William Barrow, & went in ye s^d service to St. Johns, Shambele, & Montreal and was not dismissed till the latter end of December & at No. 4, and the fifth day of January set out for Lunenburg. The Day Proved extream cold & there arose a violent snowstorm and Being lost in the woods & Destitute of any Fireworks could not come to any Inhabitance for more than forty-eight Hours in which time your memorialist was taken by the surgeon & others. He lost both his Feet which came off in three weeks from that time & he ever since is obliged to Go upon his knees & Draw his Legs behind him which are yet Running sores : & so Has Received his support by the charity of Tender hearted & well meaning People. But now Being in Needy & Distressed Surcomstances Humbly Prays your Excellincy & Honors would be pleased to take His case into your wise consideration, to make such supplys for his Relief as you in your Grate wisdom shall see meet, & your humble servant shall as in duty bound ever pray.

his mark
JOHN + BEVERLY."

It appears from the action of the Court on this petition that John Beverly was a minor, was entirely incapable of taking care of himself and (as the court states) "that his master Isaac Blunt, of Andover to whom said Beverly some years ago was put an apprentice by the selectmen of Andover, refuses to take any care of him and that Capt. William Barrow has drawn the said minor's wages," etc.

It was voted that "the selectmen of Andover should take the wages and provide a suitable place that he may learn the Taylor's trade at which calling he may be serviceable."

In 1763, the General Court granted him a pension of six pounds per annum, enough, one would think, to support him

---

[1] *Mass. Archives,* vol. lxxx., p. 650.

with such aid as would be readily afforded by the charity of the town or individuals to a deserving person.

In the Essex Gazette in 1775 appeared a notice, dated Andover, March 31, 1775: —

"It is desired by the selectmen of Andover that no person would have any dealings with one John Beverly, a person of bad character. He may be known by his going about upon his knees, having lost both Feet."

Another notice appears later, setting forth more fully his case: —

"This is to desire all persons not to trust or to have any Dealings with one John Beverly, a person of no Property and under the care of the Selectmen of Andover, who are determined not to pay any Debts of his contracting. He may be known by his going about upon his knees, having lost both feet.

BENJ. STEVENS, 3d, } *Selectmen*
NATHL LOVEJOY, } *of*
JOHN INGALS, } *Andover.*

The life of this troublesome citizen of Andover was remarkably prolonged, considering his infirmities and distresses. It seems longer than it was in fact, because of the frequent mention of his name in the town records and the General Court. He was a persistent petitioner for more than forty years. In 1801, February 6, the House of Representatives had his case under consideration: —

"On the petition of John Beverly of Andover, showing that he had lost both his feet in the service of his country as a soldier in the year 1760 & that the General Court in the year 1763 granted him a pension of six pounds annually, that he is now advanced in years, extremely indigent, and unable to labor, and that from the rise of the prices of the necessaries of life since his pension aforesaid was granted, it has become insufficient for his comfortable subsistence, Resolved that his pension be increased to forty dollars a year and that there be allowed and paid out of the Treasury of the town of Andover annually from this time during the life of said John and for his use the sum of fifty dollars to be disposed of by the overseers of said town for his benefit.

" In senate read & concurred in. Approved."

There is before the writer a book, " History of the American Revolution," which has on its fly-leaf the name of John Beverly. It is not unlikely that he parted with it in his destitution, either for the necessaries of life or for strong drink. However that may be, it was well kept, and yet it bears evidence of having been much read. It is written in the form of Chronicles like those of the Old Testament Scriptures, and doubtless, the quondam soldier, who was debarred by his infirmities from military service in the Revolution, solaced his misfortunes by reading exploits of his friends and countrymen at Ticonderoga, Crown Point, and other places familiar to him.

Beverly was a frequent guest in the kitchens of hospitable housewives of Old Andover, and had a reputation for capacity of eating and drinking. He could drink the "hardest" cider which the cellars had stored, and at one place the family kept a barrel especially for him. He happened to discover the plan from hearing one of the servants, who was to draw cider for him and another visitor of the same stamp, inquire, in an undertone, if she should get it from "Beverly's Barrel." "No," exclaimed he indignantly, "get it from the other barrel!"

A relic of the campaign of 1761 remains, a leaf of a diary kept by Isaac Noyes, a brother of Dr. Ward Noyes. There are only a few lines on a leaf of a small note-book, which has been used for various purposes, and now after all its wanderings and vicissitudes is doing domestic service in an Old Andover kitchen as a cookery recipe-book. In its day, at campfire or by chimney-corner of the inns where its owner tarried, it has seen many a savory, and perhaps many an unsavory meal made ready where bayonets gleamed and powder flashed over frying-pan and kettle, but now the most stirring scenes in which it figures are the concoctions of church-conference puddings and pies or tea-party cakes and doughnuts.

The entire fragment, which has little of the military flavor, save the marching, is as follows: —

"*Aug.* 27, 1761. I set out from Billerica and marched to Concord and Lodged at Howards'.

"28*th*. I marched to Shrewsbury and lodged at furnishes.

"29*th*. Marched to Brookfield and lodged at Adriatic House.

"30*th*. I marched to Kingston and their overtook part of the company.

"31st. I marched to Blandford and Lodged at Knoyes.
"13th. I marched to ——— and lodged at the widow Jackson.
"14th. Marched to   lodgings"

The expenses of the Province for these wars were heavy. In the year 1753, the tax levied was twenty thousand, seven hundred, forty-two pounds. Andover was apportioned eighty-one pounds. The warrant received by Mr. John Abbot, constable, for its collection, authorized him in case of non-payment to "distreyn the Person or persons so refusing or neglecting .... by his or their Goods or chattels, to keep the Distress or distresses so taken for four days at the cost of the owner," and then, if payment were not made, to sell them "at an Outcry," for payment, the overplus, after paying all charges, to be restored to the owner. "If no sufficient Distress can be found, then the Person or Persons were to be committed to the Common Goal as the law directs."

The following list presents the names of the principal officers in service in the French War: —

LIST OF OFFICERS.
1745-1763.

Col. Joseph Frye.
Lt.-col. James Frye.
Adjt. Col. Moody Bridges.
Surgeon Ward Noyes.
Surgeon Abiel Abbot.
Capt. John Farnum.
Capt. Thomas Farrington.
Capt. Abiel Frye.
Capt. Asa Foster.
Capt. Henry Ingalls.
Capt. Peter Parker.
Capt. James Parker.
Capt. Thomas Poor.

Capt. Jonathan Poor.
Capt. Asa Stevens.
Capt. James Stevens.
Capt. John Wright.[1]
Capt. Isaac Osgood.
Lieut. John Peabody.
Lieut. Nathan Chandler.
Lieut. Jacob Farrington.
Lieut. Nicholas Holt.
Ensign Nathaniel Lovejoy.
Ensign George Abbot.
Ensign John Foster.
Ensign William Russ.

Capt. Thomas Farrington entered the service in the Revolutionary War,[2] and the following testimony to his merit as

[1] Lieutenant at Andover, 1748. 1758 at Georgetown.
[2] He then commanded a company from Groton.

an officer is made by James Otis in recommending him with others to General Washington as candidate for a commission: —

COUNCIL CHAMBER,[1] *Nov.* 4, 1775.

"SIR: The Board beg leave to inform your excellency that from the best authority it appears that Capt. David Parsons, Thomas Farrington & Simon Stevens were employed in the service of their country in the late war from the year 1755 to the Reduction of Canada, in the course of which time they were advanced by their own personal Merit from private to the command of companies, and having Signified to the Board their Desire of entering into the present service of the United Colonies and considering that many vacancies have or may happen by Death and Resignations we would therefore recommend them to your excellency as candidates to fill such vacancies in the army as your excellency upon examination shall find their abilities to deserve.

"In the name of or by order of y* council.

"*His Excellency* JAMES OTIS.
"GEORGE WASHINGTON."

Captain Farrington submitted with this paper a record of his service.

As the companies, in service in this war, were not usually made up from men of the same town, and often the names of residence are not given in the muster rolls, it has not been thought best to attempt to collect the names of the soldiers in service.

The men of Andover who during this period represented its interests, and expressed its sentiments in the General Court, may be not inappropriately noticed in this connection. They were active in attending to the welfare of the soldiers, and, to their exertions was due the success of many of the petitions.

A List of Representatives to the General Court, First Quarter of the Town's Second Century.

1746.	Capt. Nathaniel Frye.	1750.	Capt. Joseph Fry.
1747.	Capt. Nathaniel Frye.	1751.	Capt. Joseph Fry.
1748.	Capt. Nathaniel Frie.	1752.	Capt. Joseph Fry.
1749.	Capt. James Stevens.	1753.	Capt. Joseph Fry.

[1] *Mass. Archives*, vol. clxiv., page 176.

1754.	Major Joseph Frye.	1761.	Samuel Phillips, Esq.
1755.	Mr. Joshua Frye.	1762.	Joseph Frye, Esq.
1756.	Mr. Joshua Frye.	1763.	Samuel Phillips, Esq.
1757.	John Osgood, Esq.	1764.	Joseph Frye, Esq.
1758.	John Osgood, Esq.	1765–1771.	Samuel Phillips, Esq.
1759.	Samuel Phillips, Esq.		
1760.	Samuel Phillips, Esq.		

Justices of the Peace.

1761.	Samuel Phillips, Esq.	1765.	Joseph Frye, Esq.
1761.	John Osgood, Esq.	1772.	Stephen Barker, Esq.
1764.	John Osgood, Jr., Esq.		

A relic of the military service of Rev. Jonathan French, in this war, has been found among his papers, in possession of his descendants at Andover, — an Almanac which has his name and "Castle William" written on it. It is for the year 1761. It contains the following verses on the victories of our arms, which, no doubt, thrilled the sensibilities of the then Sergeant French : —

> "How shall my muse in proper lines express
> Our Northern Armies Valour and Success?
> While I am writing comes the joyful news
> Which cheers my heart anew inspires my muse.
> Our three brave armies at Montreal meet,
> A conquest of New France they three compleat.
> To God we owe the Triumphs of the Day ;
> New France submits to George's gentle sway.
> May Lewis that proud tyrant never more.
> Bear any rule upon this northern shore !"

A few notes may here be added respecting the manners and customs, and peaceful avocations of the town in this period. The marchings hither and thither of so many soldiers made the town more or less active and bustling. There are frequent accounts of charges for ferrying soldiers across the Merrimack, and bills for their entertainment at the taverns of Andover. Henry Abbot, innholder, had charges for fifty-one meals, of soldiers who belonged to different companies, one or two of whom at a time seem to have tarried at his house on their way to and from their respective companies. Mr. Daniel Ingalls was also an innholder of this period (1761), and Capt. James Frye. The traders and retailers also did a thriving business. Mr. Samuel Phillips, in the North Parish, and Mr. Isaac Abbot, in the South Parish, have large bills for various articles of merchandise furnished for soldiers. A relic of one of the taverns familiar to Andover men, and an illustration of the customs of the time, is the following petition : —

"*The Petition*[1] *of James Kittredge Jr of Tewksbury in the county of Middlesex*, humbly sheweth —

"That his Father James Kittredge of said town kept a Tavern for many years in the same, his House being situated on the Country Road leading from Andover to Billerica: Travellers have allways Depended upon being entertained there, but ever since the twenty-third day of Jany last people could have none there by reason at that time your Petr's father was taken away by Death and altho' he left considerable of Spirituous Liquors in the House and your Petr. living in the same, yet he dare not let travellers have any, his father's license being no warrant to him in that case, and as its a damage not only to Travellers but to your Petr. to have the stock lay Dead on his hands, he therefore himself prays your excellency and hons. would be pleased to Impower the Justices of Gen. Sessions of the Peace for the county of Middlesex at their next sessions to grant him License to keep a Tavern in s^d House, that those Inconveniences may have a spedy Remedy, and as in Duty bound will ever Pray   JAMES KITTREDGE."

"*Apr.* 21, 1754. It was granted in the House of Representatives.

"Granted to empower the Court of Sessions to give a license to James Kittredge jr."

The physicians and surgeons were also kept busy, not only those who followed the army into field, but also those at home ; for the wounded and sick soldiers were constantly returning, for treatment, to their own homes, or tarrying at the houses of the surgeons. The case of one who stayed four months with Dr. John Kittredge has already been alluded to. The following petition is a still fuller illustration of the customs of the period, in the surgical practice occasioned by the wars : —

[1] *Mass. Archives*, vol. cxi., p. 299.

"These[1] may certify whom it may concern that I, John Kittredge of Andover aforesaid, sometime in the month of August last I saw Lieut. Simon Wade of Medford at the House of my father in Tewksbury which I found in dangerous circumstances by reason of a wound (as he enformed he Received at Fort William Henry in the Late Expedition to Crown Point). My father enformed me that he was doubtful whether he would recover of his wound & to all appearance his wounds looked Incurable. About the term of three weeks (as my Father enformed me) he continued with him, during which time my father enformed me that the canker had taken his sore & it eat to a Great Degree & caused his sore to Bleed half a pint in one night & that he Despaired of his recovery. sometime in the month of Sept' last Mr. Wade put himself under my care (by reason that my father was labouring under bodily Indisposition) & from s^d month of Sept. to the Day of the Date hereof s^d Wade hath been under my care & for the greatest part of the Time his wound was very Bad. I was obliged to take several pieces of Bone out of his Leg & even now Judge him to be quite Incapable of military Duty. JOHN KITTREDGE.

"ESSEX, ANDOVER, *June* 19, 1757."

"Doctor John Kittredge personally appeared and made oath to the above Declaration before me.

JOHN OSGOOD, *Just. Peace.*"

The wars seem, therefore, the principal event of the times. Physicians, clergymen, all classes, were brought into connection with the military affairs. The schools felt the depressing effects of so much military service, especially when the youth, the very flower of the towns, were drafted into the king's service, and even school-boys quitted their Latin accidence for the military manual, the gun, and knapsack. Every class of the community, every trade and industry, was more or less affected ; so that, notwithstanding all that is said about the magnifying of war on the page of history, it is impossible that it ever should be magnified there beyond the reality which it is in a community on which its baleful shadow falls. Perhaps one reason why its incidents are more often recited than those of peace, is that besides their more dramatic and thrilling interest there have been kept fuller

---

[1] *Mass. Archives*, vol. lxxvi., p. 241.

materials for details. Muster-rolls and petitions remain in the archives, memoranda of deaths in the town register, commission and letter, and musket and bayonet, among family heirlooms, while few traces exist of the peaceful avocations of the citizens in the mean time. The same facts are emphatically true in regard to the part which the women of the past took in its history. Except in regard to a very few exceptional women, wives of ministers or eminent men, or women of some very marked individuality, few records exist. The names of women petitioners, for friends and relatives killed or wounded in the wars, show to some extent what their peculiar part was, then (as it has always been, and to a great degree will probably always be), — to endure with patience and fortitude the inevitable. Some women of this time scarcely knew what it was to pass a year without anxious suspense for the fate of husband or son, brother or lover, in the wars. That they bore cheerfully these privations, and in some instances even made great sacrifice for the sake of the suffering, the scanty records show.

Witness the following testimony from the selectmen of Andover, in regard to an Andover woman's hospitality to a stranger soldier : —

"*The Petition*[1] *of the selectmen of the Town of Andover* hereby sheweth : That Jeremiah Burnum of Ipswich, who was in the last year in His Majesty's service at the westward in the Regiment under Col. Joseph Ruggles and company under Capt. Bailey. Upon his return from s^d service he the s^d Burnum was taken sick with the small-pox in said Andover on the 4th of December last. Being utterly unable to Travel any further did then and there cast himself upon the pity and charity of one Mrs. Lidia Tyler, who out of pure compassion to a fellow mortal tho' an utter stranger and with Great inconvenience & Danger to Herself and Numerous Family of small children did Admit said Burnum to her House and after making all Necessary provision for His Comfort that was in her power, any ways consistent with Her and children's safety, did forthwith apply to your petitioners for Relief under her distressed situation. Your petitioners did then take the s^d Burnum into their care and make the Best provision as to Doctor, Nurses, House

[1] *Mass. Archives*, lxxix., p. 456.

Room, &c., that was in their power, which was attended with considerable charge & expense, the Particulars whereof are as follows, viz," etc. [Total nine pounds.]

"ANDOVER, *Feb.* 15, 1761."

In comparing this period of our town's history with the present, it is impossible to avoid the conviction that the long period of military service, and the consequently varied life and many vicissitudes experienced by a large number of citizens, must have contributed to increase the intelligence and mental activity of the community. Distant places became familiar, and many phases of life were known to the Andover yeoman, who had roughed it in camp and field from Nova Scotia to Ticonderoga, had slept beside the Indian in his wigwam, heard mass from the lips of the Jesuit missionary, and been comrade-in-arms of His Majesty King George the Second's Regulars. When we reflect that some of the men were thus trained who fought the battles of the Revolution, we shall not be surprised at the energy and perseverance which carried through successfully that hazardous undertaking of separating from the British government.

The every-day life of the pre-Revolutionary period — this time of the French War — was quite unlike that of a few years later, when "liberty, equality, and fraternity" had changed the social customs.

The early colonial period was of necessity one of simplicity. Few families had wealth, and still fewer had luxuries and elegances. But a hundred years had made great changes. In 1651 the representative to the General Court from Andover, dying, left an inventory of household goods in which not a piece of silver was named, and of which everything was humble in the extreme. But in the valuations and inventories of 1751 to 1771 are mentioned silver plate and chaises and slaves ; and there are families which have relics of that period, heirlooms of silver and mahogany and tapestry, family portraits and wardrobes which show wealth and refinement, and indicate the elegance of apparel and furniture then indulged by persons of social rank. The distinctions in style of living and dress were great, and the humbler classes, even the well-to-do farmers, had the idea firmly implanted in their minds that any attempt to imitate the fashions of the "gentlemen" was foolish and wicked. Yet there was thrift and comfort in many houses where there was no attempt at "style." The following extract, from a will made by one of the rich farmers of North Andover (on the Boxford [1] line), in 1771, is an interesting relic, and illustration of the style of living of the rich farmers. The writer of the will was Mr. John Peabody, father of Capt. John Peabody, of the Revolutionary service, of Lieut. Oliver Peabody, and Rev. Stephen Peabody : —

"As my well beloved wife Sarah Peabody is so far advanced in years as renders her unable to Improve the third part of my Real Estate which by Law she will be Intitled to I have thought that an Annual Supply of the Necessaries and Comforts of Life will be more agreeable to her than the Improvement of a Third of my said Estate can possibly be. Therefore It's my Will and I do hereby order that my three sons shall annually provide and deliver to Her the following articles, viz. Twenty Bushels of Indian Meal, three bushels of wheat meal or Floure equivalent thereto, three hundred Pounds of Porke, one hundred pounds of Beef, fifty pounds of fresh Meat to be either Lamb or Veal as she shall choose, eighty pounds of Butter, one hundred pounds of Cheese, as much new milk as she shall have need of for her own use, or in lieu of the Butter cheese & milk above mentioned to keep her two good milch cows if she shall choose it. Also as much salt & spices of every sort as she shall need for her own use. Likewise six barrels of Cyder, Six gallons of Molasses, four gallons of Rum, fifty six pounds of Sugar, two bushels of Malt, twelve pounds of Sheeps wool, thirty pounds of flax, & as much fire wood as she shall need to be cut fit for her fire and not only brought to her Doore but brought into her Dwelling-Room or Rooms as she shall want it. Also as many apples (such as she shall choose) in my orchard and as many Cabages, Turneps, Potatoes, Carrots, Parnsneps, Beets, green & drie Beans & Pease as she shall want for her own Consumption ; and keep her a good horse, and my chaise in good order Ready at her command whenever she may want to ride to Meeting or elsewhere, and whenever she may be exercised with Sickness or lameness she shall be provided with a good nurse & able Physician as her case may require.

[1] The homestead of the late Daniel R. Gage.

"I give to my said wife the Improvement of Two Rooms in my dwelling house, together with as much liberty in my wash-house as she shall have occasion for, ... the use of my Household goods of every Denomination .... also she shall have sufficient Room in my Pew in the North Meeting-House, in Andover aforesaid, whenever she attends the Publick worship of God there." ....

In some households negro slaves were still kept, and sales were occasionally made, although public sentiment was against it. The apprentice system of labor prevailed, and young persons were bound out to trades and to housework.[1] The mode of travelling had changed largely from the saddle and the pillion to the more comfortable, though less picturesque, family chaise; or for public conveyance, the stage-coach had been introduced. There are among the papers of many families, certificates of taxes, paid at this period and later, for the chaises kept. The stage-coach did not come into general use, except for long routes, as Boston to Portsmouth, until somewhat later, during and after the Revolution.

This pre-Revolutionary and provincial period, when the people were all loyal to King George's government, and when, to a great degree, the aristocratic ideas and customs of the old country prevailed, is a pleasant picture on the page of history, and we cannot help lingering a little regretfully before turning the leaf which opens upon change and commotion and bloodshed, and transforms our townsmen from loving subjects of the sovereign lord, the King of Great Britain, France, and Ireland, to free and independent citizens of the United States of America.

[1] See Chapter I.

CHAPTER V.

THE PART OF ANDOVER IN THE REVOLUTIONARY WAR.

The French War had hardly come to a close before the mutterings of the Revolutionary storm began to be heard, and at no place sooner than at Andover. The town had cheerfully contributed men and money, so long as these were needed, to defend the Province from French aggression, and her proportion of the taxes which followed she bore patiently. This burden was not light, for the levy was chiefly on real estate, in which the wealth of the town principally consisted. Yet, though ready to bear her just part of the common burden, Andover early showed a jealousy of any measure of taxation which looked toward an infringement of the rights of individuals or involved surrender of important principles. Even though for the time the measures might operate to the pecuniary advantage of the community, it was clearly discerned that the temporary gain might prove an eventual loss and permanent harm.

Thus, when the General Court proposed an excise on spirituous liquors, which would lighten the tax on real estate, and the bill was greatly favored by many of the agricultural towns, Andover joined her voice to that of Boston and the sea-board cities against it. It involved the right of search of private houses and conferred powers which were thought to be dangerous and subversive of liberty. When the British Parliament began the series of acts of taxation, and the colonies the acts of resistance which culminated in rebellion, Andover was one of the most uncompromising foes of the oppressive measures.

The passage of the Stamp Act called forth the following declaration of the sentiments of the town, which was given as "instructions" to the representative to the General Court, Mr. Samuel Phillips, Sen. : —

.... "That you do not give your assent to any act of Assembly that shall signify any willingness in your constituents to submit to any internal taxes that are under any color imposed otherwise than by the General Court of this Province agreeable to the constitution of this Government."

The resolution also expressed fears : —

"That by sundry acts, especially by an act commonly called the stamp-act, we are in danger of being not only reduced to such indigent circumstances as will render us unable to manifest our loyalty to the crown of Great Britain, as upon all occasions we have hitherto done by cheerfully exhibiting our substance for the defence of the British dominions in this part of the world, but of being deprived of some of our most valuable privileges which by charter and loyalty we have always thought and still think ourselves justly entitled to."

Furthermore the town charges its representative to strive for the repeal of the obnoxious act : —

.... "To join in such dutiful remonstrances to the king and parliament and other becoming measures as shall carry the greatest probability to obtain an alleviation of the embarrassments the commercial affairs of this province labor under by the vigorous execution of the acts of Parliament respecting the same."

But, while enjoining this upon their representative, the town was careful to express disapproval of the violent measures taken in some places, and urged that the representative should give his influence against them : —

"That you would use your best endeavors in conjunction with the other members of the General Court to suppress all riotous unlawful acts of violence upon the persons and substance of his majesty's subjects in this quarter."

When the excitement increased, and there were hangings-in-effigy, tarrings and featherings, destruction of property, and danger to life, from the too zealous "sons of liberty," the town of Andover did everything possible, to check such unlawful demonstrations ; voting "utter detestation and abhorrence of all such violent and extravagant proceedings," and giving orders to the selectmen, the militia officers, and the magistrates, to coöperate to prevent such disorders ; engaging that the freeholders and other inhabitants should support them in maintaining quiet and order. Indeed, so dispassionate was the general sentiment of the town that it was voted to instruct their representative to use his influence in the General Court to have reparation made to the sufferers in Boston, tories or loyalists, for the losses sustained by them from the violence of the "Sons of Liberty."

Yet the determination to pursue a course of resistance to oppression was strong. The town in 1768 chose a committee to consider what measures could be adopted suited to the exigencies of the time. The members were Samuel Phillips, Esq., Capt. Asa Foster, Capt. Peter Osgood, George Abbot, Esq., Col. James Fry, Capt. John Foster, and Mr. Joshua Holt. They recommended especially "the suppression of idleness, extravagance, and vice, and the promoting of industry, economy, and good morals, and by all prudent means to endeavor to discountenance the importation and use of foreign superfluities and to promote and encourage manufactures in the town."

This report was primarily designed to promote independence of British manufacturers and imports, in resistance to and retaliation for the unjust taxation.

Then it became fashionable to dress in homespun instead of broadcloth and brocade, to practise at the spinning wheel and the loom instead of the embroidery frame and the sampler. Even the students of Harvard College in their patriotic ardor voted "to take their degrees in the manufactures of the country."

The students from Andover, Samuel Phillips and David Osgood, were among the most forward in helping on the patriotic or rebellious spirit, as it was variously styled. Samuel Phillips, for one of his themes, took the subject "Liberty," and wrote his sentiments in regard to British oppression: "We should watch against every encroachment and with the fortitude of calm, intrepid resolution oppose them. Unborn generations will either bless us for our activity and magnanimity, or curse us for our pusillanimity."

While the youth were writing themes and declaiming patriotism, their elders were speaking and acting, where words and action were more perilous and more important. Their action was not, however, always so impetuous as would have been acceptable to young and fiery spirits.

The Convention of Delegates, to which Samuel Phillips Esq., was sent, was moderate and conciliatory in tone, declared their desire to be peace and order, and drew up a humble petition to the King. But before the Convention adjourned, two regiments of the King's troops had arrived in Boston, September, 1768. Doubtless the representative from Andover saw them march up to the Common. At any rate, his son saw them when he came over from Cambridge, as he records in his journal, and his indignation kindled at the sight. The General Court would not transact business under the overawing of British bayonets, and the Governor was obliged to adjourn it to Cambridge. The Boston people became irritable and exasperated and finally desperate, with the "redcoats" always at hand. The mob taunted the troops, the troops fired on the mob.

The Boston Massacre aroused the whole country. Andover voted, May, 1770, "to sustain Boston in repelling tyranny and oppression and establishing those rights which they are entitled to as men and as Englishmen."

The town took a determined stand with regard to any who should refuse to join heart and hand in opposing the acts of the British Government. No man should be harmed by a lawless mob, but all should be punished legally and condignly. All persons who refused to sign the non-importation act were declared to be " enemies of the Country, divested of every public virtue and even of humanity itself, regardless of and deaf to, the miseries and calamities which threaten the people, preferring their own private interest to the liberty and freedom of the community, and sordidly endeavoring to counteract such benevolent and salutary agreement."

With such persons, the lovers of liberty voted to have no commercial or social connections, directly or indirectly. Whoever such persons were, many or few, high or low, they seem to have been effectually silenced and subdued. For, while in almost all the large towns, as Cambridge, for example, tories were numerous, no records of any have been found at

Andover. At the town meetings, every measure was carried *nemine contradicente*. Although the representative from Andover, Samuel Phillips, Sen., Esq., was conservative and cautious, less ardent than some of his constituents, his affiliations were with the prime movers of the Revolution. May 28, 1772, occurs the following in the Records of the General Court: —

"The Secretary went down to the House of Representatives with a message from his Excellency the Governor to desire that they would send up John Hancock and Samuel Phillips, Esq., two of the members of the House who were chosen yesterday Councillors, that they may take the proper oaths and their seats at the Board."

The representative elected as the successor of Mr. Phillips was of a more ardent temperament and fervid oratory. His "instructions," not unlikely to have been of his own composing, are grandiloquent, and were no doubt inspiring to the constituents who heard them read in town meeting: —

"To Mr. Moody Bridges,[1] *Representative for the town of Andover, Sir:* We cannot but be possessed with thoughts pregnant with the deepest sorrow, when on every side we behold the most bold innovations made upon our civil rights. Resentments against the daring invader and distress of mind for the wound liberty had received alternately perplex our anxious hearts, — that liberty which we cannot view but it points us to the Dangerous methods by which it was purchased. How many of our Distant Relations led on by an insatiable thirst for Liberty freely exchanged the crimson stream of Life for her and strictly enjoined it upon Posterity to esteem them as inseparable companions. And now by adhering thereto they have produced ferments and contention. But should our Rulers for that reason be left to do what they please without control? If a Man's house is attacked, he has certainly a right to alarm the neighborhood, and if any bad consequences should ensue upon it, is he to be blamed for them? But to whom must the excess of this warmth and Resentment be imputed? To those who found themselves under the unhappy necessity of standing up courageously in their own Defence or to him who reduced them to that disagreeable necessity. Who may most properly be said to inflame the Mind of the People, those who opposed an un-

---

[1] *Town Records.*

natural scheme which they justly apprehended to be big with their own destruction, or he who projected and persisted in it till it created tumults that threatened the peace and tranquillity of the Province? Therefore, we advise you, sir, to oppose, not with an indifferent coolness, but with unremitted resentment everything that threatens the peaceful and quiet enjoyment of our Liberties.

"We already see the subject deprived of his essential rights to a tryal of juries; his house and business exposed to a parcel of low-lived officers under the absolute direction of the crown and our civil magistrates dependent on the same for their support. We have seen a native of this Province invested with Power resembling that of a Spanish Inquisition. To be condemned to dig half-starved and chilled in Mines where Hope and Daylight never visit the poor wretches could not inspire a true Englishman with more resentment and detestation than this newly invented and alarming Tribunal in a sister Province. May all that is dear in Nature defend us, and not only us but our Domesticities that are possessed of the least degree of feeling, from such an Inquisition. To you we present our tender offspring. Upon you their as well as our own happiness or Misery depend in part, for which you will in future ages receive their unbounded gratitude, or most exasperated imprecations. We further enjoin you to return our sincere thanks to the town of Boston for their unwearied exertions in the cause of Liberty, inform them that although we did not answer their letter personally, yet we received it thankfully, perused it, and united in sentiment with it."

The measures of General Gage, in 1774, were such as to justify the strong expressions of these and other similar instructions to the representatives. He collected at Boston stores and ordnance, seizing all which he could find in the vicinity, fortified Boston Neck, thus cutting off the country people from communication with their friends in the city, and dissolving the General Court, he governed by a Council wholly pliant to his purposes. Thirteen of the councillors elected by the General Court he rejected. Among these were two, well known at Andover, the Hon. Jedediah Foster and Hon. William Phillips. Though not residents of the town, they were closely connected with its interests, and their rejection by the Governor was greatly resented. The people began to talk openly of using force, resorting to arms to maintain liberty.

The First Provincial Congress met at Salem, September, 1774. Mr. Moody Bridges was sent from Andover. The Congress directed a committee to see about organizing the militia to ascertain the quantity of arms, cannon, and gunpowder in the Province, and to encourage military discipline.

Andover had already anticipated this action. In town-meeting, June, 1774, the question being put, "Whether the town will direct the selectmen to make enquiry into the Town-Stock of ammunition and if found deficient to make such additions as the law requires," it passed in the affirmative. This meeting also chose a committee of nine to consider what was best to be done in the embarrassment and distress of the Province, and though, as they say, in view of the approaching Congress in whose wisdom and fidelity they place great confidence they do not wish to commit themselves to any action, to go into "any decisive, binding engagement previous to that Congress, they desire to assure their brethren through the continent of their hearty good wishes to the common cause of liberty and our Country." Thus, high and clear, rang out the voice of old Andover, among the very first to join, or rather to start the chorus that soon swelled strong for liberty and independence.

During the session of the Provincial Congress, the Continental Congress was also in session. The latter was upheld and sustained by the action of the former, and, as the Continental Congress derived encouragement and support from the assemblies of the Provinces, so these in turn were urged on by the patriotic action of the towns. The little gatherings of freeholders and inhabitants in the meeting-houses of Massachusetts, of homespun garb and rustic manners, but of sagacity born of generations of intelligent freeholding and voting, of sobriety from generations of Bible-reading and prayer, and of unfaltering faith in the God of nations, exhibited a firmness and dispassionateness unparalleled in the history of revolutions.

The action and utterances of Andover were among the most determined and dignified. It is impossible to read through the records of our town at this period without feeling pride in the possession of such a heritage. Besides the

HOME OF COLONEL SAMUEL JOHNSON

sturdy patriotism of the yeomanry, the bone and sinew of the town's strength, there was at Andover, more than in most country towns, an element of scholarly culture, a fine sense of propriety, a consciousness of influence.

The town spoke as though her voice was sure to be heard, and as though sensible that her words ought to be well considered and carefully chosen. In Mr. Samuel Phillips, Jr., who, immediately after his graduation, became active in affairs, the town had a valuable acquisition to its counsels. His speeches carried conviction. Says his biographer:[1] "For mere rhetorical declamation he had no aptness and no taste. His was the practical and solid oratory of a calm, far-seeing mind deeply moved yet never swayed by simple emotion."

Here, too, was the elder Phillips, inflexible, conservative,[2] but with his conservatism in the direction of holding to constitutional rights and charters antecedent to Lord North's Parliament and King George the Third, and his inflexibility never to yield to oppression.

Here, too, was Samuel Johnson, the afterward Colonel of the Fourth Massachusetts Regiment, a man of persuasive eloquence and ardent patriotism, and of remarkable personal influence; also preëminent was the Hon. Samuel Osgood, whose voice was listened to with respect by councillors; and there was, moreover, the popular oratory of Moody Bridges, which thrilled the multitude; and the off-hand, rough, but effective speech of Col. James Frye, who, priding himself on being a fighter, and not a maker of phrases, when he had anything to say said it with an emphasis, and elicited applause.

There were, too, in Andover many others who would have been conspicuous where there were fewer distinguished men, of ability above the average of rural towns. A Committee of Circumspection, chosen by the town, June, 1774, included the following names: "Mr. Moody Bridges, Samuel Phillips, junior, Samuel Osgood, junr., Capt. John Farnum, Mr.

---

[1] *Life of Judge Phillips*, by Rev. John L. Taylor.
[2] It was sometimes said he was not in full sympathy with the Revolution, but there is no evidence of his having been ever lacking in patriotism.

Joshua Holt, Capt. Asa Foster, Mr. Asa Abbot, Mr. Nehemiah Abbot, Lieut. Henry Abbot, Dea. Joseph Abbot, Capt. Samuel Johnson, Ensign Josiah Blanchard, Ensign John Barker, Col. George Abbot, Col. James Frye, Lieut. Nathan Chandler, Mr. Benjamin Poor, Capt. Isaac Osgood, Doct. Joseph Osgood, Mr. David Abbot, Lieut. John Ingalls, Mr. Barachias Abbot, Ensign Stephen Holt, John Abbot 4th, Sergeant John Abbot, Mr. William Foster, Mr. Ebenezer Poor, Dea. John Dean, Mr. Benjamin Farnum, Mr. Samuel Frye."

The duty of these was defined to be as follows : —

. . . , " Till there may be a meeting of the town in consequence of the result of the continental congress, to embrace all convenient opportunities by precept and by example to inculcate and urge on the inhabitants the importance and necessity that each individual employ his influence to discountenance every practice that may appear unfriendly to the prosperity of the community, and equally exert himself to encourage those of a contrary tendency and to give them that attention which the nature of their office may require."

Agreeably to the advice of the Continental Congress, the town entered into a "solemn [1] league and covenant to con-

[1] The enemies of their country would have been cordially treated and heartily applauded in Andover of the old country, as appears from the following address [1] : —

"To the King's most excellent Majesty, the humble Address of the Bailiff, Steward, Approved-Men and Burgesses of the Borough of Andevor in Common Council assembled   Most Gracious Sovereign:

"We your Majesty' most dutiful subjects, the Bailiff, Steward, Approved-Men and Burgesses of your ancient Borough of Andover, beg leave to approach your royal person, to testify the abhorrence we have of the rebellious revolt of many of your American subjects, under the false pretence of asserting rights they never had, but in reality with a design of casting off their allegiance to your Majesty, and their dependence in the British Empire of which they are an undoubted part.

" We have too much reason to fear that the spirit of disobedience now raging in this distant part of your Majesty's Dominions with all the madness of arbitrary riot and cruelty hath been worked up to its present alarming crisis, by the artful insinuation of some designing leaders, who have themselves other pursuits in view than what their deluded followers may perhaps as yet suspect.

" We trust and do most sincerely hope that this will eventually turn out to be the case, and that these unhappy and misguided men will soon see the fatal tendency of their rash proceedings and return to their duty."

[1] Force's *American Archives*.

form to the act for non-importation, non-exportation, and non-consumption of British goods." All the persons in town, over twenty years of age, who refused to sign this were to be published in the "Essex Gazette" as enemies[1] of their country, and their names entered on the town records.

A Committee of Inspection for the town was chosen January 2, 1775, "to see that the Resolves of the Continental Congress and Provincial Congress were adhered to — to inspect the merchants and traders in this town," and get inventories of their merchandise, and see that they complied with the orders issued ; also " to *inspect the conduct of every person in the town* touching the aforesaid association."

The names of this committee were : Col. James Frye, George Abbot, Esq., Col. Samuel Johnson, Ensign Joshua Holt, Capt. John Farnum, Mr. Nehemiah Abbot, Mr. Moody Bridges, Ensign Stephen Holt, Messrs. Asa Abbot, Samuel Frye, and Lieut. John Ingalls.

In the December previous, a Committee of Safety had been chosen to maintain " peace and harmony hitherto so happily continued, to suppress all unwarrantable mobs and riots, to promote good will and affection toward one another and more especially by their life and conversation as well as by their prudent and seasonable advice to recommend a reformation in life and manners so much to be wished for, and earnestly supplicated by all good men."

The names of this committee were : " Hon. Samuel Phillips, Esq., Capt. Peter Osgood, Deacon Samuel Barker, Doct. Joseph Osgood, Col. George Abbot, Capt. John Farnum, Capt. Asa Foster, Col. James Frye, Capt. Henry Ingalls, Lieut. Nathan Chandler, Ens. Josiah Blanchard, Ensign Joshua Holt, Deacon Joseph Abbot, Mr. Barachias Abbot, Capt. John Abbot, William Abbot."

Before the year 1775 came in, the military companies had been, by vote of the town, ordered to meet every week, and the moneys collected by the constable, or collectors, were ordered to be withheld from the treasurer under the Governor's control, and to be placed at the disposal of the Receiver-general appointed by the Provincial Congress.

[1] No such names are found.

So, in vigilance and circumspection, in anxiety and preparation, the old year went out and the new year began, — the year whose close would see the soil of Massachusetts stained with brothers' blood, and many homes of Andover desolate ; fathers, brothers, and sons doing duty in a distant camp, or at rest in a soldier's grave.

In February, the town records begin to look like work in earnest : —

"*Voted*, that the enlisted soldiers be furnished with bayonets at the expense of the town. *Voted*, that a committee be chosen to collect the bayonets now in the hands of individuals in this Town and provide such a number of new ones as will be sufficient to supply the minute men. *Voted*, that the Committee chosen at the last meeting to procure bayonets collect as many as they can of those belonging to the Province by next Wednesday, two o'clock, P. M., that they procure one hundred more to be made as soon as possible and supply those firelocks that are effective which belong to the minute men with good bayonets as soon as may be."

What the people did outside of town-meeting, and how the enlisted men referred to had been enlisted, we learn from a letter in the "Essex Gazette," contributed from Andover. It was not then common as now to have correspondence and reports from the several towns, and the publication of this shows that the action of the town was regarded as exemplary and important to be widely known : —

"ANDOVER, *Feb.* 2, 1775.

"Last Tuesday at 2 o'clock P. M. the town foot-companies of the 4th regiment of Militia in the County of Essex, Inhabitants of the North Parish in Andover, being mustered (after attending prayers for the direction of the God of armies), Col. Samuel Johnson, lately chosen first officer of said regiment, addressed himself to the companie and with great zeal recommended to them the necessity of enlisting themselves into the service of the province and in a short time fifty able-bodied effective men, being one quarter part of said companies — more than a third part of whom are heads of families and men of substance and Probity, willingly offered themselves: they were then escorted to an Inn, where they made choice of Capt. Thomas Poor, junr, for their captain, Ensign Benjamin Farnum first lieutenant, and Samuel Johnson junr. for second lieutenant. They then subscribed a covenant obliging them to conform to the Resolves of the former or any future Congress or General Assembly of the Province that hath or may have Relation to their Duty, and by said Covenant subjected themselves to martial discipline for the term of one year from the time of their enlisting. And this day the two companies in the South Parish in this town were mustered at two o'clock afternoon, when after attending prayers for direction, Col. Johnson enlisted forty-five able-bodied men as aforesaid and of the like condition and probity, being one quarter part of said companies last mentioned, who immediately proceeded to make choice of Capt. Benjamin Ames for their captain, Lieut. David Chandler first lieutenant and Isaac Abbot for second lieutenant, and subscribed the covenant aforesaid. All being performed with great unanimity, seriousness and decorum, and the soldiers seeming rather to be animated than disheartened by the late disagreeable news contained in the king's speech."

It will be seen from the above that there were at this time four militia companies at Andover, containing in all four hundred men. The two companies, commanded respectively by Captain Poor and Captain Ames, appear in the muster-rolls of the "Lexington Alarm," in the regiment of Col. James Frye. They are, doubtless, the same referred to here. Although Colonel Johnson enlisted the men they were regimented under Colonel Frye.

The roll[1] of these companies, the names of the men of Andover who first responded to their country's call, is as follows:—

"*A Muster Roll of the Minute Men under the Command of Captain Thomas Poor of Andover in Colonel James Frye's Regiment From the Nineteenth of April, 1775, to the 25th of sd Month.*"

Thomas Poor, Capt.	Benjamin Parker, do.	William Gordon.
Benjamin Farnum, Lieut.	Nehemiah Abbot, Privet.	Joshua Johnson.
Samuel Johnson, 2 do.	John Barker, jun.	Phineas Johnson.
John Chickering, Sergt.	John Barker, 3rd.	Isaiah Ingalls.
Cyrus Marble, do.	Jacob Barnard.	Peter Johnson.
Philip Farrington, do.	Ingalls Bragg.	Phineas Ingals.
William Johnson, do.	John Clark.	Abiel Lovejoy.
Joshua Frye, drummer.	Zechariah Chickering.	Ephraim Lasey.
Joshua Long, fifer.	Thomas Clark.	John Nichols.
John Parker, corporal.	Stephen Farrington.	Timothy Noyes, jr.
Peter Farnum, do.	John Farrington.	Asa Osgood.
John Johnson, do.	Jonathan Gardner.	Abraham Poor

[1] Secretary's office — State House.

Michael Parker.
Stephen Poor.
Timothy Poor, jr.
Enoch Parker.
Daniel Poor, jr.
Peter Poor, jr.
John Parker, jr.

Jonathan Roberson.
Jonathan Stevens.
David Stevens.
Darius Sessions.
Amos Stevens.
James Stevens.

John Tyler.
Simon Wardwell.
James Wiley.
John Wilson.
Samuel Carlton.
Timothy Carlton.

"Each of the above named persons equipt themselves with fire arms and all accoutrements. THOMAS POOR, *Captain*." [1]

"*A Muster Roll of Capt. Benjamin Ames's Company as Minute Men in Col. James Frye's Regiment From the 19th of April, 1775.*

Benjamin Ames, Capt.
David Chandler, Lieut.
Isaac Abbot, Lieut.
Benjamin More, Sergt.
Joshua Lovejoy, Sergt.
William Chandler, Sergt.
Thomas Boynton, Sergt.
David Blunt, Corporal.
Bixbe Abbot, Corp.
Eben'r Holbrook, Corp.
Moses Boynton, Corp.
Joshua More, Drummer.
Caleb Abbot, Rank and File.
Nathaniel Abbot.
Samuel Blanchard.
Jonathan Boynton.
Peter Chandler.

Jonathan Commins.
Nathan Chandler.
William Chamberlin.
Joseph Chandler.
William Dane.
Joseph Dane.
Amos Durrant.
Abiel Falkner.
Theophilus Frye.
George Holt.
William Haggit.
Joshua Holt.
Jesse Holt.
Humphrey Holt.
John Herrick.
Ephraim Johnson.
Josiah Johnson.

Josiah Jones.
Nathan Lovejoy.
David Lovejoy.
Obadiah Lovejoy.
William Lovejoy.
Samuel Martain.
Perley McIntire.
Phineas Osgood.
Joseph Parker.
Carlton Parker.
John Stevens.
Nathaniel Toy.
James Turner.
Jeremiah Wardwell–Pembrook.
Ezekiel Wardwel.
James Johnson.

BENJ. AMES, *Capt.*" [2]

Colonel Johnson was indefatigable in his labors to enlist men for the service. On the 22d of February he was at Boxford, and there, as the "Gazette" records, "he addressed himself with great zeal to the two foot-companies of the Fourth Regiment, recommending to them the necessity of enlisting themselves into the service of the Province, and in a short space of time fifty-three able-bodied and effective men willingly offered themselves to serve their Province in defence of their liberties."

Other towns, Haverhill, Methuen, Bradford, were visited, with the same results. A specimen of Colonel Johnson's mode of address to his regiment is given in a manuscript

---

[1] *Lexington Alarm Rolls*, vol. xiii., p. 42.
[2] *Ibid.*, vol. xi., p. 189.

preserved among his papers. It is the first draft of an address or circular to the regiment. It is crossed off and re-written in some places, and bears no signature, but is perfectly legible, and unmistakably the handwriting of the Colonel: —

"To THE OFFICERS AND SOLDIERS *of the Regiment under my command*, with my sincere Regards to your person, and as a well-wisher to your Interest and Welfare and that also of the whole community, I present to you the following address.

"Considering ourselves under Indispensable obligations to Defend our lives and Liberties against a Potent, Avaricious, Tyrannical Enemy who are incessantly contriving and Thirstily pursuing our utter Ruin, it Becomes us to be diligent in the use of all outward means for Defence, without which we cannot expect Divine Protection; and I would Recommend to soldiers, as they would preserve their lives and liberties and everything dear to them, that they attend to such orders of their officers as they shall receive, and in particular not to fail of Giving their attendance whenever notified to muster, which Duty I fear, according to what information I have had from some companies in the sd regiment, has been too much neglected."

Nor does the Colonel hesitate, while urging faithfulness, to administer needed reproof: —

"Officers giving way to indulgence for some reasons rather than to take such measures as the time points out, fills me with fear that Military Authority will soon be brought into contempt, and who would not shudder at the thought of the Consequence. I therefore enjoin it upon the officers of my regiment that they see their orders punctually obeyed, although they should be obliged to take such measures as the law directs. In order hereunto, Military preparations are the only Measures wherewith we may expect to meet our enemy with safety and success."

After thus encouraging the hearts of the wavering (if there were any who wavered), he goes on to exhort the soldiers to be themselves inspirers of their fellow-citizens: —

"I earnestly call upon all officers in my Regiment to exert themselves in their several places to cultivate a marcial spirit and Disposition and to maintain their sincerity and activity therein by frequent mustering according as the Legislative Assembly has required."

The men enlisted, many of them untrained to subordination, were, perhaps, somewhat reluctant to the implicit obedience necessary for military discipline. But their commanding officer knew that he could appeal to their good sense, that they would yield to moral motives, and submit of their own free will. "Who is the man," he exclaims, "that wants the Law to quicken him to his Duty at such a time as this!" He then gives some directions respecting equipments, and he adds what shows his confidence in the goodwill of the regiment: "Compliance with the above advice & Injunctions will, I trust, tend not only to your Real advantage, but to the joy and satisfaction of your — [commander]."

In March came news of the actual invasion of Essex County by an armed British force. To seize stores at Danvers, they were marching by way of Salem, when their passage over a bridge was disputed by Colonel Pickering's militia. Bloodshed was only averted by the interposition of moderate men, who had influence with both of the opposed parties. The Rev. Thomas Barnard, the grandson of the former minister of Andover, was principal in effecting a compromise. Whether some of the more zealous acquaintances at Andover did not think worse of him for his peace-making may be questioned; for the "martial spirit" had been cultivated to good purpose, and the people were ready to have things brought to the test of the bayonet.

April came in; a remarkably early spring covered the land with verdure, bringing tree and flower into blossom, and starting the tender grain, — the grass and grain and flowers soon to be trampled down by the tread of hurrying troops, and drenched with the blood of combatants. The farmers went to their labors in the field, as usual, but prepared at a minute's notice to quit them. The women did their household duties in a spirit of self-abnegation, awaiting the time when the duties would be unnecessary, the household being broken up. Life was real and intense in those days of waiting. At last the summons came. Who brought it, — what messenger galloping through the night, neither history nor tradition tells; but old men remember how their fathers have described the ringing of the meeting-house bells in the early morning,

April 19, 1775, the beat of the alarm-drum, the hurrying hither and thither of breathless messengers, — how oxen were left standing in the field, ploughs in the furrow, the hammer dropped on the anvil, the shuttle at the loom, the corn left unground at the mill, the food untasted on the table, — how men seized musket and bayonet, and with hardly a good-by or a God-bless-you, were off.   Col. James Frye's eldest son was a farmer living across the Merrimack, in the town of Methuen.   He was ploughing in the field near his house when the news came that the minute-men were ordered to march. His wife, knowing that he would lose no time, hastened out of the house to bid him good-by, but she found only the oxen and plough standing there.   Hurrying down the road toward the town, she could from the top of the hill just descry her husband in the distance running at full speed.   At her loud call he waved his hat, and was soon out of sight.[1]   From Boxford, Lieutenant Peabody, also at his field labors, heard the North Andover meeting-house bell, and, bidding a hasty farewell, left his family, not to return to them for months.

The names of the captains who marched in command of companies on that day have been variously reported.   Those given here are made up from the State muster-rolls of the "Lexington Alarm Rolls."   There is something thrilling in the very names of the great folio volumes, which are crowded with the lists of the long-forgotten dead.   From the silent pages sounds out to us through the centuries the cry which penetrated not alone to "every Middlesex village and farm," but which awoke the echoes of all the adjoining counties and towns and summoned their citizens to the conflict.

Besides Capt. Benjamin Ames's Company and Capt. Thomas Poor's, there are rolls of companies acting under Capt. Peter Poor, First Lieutenant of Capt.[2] James Sawyer's Company, Capt. Henry Abbot, Capt. Nathaniel Lovejoy's Company, under Lieut. John Adams, Capt. Joshua Holt.

The following are copies, the particulars of pay, time of enlistment, etc., omitted.

[1] Frye Genealogy, MS., by Mr. Theophilus Frye.
[2] Not of Andover.

"*Muster Roll of Company Marched from Andover to Cambridge, 55 miles, Apr. 19, 1775.*"[1]

Peter Poor, Lieut.	Saml Chickering.	Thomas Kinne.
Tim⁰ Osgood, Lieut.	David Chadwick, jr.	Stephen Messer.
Jedediah Holt, Sergt.	Joshua Chadwick.	Peter Marston.
John Philips, Sergt.	Eben Clarke.	Daniel Osgood.
Andrew Peters, Sergt.	David Chene.	Daniel Page.
Phineas Barker, Sergt.	Thomas Emes.	Benja. Peters.
Benj⁰ Abbot, Drummer.	William Frye.	John Poor 3d.
John Abbot.	Abijah Fuller.	William Peabody.
Spofford Ames.	Simeon Farnum.	John Stickney.
John Bridges.	Jacob Grainger.	Timothy Stevens, jr.
James Bridges, jr.	Samuel Holt.	Jacob Stiles.
Asa Barker.	David How.	Jacob Tyler, jr.
Isaac Barker.	Tim⁰ Johnson.	Joshua Wilson.
Benj. Barker.	Henry Ingals.	Obadiah Wood.
Isaac Carlton.	John Kittredge.	Sam Fowler.

"*Dec.* 29, 1775. Capt. Peter Poor made oath to the truth of the written roll. PETER POOR, *first Lieut.*

"*A True Roll of the Travel and Service of myself and the Men under my command who marched in consequence of the alarm made on the 19th of April, A. D. 1775.*"[2]

Captain Henry Abbot.	Abiel Holt.	Joseph Jackson.
1. Lieut. William Foster.	Thomas Holt, junr.	Jonathan Lovejoy.
2. Lieut. John Abbot.	Zela Holt.	Daniel Lovejoy.
Sergt. Darius Abbot.	Jacob Holt.	Joseph Lovejoy.
Clerk Moses Abbot.	Simeon Holt.	Abraham Mouar.
Sergt. Samuel Jenkins.	Asa Holt.	Thomas Manning.
Sergt. Joseph Holt.	Ezekiel Hardy.	Daniel Poor.
Sergt. Jonathan Abbot.	David Holt.	John Patten.
Nathan Abbot.	Edward Herrick.	James Parker.
Asa Abbot.	George Holt.	Uriah Russel.
Nathan Abbot, jr.	Dane Holt.	Jedediah Russel.
John Lovejoy Abbot.	Timothy Holt, junr.	James Turner.
Samuel Burnap.	Nathaniel Holt.	Oliver Whiting.
James Burnap.	Peter Holt.	Solomon Wardwell.
Philemon Chandler.	Jabez Hayward.	Samuel Woodbridge.
John Chandler.	Humphrey Holt.	Peter Wardwell.
Jonathan Cummings, jr.	Joel Jenkins.	Daniel Wardwell.
Ebenezer Dale.	Samuel Holt.	Pomp Lovejoy.
Jacob Foster.	Abijah Ingals.	Benjamin Eaton.
William Goldsmith.		

[1] *Lexington Alarms*, vol. xiii., p. 62.
[2] *Ibid.*, vol. xl., p. 193.

"Capt. Henry Abbot appeared and made oath of the truth of the foregoing before me.   SAMUEL PHILLIPS, *Jus. Peace.*

"*Feb.* 14, 1776."

"*A Muster Roll of Capt. Nathaniel Lovejoy's Company in Col. Samuel Johnson's Regt. that marched April 19, 1775, under the command of Lieut. John Adams.*"[1]

John Adams, Lieut.	Joseph Faulkner, jr.	Saml Sessions.
John Frye, Lieut.	Simeon Foster.	Cyrus Stiles.
Saml. Barker, Sergt.	Benja. Fisk.	Phineas Tyler.
Nathan Town, Sergt.	David Fisk.	Aaron Town.
Samuel Farnum, Sergt.	Lemuel Holt.	Peter Town.
Josiah Long, Drum.	Daniel Holt.	Moses Town.
Paul Averil.	David Ingalls, Jr.	William Wilson.
David Beverly.	Nathan Ingalls.	Joshua Wood.
John Berry.	Edmund Ingalls.	Joshua Wardwell, jr.
Joseph Batchellor, junr.	Stephen Johnson.	Ebenr Thompson.
Danl Batchellor.	Danl Kimball.	Danl Carlton, jr.
Uzziel Batchellor.	Amos Kimball.	Benj. Farrington.
Elijah Barker.	Asa Lovejoy.	Benj. Berry, jr.
Joshua Barker.	Moses Lovejoy.	Thomas Gray, jr.
Christopher Carlton, jr.	Stephen Long.	Thomas Farnum.
James Fry, junr.	Solomon Martin.	Joshua Holt.
Benjamin Fry.	Peter Stevens.	

"N. B. The company marched from Andover to Cambridge by ye way of Billerica.   JOHN ADAMS."

"*In this Role*[2] *is contained the Names of those belonging to the fourth foot company of Andover who marched in consequence of the alarm on the 19th of April A. D. 1775 Under the Command of Joshua Holt with an account of Travel from their Alarm Post to Cambridge & from Cambridge to the Place again with the expence and service Set in Distinct Colums as follows :*"[3] —

Capt. Joshua Holt.	Ezra Anice (?)	Moses Kimball.
Lieut. Nehem. Abbot.	Obadiah Johnson.	Isaac Osgood.
Ensign Jonathan Abbot.	Saml. Frye.	Daniel Ordway.
Sergt. Moses Bailey.	Philemon Dane.	Nathaniel Sawyer.
Sergt. Ephraim Abbot.	Francis Dane.	Charles Furbush.
Sergt. Jeduthan Abbot.	Abiel Stevens.	Jeremiah Blanchard.
Sergt. Benjam. Ames.	Jeremiah Lovejoy.	Samuel Bailey, jr.
Clerk John Mooar.	Josiah Blanchard, jr.	Ebenezer Dow.
Samuel Phelps.	Josiah Johnson.	Nathan Chandler, jr.
Obadiah Foster.	Samuel Lovejoy.	Joseph Shattuck.
Shemuel (?) Griffin.	Thomas Peavey.	Joseph Shattuck, jr.

[1] *Lexington Alarm*, vol. xi., p. 188.
[2] *Ibid.*, vol. xii., p. 136.
[3] The " expence and service " are here omitted.

Aaron Blanchard.	Zebad[a] Abbot.	Simon Crosby.
Ezra Anice, jr.	John Foster.	Zebad[a] Chandler.
Isaac Chandler.	Daniel Blanchard.	Jonathan Buxton.
Isaac Chandler, jr.	Benj. Buxton.	Gideon Foster.
Joshua Chandler.	Samuel Stevens.	Nathan Bailey.
William Blunt.	Samuel Stevens, jr.	James Anice.
Samuel Fealds, jr.	William Clark.	Isaac Ingalls.
Daniel Dane.	John Wood.	James Barnard.
Peter Martain.	Benj. Wood.	Thomas Smith.
Joseph Chandler.	Israel Wood.	Joseph Blanchard.
Kendal Parker.	Thomas Haggit, jr.	Abijah Clark.
Jacob Osgood.	Joseph Burt.	Samuel Kittredge.

"*Jan.* 13, 1776, Made oath Joshua Holt before S. PHILLIPS."

The roll of Capt. Joshua Holt's company has appended to it the following statement:—

"There were also in the aforesaid company a number of aged men and some unable to bear arms who rode to Cambridge on the day of said alarm and the day following to carry provisions for those who stood in need, who humbly ask the same allowance for time and travel that is made for others, having made no charge for the provisions they carried. their travel to and from Cambridge is generally about thirty-six miles.

DEA. JOHN DANE.	SAML. FIELDS.
THOMAS BLANCHARD.	JAMES HOLT, JR.
JOSEPH DANE.	EBENEZER RAND.
BENJ. MOOAR.	WILLIAM DANE."

It has been often written that Benjamin Farnum commanded a company on the 19th of April. But he was then Lieutenant of Capt. Thomas Poor's company. In May, he was promoted to the rank of captain.

Two other citizens of Andover were in important service at this time, Mr. Bimsley Stevens and Mr. Samuel Osgood. Mr. Bimsley Stevens went to Cambridge on the alarm, and was invited by General Ward to serve as his adjutant. The following is Mr. Stevens's record [2] of the fact:—

"*Nov.* 8, 1775. Petition of Bimsley Stevens begs leave to relate that on the 19th of April last, having come to Cambridge on the alarm occasioned by the Invasion made by the king's troops, General Ward requested your petitioner to serve the army in the ca-

---

[1] *Lexington Alarm*, vol. xii, p. 136.
[2] *Records of General Court*, also *Mass. Archives*, vol. ccvii., p. 174.

pacity of an adjutant General, in which department he consented to subject himself to great labor and peculiar fatigues arising from the unsettled confused state of the Regiments and exerted himself to render the best service in his power. In this station he continued till the 28th of June," etc. [Praying for compensation for services.]

In 1776 Mr. Stevens was adjutant in the Fourth Regiment. Mr. Osgood[1] was appointed, April 20, aid-de-camp to General Ward. He had been a member of the Provincial Congress, which sat at Concord, and which was dissolved April 15th. He says (in his autobiography) that on the 19th of April he marched to Lexington as captain of a company of minute-men, of which he had been some time in command. But no record of any such company has been found in the rolls. This might be accounted for from the fact that on the 20th of April he was appointed aid to General Ward. His testimony is explicit in regard to his part in the Lexington fray: —

"April 19 the Battle of Lexington took place. He [Mr. Osgood] had for some time been a captain of a company of minute men. He marched with them on that day about twenty miles to Lexington and from thence to Cambridge, about 15 miles more, in pursuit of the British troops. The American army immediately collected together at Cambridge and the commander-in-chief Gen. Ward appointed him one of his aids, in which situation he continued till Feb. 1776, when he quitted the army, not having much taste for military matters. The offer of the command of a Regiment had no effect on his mind. He returned to private life, but the town of Andover would not permit him to enjoy it. He was immediately sent to the State Congress, who appointed him a member of their Board of War."

Among the private papers of Mr. Osgood are several letters from a British officer, a prisoner, who had been captured April 29th, at Cambridge (on his way to Boston from Canada). This officer, Major Dunbar, had served in America, in the French and Indian war, and was, at the breaking out

---

[1] Ward's *Register* — Appendix. Also Petition for allowance for service of Samuel Osgood, as Major of Brigade, from 19th of April. — *Records of General Court*.

of the Revolution, Mayor of Quebec. With the desire (as he says in one of his letters to Mr. Osgood) to see a part of America he was unacquainted with, and to meet some of his old friends and acquaintances then brought by the fortune of war to Boston, he had set out for General Gage's headquarters, when he was intercepted at Cambridge. He was placed on parole, first at Woburn, afterward at Newbury, and remained a prisoner some months. He wrote a series of letters to Mr. Osgood, in all of which, except the last, he manifested the greatest regard and gratitude for the kindness shown him by Mr. Osgood in obtaining mitigation of the severities attending his condition as a prisoner. Having, however, been at length exchanged, he adopted a more distant and dignified address, as perhaps became an "enemy of war," although it savors of ingratitude. When he was on his way from Woburn to Newbury he took the opportunity to pay his respects to the wife of Mr. Osgood, at Andover. Regarding his visit he writes : —

"On my journey hither I did myself the pleasure to call on Mrs. Osgood at Andover, who by her behavior confirmed any good opinion her husband may have of me. We compared notes together and both seemed to be unhappy enough from the present melancholy situation of affairs."

Mrs. Osgood (Miss Martha Brandon) was at this time only four months married. She was the niece of Madam Phebe Foxcroft Phillips, and had been brought up with that lady in the family of her grandmother, Madam Foxcroft, of Cambridge. She had had all advantages of social culture and education, and her letters show that she was remarkably gifted in easy and graceful writing. She is said to have been a great favorite, the life of the social circle, charming in manner, and of much personal beauty. Her early death, only three years after her marriage, was deeply mourned. Mr. Osgood writes of her : —

"She was of one of the most ancient, respectable, and pious families in the state. In beauty and merit she was surpassed by none. In piety by very few of her age. In Aug. 1778 she received intelligence that her uncle in Cambridge, in whose family she had been brought up, was very ill. Her affection for him, for she was his greatest favorite, would not permit her to hear of his sickness and not visit him. She went and never returned. She was seized with dysentery and died after a few days' illness, never having had any children. Her education was excellent. The softness of her manners and her sympathetic tenderness insured her the affection of all who knew her. Time alone blunted the edge of this almost insupportable affliction."

The companies which went from Andover to Lexington marched through Tewksbury and Billerica toward the scene of action, but, learning of the fight and the retreat of the regulars, they turned and took the road in pursuit. They did not, however, overtake the enemy. All they saw was the straggling line of the fleeing, the wounded and dying left by the road-side, and the burning houses and ravaged farms on the track. The march of Captain Poor's company is thus described in the Journal of the then Lieutenant Benjamin Farnum : —

"*April* 19, 1775. This day, the Mittel men of Colonel Frye's regiment were Alarmed with the Nuse of the Troops marching from Boston to Concord, at which Nuse they marched very quick from Andover, and marched within about 5 miles of Concord, then meeting with the Nuse of their retreat for Boston again with which Nuse we turned our corse in order to catch them. We retreated that Day to Notme [Menotomy] but we could not come up with them. The nit coming on, we stopped; the next day we marched to Cambridge."

From this point to March 28, 1777, the leaves of the Journal are missing. Only a few memoranda for May and June remain on the inside of the cover, on which also this account of the Lexington alarm is written.

Many legends and traditions are told of the events of that day, and the scenes witnessed by various soldiers. Charles Furbush,[1] a private (afterward captain) of Capt. Joshua Holt's Company, and another, said to have been Captain Ford, of

[1] Of West Parish, near Wood Hill. A part of Captain Charles Furbush's farm, given by him to his son, Simeon Furbush, is now owned and occupied by a grandson of the latter, Mr. Simeon Bardwell, whose mother, Rachel Furbush, was the wife of Rev. Horatio Bardwell, D. D., one of the first missionaries to India.

Chelmsford, were fired upon by a British officer from a house which he was plundering. They rushed in and killed the man. They were used to the sight of blood, having served in the French war, but though veterans in the horrors of war, their souls revolted at some of the dreadful sights of that day. They related [1] that our men seemed maddened with the sight of British blood, and infuriated to wreak vengeance on the wounded and helpless. A fallen grenadier had been stabbed again and again by the passers-by, so that the blood was flowing from many holes in his waistcoat. Furbush and his comrade, cooler and more compassionate from experience in regular warfare, and, perhaps, remembering the days when they had called these men companions-in-arms, gently lifted up the dying soldier and gave him water to drink, for which he eagerly begged.

Another Andover soldier, Thomas Boynton, of Captain Ames's company, kept a journal of these days. A leaf of it was printed, 1877, in the " Proceedings of the Massachusetts Historical Society " : —

"ANDOVER, *April* 19, 1775.

"This morning, being Wednesday, about the sun's rising the town was alarmed with the news that the Regulars was on their march to Concord. Upon which the town mustered and about 10 o'clock marched onward for Concord. In Tewksbury news came that the Regulars had fired on our men in Lexington, and had killed 8. In Bilricke news came that the enemy were killing and slaying our men in Concord. Bedford we had the news that the enemy had killed 2 of our men and had retreated back ; we shifted our course and persued after them as fast as possible, but all in vain ; the enemy had the start 3 or 4 miles. It is said that their number was about 1500 men. They were persued as far as Charlestown that night ; the next day they passed Charles River. The loss they sustained as we hear were 500 ; our men about 40. To return, after we came into Concord road we saw houses burning and others plundered and dead bodies of the enemy lying by the way, others taken prisoners. About eight at night our regiment came to a halt in notime. The next morning we came into Cambridge and there abode."

Still another soldier's journal has been found, that of pri-

[1] The story is told by the grandson of Captain Furbush.

vate James Stevens, in Capt. Thomas Poor's company. It begins April 19, 1775, and continues to June, 1776. From it we learn that the news of the march of the British ("that the Reglers was gainst Conkerd"), reached Andover at seven o'clock in the morning, and that Captain Poor's company gathered at the Meeting-house, and marched "through Tewkesbury & Billerica." "We stopped to Polerds & eat some bisket & Ches on the common." At Lexington, says the Journal, they came "to the destruction of the Regelers," — the traces of the bloody work made when Major Pitcairn ordered the troops to fire: —

"They killed eight of our men & shot a cannon ball through the metin-house. We went along through Lexington & we saw several regerlers ded on the rod & some of our men & three or fore houses was Burnt & som hoses & hogs are kild, they plundered in every house they could get into, they stove in windows & broke in tops of desks, we met the men a coming back very fast."

The march to Boston is described, and the arrival at Cambridge. The Journal then goes on as follows: —

"*Thursday*, y' 20, this morning we had alarm about day, we imbodied as soon as possible & march into the comon; we herd that the regerlers was gon to Boston, we staid on the comon a spel & then we retreted back to the hills & expected them out on us. we herd severl small arms & one or two swevels from a tender. We staid awhile, ten or aleven a clock, & then come down & got some refreshment & men come in very fast."

The "refreshment" here alluded to may have consisted in part of supplies from home, provided by the solicitude of friends, for the town records of Andover show that provisions and clothing and arms were sent to camp: —

"To pay Andrew Peters for a Barrel of Pork delivered April 20, 1775, to send to Cambridge to the militia and minute men of Cambridge belonging to the town." — "To pay Lieut. John Adams for making six pairs of shoes." — "To pay Capt. Wm. Peabody for making two bayonets."

The Journal is thus continued: —

"*May* 1, Lieut. Farnum come this morning very early & praded with us, the image of General Gage was burned on the common."

"*May 4th.* Brag & Roberson & Ben Parker & I went up to the upper yard and sarsh a little Pond after some regelers guns, for they sed that they threw in som."

Life in camp was not eventful; now and then it was varied by a visit from friends : —

"*Fryday 5th.* Stephen Barker came and brought us some nus. I watched with Osgood — Asa — Saturday I staid with Asa Osgood all day — his brother come down to se him.

"*Sunday ye* 7, forenoon I went to the meting-house [1] and herd the President preach from Matthew the 10th & 28th vers.[2] In the afternoon I went about a mile and a half tords home & herd a sermon from numbers the 1st (?) 13 vers.

"*Wednesday ye* 10. We got our breakfast & then went on the pread in the morning & Capt. Poor come out & spok very rash concerning our chusing a sargent & said that we had no right to, which displeased the soldiers very much ; they went up & did no duty that Day ; about seven o'clock we praded & Capt. Poor come & said that he was misunderstood & the company setled with him by his making som recantation."

It was not long after this that Lieutenant Farnum was put in command, and Captain Poor was commissioned Major of the regiment. The Journal chronicles various other events of little general interest, and continues thus : —

"*Thursday* 11. It was fast. I went to meeting & herd Mr. Adams preach. Afternoon I staid at home to cuk."

On Monday, the 15th, James Stevens and his comrades Wiley and Enoch Parker obtained a pass to go to Andover : —

"We sot off for hom about a leven a clock ; we got hom about eight a clock . . . . Tuesday I staid at hom this forenoon & mad a par of feters for my mare."

The soldier seems to have spent a good deal of time visiting, going "to father Peters, to Jedediah Farnums, to Bradford, to Boxford, to decon hoveys ; " and on Thursday " got ready very early to go to the army." He was, doubtless, the hero of the hour, and if he talked as fluently as he wrote,

---

[1] He was a devoted attendant on divine service.
[2] "And fear not them which kill the body," etc.

must have entertained his friends with full descriptions of his adventures since his departure on the day of the alarm.

On Saturday, the 27th (?) May, James Stevens was called on to show his courage under fire. An alarm came that the regulars were landing troops from a vessel of war, and a detachment of the American forces was ordered to the spot. They marched to Chelsea, within a quarter of a mile of the ferry : —

"As soon as the reglers saw our men they fired on them, the firing begun on both sides & fired very warm, there com a man & ordered us over a nol rit into the mouths of the cannon. we got onto the top of the nol & the grap shot & cannon bauls come so thick that we retreated back to the rode & then marcht down to the ferry, the regerlers shouted very much. our men got the cannon & plast them & gave them two or three good broad sides & the firing sest in a measure & there was a terrabel cry amonst the regelers, they fired onst in a while all night. about ten o'clock the scooner ran on the ———— & stuck fast; there cum a slup for her relief & they left the sconer.

"*Sunday ye* 28, this morning about day they com with thare barges to bord the sconer. Cornel Putnam com & ordered us down to the wharfe & we fired so that they retreted back to the sloop our men run down & fired the sconer it burst very fast, the slup begun to of in about three quarters of a our after it was sot on fire, the magersene Blod up & blod out som plunder, they fired from Nodles iland on us about an hour . . . . we are retren back to our packs & go at our Brekfast, the slup drad of to Boston. there was of our men wounded fore non cild."

In another part of the Journal is —

"*A List of the names of the Men belonging to Mager Poor's company that was at the taking of the Schooner.*"

Jno. chickering.	Jacob Tyler.	Simon Wardel.
Wm. Johnson.	John Barker.	Jno. Turner.
Peter Farnum.	Josh. Wood.	Jonath Gardner.
Jno. Johnson, jr.	Daras Sessions.	Saml Wiley.
Josh. Johnson.	Tim. Carlton.	James Stevens.
Micah Parker.		

The honorable record of Major Poor's service, and his promotion to the rank of colonel, are noted in an obituary in the "Haverhill Observer," October 2, 1804 : —

"Died at Methuen,[1] Sept. 24, Col. Thomas Poor, aged 72. In his youth he led a company against the French army in Canada. In the war of '76 by his valor and integrity he honored the several commissions of Captain, Major, and Colonel."

"In peace he served his country as a legislator and has ever since been a promoter of good order, honor and integrity by his life and conversation."

The list of names of the men, at the taking of the schooner, is followed by some verses, which were doubtless familiar as an army song to the ears of Andover soldiers:—

"A SONG.

"Americans, to arms repair!
Honour & glory beat to war;
Exert yourselves with force & might
And show how American Boys can fight
For to maintain their charter right.
 Huzza, Brave Boys!

"Hark, how the Warlike trumpet sounds
Whare there is Nought but Blood & Wounds:
The Drums a beating, Colours fliing,
Cannon roring, tories Dieing,
These are the noble effects of War!
 Huzza, Brave Boys!

"Ye that Rain masters of the serf
Shake off your youthful sloth & ese;
We'll make the hauty torys to know
The torters they must undergo
When they engage their mortal foe.
 Huzza, Brave Boys!

"Display your colours, mount your guns,
Bater their castels, fier their towns!
United sons of American fame
Let not your courage tame,
We'll drive the tories back again!
 Huzza, Brave Boys!

[1] The residence of Colonel Poor, while he lived at North Andover, is supposed to have been near the Shawshin, the ancient house now standing on the old road to Lawrence, on the east bank of the river.

> "Why then should we be Daunted at all
> Since we are ingaged in such a caus,
> As fiting for our rights & laws;
> Enduring in so just a cause
> We 'll prove their fulle overthrow !
>   Huzza, Brave Boys !"

The anxiety and distress of those who were left at home on the day of the Lexington alarm, after the able-bodied citizens, and not a few of the feeble and decrepit and many of the boys, had departed to the scene of conflict, can be readily imagined. Everything had been for a few hours in hurry and confusion; the bells ringing, drums beating, the roads alive with the gathering of troops, the houses filled with the bustle of preparation and the voices of farewell. Now all was still again. But it was not the same stillness as before the alarm, — the peace of a spring morning in the country, broken only by the cheerful sounds of labor, nor yet the hush of the Sabbath, the assembled village at prayer in the sanctuary or in subdued social converse in the family circle. It was the silence of desolation, the stillness that oppresses when war or pestilence have swept over happy communities. The fortunes and the feelings of those who marched forth that day at their country's call have been often described and imagined. But the records and the legends of the events and scenes in the deserted villages and towns are comparatively few. A lady of North Andover relates that her grandmother told her of a panic in one neighborhood, a rumor that the regulars were coming to plunder the town. Valuables were packed, and some of the people were about to flee with them to the woods near Den Rock, where they thought to hide and find shelter, when word came that this was a false alarm.

But we are not limited to imagination and tradition for our knowledge of the scenes of distress on that day. The following extract[1] from a letter of Mrs. Winthrop, wife of Professor Winthrop, to Mrs. Mercy Warren, puts us in possession of some of the actual facts. She fled from Cambridge to Andover with her husband, who was sick: —

[1] *Mass. Hist. Soc. Proceedings*, 1875-1876.

"It seemed necessary to retire to a place of safety till the calamity was passed. My partner had been a fortnight confined by illness. After dinner (19th) we set out not knowing whither we went. We were directed to a place called Fresh Pond, about a mile from the town, but what a distressed house did we find there, filled with women whose husbands were gone forth to meet the assailants; seventy or eighty of these with numbers of infant children, crying and agonizing for the fate of their husbands. . . . . Another uncomfortable night we passed, some nodding in their chairs, others resting their weary limbs on the floor. . . . . To stay in this place was impracticable. . . . . Thus with precipitancy were we driven to the town of Andover, following some of our acquaintance, five of us to be conveyed by one poor tired horse-chaise. Thus we began our pilgrimage, alternately walking and riding, the roads filled with frighted women and children, some in carts with their tattered furniture, others on foot fleeing into the woods. But what added greatly to the horror of the scene was our passing through the bloody field at Menotomy, which was strewed with the mangled bodies. We met one affectionate father with a cart looking for his murdered son and picking up his neighbors who had fallen in battle, in order for their burial."

The quiet and repose of Andover's serenity, after these scenes of horror, was a benediction to the wanderers. Mrs. Winthrop writes:—

"I should not have chose this town for an asylum, being but twenty miles from sea ports where men of war and privateers are stationed; but in being fixed here I see it is not in man to direct his steps. As you kindly inquire after our situation, I must tell you it is rural and romantically pleasing. Seated in a retired spot, no house in sight, within a mile of neighbors thinly settled; the house decent and neat stands under the shade of two venerable elms on a gentle rising, one flight of steps with a view of a spacious meadow before it, a small rivulet meandering through it, the grassy carpet interspersed with a variety of flowering shrubs, several little mounts rising in the conic form intersected with fertile spots of waving grain, the horizon bounded with a thick wood, as if nature intended a barricade against the cannonade of some formidable despot. But here all is perfect silence, nothing is heard but the melody of the groves and the unintelligible language of the animal creation. From the profound stillness and security of this woody region, I can almost persuade myself we are the only human inhabitants of creation, and, instead of losing my fondness for society, I shall have a higher relish for the pleasures of friendly converse and social endearments," etc.

But, although our town seemed so secure and peaceful, rumors were rife of the approach of the regulars from this time, and, as has been said, even before this time there had been anxiety lest they should make an invasion.

The utmost vigilance was maintained in the town to defend it from foes both within and without.

May 29th, it was voted in town-meeting that a watch should be kept, and sentinels should challenge every person abroad after nine o'clock in the evening, and inquire his business. If any refused to answer, the sentinel should, "with a strong voice," order him to stop, and should forthwith have him arrested.

The town also took action at this meeting on the following communication received from the Provincial Congress, then just dissolving, to which Samuel Osgood, Esq., had been their representative : —

"WATERTOWN, *May* 5, 1775.

"*Whereas*, his Excellency General Gage since his arrival into this colony hath conducted as an instrument in the hands of an arbitrary ministry to enslave this people, and a Detachment of the troops under his command has of late been by him ordered to the Town of Concord to destroy the publick stores deposited in that Place for the use of the Colony and the citizens, without any provocation given by them, have been illegally, wantonly and inhumanly slaughtered by the troops, therefore

"*Resolved*, That the said General Gage hath by these and many other means utterly disqualified himself to serve the colony as a Governor and in every other capacity and that no obedience ought in future to be paid by the several towns and Districts in the colony to his Writs for calling an Assembly or to his Proclamation or any other of his acts or Doings, but that on the other hand he ought to be considered and guarded against as an unnatural and inveterate enemy to the country.

"JOSEPH WARREN, *President P. T.*"

The action of Andover is thus recorded : —

"In pursuance of the Within Directions we have called the Town together and made choice of Mr. Samuel Phillips, Jr., to Represent them in Provincial Congress to be held at the meeting house in Watertown on Wednesday the thirty-first day of May Inst.

> ASA ABBOT,
> NATHAN LOVEJOY,
> ZEBED. ABBOT,
> JOHN INGALLS,
> BENJ. STEVENS,

} *Selectmen of Andover.*"

Respecting the position which the Andover representative took in the Congress, his biographer says [1]: —

"This memorable Congress held four protracted sessions before it was finally dissolved on the 10th of May, 1776. During this period Mr. Phillips was twice on a committee to confer with General Washington upon points connected with the war, he was also in rapid succession upon committees to countersign the colony notes emitted by the Continental Congress and the notes of the Receiver General, to direct the mustering and paying of one militia company, to muster and pay another, etc., etc. In it all he distinguished himself and did honor to the town whose name he represented."

About the last of May, there arrived in Andover a distinguished visitior, the former citizen, Col. Joseph Frye. He had been for five years living at Fryeburg, the township granted him for his services and sufferings in the French War. He had left his plantation for the purpose of procuring a supply of ammunition; the town being apprehensive of an attack by the British from Canada. Undoubtedly, too, the veteran burned to be nearer the seat of war, and to share in the conflict. Not being able to get at any powder in all the trading towns, he arrived at length at his old home in Andover. Here, says his memorial to the General Assembly, he heard of the expected arrival at Watertown of a large supply of gunpowder.

He "tarried," therefore, at Andover some days, waiting the news of its arrival. His visit could hardly fail to be a matter of great interest in the town. He had been identified with its affairs for many years, and was a universal favorite, the hero of military romance as well as the trusted citizen and practical man of business. He it was who had presided at those stormy

---

[1] *Life of Judge Phillips*, by Rev. John L. Taylor.

but unanimous town meetings about taxation and the Stamp Act ten years before, and now, we may be sure, the people flocked around him to get his opinion of the state of the country and to tell him of the part which Andover had taken in the late alarms and fight. Also there would be much to inquire about from Fryeburg, for many Andover men had joined the settlers there, and to hear from their relations and friends by the voice of their common benefactor would afford to the citizens great gratification.

While Colonel Frye was at Andover, events happened which made, for the time being, gunpowder for the remote plantation in York appear of secondary importance. No rumor of any immediate movement in the army seems to have reached the town, although it is probable that the representative to the Provincial Congress must have known that something was on foot. On Saturday, the 17th of June, the booming of cannon announced that fighting was begun, and soon the news came that Andover companies were in the detachment engaged, that reënforcements were wanted and provisions. Then, as on the day of the Lexington alarm, there was mounting in hot haste and hurrying to and fro, and pale cheeks and trembling hearts. Mustering troops and beat of drum blocked and made noisy the highways, and, behind the marching line of soldiers, streamed a motley throng of civilians, hastening to the succor of their townsmen, or to see what the day would bring forth. In the houses, women were busy cooking provisions, mixing cordials and medicines, ransacking for stray muskets and ammunition, and, later (as the thunder of the cannonade grew louder and more incessant and the messengers of bad tidings began to come in), cutting up their choice linen into bandages, scraping lint and making ready to receive the wounded or the dead. The Andover companies detached with the working party which fortified Bunker Hill, were Capt. Benjamin Ames's, Captain Farnum's, and Captain Furbush's. The first two belonged to Col. James Frye's regiment, the latter to Col. Ebenezer Bridge's. A muster roll of Captain Ames's company, giving the list of eight months' men enlisted from October 6, 1775. marks the names of certain soldiers as having been among those "killed on the

17th of June." It may therefore be presumed that this roll presents a pretty correct showing of the men of the company who fought at Bunker Hill. It will be noted that this roll differs in some names from that of the company on the 19th of April. It seems still more probable that this was the roll of the company as at Bunker Hill, from the fact that no other earlier muster roll is found, and also that the following petition indicates the loss of the earlier rolls or their failure to reach the proper authorities: —

"*Aug.* 31, 1775.[1] TO THE HONOURABLE THE COUNCIL AND HOUSE OF REPRESENTATIVES OF THE COLONIES OF THE MASSACHUSETTS BAY IN GENERAL COURT ASSEMBLED, — Your Petitioner, a Captain in Col. James Frye's Regiment, begs leave to relate that the Company which he has the Honor to Command, consisting of fifty seven non-commissioned officers & soldiers, came into Camp at Cambridge on the 19th of April last, that since that time said company has regularly done duty, but though they have been in the service of this colony above three months, not one Man has received any part of the Forty shillings which a late Congress promised should be advanced to them, That these soldiers with many of their families have suffered difficulties that are not small by reason of this delay. Their necessities have been growing daily more urgent, till at length I am able to withstand their Importunity no longer. I am therefore constrained most earnestly to entreat of this Honble Court that relief to which your humble petitioner presumes he has some claim in justice, & your Petitioner as in Duty bound shall ever pray. BENJⁿ AMES.

"CAMP IN CAMBRIDGE, *Aug.* 2, 1775."

The following was the action of the Court: —

"IN THE HOUSE OF REPRESENTATIVES, WATERTOWN, *Aug.* 2, 1775.

"*Ordered* that Mr. Samuel Phillips be directed to Muster the Company of Capt. Benjamin Ames in Col. Frye's Regiment (if not already mustered) and that he be also impowered to draw out of the Publick treasury of this colony the sum of forty shillings as advanced wages to each of the non commissioned officers & private soldiers belonging to the above Company, if they have not been paid," etc.

[Concurred in and assented to.]

[1] *General Court Records*, also *Mass. Archives*, vol. ccvi., p. 161.

ANDOVER IN THE REVOLUTIONARY WAR.   319

Captain Benjamin Ames's Company (presumably) at Bunker Hill.[1]

Benjamin Ames, Capt.
David Chandler, Lieut.
Isaac Abbot, Lieut.
Benjamin More, Sergt.
Joshua Lovejoy, Sergt.
Thomas Boynton, Sergt.
William Chander, Sergt.
David Blunt, Corporal.
Bixbe Abbot, Corporal.
Ebenezer Holbrook, Corporal.
Moses Boynton, Corporal.
Joshua More, drummer.
James Chandler, do.
Caleb Abbot.
Nathaniel Abbot, dischg. Aug. 20.
Solomon Ames.
Philip Abbot, killed in battle, June 17.
Samuel Blanchard.
Jonathan Boynton.
Peter Chandler.

Timothy Chandler.
Jonathan Cummings.
Nathan Chandler.
William Chamberlain.
Joseph Chandler, killed in battle June 17.
Stephen Chandler.
William Dane.
Joseph Dane.
Israel Herrick, Lewiston.
Amos Durant.
Simeon Dresser.
Abiel Faulkner.
Theophilus Frye.
George Holt.
William Haggit, killed in battle June 17.
Joshua Holt.
Israel Holt.
Jesse Holt, died June 21.
Humphrey Holt.
William Holt.
John Herrick.
James Johnson.

Ephraim Johnson.
Josiah Jones, Londonderry.
Nathan Lovejoy.
Obadiah Lovejoy.
David Lovejoy.
William Lovejoy.
Samuel Martain.
Peter Martain.
Perley Mackintire.
Christopher Osgood, Blue Hill, Me.
Joseph Parker.
Carlton Parker.
Salem Poor.
John Stevens.
Jonathan Stevens.
Nathaniel Toy.
James Turner.
Jeremiah Wardwell, Pembrook.
Ezekiel Wardwell.
Israel Herrick, Lewiston.

Capt. Charles Furbush's Company (presumably) at Bunker Hill.[1]

"*A Muster Roll of the Company under the command of Captain Charles Furbush in Col. Bridge's Regiment to the first of August, 1775.*"

Charles Furbush, Capt., Andover.
Jeremiah Blanchard, Lieut.,[2] Andover.
James Silver, Lieut., Methuen.
Joseph Frost, Sgt., Tewksbury.
Daniel Silver, Sgt., Salem.
William Smith, St., Salem.
Hugh Riley, St., Danvers.
Jeremiah Morrel, Corporal, Andover.
William Moorland, Corporal, Salem.
Jacob Amas, Corporal, Andover.
Thomas Smith, Corporal, Andover.
Simeon Furbush, drum, Andover.
Abraham Stickney, fifer, Tewksbury.

John Baldwin, private, Andover.
William Bailey, Andover.
John Craford, Andover.
Jeremiah Blanchard, Andover.
David Clough, Dracut.
London Cittizen, Andover.
Theodore Emerson, Methuen.
Samuel Farmer, Tewksbury.
Isaac Foster, Tewksbury.
Charles Furbush, Jr., Andover.
William Gorden, Salem.
Elijah Hildreth, Dracut.
Israel Hunt, Tewksbury.

[1] This return was made October 6, 1775, for the purpose of showing the men who had been eight months in service, and were, therefore, each to receive a coat as bounty. They enlisted February, 1775. See *Coat Rolls*, "Col. James Fry's Regiment," p. 10.

[2] *Muster Rolls*, vol. xiv., p. 95.

Keto Hubbard, Tewksbury.	Danl. Petengel, Methuen.
William Kemp, Billerica.	Cuff Blanchard, Andover.
John Hancock, Methuen.	Cesar Porter, Andover.
Thomas Hadley, Boston.	Abraham Silver, Methuen.
Danl Longren, Andover.	Marcus Shedd, Tewksbury.
Thomas Hagget, Andover.	David Silver, Salem.
John Morrison, Boston.	Nathan Tyler.
Josiah Mecom, Boston.	Abiel Upton.
Isaac Melvin Kidah, Methuen.	Benjamin Clark, Reading.
Nehemiah Ridale, Methuen.	Samuel Bealy, Andover.[1]
Joseph Petengel, Methuen.	John Boughton, Andover.

Among the "Coat Rolls" of Col. Ebenezer Bridge's regiment is a copy of a paper which contains the same names as the foregoing, with a few exceptions. Five additional ones appear, namely, Ezra Anes, John Loyd, Joshua Ball, David Merril, Alexander Silver.

The paper without the names is as follows:—

"CAMP AT CAMBRIDGE, *Nov. the* 21, 1775.

"TO THE HONOURABLE THE COMMITTEE OF CLOTHING *sitting at Watertown.* Please to deliver to the Bearer Capt. Charles Furbush a coat for each one of us the subscribers, being soldiers in Capt. Furbush's company in Col. Bridge's Regt." . . . .

"These may certify that the soldiers within named belong to my company and have not received the coats within mentioned nor the money.   CHARLES FURBISH, *Captain.*"

Captain Benjamin Farnum's Company (presumably) at Bunker Hill.[2]

Benjamin Farnum, Capt.	John Johnson, *o.*	Thomas Clark.
Saml. Johnson, Lieut.	Benjm. Parker.	Zachariah Chickering.
Cyrus Marble, Lieut.	Ephraim Lasey.	John Dillaway.
John Chickering, *o.*	Nehemiah Abbot.	Stephen Farrington.
William Johnson.	Spofford Ames.	John Farrington.
John Parker.	George Abbot.	Samuel Fowler.
Saml. Carlton.	John Barker.	Jonathan Gardner, *o.*
John Barker.	Ingalls Bragg, *o.*	William Gordon.
Joshua Frye.	Jacob Barnard.	David How.
Joshua Long.	Timothy Carlton.	Phineas Johnson, *o.*
Peter Farnham, *o.*	John Cross.	Peter Johnson.

[1] Killed June 17.

[2] This company was formed of men of Capt. Thomas Poor's, and some other companies, in May. They were enlisted in February. See *Coat Rolls,* "Col. James Fry's Regiment."

Isaiah Ingalls.	Timothy Poor.	Ebenezer Thompson.
Phineas Ingalls.	John Parker.	John Wilson.
Samuel Lasey.	Stephen Poor.	James Wiley.
Stephen Long.	Enoch Parker.	Simon Wardwell.
Thomas Kenney.	Jonathan Robinson.	Joshua Wood.
Dudley Messer, Methuen.	Jonathan Stephens.	Frederick Frye.
John Nichols.	James Stephens.	Phineas Parker.
Timothy Noyes.	David Stephens.	Cato Negro.
Asa Osgood.	Darius Sessions (taken captive at Bunker Hill).	Amos Stephens.
Jacob Osgood.		Philip Farrington.
Michael Parker, *a*.	John Tyler.	Jacob Tyler.
Danl. Poor.	John Turner, Deserted, *a*.	

There is in a manuscript memorandum of Captain Farnum a list of names of men who received pay in his company. It differs in some respects from the foregoing roll. The names marked *a* in that roll are absent from it, and the following additional names [1] appear: —

William Parker.	Peter Poor.	Benjamin Abbot.
William Dilloway.	Stephen Messer.	

At sunset, on the night of June 16th, the detachment for intrenching at Bunker Hill was ordered to be drawn up on Cambridge Common. Whither they were to go, or what duty to perform, was a profound secret to the men. They were paraded, and then a fervent prayer was offered by the Rev. Dr. Langdon, the patriotic President of Harvard College. The occasion was impressive, for all felt that some perilous enterprise was before them, and that this might be the last prayer which some of them would ever hear on earth.

The night's march and work are familiar to all, but the description of it by one of the Andover men will be read with interest. Thomas Boynton was Sergeant of Captain Ames's company. He writes:[2] —

[1] There were also Andover men in companies from other towns. The place of residence is not always given in the rolls, and the rolls, moreover, are only partial records, such as chance to have been preserved. Therefore were every name of Andover searched out, we should not know all the Revolutionary soldiers of the town.

The writer has preferred to attempt to show the companies as a whole in their more important service. This method, although it repeats some names and omits some, is believed to give more graphic and even historic interest; for, by it the past is more truly brought before the majority of readers, even though family or individual curiosity in respect to some particular soldier may not be gratified.

[2] *Mass. Hist. Soc. Proceedings*, 1877.

"Three regiments were ordered to peraid at 6 o'clock in the afternoon, namely: Conl. Fryes, Conl. Bridgs's and Conl. Prescotts, after which being done we attended prayers and about 9 at night we marched to Charlestown with about a 1000 men and at about 11 o'clock we began to intrench in sight of Boston and the shiping."

"It was a warm, still summer night," says Washington Irving in his description of the battle, "the stars shone brightly, but everything was quiet. Boston was buried in sleep. The sentry's cry of 'All's well' could be heard distinctly from the shores, together with the drowsy calling of the watch on board the ships of war, and then all would relapse into silence."

But of the stars, or the stillness, or the sleeping city, the poetry of the scene, Sergeant Boynton tells nothing. He was, doubtless, too hard at work to watch the heavens, or if he glanced above at the stars, while pausing from his labor in the trenches, it was to think how these same stars were shining down on the homestead at dear old Andover, and to wonder if any eyes were there watching them, and what the sleeping household at home would think if they could see him at his midnight toils. The night was hardly long enough to finish the work of intrenchment. As soon as the day broke, the British discovered what had been done and began their firing. Sergeant Boynton describes it as follows:—

"At the sun's rising, they began to fire upon us from the shiping, the 3^d or 4th shot they kild one man, and many others escaped very narrowly. At length they ceased their fire. Our work went on continually; they began about 8 or 9 o'clock from Corps Hill and continued a hot fire."

The history of the battle of Bunker Hill is in all the books. Nothing needs to be told to add to the knowledge of it, yet a description of it, as it appeared to one of our own townsmen,[1] is too interesting to be omitted. Boynton's journal continues:—

"About 2 or 3 o'clock the enemy landed and advanced toward us, its thot to the number of 2000 men, and soon planted their cannon and began the fire and advancing up to our Fort. After they came within gun shot we fired, and then ensued a very hot engagement.

[1] An English born citizen of Andover is grandson of a soldier who fought at Bunker Hill in the King's service.

After a number of shots passed, the enemy retreated, and we ceased our fire for a few minutes. They advanced again, and we began a hot fire for a short time. The enemy scaling our walls and the number of our men being few, we was ordered to retreat, at which time the enemy were allmost round us, and a continual firing at our heals."

Colonel Frye was not with the working party, or on the field, at the beginning of the action, being occupied, it is said, with a court martial.[1] Learning that the battle was going against our forces he, in the midst of the action, galloped to the field. Overtaking troops halted on the road, he rode up to the officer in command and impetuously demanded why there was any halting at such a time. Then cheering on the soldiers, he shouted, "This day thirty years I was at the taking of Louisburg. This is a fortunate day for America, we shall certainly beat the enemy!" Later in the day, after the British had carried the redoubt and our troops were retreating, the enemy in pursuit, Colonel Frye was wounded in the thigh by a musket ball, which passed through the saddle and lodged in the back of his horse. He dismounted, extracted the ball, and rode on, with the remark, "The Regulars fire damned careless!" Many other incidents are told of the bravery and coolness of Andover men. A private, John Barker, seeing his captain and friend, Benjamin Farnum, lying wounded in the path of the retreat, took him upon his shoulders, and steadying him by putting his gun across under his knees, bade him hold fast, and started off on the run, calling out, "The Regulars sha'n't have Ben." This is told by descendants of Captain Farnum, and by some of the neighbors. On the other hand it has been the tradition in the Abbot family, and the Barker family, that Lieut. Isaac Abbot was the man rescued from the "Regulars." Since the claim is made for the two, it is undoubtedly true that one or the other was carried off.

There is a tradition in regard to the bravery of a negro servant in the battle, which is also confirmed by the State records. The story goes that "Salem Poor," a slave, owned by Mr. John Poor, shot Lieutenant-colonel Abercrombie. As

[1] MS. pedigree of the Frye family.

that officer sprang on the redoubt, while our men were in retreat, and exclaimed, "The day is ours," Salem turned and took aim and fired. He saw the officer fall. The record in the Archives[1] is as follows: —

"RECOMMENDATION OF SALEM POOR, A NEGRO, FOR BRAVERY.

"TO THE HONL. GENL. COURT OF THE MASSACHUSETTS BAY. The subscribers begg leave to Report to your Honble House, which we do in justice to the Caracter of so Brave a Man that came under our observation. We declare that a Negro Man called Salem Poor, of Col. Frye's Regiment, Capt. Ames' company, in the late battle at Charlestown behaved like an experienced officer as well as an excellent soldier; to set forth Perticulars of his conduct would be tedious. Wee would only begg leave to say, in the Person of this sd. Negro centres a Brave & Gallant soldier. The Reward due to so great and Distinguished a Caracter wee submit to the Congress.

"CAMBRIDGE, *Dec.* 6, 1775.

JONA BREWER, *Col.*
THOMAS WINON, *Lt.-col.*
WM. PRESCOTT, *Colo.*
EPH^m CARY, *Lieut.*
JOSEPH BAKER, *Lieut.*
JOSHUA REED, *Lieut.*"

The descendants of Captain Furbush relate[2] that he was disabled at the beginning of the action, and carried to the rear, and that Samuel Bailey, the lieutenant, took the command, and was rushing forward, cheering the men, when he was shot dead by a cannon ball. The first tidings that reached Andover were that both Captain Furbush and Samuel Bailey had been killed. Their wives, who were friends,

---

[1] Vol. clxxx, p. 241.

[2] See "Revolutionary Reminiscences," *Lawrence American*, 1875. The writer finds no evidence to show that Samuel Bailey held the rank of lieutenant, although it is a family tradition that he did, and that he came within one vote of being chosen captain. The first roll found of the company has a *blank* in the first lieutenant's place. The roll for October has the name of Jeremiah Blanchard, lieutenant, and also as private, indicating that he may have been promoted after the death of the lieutenant. The name of Samuel Bailey, Jr., is given among the privates as "killed June 17, 1775." Samuel Bailey, Jr., was the son of Samuel Bailey, who, in 1733, bought a quarter section of land (250 acres) in the west part of Andover, near the Merrimack River, and the borders of Tewksbury (first of the name in town). He was great-grandfather of the writer of these sketches.

had met to mourn together when news came of the Captain's safety. He had the bloody clothes of his comrade-in-arms cleansed and sent home. The son of the deceased, a lad of sixteen, was on the field and recovered his watch.

The following action was taken in the General Court, in March, 1776, in regard to the petition of representatives of the deceased for compensation for his loss of gun, etc.: —

"On the account of the loss of Samuel Bailey, Jr., deceased, of a Gun and sundry other articles in the Battle on Bunker's Hill —

"*Resolved*, That there be paid to the Heirs of the said Samuel Bailey, Junr., deceased, the sum of seven pounds sixteen shillings and eight pence in full of said account."

Again, in June, further action was taken as follows: —

"*June* 14, 1776. Whereas, at the sessions of the last General Court of this Colony, an account of losses sustained by Samuel Bailey, Junr., at the Battle at Bunker's Hill was exhibited to said Court and by a resolve of the said Court of the 15th of March last, the sum of seven pounds sixteen shillings and eight pence was ordered to be paid to Joseph Bailey in full of said account, which resolve passed all branches; and whereas it appears evident that it was through mistake that the sum aforesaid was ordered to be paid to the said Joseph and that it ought to have been made payable to the administratrix on the estate of said Samuel, therefore it is resolved that the resolve aforesaid be and hereby is declared null and void, and that the sum of seven pounds sixteen shillings and eight pence be paid to Hannah Bayley administratrix on the estate of the said Samuel Bailey, junior, Deceased, in full of his account for losses at the battle at Bunker Hill."

[Read and concurred — consented to.]

It is sometimes supposed by persons unacquainted with the facts that accurate and careful records are on file in the State Archives in regard to the soldiers who fought in the battles of the Revolution; that the names of the killed and wounded in any battle are readily to be found. But such is by no means the case, as every one knows who has had occasion to make search. The rolls were returned mainly for the purpose of obtaining the pay due the soldiers, and they are often deficient in particulars of residence and in other respects; and moreover, they do not cover the entire service, but are fragmentary and imperfect, and, to a great extent, without chronological arrangement.

The only roll found which shows the losses sustained of the men at Bunker Hill is one of the company of Captain Ames, containing a list of names, and "guns that is lost," "coats that is lost," "Blankets that is lost," "great Coats that is lost," "Knapsacks that is lost." This indicates the panic and haste in which the fleeing men dropped whatever impeded their retreat.

Boynton's journal says : " We lost William Haggot, Joseph Chandler, and Philip Abbot. Wounded, Lieut. Isaac Abbot, Sergt. Joshua Lovejoy, James Turner, Jeremiah Wardwell, Stephen Chandler, and Israel Holt, of our company."

An account of moneys paid to Mr. Samuel Phillips for several Andover men for their losses has the following names : [1]—

Cyrus Marble	£2 5 4
Isaac Abbott	2 8
Stephen Farrington	2
Benjamin Farnum	3 13
John Barker 3d	2 16

To Captain Farnum's [2] family came, on the day of battle, the news that he was wounded, and they took measures to

[1] Other names are found (*Mass. Archives*, vol. cxxxviii., p. 381), on a list from Andover and vicinity, the towns not specified. The following seem to belong to Andover.

Timothy Johnson	£1 14 8
Timothy Carlton	2 16
Spofford Ames	2 4
Jonathan Stevens	2 10
Thomas Kenney ⎫ Jacob Osgood ⎪ Simon Wardwell ⎪ Ingalls Bragg ⎬ Eph. Lacey ⎪ Joshua Wood ⎪ Timothy Noyes ⎪ Saml. Carlton ⎪ Tho. Clark ⎪ John Parker ⎪ Jacob Barnard ⎭	2 0

[2] Resident of North Andover. The estate owned now by Jacob Farnum, in the Farnham District.

have him brought home. A sort of litter was placed on poles, and fastened to two chairs, and drawn by horses harnessed tandem. The Captain never wholly recovered from this wound, though he served during the whole war, and lived to a remarkable age; the sore made by the bullet continued to fester and be painful. Pieces of bone and the bullet that were taken from it were long kept, ghastly trophies of his first battle. The following notice of this veteran patriot appeared in the "Essex Gazette," June, 1829: —

"Observing in a late Boston *Patriot*, since the death of Gen. Dearborn, that he was the last surviving captain who was at the ever memorable battle of the 17th June 1775 on Bunker Hill, and of the only five who were present at the laying of the corner stone of the monument in 1825, I would state that I am informed that Capt. Benjamin Farnum commanded the Andover Infantry Company on that memorable day and was on the same spot fifty years afterward, and is now also alive and in his eighty-third year. Although some infirm and lame from the wounds received in the action by two balls in his thigh, one of which has been extracted and he still keeps it as a valuable relict of that eventful day's carnage. Capt. Farnum still sustains the office of deacon of the North church in *Andover* which he has honorably and respectably filled for nearly forty years.[1]

"ANDOVER NORTH, 17*th June*, 1829."

The day of the Battle of Bunker Hill and the night which followed, were full of terrible anxiety and suspense to the friends trembling for the fate of their kindred and townsfolk. From the high hills they strained their eyes to catch a glimpse of coming messengers, and watched the lurid fires of the burning city stream up on the horizon, while the incessant booming of the cannon made even stout hearts quail and all tremble for the fate of friends on the battle-field.

The next day was the Sabbath; but who could sit down in the meeting-house and listen to sermons, or compose his mind for the duty of public prayer, however devout he might be! Concerning the state of things, the pastor of the South Church, the Rev. Jonathan French, writes: —

[1] A memorandum in Deacon Farnum's note-book is as follows: "The First Church in Andover to Benj. Farnum, *Dr*., For Bread and wine to supply the Communion table for six sackrements in the year 1791, £4 3*s* 9*d*.

"Our houses of public worship were generally shut up. It was the case here. When the news of the battle reached us, the anxiety and distress of wives and children, of parents, of brothers, sisters, and friends was great. It was not known who were among the slain or living, the wounded or the well. It was thought justifiable for us who could to repair to the camp to know the circumstances, to join in the defence of the country and prevent the enemy from pushing the advantages they had gained, and to afford comfort and relief to our suffering brethren and friends."

With surgical instruments, for he was a practical surgeon, and musket, for he was a trained soldier, and Bible, as became his profession, the Rev. Dr. French made his Sabbath day's journey to the camp, and rendered valuable aid there in ministering to the wounded and the dying.

There were two other officers at Bunker Hill whom Andover might justly claim as among her sons. One of these was Colonel (afterward General) Enoch Poor, of Exeter, a brother of Major Poor, of Andover. He commanded one of the New Hampshire regiments under General Stark. The chaplain of one of these regiments was our townsman, the Rev. David Osgood. He had been less than a year settled in Medford, and from that place (through which marched the New Hampshire troops) joined the service. The horrors of the day made a deep and lasting impression on his mind, and led him to deplore war as a great, if sometimes necessary, evil. He strongly opposed, in his old age, the War of 1812. In a sermon, written against this war, he thus describes his feelings during the Revolution: "I have not forgotten, nor can I ever forget while consciousness abides with me, my own mental sufferings during the period of our former war. Through the eight long years, whose slow, lingering pace, while hope was deferred and the heart sickened with pain and anguish, seemed without end, a burden lay upon my spirits, by day and by night, almost too heavy for frail mortality to sustain. During the hours of repose, visions of horror rose in my imagination, and disturbed my rest; through the long-lived day the distresses of my country and the dangers and disasters of my friends harassed my thoughts. In the meanwhile, the course of nature moved on tranquil and serene, without suspension or interruption. The delightful vicissitudes of day and night, the cheery rotation of the seasons were what they had been before, and what they have continued to be since, but to my feelings they were not the same, and brought not the accustomed pleasure. . . ."

After relating the course of meditation which filled his mind on the strange contrast between the peace and beauty of nature and the passions and strife of man, he says: —

"Thus daily lamenting and praying against the miseries of war, I passed through that most gloomy portion of my past life, from 1775 till the transporting sound of peace, in 1783."

Yet David Osgood was, like his classmates in college, Samuel Phillips and Jonathan French, a zealous advocate of the Revolutionary measures. Respecting his position, in regard to this war, he says: "I entertained the sentiment in which my fellow-citizens were universally, almost to a man, agreed, that on our part it was necessary, and from this conviction I composed and preached frequent discourses to animate and encourage its prosecution."

Besides being favored with excellent religious advisers, and the sympathizing attendance of their minister, the Andover soldiers had also the advantage of the medical service of one of their own townsmen. Dr. Thomas Kittredge was the surgeon of Col. James Frye's regiment. He was in the battle, and doubtless did much to alleviate the sufferings of the wounded, who were his acquaintances and friends. He was remarkably well fitted for his position, by his familiarity from childhood with such practice. His father, Dr. John Kittredge, had been famous in all the country around Andover, and had had staying in his house for treatment, soldiers of the French War. His grandfather, also Dr. Kittredge, of Tewksbury, was a physician of repute, and his great-grandfather is said to have been a physician of the Old Country. To these advantages of inherited professional talent, Dr. Kittredge joined ample education. Moreover, he enjoyed exceptional facilities for procuring the supplies needful for alleviating suffering, being not only himself a man of wealth, but intimately connected with the most influential officers in camp, and brother-in-law to Maj. Samuel Osgood, who had charge of the department of supplies.

The following letter, found among Dr. Thomas Kittredge's papers, is of interest. If the answer to it could be found, it would be still more valuable.

"ROXBURY, *June* 8, 1818.

"To Dr. Thomas Kittredge:—

"*Sir:* Understanding you were in the Battle of Bunker Hill, I will thank you to answer the following questions: Where were you stationed during the battle and what were the general occurrences during the engagement? Did you see Genl. Putnam on the battle ground while the action continued? Did you see Genl. Putnam during the 17th of June, 1775; if so when was it and what was he doing? When the Americans retreated did you see Genl. Putnam on foot or on horseback on Bunker Hill or Charlestown Neck? Have you seen Genl. H. Dearborn's account of the Battle of Bunker Hill? If so what is your opinion of it? You will much oblige me by returning a letter containing your answer, an account of the battle so far as you were acquainted with the circumstances of the day. With due respect,

Your obt servt,

H. DEARBORN."

The soldiers of few country towns (it is safe to hazard the statement) were more influentially represented in the camp at Cambridge, in the year 1775, than were those of Andover. To recapitulate: there were more or less at camp, besides the captains of the companies, Maj. Samuel Osgood, Maj. Thomas Poor, Col. James Fry, Gen. Joseph Fry, Adjutant-general Bimsley Stevens, Hon. Samuel Phillips, Sen., Samuel Phillips, Jun., Esq., Rev. Jonathan French, Dr. Thomas Kittredge, Col. Samuel Johnson, with Col. Enoch Poor, of New Hampshire, Rev. David Osgood, Mr. William Phillips, of Boston, all natives of the town. Any of these would have the ability and the disposition to befriend a townsman in his country's service; and it is therefore reasonable to believe that Andover soldiers suffered less than many others for lack of the necessaries and comforts of camp-life.

In mentioning the surgeon of the First Regiment, it may be suitable also to notice briefly the other physicians in practice at Andover in Revolutionary times. Dr. Ward Noyes, the surgeon of the French War, lived through the Revolution, and did service for soldiers.

Dr. Joseph Osgood, a trader and apothecary, also prescribed, and had a large practice, and was succeeded by his son, Dr. George Osgood. To Dr. Osgood, one of the soldiers, James Stevens, at home from camp on furlough, applied for medical treatment, as he records in his journal.

Dr. Abiel Abbot, too, of French War service, was still in practice in Andover. Also, Dr. Daniel How, son of Dr. Israel How, the first physician of Andover (1718), was in practice, especially in treatment of the insane.

The Provincial Congress, June 14, 1775, passed the following resolve, in regard to Dr. How: —

"Whereas the committee are informed that Dr. How of Andover is prepared to receive insane patients and is well skilled in such disorders, resolved that Daniel Adams, a lunatic now at Woburn, be carried to the town of Andover and committed to the care of Doct. How and the said Dr. How be hereby desired to take proper care of the said lunatic at the expense of this colony."

It is possible that the reputation of this physician may have had something to do with the subsequent selection of Andover as the place of retreat for the patriot James Otis, when his mind became clouded and deranged.

The Sunday morning following the day of the battle of Bunker Hill, Col. Joseph Fry left Andover for the camp at Cambridge. He spent the night at Medford, and arrived on the 19th in camp. His old friends flocked around him, — the officers and soldiers of his former campaigns. They importuned him to stay and accept a command. He says that, "finding his services so generally desired, he consented to serve his country accordingly, the distresses of his exposed plantation notwithstanding. The Honorable the Congress of the Colony were pleased to honor him with a Major General's Commission date June 21." However, when the Continental Congress adopted the army at Cambridge, and appointed the officers, some mistake or delay occurred about Colonel Frye's commission. He ultimately received a Brigadier-general's commission, presented to him by Washington in person, 5th February, 1776. He stayed in camp during June and July of 1775, then returned to Andover and "tarried here till November,"—then was put in command of a force in Cumberland for defence of the sea-coast.[1] His connection with Andover, so far as we know, now ceases, his place of residence being the town of Fryeburg.

The Battle of Bunker Hill, and the consequently increased discomforts to the patriots of living in Boston, brought some other residents to Andover during the summer of 1775. Mr. William Phillips, a nephew of the Rev. Samuel Phillips, of Andover, was a merchant of Boston. He had married Miss Margaret Wendell. Her brother, Mr. Oliver Wendell, and his partner, Mr. Nathaniel Appleton, were also in mercantile business. These gentlemen both left Boston, Mr. Wendell going to reside in Newburyport and Mr. Appleton coming to live at Andover. These statements will serve to explain the allusions in the following letters. Three days after the battle, Mr. Appleton writes from Andover to Mr. Wendell, whom he addresses as "Brother pilgrim":—

"ANDOVER,[2] *June* 21, 1775.

"This informs you that (Mother Rowlandson like) I have made a second remove, have got a very commodious house, considering the times, about 2 miles from the grand country road. If you come to see me, take your directions of Mr. French, or if you write, direct to his care.

"I have been hoeing my Potatoes and Beans today. You 'd say, brother Nat is in good spirits, but be assured he is extremely anxious for our public affairs. I went to Cambridge last Friday. Father remains poorly, but we removed him to your good sister Phillips's that afternoon. Next day, as wife and I were returning home through Cambridge, met the express góing to Congress informing the regulars had landed at Charlestown; we tacked about, went through Woburn to Salem, and was constantly presented with the melancholy appearance of the fire at Charlestown. . . . .

"Late at night, candle going out.   Yr. friend."

Various other letters are written from this time to November, when Mr. Appleton comunicates good news, the birth

[1] These facts appear in various petitions to the General Court found in the records and archives.
[2] *Hist. Coll. Essex Institute*, vol. xiii.

to him of a son, and, in patriotic strain, he adds: "The boy I named last Sabbath George Washington."

From another letter, which follows this, it may be inferred that this "naming," probably by baptism, of his son for the "rebel" leader, was obnoxious to some of Mr. Appleton's loyalist acquaintances, and that the British general showed his spite by increased severity toward some of Mr. Appleton's friends in Boston: —

"Why you should attribute How's treatment of the Deacon[1] to *poor little George* I can't conceive, as we are all rebels. . . . . And you say they hate me. Who? Surely amidst the ten thousand of Israel little N. A. in Andover woods, can't be of importance enough to be inquired after."

Patriotic christenings were fashionable at Andover, in 1775. The "Boston Gazette," Monday, November 27th, records: —

"The 19th Inst. Mr. Joseph Hall late of Boston but now of Andover had a child christened by the Rev. Mr. French of that place by the name of Joseph Warren, to perpetuate the memory of Major Genl. Joseph Warren who was slain on Bunker Hill in the ever memorable battle on the 17th of June, 1775."

Such "christenings" were no doubt performed with an unction by the patriotic parson French. And the fervent appeals which he made on such occasions of consecration no doubt inspired and strengthened many parents for the dedication which they made so cheerfully to their country of the children whom God had given them. From the meeting-house to the camp, and from the camp to the meeting-house, as appears from the diary of our townsman James Stevens, our soldiers went, in the true Cromwellian spirit, to "trust in God and keep their powder dry."

Besides the eminent and influential residents of Boston who made Andover a place of refuge, there were others less known to fame: —

"Died[2] at Andover, the 12th Inst., Mrs. Lydia Smith, aged 64. She was formerly a schoolmistress in Boston, but lately drove from that unhappy town by the cruel hand of Tyranny. By her life and

---

[1] Perhaps Mr. Lovell, the business agent left, who was imprisoned.
[2] *New England Chronicle*, for year 1776.

conversation we must draw the conclusion that she is departed to that happy Place where the wicked cease from Troubling and the weary are at rest."

Some of the poor of Boston were also assigned to Andover in the distribution made of them among the towns.

Andover was selected as a place of safety for the library of Harvard College. At first the Provincial Congress voted to send the whole library here, but afterward it was decided to distribute it in various towns. Mr. Samuel Phillips, Jr., was packing the books on the day of the battle of Bunker Hill, and says he was so busy that he did not hear the sound of the battle : —

"Amid all the terrors of battle I was so busily engaged in Harvard Library that I never even heard of the engagement (I mean the siege) till it was completed."

On the 15th of June, 1775, the Congress had taken the following action : [1] —

"*Resolved*, that the Library apparatus and other valuables of Harvard College be removed as soon as may be to the town of Andover, that Mr. Samuel Phillips, Mr. Daniel Hopkins and Dummer Jewett Esq. be a committee to consult with the Revd. the President, the Honble Mr. Winthrop, and the Librarian or such of them as may be conveniently obtained and with them to engage some suitable Person or persons in said town to transport, receive and take the charge of the above mentioned Effects, that said committee join with other gentlemen in employing proper persons for packing said Library apparatus and such other Articles as they shall judge expedient and take all due care that it be done with the greatest safety and despatch and as the Packages shall be completed that they give notice to those engaged to receive them."

On the 23d of June, this resolve was reconsidered and it was voted to engage some suitable person, in the town of Andover and *such other places as they may think best*, to receive and take the charge, etc.

The following accounts which are found of the expenses of this removal indicate the places where the books were kept in Andover : —

[1] *Records of General Court.*

"*Bill for Carting Books from Cambridge to Andover.*

"ANDOVER, *July* 22, 1775.
"Colony of Massachusetts Bay to the following persons, viz.
"To Josiah Blanchard, jr.
"To carting one load of Books belonging to Harvard College from Menotomy to Mr. Samuel Osgood's in Andover,[1] 20 miles £1. o. o Dr.
(Signed) JOSIAH BLANCHARD."

"Colony aforesaid to John Lovejoy Abbot Dr.
"To carting one load of Books from Menotomy to the house of George Abbot, Esq.,[2] in Andover, 17 miles £0. 17. Dr.
"(Signed) JOHN L. ABBOT."

Also there are bills of Benjamin Ames, Jr., and Philemon Dane, for carting books the same distance as the first named lot, at the same price, namely one pound. This would indicate that three loads were brought the twenty miles to the house of Mr. Samuel Osgood. A receipt follows from Mr. Phillips: —

"ANDOVER, *July* 22, 1776.
"This may certify that the within named Josiah Blanchard, Benj. Ames Jr., Philemon Dane, John Lovejoy Abbot did the within mentioned service by my order. . . ."

"WATERTOWN, *May* 12, 1776.
"Received the sum of three pounds seventeen shillings in full of the above account.
"(Signed) SAMUEL PHILLIPS JR."

The journal of James Stevens gives a glimpse of Andover on the day of the battle of Bunker Hill and also a picture of the camp life of the soldiers about Boston in the first year of the war, their journeyings back and forth between Cambridge and Andover, and the sort of life they led while on duty. At the time of the battle, the writer of the journal was on furlough for sickness. On the 15th, he had a pass to go home: —

"I was not abel to do my duty. I went up to farington's & there I had his horse, & his wife went with me & Jonathan Gard-

[1] North Andover.
[2] Phillips Street, west of Latin Commons, afterwards occupied by Judge Phillips.

ner. We got hom about ten a clock. I staid all night at brothers.

"*Fryeday* y*e* 16. This morning I went to Docter Osgood's & he gave me a puk. I went home & in the afternoon I tuk it.

"*Saturday* y*e* 17. I went after my hors up to ———— I herd that our men was gon to bunker hill to intrench and that they shot won of our men, won polerd of Bilrica. we saw a lit tords Charleston.

"*Sunday* y*e* 18. this morning I went to doctor Osgood & there was a larum, they said that the regerlers had com out & we herd that our men was gon on to bunker hill to intrench & that the regelers was com over & had cild a hundred of our men & wounded a great many more. in the afternoon I went to Boxford meeting ;[1] after meeting I went to town to se what nuse. the men was a coming back.

"*Tuesday* 20. This morning I went up to Captain Varnum's to se him. he was wounded in two places in his leg.

"*Thursday*. this morn I started for Cambridge about nine a'clock. I met Timothy Carlton at deacon barlerds. he was wounded in the nek. I got down to Cambridge about sunset."

Nothing more of marked interest is chronicled till Saturday, July the 1st, when the arrival of General Washington is expected : —

"We preaded to receive the new general Washington but he did not com.

"*Sunday* y*e* 2. This morning we preaded to receive the new jineral. it rained & we was dismissed. the jeneral com in about nine. There was *no meting*. In the *afternoon I went* to the *colidge & heard a sermon*."

The fourth of July, not yet "Independence Day," brings visitors to camp, come partly for the sake of seeing the new general : —

"*Afternoon*. Mr. Stephen Barker & his wife, Sarah & Major Poor's wife, & Jonathan Stevens' wife & Phineas Johnson's wife, they all come down.

"*Thursday*, 13. I went to her prayers.[2] Jonathan Gardner came from Andover & told us that Cor. Osgood was ded."

[1] Nothing interfered with his observance of his religious duty.
[2] This phrase to " hear prayers " first occurs in the journal after Washington took command.

On Tuesday, August 1st, James Stevens has a little variety in his round of duty. He is one of a company detailed to march to Worcester, as a guard of some thirty prisoners: —

"About nine we went to Concord & staid all night. we put the prisoners into jail, we got our supper & sot a sentry."

The journal states that they marched through Littleton and Lancaster, and at the latter place stayed all night, where the "towns peapol stod sentry over" the prisoners and relieved the soldiers. They arrived safe in Worcester, and lodged their prisoners in the jail. These prisoners were tories. How they were dealt with for their toryism by the zealous sons of liberty, appears from the memoranda of this diary: —

"The toris went with their hats under thar arms & we returned them to the prison — the *tories went in to the dungeons.* . . . .
"We got some vitels & then sot of for hom."

James Stevens and his comrades now in camp again, he devotes himself to the nursing of a sick friend, Asa Parker, and is himself also sick for a time. But as often as Sunday comes he goes to meeting. The sermons which he mentions as having heard would make a volume. Now it was President Langdon, and now Dr. Appleton, and then "won Mr. Emerson," and Mr. Osgood and Mr. Cleveland.

In September he was at home on a visit, and the 30th made "a apel chest for grandfather."

Sunday, October 1st, "I went to Andover meeting & herd Mr. Syms." On the 7th of October he was enlisted, under Captain Pollard, and at work as a carpenter on the barracks: —

"*Sunday, Dec.* 10. Captain Polerd com out & said that our wages was cut down to eight pence, the men all Left of worke, in the forenoon Cap. Polerd com & said that we was all Dismissed there was a great many of the militia coming.

"*Monday.* This morning Cap. Pollerd com out & said if we would go to worke we should have seven pounds ten a month.

"*Wednesday, Dec.* 20. I got a man to cuk for me & I set of for home. I got to Andover about aleven a clock at night. I went to John Barker's to carry some things to uncle John.

"*Dec.* 25. This morning I got up a little afore Day & yoket up fore oxen for uncle John & set off for Cambridge. I got to Cambridge about Dusk & then went to roxbury & got there a little after eight."

A good day's work this was, in the dead of winter, — yoking up oxen before daylight, and travelling all day over such roads as there were a hundred years ago. At the end of the month the company were dismissed (their time having expired), and their "guns were taken away."

James Stevens stayed a few days "to work," and on the 7th of January, at five o'clock in the morning, set off for home. It was Sunday, and, true to his principles, he stops (within three miles of home) and goes "to Mr. French's meeting," and, travelling on a piece toward home, in the afternoon goes to Mr. Symmes' meeting. The next Sunday he was at Cambridge, and for two Sundays he "worked" on General Putnam's store. (This was not according to his ideas of Sabbath-keeping.) He says, "I *was obleaged* to work at the store." . . . . "Sunday, March the 11, We did not worke. I *went* to *meeting* in the forenoon. In the afternoon I went on to the hils, & sold my gun for ten Dolers." He records a feat of two of his fellow soldiers and its result, thus : —

"There was a man ciled himself a Drinken jin. There was two men Drinkt forty-fore glasses — won Died."

In March he is "at hom." Sunday, the 17th, he goes "to meetin to Boxford," and hears "Mr. Holihok." . . . . "Monday, Mar. 18. This Day I went up to town & got my hair Drest, & then went to Deacon Chadwick's to se the Boxford officers chose." But although his time was out, he could not be easy at home. He has to go to camp to see what is doing. He hears of the evacuation of Boston by the British : "They told us that our peaple had tuck possession of Boston. The regerlers lie in sight."

He stayed about Cambridge doing duty as a substitute for a month, and in April returned to Andover. The journal leaves him going to meeting, hearing Mr. Adams preach, or Mr. Symmes, on Sundays, and on week-days working at splitting rails, and helping "uncle John work on his hous."

In regard to the events in camp at Cambridge, a few other relics and traditions of Andover men are preserved. A souvenir of the courtesies of General Washington was long kept by the descendants of Captain Furbush — an invitation to a dinner party. It is thus described by the Captain's grandson : —

"This Invitation is written on figured paper, a strip six inches long and three wide folded once lengthwise and then by four angles into a square and addressed to Capt. Furbush, Col. Bridge's Regiment. The contents are as follows: 'Gen. Washington's Compliments to Captain Furbush and requests his company to dinner to-day."

There is a tradition of an interview of another Andover officer with the commander-in-chief, somewhat less agreeable, than this dinner-party may be supposed to have been. The General was in conference with the field officers, respecting various important and perplexing questions of organization and discipline, of which there were so many at this time. He was rehearsing the difficulties and embarrassments of his position, in command of an army undisciplined, poorly equipped, and enlisted only for a short period of service. With a view, doubtless, to animate the patriotism of the officers and to induce them to forego any petty jealousies or personal considerations, he dwelt at length on his own sacrifices, and emphasized the statement that he had left his comfortable home and come to Cambridge to take command, from no motive of ambition, but influenced solely by love of country and a desire to serve the public interests. Nettled at what he conceived to be an affront to the Provincial officers, and conscious of his own singleness of purpose, Col. James Frye sprang to his feet, and facing General Washington, interrupted his discourse, — "Sir, what do you think *we* came here for ? "

Notwithstanding the commander's despondency and Colonel Frye's irascibility, the work of reorganizing went on successfully. Difficulties were overcome in a manner that seems almost miraculous. " Search the vast volumes of history through," wrote Washington, "and I much question whether a case similar to ours is to be found, to wit: to maintain a post against the flower of the British troops for six months together, without powder, and at the end of them to have one army disbanded and another to raise within the same distance of a reënforced enemy." Everywhere, however, he was sustained. The towns sent in supplies to the extent of their ability, and the work of enlisting went on briskly, although it seemed often to the anxious officers to be but slowly. Andover sent fifty pounds of powder and also another company of soldiers. Capt. John Abbot's memorandum, — "Perticular Allowance I have Rec'd for my company, since we arrived at Head Quarters at Cambridge," shows that the company arrived December 9, 1775. The note book has various memoranda: as "Draw'd one Day's allowance of Bread & Meat. .... Draw'd allowance of Molasses, Sope & Candles for 7 days." ....

The following list of names of the company is made up from this note book.

The other muster roll of Benjamin Farnum's company is added to show the changes of officers in the regiment within the year. Capt. John Peabody, the roll of whose company follows, is sometimes reckoned from Boxford, sometimes from Andover.

Captain Peabody served as adjutant to Col. Isaac Smith early in the year, in the army about Boston.[1]

"*Captain John Abbot's Company. A Reinforcement to the Army at Cambridge, Dec. 9, 1775.*"

Captain John Abbott.	Elijah Barker.	Simeon Farnum.
Lieut. John Peabody.	Isaac Barker.	John Field.
Lieut. Benj. Poor.	Uzziel Batchelder.	David Fish.
Sergt. Stephen Abbot.	John Bejom.	Joseph Foster.
Sergt. Daniel Poor.	Philip Bejom.	Isaac Foster.
Corporal Philip Abbot.	John Blunt.	John Frye.
Corporal Isaac Carlton.	Benj. Carlton.	Abijah Fuller.
Ephraim Abbot.	Ebenezer Clarke.	Jacob Grainger.
Nathan Abbot.	John Chandler.	Thomas Gray.
Nehemiah Abbot.	Nathian Coburn.	Jeremiah Goldsmith.
Andrew Allen.	Francis Dane.	Edward Herrick.
Benjamin Barker.	William Dennice.	David Holt.

[1] See Force's *American Archives*.
[2] See also, *Mass. Rev. Rolls*, vol. xxviii., p. 124.

Samuel Holt.
Lemuel Holt.
Daniel Ingalls.
Edmond Ingalls.
Henry Ingalls.
Joel Jenkins.
Obed Johnson.
Thomas Kimball.
Daniel Lovejoy.
Moses Lovejoy.

Samuel Lovejoy.
John Lovejoy.
Jacob Mackentire.
James Marshal.
Saml Marshal.
Isaac Mooar.
Aaron Parker.
John Phillpes.
Joseph Russel.
Jedediah Russel.

David Russel.
Isaac Russel.
Jacob Russel.
Nathaniel Sawyer.
Phineas Spafford.
Ephraim Swan.
Joseph Shattuck.
Oliver Whiting.
Joseph Wilson.
Benjamin Wood.

"*Roll of Capt. Benjamin Farnum's Company. A Reinforcement to the Army near Boston, Feb. 1776.*"

Time of Service 66 days.

Benj⁰ Farnum, Capt.
Eliphalet Hardy, 1st Lieut.
Ebenezer Peabody, 2nd Lt.
Joshua Chandler, Ensn.
Stephen Messer, Sergt.
Andrew Peabody, do.
Jeduthan Abbot, do.
William Bacon, do.
Timothy Carlton, Corpl.
Elijah Clark, do.
Jonathan Lovejoy, do.
Allier Perley, do.
Jonathan Buxton, Drum.
John Wilson, Fifer.
John Welch.
Jeremy Robinson.
Peter Robinson.
Samuel West.
Benja. Frye.
Nathan Ingals.
Jacob Barnard.
Jonathan Ballard.
Abiel Abbot.
Jacob Stiles.
Joseph Parker.
Abijah Ingals.
John Chandler, jr.
Joseph Chandler.
John Farington.

Timothy Johnson.
Jonathan Darrow.
David Dorrant.
Daniel Blanchard.
Isaac Smith.
Phineas Parker.
David Porter.
Phineas McIntire.
Daniel Ingals.
Jotham Barrow.
Joseph Abbot.
Jacob Johnson.
Isaac Holt.
Jabez Haywood.
Israel Farnum.
Nathaniel Frye.
David Beverly.
John Nichols.
Daniel Kimball.
William Lovejoy.
John Poor.
Daniel Poor.
James Bridges.
Spofford Ames.
Abiel Upton.
Josiah Hardy.
John Macloyt.
Henry Hardy.
William Marden.

Free Parker.
Jabez Gage.
Aquila Kimball.
Edmond Herrick.
Dudley Bixby.
Edmund Cheney.
Nathaniel Griffin.
Uriah Gage.
Daniel Cheney.
Dudley Hardy.
Amos Bayley.
Robert Savery.
Ebenezer Hardy.
Jonas Hardy.
David Hale.
Amos Head.
Jonathan Woodman.
Nathaniel Hale.
Jonathan Porter.
Thomas Dwinell.
Ephraim Matthews.
Samuel Stiles.
Tyler Porter.
Amos Hovey.
Thomas Chadwick.
Rufus Burnam.
David Cheney.
Samuel Lovejoy.
David Farnum.

"*A Pay Roll due to Capt. John Peabody's Company in Col. Ebenezer Francis's Regiment, being for travel into camp and home again, at one penny per mile, also for one day's pay for every twenty Miles Travel home from Camp and their Gun and Blanket money. The said company being draughted from the Towns of Salisbery, Newburyport, Bradford, Haverhill, Methuen, Boxford, & Andover.*"

Capt. John Peabody, Andover.
Lt. Moses Greenleaf, Newburyport.
Lt. Reuben Evans, Salisbury.
Ens. Samuel Hazeltine, Haverhill.
Sergts. Phil[a] Lahaman, Boxford.
Jno. Richardson, Methuen.
Rich[d] Bayley, Haverhill.
James Chase, Newburyport.
Corps. Richard Merrill, Bradford.
Nathan Abbott, Andover.
Josh Somerby, Newburyport.
Josh Stevens, Salisbury.
Drum. Jacob Quhn, Newburyport.
Fife, Asa Wood, Bradford.

Jonathan Noyse, Newburyport.
[42 names. Newburyport, Bradford, Haverhill, Methuen.]
Uzziel Bachelder, Andover.
Obed Barker, Andover.
Jonath Ballard, Andover.
Saml Cogswell, Andover.
Peter Carlton, Andover.
Seth Emerson, Andover.
James Frye, Andover.
William Hopping, Andover.
Solomon Wardwell, Andover.
William Bodwell, Andover.

DORCHESTER HEIGHTS, 1776.[1]

The scarcity of gunpowder was one of the greatest sources of embarrassment to the military operations. At the close of the year, 1775, there seem to have been no mills in Massachusetts which were available for the manufacture of powder, although there were the remains of mills which had been erected in early colonial times but had long been disused. It became therefore of prime importance to revive this manufacture. Accordingly in November, 1775, the General Court voted to build mills, and, after some indecision as to the place of location, selected Stoughton, and ordered the work of repairing and putting in order an old mill there to proceed with expedition. Meanwhile Mr. Samuel Phillips, Jr., of Andover, with the sagacity which characterized him, foresaw the advantages of this manufacture both as a private enterprise and a public necessity. He made a proposition to the Court that he would, with sufficient encouragement from the State,

[1] Time, two or three days, miles thirty-seven to sixty. *Mass. Rev. Rolls*, vol. xxi., p. 195.

erect a mill at Andover, at his own expense. His proposal was accepted. It was agreed to furnish him with saltpetre and sulphur at cost for a year, and to pay him at the rate of eight pence per pound for all the gunpowder which he should manufacture, he agreeing to "keep a good and sufficient Guard about the mill at all time to prevent any wicked and designing persons from destroying the same," and also to cause to be published all the discoveries which he shall make relative to the construction of said mill and the manufacturing Powder as aforesaid."

Mr. Phillips lost no time in beginning operations. On the 2d of January, he despatched a letter[1] to a builder, one Mr. Samuel Cunnable, who has been recommended as "a person of Great Integrity and proper to be employed in the undertaking." Also he obtained an order from the General Court permitting him to employ the master-workman of the powder-mill erecting for the colony, at Stoughton, — one Mr. Harling.

Mr. Phillips then called a meeting of the citizens of Andover, placed before them his projects, explained the necessity of despatch, and engaged large numbers of them to join in the work of digging the mill-race, agreeing to pay them if the manufacture should pay him. It is said that to stimulate their ambition and hasten the work he himself worked with the company.

By this prompt and energetic action, the mill[2] at Andover was completed and in operation in March, nearly three months before the one at Stoughton was ready for work.

Witness the following item from the "Massachusetts Spy," May 31, 1776: —

"WATERTOWN, *May* 20.

"The Public may rely on it as a fact that there has been made at the Powder-mill, at Andover, within these six weeks past about one thousand pounds weight of good Gunpowder per week.

"The powder mill at Stoughton will begin to go in a few days."

---

[1] Some of these letters are found among the private papers of Mr. Phillips, and some in the *Mass. Archives*.
[2] On the Shawshin, north of the Marland Mills, or Andover Mills.

This newspaper statement is confirmed by the testimony of Professor Winthrop.

"*May* 23, 1776.

"Last week I was at the Powder Mill at Andover. They go briskly on and turn out, as they told me, twelve hundred pounds per week, and shall soon turn out considerably more."

Great care was taken and every precaution used to prevent the entrance of visitors to the mill who would be careless or do damage on the premises.

The General Court ordered that there should "be placed round the mill and every building belonging thereto that shall contain any gunpowder, a Pole or Line at the Distance of one Rod at least; And if any person shall enter within such bounds as have been herein mentioned at any time between sunsetting and sunrising and refuse or neglect to depart therefrom, after having been three times called upon audibly by any Person that may be on guard, by consent of the said Phillips, in such case it shall be lawful for the said Guard to fire on any person so neglecting or refusing."

The difficulties of procuring materials were great. The supply of saltpetre being very insufficient, it became necessary to pull up the floors of sheds and buildings, to obtain earth from which to extract saltpetre, before facilities were afforded for its better manufacture. In this department of the work, Mr. Eliphalet Pearson, the afterward preceptor of Phillips Academy, by his inventive genius and practical knowledge of chemistry, rendered valuable aid.

The utmost capacity of the mill was not equal to the demand for powder, although it was run day and night, and on Sunday as well as week-days.

Just as things were going on well, the foreman of the mill, Joshua Chandler, was drafted or enlisted to make up a company for the reënforcement of the troops at Dorchester; also the next most important man of the mill, Josiah Johnson, was summoned to military duty. Mr. Phillips at once petitioned the General Court to exempt these men from military service and to treat the men in his employ "as though they were in publick service as really as those in the continental army."

Among other considerations he adduces the following reasons for requesting this favor of the Court: —

"When your Petitioner considers the distress this state has suffered for want of this article of Gunpowder, the danger it is still exposed to through the still remaining deficiency, That the anxiety of the Assembly on this account was such that they lately requested that this mill should be kept employed by night as well as day: and not on the week time only, but also on the Sabbath, and at the same time reflects how much the manufacturing will be retarded by changing hands, and also the difficulty of making Powder of so good a Quality, and the Impossibility of improving the stock to so much Advantage for the State, he thinks it his Duty in regard to the Publick interest as well as his own to make application to the Honble Board, as having the first command, that the aforesaid Foreman, Joshua Chandler by name, may be discharged from his enlistment, and that the men necessarily employed in that manufactory be excused from all military service during their continuance therein," etc.

The petition was granted, and it was ordered to discharge Joshua Chandler. Everything in the town which could help on the work was put into requisition for the mill. Even the meeting-house furniture was not spared.[1] "Without I can have one of those stoves[2] in the meeting-house," writes Mr. Phillips to his friend Richard Devens, Esq., Commissary-general, March, 1776, "my Powder works must be retarded. I can place another in its stead that may serve that purpose as well, tho it wont answer for my use on account of being cracked. I would wish for your advice whether it is not best to take one without waiting for the leave of the House as I have an opportunity tomorrow to convey it, and waiting to ask the House will probably retard the whole business at least one day and perhaps more. . . . ." Again, March 29th, Mr. Phillips asks for more saltpetre, and says : "All the saltpetre is worked up. My pestles must stand still till I receive more." Mr. Zebadiah Abbot, a trader of Andover, was chosen by the committee of the House to receive and examine saltpetre.

This experiment of the manufacture of gunpowder, upon whose success hung the greatest issues, was watched with solicitude by patriots all over the country.

[1] *Mass. Archives*, vol. cxciv., p. 309.
[2] A letter of Mr. Phillips to Mr. Timothy Pickering also says that the selectmen of Marblehead have given him the use of their stove.

Mr. Phillips received letters from various men of position and influence, congratulating him on his having undertaken the work, and expressing hopes for his prosperity in it.

One of these letters, from Mr. B. W. Paine, dated Philadelphia, September 25, 1776, speaks of the failures to make satisfactory gunpowder, and says there had been "some miserable trash turned out for gunpowder," and adds that it would be "a most cruel vexation in the day of decision for Liberty or Slavery to have the scale turn against us merely through the defect of our own powder."

But, notwithstanding the energy displayed and the pains taken, the gunpowder was not wholly satisfactory. Witness the following letter [1] from General Washington to General Heath, who had complained of the gunpowder made in Massachusetts:—

"*April 8th*, 1777. There must certainly be either roguery or gross ignorance in your powder-makers, because the powder made in the other states is esteemed better than that imported from Europe. . . . . It is a matter of so much importance that it should be strictly inquired into."

In July following, the House of Representatives ordered "that as some of the gunpowder made at Andover and Stoughton had been found defective, arising from want of experience in this new manufacture, all such defective powder should be received back into the mills and good powder furnished the Government instead. An inspector, Colonel Burbeck, was also ordered to visit Andover, in June, "for a trial of the powder and to make experiments of divers mixtures [2] and ingredients of gunpowder and various methods of drying."

Besides the discouragement from the difficulty of making good gunpowder, there was another still more serious and distressing,—an explosion, June, 1778, at the mill, the blowing up of the building and killing three men. This caused great excitement and consternation in the town. The General Court, June 10th, ordered a committee of investigation,

---

[1] *Mass. Hist. Coll.*, Fifth Series, vol. iv.
[2] *General Court Records*, vol. xxxvii., p. 136.

and to consider the expediency of continuing the business. This committee reported, June 12th, that the "late misfortune in blowing up the two buildings at said Andover was not owing to any Imprudence in Mr. Phillips but to mear accident, also that in their opinion the public service requires that Mr. Phillips should still proceed in the manufacturing of Gunpowder."

But there was considerable local feeling about the danger of the mill, and for some months operations were suspended. In October, the General Court passed a resolve for the encouragement and aid of Mr. Phillips in repairing the mill, ordering that if the powder-mill should again suffer damage by accident, that half the expense of repairing should be refunded by the State.

Measures were also taken for procuring the service of experts in the manufacture. Two French gentlemen,[1] Mons. Nicholas Fouquett, and his son, Mons. Mark Fouquett, who were "to propagate the art of making powder in these States," were ordered to come to Andover to give the necessary instructions.

An interesting letter from Mr. Phillips to Colonel Pickering, gives an account of their visit, and expresses his good opinion regarding their ability for the work. "I found he very well answered the character you gave of him. His method of forming the Morter is very ingenious and of great utility and his acquaintance with the manufacture of Gunpowder such as well qualified him for his undertaking."[2]

Yet although Mr. Phillips expresses his approval of Mons. Fouquett, and his sense of the value of his advice, he seems to think that in some respects the Andover powder-makers were as competent as their instructor: —

"I think it must be acknowledged he has done much good, yet he promised rather more from his construction of a Mill than it would perform. Instead of its answering best to put all the materials whole into the mortar, I find my Pestles will not in that way make the Sulphur or salt petre fine enough, and that it is necessary to reduce both to a powder before the ingredients are mixed."

[1] Private papers of Mr. Phillips.
[2] *Pickering Papers* — *Mass. Historical Society.*

In this letter Mr. Phillips also mentions the fact that many British prisoners of war had been employed in the powder-mill, and that the government was now contemplating taking them away with a view to exchange. He says this will seriously embarrass his work, and further, that he thinks these men would prefer to stay in Andover, where "some have married, had children, taken the oath of allegiance, paid taxes, and become useful members of society." He says one man in particular is so trustworthy that the whole charge of the powder-mill has been committed to him.

After the close of the Revolution, and the establishment of the Government on an apparently sure foundation, Mr. Phillips began to think of giving up the manufacture of gunpowder, and turning his attention to the manufacture of paper, which was in great demand. But he made the change gradually, and continued the gunpowder making longer than he at first contemplated, — down to about 1797. It seems, from letters written to Mr. Phillips, in June, 1789, that the work of transforming the powder-mill into a paper-mill had even then begun. The paper-makers and the powder-makers came into collision, there having been some misunderstanding, and the foreman of the powder-mill began preparations to fill an order for gunpowder, and ordered the engines for the paper-making to be removed. So serious was the difficulty that the superintendent of the paper works threatened to leave. Mr. Phillips settled the difficulty, for both manufactures were continued, additional buildings being put up. An explosion took place again, in 1796, October 19th, by which two men were killed. For a time the manufacture was suspended, if it was not at once relinquished. It is stated [1] that no more powder was made after the explosion. A letter written by Mr. Phillips shows that there was some intention (if it was not actually carried out) of continuing, at least long enough to use up the stock on hand, after the excitement had subsided. He says that Mr. Hardy and Mr. Holt are both willing to go on, and he thinks it might be well, instead of selling the stock of saltpetre, to retain as much of it as they have not promised, since the continuance of "the war" (in France) would create a demand for powder.

[1] Abbot's *History of Andover.*

The termination of the powder-making may be said to have been practically made at the time of the explosion in October.

The following epitaph on a gravestone, in the South Parish Burying Ground, is the latest relic remaining, which is evidently connected with the powder manufactory : —

In memory of
MR. DAVID HALL who
was killed at the explosion
of the powder house in
Andover Oct. 17th 1796
Aged 32 years & 8 months.

We mourn thy sudden swift remove,
From earth and all enjoyments here;
When Christ commands, we must obey
Without a murmur or a tear.

To return to the military events and condition of things in the first winter of the war. The winter of 1775 was a time of the deepest anxiety at Andover, as well as throughout the country. Aside from other sources of distress, the mere absence from home of so many able-bodied men was severely felt, perhaps even more so during the winter than it had been in the summer and autumn. They had been much missed in the planting and the harvest, but when the blocking snows set in, women and children on remote farms were in many instances cut off from the comforts and even the necessaries of life, and shut in from the sympathy of friends and the tidings of the progress of events.

There are only a few items of information found additional to those already noted in the journals quoted, respecting the soldiers in camp at Cambridge and Dorchester. In November, the soldiers who had been in service eight months each received a coat, according to a vote of the Congress: —

"We the subscribers, officers and soldiers in captain Benjamin Ames's company, in Col. James Frye's regiment, pray you Gentlemen to Deliver to Lieut. David Chandler or Lieut. Isaac Abbott the coats we are entitled to by vote of a late congress, and their Receipt shall be your discharge for the same.
"CAMBRIDGE, *Nov.* 14, 1775."

"TO THE COMMITTEE OF CLOTHING *at Watertown.* Received 45 coats for the within mentioned men.   DAVID CHANDLER."

Captain Farnum's company did not care for the coats, being already comfortably provided, and petitioned for money in lieu of the coats.

In January, 1776, the town and the army sustained a great loss in the death of Col. James Frye. Concerning his death and funeral rites, nothing more has been learned than the record on his gravestone in the North Andover Buryingground: —

> In Memory of
> COLONEL JAMES FRYE
> who departed this life
> Jany the 8th 1776
> *Ætatis* 66
> while
> in the continental service
> supporting the Independence
> of the United States
> of America.
> *Homo fuit.*

Although anticipating, it may here be mentioned, that not far from the grave of Colonel Frye sleeps his brother officer, Col. Samuel Johnson, who passed through the whole six years of the Revolutionary service unscathed, though he was in several hot engagements, and did valuable service. He died November 12, 1796, aged eighty-four.

Also, near by these officers' graves is the grave of the good captain who did duty under both Colonels, but who so long survived their day and generation, and served so faithfully (as is elsewhere related) in peaceful labors that his military title was finally exchanged for that of his ecclesiastical office. The epitaph merely states that Dea. Benjamin Farnum died December 4, 1833, aged 87.

The evacuation of Boston by the British, although it was cause for general rejoicing, was, in the end, the occasion of sorrow to many individuals, for it transferred the soldiers from service within easy access of home to distant fields, to and from which letters and messengers were necessarily infrequent and irregular. While it was possible in a few hours' ride to visit friends in camp, and while influential citizens of Andover were in the near neighborhood of the army, there seemed less cause of anxiety for the welfare of the soldiers.

But their beloved Colonel, the sharer of the soldier's fortune and the animator of the soldier's courage at Louisburg and Bunker Hill, was asleep in the old Andover Buryingground ; the Andover men who had served under his command, with the exception of a few put into Col. Samuel Johnson's regiment, were under the orders of a stranger, and in place of being within calling distance of their representative, and within sight of the metropolis, and favored with Sunday sermons from the professors of Harvard College, our townsmen soon were marching painfully through northern forests, afloat on unknown rivers and lakes, garrisoning lonely forts which recalled legends of Indian barbarities, French duplicity, and British negligence. Ticonderoga, Crown Point, and all the names of that region known to the veterans of the French war, now became familiar to their children, some of whom were accompanied in the campaign by their fathers of the old-time "service under the king."

The following is a roll of Colonel Johnson's regiment,[1] March, 1776 : —

"*Agreeable to the Direction of the Honorable Counsel, We have divided and set off the Companies in the Fourth Regiment of Militia in the County of Essex who have made choice of the several Persons hereafter named for their officers, and the Rank of the said companies are as followeth :* —

[1] *Mass. Rev. Rolls*, vol. xxxii., p. 269.

Rank of Companies	Towns	Captains.	First Lieutenant.	Second Lieutenant.
1	Andover.	John Peabody.	Samuel Johnson.	Cyrus Marble.
2	Haverhill.	Nathl. Marsh.	Israel Bartlett.	Ebenezer Gage.
3	Bradford.	Nathl. Gage.	Daniel Kimball.	Joseph Mulliken.
4	Boxford.	Jacob Gould.	John Dorman.	Jedediah Stickney.
5	Methuen.	John Bodwell.	John Huse.	Saml. Cross.
6	Andover.	John Abbot, Jr.	Moses Abbot.	Saml. Jenkins.
7	Haverhill.	Saml. Merrill.	Stephen Webster.	Saml. Crowel.
8	Bradford.	John Savory.	Thomas Stickney.	Moses Herriman.
9	Andover.	Nathl. Lovejoy.	John Adams.	John Frye.
10	Haverhill.	Timothy Johnson.	Ephraim Eliot.	John Page.
11	Andover.	Joshua Holt.	William Dean.	Jonathan Abbot.
12	Methuen.	James Jones.	Nathaniel Messer.	Stephen Webster.
13	Boxford.	John Cushing.	Samuel Runnels.	Asa Merril.
14	Haverhill.	Joseph Eaton.	Isaac Snow.	Samuel Hazeltine.
15	Methuen.	David Whitier.	James Mallon.	John Parker, Jr.

Samuel Johnson, ⎫
John Whittier, ⎬ *Field officers.*
Samuel Bodwell. ⎭

"ANDOVER, *Mar.* 26, 1776."

There are only scanty records of any service of Andover men about New York, or in the middle department. Capt. Nathaniel Lovejoy's manuscript (quoted in Abbot's "History") mentions that ten men of his company were "in service at New York, 1776." A return, among the rolls, also indicates such service "on the North Rivour, under General Warner," but no names are specified, merely the number, "nineteen men from Andover."[2]

Fuller accounts are found of the Andover men ordered to the northwest. June 20, 1776, Capt. Samuel Johnson[3] was put in command of seventy-five men (sixty-four of whom were from Andover) for the "reinforcement of the Continental army."

[1] *Mass. Rev. Rolls*, vol. xxxii., p. 285.
[2] *Ibid.*, vol. xliii., p. 101.

ANDOVER IN THE REVOLUTIONARY WAR. 353

The company of Capt. Samuel Johnson, in Colonel Wigglesworth's regiment, was sent to the northward, as part of a force to defend Ticonderoga against Sir Guy Carleton's expected attack; but that officer's power being broken by Arnold's vigorous action on Lake Champlain, and the fort no longer menaced, the troops were ordered back to Albany to spend the winter. Some of those whose time had expired returned to Boston to be discharged. The following is the roll of Captain Johnson's company [1]: —

"*A Role of the Travel of Capt. Saml. Johnson's* [2] *Company in Col. Wigelsworth's Regiment from Albany to their Respective Homes — 1776.*"

Capt. Samuel Johnson.	Samuel Currier.	Peter Marston.
Lt. Isaac Chandler.	William Dillaway.	Jeremiah Morel.
Lt. John Parker.	Charles Danolson [dead].	James Maglathlon.
*Ens. James Lunt.	Eliphalet Emery.	*Ruben Nola.
Sergt. Solomon Ingals.	John Ellet.	Andrew Otis.
Sergt. William Peabody.	Simeon Farnum.	David Porter [dead].
Sergt. David Stevens.	Abijah Fuller.	Joseph Parker.
Sergt. Ebenezer Davis.	Thomas Fisher.	*Umphrey Purington.
Corp. Isaac Carlton.	Nathaniel Grenough.	*Thomas Pool.
Corp. Jacob Marshall.	Samuel Hazelton.	John Rollins.
Corp. John Morrel.	Lemewel Holt.	Joshua Shaw [deserted].
Corp. Nathl. Ingals.	Daniel Holt.	Jacob Stiles.
Drum. Isaiah Ingals.	Thomas Abbot.	Thomas Stevens.
Fifer William Peabody.	Zebediah Holt.	Ephraim Swan [dead].
David Beverly.	Zaley [Zelah] Holt.	Joshua Swan.
Philip Bagley.	Paul Hardey.	Joseph Shattuck.
John Baldwin.	*David Hinkley.	Joseph Sandborn.
*Enoch Brown.	Phineas Ingals.	Edward Thomas.
*John Barker.	John Johnson.	Abiel Upton.
William Collens.	Abijah Ingals [dead].	*Samuel Neasey.
Joshua Chadwick.	Thomas Kimbal.	John Whitehorn.
Peter Cummens.	*Cornelius Shiff.	Samuel Woodbridge.
William Cabley.	Ezra Annes.	Robert Williams.
William Chamberlain.	William Lovejoy.	Isaac Smith.
Jonathan Carlton.	Saml. Lovejoy.	William Goodwin.
Timothy Chandler.	Stephen Messer.	

Captain Johnson made a memorandum in his note book of

[1] *Mass. Rev. Rolls*, vol. xx., p. 105.
[2] The distance of travel is given 210 miles, from Andover. The names marked * were of men from "Caskobay." They travelled 300 miles.

the places at which he stopped on this march. Most of the writing is now faded and illegible. A fragment is as follows : —

"TICONDEROGA, *November* 23d, 1776.
"This day at three of the aklock we struck our tent, and at Sunset we Barked on Bord the Bote and arived at Skeem-borer, 34 milds, at twelve aklock at night. — 24 Day. it was Raney So that we did not march. — 25. Marched from Skeem to forte an, fortene mils. — 26. from forte an to fort Edward, fortene mils. — 27. from fort Edward to Saratoga, forteen mils. — 28. from Saratoga to half moon, 28 miles. — 29. from half-moon to Albany, 12 miles. — 30. Staid in Albany on night ; it was Raney. — Sunday morning. we marched from Albany. — December 2. Loged at Canter hook ——— mils. on the 3. Loged in Nobletown, the Last tavern in York Government. . . . . Thro Glasko and through Westfield over into Springfield ; there loged ; from Springfield to Brookfield."

While military operations were going forward diligently, the great and decisive step was taken that made retrogression impossible. Massachusetts had practically anticipated the Declaration of Independence when she organized a House of Representatives and Council, and gave orders to ignore all public documents and orders of the royal governors. When the formal Declaration of Independence was under discussion by the State, in Andover, in town-meeting, June 12, 1776, "the question being put whether, should the Honourable Congress declare them independent of the kingdom of Great Britain, you will solemnly engage with your lives and fortunes to support them in the measure," it passed in the affirmative unanimously.[1]

The Declaration of Independence made necessary the adoption of a form of government for the provinces, some of which, up to this time, were nominally under the rule of the officers of the crown. But Massachusetts was in no pressing need of a change, having already settled satisfactorily, for the time being, the administration of affairs ; the House of Representatives as the legislative, and the Council as the execu-

[1] The Declaration of Independence is copied in full into the Town Records of Proceedings.

tive power, managing with efficiency. Accordingly, many prudent men deprecated calling up new questions to complicate and perhaps retard military operations.

Yet, when the subject came up, Andover voted, October 3, 1776, that "it is the consent of the town to intrust the matter of framing a constitution to the House of Representatives, together with the Council."

There had, however, arisen in some quarters a strong feeling against committing to the legislative body the framing of a constitution. Boston took decided ground against it, and advocated a Convention of Delegates for the purpose.

Most of the towns in the State, however, instructed their representatives, with a special view or an implied consent, to the framing of a constitution by the House.

At this juncture, Andover joined her voice to the opposition, not, however, advocating so much the Convention of Delegates, in distinction from the House of Representatives, as opposing all action at this time on the matter of a form of government. The town elected as its representative Col. Samuel Johnson, and instructed him to oppose any action in regard to a constitution, to advocate the vigorous prosecution of the war, and the postponement of questions of government to a future decision. The reasons alleged are, that "some of the ablest men, who have a peculiar right to a voice, are absent in the field or at Congress," and further, that it is no time when "foes are in the midst of us and an army at our Doors to consider how the country shall be governed, but rather to provide for its Defence."

This letter of "instructions" is among Colonel Johnson's private papers, and it is not improbable that it expressed fully his views, if it was not his own composition. It is an interesting paper, but too long for full quotation here. It closes by saying: "We, therefore, conclude that to set about the forming a New Constitution of Government at this time is unnecessary, impolitic, and dangerous; and it is accordingly our direction that you oppose it with those solid arguments of which the subject is so fruitful, and that you do it vigorously and perseveringly."

But, notwithstanding the opposition, the House of Representatives chose a committee to draft a constitution. This draft was submitted to the towns, and they voted [1] against accepting it. Therefore, in September, 1779, a Convention of Delegates met at Cambridge. The delegates from Andover were the following : [2] Samuel Osgood, Esq., Samuel Phillips, Jun., Esq., Mr. Zebadiah Abbot, Mr. John Farnum, Jr. "To this Convention," says Mr. Winthrop, "there were as great a number of men of learning, talents, and patriotism as had ever been assembled here at any earlier period." Mr. Phillips was one of the committee chosen by the Convention to draft the constitution. The form drafted was again submitted to the towns. In a town-meeting at Andover (May 1, 1780), of which the Hon. Samuel Phillips, Sen. (then sixty years old) was chosen moderator, a committee was chosen "to join with the members of the Convention for said town, to make such remarks and amendments in the Form of the Constitution as they shall think proper, and lay the same before the town at the adjournment of this meeting for their Consideration."

This committee consisted of the following : Rev. William Symmes, Mr. Jonathan French, the Hon. Samuel Phillips, Dea. Joshua Holt, Capt. John Farnum, Mr. Nehemiah Abbot, Mr. Moody Bridges, Mr. Asa Abbot, Capt. Peter Osgood, Mr. Philemon Chandler, Lieut. Oliver Peabody.

At the adjourned meeting, the town voted to approve the constitution, with the exception of certain articles which were taken up separately for discussion. Among these was the third article of the Bill of Rights, in regard to taxation for the support of public worship.

The town of Andover was in favor of taxing all citizens for the support of some form of worship, but allowing each to choose to what church his tax should be applied ; and in case of his declining to make any choice, the tax should be applied to "the support of the Teacher or Teachers of the Parish or Precinct" in which the moneys are raised.

The city of Boston was in favor of larger toleration, and

---

[1] The vote of Andover upon "the late Form of Government" was 33 for, 32 against.
[2] Colonel Johnson was now engaged in military duty.

of taxing no man for the support of a form of worship which he did not choose to attend, but to appropriate the tax collected from non-attendants of the prevailing worship to the support of the poor, or to objects of public utility.

Andover was strongly in favor of religious tests in regard to candidates for public office. It was voted, 180 affirmative, 1 negative, that "the Governor, Lieutenant-governor, Counsellors, Senators, and Representatives ought to be of the Protestant Religion, and that this restriction should be made."

To return now to the military affairs of 1776: The siege of Boston was vigorously pressed, and some Andover men were engaged in the various operations, offensive and defensive.

Capt. Nathaniel Lovejoy's[1] MS. notes service of his men[2] at Prospect Hill and at Dorchester, from February, 1776. The occupation of Dorchester Heights, on the 4th of March, the suspense of the week when the British were expected to storm the fortification, and another Bunker Hill fight was feared, the rejoicings when the enemy evacuated Boston and our army entered the city, were all, no doubt, fully described by tongue and pen of Andover men, eye-witnesses and participants of the events. But no record or tradition has come down to the present generation.

In 1777, the evils arising from the short terms of enlistment became so great that it was urgently pressed that men should enlist for three years or the war. This was difficult to secure; for the men, though willing to fight, if occasion required, were averse to pledging themselves for so long a time. In addition to the regular pay of the troops, the towns offered bounties. The town of Andover was remarkably liberal in these bounties, and also in providing for soldiers and their families. It has already been seen that when coats were given to the soldiers who had been eight months in the service, in 1776, one of the Andover companies (Captain Farnum's) did not wish to receive them, being well supplied. The difficulty of enlisting men led to levies. It is noticeable

---

[1] Captain Lovejoy of the militia does not appear to have been in active service.

[2] See *Abbot's History*.

that, while many towns were deficient, Andover's quota was always complete, and sometimes in excess.

Following are lists of men in the Continental service, 1777–1781:—

"*An exact account of all the men enlisted to serve in the continental army for the term of nine months, agreeable to a resolve of the General Court of the 26th of April, who belong to the Fourth Regiment of Militia in the County of Essex, of which Samuel Johnson, of Andover, is Colonel. Andover, June 2d, 1778.*"[1]

Names.	Age.	Complexion.	Height.	Compy. Capt.	Regt.	Town.
Frederick Ballard	16	Dark.	5.0	Lovejoy.	Johnson.	Andover.
Daniel Young	30	do.	5.10	do.	do.	do.
William Wilson	40	do.	5.6	do.	do.	do.
John McCoy	17	Olive.	5.5	do.	do.	do.
Aaron Readington	16	Sandy.	5.5	do.	do.	do.
Samuel Stickney	43	Light.	5.8	Holt.	do.	do.
Timothy Chandler	40	do.	5.10	do.	do.	do.
John Macoy	20	do.	5.8	do.	do.	do.
Aaron Parker	19	Dark.	5.6	do.	do.	do.
John Montgomery	40	do.	5.8	Johnson.	do.	do.
Alexander Montgomery	17	do.	5.3	do.	do.	do.
Aaron Wood	16	Light.	5.3	do.	do.	do.
Nathaniel Frye	18	Dark.	5.3	do.	do.	do.
James Parker	18	Dark.	5.3	do.	do.	do.
Simeon Dresser	19	Light.	5.9	Holt.	do.	do.
Ephraim Abbot	19	do.	5.7	do.	do.	do.
Elijah Knight	19	Dark.	5.8	do.	do.	do.
Robert Gray, jun.	17	Dark.	5.9	do.	do.	do.
Carlton Parker	24	do.	5.10	do.	do.	do.
Dudley Pettengel	25		5.11	Bodwell.	do.	Methuen.

The other names, thirty-eight, are of Methuen, Bradford, Haverhill.

"*A Return of those Men Inlisted into the Continental Service for the Term of three years or during the War, and Returned for the Second Foot company in the Town of Andover.*"[2]

Benj. Wild.	Jacob Russel.	Isaac Lovejoy.
Silus Blunt.	Isaac Russel.	James Turner.

[1] *Mass. Rev. Rolls*, vol. xxviii., p. 165½. [2] *Ibid.*, vol. xli., p. 64.

ANDOVER IN THE REVOLUTIONARY WAR. 359

James Turner, jr.
Thomas Day.
Palfrey Downing.
Benj. Webb.
Daniel Holt, jr.
Edward Herrick.

Mark Winter.
George Blunt.
Cesar Cogswell.
Cato Foster.
John Crosby, Boston.
John Quin, Boston.

Benj. Eaton.
John Knights.
Jonathan Hutchinson.
Caleb Abbot.
James Parker.

JOHN ABBOT, JR., *Capt.*

"ANDOVER, *Feb.* 16, 1778."

Continental Service, 1779.[1]

Names.	Age.	Height.	Complexion.	Company Captain.	Captain to whom delivered.
Asa Parker	19	5.6	Light.	Johnson.	Marshall.
Eben Clark	26	5.6	do.	do.	do.
Asa Town	16	5.2	do.	do.	do.
Nathl. Frye	20	5.4	do.	do.	do.
Jacob Dascombe	19	6.1	do.	Lovejoy.	do.
Michael Carlton	18	5.8	Brown.	do.	do.
Daniel Gray	18	5.7	Light.	do.	do.
David Stevens	18	5.10	do.	do.	do.
Wm. Harris	21	5.11	do.	do.	do.
Wm. Richardson	20	5.3	do.	do.	do.
Daniel Blanchard	19	5.9	do.	do.	do.
Isaac Blanchard	16	5.4	do.	do.	do.
Saml. Holt	17	5.8	Dark.	Abbot.	do.
Abiel Holt	33	5.7	Light.	do.	do.
John Fry	24	5.8	do.	do.	do.

A *Return*[2] *of Men raised for three years from Dec.* 2, *1780.*

Jacob Annes.
John Stevens.
Jesse Hagget.
Joseph Armstrong.
Peter Cummings.
Amos Blanchard.
Joseph Blanchard.
Matthew Lillies.
Dudley Woodbridge.
Thomas Abbot.
Thomas Andrews.
David Beverly.
Frederick Frye.
Isaac Lovejoy.

Allen Richards.
William Wilson.
Scipio Weare.
Jona Holt.
Abraham Moore.
Darius Holt.
Jacob Jones.
John Holt.
March Farrington.
Cesar Russell.
Isaac Russell.
Peter Martin.
Thos. Smith.
Zebediah Holt.

David Osgood.
Jacob Dascome.
Abiel Wilson.
Jona Ballard.
Joseph Pettengel.
Nathan Osgood.
Christopher Osgood.
Joseph Frost.
William Baxter.
James Hicks.
Peter Willis.
James McFarland.
Daniel Blanchard.
William Holt.

[1] *Mass. Rev. Rolls,* vol. xxix., p. 43. [2] *Ibid,* vol. xxviii., p. 181.

"*A Return*[1] *of Men belonging to Town of Andover, Jany, 1781, in the Continental Army, for 3 years or during war.*"

Dudley Messer.	Palfrey Downing, Corpl.	Asa Towns.
John Mabury.	Elias Heath.	Nathaniel Frye.
John White, Sergt.	Daniel Lindsay.	Benj. Webb.
James Turner.	Benj. Abbot, Drummer.	Benj. Berry.
Cato Foster, Drum.	Mark Winter.	Cesar Cogswell.
Joseph Wardwell, Sergt.	John Cross.	Asa Osgood, Sergt. Major.
Joseph Foster.	Ebenezer Johnson.	Joseph Frost.

A List[2] *of Three Years' Men, from 1777 to 1780. Enlisted in Essex and Middlesex Counties, belonging to Andover.*

Abbot, Benjamin.	Farnum, David.	McFarland, James.
Abbot, Caleb.	Frye, Nathl.	McFarland, James, jr.
Ames, Prince.	Feald, John.	Noyes, Timothy.
Anice, Jacob.	Fisk, Benjamin.	Parker, James.
Arbunile, Samuel.	Frye, Prince.	Parker, Benjamin.
Abor, Thomas.	Frye, Cato.	Parker, William.
Allin, Davis.	Gordon, William.	Poor, Salem.
Blunt, Silas.	Holt, Daniel, Jr.	Phelps, Thomas.
Blunt, George.	Herrick, Edward.	Pevey, Peter.
Beverly, David.	Hutchinson, Jonathan.	Russel, Jacob.
Barker, Joshua.	Holt, Samuel.	Russel, Isaac.
Barker, Obed.	Holt, Daniel.	Stevens, Thomas.
Berry, Benjamin.	Hagget, Thomas 3d.	Stevens, Bimsley.
Ballard, Jonathan.	Holt, Israel.	Stone, George.
Baldwin, John.	Herrick, Edmund.	Salter, Bosenger.
Boynton, Jonathan.	Ingals, Daniel.	Savory, Isaac.
Carlton, Timothy.	Ingals, Moses.	Shattuck, Joseph, jr.
Cummings, Peter.	Johnson, James.	Stevens, John, Jr.
Day, Thomas.	Knight, John.	Stiles, Hezekiah.
Douglas, John.	Kittredge, Peter.	Turner, James.
Dilaway, Benjamin.	Lovejoy, Isaac, jr.	Turner, James, Jr.
Eaton, Benjamin.	Long, Joshua.	Tite, a negro.
Farnum, Israel.	Lerabee, Ezekiel.	Tobey, a negro.
Frye, Joshua.	Lindsay, Daniel.	Weld, Benjamin.
Frye, Sampson.	Lovejoy, Obadiah.	Webb, Benjamin.
Farington, Thomas.	Lovejoy, John.	Winter, Mark.
Frye, Benjamin.	Mark, a negro.	White, John.
Farnum, David.	Mallon, John.	Welch, John.
Frye, Benjamin.	Martin, Peter.	

[1] *Mass. Rev. Rolls*, vol. xxix., p. 101. — Most of the men were enlisted in 1779.
[2] *Ibid.*, vol. xxvii., pp. 109-130. — These are mostly additional to those already given.

"Six Months Men[1] in Continental Service, 1780-81."

Adams, Nathaniel.	Hazelton, Elijah.	Pemberton, James.
Annis, John.	Holt, Abiel.	Poor, Daniel.
Abbot, Benjamin.	Holt, Daniel.	Porter, Nathl.
Ballard, Jona.	Ingals, Eben.	Pemberton, James.
Carlton, Stephen.	Jameson, John.	Parker, John.
Carlton, John.	Kenney, Thomas.	Poland, Asa.
Clough, Daniel.	Kimball, Benjamin.	Quarles, William.
Chandler, Samuel.	Knowlton, John.	Russel, Jacob.
Cowan, Isaac.	Knowlton, Nathl.	Ramsay, Thomas.
Chandler, James.	Knowlton, Thos.	Shattuck, Abiel.
Cady, James.	Long, Nathl.	Shattuck, Nathl.
Davis, James.	Lovejoy, Jeremiah.	Teague, Nathl.
Edes, Thos.	Lovejoy, Peter.	Thompson, James.
Foster, Simeon.	Lovejoy, Isaac, jr.	Thompson, John.
Foster, Danl.	Lovejoy, Joshua.	Townsend, Dennis.
Farnum, Asa.	Macoy, Barnabas.	Wilson, William.
Frost, Joseph, jr.	Osgood, David.	Wilson, Thomas.
Gibson, William.	Parker, William.	Walters, Benjamin.
Grant, Nathl.	Parker, John.	Walters, James.
Harris, John.	Parker, James.	

The military operations of the Massachusetts regiments, of the year 1777, were directed mainly toward the reënforcement of the northwestern department of the army, under command of General Schuyler, and its defence against any invasion by way of Canada. These operations are familiar to the reader from the general histories of the Revolution. The relation of them to Andover it is our province to trace.

One of the first companies ordered to this service was that of Capt. Benjamin Farnum, which was a part of the regiment of Colonel Francis.

The troops were sent to reënforce Fort Ticonderoga. The following is a list of the men in this expedition, in Captain Farnum's company: —

---
[1] Found on Town Record of Bounty, also *Mass. Rev. Rolls*, vol. iv., p. 37; xxvii., p. 8; xxv. p. 220.

"*Abstract*[1] *for the Reashans of a Company of Men whereof Benjamin Farnum is Captain, in the Battalion whereof Eben[r] Francis, Esq[r]., is Colonal, in the service of the United States of America, from there Inlistment till there Arrival at Bennington, allowing them to march the 28th Instant.*"

Benjamin Farnum, Capt.	John Stevens.	John Cross.
Stephen Abbot, Lieut.	Hezekiah Stiles.	David Farnum.
James Turner, Jr.	Thomas Haget.	Benj[a]. Abbot, Jr.
Isaac Lovejoy.	John Bauldwin.	David Beverly.
Isaac Russel.	James McFarland.	Joshua Frye.
Edward Herrick.	James McFarland, Jr.	Israel Farnum.
Daniel Holt.	John Welch.	Thomas Day.[*]
Cesar Cogswell.	Thomas Smith.	Benj. Webb.
George Blunt.	Thomas Phelps.	Palfry Downing.
Obadiah Lovejoy.	Jona. Hagget, Tewksbury.	Cato Foster.
John Lovejoy.	Daniel Linsey.	Mark Winter.
Peter Marten.	Wilm Parker.	Thomas Stevens.
Prince Ames.	Benj[a] Abbot.	Nehemiah Carlton, Bradford.
Joseph Shattuck.	Jona. Ballard.	
John Fields.	James Wiley.	Thomas Fuller, Salem.

Captain Farnum's diary has been preserved. It begins the day when the troops marched: —

"*28th Mar.* 1777. This day Lieut.[1] Stephen Abbot, with about 40 men, marched from Andover in order for Bennington. The 10 men that marched with me set out."

They arrived April 25th at Fort Edward. Captain Farnum makes the following memorandum: —

"*April* 26. Set as President on Cort Marshal. tryed five of Capt. McCraken's men, three of which were sentenced to be whipte (two set free, one pardoned by the commanding officer of the garrison), the other two Rec'd. 39 Lashes on the bare back.

"28*th*. Myself with 7 men marched to Fort George.

"30*th*. marched to Ticonderoga & Mt. Independence."

He stayed at this place till the 2d of May and then crossed Lake George and marched back to Fort Edward. The journal continues: —

"*May* 5*th.* 28 wagons garded from this garrison to Fort George.

"*May* 6*th.* A cort Marshall sot on one of the wagners, being guilty of stealing Pork out of Dr. Smith's Pot ; found guilty ; sents 29 lashes on the bare back, which he has rec'd, *well put on.*"

[1] *Mass. Rev. Rolls*, vol. ii., p. 35.   [*] Commissioned captain in 1778.

Captain Farnum, notwithstanding his apparent relish for the chastisement of offenders, and his occupation in the business of courts-martial, had a taste and found time for other recreations, as appears from some entries in his journal. We may imagine him arrayed in his best military style and quite another man from the one who sat on the court-martial and sentenced stripes for soldier's backs, when, May 12th, "I Rode with Mr. Halle and wife, Lieut. Donne and wife and others to the wider Hareses in a wagen." Still more suave, doubtless, was the captain when, May 15th, "Went down the River to Esq. Tutels with the wider McNeal and Mis Jeney with 3 men to row."

We may here anticipate events somewhat, to inquire who these ladies were with whom the captain was sailing down the Hudson in the May days of '77. He has another note regarding them, Sunday, July 27 : —

"Nuse that the Widder McNeal & the young woman that was with her at her house ware taken out of the seller & carried of by the enemy aboute a Mile and barbarously treated, then kiled and skalped."

These were the ladies whose melancholy fate has formed the theme of so many tales of history and romance, and been so variously related.[1]

" Mis Jeney," as Captain Farnum calls her, was Miss Jane McRea, the daughter of a Scotch Presbyterian clergyman of New Jersey. Her father was dead, and she lived with her brother on the Hudson River a few miles below Fort Edward. Her brother was an ardent patriot ; but Miss McRea was engaged to be married to a young man, David Jones by name, who had taken sides with the Tories, enlisted in the British army in Canada, and become a lieutenant in General Fraser's division. Between her brother's patriotism and her lover's toryism, Miss McRea found her position a trying one. The fortunes of war brought Lieutenant Jones back to the neighborhood of his home and to the near vicinity of his betrothed, who was visiting Mrs. O'Neil ("widder McNeal,") a Tory sympathizer. The brother of Miss McRea, after the invasion

[1] The version of Washington Irving is here followed.

of Burgoyne, in July, prepared to remove to Albany and sent several imperative messages to his sister to come home from her visit that they might be gone before it should be too late. But she delayed, loth to leave the neighborhood of her lover's encampment and thinking herself safe because of the loyalty of Mrs. O'Neil to the British cause. She had, however, reluctantly made ready and was to depart that day on a bateau bound down river, when a party of Burgoyne's Indian allies marauding broke into and plundered the house and took the inmates prisoners. Miss McRea, says tradition, told them her relation to Lieutenant Jones and promised them a large reward if they would take her safely to him in the British camp. This they agreed to do, but on the way they fell into a dispute about the reward and, to settle it, one of them in a rage killed Miss McRea on the spot.

"Her scalp, with its long silken tresses," says Irving, "was secured by her lover, who brooded over it in anguish and preserved it,—a sad but precious relic. Disgusted with the service, he threw up his commission and retired to Canada, never marrying, but living to be an old man, taciturn and melancholy and haunted by painful recollections. A stone, with her name cut on it, still marks the grave of Miss McRea near the ruins of Fort Edward, and a tree is pointed out near which she was murdered."

Captain Farnum, after his boat ride with the ladies (so unconscious in their gayety of the dreadful fate before them), chronicles nothing of marked interest, merely makes notes of journeys to and from Fort Ticonderoga, "making muster rolls of my company — writing letters to send to Andover," etc. None of his letters have been found, but there are a few relics of the correspondence of soldiers of his company. One of these written by a mother to her son was received by him at Fort Edward, carried through all his campaigns, and finally brought back to the home whence it had been sent, and where it has been kept till now. The letter is dated Andover, July 5, 1777, and signed : —

"Your loving father and mother till Death.

JOSEPH SHATTUCK.
ANNA SHATTUCK."

The receiver of the letter was Joseph Shattuck, Jr., corporal in Captain Farnum's company.

Joseph Shattuck whose name is signed to this letter was the son of Joseph Shattuck, who, in 1728, bought a farm in West Andover near the Merrimack River. His wife was Anna Johnson, daughter of Cornelius Johnson, of Haverhill. Her letter shows her to have been a remarkably well educated woman for her time, the composition and spelling being noticeably correct. Joseph Shattuck, the soldier, after his campaigns, settled on a farm on the banks of the Merrimack where he lived to be almost ninety years old (dying in 1847), a venerable and good man. His first wife was a daughter of Joshua Chandler, Esq. She died at the age of twenty, leaving no children. He married again Phebe Abbot, daughter of Capt. Jonathan Abbot. She lived to be almost eighty-three years old. The writer remembers this aged couple (they spent nearly fifty-eight years together), as they sat at the fireside or at the round tea-table (the wife at her husband's right hand), "grandsire" with his long white hair neatly braided in a queue and tied with a black silk band, "mother," with her snowy cap and smoothly folded neckerchief setting off to advantage a face benign and (as it seemed to the young folks whom she loved to welcome to her hospitable board and her well-stored pantry of goodies) beautiful to look upon.

The eldest son, Capt. Joseph Shattuck, and his only brother, Capt. Nathan Shattuck, lived within a mile of each other, the former on a part of the ancestral estates. Both were respected citizens, selectmen many years, and representatives to the Legislature.

Captain Farnum on the seventeenth of June, 1777, stirred by the memories of the day, makes a record in his diary : —

"*June* 17. This day two year I was wounded in the batel at bunkers hill."

"*June* 20. Departed this life, Thomas Hagget, a soldier in my company.

"21. Lieut. Abbot took an inventory belonging to Thomas Hagget, lately Deceased."

Sunday, June 22d, Captain Farnum writes : "An officer

from Ticonderoga, the 21 — but has no nuse of the enemy." Yet at this very time the enemy were close at hand, — Burgoyne with about four thousand British, three thousand Germans, two hundred Canadians, four hundred Indians — besides artillery, in all nearly eight thousand strong, under command of the able officers Generals Frazer, Powel, Hamilton, and the Major-general the Baron de Reidesel in command of the Germans.

The commander of the American forces at Ticonderoga, General St. Clair, had witten to General Schuyler that he could easily hold the fort, but when the enemy appeared he changed his mind and sent off dispatches : —

"There is no prospect of being able to defend Ticonderoga unless militia come in."

By the time the news of the General's first dispatch had reached General Washington the fortress had been surrendered. It is needless to detail particulars, how passes were left unguarded, and commanding heights unnoticed, till the enemy held them and from Mount Defiance could rake the fort. Capt. Farnum puts it all into a half dozen words, this work of nights and days, of British energy and victory and American negligence and defeat.

"*Sunday*, 6 *July*. Nuse of Ticonderoga & Mount In Dependence being Vequeated. this evening the retreating parte begun to come into this Garrison.

"*July* 9. Myself, with the men belonging to Col. Francis's regt., marched to Mr. Gillet's and incamped. Nuse that the body of our army that came from Ticonderoga are coming by white crick & are expected here soon.

"*July* 10. Nuse that Col. Francis was killed at Hubeton (Hubardtown), 22 miles from Tyconderoga in a batel with our rear and the enemy. Nuse that Col. Warner & Col. Titcomb are wounded in the same batel.

"*July* 14. Nuse that 80 of our wagons are cut off Between Fort Edward and Fort George.

"16*th*. Nuse that the enemy Drive a great many catell from White Crick.

"17*th*. Fort George Vequated. . . . .

"23*d*. Veaquated Fort Edwards after moving all the stores and burned the barracks."

In the midst of this flight and confusion, Captain Farnum receives the sad news of the murder of the ladies of his pleasure-boat party.

He with his company were now on an island in the Hudson River, between Fort Edward and Saratoga. They soon broke up camp and shipped their stores down river; and the troops marched to Saratoga. On the third of August they were ordered to march to Stillwater. Their arrival is thus noted: —

"Arrived about one o'clock at nite; lodged on the wet ground. In the morning the ground was laid out for each brigade to camp in. We got our boards out of the river & made our huts. those that had tents pitched them.

"*August* 11*th*. received nuse from my friends at Andover; ware dated the 10th of May."

By the return post, Corporal Shattuck sent a letter which confirms the notes of Captain Farnum's diary regarding the movements of the army: —

"Honored father and mother, after my duty to you I would inform you that through Divine Goodness I am in Good health at this time. . . . . I would inform you that our armey is Retreten and we Dont know where we Shall mak a Stand."

The retreat was soon arrested by the news of the battle of Bennington, followed by further news of the check given to Burgoyne's tide of victory by the operations of the Massachusetts militia sent on as a reënforcement.

Captain Farnum thus records the battle of Bennington: —

"19*th*. The following is just from Bennington by express: that the battel their has turned in our favor, that our army has kiled & taken 936, that the loss on our side 20 kiled and 80 wounded. 4 brs. field Peaces taken from the enemy."

The surrender of Fort Ticonderoga, although it could not have been foreseen by General Schuyler, he incurred the blame of, and it completing his disgrace in the eyes of the people, he was superseded by the favorite General Gates. Captain Farnum notes the event: —

"*Aug.* 20. This evening the honourable Gen. Gates arrived here."

As all readers of history know, we are now arrived in this narrative at the point of the decisive battle of Stillwater, which resulted in the surrender of General Burgoyne. The retreating American army, encouraged by the victory of Bennington and aided by other operations of the reënforcements of militia in the North which will be hereafter related, made a stand and gained the victory which produced such rejoicing throughout America.

There is only a brief record of the first battle, — " A smart batel with the enemy," — as Captain Farnum was then sick in Albany. His account of the second battle is as follows: —

" *Oct. 7th.* This day a batel begun about t'o o'clock in the afternoon, which held til dark. Mager Lipko, Adj. Francis, Ensign Round, an a number others were wounded, and a number kiled. we tuck 8 cannon and a Number of prisoners, about 200. The batel was much in our favour.

"*8th.* This day a constant firing cept by our People on the enemy's lines."

This "constant firing" referred to by Captain Farnum is spoken of by all the historians. It was merciless and terrible, endangering even the British chaplains engaged in burial rites of their dead officers. General Burgoyne said of it, in description more graphic than that of our Andover narrator: —

"The incessant cannonade during the ceremony [1] the steady attitude and unaltered voice with which the chaplain officiated, though frequently covered with dust, which the shot threw upon all sides of him, the mute but expressive mixture of sensibility and indignation upon every countenance, these objects will remain to the last of life upon the mind of every man who was present."

Capt. Farnum's diary goes on describing the surrender: —

" *14th.* Ordered that there be no fireing on the enemy: flags exchanged between Genl. Gates and Mr. Burgoyne.

" *15th.* This day the generals are a tryin to settle the terms that Burgoyne shall Render himself & army Prisoners of War.

" *16th.* This day the terms agreed on; the writings drone, & signed, seld, and Delivered.

" *17.* This morning ordered to strike tents and march; we

[1] For General Frazer's burial.

marched to Saratoga meeting-house. The army perade and ginl. burgoine, with his army, marched out, after grounding their armes, & Serender them* Prisoners of war.

"18*th October*. This morning I wente to see the Lines that the enemy lefte. Returned to my tent, eat Bexfast."

Thus jotting down with equal conciseness the surrender of armies and his eating breakfast, the Captain continues his diary till he comes to Albany. There he wrote a letter home on the 22d, and on the 24th, "received a letter from my wife." 26th, "attended divine seryice," 28th, "Rote a letter to my daughter." He notes that Colonel Tupper took command of the regiment the 27th.

The brief season of rest in a pleasant city among the peaceful habitations of men, after the forest life and lonely garrison, was, no doubt, a great refreshment, but it was soon over:—

"30*th*. Strike tents and march down to the wharf, went abord the ships, sailed down 12 miles, landed and camped witbout tents that nite."

The weather was cold and snow had already fallen. The hard marches and exposure told upon the soldiers.

"*Nov. 4th*. This day Corporal Shattuck, with a number of other sick men, were sent to Albany."

On the fifth of November the captain performed an agreeable duty: "Drew 13 pairs of Breaches, 73 pear of shus, 4 shirts . . . . in part of clothing for my company."

Soon the company are sailing down river "all nite" forty miles from Albany past forts Constitution and Montgomery, and on the 11th of November they land at King's Ferry. They are on their way to join the army of General Washington near Philadelphia.

"20*th Nov*. Cross the ferry, then pitch tents in Penselvenea.

"21*st*. March through Crucked Billet,[1] & march within 5 miles of ginl Wa hington's head-quarters.

"22*d*. March to Whitemarsh, near headquarters, and in camp nuse that Red bank forts is veaqueated.

"28*th*. Thomas Stevens sent to Plumton (?) among the sick of the regiment.

[1] "Crooked Billet," a town near Philadelphia, so named from the sign of an ancient inn.

"*29th Nov.* Died, Mr. Thomas Stevens; he was nine miles from camp.

"*Dec. 2.* Corporal Cross went after Mr. Stevenses cloaths.

"*3d Dec.* This morning we was a Larmed at Day break. Marched to the alarme post but saw no enemy.

"*5th.* Larmed at two o'clock. We tuck our alarme poste; the enemy came out to Germantown; the scouts had some scurmishing; all ower bageg sente to 24 mile aton.

"*6th.* Parade at Day Breake; lay on our Larm poste til 4 o'clock; the enemy lay on Chestnut hill, within 2 miles, but no attack this Day.

"*Sunday, 7th.* Parade at 6 o'clock, lay on the lines all day; at 2 o'clock, scurmishing begun by small parties held til Dark.

"*8th.* The enemy retreated to Phalled'-a [Philadelphia]; our Scouts and Rifelmen followed their Rear. Col. Tupper's regiment ordered to march no further than head quarters by hearing that the enemy had got into the Site [city]."

Soon our journalist is getting ready for the winter encampment at Valley Forge, that winter of suffering, and sorrow, and discouragement, when Washington, censured by his countrymen for inactivity, beheld his men dying around him for lack of shelter from the cold and of food to keep them from starving. There were about eleven thousand soldiers in camp in huts of wood, fourteen men in each hut. Captain Farnum writes: —

"*Dec. 22.* Lay out the camping ground. *25th,* cutting timber for the huts. 29, 30, & 31, at work building a hut. *Jan.* 1, 1778. This day moved into our hute. *3d,* built cabens in our hut. *Sunday,* rote letters home."

Such life was hard, and it is no wonder some poor fellows were homesick and tempted to get away from such a wretched place — where the snow was marked with the blood of the soldiers' sore and frozen feet, and groans and curses too often made the huts unendurable. But the penalty for desertion from even such quarters was death, and death not as became a soldier, but by hanging: —

"*Jan. 9th.* This morning at 10 o'clock, 4 men from each Brigade wore Praded to see a Deserter shote. He was reprieved for one day.

"10th. This day at 11 o'clock, John Rilee was hanged for Desershon.
"11th. A snow storm. . . . .
"23d. Went to the Peste House & tuck the Small Pocks with Col. Litel, Dr. Parker, & others.
"24th. Tuck fisick. *Sunday,* 25th. Made out Returns of my company & Capt. 'Greenleaf's, to send to the cort of M T B.
"26th. Tuck fisick in preparation for the S¹ Px.
"27th. On fatege at the Lefte Radout.
"28th. Tuck fisick.
"31st. Went out of the campe on wa . . . [illegible] with the small pox."

This closes the captain's diary.

The camp at Valley Forge is thus described by Hildreth: —

"Such was the destitution of shoes that all the late marches had been tracked in blood. For want of blankets many of the men were obliged to sit up all night before the camp fires. More than one quarter part of the troops were reported unfit for duty, because they were barefoot and otherwise naked."

In this deplorable condition of things Massachusetts took measures to relieve the soldiers from this State. Returns of the state of each company were ordered.

The return of Captain Farnum's company is here given. It shows [1] much less destitution than existed in other companies. Undoubtedly the town of Andover and individual friends of the soldiers provided for their necessities : —

"*A Return* [2] *of the State of a Company commanded by Capt. Benjamin Farnum, in a Regt. Raised in the State of Massachusetts Bay, for the Defence of the United States of America, Commanded by Col. Benj. Tupper, Jan. 24, 1778.*"

Benjamin Farnum, Capt.	David Beverly, (?) Corpl.	Jonathan Ballard.[b]
Stephen Abbot, Lieut.	John Cross, Corporal.[b]	Benj. Barry.[d]
David Farnum, Sergt.	Benj. Abbot, Drummer.	Nehemiah Carlton,[e] Bradford.
Obadiah Lovejoy, Sergt.	Joshua Long,[e] Fifer.	
Joshua Frie, Sergt.	Benj. Abbot, Private.	Cesar Cogswell.[d]
James Willey, Sergt.	Prince Ames.	Thomas Day.
Joseph Shattuck, Corpl.[a]	George Blunt.[d]	Palfrey Downing.
Asa Osgood, Corporal.	John Baldwin.	Thomas Fuller, Salem.

[1] The articles lacking are specified with the names.
[2] *Mass. Rev. Rolls*, vol. xi., p. 76.

Israel Farnum.[a]	John Lovejoy.	Hezekiah Stiles.
John Fealds.[a]	Daniel Linsey.[b]	Thomas Smith.[g]
Cato Foster.[d]	Peter Martin.	Bimsley Stevens.[d]
Samson Frye.	James McFarling.[b]	Thomas Stevens.[f]
Daniel Holt.[a]	James McFarling, jr.[b]	James Turner.[h]
Edward Herrick.	Thomas Phelps.[c]	James Turner, jr.[d]
Thomas Haggit.[f]	William Parker.[b]	Mark Winter.[h]
Jonathan Haggit,[e] Tewksbury.	Peter Pevey.	John Welch.
	Isaac Russel.	Benj. Webb.[h]
James Johnson.	John Stevens.	Titus Chickren.[d]
Isaac Lovejoy.[d]		

[a] Sick at Albany. [b] Not fit for duty for want of shoes. [c] Discharged. [d] Unfit for duty for want of clothes. [e] Sick at Morristown. [f] Dead. [g] Lame at Crooked Billet. [h] On furlough.

Accompanying the returns of his regiment is a letter from Colonel Tupper, appealing to the State for relief, and saying he would rather leave the service than be the witness of such sufferings as the soldiers at Valley Forge were then undergoing.

Leaving now the camp at Valley Forge and Captain Farnum sick with his taking of the small pox, we return to trace other events which were prior to the surrender of General Burgoyne and contributed to hasten it, and in which one of our Andover officers acted a distinguished part.

Immediately upon the news of the fall of Ticonderoga, reenforcements had marched from Massachusetts to join the troops under the command of General Lincoln. A part of the force was commanded by Col. Samuel Johnson of Andover. There were some five hundred men from different regiments under his command.

Following are rolls of the regiment of Colonel Johnson, and of companies which were in service during the whole or a part of the time from August 14 to the last of November: —

"*A Pay Roll*[1] *of the Field and Staff officers of Col. Saml. Johnson's Regiment of Massachusetts Bay Militia.*"

	Establishment per Month.
Saml. Johnson, Col.	£22 10 s
Ralph Cross, Lt.-col.	18 0
Eleazer Crafts, Major	15 0

[1] Date of years not given, but from dates of months and time of travel evidently that of the reenforcement of 1777, for the Northern Army.

ANDOVER IN THE REVOLUTIONARY WAR. 373

Bimsley Stevens, Adjt.	£12 0 1
Caleb Cushing, Q Master	8 50
William Bacheler, Surgeon	18 0
George Osgood, Sur. Mate	9 0

"*A Pay Roll*[1] *of Bounty Granted by the Great and General Court of the State of Massachusetts Bay to the Non Commissioned officers and Soldiers of Capt. John Adams's company in Col. Samuel Johnson's Regiment of Militia, commanded by Maj^r Gage, to Reinforce the Northern army, According to a Resolution of the said Court of the twenty-second of Sept. Last.*"

Solomon Ingals, Sart. Majr.	John Barnard, jr.	Zebadiah Holt.
William Johnson, Sargt.	John Carlton.	Daniel Ingalls.
John Barker, do.	Daniel Carlton.	Francis Ingals, jr.
Peter Farnum, do.	Benjamin Carlton.	Ebenezer Ingals, jr.
John Barker, Junior, do.	Michael Carlton.	John Ingals, jr.
John Poor, Corpl.	Samuel Chickering.	Solomon Martin.
Timothy Carlton, Corpl.	Jonathan Downing.	Timothy Poor, jr.
Daniel Poor, do.	James Davis.	Benjamin Poor, jr.
Daniel Granger, Drum.	William Foster.	Timothy Stevens.
Daniel Poor, jr., Fifer.	Timothy Farnum.	Abiel Wilson.
Asa Barker, Private.	John Frye, junr.	Cesar Barker.
Jacob Barnard.	Daniel Poor, jr.	Nehemiah Abbot.
	John Frye, 3d.	Saml. Spofford.

"*A Pay Roll*[1] *of Bounty Granted by the Great and General Court of the State of Massachusetts Bay to the Non-Commissioned officers and soldiers of Capt. John Abbot's company in Maj^r Gage's Regiment of Militia, according to a Resolution of the said Court of the Twenty-second af Sept. last.*"[3]

John Abbot.	John Blunt.	Ebenezer Jones.
Moses Bailey, Sargt.	John Bailey.	Isaac Lovejoy.
David Blunt, do.	Saml. Blanchard.	Thomas Merrill.
John Russell, do.	Daniel Blanchard.	Saml. Marshall.
Abiel Stevens, do.	Josiah Chandler.	Isaac Mooar.
John Wood, Corpl.	Zebadiah Chandler.	Joses Ordway.
John Mooar, do.	Nathan Chandler.	Jonathan Russel.
Robert Day, do.	Simon Crosby.	William Shelden.
Daniel Chandler, do.	Simeon Dresser.	Nathan Shattuck.
Abiel Chandler, Fifer.	Francis Dane.	Abiel Shattuck.
John Abbot.	Jeremiah Goldsmith.	Saml. Stevens.
Nathan Abbot.	Robert Gray.	Abiel Upton.
Ebenezer Abbot.	Saml. Holt.	Dudley Woodbridge.

[1] *Mass. Rev. Rolls*, vol. xvii, p. 13.
[2] *Ibid.*, vol. xvi, p. 84.
[3] The time of service in the roll was from September 30, 1777, to November 6, 1777. Service "in Northern Army."

"*A Pay Roll*[1] *of Capt. Samuel Johnson's company, in Col. Johnson's Regiment of Militia, Belonging to the State of Massachusetts, being in the army to the Northward, Nov. 30, 1777.*"

Samuel Johnson, Capt.	Phineas Carlton.	Nathaniel Marshal.
James Mallon, Lieut.	Ezra Chandler.	John Nichols.
John Fry, 2 Lieut.	William Cross.	Daniel Osgood.
Jeduthan Abbot, Sergt.	Abijah Cross.	John Parker.
Solomon Jennes, Sergt.	Asa Colburn.	Asa Parker.
William Chandler, Sergt.	William Davis.	James Parker.
Joseph Bachelder, Sergt.	Jacob Deakum.	William Parker.
John Richardson, Corp.	James Darrunt.	Andrew Richardson.
Zebediah Barker, Corp.	Jonathan Evans.	Peter Roberson.
Daniel Mors, Corp.	Simeon Farnum.	Moody Spofford.
Joseph Dean, Corp.	Nathaniel Frye.	Jonathan Stevens.
James Chandler, Fifer.	Joseph Foster.	Ebenezer Serjant.
Thadeus Ladd, Drum'.	Phineas Goodhew.	William Swan.
Spofford Ames.	Jacob Granger.	William Wilson.
Ephraim Abbot.	Thomas Gray.	Benjamin Wood.
Samuel Austin.	Zelah Holt.	Benjamin Webber.
Solomon Austin.	Isaac Ingals.	Joshua Wardwell.
Frederick Ballard.	Mical Ladd.	Joseph Wardwell.
James Baley.	William Lovejoy.	Elisha Webber.
Peter Barker.	Nathaniel Lovejoy.	James Williams.
William Burbank.	Nathaniel Ladd.	William Harris.
Isaac Barker.	Jacob Makentire.	Simeon Stevens.
Moses Bienlan [Brentun].	James Messer.	Jonathan Pettengel.
Asa Cummins.	Joseph Merrel.	Joshua Stevens.
Jonathan Cummens.	Obediah More.	Nehemiah Abbot.

"ANDOVER, *Jan.* 15, 1778. Continental Pay Roll."

The date of engagement, August 14, 1777. The date of discharge, last day of November, 1777.

The troops marched by way of Bennington and stopped there. The recent victory of Colonel Stark had animated the courage of the people of that vicinity and the officers of the Massachusetts Militia caught the enthusiasm. It was determined that before marching to join the retreating army, whose course we have just followed, they should strike a blow and attempt to retake Fort Ticonderoga[2] and Mount Independence. The enterprise was intrusted by General Lincoln to Colonels Brown and Johnson.[3] It was a very

---

[1] Private manuscript. Pay Rolls nearly corresponding with this are found in the *State Rolls*, vol. xx., p. 130; also, vol. xx., p. 102.

[2] These were directly opposite each other.

[3] Colonel Johnson calls it a "private expedition."

bold and even desperate undertaking, for the fort was almost impregnable and strongly garrisoned. But by the conduct and courage of the officers it proved, although not wholly successful so far as taking the fort, a great advantage and victory. Large supplies and stores of the enemy were captured and their communication cut off so that General Burgoyne was impeded in his operations and pushed to his final surrender. The details of the expedition are somewhat variously related in the histories. Colonel Johnson wrote a full narrative of the movements of the troops under his command in letters to his family at Andover. From it the following is compiled. He says: "There were fifteen hundred men in three parties, Col. Brown with five hundred to attack Ticonderoga, myself with five hundred to attempt Mt. Independence, and Col. Woodbridge with the same number stopped at Skenesboro to cover Col. Brown's retreat."

Skenesboro was the place at which St. Clair's fleeing army had halted when he abandoned Ticonderoga; indeed Colonel Johnson's march all the way was through the very places where our retreating troops had passed a few weeks before. Traces of the battles and the flight were all along their route: —

"Marched the thirteenth day of September; arrived at Castleton, waited there one day for Col. Brown to get forward, then marched to Hubbardton."

The last named town was where the gallant Colonel Francis had fallen, July 7th, and the place also where Major Ackland, a British grenadier, was wounded, and whither his heroic wife and her friend, the Baroness de Reidesel, came to join the British army. But in respect to all these facts the letters of Colonel Johnson are silent. He simply gives the details of his own expedition: —

"At Hubbardton I formed my detachment into three divisions. Col. Safford commanded the first, Col. Barret the second, Major Cross the third."

The letter goes on to say that marching all day they arrived about eight o'clock in the evening (September 16th) within two miles of Mount Independence (which was just across the narrows of the lake from Fort Ticonderoga), that soon after their arrival Colonel Johnson was waited upon by two messengers, who had swum the lake bringing letters from Colonel Brown. This officer had arrived and encamped before Ticonderoga. The letters arranged for a united attack on the fort just before day. But about one o'clock Colonel Warner arriving at the camp of Colonel Johnson, it was determined in a council of war that it would not be best for them to attempt to force the enemy's lines, but, rather, to make a feint in order to draw attention from Colonel Brown. This was, therefore, done, and it seems to have succeeded in the object intended. Colonel Johnson says: "We surprised the enemy at break of day, driving in their piquet guard, and immediately ensued a considerable fire from their shipping and lines, and we continued to return their fire the chief of that day" (September 17th). Meanwhile Colonel Brown (attention thus being diverted from his movements) "attacked the Landing at Lake George, the mills, and mount Defiance, also the French lines, and carried them;" he relieved, says Colonel Johnson's letter, nearly a "hundred American prisoners, took twelve British officers, and 143 non-commissioned officers and privates, 119 Canadians, and 14 artificers, several hundred stands of armes, besides a great quantity of baggage, with the loss of only two killed and three or four wounded."

Being obliged to send a considerable number of his force to guard the prisoners, and get off the baggage and stores taken, Colonel Brown called on Colonel Johnson for two hundred men to reënforce him. Deciding[1] that it was not best to storm the Fort (as they had learned from a deserter of its great strength), he made haste to secure what stores he could, and retire before he should be attacked, intending to proceed up the lake and surprise Fort George (formerly Fort William Henry). He collected a large number of bateaux, seventeen gun-boats, and one armed sloop, and embarked his men. In command of men on one of these boats was Capt. Samuel Johnson — probably being one of the two hundred sent as a reënforcement by Colonel Johnson.

[1] Hildreth's *History* says there was a four days' siege, but it seems otherwise from this letter.

But the garrison at Fort George had been apprised by a tory of their approach, and immediately on their arrival at Diamond Island, September 23d, opened fire upon them " with such effect," says the letter of Colonel Johnson, that every boat was shot through, except the one which Captain Johnson commanded.

Destroying the boats and stores, Colonel Brown then hastily retreated from Fort George and marched to Skenesborough. There Colonel Johnson joined him, having marched from Mount Independence.

The next morning they started for Pawlet, where, says Colonel Johnson, we "arrived the 27th, and still remain."

The letter of Colonel Johnson and with it Colonel Brown's letter, and probably many other letters, were sent to Andover. One letter from a private of Capt. Samuel Johnson's company has been preserved: —

"PAWLET, *October y⁰ 1ˢᵗ*, 1777.

"LOVING SISTER, — These will inform you that I am very well at present, and have been so ever since I came from home, and I hope you and all my friends enjoy the same state of health.

"We have been up to Ticonderoga and took almost four hundred prisoners of the British army, and relieved one hundred of our men that were prisoners there.

"Our army have come from Ticonderoga down as far as Pawlet, about sixty miles, and expect to march to Stillwater very soon.

"So no more at present. I remain

"Your Loving brother,

"JONATHAN STEVENS.

"To THE WIDOW LYDIA PETERS *in Andover.*"

Although this expedition had not, as was hoped, succeeded in capturing Fort Ticonderoga, and Colonel Johnson in his letter makes no claim to a brilliant achievement, the news of it spread joy through the American army on the Hudson, and struck dismay to the heart of Burgoyne : —

"On the 21ˢᵗ," says Irving, "the British general heard shouts in the American camp, and in a little while their cannon thundered a *feu de joie*. News had been received from General Lincoln that a detachment of New England troops under Colonel Brown[1] had sur-

---

[1] Hildreth says "and Colonel Johnson."

prised the carrying place, mills, and French lines at Ticonderoga, captured an armed sloop, gun-boats, and bateaux; made three hundred prisoners, besides releasing one hundred American captives, and laying siege to Fort Independence."

The siege of Fort Independence, as we have seen, alone enabled Colonel Brown to achieve his exploits, and Colonel Johnson's prompt reënforcement helped him in effecting the removal of the stores and prisoners. Colonel Johnson's labors were incessant. "I have not had my clothes off this fifteen days," he writes. His cheerfulness and courage were unfailing. "Through the goodness of God I have enjoyed my health as well as ever, although the fatigue of the army is hard to undergo, yet do not doubt that through the goodness of God we shall be able to surmount all the hardships we shall have to pass through."

In his letter, too, the Colonel takes pains to give information regarding the Andover soldiers, which he thinks will be cheering to their friends. The troops marched from Pawlet to Stillwater, and were there in time to share in the battle on the 7th of October.

The name of a soldier on the roll of Captain Johnson's company is found in connection with a petition[1] to the General Court. He was at the time a resident of Methuen: —

"*The Humble Petition of William Parker, of Methuen, in the county of Essex in said state,* humbly sheweth: That your petitioner was an Inlisted soldier in Capt. Saml. Johnson's Company, in Col. Samuel Johnson's regiment. That your petitioner was in the Battle near Stillwater on the seventh of October Last, and was there Badly Wounded with a Musquet Ball from the Enemy; Shot through one of the s^d William's Hips; Was carried out of ye Battle by some of his Friends, his life much Despaired of. That after Carefull Dressing of his Wounds In the Army he so far Recovered in about one month as to be Conveyed, at his own Expense, In a shay carriage, home to Methuen, which is about Two Hundred Miles. That I then Bore my own Expense for myselfe & assistance in my journey home, and my Horse hire & carriage, & have borne the expense of Doctors & Nursing about six months. That I am capable of Doing some Labour, but remain a Cripple, and

[1] *Mass. Archives,* vol. clxxxiv., p. 236.

greatly fear I always shall. That when I fell with my wound I lost my firelock, which was an exceedingly valuable one. That I lost my hat, which was then almost new, & what was called a Good fur hat, wh. firelock & hat was not lost through carelessness or negligence, but by our being at that time forced from the ground where I was wounded, & the enemy Immediately took possession of ye same.

"Wherefore your humble petitioner most humbly prays that this honorable Court in your wonted justice, clemency, & Goodness will take your petitioner's grievances under your wise consideration, and so grant and Direct therein that he may be allowed for his loss of Time, for his Doctors & nursing, for his Reasonable & Necessary Expenses In his being conveyed Home, & for the Loss of his Firelock & hat, & such further allowance for his being at present, and according to all human probability likely to remain a cripple for the Future. That he may in some measure be Considered in the number of Pensioners who have jeoparded their Lives & Lost their Limbs in the Defence of their Country under such Limitation & Restriction as in your wisdom & justice you shall think fit, & your petitioner, as in duty bound, shall ever pray.

WILLIAM PARKER.

"METHUEN, *Sep* 16th, 1778."

"This may certifye to the Honble Cort that William Parker, as above mentioned, was wounded at Stillwater with a Musquet Ball threw one of his hips; was Brought home to methuen in a carig, as soon as he was abel to Ride, at his own expense. after he came home he applied to me as surgeon to cure his wound and Lameness, which I attended till his wound healed up; But his Lameness remained for a Long while Before he was fit for any Labour; But he still remains lame, and I fear never will outgrow His Lameness, By reason of Sum Nerves Being wounded. Therefore I think he ort to be considered. . . . . SAML. HILDRETH."

"ANDOVER, *Sept.* 14, 1778.

"This may certifie that William Parker befor menshioned was an inlisted soldier in my company, and that sd Parker was in the Battel as before mentioned, and Did Loos his firelock and other things by Reason of his being wounded.

"SAML. JOHNSON, *Capt.*"

Notwithstanding this accumulation of arguments, and the petitioner's confident belief in the justice of the court, he was left unaided.

"The committee report that the petitioner have leave to withdraw."

The honorable part of Colonel Johnson in the battle is borne witness to in an obituary notice, 1796: —

"In 1777 he commanded a regiment detached from the county of Essex, and led them to victory and glory in the memorable action on the 7th of October, where his firmness and courage was particularly distinguished. His regiment was a part of that respectable yeomanry whom General Burgoyne honored as the owners of the soil, men determined to conquer or die. This was the Fourth Massachusetts Regiment which Col. Johnson commanded through the war, and with promptness and punctuality answered the requisitions of Government in a manner highly satisfactory to the several corps which composed the regiment."

It would not be proper to pass by the battle of Stillwater, of October 7th, without allusion to one of the most prominent and gallant of the American officers on the field, Gen. Enoch Poor, who commanded the New Hampshire regiments. General Poor was an Andover man, a brother of Col. Thomas Poor. About ten years before the war he had removed to Exeter, where he became an influential citizen. A brief sketch of his life and services in the Revolution is given in a historical sketch of Exeter.[1] Although it interrupts somewhat this narrative of events, it is of sufficient interest to be here introduced: —

"Enoch Poor was one of the most active business men of Exeter when the war began. He had come here some ten years before from Andover, Massachusetts, his native town, and had engaged in trade and ship-building. He showed himself to be decided 'bold' and fitted for command, and 'as he was an ardent friend of liberty' he was regarded at an early period as a leader in organizing resistance to the British authority. . . . . He was at once made colonel of the second regiment of New Hampshire troops, and thenceforward until his death he shared the fortunes of the American army. He was in command of his regiment in the Canada expedition, and was appointed a Brigadier-general in 1777, in which capacity he did excellent service in Gates's army in the battles which resulted in the capture of Burgoyne. He was at Valley Forge and in the

[1] *Exeter in 1776*, by Charles H. Bell.

battle of Monmouth; won distinction by his efforts in retrieving the fortunes of the day, at first imperilled by Lee's ill-timed retreat. In 1780 he was in command of a brigade of light infantry under Lafayette, who had a high opinion of him. . . . . Washington wrote of him in high terms of commendation."

Lafayette, on his visit to America, paid a tribute to his memory by giving as a sentiment on public occasions: "The memory of Light Infantry Poor and Yorktown Scammel."

There is a likeness of General Poor which is said to have been drawn by the Polish engineer, Thaddeus Kosciusko, upon the fly-leaf of a hymn-book in church. It represents him in the Continental uniform.

He died, after a short illness, in New Jersey, September 8, 1780. There was a rumor that he was killed in a duel with a French officer, and that this was kept secret to prevent exciting ill-feeling against our allies, the French. But the story is not credited by the best authorities.

Before the expedition to the northward, some of the Andover men had done service in Rhode Island. An expedition had been planned to drive the enemy from Newport.[1] The Massachusetts militia were ordered to march to reënforce the troops commanded by General Spencer, of Connecticut.[2] Three hundred and twenty-six men were drafted out of the Essex brigade. The men from Andover, Haverhill, Boxford, were put under command of Capt. Samuel Johnson.[3] The following is the pay-roll of the company: —

"*Pay Roll[4] for Capt. Johnson's Company, in Col. Titcomb's Regiment of Militia, from the State of Massachusetts Bay to State of Rhode Island, for two months service from their arrival at Providence in sd State, with addition of Days' Travel from their several towns to the place of Destination and the Return home to the several towns whence they come, of the State Bounty Due to sd company.*

Saml. Johnson, Capt. a.	Jonathan Barker, Sargt.	Benjamin Ordway, Sargt.
James Mallon, Lieut.	Andrew Peabody, do.	Caleb Cushon, "
Saml. Crowell, Lieut.	Jabesh Gage, "	Nathan Ingals, Corp. a.

[1] Barry's *History of Massachusetts*.
[2] Letter of Michael Farley, *Mass. Archives*.
[3] *Mass. Rev. Rolls*, vol. ii., p. 35.
[4] Men of Andover, Haverhill, Methuen, Bradford, Boxford. Those marked *a* of Andover. *Mass. Rev. Rolls*, vol. ii., p. 139.

Isaach Chandler, Corp.	Isaac How, a.	James Barker.
Aquiller Kimball, Corp.	Simeon Dresser, a.	Day Michel.
Joshua Rhay, do.	John Alley.	David Hale.
James Chandler, Fifer, a.	James Kimball.	Zechariah Baker.
John Chandler, Drum, a.	Joshua Kimball.	Jonathan Cross.
Peter Poor, Private, a.	Daniel Adams.	James Williams.
Simeon Farnum, a.	William Sergeant.	Nathaniel Smith Messer.
Joshua Johnson, a.	Daniel Mitchal.	Ebenezer Barker.
Samuel Philips, a.	Joseph Ayrs.	David Barker.
Abiel Wilson, a.	Jonathan Hayns.	Solomon Austen.
Samuel Chickren, a.	Samuel Bradbury.	Elisha Parker.
Francis Ingals, a.	Samuel Lecount.	James Parker.
Benjamin Carlton, a.	Thomas Sergant.	William Swan.
James Davis, a.	David Crowell.	Samuel Perley.
Robert Davis, a.	Simon Hereman.	John Welds.
William Lovejoy, a.	Robert Hunkens.	Seth Burnum.
Jonathan Baxter, a.	William Bradley.	Stephen Tyler.
Andrew Richardson, a.	Solomon Smith.	Samuel Stiles.
Tobe Abbot, a.	Joseph Uron.	Ephraim Matthews.
Asa French, a.	Timothy Hayes.	

"BRISTOL, *June* 27, 1777."

The expedition was unsuccessful. The British continued through the year and during the spring of 1778 in the vicinity of Newport and made frequent incursions into the country around. An expedition was formed to drive them out, and Colonel Johnson in July received orders to hurry his men to Tiverton. "Fail not as you would avoid the censure of your country," wrote General Titcomb in his dispatches, which are among Colonel Johnson's papers. Thus from place to place, North — South — far and near, the men were kept on the move, some of them scarcely stationary a month at a time. A few relics of their marchings and place of service are found. One is "A Pay Roll of Lieut. Jeremiah Blanchard's company in Col. Thomas Poor's reg. of the Mass. Bay Militia in the service of the United States of America, for the Term of eight months from the time of their arrival at Peekskill for the additional pay of forty shillings per month agreeable to a Resolve of the General Assembly lately passed Apr. 20, 1778." The men were of several towns, Andover included.

Of the movements of Colonel Poor's regiment the following[1] affords a glimpse : —

[1] *Worcester and Mixed Rolls*, vol. ii.

"William Adams, of Chelmsford, in the County of Middlesex and commonwealth of Mass., in the 79th year of my age, do testify .... that in the first part of the summer of 1778 I enlisted and went to West Point. the company that I belonged to was Capt. Asa Lawrence's Company, of Groton. the regiment was commanded by Col. Poor, of Andover or Methuen. Some part of our service was rendered at White Plains and Peekskill. this was an eight months' service. We received our discharge Feb. 1779."

Although the frequent calls upon the militia of Massachusetts were for the most part cheerfully responded to, yet at the close of the Northern campaign it was felt in many quarters that the demand had been too great for the military service of the soldiers outside of the State. As we have seen, some of the Andover companies had scarcely returned from the Rhode Island service before they were called to march to Ticonderoga. The people of Essex County were aroused by a sense of injustice when after the surrender of General Burgoyne the militia were not dismissed but were summoned to guard the prisoners of war and march to Boston. A petition was made to General Titcomb and subsequently to the Council, stating the feelings of the community and of the officers of the Fourth Regiment of militia of Massachusetts.

Captain Lovejoy, of Andover, in a forcible letter [1] set forth their grievances and said the ordering of fresh military service he regarded "dishonorable, unreasonable, unjust and highly injurious."

There seems to have been at Andover during the year 1777, some apprehension or suspicion of treason in the town, or at least, of what was regarded as treason, a spirit of opposition to the military measures. Possibly it was from the British prisoners who had become naturalized from motives of prudence, but would not be likely always to feel full sympathy with the ardor of the native American citizen.

"Captain Joshua Holt was chosen to procure and lay before the Court any evidence that may be had of the Inimical disposition to this or any of the United States of any Inhabitant or Inhabitants of this town who shall be charged by the Freeholders or other Inhabitants of sd Town as being a Person whose residence in this State is dangerous to the publick Peace and Safety."

[1] *Mass. Archives*, vol. clxxv.

The closing years of the war were perhaps attended with even more suffering than the beginning. There were fewer alarms, but there was constant distress, especially among the middle classes, — the "respectable yeomanry" whom General Burgoyne complimented. More than one good farm went to ruin ; its lands untilled, its buildings decayed, its flocks and herds dwindled away to contribute to or pay for the support of the owner's family. What was worse, more than one "steady" man, who had been a good provider and kind husband and father before the war, came home with unsettled habits and took to spending his time and his money at taverns and grog-shops ; and what with these evils and the depreciation of the currency and the heavy taxes, many once happy households were plunged into misery and disgrace. On the other hand, there were a few who made great fortunes by the war. Some traders did not scruple to charge extortionate prices for merchandise and necessaries of life, and to make gains which could not be justified by any system of ethics. If there were any such "unjust men extortioners" at Andover they got plain doctrine as to their conduct from Parson French. In a sermon which so gratified the majority of his congregation that they requested its publication, he describes one of these men who are making money out of the sufferings of their brethren. He imagines the extortioner's prayer : —

"Let his professions be what they may, to be consistent with himself, his prayers, if he ever does pray, must be something like this : —

"O thou Sovran Lord of the Universe, accept of a tribute of thanks from thy *professing worthy servant*, who rejoices that thou hast permitted those public calamities which have given so happy an opportunity for the exercise of my unbounded avaricious lusts. I congratulate myself at what I have already accumulated by extorting from others. May my merchandise still prosper, or my husbandry increase, but may scarcity and want still be the fate of my country, and more and more abound. May the time speedily come, when I shall be able to buy the poor for silver, and the needy for a pair of shoes. May all my countrymen be brought low and I be made Lord over them. O satiate my ambitious avaricious desires, which are all as unbounded as the ocean, and give me, if possible, to live always; but if this may not be granted, though I cannot bear the thoughts of ever dying, and deprecate the horrible idea of parting with my possessions, yet when I can enjoy my earthly paradise no longer, then give me the largest portion in the paradise above."

The town did all that was possible to provide for the necessities of the soldiers' families, to insure the payment of the soldiers' wages and provide for their better equipment and comfortable clothing.

In 1779 they voted to authorize the committee for supplying the families of the soldiers in the Continental army "to hire money upon the Town's credit, and immediately procure the necessaries of life for the use of the aforesaid families."

Also a committee was chosen to consult on measures to restore the credit of the currency and reduce the price of necessaries.

The town also published a price list for "Innkeepers, Labour, Teaming, and manufactures," and voted that "those who infringed should be considered enemies of the country, and dealt with accordingly."

In July, 1779, it was voted "that the town highly approves the attempts making to relieve the community of the embarrassments from depreciation of the currency," and they authorize one or two of the Committee of Correspondence and Safety to meet with others in a convention at Concord.

In July, 1780, it was voted in town meeting, of which Col. Samuel Johnson was moderator, "to provide for the three months enlisted soldiers, give obligations for their State pay, & hire money on the town's credit."

In December, 1780, it was recommended by the committee that "the Town do hereby engage to every able-bodied, effective man that shall Inlist, that in case the monthly pay of forty shillings engaged by Congress, to be paid in money of the new emission, shall depreciate from its present value, which is to be considered as now equal to $\frac{2}{3}$ of the same sum in coined silver, then the Town will fully make up such Depreciation at the expiration of each year's service. This was passed in the affirmative, *unan*."

The records of the military service of 1779 and 1780 are

few. They are mostly of duty near West Point. Capt. Stephen Abbot, in the 11th Massachusetts Regiment, was at West Point, August, 1779, and then petitioned for supplies of clothing for soldiers. In the latter part of the year 1780, after Arnold's treason, Capt. John Abbot's company were at West Point. They must have heard many a tale told at the camp-fires those autumn evenings about the traitor Arnold, and the unfortunate André. Following is a roll of Captain Abbot's company: —

"*A pay role of Capt. John Abbot's company, in Col. Nathaniel Wade's Regiment of Militia, for three months' service*[1] *at West Point, agreeable to a resolve of the Great and General Court of the Commonwealth, passed June 22, 1780, last.*"[2]

John Abbot, Capt.	Thomas Blanchard.	Alex^{dr}. Montgomery.
Cyrus Marble, Lieut.	Jesse Barker.	Ebenezer Messer.
Ephraim Clarke, Lieut.	Toney Ballard.	John Nichols.
Ezekiel Wardwell, Sergt.	Thomas Clark.	Joseph Osgood.
John Johnson, 2 Sergt.	Israel Carlton.	John Proctor.
William Whitaker, 3 Sergt.	Simon Crosby.	Elisha Parker.
Josiah Abbot, 4 Sergt.	Jacob Descomb.	Stephen Parker.
Peter Carlton, Corporal.	John Fry.	Aaron Parker.
Benj. Carlton, Corporal.	Peter Foster.	Jacob Russell.
Timothy Carlton, Corpl.	Cesar Freeman.	Zacher^b. Stevens.
Timothy Chales, (?) Corpl.	Wilm. Freeman.	Caleb Styrdevan.
Daniel Morse, Corporal.	Asa French.	Benj. Sargent.
Daniel Granger, Drummer.	March Farrington.	Jeremiah Stevens.
Joseph Morse, Fifer.	Zebediah Holt.	Simeon Stevens.
Abial Abbott.	Jon^a. Holt.	Simeon Towns.
Ephraim Abbot.	Simon Ingalls.	Abiel Wilson.
Nathl. Barker.	Flecher Ingalls.	Aaron Wood.
Thomas Barker.	William Lovejoy.	James Williams.
John Blake.	John Morrill.	Willm. Webster.
Daniel Blanchard.	Abraham Moor.	Eldad Prindale. (?)

The following are some names of militia officers commissioned, which may be of interest, as they do not appear elsewhere on the rolls in the rank specified: —

"*May* 13, 1778. Thomas Poor, Colonel to one of ye Regiments destined for Peekskill."[3]

"*Oct.* 7, 1779. Timothy Abbot, 2nd Lieut.; John Frye, 2nd Lieut.; William Johnson, 2nd Lieut."[4]

---

[1] Time of service, three months, eleven days, from October 11, 1780; number of miles 220.
[2] *Mass. Rev. Rolls*, vol. xvii., p. 1.   [3] *Ibid.*, vol. xxviii., p. 40.
[4] *Ibid.*, vol. xxviii., p. 42.

"*July* 3, 1780. William Johnson, 1st Lieut. 14th Company 4th Regt."[1]

One of the memorable events of the year 1780, although not of a military character, may here be mentioned, for it was popularly believed to be a portent of military import, and even some of those who were not prone to vulgar superstition almost believed that this might have some connection with the prophetic "last days," when there should be "wars and rumors of wars," distress and perplexity of nations.

The "dark day," May 19th, was long remembered, and has been often described. The following description is compiled from the account of the Rev. Mr. French, of Andover: —

On the morning of this dark day, at nine o'clock, the heavens were as dark as they are wont to be at the same hour of the evening. Candles were lighted, the brute creation made ready for a new night's repose, apparently unconscious of the brief time since their last awaking, chickens went to roost, cattle came home from pasture, frogs peeped, night birds took the place of the songsters of day. A sort of superstitious horror brooded over the community. "The clouds put on a strange kind of brassy copper-color, and everything conspired to make the appearance exceedingly gloomy." Toward the latter part of the afternoon the darkness lifted somewhat, but it deepened with the night, and the evening was totally black, although this was at the full of the moon. "Concern and terror," says the Rev. Mr. French, "sat upon the faces of the people." But the gloom passed away with the night, and the business of life went on as usual.

As after the gloom and oppression of the dark day, the sunlight came thrice welcome and beautiful, so after the long night of war broke the dawn of peace. Its harbinger, the glorious day of Yorktown, October 19, 1781, and the joy which hailed it, are described by an Andover young man, then a student in Harvard College, John Abbot (the son of Capt. John Abbot), subsequently Professor in Bowdoin College. In a letter to his younger brother, Ezra Abbot, at

[1] *Mass. Rev. Rolls*, vol. xxviii., p. 42.

Andover, dated Cambridge, November 10, 1781, he says, after speaking of the high prices and hard times, and the money which his winter supply of wood has cost him: —

"We have had pretty general rejoicing here this week for the capture of Cornwallis. Last Monday morning I was awaked just at break of day by the ringing of all the bells. I sprang up, supposing that a fire had broke out, and after slipping on my clothes as soon as possible hastened down to assist the distressed, but was soon informed by those I inquired of that it was only a public rejoicing. They discharged 14 guns in the morning, 13 for the United States and 1 for the King of France; the same number at noon and at night.

"The town House and Braddishes were illuminated, a fire built upon the common, and double the above number of cannon were fired."

No doubt the letter which answered this told of similar demonstrations at Andover.

The service, during the remaining years of the war, of Andover men was for the most part under captains not of their own townsmen. The soldiers were scattered about, as they were needed in different companies and regiments. Not a few slaves were sent into the service by their masters in the later years of the war. The following are some of the certificates of masters: —

"This may certify that I, the subscriber, have sent a servant belonging to me into the three years' service, named Peter Wallis, mustered by Colo. Samuel Johnson on the 22nd day of February last, being a soldier, to serve said term for class no. 1 in the North District in the Town of Andover, in Consideration of the sum of one hundred pounds Lawful money, to be paid me.

SAMUEL PHILLIPS."

"ANDOVER, *June* 17, 1781."

"ANDOVER, *Apr.* 9, 1782.

"Received of the class No. 5, in sd. Town, of which class No. 5 in sd. Town Capt. Henry Abbot is appointed Chairman, the sum of Ninety Pounds for the service of my servant Boy, named Peter, who has engaged in the service of the United States of America for the term of three years, unless sooner discharged.

JOSHUA LOVEJOY."

Also minors' wages were received by their fathers. The following is a curious receipt for pay of one young man's service: —

"I, the Subscriber, have received of Mr. Samuel Herrick the sum of nine hundred and eighty dollars, fifty eight silver dollars, a noat containin one hundred & eighty-six dolers, and a Pare of silver Bockels, which is in Full for my son, Richard Frost's hire for serven in the continental army for the said Samuel Herrick's class during the Present war Between the United States of America and Great Britain. per me JOSEPH FROST."

"ANDOVER, *July* 16, 1781.

"Attest: SAML. DOWNING,
STEPHEN ABBOT."[1]

The proclamation of peace, and the joy which it brought, are thus described by John Abbot, the Harvard student: —

"HOLLIS HALL, *May* 29, 1783.

"DEAR BROTHER, — Last Monday was kept by the town of Cambridge as a day of public rejoicing. The morning was ushered in by a discharge of cannon. An excellent oration was delivered by Mr. Thacher, & an anthem performed by the college choir. Large donations were given to prepare a public entertainment by several gentlemen in Town, particularly an ox at Mr. Fairweather's & an equal donation by Mr. Tom. Lee, which I supposed mounted to 70 or 80 dollars. In the evening there was a very curious collection of fire works of different kinds of construction. But with all these circumstances of parade & shew I could not but be heartily glad when it was over, for such public days are always attended with jargon, noise, and confusion, which are always disagreeable & disgustful to me."

Amidst the rejoicings at the return of peace, an event occurred which was of melancholy interest throughout the country and especially at Andover, the scene of its occurrence. This was the sudden death of the patriot, James Otis, from a stroke of lightning. Mr. Otis had been for nearly two years a resident of Andover, living on the homestead of Mr. Jacob Osgood[2] in the West Parish of the town. He was suffering from a mental disturbance caused by a blow on the head in-

---

[1] *Mass. Rev. Rolls*, vol. xxxii., p. 425.
[2] The early home of Rev. David Osgood, D. D.

flicted by a political opponent, which forbade any violent excitement and made seclusion a necessity. He thought himself, at one time, to be quite restored, and wrote in his journal on Sunday : " I have this day attended divine service and heard a sensible discourse, and thanks be to God I now enjoy the greatest of all blessings *mens sana in corpore sano.*" But a visit to Boston and a dinner party at Governor Hancock's brought a return of his malady. After his return to Andover he expressed a foreboding of approaching death, although he was then in excellent physical health. He pointed out a spot under a clump of trees, where he would like to be buried, and said [1] with a little touch of humor that shone forth like a bright gleam in a tempestuous sky, " You know my grave would overlook all your fields and I could have an eye upon the boys and see if they minded their work."

Six weeks after this, May 23, 1783, came his summons. A sudden shower had arisen and the family were within doors, gathered in the sitting-room watching the clouds and waiting for the rain to cease. Mr. Otis with his cane in one hand, stood leaning against the door which opened into the entry. He was in the act of telling a story when an explosion took place which seemed to shake the solid earth, and he fell, without a struggle or an exclamation, instantaneously dead. Mr. Osgood sprang forward and caught him as he fell. This flash was the only remarkable one. No other person was injured. The lightning did some damage to the house ; but " no mark of any kind could be found on Otis, nor was there the slightest change or convulsion in his features."

He had often expressed a wish that he might be struck by lightning. His death called forth many eulogies, orations, and poems. His biographer quotes some lines by the Hon. Thomas Dawes, " On the death of James Otis, killed by Lightning, at Andover, soon after the Peace of 1783." The following are the closing lines : —

> " Hark, the deep thunders echo round the skies,
> On wings of flame the eternal errand flies :
> One chosen charitable bolt is sped,
> And Otis mingles with the glorious dead."

[1] *Life of James Otis,* by William Tudor.

Following are lists of the military and the civil officers of Andover in this period : —

Military Officers in Service in the Revolutionary War.

Brigadier-general Joseph Frye.
Colonel James Frye.
Colonel Samuel Johnson.
Colonel Thomas Poor,[1]
Major Samuel Osgood.
Adjutant-general Bimsley Stevens.
Captain Benjamin Ames.
Captain Henry Abbot.
Captain John Abbot.
Captain Stephen Abbot.
Captain John Adams.
Captain Benjamin Farnum.
Captain Charles Furbush.
Captain Joshua Holt.
Captain Samuel Johnson.
Captain John Peabody.
Surgeon of 1st Regt., Dr. Thomas Kittredge.

Capt. Nathaniel Lovejoy's men were in service. No record of his being in field or camp has been found.

A List of the Civil Officers of the Revolutionary Period.
Second Quarter of the Town's Second Century.

REPRESENTATIVES TO THE GENERAL COURT.

1771.	Samuel Phillips, Esq.	1781.	Capt. Peter Osgood.
1772.	Samuel Phillips, Esq.		Capt. Joshua Holt.
1773.	Mr. Moody Bridges.	1782.	Capt. Joshua Holt.
1774.	Capt. Moody Bridges.[2]	1783.	Joshua Holt, Esq.
1775.	Mr. Samuel Phillips, jr.[3]	1784.	Hon. Samuel Osgood, Esq.
1776.	Mr. Samuel Phillips.	1785.	Joshua Holt, Esq.
	Capt. Joshua Holt.	1786.	Joshua Holt, Esq.
	Samuel Osgood, Esq.	1787.	Mr. Peter Osgood, junr.
	Mr. Nehemiah Abbot.	1788.	Capt. Peter Osgood.
1777.	Col. Samuel Johnson.	1789.	Capt. Peter Osgood.
1778.	Col. Samuel Johnson.	1790.	Capt. Peter Osgood.
	Mr. Samuel Phillips	1791.	Capt. Peter Osgood.
1779.	Mr. Samuel Phillips, jr.	1792.	Capt. Peter Osgood.
	Samuel Osgood, Esq.	1793 to 1800.	Joshua Holt, Esq.
1780.	Col. Samuel Johnson.		
	Capt. Joshua Holt.		

1780. Samuel Osgood, Esq. } Senators.
1781–1801. Samuel Phillips, jr., Esq.

1781. Hon. Samuel Osgood, Representative to Congress.
1801. Samuel Phillips, Esq., Lieutenant-governor.

1781–1798. Samuel Phillips, Justice of the Court of Common Pleas.

1770. Thomas Bragg, Deputy Sheriff.

[1] Of Methuen in the latter part of his service.
[2] Provincial Congress, October, 1774. — March, 1775. Samuel Osgood.
[3] Provincial Congress, May, 1775. General Court, July.

The heavy taxes and the drain upon public and private resources in raising and equipping the soldiers made the hardships and embarrassments very great after the close of the war. But, notwithstanding all these, and the popular clamor in many quarters, the town of Andover stood firm in opposition to all temporary expedients and make-shifts for tiding over difficulties. Far-seeing and prudent, determined to endure all present evils in order to establish the government on a sure foundation, the town expressed in strong language its dissent from the views put forth by the more timid and timeserving : —

"1785, *Oct.* 17. Whereas it has been said that a neighboring town has lately, by a public vote, expressed a disposition for a Paper currency.

"*Voted*, that Joshua Holt, Esq., be and he is hereby instructed in case any motion shall be made in the General Court for introducing a paper medium, vigorously and perseveringly to oppose the same as being a measure calculated, in our opinion, to promote idleness, dissipation, and dishonesty, and by destroying the morals of the people to bring on the ruin of the Commonwealth."

In December, 1786, the disaffection which had been spreading through the community broke out in Western Massachusetts in an armed insurrection. This found sympathizers and abettors in individual towns in the more eastern sections of the State. But although the town of Andover recognized the causes of complaint, and that there were "grievances" that demanded attention and encroachments that all good citizens ought to guard against, they declared it to be their opinion that these should be met in a regular and constitutional way. They accordingly chose (September, 1786), a committee to report on proper measures "to promote the general welfare and state what upon due deliberation appear to be grievances."

This committee consisted of Hon. Samuel Phillips, Esq., Capt. Nehemiah Abbot, Capt. Peter Osgood, Mr. Moody Bridges, Mr. Philemon Chandler, Mr. Nehemiah Abbot, Capt. Moses Abbot, Capt. John Abbot, Jr., Mr. Samuel Chickering, Jr., Lieut. Benjamin Poor, Capt. Jonathan Abbot, Lieut. Oliver Peabody, Lieut. John Ingalls, and Col. Samuel Johnson. The report of this committee specified among the grievances and causes of complaint : —

"The method commonly practised in our Courts of Common Pleas for recovering debts, it being needlessly expensive."

"The method of paying the Representatives out of the public treasury lays an unequal burden on many parts of the State, which might be alleviated by each town paying their own Representatives."

They also recommend a "thorough looking into" the salaries of public officers, and express their belief that the removal of the General Court out of the town of Boston would greatly lessen the expense of the government. They furthermore state that "we conceive it matter of just complaint that the accounts of the United States with the Commonwealth are not adjusted."

Still, whatever may be the "grievous acts of the Legislature," and however the town may deem it "the duty of a free and virtuous people at all times to keep a watchful eye against all encroachments upon their dear-bought rights, they deprecate all contentions and unconstitutional opposition to Government." They make the following dignified and yet determined utterance : —

"We esteem it our duty, at the present day, to bear our explicit testimony against all riotous and illegal proceedings and against all hostile attempts and menaces against law, justice, and good government, and to declare our readiness to exert ourselves in support of Government and the excellent Constitution of this Commonwealth. But at the same time we suppose there are many things complained of which ought to be remedied ; and it is our desire that every grievance may be in a constitutional way redressed."

Then follows the statement of grievances as above quoted.

"*Voted*, that the foregoing report be accepted by the town and transmitted to Joshua Holt, Esq., as the sentiment of the town, requesting his influence in the General Court that the same may be remedied."

Subsequently, in January, 1787, the town voted that the account rendered by the General Court to the people of the expenditure of the public money was "explicit, full, and satisfactory." Meanwhile, the militia of the eastern counties, under General Lincoln, was called for to suppress Shays's Rebellion, and Andover soldiers were again mustered into service. It is not necessary to attempt a detailed account of the military operations and the part of Andover. The following incidental minutes are found in the town records:—

"1787, *May* 3. An order to pay Capt. Samuel Johnson in part for his slay going to Worcester to carry provisions for the men that were detailed to suppress the insurgents."

"To pay Timothy Johnson for his slay going to Worcester."

"To pay Joseph Stevens for sundries delivered to the town for the use of the soldiers detailed under Genl. Lincoln to suppress the Insurrection in the western counties in the year 1787."

Although the insurrection was suppressed, there was still a strong sympathy with the discontent which had led to it, in many quarters, and not a few of the country towns expressed great dissatisfaction with the administration of the State government. The evils complained of were principally, says Hildreth, the "extortions of the lawyers, the aristocratic character of the Senate, the high salary of the governor, the sessions of the General Court in Boston, the refusal to issue paper money, and especially the recent grant .... conceded to Congress as a means of paying the interest on the federal debt." A convention of delegates of thirty-seven towns had discussed these grievances before the resort to arms. With this spirit of rebellion, Andover, as has been before said, had no sympathy. Prominent for his moderation and just counsels was the Hon. Samuel Phillips, Jr., President of the Senate, and his action and counsels were always acceptable to his constituents at Andover. The mind of the town was expressed in the following instructions to their representative to the General Court:—

"*June* 4, 1787. To MR. PETER OSGOOD, JUNR., *Representative for the Town of Andover.*

"*Sir:*—The Town by choosing you for their Representative have expressed that confidence in your ability & Integrity which supersede the necessity of any particular directions in conducting the common and ordinary concerns of Government, but they have thought in compliance with your desire to give you Instructions on certain subjects of principal Importance.

"In the first place you will exert your influence to retrieve and preserve the public credit, and bearing in mind that this is the foundation of a people's reputation & prosperity and safety. The evils which arise from the stagnation of a circulating medium will claim your serious attention, and as this is the most probable means to remove them, you will endeavor that the minds of the people be freed from all apprehensions of a probability of a paper medium, as an emission of such a medium would powerfully tend to encourage Idleness, Dissipation & Extravagance, Overreaching, Uneasiness, Jealousies, Contentions, and would in its consequences endanger the peace and safety of the commonwealth," etc.

He is instructed to favor the removal of the General Court from Boston, "but not into any County where there has been an open Insurrection," and to favor clothing the Federal Government with greater power.

Concerning the true character of the insurrection and the temper of the insurgents, the town of Andover had means of accurate knowledge. Judge Phillips had, as one of the commission to treat with the disaffected, spent a month in the discontented counties, and gained full information respecting the aims and plans of the chief conspirators. It was not, however, without obloquy that our distinguished townsman performed this duty. The feeling created by his service as Commissioner [1] caused his losing the nomination as one of the Senatorial candidates for the year 1787. But the decline of popularity was only temporary. The following year he was reinstated as President of the Senate. The anxiety felt by his fellow-citizens and by his family for his success in the hazardous duty of Commissioner was great. A letter of Madam Phillips to him breathes the spirit of patriotism which animated the people, the women as well as the men, of Andover, at the trying time : —

"*April* 3, 1787.[2] I feel exceedingly for you, judging you must be anxious on account of the aspect of public affairs, which is truly alarming, but I trust you will not suffer your thoughts to make long visits to your family. I wish you to exert every faculty for the public good. I sincerely wish the Divine blessing may attend your consultations. I am very willing to make any sacrifice, might tranquillity be restored to our deluded States. Heaven only knows when it will end."

[1] Taylor's *Life of Judge Phillips*.   [2] *Ibid.*

The town of Andover had expressed the opinion "that the Federal Government ought to be clothed with more power." This was the conclusion to which the logic of events had been pushing thoughtful minds. Public attention had been for some time directed to the consideration of measures which would at least confer power upon the Federal Government sufficient for self-preservation.

In May, 1787, a convention of delegates met at Philadelphia to revise the Articles of Confederation, and they drew up a form of Constitution, which was to be submitted to the States for their adoption or rejection. A convention was called by the Legislature of Massachusetts, to meet in Boston, January 9, 1788. The history of this Convention, and the important part taken in it by one of the delegates from Andover, has been written in a memorial[1] tribute to the first lawyer of Andover by the oldest lawyer of the town now living. To this eloquent tribute and accurate history nothing need here be added. From it the following facts are mainly compiled. The town of Andover chose to represent it in the Convention three delegates, Dr. Thomas Kittredge, Peter Osgood, Jr., and William Symmes, Esq. The sentiment of the town, like that of all the delegates, was opposed to the form of the Constitution. Among the papers[2] of Mr. William Symmes is a copy of a letter from him to Capt. Peter Osgood, giving his "reasons for objecting to the Federal Constitution." It is dated November 15, 1787, within sixty days after the adoption of the report of the Constitution at Philadelphia, and was, says Mr. Hazen, "probably the earliest review made of the entire instrument." This letter of considerable length discusses the objectionable parts of the Constitution, but, nevertheless, exhibits a candid spirit, and free from prejudice, and concludes with an exhortation to "equally shun a hasty acceptance or a precipitate rejection."

Indeed it is true that some of the most conscientious and careful thinkers were in doubt as to the wisest action, while

---

[1] *Memorial Discourse on William Symmes, Esq.*, by Nathan W. Hazen. — *Historical Collections of the Essex Institute*, 1860.
[2] See *Memorial of William Symmes, Esq.*

some, on the other hand, were clear and decided in their convictions. After listening to the debates, Mr. Symmes became convinced that the Constitution ought to be adopted, and, although he had at first given his voice against it, he spoke a second time strongly in its favor. In his first speech he made the following statement : —

"Sir, — I will not dishonor my constituents by supposing that they expect me to resist that which is irresistible — the force of reason. No, sir, my constituents wish for a firm, efficient continental government; but fear the operation of this which is now proposed. Let them be convinced that their fears are groundless, and I venture to promise in their name that no town in the Commonwealth will sooner approve the form or be better subjects under it."

This speech was made on the 22d of January. The subject was warmly and ably discussed, Mr. Theophilus Parsons and Colonel Varnum replying to Mr. Symmes. On the 30th, Mr. Parsons moved that the Convention do assent to and ratify the Constitution. The vote was, however, deferred. Governor Hancock expressed himself in favor of the adoption, moving some amendments, and several members who had at first opposed the adoption, gradually changed their opinion. At Andover, January 31st, a town meeting was held "for the purpose of expressing the sentiments of the inhabitants on the subject of the Federal Constitution." It is not improbable that the town had received information of the change of sentiment in the Convention, and that Mr. Symmes now favored the adoption of the Constitution. The question being put to vote, "Whether it is the opinion of the town that it be expedient, all circumstances considered, that the Federal Constitution now under the consideration of the Convention, sitting at Boston for the purpose of considering the same, be adopted as it now stands." One hundred and fifteen voted in the affirmative, one hundred and twenty-four in the negative. This vote showed a decided change in the sentiment of the town. There was, however, a unanimous vote not to give any instructions to the delegates.

On the 6th of February Mr. Symmes, in a speech to the Convention, avowed his change of conviction, made a strong argument in favor of the adoption, concluding with an assertion of his conscientiousness in the change of sentiment: —

"In so doing I stand acquitted to my own conscience. I hope and trust I shall to my constituents, and know I shall before God."

The vote of the members from Essex County was 38 yeas and 6 nays, the largest vote, in favor of the constitution, of any county, both numerically and in proportion to the whole number of votes. The vote of the Convention was: yeas, 187; nays, 168.

Mr. Symmes's biographer has no doubt that this majority of the Convention was largely due to the moral effect of his fearless avowal of his change of conviction.

Whatever the effect of Mr. Symmes's action, there can be no doubt as to its motives. He yielded to the force of argument, and dared to take a stand which he knew would expose him to the censures, if not to the suspicion of some of his townsmen. Says Mr. Hazen: "He knew that the majority of those who sent him there had recorded his condemnation in advance. It does not appear that he expected or conciliated favor from their minority. It is certain that he received none; he could receive none. If he had had from them a popular nomination, an appointment, or even professional patronage, it might have brought suspicion upon his integrity. But the sacrifice was complete. For the time he lost all and gained nothing. . . . . He now stands before us a patriot above suspicion, — a great man, who in the ardor of youth, full of abilities, with a capacity proved fitted for the highest posts, yet repelling at once the counsellings of selfishness and the promptings of ambition, surrendering his chosen prospects in life, the hope to acquire wealth and honor in his native town, for the sake of the people, the whole people, and expecting for it all no reward but in his own consciousness and in the approval and gratitude of whoever should stand where we do witnesses of the entire success of the Union and Constitution then formed."

We may accord with the estimate of Mr. Symmes's character and yet see how his townsmen, and especially his colleagues, the delegates to the Convention, would regard him with suspicion. He had taken side with the winning party, and his motives would, as a matter of course, be impugned. He had dissented, being a young man, from opinions held by his colleagues, old and tried counsellors of the community, and his opinions had triumphed. It could not be possible that he should at once regain their confidence. He was keenly sensitive and the more so, doubtless, that he knew the purity of his motives. At any rate he found his position in the town so uncomfortable that he removed and settled in Portland, where he rose to high rank among the lawyers of the Cumberland bar.

The ratification of the Constitution by the other States, the election of General Washington as President, and the events of his administration,[1] are familiar to all readers. Under this administration Mr. Samuel Osgood was appointed Postmaster-general. He had held for the four years previous the office of "Commissioner of the Treasury." In regard to his selection by the President as Postmaster-general he writes in his autobiographical memoranda: —

"It was not expected that he should have had any office offered him, he having been opposed for a time to an unqualified adoption of the new Constitution. Parties being highly exasperated, those who had exerted themselves in procuring the adoption of the new Constitution were to be rewarded[2] with all the offices. But General Washington had been well acquainted with him from the commencement of the war, and offered him the Postmaster General's department, which he accepted and held for about two years at a salary of $1500 a year. He had been encouraged to believe that this would be increased, but seeing no prospect of it he resigned, and continued in private life till the year 1800." . . . .

Before his appointment as Postmaster-general, Mr. Osgood had removed to the city of New York, and his history[3]

---

[1] It is not intended to include in this chapter the enterprises of his administration, but merely to conclude those of the Revolutionary period.

[2] This indicates the feeling towards Mr. Symmes.

[3] Mr. Osgood had no children by his first wife. By his second wife, Martha Franklin, he had four daughters and a son, Walter Franklin Osgood. One of the daughters was married to the Hon. Mr. Genet, French Minister at Washington.

henceforth ceases to be intimately connected with that of Andover.

An interesting relic [1] of this period, and one which shows some of the practical difficulties in the workings of the new government, is found in a letter of Thomas Houghton (the partner of Mr. Phillips in paper-making), 1792, in regard to his son's bearing arms in the State militia. Mr. Houghton was an Englishman, of Quaker bringing-up, and therefore had special objection to military service. He came to America in 1789.

"Sir, — The present is to request the favor of you to return me the paper I put into your hands containing some reasons for not letting my son carry arms in the militia of the state. I some time ago had some talk with Cap. Poor on the subject. He assured me that he acted in that affair exactly agreeable both to the Militia Laws of the State, and also what had been constantly practised towards all foreigners; on my expressing very great surprise, he asked if I had seen the Militia Laws. I replied no; neither did I wish to see them, for if they were such as he represented them they took away the Rights of Man which the Americans so much boasted of; and I further remarked that if the militia laws of this state gave the militia officers such power as he conceived, and had attempted to enforce, it was a disgrace to the country, for the Massachusetts boasted that on the late enumerations it had not any slaves in it, yet the fact was not truly stated, for every foreigner compelled to carry arms contrary to his inclination, and perhaps forced to use them against his native country, was a slave in the very worst of situations that human nature could be placed in, even worse than what the negros experience in the West Indies, however the Americans might pride themselves on the full liberty said by them to be enjoyed by every resident inhabitant in their happy country. Its true the negroes suffer great hardships in their bodies, but then their minds are free, but here on a foreigner's being forced to perform military duty his mind must be continually on the rack by not knowing the service he may be forced to act in. Perhaps it may be against his nearest and dearest relatives; if so, what signifies the pain of the body to what a sensitive mind must feel at such a period!" etc.

Shortly after General Washington's inauguration, he made

[1] Phillips Papers.

a tour of the Eastern States, visiting Andover on his return from New Hampshire, on his way from Haverhill to Lexington. His visit to Andover is thus described by the biographer of Judge Phillips: "Thursday morning (November 5th) he drove early to Andover, and breakfasted at Deacon Isaac Abbot's tavern, in the house now owned[1] by Hon. Amos Abbot. Here, as he stood in front of the house, some of our most aged citizens remember to have seen him.

"While tarrying here, he asked the little daughter of Deacon Abbot to mend his riding-glove for him; and when she had done it, took her upon his knee and gave her a kiss, which so elated Miss Priscilla that she would not allow her face to be washed again for a week."

General Washington was the guest of Judge Phillips at the mansion-house, where he met some of the principal citizens. He received the salutations of the people, as he sat on horseback on the common, near the mansion-house.

From Andover he went to Lexington by way of Billerica.

This visit to Andover, General Washington himself briefly described[2] in his journal:—

"*Thursday, 5th November*, 1789. About sunrise I set out, crossing the Merrimack river at the town over to the township of Bradford, and in nine miles came to Abbot's tavern, Andover, where we breakfasted and met with much attention from Mr. Phillips, President of the Senate of Massachusetts, who accompanied us through Billarike to Lexington, where I dined and viewed the spot on which the first blood was spilt in the dispute with Great Britain on the 19th of April, 1775." . . . .

General Washington remarked on the beautiful scenery and fine cultivation of the country.

Another distinguished tourist, the Marquis de Chastellux, who visited Andover some years before (1782-1783), also bore witness to the beauty of its scenery and its cultivated farms:—

"Nous[3] traversames South & North Andover. North Parish

---

[1] This house is now owned by Mr. Samuel Locke.

[2] *Washington's Private Diaries*, Lossing.

[3] "We passed through South and North Andover (or, if you prefer to call it so, North Parish). North Andover is a charming place. Here are seen beautiful

ou, s'il on vent, North Andover est un endroit charmant. On y voit de trés jolies maisons & en grande quantité, beaucoup de prairies & des bestieaux de la plus belle espèce."

An interesting description of Andover at this period is given in letters of the Englishman, Thomas Houghton, who came here to engage in the business of paper-making with Mr. Phillips. Although this, in a measure, anticipates and trenches upon the topics assigned to a future chapter on the history of the town's industries, it may be introduced at this point to give a general view of the state of things at the close of the Revolutionary period: —

"ANDOVER, *April* 21, 1789.

"I am now at Andover, about 22 miles nearly east from Boston. I am at the house of the Hon[ble] Saml. Phillip, junior, Esq., pres. of the Senate, one of the Judges in this State, a creditable well regulated family, and here I purpose staying some time, having agreed with this Gentleman to go into partnership in manufacturing of paper."[1]

After many statistics in regard to the country, its industries, etc., he speaks of the spirit of equality that prevails: —

"I must confess freedom is carried to what I think is too great a pitch. Here is very little subordination. All hold themselves equal in nature, & to call a Man or woman a Servant is deemed a very great affront. Even Judge Phillips addresses his servant men by the appellation of Mr. such a one, & 'pray Mr. Such a one do so & so, or don't you think it best to do so & so.' The reply in general is, 'Yes, sir, I conceive it is.' You must move y[r] Hatt to every one you meet and have any acquaintance with, and take them by the hand & ask how they do, also enquire after the family. Women are addressed in a style pretty equal to the men. One thing I must observe which I think wants rectifying, that is their pluming pride when adjoined to apparent poverty, no uncommon case."

Speaking of the comparative population in America and England, he says: —

"The country, all where I have been, is well settled, & I think as thick of inhabitants as Lincoln in England, in general good houses, and in great numbers, many fields and cattle of the finest kind." — *Voyage en Amérique.*

[1] Statements as to the mill, etc., reserved for the chapter on Manufactures.

houses. Here is two places of worship in this Town. Such places are called chapels: those at this place, much larger than Raisin Church, are generally well filled with genteel people, who dress entirely after the English fashion. They are very sensible of the impropriety of wearing & using European commodities, but custom and habit are bad to get over all at once; however the Rich & great strive by example to convince the populace of their error by growing their own Flax, having some one in the family to dress it, & all the females spin, several weave & Bleach the Linen. They also grow their own beef, pork & mutton, consequently their own wool, which they also get spun, weaved, & dyed, & both the Gentleman I am with & his father, who is a Justice of Peace, generally appear in their own manufacture in imitation of the British." . . . .

As to the laborious habits and general appearance of the farmers, he says:—

"I assure you they don't appear to me to work hard, but I am told they live well; however they appear very civil, decent, well instructed people, possest with a spirit of Religion. On Sundays they keep very close, except when at publick worship, which is forenoon and afternoon, and perhaps in the evening, at home reading to one another when not called to family prayers, in singing of Watts' Psalms & Hymns. I am told a publickan would have his license taken from him & be also fined if he was to suffer tippling on the Lord's day. These are regulations worthy of example, but I don't by any means intend to insinuate that the people are perfect here any more than in England, only it appears to me they shew fewer public vices. As to property it seems so well secured from principle in the people that here is not such use of Locks & Bolts as in England. Even where I am we have five out Doors & sixty-two Sash windows; yet all the barage on the doors is a wood catch on the door snek. At the time of fruit being ready I am told there is no occasion to rob orchards, for here is plenty of apple trees by the road-side whose branches hang into the road & in a manner invite the traveler to taste."

There are many statistics of the progress of the country, its industries and resources, and the writer thus comments on the loss to England of such colonies:—

"O what a country has Britain lost by her folly; but this is too large a field to dwell on in a letter, the subject from even poor me would easily draw forth a volume. Suffice it is that even now though they glory in their independence, & speak of the cruelties inflicted on them with the utmost freedom & even abhorrence, yet the name of an Old England man softens them instantly, but the accounts of cruelty that I have been made acquainted with were enough to shake the allegiance of any people, possest as they were of an extensive country full of resources to enable the inhabitants to be their own Legislators. They have obtained it, and past injuries keep up the present spirit of the nation, but they are already so clogged with taxes that thousands sigh on remembering the times they enjoyed formerly under the British government at the time of the peace of Paris. They have now a federal Constitution. The members are at this time sitting at New York, and have almost converted the Constitution into a monarchy, having their president, upper house, & lower house, with the speakers, &c. The populace expects redress of every grievance, & their Spirit will be greatly hurt when they find by experience their expectations disappointed; and disappointed they must be for some time, for this Country labors under evils that will require great wisdom to remove, the principal of which I conceive arises from a want of specie. The war brought them plenty of Cash & introduced foreign luxuries; the cash is gone to pay for such luxuries, and they have not a surplus of exports to bring in either cash or goods equal to the demand that such luxuries call for, & yet the Rage for finery of every kind seems almost as great as ever. I believe the populace think Congress can call down Gold out of the clouds to enable them to answer every demand."

Allusion has been made to the use of home manufactures for clothing. The town had taken action on the matter in 1787, and voted to encourage home manufactures as one means of alleviating the distress then prevailing, and lightening the burdens of taxation. Every one familiar with the portraits of the period knows that great elegance in dress had prevailed among the wealthier classes after the Revolution. One need not go out of Andover to find pictures and actual relics also of these rich but quaint costumes, — three-cornered hats, flowered satin waistcoats, velvet coats, silken hose, silver knee-buckles, ruffled shirt bosoms; and in women's attire, brocades and laces, spangled slippers, huge tortoise-shell combs. From the gilded frames in the ancient mansions and libraries, the calm, beautiful faces of the women, and the grave, dignified men, by the painter's art, glorified into their noblest selves, look down upon us, and show the present generation what their ancestors were when only the rich and great had likenesses taken, and when few artists except masters were thought competent to the work of portrait-painting. Then the few had Stuarts and Copleys. The popular likeness of those times was the profile, the black silhouette. These are familiar to all the visitors at old country homesteads, the grandfather's queue and the grandmother's high, ruffled cap effectively displayed in companion-frames, facing each other over the mantel, in the "best parlor" or "spare chamber."

Not to dwell too long upon the customs of this period, we must pass, but not without allusion, to one of its characteristic institutions, the public house, or tavern, and the stagecoach.

Travelling had undergone essential changes in the century. People, in 1789, were no doubt wont to look back a hundred years, and regarding the primitive modes of journeying of their ancestors, on horseback or in lumbering cart, or tumbril, congratulate themselves on the wonderful progress of the century which had substituted for the saddle and the pillion for long journeys the wonderful modern convenience of the stage-coach. It is true that there had been for a long time in use chaises and "chariots" for private journeying; but the great public stage was a comparatively new invention in the Revolutionary period. In 1781, a stage ran from Boston to Portsmouth. In 1776, a stage had long run [1] past Mr. Isaac Abbot's house at Andover, though to and from what places has not been ascertained.

Mr. Abbot petitioned the General Court at that time to be allowed to keep a house of public entertainment, since the house near him had been closed and he had been subjected to no small inconvenience from applications of passengers for refreshment, his house being "near the old stage" road.

This petition also speaks of the "extraordinary travel which is rendered necessary by means of the army before Boston."

[1] *Mass. Archives*, vol. ccviii., p. 180.

This gives us a hint of what was then the condition of things, as it had been during the old French War: journeys hither and thither of troops, the quiet of the country village and tavern suddenly broken by the arrival of militia, or Continental troops, hungry mouths to be fed, tired bodies to be refreshed, or wounded and sick to be soothed and cared for, jaded horses to be rubbed down and fed with the best the stable afforded; General and Colonel and Captain to be served in the best room and subordinates at the kitchen fire; great demands upon the stores of wine and strong liquors, and clouds of tobacco smoke; and wonderful stories and adventures related to the astonishment of village rustics. There was at Andover, moreover, the arrival of visitors to the new school, the eminent men of the time, coming to place here their sons to be educated for the great responsibilities to fall upon them as citizens of the new Republic. The ancient stage-coach that lumbered up to Andover houses of entertainment and rolled off once or twice a week would, if its history were traced from the beginning and all the visitors it brought and carried away were chronicled, make a volume of no common interest.

> "Who, in these days when all things go by steam,
> Recalls the stage-coach with its four-horse team?
> Its sturdy driver, — who remembers him?
> Or the old landlord, saturnine and grim,
> Who left our hill-top for a new abode
> And reared his sign-post farther down the road?"[1]

During the Revolutionary period there were public houses (besides that of Isaac Abbot), of Col. James Frye, Isaac Blunt, Hezekiah Ballard, Capt. Asa Foster, and later those of Benjamin Ames, Bimsley Stevens, and Ebenezer Poor. The opinion of the Marquis de Chastellux was not flattering in respect to the inn at which he stayed: "Une mauvaise auberge tenue par un homme nommé Foster: nous nous contentames de faire repaitre nos chevaux dans ce mauvais cabaret."[2]

The post rider at this time was a person of no small consequence in public estimation and his own. He rode on

---

[1] *The School Boy*, O. W. Holmes.
[2] "A wretched inn kept by a man named Foster. We were glad to do no more than feed our horses in this miserable tavern."

horseback "post-haste" equipped with saddle-bags and a horn which announced his approach. Letters were often sent by private conveyance. Many have been found in Andover thus sent with the names of the bearers, who did the favor or "honored" them "in conveyance," as distinguished travellers on business to the city did not scorn to do for humble friends. In 1775, a post rider was established between Boston and Haverhill and a post office at the latter place. Letters for Andover people were often advertised in the post office at Haverhill. In 1780 Samuel Bean, a post rider, carried the "Independent Chronicle" from Boston to Londonderry. Doubtless he came through Andover, then, as he did ten years later. His advertisement in the "Chronicle" of February 17, 1780, is a curious illustration of the customs of the time : —

"Samuel Bean, Post Rider from Boston to Londonderry, informs his customers that the time for which he engaged to ride expires the last week in this month. He purposes to ride another Quarter, which will begin the first week in March. The Price will be 16 dollars in Cash or half a bushel of Rye or three Pecks of Indian Corn for three months, which is as cheap as they were before the war. As there are about a Hundred, exclusive of those who agreed to pay him in Grain who had the paper the last quarter[1] and have not yet paid him, he hopes they will settle the same immediately. He would also inform them that if they are not more punctual in Payment he must quit riding at the end of the ensuing Quarter. As it is uncertain what Number of Papers to engage for with the Printer, he hopes all who intend to become Subscribers will immediately give in their names.

"P. S. If the weather should be bad or anything shall happen so as to prevent his riding the first week, he intends on the second week to carry two weeks' papers, and the Quarter to begin from the first week in order that his subscribers may receive the whole of Col. Allen's narrative."

Another relic of the travel in Andover, in 1780, is found in an advertisement of the "Independent Chronicle" of February 10 : —

"Lost on the 28th ult., between Mr. Abbot's and Deacon Ballard's taverns, in Andover, a Pinch-Beck WATCH with two cases,

[1] Several copies are found in Andover.

the outside case, Tortois-shell, with a braded worsted string in lieu of a chain. Whoever has found said watch and will leave it at either of the above taverns shall have *Fifty Dollars* Reward.

"HAMPSTEAD, *Feb.* 3, 1780." MOSES JOHNSON."

There were, during this period, several stores at Andover, the principal one being that of Judge Phillips, in the South Parish, near his mansion house; also one of Mr. Zebadiah Abbot. The only manufactories were those owned by Mr. Phillips, the powder mill and paper mill, at the present site of the "Andover Mills"[1] on the Shawshin.

The Phillips Academy was established in 1778, and the town Grammar and District Schools were kept up with more or less regularity. The two churches were crowded on Sundays and weekly lecture-days. There was a social library in the North Parish, and, on the whole, the town of Andover was as flourishing as any inland town of the Commonwealth. The civil and municipal history, after the adoption of the Federal Constitution, it is not our present purpose to consider. This summary will serve to outline the general aspect of things from the beginning of the Revolution to the dawn of the new era of the United States Government.

The death of General Washington (in December, 1799) caused a profound sensation at Andover, where he was personally known and revered by so many citizens. The anniversary of his birth-day, the following February 22d, was selected as a fitting time to pronounce a eulogy. The following indicates the action of the town: —

"*Jan.* 22, 1800. Warrant for a town meeting to see what method the town will adopt for the purpose recommended by the people of the United States by the President in his Proclamation upon the Resolve of the Congress of the said United States of the 6th day of January, and in publickly testifying their Grief for the Death of General George Washington by suitable Eulogies, Orations, or Discourses, or by publick prayers on the 22d day of February next. . . . .

"*Voted*, to assemble together as a Town on Saturday, the 22d day of February next for the purpose recommended. To meet at the North meeting-House. To choose a committee of arrange-

[1] Marland Mills.

ments. Mr. William Symmes, the Rev. Jonathan French, Mr. Nehemiah Abbot, Mr. John Phillips, Nathan Lovejoy, Doc' Thomas Kittredge, Captain Henry Abbot, Deacon Benjamin Farnum, Mr. Mark Newman, Major Samuel Johnson, Cap. Zebadiah Holt, to make arrangements upon this melancholy occasion."

On the 22d the militia, with badges of mourning on their arms, marched to the beat of muffled drum to the meeting-house, where an eloquent eulogy was pronounced by the Hon. John Phillips, of North Andover.

In this connection it is perhaps not unsuitable to record another funeral solemnity of scarcely less interest in the town, and, indeed, of more real grief to many individuals than that of the First President, General Washington.

This was on the occasion of the death of the then Lieutenant-governor, "Judge Phillips," as he was known by his townsmen. He died Thursday, February 10, 1802. Funeral services were held at Boston and at Andover. The burial was at Andover, in the South Church Burying-ground. The Rev. Dr. Tappan preached a sermon in the South Meeting-house. The Rev. Mr. French made a prayer, and an appropriate anthem was sung. The procession formed at the mansion-house, and walked to the burial-ground. First in the procession marched the students of Phillips Academy (present and past members), next the Trustees of the Phillips Academies at Andover and at Exeter, then came the bier. The pall-bearers were his Excellency the Governor, three of the Council, the President of the Senate, and Speaker of the House of Representatives. Then followed the family and relatives of the deceased, "and a very long train of mourning fellow-citizens."[1]

Respecting these solemnities the biographer of Judge Phillips says:—

"The immense concourse, the presence of so many distinguished civilians, the universal sensibility, and the impressive exercises with which her favorite son was then laid in his tomb made this a most memorable day to Andover; such as she had never seen before and will never see again."

[1] Compiled from contemporary accounts.

CHAPTER VI.

CHURCHES AND MINISTERS. — CHURCH-YARDS, OR BURYING-GROUNDS.

Of all the institutions of our forefathers, perhaps the most important, certainly the most characteristic, was the church. To its upbuilding they gave their best energies. Whatever else might thrive or perish, that must prosper, its work must go on. Whether the people lived in log-cabin or frame house, whether they built school-house or mill, whether they were few and feeble, or numerous and powerful, they failed not to build the house of God, and to meet regularly and often for the service of the sanctuary. They did not, indeed, expend time and money in church architecture, for the more these were absent, reasoned the Puritan, the more would the Holy Spirit be present to make his abode in the truer temple of the heart. Accordingly, the house of worship was simply the meeting-house, a convenient place for the people to assemble, whether to hear sermons or transact town business.

The first meeting-house of Andover is supposed to have stood near the " Old North Burying-ground ; " the English Church custom of gathering the graves of the dead about the place of prayer being retained by the colonists for at least forty years. When the meeting-house was built is unknown, but there is reason to believe that it was among the very first works of the town : —

"At a lawful Town meeting the 3^d of ffebruary, 1661, itt is ordered ' that all first comers of inhabitants that have been at the charges of purchasing the plantation and building the minister's house, the mill and meeting house, For and in consideration thereof are allowed an acre and a halfe to every acre houselott of Low and Swamp land, and every other inhabitant that have been at the charges of building the meeting-house and mill is to be allowed one acre to every acre house lott, and this land to be apportioned to the lots.'"

This first meeting-house was a temporary one, and stood only till about 1669, and then a second one was built: —

"1st Feb., 1669. It is agreed and voated that the selectmen, with three men joyned to them, that is, Nathan Parker and George Abbot, senior, and John Lovejoy, shall, and are hereby Impowered to make sale of certain parsells of land as they in their discretion shall see meet, not exceeding a hundred pounds, for the defraieing the charges about the new meeting-house."

That this "new meeting-house" was not the first which the town had had, and that this was not the same house as the one alluded to in the vote of February, 1661, is implied in two earlier votes, one in 1662, the other in 1664, in neither of which is the meeting-house then in use spoken of as "new."

In regard to the size and construction of this "new meeting-house" of 1669, nothing further is known than that it had "upper and lower galleries" built either at the first or at some later period. In 1692 it was "granted to Mr. Andrew Peters to build a seat in ye east gallery, and to Joseph Willson to build a seat over by ye north stairs." In 1696, "upper and lower" galleries are specified. The pulpit was cushioned, as appears from a vote to give George Abbot the use of a part of the parsonage lands for his services in repairing the meeting-house, he agreeing to "mend ye pulpit cushings, and to gett ye lock on ye meeting-house mended."

The first legislation found, in regard to the new meeting-house after 1669, stands recorded as follows: —

"3 ffeb. 1672. It is ordered that whatsoever doggs be in the meeting-house on the Sabbath-day, the owners thereof shall pay six pence for every time being there, and George Abbot, junior, is appointed to take notice thereof, and to have the pay for his services and to gather it up."

Also George Abbot, in 1675, was to be paid "for sweeping ye meeting house and ringynge ye bell, thirty shillings per annum." To his Sunday duties were subsequently added daily, or, rather, nightly, services as follows: —

"At a meeting of the Selectmen of Andover, ye 16 of ye 1 month,

167 6/9, we have agreed with Georg Abbot,[1] drummer,[2] to Ring ye bell at nine of the clock at night, as also to give notice by ye towling of the bell every night of ye day of the month, and his time of Ringing to begin the time of ye instant march, which he is to doe, and to be payd for his labour thirty shillings by the yeare."

This is the beginning of the record in Andover history of that important functionary, the sexton. The line of succession of sextons to the First Church is not continuously traceable, but in 1688 George Abbot's name appears again, then Nehemiah Abbot, then, October, 1689, John Abbot.[3]

The next incumbent to the office was a woman: —

"Agreed with widdowe Rebekah Johnson, this 10th of November, 1690, to sweep ye meeting-house and ring ye bell, as is exprst in ye agreement above made with John Abbot, only her yeare is to begin ye 1st of Dec. next, and ye towne to allowe her 40s. in pay for her pains."

The widow, Rebekah Johnson, served for at least eight years.

After the building of a meeting-house, the arrangement of the congregation in the pews was a matter of no small importance and difficulty. This was not left to be determined by the choice of the persons to be seated. A committee chosen by the town ranked the seats according to their eligibility. This was called "dignifying" the pews. The pews of highest rank were then assigned by a committee to those members of the congregation who were regarded as occupying the highest positions of social or ecclesiastical eminence. This was called in technical phrase, "seating the meeting-house."

The seating and ranking was a fruitful source of jealousies and hard feeling. Some of the committee would gladly have been excused from this disagreeable task; but excuses were not allowed. It is recorded that Capt. Dudley Bradstreet "protested against being compelled to serve in seating the meeting-house."

The conduct of the congregation, as well as the seats which

---

[1] George Abbot is the one "of Rowley," not "George Abbot, Senr."
[2] The person who beat the drum for the signal for service and for daily labor.
[3] Sons of George Abbot.

they occupied, came under the jurisdiction of the town officers. The records bear witness to a great deal of legislating of the selectmen in regard to "young persons." Then, as now, these appear to have been irrepressible : —

"Y⁰ 16 of y⁰ 1 month, 1679-80. .... We have ordered Thomas Osgood and John Bridges to have inspection over the boys in the galleries on the Sabbath, that they might be contained in order in time of publick exercise."

"14th March, 169¾. And whereas there is greivous complaints of great prophaneness of y⁰ Sabbath, both in y⁰ time of exercise, att noon time, to y⁰ great dishonor of god, scandall of religion, & y⁰ grief of many serious christians, by young persons, we order & require y⁰ tything men & constables to tak care to p'vent such great & shameful miscarriages, which are soe much observed and complained of."

The tything men were chosen either by the town or by the selectmen. It was their duty not only to inspect the conduct of the church-goers, but also to take note of absentees, and report the cause of absence to the authorities. Incorrigible "Sabbath-breakers" were amenable not only to the town but also to the laws of the General Court. In 1677, when Col. Dudley Bradstreet was deputy to the General Court, an act was passed authorizing a *cage* to be set up in Boston to confine Sabbath-breakers.

Those at Andover, whose behavior during divine service was regarded by the tything men as reprehensible, were liable to be "called forth" and reproved by the minister, and brought before a justice of the peace, as appears from an order of the selectmen that they shall be "punished for such crimes as y⁰ law directs."

Any one chosen to the office of tything man, and refusing to serve, was liable to a heavy fine. These officers were also obliged to see that young persons were not abroad late Saturday nights.

Thus, by pains and penalties, if devotion could not be produced, decorum was secured, and a reverence for the externals of religion maintained, which, in the opinion of many, went far toward creating the inward grace, but which in the estimation of others tended chiefly to hypocrisy and cant.

The latter was the view taken by the Quakers, Antinomians, Anabaptists, and other "heretics" who cried out upon the Puritan works of righteousness as offensive to heaven. Although no such disturbers of the peace troubled Andover church (so far as can be now ascertained), yet some of the Andover church members were prominent in the Quaker persecutions, especially Mr. Simon Bradstreet, who, in Court at Ipswich, and in the ministerial councils at Newbury, was zealous against offenders. His zeal, no doubt, highly commended him to his brethren at Andover, but it is severely stigmatized by the Quaker historians. Although it may be in a sense a digression to turn here to the consideration of the Quaker persecutions, it is, perhaps, as pertinent to the present subject as to any other department of the town's history. It was not only as a magistrate, but as a church member in fulfilment of his supposed obligations to covenant vows, that the Puritan dealt anathemas and visited penalties upon heretics. The epithets which the heretic historians and sympathizers heap upon their persecutors, and, on the other hand, the satisfaction which the Puritan writers show in what they think just and deserved penalties upon the enemies of sound doctrine and good order, attest the impossibility of dispassionate judgment in regard to such acts of religious zeal, and the danger of extremes in any coercion in matters of conscience.

The author of "New England Judged by the Spirit of the Lord," George Bishop, says, regarding the Andover magistrate and his coadjutors: "Your high priest, John Norton, and Simon Bradstreet, one of your magistrates .... were deeply concerned in the Blood of the Innocents, and their cruel sufferings, the one as advising, the other as acting." Again, he writes: "Simon Bradstreet, a man *hardened in Blood and a cruel persecutor.*"

After detailing the sufferings of Nicholas Phelps (whose chief offence was absenting himself from the established Puritan worship, and wearing his hat in presence of the court), describing how, "with a three-fold corded whip with knots," he was scourged again and again, and also how a woman was bound to the whipping-post in Ipswich, in presence of the magistrates, and most barbarously lacerated, Bishop says: —

"And in this cruelty your Major General Daniel Denison bore the greatest sway. . . . . Simon Bradstreet and William Hathorn aforesaid were Assistant to Denison in these executions, whose Names I Record to Rot and Stink as of you all to all Generations, unto whom this shall be left as a perpetual Record of your Everlasting Shame."

Neither Mr. Bradstreet nor any of the persecutors of the Quakers ever seem to have experienced remorse of conscience for their acts, as did some of those concerned in the apprehensions and condemnations for witchcraft. The Old North Meeting-house witnessed no confessions of cruelty to heretics; but, on the contrary, it, no doubt, heard many expressions of righteous indignation at their impieties, and many congratulations to the "worshipful Mr." Simon Bradstreet for his conduct as a magistrate so creditable to the zeal for truth of the Andover "First Church."

In regard to some of the disturbances and transgressions of the heretics, it must be admitted that they outraged decency, and required legal interference; but, as it seems now, in the light of history and science, the interference of pity and humanity, such as should be bestowed upon derangement of reason and excitement of imagination, and not the harsh penalties of pillory and whipping-post.

The only indication which has been found that any citizen of Andover was a troubler of the peace, or a dissenter from the prevailing views about the righteousness of the Puritan penalties, is in a presentment before the County Court, March, 1656: —

"We p'sent William Young [1] for abusive speeches, for wishing theme hanged that made that order of whipping; Then he was desired to consider what he said: Then he, the sayd Young, answered that he thought they had bin a company of rude, deboyst fellows that made it. Witnessed by WILLIAM BALLARD, ANDREW ALLEN."

So far as can now be ascertained, the church at Andover

[1] His name disappears after this from the Andover records.

passed its first half century in happy immunity from "all false doctrine, heresy, and schism," according to Puritan definition of these words. The following rhymed address to the church of Andover occurs in the "Wonder-working Providence of Zion's Saviour," published 1654. It may, in the light of the subsequent theological history of the town, receive a prophetic interpretation: —

"TO THE FIRST CHURCH AT ANDOVER.

" Thou Sister young, Christ is to thee a wall
Of flaming fire; to hurt thee none may come.
In Slippery path and darke wayes shall they fall;
His angel's might Shall chase their countless Sum;
Thy Shepherd, with full cups and table Spread,
Before thy foes in wilderness thee feeds;
Increasing thy young lambs in bosom bred
Of churches by his wonder-working deeds,
To countless number must Christ's churches reach.
The Day 's at hand both Jew and Gentile shall
Come crowding in his churches Christ to preach,
And last for aye, none can cause them to fall."

"The Church at Andover"[1] was organized October 24, 1645. The names of the ten members freeholders (required by law to constitute a church) were Mr. John Woodbridge, teacher, John Osgood, Robert Barnard, John Frye, Nicholas Holt, Richard Barker, Joseph Parker, Nathan Parker, Richard Blake, Edmond Faulkner.

A year before this time (September, 1644), a council had assembled at Rowley to organize this church, and also a church in Haverhill.[2] The reason assigned for the meeting of the council at Rowley was, that there would not be sufficient accommodation at Andover or at Haverhill for the guests who would assemble.

The churches[3] were not organized because the members refused to make "confession of faith and repentance," having done this at their admission into other churches. Therefore, nothing was effected; but the following year, October, 1645, the council meeting again, satisfactory conclusions were

[1] North Andover.
[2] Hubbard's *History of New England*.
[3] Winthrop's Journal.

arrived at, and Mr. John Woodbridge [1] was ordained minister of Andover, and Mr. John Ward minister of Haverhill. The Rev. William Symmes, of Andover, in a historical sermon, states that "Mr. John Woodbridge was the first, strictly speaking, that was ordained a minister of the gospel in this County, and the second in New England." Immediately previous to his coming to Andover, he was master of the Boston Latin School.[2] His seeking ministerial ordination is said to have been due to the influence of his father-in-law, Gov. Thomas Dudley, who "stirred him up to seek advancement as a minister." He was not only a scholar, but was also versed in practical affairs. He was, as has been said, chief in negotiating the purchase of the Andover plantation from Cutshamakin. He was a man well suited to share the fortunes of a new settlement, — versatile in expedients, ready to lend a helping hand to every enterprise, and accurate and methodical in whatever he undertook. To these qualities his official documents and records, as magistrate for the town of Newbury, bear witness. His residence after he left Andover was chiefly (except some years in England) in that town (in which he had lived on his first coming from England to America). Cotton Mather, in the "Magnalia," in his "Lives of those Persons who have been the Minysters of the Gospel that fed the Flocks in the Wildernesse," gives a biography of Mr. Woodbridge.

"CLASSIS SECOND — Of *young scholars whose education for their designed Ministry not being finished, yet came over from England with their Friends and had their Education perfected in the Country, before the College was come into Maturity, enough to bestow its Laurels.* 14, Mr. John Woodbridge, of Newbury."

This biography is not exceeded in fulness or in interest by any subsequent ones. No apology is needed for presenting it here, verbatim : —

"But he that brings up the Rear is Mr. John Woodbridge, of whom we are able to speak a little more particularly. He was

---

[1] Hubbard's *History of New England*.
[2] *Catalogue of the Latin School*, based on a record of the town of Boston, 1644, that "*Mr.* Woodbridge" was master (presumably Mr. John Woodbridge).

born at Stanton, in Highworth, in Wiltshire, about the year 1613, of which Parish his father was Minister, and a Minister so able and Faithful as to obtain an high esteem among those that at all knew the Invaluable worth of such a Minister. His mother was daughter to Mr. Robert Parker, and a daughter who did so virtuously that her own Personal character would have made her highly esteemed, if a Relation to such a Father had not farther added unto the Lustre of her character.

"Our JOHN was by his Worthy Parents *trained up in the way that he should go* and sent unto *Oxford*, where his education and Proficiency at school had ripened him for the University, and kept at Oxford until the Oath of Conformity came to be required of him, which neither his Father nor his Conscience approving, he removed from thence unto a Course of more *Private Studies*. The Rigorous enforcing of the Unhappy *ceremonies* then causing many that understood and regarded the *Second Commandment* in the Laws of Heaven to seek a *peaceable* Recess for the pure worship of the Lord Jesus Christ in an *American Desart*, Our young Woodbridge, with the consent of his Parents, undertook a voyage to New England about the year 1634, and the company and assistance of his worthy uncle, Mr. *Thomas Parker*, was not the least Encouragement of his voyage. He had not been long in the country before Newberry began to be planted, where he accordingly took up lands and so seated himself that he comfortably and Industriously Studied on, until the Advice of his Father's death obliged him to return to England, where, having settled his affairs, he returned again into New England, bringing with him his two brothers, whereof one died on the way. He had married the daughter of the Honble Thomas Dudley, Esq., and the town of Andover then first peeping into the world, he was by the hands of Mr. Wilson & Mr. Worcester, Sep. 16, 1644, ordained the teacher of a Congregation There. There he continued with good Reputation discharging the Duties of the Ministry until upon the Invitation of Friends he went once more to England."

The vicissitudes of Mr. Woodbridge's fortunes were many. From being deputy to the General Court (1641), surveyor of arms, justice of the peace, schoolmaster, trader with Indians, religious teacher in an " American Desart," he became familiar with camp and court, — so far as there was " court," when royalty was in enforced exile. He was chaplain of the Commissioners who treated with the banished monarch Charles

I., at the Isle of Wight, and was afterward settled over a parish in Andover, Hampshire County. But when the restoration of the old *régime* came, Mr. Woodbridge for his nonconformity lost his living, and for the same offence was ejected from a school of which he became master at Newbury. It is noticeable that the two towns of his abode in Old England were of the same name as those in which he lived in New England. Dr. Calamy, in his account of the ejected ministers, names with respect Mr. John Woodbridge.

After thus losing his prospect of comfortable abode in the old country, he, in 1663, come over again to the colony and settled in Newbury, becoming the assistant in the ministry of his uncle, the Rev. Thomas Parker. His biography is thus continued by Cotton Mather: —

"The Church of Newbury solicited him to become an Assistant unto his Aged uncle, Mr. Parker, and in answer to their solicitations he bestowed his constant, Learned, and Holy Labours upon them. At last there arose little Differences between him and some of the People upon Certain points of Church Discipline, wherein his Largeness and their Straitness might perhaps better have met in a Temper; and these Differences ended not without his putting anend unto his own Ministry among them."

These "differences" of the church with him and his colleague were on the ground of their having too little sympathy with the Congregational Church government,[1] and holding high ideas of the minister's prerogative and powers akin to those of the English Church.

Mather goes on to say that Mr. Woodbridge continued to live in Newbury, was greatly respected, was "chosen Magistrate, and afterward Justice of the Peace." He thus sums up Mr. Woodbridge's Christian virtues: —

"A Person he was of truly an Excellent Spirit; a Pious Disposition accompanied him from his early childhood, and as he grew in years he grew in the Proofs and Fruits of his having been Sanctified from his infancy. He spent much of his Time in Holy Meditations, by which the Foretastes of Heaven were Continually Feeding of his Devout Soul, and he abounded in all other Devotions of

[1] Coffin's *Newbury*.

Serious, Heavenly, Experimental Christianity. He was by Nature wonderfully composed, Patient, and Pleasant; and he was by grace much more so. He had a great Command of his Passions, and *could* and *would* and *did* forgive Injuries at a rate that hardly can be imitated.

"It was rarely or never observed that Worldly Disappointment made any Grievous Impressions upon his Mind. . . . . Only he was observedly overwhelmed by the Death of his most Religious, Prudent, and Faithful Consort when she was, July 1, 1691, Fifty years after his first marriage unto her, torn away from the Desire of his Eyes. His value for the whole world was after a manner extinguished in the Loss of what was to him the best part of it, and he sometimes declared himself desirous to begone whenever the Lord of Heaven should please to call him thither."

Mr. Woodbridge died 1695, "and (says his biographer) he who had been a Great Reader, a Great Scholar, a Great Christian, and a Pattern of Goodnesse in all the successive stations wherein the Lord of Hosts had placed him, on March 17, the Day of the Christian Sabbath, after much Pain, went unto his Everlasting Rest, having a few minutes before it refused a Glass of offered wine, saying, '*I am going where I shall have better.*'"

Mr. Woodbridge was eighty-two years old. His companion for fifty years, the wife whom he so deeply mourned, was Mercy Dudley, the daughter of Gov. Thomas Dudley, and sister of Mrs. Anne [Dudley] Bradstreet. She was the mother of twelve children, "whereof," says Mather, "eleven lived unto the age of Men and Women. He [Mr. Woodbridge] had the consolation of seeing Three sons with two sons in Law Improved in the ministry of the Gospel and Four Grandsons happily advancing there unto." One of these children, Lucy Woodbridge, who lived at Andover when about three years old,[1] was married to her cousin, the Rev. Simon Bradstreet, minister of New London. The eldest son of Mr. Woodbridge, the Rev. John Woodbridge, of Killingworth, Conn., is thought by some to have been born at Andover, Mass.[2]

The REV. FRANCIS DANE, the second minister of Andover,

[1] She was born 1642.   [2] *Mass. Hist. Coll.*, Fifth Series, vol. v.

is also named by Cotton Mather among the young men who finished their studies in the colony before the college conferred degrees. His name is found among the early residents of Ipswich, 1641. "He removed to Andover, 1648," says Felt's "History of Ipswich." He was son of John Dane, settler in Ipswich and Roxbury. No contemporary biography of him has been found. His name does not occur in Sprague's "Annals of the American Pulpit," although he had an important part in the colonial history. He was pastor at Andover over forty-eight years (1649 to 1697). No church records of his ministry are preserved. The history of his pastorate is chiefly gathered from the town, county, and colony records, and, therefore, pertains rather to his secular than to his spiritual influence and interests, but his notebook recently brought to light has some fragments of interest, among them a creed evidently of his own composition, or rather compilation. It is, though moderate in doctrine, in substantial agreement with the creeds accepted in New England. One clause is as follows: —

"I believe y^t ye Catholic or universall church consists of all those throughout the world that doe profess ye trew Religion, together with their children, and in ye Kingdom of ye Lord Jesus, and ye house and family of God, out of which there is no ordinary possibility of obtaining Salvation."

In reference to the pastoral relations of Mr. Dane, Abbot's "History of Andover" says: "From the town books it appears that he was respected, that harmony prevailed, that the worship and ordinances of religion were well attended." This is true. The town books show no evidence that this "harmony" was ever interrupted. But it is a noticeable feature of our town records that everything like record of controversy seems excluded, and, indeed, almost everything of human interest; land grants, perambulations of bounds and privileges of occupation being the chief subjects noted. Accordingly, the reader, from the records of Mr. Dane's ministry, is led to conclude that forty-eight years of uninterrupted peace between pastor and people were spent in the old Andover church, an inference not only incorrect but disheartening as a commentary on the fruits of two hundred years of gospel preaching. To learn, in these days of feuds and divisions of churches, that the old times had also their dissensions is not without value. The happy sequel of the first known church controversy of Andover,— the parties reconciled, the pastor spending an honored old age in the community of his youthful choice, and defending it at personal risk from injurious aspersions, is honorable to pastor and people, and suggestive to their posterity of valuable lessons in the settling of church dissensions.

The full account is found in the "Records of the General Court." The summary of it is as follows, omitting some minor details: —

The General Court having been applied to by the Andover church, sent a committee to Andover and "convened the people of the church and town together, with their pastor," and proceeded to hear their "several plans, pretensions, and allegations as to the matter of their difference." The substance of these was that, Mr. Dane being infirm and needing a colleague, they had "invited and procured a young man to be helpfull to them," and were not willing to pay the older pastor "his wonted maintenance." They thought as he was in comfortable circumstances he might "subsist without being burdensome to them."

But the General Court, in consideration of the fact that the pastor "hath for a long time been an officer among them," advised the Andover church to pay him, at least, thirty pounds per annum, and "if his necessity should require a fuller supply," they express hope that the people will "not be wanting to testify their respects to him upon that account."

They advise Mr. Dane to "improve his utmost diligence to carry on the public worship of God," and to encourage the young man, his colleague, by his aid. And further, they advise him "to carry it to his people with that tender love and respect (forgetting all former disgusts) as becomes a minister of the gospell."

The young man referred to was the Rev. Thomas Barnard, of Hadley, a graduate of Harvard College, 1679. In January, 1681-2, the town voted to give him a call, and to "pay for his diet so long as he shall remain a Single man among us."

There are few records of the joint labors of the colleagues in the pastoral office. It was finally voted to pay [1] Mr. Barnard fifty pounds, one quarter of it in money, the use of the parsonage and his firewood, so long as Mr. Dane "should carry on a part of the work," and whenever Mr. Dane should cease to aid him he should receive eighty pounds per annum.

Andover had great reason to be thankful for the adjustment of the difficulties with their pastor. Mr. Dane "forgot his disgusts" according to the advice of the Court, and devoted himself to the interests of his people, so far as the infirmities of age permitted. When the community was frenzied with the witchcraft delusion, Mr. Dane was one of the few men whose judgment remained unshaken, and whose courage was not daunted by fear of personal danger. "The Rev. Francis Dane deserves," says Upham, "to be recognized preëminent, and for a time almost alone, in bold denunciation and courageous resistance of the execrable proceedings of that dark day."

Every record goes to prove Mr. Dane to have been a man of strong sense, fearless courage, and withal of Christian fortitude. Out of his manifold afflictions in the witchcraft time, when almost every member of his family was under arrest or suspicion, he said, " The Lord give us all submissive will, and let the Lord do with me and mine what seems good in his eyes."

Mr. Dane died February 17, 1697, aged eighty-one years. He was married three times: to Elizabeth Ingals, before 1645, who died 1676; to Mary Thomas, 1677,[2] who died 1689; to Hannah Abbot, widow of George Abbot, 1690; she died 1711. He had two sons, Nathaniel and Francis, and four daughters, Elizabeth (Johnson), Hannah (Goodhue), Phebe (Robinson), Abigail (Faulkner). He willed his house to his son Nathaniel, and also gave him a silver cup. His son, Lieut. Francis Dane, was one of the original members

---

[1] Some men of Haverhill and Boxford were tax-payers. Quartermaster Moses Tyler and John Chadwick, of Boxford, had been allowed "to set up a house for their convenience, for families and horse, on Sabbath days," and paid three shillings rate per annum.

[2] By Mr. Danforth. — *Town Records.*

of the South Church. He died 1738, aged eighty-two. The grandson of Lieut. Francis Dane, John Dane, was deacon of the South Church thirty-nine years, 1755 to 1794, and a member till his death, 1801, at the age of eighty-four. He used to read the psalm line by line for the congregation to sing. Rev. John Dane, son of Daniel Dane, was a graduate of Dartmouth College, and ordained minister of Newfield, Me., 1801.

There is no trace of the minister's grave, nor any sermon or memorial of his ministry, except a manuscript record book, and an autograph letter or petition regarding the witchcraft.

The record book contains a rhymed account of his difficulties and perplexities in search of a second wife: —

> ". . . . Long have I looked about
> But could not I ye Matron yet find out
> But some objections crosst my purpose so
> As yet I sayd I know not wt to doe . . . .
> I sometimes heere and sometimes there have sought
> To see if I the thing could bring about
> That might best suite mee in my pilgrimage,
> And match to one who's sober, chaste, and sage,
> That's Loving, meeke, no Tatler, not unruly
> That loveth goodness & yt hath a mind
> To Conjugal subjection inclined ;
> In such a blessing may I have a share
> For other things I need not much a whit to care.
> A vertuous wife's her husband's crowne & shee
> With immortality shall { crowned } bee.
>   { cloathed }
> Who doth her find hath gret cause to confesse
> The Ld's free favour & his name to bless.
> Let every Xhian ply ye throne of Grace
> That with a meete help hee may run his Race.
> I bow my knee & humbly do implore
> God's tenderness towards mee therefore."

Before proceeding to consider the life and ministry of the third minister of Andover, we may turn attention for a little to the young men of the First Church of Andover who during the time of these three pastorates were prepared for and ordained to the ministry. There were not many, but perhaps in proportion to the town's population they were as many as there have been at any time since.

Rev. John Woodbridge, Jun., son of the first minister of Andover, graduated at Harvard College 1664, settled in Killingworth, Conn., removed thence to Weathersfield, 1679, and was pastor there till his death, 1690.

Rev. Simon Bradstreet, son of Gov. Simon Bradstreet, was born at Ipswich, graduated at Harvard College, 1660, was ordained minister of New London, Conn., 1670. He married his cousin, Lucy Woodbridge, daughter of the Andover minister. He died 1683.

Rev. Simon Bradstreet, son of Rev. Simon Bradstreet, born 1671, lived, probably after his father's death, at Andover, for he became a member of the church here. He graduated at Harvard College 1693. When he was called to be pastor of the church in Charlestown some of the Boston ministers did not approve, because they thought him of heterodox belief and they doubted his regular standing in the church at Andover. "It is unknown to us how far or in what way he became a member of the church therein." Other ministers, however, expressed opinion that he was "orderly dismissed or Recommended from the church of Christ in Andover."

Mr. Bradstreet was ordained October 26, 1698, and served forty years in Charlestown with acceptance, although he was suspected by some of a leaning to Arminianism; and his admiration of Archbishop Tillotson's sermons was a grief to the more rigid Puritans. He was a man of some eccentricities, but a great scholar. "Here is a man who can whistle Greek," said Lieutenant-governor Tayler, in introducing Mr. Bradstreet to Governor Burnet.

Rev. Joseph Stevens, son of Deacon Joseph Stevens, of Andover, in the twenty-fifth year of the Rev. Simon Bradstreet's pastorate at Charlestown, was ordained his colleague.

This ordination deserves to receive special mention. The position and character of the young pastor made it of general interest at the time, and the sundering of its ties after a brief period by the sudden and distressing death of the pastor and nearly all his household has served to give to this ministry a prominent and a sad interest in the early church history.

Of all the young ministers who had connection, either by birth or residence, with Andover in the Colonial days, there was none who could be so fully claimed as an Andover man as Joseph Stevens. The Bradstreets had received more or less of their education in other towns, and the family was so widely connected in various parts of the colony, that scarcely one of its members is exclusively identified with Andover during his youth. But Joseph Stevens was born and brought up at [North] Andover. His father, Deacon Joseph Stevens, was a native of the town, and his grandfather, John Stevens, a first settler. So far as is known both these ancestors of the Rev. Joseph Stevens lived entirely in Andover [North] during their citizenship, not being called by private or by public business to much association outside of their own community. What Andover could produce of physical, mental, and moral development is therefore seen exemplified in the person and character of this young man. In regard to him, wrote the Rev. Dr. Colman in a biographical sketch (prefixed to a sermon by Mr. Stevens), published not long after his death: "We scarce ever saw a more beauteous mind and body united than in the Person of Mr. Stevens. A fulness of Life and vigour, with all the soft charms of goodness and sweetness, met in his grave and florid countenance, and commanded respect and Love. Humility and meekness guarded and adorned his bright and fervent conversation, and modesty gave a very singular grace to that superior air which was natural to him."

Joseph Stevens was born in 1682, June 20, during the ministry of the Rev. Francis Dane and the Rev. Thomas Barnard, whose religious and whose classical teaching he doubtless enjoyed. He graduated at Harvard College at the age of twenty-one, in the class of 1703, and afterward was a tutor in the college.

Respecting him as a preacher Dr. Colman says: "But it was in the Desk that he eminently shone, where his eyes as well as tongue were wont to speak with a majesty and solemnity that very much commanded the ears and hearts of the audience. In short, the Gentleman, the Scholar, and the Christian met in him, and as they formed a very accomplished Divine, so would they as well a judge for the bench or a commander for the field had Providence so called him."

He was ordained October 13, 1713. Fifty pounds were appropriated to defray the expenses of the day, more money than som: ministers of repute received for a year's salary. The estimation in which the candidate for the sacred office was held is seen by the rank of the ministers selected to officiate. The Rev. Increase Mather, then seventy-four years old, gave the charge, and his son, the Rev. Cotton Mather, the right hand of fellowship.

The ministry thus auspiciously begun was cut short after the, as it was then considered, brief term of eight years. Mr. Stevens was suddenly smitten down with the small pox which raged in Boston and vicinity with violence. Himself, his wife, son, and daughter died in one month.

Only one of the household survived, an infant son seven months old. This babe was carried, with its nurse, to Andover. The child grew and throve, and, nurtured amid the same influences which had developed his father's character, proved a son worthy of such a parent, and became one of the most eminent ministers of his time. The REV. BENJAMIN STEVENS graduated at the age of nineteen at Harvard College, 1740. He was at one time candidate for the Presidency of the college. He had rare scholarship, elegant manners, and was, says Chief Justice Parsons, "a man of whom one may say everything good." In his parish at Kittery, Maine, he preached to Sir William Pepperell, and was an honored guest in the old Province families of that region.

REV. DUDLEY BRADSTREET, son of Col. Dudley Bradstreet, graduated at Harvard College 1698, taught the Andover Grammar School two or three years, was ordained minister of Groton 1708. He was a thorough classical scholar. He resigned his ministry at Groton after a few years, went over to England and took orders in the Established Church. He died 1714.

REV. JOHN BARNARD, graduated at Harvard College 1709. [See page 432.]

When the Rev. Thomas Barnard, who was ordained with Mr. Dane, 1682, had by the death of his colleague, in 1697, become the sole pastor, the church, or rather the town of Andover, began to make provision for his increased comfort and dignity. It was voted in town meeting to "build a leantoe to the parsonage house," and "inlarge the minister's wive's pew the breadth of the alley," and finally in October, 1705, to "build a new meeting-house as sufficient and Convenient for the whole town as may be." In May, 1707, it was voted to build a "meeting-house for ye inhabitants of Andover of these following dimensions, viz: of sixty-foot long, and forty-foot wide and twenty-foot studd and with a flatt roofe."

The location of this new meeting-house gave rise to much voting and altercation.

Many letters and petitions passed back and forth which need not here be cited. One of them, signed by Mr. Samuel Osgood and Mr. James Bridges, suggested that the General Court order the town to build one meeting house for the whole town for ten years and to allow them after that time to have two houses of worship.

In vain it was sought to come to an agreement or compromise between the contending factions. The town a second time voted, October 12, 1708, to build in the place first decided on. This was quite remote from the residence of the minister, which was now in the house which had been the house of Col. Dudley Bradstreet [1] (deceased).

A vote in October, 1708, in regard to the new meeting-house, although it differed not from the former as to location made some changes of dimensions and construction, — "fifty-six foot long, fifty foot wide, and twenty-two foot studd and with a square roofe without dormans with two Lucoms on each side."

What sort of a meeting-house "roofe" was suggested to the worthy clerk who recorded the vote we may imagine by translating his orthography into "dormer" and "Luthern;" and perhaps from this incidental record it is safe to form an idea of the third Andover meeting-house, which, built in 1709, stood till 1733. This was not, however, built by or for the whole town, nor according to the former vote. The General Court, after finding that the inhabitants of Andover refused to come to any agreement or compromise, complied with the petition of the south part of the town, divided it into precincts (January, 1709), ordered each precinct to support a minister and have a meeting-house, and gave to Mr. Barnard his choice of precincts. The South precinct forthwith began to build a meeting-house "at [2] ye Rock on the West side of Roger's brook." This was used for worship in January, 1710. As late as November 7, 1710, the Rev. Mr. Barnard had not signified which precinct he would live in and minister to, and the South precinct petitioned the General Court to direct him

---

[1] The parsonage had recently been destroyed by fire, as appears from the following votes: —

"26 May, 1707. Voted and passed that there be a committee on Rev. Mr. Barnard's settlement in some convenient house till a house can be built for him. — 5 July, 1707, — that there be some convenient fortification made with bords and timber about the house where the Rev. Mr. Barnard is for the present shrouded, and that some of the bricks from his house that was burnt be taken."

[2] East of the present site of the South Church.

to make choice. This was done and he was requested to decide before the eleventh of December, and, if he should not then have decided, the South Precinct were ordered to provide for themselves. On the tenth of December, the South Precinct unanimously voted "that Mr. Samuel Phillip' shall be our pastor." By the division, the North Parish lost eighty freeholders and thirty-five members of the church. It was a trying time for the Rev. Mr. Barnard, who, while the matter was pending, had been cut off from his salary, the factions refusing to pay the minister's rates. Moreover, he lost some who preferred to stay in the North Parish, and pay taxes there. In this difficulty he addressed a letter to the Governor, which is in the State Archives now.[1] It is too long for insertion here, but is of considerable interest, not only as being an autograph composition of an Andover minister, from whose pen there are no known printed compositions, but also because it gives a statement of the grievances of the North Precinct, in the division. "The north part of the town that was the first settlement," he says, "are dissatisfied that they are made the lesse part;" and also that in these circumstances, the General Court orders them to "perform obligation of the whole town" (that is, pay full salary to their minister). And further he says, it is peculiarly unjust because some families which would prefer to pay taxes for his church are compelled to belong to the South Parish, and be rated there.

These families, John Stevens and John Lovejoy, were at last allowed to remain in the North Parish, and about 1711, a final and satisfactory settlement was made.

The South Parish voted "to pay their minister sixty pounds in money while he is an unmarried state and ten pounds more when he shall see reason to marry." The North Precinct, though reduced in numbers more than one half, voted to pay their minister "forty-two pounds in money and to build a new meeting house." This although the General Court had advised them "to take the present meeting-house and repair it and add to it."

The salary paid was in accordance with a proposition of

[1] Vol. ii, p. 183.

Mr. Barnard, that he would receive forty-two pounds in money, instead of sixty in corn.

Though their number was diminished, the North Parish made their meeting-house nearly as large and as costly as that voted in 1708 for the accommodation of the whole town.

"*Voted*, that the meeting-house be of the following D.mentions, viz: Fifty foot long, Forty-five foot wide, and Twenty-four foot between Joyntes, and with a Roofe like Salem-village meeting-house .... ye model of ye seats to be like Bradford meeting-house seats."

They were not, however, regardless of expense, for they voted that "ye old pulpit in the North Precinct shall be set in our new meeting-house."

The question of the site of the meeting-house of the North Precinct occasioned again considerable "voating." One vote was to set it "at ye oack by Capt. Benjamin Stevens, his barn;" but afterward this was declared "nuled and void," and the final vote was, "that the new meeting-house be set up at the apel tree[1] in Joseph Parker senior his land whear the Bulk of the Timber lyeth for sd meeting-house."

So, in the forest shades the foundation was laid, and the woodman began to fell the strong and beautiful trees which, to our ancestors, were simply "timber" and "woods," valuable for meeting-houses and fuel.

Before the edifice was raised and finished and seated, there was much voting and nulling and making void; but finally all was done, and the new house occupied, to the delight of the parish.

During the controversy, the Rev. Mr. Barnard bore himself with dignity and discretion. He gave a cordial welcome to the minister selected by the South Parish, and these brother-ministers lived always on terms of friendship. After the death of Mr. Barnard, Mr. Phillips said in a sermon:—

"I have always esteemed it a favor of Providence that my lot was cast in the same town with that holy man of God, who was pleased to express the kindness of a father to me, and where I had for some years the advantage of his guidance and example. He was

[1] Near the site of the present Unitarian Church, North Andover.

really one of the best of ministers, had the tongue of the learned, was a sound and eminent divine, delivered excellent sermons, and had the spirit as well as the gift of prayer, was gentle as a father, yet maintaining government and discipline in the church, very obliging towards all men, and always studied the things that make for peace." . . . .

If anything were needed to corroborate the truth of such a statement from so eminent a minister, it would be enough to add, to show the character of the Rev. Thomas Barnard, that he reared a son who succeeded him in the same parish, and ministered to the church thirty-eight years; the father and son governing the affairs of the North Parish of Andover during seventy five years. The death of Mr. Thomas Barnard was sudden, — on the 13th of October, 1718. The afflicted Parish set apart a day of "fasting and prayer to all mytie God that the Lat and afull Strok in Taking away their Reverend Pastuer by so sudden a death [might] be sanctified to His flock Left Destitute of a Teacher."

The parish appropriated twenty-four pounds to pay the funeral expenses. This large sum, near half a year's salary, shows that the burial must have been with considerable pomp. The gravestone is unpretentious. An upright slab, bare of ornament and without even a "holy text" to illustrate the virtues or suggest the rewards of the faithful minister. Several facts go to indicate that this absence of eulogistic inscription was due to the wishes and taste of Mr. Barnard himself. It characterizes all the memorial tablets of his family.

Mr. Barnard married three times: Mrs. Elizabeth Price, 1686; Mrs. Abigail Bull, 1696; Mrs. Lydia Goffe, 1704.

He had three sons. The eldest died before him without children, the second was the Rev. John Barnard, his successor in the North Church pastorate; the third, Mr. Theodore Barnard, whose daughter Elizabeth became the wife of the Rev. Mr. Phillips's son, Hon. Samuel Phillips, of North Andover, the founder of Phillips Academy.

Thus the town's controversy about the meeting-house resulted ultimately in a union of the families of the two pastors, which conferred on the town signal and lasting benefits. The son of Elizabeth Barnard and Samuel Phillips, Sen., was Lieutenant-governor ("Judge") Samuel Phillips, whose name is so widely known.

The Barnard name was continued in the west part of the town by descendants of Theodore Barnard, but never has been prominent in the town history.

The fourth pastor settled in Andover was the Rev. Mr. Phillips, of the South Parish; but as his ministry outlasted that of Mr. Barnard's successor, its history is deferred until after that of the First Church minister.

The REV. JOHN BARNARD, the son of the late pastor of the North Parish, was invited to fill his father's place, December, 1718. He was then twenty-eight years old. He was born at Andover, 1690, graduated at Harvard College, 1709. He was for some time master of the North Grammar School in Boston, and of the Andover Grammar School. He was ordained pastor of the First Church of Andover, 1719. He records his ordination in the church records:—

"I was ordained Pastor of the first church of Christ in Andover, April ye 8th, 1719. The Rev. Mr. Capen, of Topsfield, gave me my charge, and the Rev. Mr. Stevens, of Charlestown, gave me the Right hand of fellowship. The Revd. Mr. Thos. Symmes preached a sermon. The Rev. Mr. Rogers and the Rev^d. Mr. Phillips assisted in Prayer."

The meeting-house was undoubtedly filled to its utmost capacity on this occasion, on which were gathered the learned and pious ministers of the neighborhood to take part in the exercises. Such a stir was seldom seen in town as that caused by the ordination days. The concourse of vehicles and horses made no small bustle of itself alone. Not then, as now, did public conveyances deposit travellers and move on. Whatever conveyance brought the visitors to town stayed also till the visit was over. "Entertainment for both man and beast" must, therefore, be had. To provide bountifully for guests was ordination etiquette. The inns or public houses were all open wide with abundance of good cheer of food and drink. The great houses of the town, the dwellings of the local aristocracy, were filled with invited guests, ministers, magistrates, and dignitaries. The dinner for the clergy was no slight solicitude to housewives, as well as to their husbands, whose best produce of farm and garden, flock and herd, had been put under contribution; kitchen fires blazed high, spits turned, unnamable decoctions simmered while the prayers and sermons were going on in the meeting-house, silver-chest and linen-press yielded up their treasures, and the hospitable board shone resplendent in delft and damask, tankard and punch-bowl, when the throng, issuing from the house of God, dispersed and repaired to the various places appointed for these concluding festivities.

Nor need we think these details trivial. They present to us an aspect of the Puritan life, as much a part of it as its graver and more commonly described occasions. The Puritans had their relaxations [1] of this sort much more than we are wont to think. In reading the diaries of the great men of colonial days, one cannot help remarking the frequency of their festivities, in which abundant good cheer and religious devotion were mingled. Enjoying the good gifts of God, eating and drinking in company of friends, praying, singing psalms, thinking of the entertainment of the Celestial City and the bliss of Paradise, our ancestors blended with their gravity and solemnity a practical cordiality and good-fellowship

---

[1] The following are selected from Judge Sewall's diary (italics not in original): "Nov. 4, 1690. Had a *sumptuous* feast. — Dec. 1690. *Dined* with me at the Royal Exchange, Sir William Phipps, Mr. Sam¹ Willard .... twelve in all. — Dec., 1691. Went to the house of Joshua Gardener .... had a *very good Dinner*. Mr. Walter craved a blessing .... The Lord fit me for his *Entertainment* in Heaven. — Nov. 15, 1692, Mr. Cook keeps a Day of Thanksgiving, for his safe arrival, Mr. Bradstreet and Lady, Maj. Richards and wife [twenty in all]. Mr. Allen preached. .... Sung after Diner. — Nov. 19 *invited his Excellency* to *drink* a *Glas* of *Brandy* which was pleased to doe with Capt. Greenough, etc. — Dec. 27. Got to Watertown meeting house about eleven aclock. Spent several hours in Debate .... about settling a minister. After this went to Nevisons and *took a very good dinner* provided for us by the selectmen. May 20, 1695. Rode to Newbury I *treat* Mr. Danforth — &c., *with salmon* at Capt. Serjeants. — Aug. 27, 1695. Went to Dorchester Lecture .... with whom sat *down* to *dinner*. Several young *Gentlewomen* sat *down afterward* .... Sept. 1695. Gov. Bradstreet *drank* a *glass* or two of *wine*, *eat some fruit*, *took a pipe* of *Tobacco*, in the New Hall. *wished me joy* of the *house* and *desired our prayers* .... Sept. 18, Mr. Torry and his wife, Mr. Willard and his wife and Cous. Quinsey *dine with us* .... was much pleased with our painted shutters; in *pleasancy* said he thought he had been got into Paradise."

which relieved the sombreness and relaxed the intensity that would otherwise have been insupportable. This mingling of the social and the serious elements was especially manifest at ordinations.

The Rev. John Barnard's ministry was a period of stirring events in the religious world and in the provincial history, and yet this would not appear from the church and parish records. Then, notwithstanding the prominent part of members of the parish in the Indian and French wars, and the connection of the pastor with the controversy in regard to the Rev. George Whitefield and the Great Awakening, nothing more exciting appears on record than building and seating the meeting-house, buying silver for the communion service, and clock and bell for the meeting-house. Mr. Barnard was not in sympathy with Mr. Whitefield. He did not believe in itinerancy, he was no enthusiast, but had a supreme regard for propriety. He was himself regarded by some of the clergy as belonging to the party of doubtful orthodoxy.[1] But, whatever his theology, he disapproved the fanaticism, as he thought it, and abhorred what he regarded as the irreverence and impiety of the great evangelist, who denounced the dignitaries of the commonwealth and hurled anathemas at its ancient and venerable seats of learning, Harvard College and her younger, but also honored, sister, Yale College. Nor could Mr. Barnard, like some of his brother ministers, overlook the evil and find the good in the movement. His name, therefore, heads the list of one of the two Neighboring Associations of Ministers in the county who addressed a letter to the Associated Ministers of Boston and Charlestown, remonstrating on the admission of Mr. Whitefield into their pulpits.

The North Church prospered in Mr. Barnard's hands. Five hundred new members were added, and there were twelve hundred baptisms during his ministry.

In 1753 the North Parish built another new meeting-house. Pews sold, January 1, 1754, for £667 15 s. 8 d. Silver was procured for the Communion service, and the pewter "plate" formerly used was given to the church in Methuen.[2] The

[1] *South Church Manual*, p. 98.
[2] *Parish Records*.

word plate refers, probably, not to the drinking vessels, for before this time the church had silver.[1]

A new bell was obtained 1755. "Abbot's History" says it was presented to the parish by Capt. Nathaniel Frye. The Parish records have a vote of thanks to Mr. William Phillips of Boston "for his bounty in giving them the purchase of a bell."

The church records are carefully kept during the pastorates of the Rev. Mr. Thomas and Mr. John Barnard. They are for the most part of little interest for the present generation, and yet, to run over their pages is not without instruction. They show what careful scrutiny of conduct was kept up as a part of Church discipline, how common it was for members in good standing to be publicly admonished. To come before the church and confess moral obliquities was an every day occurrence. At almost every meeting some offender was dealt with. To omit all mention of these facts would be to give a partial view of the life of the past, to create an erroneous and a discouraging impression of the superior excellence of the former times as compared with the later days. The biographies of eminent men and women present them for the most part on state occasions, and their unflawed perfection strikes us as impossible. It is beneficial, therefore to get a glimpse of the masses of men and women, church members, in their every day life when they are beset and often overcome by temptation, and to see how their frailties and falls were dealt with by their brethren. A few selections have therefore been made to illustrate the earlier church discipline. The grosser and more revolting memoranda, some of which the ministers have thought fit to put on record in the Latin, rather than in plain English, it has not been thought necessary to present. But for truth's sake it must be said

[1] The silver is massive and elegant. It consists of eleven tankards with covers, and two flagons. The oldest tankard was given by Mrs. Sarah Martyn, of Boston, 1724. The others were the gifts respectively of Benjamin Stevens, Esq., 1728; Mrs. Mary Aslebe, 1739; Ebenezer Osgood, 1745; Peter Osgood, 1751, in fulfilment of the desire of his grandfather, Timothy Osgood; widow Elizabeth Abbot, 1756; Capt. Timothy Johnson, 1761. There are three inscribed "For the Use of the First Church of Christ in Andover, A. D. 1728," one "1729." The two flagons were given, one by Benjamin Barker, 1765, the other in 1801, by Capt. Peter Osgood.

they are not a few. But bearing in mind that the church to some extent exercised the functions of a local court and police, and that offences then received harsher names than they now receive, we may correct our possibly too severe judgment of the morals of the church in the early part of the eighteenth century.

Another matter of surprise in reading the record of these times, in regard to the church discipline, is the indiscriminate way in which the censure of trifles is mixed up with that of flagrant offences; a harsh criticism of a minister or a church officer, or an indolent disposition, subjecting a member to as severe treatment as some outrage of the moralities of society : —

"*Voted* (1729), that Lawrence ——— shall make a Publick confession for his neglect of the Publick worship, and for the Idle, lazy life he has lived for these many years."

The above-named offender was repeatedly admonished; he confessed again and again, with promises of amendment, but at last was "suspended for neglecting to labour and ye publick worship."

"*Voted* [1731], that I [the pastor] dispense admonition in the name of the church, to the wife of Joseph ———, who has for some years been under suspension for her intemperance."

This case was several times brought up, and "essay made to bring her to the sight of her sins that her excommunication may be prevented." It is noticeable that the step of excommunication was rarely and reluctantly taken, except for heresy or long absence from divine worship. Something of the spirit of the ancient church seemed to linger even in the Puritan colonies, which invested excommunication with a peculiar solemnity, and made them hesitate to pronounce a sentence which might be far-reaching in its consequences. Drunkenness was a crying sin of the time. Men and women were alike guilty, and often disciplined : —

"*Feb.*, 1746. The church voted on the case of William ———'s wife, accused of being distempered with drink on the last Thanksgiving Day. Suspended from communion till publick satisfaction be made."

It is to be observed that the grossest sins were treated as atoned for by confession : —

"Elizabeth ——— and Hannah ——— confessed . . . . in Publick, upon which ye church restored them to church privileges."

"*Voted*, that ——— be allowed to make a confession for unlawful and filthy conversation. . . . . *Voted*, the confession to be full and satisfactory.

"*Voted*, that communicants who have fallen into scandalous transgressions shall forbear coming to ye sacrament for some time after their confession.

"——— made her confession for scandals. The church accepted her confession. *Voted*, that the two above-mentioned shall have liberty to come to ye Lord's table."

Of many offenders, one severely dealt with and held up to reprobation by the pastor's memorandum was Timothy ——.

"*Voted*, that Timothy ———, jr., make a publick confession for his false and uncharitable reflexion upon me [Mr. Barnard] in a complaint, and for sinful passion and expressing himself prophanely and uncharitably."

Such an offence as an "uncharitable reflexion" upon the minister was deemed deserving of grave treatment. Three ministers from neighboring churches were called in, with a brother from each church. After a great deal of voting and admonishing, the offender made confession and was "restored to full communion."

A passer of counterfeit money was less severely dealt with : —

"1739. Joseph ——— is suspended for Feloniously uttering two 5 pound Bills counterfeit of the Colony of Rhoad Island. 1743, acceptance of acknowledgment of Joseph ——— and *voted* restoration to his former church Privileges."

One of the methods of visiting the sins of the fathers upon the children seems (considering the prevalent doctrine that the unbaptized had no promise of salvation), to savor of injustice and cruelty to the innocent : —

"*Voted* (1731), that Saml. ——— for abusing Nathan Parker at the Tavern shall be deprived of the Priviledge of bringing his children to Baptism. — 1735. The above satisfied the church, and was admitted to bring a child to baptism."

Some of the members of the North Parish of Andover were, in 1740, set off to the North Parish in Boxford, and permitted to pay their parish rates there, but to do this they were obliged first to get the sanction of the General Court, so intimate was the connection of church and state, even down to a comparatively recent date. The members who petitioned to go to the Boxford church were Ephraim Foster, Joseph Robinson, John Foster, David Foster, Moses Foster, Joseph Robinson, Jr., Timothy Sessions, also, in 1746, John Barker, Sen., John Barker, Jr., Nathan Barker, Widow Lacy:

The Rev. John Barnard ministered thirty-eight years in the North Parish of Andover. He died suddenly, June 14, 1757, aged sixty-seven years. The parish appropriated twenty pounds to defray his funeral expenses.

Mr. Barnard was married, 1725, to Miss Sarah Osgood, by Mr. Samuel Phillips. At the time of his death he had two sons settled in the ministry: Mr. Thomas Barnard, the eldest, had been seventeen years before ordained pastor of the church in Newbury, and in 1755 had settled as pastor of the First Church in Salem. Mr. Edward Barnard had been fifteen years pastor of the First Church in Haverhill. Both these sons of the Rev. John Barnard, of Andover, were among the eminent preachers of their day. The son of the Rev. Thomas Barnard, of the First Church of Salem, of the same name as his father, also settled as a minister in Salem, over the North Church, where he lived till 1814. Thus from the Rev. Thomas Barnard, the first, of Andover, 1682, to the Rev. Thomas Barnard who died at Salem, 1814, there was an unbroken line of ministerial succession in Essex County of one hundred and thirty-two years. The Rev. John Barnard had one daughter, wife of the Rev. Dr. Tucker, of Newbury, also a son, John Barnard, who died while a student in Harvard College.

The gravestone of Mr. John Barnard is as devoid of funeral eulogium as was that of his father. But though the parish and the family of the pastor, either by his request or their own choice, refrained from monumental inscriptions of praise, they have not left their minister without a memorial.

The book of "Records for y⁹ North Precinct of y⁹ Towne of Andover" has a memorandum in the clear, beautiful handwriting of the then parish clerk, Dea. (the Hon.) Samuel Phillips: —

"*The Character of y⁹ Revd. Mr. Jno. Barnard, Decd. Taken from y⁹ Publick Prints, viz.:*

"ANDOVER, *June* 20, 1757.

"Last Sunday, being y⁹ 14th Instant, Dec'd here of a Violent Fever, of a few days' continuance, the REVD. JOHN BARNARD, Pastor of y⁹ first church & Congregation in this Town in y⁹ 68th year of his age and 39th of his Ministry. He was second son of the Revd. Tho'. Barnard, whom he succeeded in y⁹ pastoral office. He was a man of strict piety towards God, which shone in a peculiar manner, as it was attended with every social virtue, — Benevolence, Friendship, & Hospitality in an Eminent Degree. He was a sound Divine, Laborious in every part of his sacred office. Nor was his usefulness confined to the Ministerial work. But being a thoro' classic schollar he was in his youth for divers years Master of the North Grammar School in Boston, and thro' y⁹ Greater part of his life educated members for y⁹ College: So that he formed many for Service who now make a Conspicuous figure in y⁹ church and Commonwealth. The Bereaved Flock are Hearty and Sincere Mourners. The flock who for seventy years, during his Father's ministry and his own, have Enjoyed a Series of Peace & Love, perhaps beyond what is common. He has left a sorrowful Widow and Three children, and had y⁹ comfort to see his offspring agreeably settled before his Departure."

The friendship between the Rev. Samuel Phillips of the South Parish and Mr. Barnard was cordial. When, on the death of a young man of promise, Mr. Barnard preached, and subsequently printed, a funeral sermon, the Rev. Mr. Phillips prefaced it with some remarks upon the author, and his own relations to him, expressing his opinion that the son made good the place of the father, as far as any man could.

The printed discourses of the Rev. John Barnard were, besides the one on the death of Mr. Abiel Abbot, one at the ordination of the Rev. Timothy Walker, of Concord, N. H., and an election sermon, 1746.

During the pastorate of Mr. John Barnard, several young men were ordained to the ministry. Following are brief memoranda of their life and ministry.

"CHAPLAIN JONATHAN FRYE, son of Capt. James Frye, graduated at Harvard College, 1723. His tragic fate, being wounded in Lovewell's fight with the Indians, and dying alone in the woods, has been described in a previous chapter.

REV. ANDREW PETERS, son of Samuel Peters, graduated (H. U.) 1723. He was teacher of the Grammar School at Andover, ordained the first minister of Middleton, October, 1729. He died 1756. He was a large muscular man, and sometimes enforced his preaching by action. Once, being roused by an assault on his negro servant, he threw off his coat and proceeded to inflict condign punishment on the assailant, exclaiming, "Lie there, Divinity, while I chastise this rascal."

REV. JOHN BLUNT, son of William Blunt (South Parish), graduate of Harvard University, 1727, was ordained minister of Newcastle, N. H., 1732. He was honored in his parish, and continued his ministry with them until his death, which occurred in 1748, when he was forty-two years old.

REV. JAMES CHANDLER, son of Thomas Chandler, graduate of Harvard College, 1728, was ordained minister of the second parish of Rowley (Georgetown), 1732. He was minister of this parish more than fifty-six years, and lived to the age of eighty-three years.

REV. THOMAS BARNARD, son of the Rev. John Barnard, graduated at Harvard College, 1732, was ordained pastor of the Second Church, Newbury, 1738, and afterward of the First Church in Salem. He had some difficulties in his first pastorate on account of doctrinal opinions, and gave up preaching. He then studied law and practised for a time, but returned to the ministry, and in 1755 accepted the call to Salem, where he was greatly beloved and respected. His son, Rev. Thomas Barnard, became minister of the North Church, Salem.

REV. PHINEAS STEVENS, son of Ebenezer Stevens, was a graduate of Harvard College, 1734. He was ordained minister of Boscawen, N. H., 1740.

HON. JOHN PHILLIPS, graduate of Harvard College 1735, founder of Phillips Academies, Exeter and Andover; preached for a time, but was not ordained. His relinquishing his design of being a minister is said to have been due in part to distrust of his ability to perform the duties of the office after he had heard them described by the evangelist, George Whitefield. But he devoted his money to founding religious and educational institutions for training youth in piety and virtue.

REV. SAMUEL CHANDLER, son of Josiah Chandler, graduated at

Harvard College, 1735, was ordained pastor of the Second Church, York, Me., 1742, and in 1751 colleague pastor of the First Church in Gloucester, of which he became sole pastor 1760. He died 1775.

REV. EDWARD BARNARD, son of the Rev. John Barnard, graduated at Harvard College, 1736, was ordained in Haverhill, 1743. He also suffered some reproach for his docirinal beliefs, but was sustained by the majority of his parish. "The good scholar, the great divine, the exemplary Christian and minister, eminently a man of prayer, as a preacher equalled by few, excelled by none," is the epitaph which describes his character. He died 1774, aged 53.

MR. ABIEL ABBOT, son of Dea. John Abbot, of the South Church, a student of Divinity, was a graduate of Harvard College, 1737. He died 1739. The sermon preached on his death is the first printed memorial discourse found in the town. It was preached by the Rev. John Barnard, with a preface to the printed discourse by the Rev. Samuel Phillips. It pays a high tribute to the character of the deceased.

REV. JOHN CHANDLER, son of Thomas Chandler, graduate of Harvard College, 1743, was ordained minister of Billerica 1747.

MR. ABIEL FOSTER, son of Capt. Asa Foster, was a graduate of Harvard College, 1756, ordained minister of Canterbury, N. H. After a time he relinquished the charge of a parish, and became prominent in civil affairs in his adopted State, being successively representative to the Legislature, State Senator, and member of Congress.

NATHAN HOLT, son of Nicholas Holt, graduated, 1757, at Harvard College, was ordained minister of the Second Church at Danvers 1759, Mr. Phillips preaching the sermon.

JACOB EMERY, a graduate of Harvard College, 1761, was ordained at Pembroke, N. H., 1768.

MOSES HOLT, a son of Jonathan Holt, graduated at Harvard College, 1767; preached a short time; entered into business at Portland.

We turn now to the pastorate of the first minister of the South Church, the Rev. Samuel Phillips. While the North, the First Church of Andover, was prospering and increasing, the South or Second Church [1] was likewise in a flourishing condition. Its history [2] having been already written by one of

[1] First church in the present town of Andover.
[2] *Manual of the South Church*, by Rev. George Mooar.

its pastors, himself a native of Andover, to enter into minute details here would be needless. Indeed, the growth of one of the early churches is similar to the growth of all. Many of the facts of this sketch are taken from the "South Church Manual," while some are derived directly from the parish records, which are remarkably clear and accurate.

The first meeting-house was occupied for worship January, 1710. It was built at a cost of £108. "No account of its size and style is preserved in the parish records," says the "Church Manual"; but it has seemed to the writer of these sketches that inference may be made in regard to the style of the meeting-house from the vote in the town records. The style and size of the meeting-house had been decided on before the division of the parishes; the only difference of opinion, then, being as to the location. Therefore, the meeting-house was probably built as the vote had been for its construction before the dispute began, namely: "fifty-six foot long, fifty foot wide, and twenty-two foot stud, and with a square roof without dormans with two Lucoms on each side."

This meeting-house stood till 1734. Then a second house was built, "after the same form and fashion as the old, fifty-six feet long, forty-four feet wide, thirty feet between plate and sill."

The same amount of voting and seating attended the building of this meeting-house that has been described in connection with the North Parish. The meeting-house was dedicated May 19, 1734. It was occupied for worship until 1787. It was preëminently a historic meeting-house. When, by the growth of the parish, the establishment of institutions of learning, and the distinguished part taken in public affairs by the sons of its minister and their descendants, Andover became a name of note in the Commonwealth, the South Meeting-house welcomed to its pews many an occasional visitor of distinction and many regular attendants of learning, piety, and patriotism. To name the men who occasionally sat in its pulpit or pews would be to make a list of professors of Harvard College, governors of the Commonwealth, judges, theologians, patriots, and officers of the Revolution. There is scarcely one of the prominent Massachusetts men, actors

OLD SOUTH VESTRY HOUSE

in the Revolution, who might not, without violating probability, be imagined at some time to have stood within the South Meeting-house. And of eminent men, prospective, there were many in the troops of boys and youth who occupied the "three back seats" in the lower front gallery, — students of Phillips Academy.

One of these students, the Hon. Josiah Quincy, President of Harvard College, has given a graphic description[1] of the meeting-house, as he remembered it at the time when he wrote, after the lapse of a half century. He describes the people trooping to church in great crowds, the "innumerable" horse-blocks around the meeting-house, where the women dismounted from their seats on the pillion behind their male escort; and then the meeting-house itself, a three-story building which, to the child's mind, seemed a vast and mighty structure, its two tiers of galleries and their occupants, the tything-man with his long pole, or rod of office, with which he would rap on the wall ever and anon, to the terror of mischievous boys and sleeping elders, — all the Sabbath-day scenes of those ancient times at Andover are vividly delineated by the pen of a master.

At the time of the erection of the meeting-house, a parsonage was also built (the gambrel-roofed house southeast of the church), forty-three feet long, twenty feet wide, and fourteen feet stud. It is no longer used as a parsonage, but occupied as a private residence. Its quaint construction and its pleasant situation, the beautiful lawn and arching elm trees, as well as its historic associations, make this one of the most interesting places in Andover.

The parsonage lands — fifty-four acres — were sold after the death of the second pastor, and by the sale the "Ministerial Fund" was obtained.

The REV. SAMUEL PHILLIPS, the first minister of the South Parish, was son of Samuel Phillips, goldsmith, of Salem, grandson of Rev. Samuel Phillips, of Rowley, and great-grandson of Rev. George Phillips, who came to the colony in 1630, and was the first minister of Watertown. He graduated at Harvard College, 1708, and was for a time a teacher.

[1] See *South Church Manual*.

He preached for a year before he was settled. In 1711, October 7th, he was ordained, and the church organized. It consisted of thirty-five members, all but three of whom were from the First Church and Parish. There were fourteen male members. Rev. Samuel Phillips (the pastor), Christopher Osgood, Dea. John Abbot, George Abbot, Dea. William Lovejoy, Francis Dane, John Russ, William Johnson, Ralph Farnum, Thomas Chandler, Nehemiah Abbot, John Johnson, William Foster, William Chandler.

During the ministry of Mr. Phillips, fifty-nine years, 574 communicants were added to the church, and 2,143 baptized.

The same remarks which have been made in regard to the discipline of the North Church are generally true of the South Church. Says the author of the "South Church Manual" in regard to this subject: "The chief causes for discipline for one hundred and twenty-five years were fornication and drunkenness. He who investigates the records of this or any other church for the same period will be astonished at the comparative prevalence of those vices as compared with the present time. Numerous confessions of these sins are preserved. Many of them, especially of the former class, are from those who belonged at least to the middle class of the community. . . . . For many years after the organization of the church a case of final exclusion seldom occurred."

One "sin," as Mr. Phillips named it, he preached against, which seldom at the present day receives such rebuke as he thought necessary to administer, but which is now of much more frequent occurrence, — the day (whether for good or for ill) having gone by when an Andover audience would listen to with approval, and request the publication of, such a discourse as that in 1767 upon the death of one of their townsmen: "His name," says his pastor, "as many think, had best to be buryd in oblivion," for "he yielded to the temptation of the enemy of souls, kept the devil's counsel concealed, nor did any person suspect that he was under the said temptation, until, being missed, he was found *hanging in his own barn*."

The deceased was one of the most respected citizens of

the town, a member of the church, a man of unblemished character, and a remarkably gentle and sensitive nature, and not infrequently, as such persons are apt to be, inclined to despondency.

He had some difficulties and perplexities in regard to his lands and estate, and had fallen into a melancholy state of mind, but not enough so to create apprehension, or even to attract special attention until after the sad event of his death.

This was the first instance, Mr. Phillips said in his sermon, of such an occurrence during his ministry. "An occasion *quite new* as well as *very awful*, such as, I think, has not occurred among us till now, since I came into this place, and I pray God that we may never see the like again." [1]

Mr. Phillips's sermon, printed with a ghastly title-page, headed with skull and cross-bones, and bordered with black, although terrible to the friends of the deceased, was, perhaps, in some respects salutary for the reflection of the community. In other respects its effects were permanently harmful, and did an injury to the family of the deceased which their pastor was the last man to have wished; for he himself cautioned his hearers against any such result, begging them to be careful of wounding the feelings of the bereaved. Yet such was the sentiment of the community, pastor and people, that the deceased was not permitted to be buried with the family in the burying-yard of the South Church, but was laid in a lonely grave on the farm under an oak tree; and such a horror of the deed brooded over the household that the name of the father was no more mentioned, and his son's son, born and brought up on the ancestral homestead, never heard the name of his grandfather, or allusion made to him, by the family, and only learned the story of the solitary grave from an old servant.

Mr. Phillips did not hesitate to address his hearers, after the fashion of the time, upon the subject of their behavior in church. In a sermon delivered after the great earthquake in

---

[1] A few years afterward, one of the principal citizens of the North Parish, a former representative to the General Court, committed suicide in despair in regard to his eternal salvation.

1755 he admonished the congregation upon the duty of watchfulness, and of being ready to meet the summons of the Lord; and he especially rebuked some for their inattentive manners in the House of God: "Sleeping away great part of sermon-time. But," he says, since the "Glorious Lord of the Sabbath" has "given them *such a shaking* of late," he hopes to see no more sleepers in meeting-time.

Among his private papers is one that shows his determination to have good order. It is a warrant signed by the justice, Peter Fry, at Salem, 1769, for the arrest of a youth who in time of divine service "sported and played, and by indecent Gestures and Wry faces, caused laughter and misbehavior in the Beholders, and thereby greatly disturbed the Congregation."

The pastor of the South Church was, says the Rev. Dr. Mooar, a "decided and zealous Calvinist, in strictest conformity to the Westminster Catechism, ... yet with these strong doctrinal opinions, he was able to unite his own people, and to maintain fellowship with the neighboring clergymen of a looser and dangerous creed." He was very just, and demanded justice from his people in their dealings with him, instructing them when they were delinquent in payment of his salary, that it was no excuse for their delinquency that he was not absolutely dependent on it for support, — as he says, "that through the mercy of God I have some small means of my own." He was rigidly economical in his household. It is said that he blew out the candle when he began his evening prayer, and relighted it at the conclusion, which, no doubt, in the course of a year would amount to a considerable length of time saved in the burning.

He married Miss Hannah White, daughter of the Hon. John White, of Haverhill. She was a lady of dignity and shared with her husband his parochial charge, going with him to make annual visits, riding on a pillion on the same horse. Madam Phillips was for almost sixty years her husband's companion, and outlived him two years, dying 1773, aged eighty-one years. When they went to meeting on Sunday Madam Phillips walked, leaning on her husband's arm, from the parsonage to the meeting-house, Mr. Phillips having his negro man-servant at his right hand, and Madam Phillips her negro maid-servant on her left hand. The family followed them in procession, according to age. The male members of the congregation who had been standing outside, as soon as the minister's family appeared hastened into the meeting-house, and when the pastor entered, the congregation arose and remained standing till he reached the pulpit and took his seat. Also at the close of service the congregation stood until the pastor and family had passed out.

The Rev. Samuel Phillips died June 5, 1771. He was buried in the South Burying-ground. The ancient tombstone has been replaced by a modern one. Six ministers were pall-bearers. They received presents of rings and gloves.

Mr. Phillips had three sons and two daughters: —

The daughters: Mary, born 1712; married to Mr. Samuel Appleton, of Haverhill. Lydia, born 1717; married to Parker Clark, M. D., of Andover.

The sons: Hon. Samuel Phillips, born 1715, died 1790. Hon. John Phillips, LL. D., born 1719, died 1795. Hon. William Phillips, born 1722, died 1804.

Mr. Phillips's published discourses were more than all those of his predecessors and contemporaries, — some [1] twenty or more sermons and tracts.

Nearly thirteen years before the death of the Rev. Mr. Phillips the fifth minister of the North Church was settled. Mr. Phillips thus being the contemporary and friend of three successive ministers of the North Parish.

The REV. WILLIAM SYMMES, D. D., the fifth minister of the First Church, stands out a conspicuous figure on the background of the past. His long pastorate of nearly a half century, covering almost the entire period of the French and Indian war and the Revolution; his prudence and moderation during the heated feeling, and often injudicious action, of his brother ministers of those trying times; his patience under the privations that resulted to him personally from the depreciation of the Continental currency in which his salary

[1] See *South Church Manual.*

was paid; his patriarchal rule of mingled dignity and simplicity; his honorable descent, and his distinguished posterity, make his name one of the most memorable in the ecclesiastical annals of the Parish.

Dr. Symmes was son of William Symmes, of Charlestown, and great-grandson of the Rev. Zechariah Symmes, the first minister of Charlestown. He was nephew to the Rev. Thomas Symmes, minister of Boxford and of Bradford (1702–1725). He was born 1728, graduated at Harvard College 1750, and received the degree of Doctor of Divinity from this college, being the first minister of Andover on whom it was conferred.

He was tutor of Harvard College three years before his settlement at Andover. He was married 1758, November 1.

A copy of the sermon preached at his ordination, and printed in Boston, has been preserved in the Parish. It is marked with the name of a citizen who, doubtless, heard it preached, "Timothy Noyes, His Book, 1759." The preacher was the Rev. Mr. Cooke, pastor of the Second Church, Cambridge.

The Parish voted to pay Mr. Symmes seventy pounds salary, to be increased to eighty after ten years' service; also wood and use of parsonage lands. After the depreciation of the currency they voted to make an appropriation to reimburse him for his losses, but he relinquished a large part of it.

The theological tenets of Mr. Symmes were even less of the Calvinistic school than those of his predecessors. He, it was said, inclined to Arianism, yet he maintained friendly relations with ministers who disagreed with him in some points of doctrine, and rarely engaged in controversy. He and the Rev. Mr. French, of the South Church, exchanged pulpits monthly for a course of lectures.

The printed discourses of Dr. Symmes are: "A Lecture on Psalmody," a Thanksgiving sermon, the Election Sermon, 1785.

All Dr. Symmes's manuscripts were, by his order, destroyed before his death. He died May 3, 1807. The funeral sermon was preached by Dr. Cummings, of Billerica.

The tombstone or monument of Dr. Symmes is in the Old

North Burying-Ground. It was erected by his son-in-law, Mr. Isaac Cazeneau, and was similar in style to the monument of the Hon. Samuel Phillips, an oblong pile of masonry surmounted by a transverse stone slab, bearing an inscription in memory of the pastor, also of his "Relict," Mrs. Susanna Symmes.

MRS. SUSANNA SYMMES,[1]
Relict of the late Rev. William Symmes, D. D.,
Who departed this life
July 26th, 1807,
aged 79 years.

Dr. Symmes married for his first wife (1759), Anna, daughter of the Rev. Joshua Gee, of Boston. She died 1772, aged thirty-three. She was the mother of nine children, all but two of whom died before the death of their father. Four are buried beside her: Convers, aged one month and eleven days, died September 4, 1770; Lydia and Charlotte, twins, born December 29, 1771, died the next day; and Miss Elizabeth Symmes, aged nineteen years, died August 13, 1784. William Symmes, Esq., the eldest son, was born 1760. He was a graduate of Harvard College, 1780, and was counsellor at law, Andover, the first lawyer in practice in the town. He removed to Portland, and died 1807, January 14, four months before the death of his father.

Dr. Joshua Gee Symmes, Surgeon of the U. S. Sloop *Portsmouth*, died at sea 1799, and was buried on the Island of Tobago.

Dr. Theodore Symmes was a physician at Falmouth and New Gloucester.

Anna, Mrs. Isaac Cazeneau, lived in Andover. She died 1849.

Daniel Symmes removed about 1791 to Pendleton, South Carolina. His son, Dr. Frederick William Symmes, was editor and proprietor of the "Pendleton Messenger."

A son of the latter is Whitner Symmes, Esq., Greenville, S. C., who was an officer with the rank of Major in the Confederate service.

Not a few aged persons now living remember "Parson

[1] Susanna Powell.

Symmes," as he looked in the later years of his ministry, his corpulent figure, his white bush-wig, his stately bearing, as he stood in the pulpit under the great sounding board, and surveyed the congregation like a venerable parent, looking down benignantly upon his children. Many are the anecdotes told of his somewhat austere rule of his household, and the devices of the young folks to carry out their plans of party-going without their father's suspecting what was on foot; for Parson Symmes, though counted lax in doctrine, was fully up to the Puritan standard in regard to amusements and festivities, especially for ministers' sons and daughters.

A story of one of Dr. Symmes's wedding services is related on the authority of a clergyman, whose father, a medical student with Dr. Thomas Kittredge, heard it from the family.

A colored servant in the household, Cato (the narrator thinks this was the name, but whether Cato, or Cæsar, or any other namesake of the ancient Romans does not affect the story), was about to be married. Dr. Symmes had been asked to perform the ceremony, and the whole family and other guests were there to grace the occasion. Cato had been presented by his master with a suit of small-clothes, and a piece of money for the wedding fee, a half crown. Impressed with the responsibility of the money, and not knowing just when and where the fee was to come in, Cato kept eyes and ears open for the minister's every word and action. "Let us pray," said Dr. Symmes, stretching out his hand as he spoke, as is a manner of some ministers. "Let us pay" heard the nervous bridegroom, and thrusting his hand into his pocket he brought out the half crown and placed it in the minister's outspread palm, before the voice of supplication awoke him to the consciousness that the summons was not to paying but to praying.

The Parish Records during Dr. Symmes's pastorate contain little that is essentially different from the customs and methods of the preceding pastorates.

In 1766 it was voted that "All the English women in the Parish who marry or associate with Negro or Melatto-men be seated in the Meeting-House with the Negro-women."

In 1769 a grave matter occupied the parish mind, namely (as it is indexed on the records), "WOMENS HATS:"—

"Being put to vote whether the parish Disapprove of the Female Sex seting with their Hats on in the Meeting-house, in the Time of Divine Service, as being Indecent. It passed in the affirmative."

In 1771 the parish voted their thanks to "Mr. Nathan Barker and Mr. John Pearson, for their good services as Quiristers for many years past, and Messrs. John Peabody, John Willson, John Abbot, 3^d, Thos. Spafford, John Adams, John Ingalls, Jacob Stevens, and James Bridges, Junr., were chosen to lead in singing for ye future."

In 1798, "chose a committe to consult the Rev. Mr. Symmes about having a vial in the meeting-house on days of public worship," and the committee report "*he's no objection.*"

Dr. Symmes preached a sermon, or lecture, on "Church Psalmody," and during his ministry the old singing-books of Brady and Tate, which had succeeded Sternhold and Hopkins, were superseded by Belknap's.

The old meeting-house, although it stood long after Dr. Symmes's day (till 1835), was really a relic of the ancient time. Its demolition may, therefore, be fitly mentioned in connection with the minister, who, for almost fifty years, occupied its pulpit. The description is from an anonymously published pamphlet, "The Old Parish Church:"—

"It chanced that on a summer's day
We youngsters left our work or play
And sallied out to help the people
Pull down the good old Parish Steeple.
The house unto its bones was stripped, —
The tower-braces were out-ripped,
And many a stout foundation-stone
From underneath its feet was gone, —
And tower and spire now stood alone.
We pulled and shouted — but no fall ;
The tower would shake, but that was all.
At last a bold mechanic pried
The last sustaining stone aside :
A thrill went up from base to spire ;
Was it of horror or of ire?
Slowly the spire forsook its trust,

> Then head-long plunged against the plain,
> Dashing to chaos and to dust :
> While we who long had watched the vane,
> A large gilt Rooster, rushed to see,
> Soon as the dust could blow away,
> Where his carcase huge might be.
> Perhaps deep down in mother clay !
> For we had oft and oft been told
> By the town's ancient men and wise
> That an ox-wagon scarce could hold
> The bird, so monstrous was his size.
> Well, after search, we found him out,
> But then no grand triumphant shout
> Went up to verify our tale.
>
> . . . .
>
> We found his roostership to be
> Like many fallen from high degree,
> But little less than vanity."

This ancient edifice of the First Church was the longest lived of any of the old Andover meeting-houses. More than four-score years its walls stood. Its bell rang the day of His Majesty George the Third's ascension of the throne, summoned the minute-men to oppose the tyrannical officers ; pealed the Declaration of Independence, and the election of the first President of the United States and of seven successive presidents, and still the ancient building showed no signs of decay, but was only out of date. " If they had let it stand," said an old man to the writer, " it would have been better than the one they have now." Its porch removed to the manufacturing village near the Merrimack, and fitted up for a part of a dwelling-house, is still doing service. The pew walls (which were carved at the top into rounds like some ancient chair-backs) made a good and unique fence for the front yard of a neighboring house, west of the Common. They have now disappeared. One of the high-backed chairs is still kept in a house near the church.

Contemporary with the latter part of Mr. Symmes's ministry was that of the REV. JONATHAN FRENCH, in the South Parish, 1772 to 1809. Mr. French was born at Braintree, January 30, 1740. He was of the Pilgrim stock, his mother being a great-granddaughter of John Alden. Bred on a farm, he at seventeen enlisted as a private in the French War, and was sent to Fort Edward. Thence, after a few months, he came back to Boston on account of ill health, but not without having done some valorous deeds in Indian fighting. He was stationed at Castle William, with the rank of Sergeant. Fond of books, he took to studying medicine here and practised surgery, but finally, by advice of friends who discovered his talent, he resolved to enter the ministry, and to that end set about fitting for college while still doing military duty. This he accomplished, and delivered up his sword only on the day when he entered a Freshman at Harvard. He was then twenty-seven years old. He graduated at the age of thirty-one. He had intended to be a missionary to the Indians (perhaps from compunctions derived from his experience and observation in the Indian fighting by Christians), but his plans were changed by his receiving a call to supply the pulpit of the South Church at Andover. This was given through the influence of Samuel Phillips, Jr., Esq., a classmate in college of Mr. French, with whom he had formed a warm friendship. At the age of thirty-two Mr. French began his pastorate, which continued thirty-seven years. He was an acceptable preacher in the parish. Less nice than his predecessor had been about fine points of doctrine, he sought rather to exercise his people in practical virtues than in subtleties of speculation, or than to ground them in doctrine. He was, therefore, by some suspected of being not quite sound in the faith. He, however, was a diligent catechist of the children, and visited the schools often to see that the duty of learning the catechism was not neglected.

An active participant in town affairs, a zealous patriot, and a promoter of every proper measure of Revolutionary tendency, he showed even in his peaceful profession his military training and ardor. In this respect he differed from the minister of the North Parish, who was "conservative" (to a fault, some people thought), but who, after the struggle fairly began, seems to have been a patriot in his sympathies, although he regarded it as not a necessary part of a minister's duty to take interest in political matters. But Parson French could not be inactive. On Sunday morning, when news of the battle of Bunker Hill came, he took no scrupulous counsel concerning Sabbath-breaking, but started for the battle-field with his musket in hand, and his case of surgeon's implements and medicines, and, no doubt, as became a minister, with his Bible also. He rendered valuable aid that day, caring for the wounded and administering comfort and consolation, physical and spiritual.

Mr. French, like the other clergy of his day, had almost always in his family some young men as students, both those who were in the Academy and others who were preparing for the ministry. The charming pictures of an aged clergyman's friendship for a boy, drawn by the author of "Wensley," are, doubtless, derived from the reminiscences and traditions of the Hon. Josiah Quincy, told in his family regarding Parson French.

Mr. French's home was noted for its hospitality, although frugal, as was necessary in the "hard times," into which the country was brought after the war.

Mr. French married Abigail Richards, daughter of Dr. Benjamin Richards, of Weymouth. An incident of their courtship has been related to the writer by a granddaughter of Mr. French.

When he decided to study for the ministry, he was engaged to Miss Richards; but, taking into consideration the long time which would elapse before his studies were finished and the changes that time might make, etc., they mutually released each other from their promise for seven years (so the tradition goes), but they agreed that if, at the expiration of that time, eitehr wished to renew the engagement, he or she should communicate with the other. The years rolled round. Mr. French remained of the same mind, and wrote a letter to that effect to Miss Richards. He entrusted the letter to the captain of a coasting vessel to carry to Weymouth. It chanced that the captain was either a rejected suitor of Miss Richards or at the time an aspirant for her favor. A letter from the young minister to her was too much for his jealousy and curiosity. He broke the seal, read the letter, and threw it into the ocean. A brother of Miss Richards, while that day bathing in the surf, saw a paper floating on the water, secured it, and, to his amazement, found it to be addressed to his sister. Thus the lover's letter reached its destination. The sequel we know.

In his household, Mr. French was often subjected to no small inconvenience by the neglect of the people to pay his salary, — he not having, as had the former pastor, means of his own. He was obliged, again and again, to expostulate with the parish in regard to their delinquency, and in doing this he sometimes showed no little shrewdness. It was customary to pay him partly in firewood, or rather to supply him with firewood. On the Sunday when he had read the proclamation for Thanksgiving, he remarked: "My brethren, you perceive that his Excellency has appointed next Thursday as the day of Thanksgiving, and, according to custom, it is my purpose to prepare two discourses for that occasion, *provided I can write them* WITHOUT A FIRE." He was enabled to write the sermons the next day.

The published discourses of Mr. French were nine[1] sermons and lectures.

Mr. French had one son, the Rev. Jonathan French, D. D., born August 16, 1777, minister of North Hampton, N. H. A son of the latter (Jonathan French) and daughter (Mrs. Sereno T. Abbot) live in Andover.

Mr. French had two daughters: Abigail, born 1776, wife of Rev. Samuel Stearns, Bedford; Mary, born 1784, wife of Rev. Ebenezer P. Sperry, Wenham.

During the pastorate of Mr. French, 1788, a new meeting-house was built. The pews were square, there were seats near the pulpit for the deacons and the old people. A sounding-board over the pulpit was inscribed: "Holiness becometh thine house, O Lord, forever." This house stood till 1833, without any essential changes; then it was remodelled, and the square pews were taken out. Stoves[2] were put in for heating the house, in 1821. There was also a building called the "noon-house," where the members of the Parish

---

[1] See *South Church Manual*.
[2] During the Revolutionary War, Mr. Phillips asked to have the "*stoves*" from the meeting-house to use in his powder-works, because his stove was cracked. He also wrote to Colonel Pickering that the selectmen of Marblehead had consented to his using their stove, and will send a team to " bring the stove, if it can be got over to Salem." What these "stoves" were has not been ascertained; but it would seem that they were more than mere small tin foot-stoves, such as were used later.

who came from a distance ate their luncheon, and in winter warmed themselves and filled their foot-stoves for afternoon service in the cold meeting-house, with live coals from the great wood-fires kept blazing at both ends of the house. In order to avoid the danger of too much gossip and waste of time, a plan of reading was devised for the intermission. Some layman of dignity and learning was selected to read aloud a sermon or devotional exercise. So valuable was this custom of reading thought to be by Judge Phillips that, at his death, he gave a silver flagon to the church as a memorial of his sincere affection and esteem, and of his earnest request that " the *laudable practice* of reading in the house of public worship between services may be continued so long as even a small number shall be disposed to attend the exercise."

Samuel Abbot, Esq., also presented a flagon as a token of his appreciation and encouragement of this practice of reading.

It is hardly necessary to say that, next to the minister, Judge Phillips was the principal spiritual as well as secular director of the South Church. His grandfather had been the pastor, his influence had placed his class-mate, the Rev. Jonathan French, in the South Church pulpit, and though the minister never compromised his manliness and official dignity by undue deference to his distinguished parishioner, it was his pleasure and advantage to be largely influenced by a man who was preëminently suited to advise in church matters.

Samuel Abbot, Esq., also one of the founders of the Theological Institution, was a leading member of the South Church for fifty-nine years (1753-1812). His labors for its welfare were great, and his gifts numerous. He gave, besides the flagon, to encourage reading, a silver tankard, a bell, a clock, large sums for the benefit of the poor of the parish, money to lengthen the district schools of the South Parish, and thousands of dollars to young men fitting for the ministry. But he gave besides, that which makes his other gifts preëminently significant and valuable, the example of a noble life. To quote the expressive words of Dr. Woods in the funeral sermon, May 3, 1812: "A man of God has been among you, and by divine grace shown you how to use this world, how to live and how to die."

Mr. Abbot was eighty years old when he died. The improvement of time had been one of the special aims of his long life. In presenting a clock to the South Church he wrote: "May it prove a convenience to you and your children in the business of life, and a salutary monitor of a careful improvement of that time which is continually passing away and can never be recalled."

Another member of the South Church, who exercised a controlling influence during the ministry of Mr. French, was Samuel Farrar, Esq. He was one of the committee appointed by the pastor's request to assist the deacons and supplement their office. Mr. Farrar united with the church of the Theological Seminary at its establishment in 1816, he being treasurer of the Board of Trustees. His philanthropic labors were chiefly in connection with the educational institutions, to which he was a generous benefactor. He continued through life to cherish a deep interest in the South Church, and the last time he attended divine service was at the South Meeting-house, on Fast Day, 1864. He was ninety-one years old when he died, and had lived in Andover sixty-seven years. His influence as a Christian gentleman was hardly second to that of any man in Andover.

In the pastorates of the three contemporary ministers of Andover, Dr. Symmes, Mr. Phillips, and Mr. French, several young men [1] were trained for the ministry who exerted a marked influence in their time, and have left a permanent name in the ecclesiastical annals of the Commonwealth. Following are some memoranda of their life and ministry: —

REV. STEPHEN PEABODY, son of Capt. John Peabody, graduated at Harvard College 1769, was ordained at Atkinson, N. H., 1772. He was pastor there forty-seven years, till his death, 1819.

His name is famous in all the ecclesiastical traditions of the region about Atkinson. His connection with Atkinson Academy and his patriotic stand during the war of the Revolution are alluded to

[1] The names of Jacob Emery and Moses Holt (page 441) strictly belong to this period.

in other chapters of this history. As a preacher and pastor he was greatly revered, and his word in the parish was law. He was majestic yet kindly in manner, and though he exacted the deference due to his ministerial rank, he was condescending and sympathetic. He is generally believed to have been an Arminian in creed, but there are different opinions among his biographers in regard to this point, as there were also among his contemporary ministers, and as there always are in regard to men who take middle ground on questions of doctrine.

Parson or "Sir" Peabody, as he was called, was remarkable for his musical ability; he had a rich voice which he used to exercise in singing (as he rode on horseback through the woods) snatches from oratorios of Handel, and the old anthems then in vogue. He also taught his dog to make musical sounds with him, and it is said that one Sunday the dog, having followed his master to church, joined in the singing, to the great mortification of the pastor.

REV. DAVID OSGOOD, D. D., graduate of Harvard College in 1771, was for forty-eight years pastor of the church in Medford. He went to college at the same time with Lieut.-gov. Samuel Phillips. The two young men were put to room together, as young Phillips wrote home, in chamber No. 26, Hollis Hall. The advantages for college preparation of the two class-mates had been very different. Everything that wealth and family connection could do for the one had been done, to place him with the best masters and to ensure his standing in the college. The other had his own way to make. His father was a plain though intelligent farmer, who lived in a remote district in the west part of the town, far from schools and means of culture. But the desire of the lad finally triumphed over obstacles. The daughter of the Rev. David Osgood thus writes [1] regarding her father's efforts to gain his preparation for college: —

"Upon a Saturday night, as he has often told us, he at length won his father's reluctant consent to his proposal, and at break of day on the following Monday morning he walked three or four miles in pursuit of a young schoolmaster with whom he was slightly acquainted, that he might consult him in regard to the books which it would be necessary for him to procure and study. From him he heard for the first time of the Latin Accidence, and obtained the loan of it. This he mastered in a short time, and in a few weeks placed himself under the care of the Rev. Mr. Emerson, of Hollis, who was in the habit of receiving youths into his family."

[1] Sprague's *Annals of the American Pulpit.*

In sixteen months this earnest student was fitted for college. Dr. Osgood was one of the ablest ministers of his time. He took an active interest in all the stirring political events, was an ardent patriot, a volunteer chaplain at the battle of Bunker Hill, in Colonel Stark's regiment, which was quartered at Medford. Yet he abhorred war in itself, and spoke fearlessly his sentiments against the war with England in 1812.

He was a good writer, and his eloquence in the pulpit and extemporaneous speaking was remarkable. He was catholic in his doctrinal creed, and was blamed by some zealots for being too Calvinistic and by others for being too much an Arminian. He was a firm believer in the right of freedom of thought. He died 1822, aged seventy-five.

PROF. JOHN ABBOT, son of Capt. John Abbot, was another scholar of fine culture. He was a graduate of Harvard College 1784; instructor in Phillips Academy and tutor in Harvard College five years. He studied divinity, but on account of the state of his health was unable to preach. He was Professor of Latin and Greek in Bowdoin College fourteen years. His health and strength, physical and mental, becoming seriously impaired, he retired from his profession, and was under medical treatment for some time. Shortly before his death, he returned to Andover, to the home of his childhood and the abode of his ancestors of six generations, where he found solace and rest. He died in 1843, aged eighty-four, — a scholar, a gentleman, and a Christian. He was honored and beloved by a large circle of acquaintance, and his memory is tenderly cherished in the institutions in which he was instructor, and in the community of his birth and death.

REV. JONATHAN FRENCH, D. D., son of the pastor of the South Church, at the age of twenty-two preached his first sermon in the South Church pulpit. He graduated at Harvard College 1798, was a teacher in Phillips Academy, ordained minister of North Hampton, N. H., 1801. He was a respected preacher for more than fifty years. He died 1856, aged seventy-eight.

REV. ABIEL ABBOT, D. D., son of Capt. John Abbot, brother of Prof. John Abbot, was a minister greatly esteemed throughout Essex County. He was eight years pastor of the First Church in Haverhill, and twenty-four years pastor of the First Church, Beverly. He graduated at Harvard College 1792. He was teacher in Phillips Academy, and was offered the Principalship, but preferred to enter the ministry. He was a man of simple, unostentatious manners, free from cant or bigotry, yet of a deeply religious spirit. He was unwearied in his labors for his people. His parish was one of those which, in the separation of the Congregational body took the Unitarian name. Of Dr. Abbot's creed his brother minister and kinsman, Rev. Abiel Abbot, D. D., of Coventry, says: "He called no man master. He belonged to no sect but that of good men; to no school but that of Jesus Christ; and he was liberal in the best sense of the term. He never thought himself called upon to denounce the opinions of others, and rarely to obtrude his own, upon the controverted points of the day."

Rev. ABIEL ABBOT, D. D., minister of Coventry and Peterborough, and author of the "History of Andover" (1829), was descended from the first settler, George Abbot, of Andover. He was cousin of Prof. John Abbot and Rev. Dr. Abbot, of Beverly, and married their sister. He was a native of Wilton, N. H., graduated at Harvard College 1787, taught in Phillips Academy, and during the intervals of his pastorates was a resident on the old Abbot Homestead, and in the ancient house. He often said that its domestic and historic associations awakened his interest in studying and writing the town history. He was ordained pastor of a church in Coventry, Conn., 1795, but after a time the theological bitterness of the day caused disturbance of his pleasant relations with his people. For "heretical" doctrines he was deposed in 1811. Through this trying ordeal he bore himself with dignity and charity. After his withdrawal from Coventry he took charge of Byfield Academy. In 1819 he came to Andover, where he spent some years. In 1827 he was installed minister in Peterborough, N. H., where he continued till the infirmities of age compelled him to resign his charge. He outlived all the members of his class in college, being ninety-four years old at his death, February 4, 1859. He died at West Cambridge, where he was living with his grandson, Rev. S. A. Smith.

Rev. THOMAS MERRILL, D. D., son of Deacon Thomas Merrill, was a native of Andover, but removed at the age of six years with his parents to Deering, N. H. He was a graduate of Dartmouth College 1801, pastor of a church in Middlebury, Vt., and Treasurer of Middlebury College.

Rev. ROBERT GRAY, son of Robert Gray, graduated at Harvard College 1786; was ordained minister of Dover, N. H., February, 1787; dismissed May, 1806; died 1822, aged sixty-four years.

Rev. PETER HOLT, son of Joshua Holt, Esq., graduated at Harvard College, 1790; was minister of Epping, N. H., and Peterborough.

REV. JOHN LOVEJOY ABBOT was a graduate of Harvard College 1805, librarian of the college, and in 1813 ordained pastor of the First Church, Boston. He died after a year's pastorate, October 14, 1814, aged thirty-one.

There were some who studied for the ministry, but entered into business or professions. The names are in the chronological list at the end of this chapter.

Thus we see that from the beginning Andover furnished ministers for the important churches of New England. The ancient parishes of Charlestown, Salem, Boston, found talent in this inland plantation equal to the demands of city pulpits; and the other venerable and influential towns of the Commonwealth, — Groton, Haverhill, Beverly, Medford, — and others more remote, as York, Me., New London, Conn., received from Andover, before the establishment of the Theological Seminary, ministers whose names adorn their ecclesiastical annals.

The contemporary pastors in Andover, of the territorial parishes in the next half century were, in the *North Parish*, REV. BAILEY LORING (1810–1850), in the *South Parish*, REV. JUSTIN EDWARDS, D. D. (1812–1827), REV. MILTON BADGER (1828–1835), REV. LORENZO L. LANGSTROTH (1836–1839), REV. JOHN L. TAYLOR, D. D. (1839–1852); in the *West Parish*, its first minister, the REV. SAMUEL C. JACKSON, D. D. (1827–1850).

The above names represent the three recognized "parishes" of Andover, whose territorial lines of demarcation regulated the church attendance and taxation of their residents. At the beginning, such attendance and taxation within the prescribed limits were rigidly enforced. No persons could, without peril, assemble for worship anywhere except in the regular parish meeting-house, or under the sanction of the town or parish pastor. And even after other forms of Christian worship were legalized, the public sentiment, in some places, was so strong against any but the prevailing faith that persons of other creeds were in some towns subject to great annoyance and were not infrequently compelled by the local officers to contribute[1] to the support

[1] This seems to have been the case in Andover. The South Parish, in 1791,

of the parish churches, or to resort to tedious processes of law to obtain redress of grievances. But, in the progress of things, all these restrictions were taken off. The parish lines ceased to have any necessary connection with the church and denominational lines, and persons were taxed only for the support of such worship as they voluntarily contributed to. Hence it came to pass that Andover, from having at first one minister supported by the whole town, had, in 1710, two pastors whose rates were gathered by the two respective constables of the North and the South Parishes, and, in 1826, three ministers, each limited in his jurisdiction (this word, then, not incorrectly represented the pastor's official relation), to the part of the town marked off and designated by the lot-layers and perambulators. At this time, no other rivals disputed the territory with the three clergymen of Andover. The Church of the Theological Seminary, formed in 1816, and having no pastors aside from the Professors in that institution, was not intended in any way to infringe on the regular parochial rights and duties of the parish ministers. It, however, in the end, came to be one of the chief church organizations of the town, and to number among its members many of the residents not directly connected with the Seminary and Academy. The organization of this church was unique and anomalous. It is a somewhat curious fact, that a church of just such a character should have grown up in Andover, and especially that the first movement in the direction of breaking down the ancient system of parishes should have come from the Theological Seminary. The Seminary Church [the account is compiled, mostly quoted, from a Memorial Discourse, by a Professor [1] of the Seminary, also once a pastor of the South Church], was at first "an *anomaly*, in its structure, neither properly Congregational nor Presbyterian, but partly both." It was not organized by an ecclesiastical council, but under a vote of the Trustees in accordance with

voted to "*dismiss*" the 14th article in the warrant, which was "to see if the parish will relinquish the tax that has been assessed on Sam[l] Flint, and others, since the time of their severally joining a Baptist Society, and exempt them from all future assessments in s[d] Parish so long as they shall continue members of s[d] Baptist Society."

[1] A *Memorial Discourse*, by Prof. John L. Taylor, October 1, 1876.

the report of a committee of the board appointed the year before. The church could neither elect nor remove its pastor, could pass no censure on its pastor or on any Professor in its membership, without the previous approbation and sanction of the Trustees. The members of the Board of Trustees, who were also members of the church, were *ex officio* ruling elders in its discipline, each Professor being also *ex officio* pastor.

The members of the church were at the outset seventeen only, but they were names of distinction: Ebenezer Porter, Leonard Woods, Moses Stuart, John Adams, Samuel Farrar, Samuel C. Aiken, Joel Hawes, Willard Holbrook, Edward W. Hooker, Jonathan McGee, John L. Parkhurst, Levi Parsons, Ebenezer B. Wright, Amzi Benedict, Alvan Bond, David L. Ogden, Levi Spaulding.

The Seminary Church continued according to its first organization for fifty years. "When it reached this crisis," to quote the Memorial, "the record of its half century of life shows a total of eight hundred and eighty-six names on its roll; and *what* names do we here find, by scores and fifties, of men whom the church has loved and honored at home and abroad, a very large percentage of the list being preachers of the gospel, and of these not a few eminent as missionaries."

This church, in its anomalous ecclesiastical organization, seemed unsuited to the progress of ideas in a Congregational theological seminary. On the 1st November, 1865, it was set aside, and a properly Congregational Church of seventy members was duly organized by a council to take its place. "But by the terms of its chronic decease" (says the Memorial), "the old church will not be extinct till the unrecorded date of the death or dismission of its last solitary member."

Through the munificence of one of the founders, the Hon. William Bartlet, a chapel for worship was erected. It was dedicated September 22, 1818. The dedication was an event of general interest; the schools throughout the town being closed, and crowds of people attending the exercises. The chapel,[1] which has not in late years been regarded as a model of architecture, was described by a newspaper of the time as

[1] It has been recently modernized by adding a tower.

"vieing in elegance with any in the United States." The present chapel was built in 1876. It is in the Gothic style of architecture, of stone from West Andover, with trimmings of Connecticut red sandstone and Ohio stone. It was dedicated October 2, 1876; sermon by Prof. Egbert C. Smyth.

The establishment of the church of the Theological Seminary seemed to pave the way for a series of churches and societies. The first was connected with a new parish proper. In 1826, a third territorial parish was marked off and the bounds perambulated, and although this was the last topographical division made under ecclesiastical sanction, there soon began to spring up other religious societies, until from one there were, before the division of the town of Andover in 1855, some dozen or more churches. We are, therefore, entering on a period of the ecclesiastical history, when a change began, and a new and different order of things was gradually established. Manifestly, this later condition of affairs gives a very different relative importance to the clergy and the churches of the old and of the new time, so far as they are connected with the town history. When the principal business of the town meeting was to vote in regard to the minister's salary and the assessment of the rates for the church's support, the history of the church was, in a sense, the history of the town. And, even after these days were gone, and the parishes transacted business each for itself, the ministers were much more prominent and directing in town affairs than they are now. Therefore, the earlier churches properly claim fuller notice than those of modern date.

Beginning the transition period with the First or North Church, the Rev. Dr. Symmes may be regarded as the last of the old-time ministers, although many of the old customs continued to a later day. When, after the death of Dr. Symmes, the parish came together to ordain the minister whom they had called, the Rev. Samuel Gay, it proved that the views of Christian doctrine which he expressed were not satisfactory to all the officers of the church and parish, being more rigidly Calvinistic than they approved. The ordination services were, therefore, broken off. Some delay ensued before the parish could agree upon another candidate. Several eminent men preached here at the time as candidates, among them the Rev. Timothy Alden and the Rev. Samuel Osgood, D. D., of Springfield. The parish were about to extend a call to Mr. Osgood, when he received and accepted a call to Springfield, although, as he wrote, he "was strongly prepossessed in favor of the church at Andover." The Rev. Timothy Alden received, but declined, the call.

The parish, finally, by a vote of 101 to 3, extended a call to the Rev. Bailey Loring, who accepted it, and was ordained September 19, 1810.

Mr. Loring was born in Duxbury, Mass., December 10, 1786, son of William and Alithea (Alden) Loring. His mother was a great-granddaughter of the pilgrim John Alden. He was a graduate of Brown University, 1807. He studied divinity with Dr. Allyn, of Duxbury. He was twenty-three years old when he received the call to North Andover. He was a resident of the parish fifty years, pastor almost forty years. His resignation took effect February 27, 1850.

It is noticeable as showing how this pastorate was a link between the old times and the new that, of the committee to consider the preliminaries of his settlement, four had been officers in the Revolutionary War: Dr. Thomas Kittredge, Surgeon, Maj. (Capt.) Samuel Johnson, Capt. Benjamin Farnum, Capt. (Lieut.) William Johnson.

Mr. Loring was not a Calvinist. His theological education had been under the Arminian school of belief. But, like his predecessors, he was catholic in his sympathies, and maintained throughout his ministry friendly relations with his brethren of various creeds. He continued to exchange pulpits with those of similar tolerant principles, even after the partition walls had been built up between the two divisions of the Congregational order, and when this breaking through was censured by the more dogmatic of both parties. For twenty years the harmony of the church and the unity of the parish were preserved; but, as in process of time the public sentiment tended more and more to sharp distinctions and precise definitions, it became impossible to hold together the various elements to mutual profit. Accordingly, in 1834, a few members [1] of the church withdrew, and, uniting with fourteen members from the South Church, formed "The Evangelical Church in North Andover," and established religious worship in a meeting-house which had been built by subscriptions of the Evangelical churches of Essex County.

Immediately after the dedication of the meeting-house of this new society, the First Church and Parish took action in regard to a new meeting-house, and voted to appropriate $7,000 to build. The house was finished and dedicated June 1, 1836. The entire cost of building was $11,500. The old meeting-house, as has been before said, was taken down. The ancient clock was, however, kept and put in repair; the society, on account of the associations connected with it, deciding to repair it at considerable cost: —

"*Resolved*, That whereas, in 1762, Mr. Benjamin Barker, a worthy citizen in the North Parish in Andover, did present to the said Parish a clock for the meeting-house: in grateful Remembrance of the said Benjamin Barker, the Inhabitants of said parish, for the purpose of keeping in repair the said clock, have expended three hundred dollars upon the same, under the direction of Mr. Simon Willard, clock-maker, in Boston."

The parish also returned thanks, through the Rev. Wilkes Allen, to Dr. Rufus Wyman (father-in-law of Mr. Allen) for the "gift of a very elegant Bible, for the pulpit of the new meeting-house."

During the ministry of Mr. Loring, the First Church of Andover became distinctly recognized as among the Unitarian Congregational churches, and maintained honorable eminence in the denomination. A preacher of no mean ability, more than ordinarily gifted in the expression of tender and chastened feeling, of uncommon sweetness and seriousness of manner, Mr. Loring both convinced the judgment and moved the hearts of his hearers. His preaching was not in the technical sense doctrinal, yet his opinions were decided and outspoken, and they identified him unmistakably with

---

[1] Seven members (one male and six female), also ten or less, who were communicants and residents, but had not removed their connection from other churches in former places of residence.

the Unitarians of his time, though, in his later years, with the more conservative school of thought. He was an acceptable exchange in the leading pulpits of the denomination, and during his ministry the First Church heard many a discourse of the finest culture of New England.

At his resignation, the parish passed resolutions expressive of regret at the separation, and when he died, the following action was taken to honor his memory : —

"*Resolved*, 1st, That the members of this Religious Society are deeply sensible of the loss they have sustained by the death of the Revd. Bailey Loring, who for nearly forty years was their Spiritual Instructor and Guide, and for nearly a half century an esteemed and respected citizen of the town.

"2d, That during the long period in which he officiated as our minister he displayed in an eminent degree all the virtues and graces that belong to and adorn the character of a Christian Divine. That as a preacher he was always found faithful to the cause of his Master, in expounding the doctrine and enforcing the precepts of his Holy Word, reproving and rebuking sin wherever it was to be found, and inciting his hearers, by the most alluring and weighty considerations, to the love and practice of the Christian virtues. That as a pastor he was 'instant in season and out of season' in visiting the sick and relieving the distressed, so that every member of his society was sure of finding at all times and under all circumstances of life a friend, adviser, and comforter in his minister; and that by his death the cause of education, morals, and religion in this society and community has lost one of its strongest advocates and most sincere supporters.

"3d, That the interest he manifested in the welfare of this church and society after his official connection with it was dissolved, and especially his regard for the intellectual improvement of his successors in the ministerial office by the donation of his theological library for their use and benefit will always be remembered by us with the most lively emotions of gratitude.

"4th, That these resolutions be placed upon the parish records and communicated to the family of the deceased."

The published discourses of Mr. Loring, so far as has been ascertained, were only two sermons, bound in one pamphlet, 1829. The subjects: "Gratitude," a Thanksgiving discourse, and "Profanity." They were published, by special request of the North Parish Association for Mutual Improvement. Mr. Loring was averse to having his sermons printed, and he did not approve of preaching funeral and memorial discourses.

Mr. Loring married, 1816, Miss Sally Pickman Osgood, a daughter of Isaac Osgood, Esq., a lady of rare social and intellectual endowments. She died 1835, leaving four sons, between the ages of eighteen and eleven years.

These are: Hon. George B. Loring, of Salem; Isaac O. Loring (deceased), of North Andover; Gayton P. Loring, apothecary, of Boston; John A. Loring, Esq., counsellor-at-law, Boston.

The succession of the ministers of the First Church and Parish, all of whom are now living, is as follows: —

The seventh minister was the REV. FRANCIS C. WILLIAMS. He was ordained February 27, 1850, and continued in office to May 27, 1856. He resigned to accept a call to Brattleborough, Vt. He left many warm friends in the parish.

The eighth minister was the REV. CHARLES C. VINAL, ordained May 6, 1857. He continued in office thirteen years, to March, 1870. During his pastorate a parsonage was built, the parish having received for that purpose a testamentary bequest of $6,000 from the late William Johnson, Esq.

In accepting this donation the following resolutions were passed, expressive of respect and gratitude to the memory of the donor: —

"*Resolved*, that by the death of the late Hon. William Johnson, this Christian Society has lost one of its most valuable, efficient, and devoted members; that the community is deprived of a man and a citizen who performed all the duties of life with integrity and honor; who by his affable manners and dignified deportment secured universal esteem and respect; and that we shall long cherish the memory of his many virtues, his excellent qualities, and his useful abilities."

Mr. Vinal, in 1870, accepted a call to the Unitarian Church in Kennebunk, Maine, where he is now pastor. His resignation was received with regret, and he is kindly remembered in the parish.

The parsonage was destroyed by fire while it was unoccupied, in 1870, and the parish library and the later Church Records were burned. The new parsonage was built in 1871.

The ninth and present pastor, REV. JOHN H. CLIFFORD, was ordained August 29, 1871. He and the two preceding pastors were graduates of the Cambridge Divinity School.

The deacons of the First Church, during the one hundred and eighty-nine years in which it was the only church in the North Parish, and who sat in a special seat in front of the pulpit, were the following: John Frye (elected 1——?), John Barker (1693), Joseph Stevens (1694), John Osgood (1719), John Farnum (1727), Samuel Barker (1736), Samuel Phillips (1748), Joseph Osgood (1763), Joseph Barker (1766), Benjamin Farnum (1790), John Adams (1797), George Osgood 1797), Joshua Wilson (1813), Jedidiah Farnham (1824), William Frost (1824).

There are few memorials of the church work, or religious character of the members of the North Church and Parish, its ministers, for the most part, not having made it a practice to preach memorial discourses.

The veil of reserve which the pastors have chosen to keep drawn over the motives and purposes of the members of this religious society, which included many of the most honored citizens of North Andover, it is not for other hands to attempt to put aside. There is much to be said in favor of the reserve, as also much in favor of giving to the community the inspiration and help which come from the contemplation of noble lives.

Within the present pastorate of the First Church there have terminated three lives of such exceptional interest as to have won by common consent the tribute of special commemoration. They were of the young man in the prime of manhood; the matron in the crown of nearly fourscore years and four and the blessing of many children; and the single woman, in the self-abnegation and devotion to others of a life also extended beyond the period pronounced to be "la bor and sorrow."

Horace N. Stevens died at North Andover, May 1, 1876, at the age of thirty-eight.

He was the youngest son of Capt. Nathaniel Stevens, and junior partner of the manufacturing firm of Moses T. Stevens and Brothers. From a memorial address by the Rev. John H. Clifford, the following extracts are selected: —

"There is indeed much concerning him that belongs to us all, to this religious Society, to these Masonic orders, to the whole community .... a priceless legacy. .... He was of the very flower of our best manhood. He united a delicacy and strength, a force and gentleness which made him, although his life among us was so quiet and humble, a person of rare influence in our midst. .... What he was to this religious society you all know by longer acquaintance than I have had. If we have pillars to our church, he was surely one, not merely resting upon material foundations, but still more truly a spiritual pillar planted firmly in the solid ground of character. .... That a man so young, scarcely entered upon middle life, and of so private and withal so modest a habit of living, should have all unconsciously (for I believe he was utterly unaware of it) drawn to himself the fond reverence of people of every sort and condition, this is enough were anything wanting to justify all that I have said of him, and to prove how far short I have fallen of his deserts. Society has sore need of such men to-day — as when has it not? Such as he, quietly faithful in private spheres, are the world's truest helpers and reformers."

Mrs. Hannah Hodges Kittredge died July 1, 1877, aged eighty-three years. She was the widow of Dr. Joseph Kittredge, Sen., and mother of Dr. Joseph Kittredge, Jr., whose lamented death followed within a year of her own. Her life was filled with active usefulness in the domestic circle and in the parish. She was for many years President of the Ladies' Benevolent Society, and her house was a centre of radiation of unobtrusive charities. A tribute to her memory by her pastor are the following lines: —

MRS. H. KITTREDGE.

Died July 1st, 1877; Aged 83 Years.

"O Mother! who hast bravely pass'd
Thy bound of four-score years;
We greet thee, in thy freedom vast,
Through mist of grateful tears.

"Thy path of life was nobly trod;
   With trust we follow on;
And plainer grows the road to God,
   Since thou the way hast gone.

"For, when the earth no longer gave
   Thy soul its vital breath,
And, thine immortal flame to save,
   Appeared God's servant, Death;

"We saw the beauty of thy life
   Diviner beauty crown,
As, calmly, thou renounc'dst the strife,
   And laidst thy burden down.

'Sweet burden! sweetly raised and borne:
   Faith, Sacrifice, and Love!
Its earthly weight no longer worn,
   That thou mightst rise above!

"To us the Comforter is come,
   And in the house abides:
O'er all the sanctities of Home
   The Mother still presides."

Miss Susan Osgood died November 12, 1878, aged eighty-four. The following is an extract from an unprinted memorial by her pastor:—

"A life such as that which during fourscore years and more has filled so remarkably both its unusual measure of years and its rare allotment of duty, though it has been largely withdrawn from public view, yet has an important part in the generations almost three, through which its pure influence has run. . . . . It is said that the loveliest flowers bloom on mountains, and the sweetest honey comes from hilly countries, and so it sometimes seems that the most beautiful characters and the gentlest spirits are nurtured among the rugged heights of solitary devotion, to which but few are called, and for which fewer still are the chosen of Nature, fitted by a temper of calmness, a love of self-abnegation and sacrifice to bear the cross of duty without claiming the crown of reward. She was so blithe of spirit, so elastic of body, so bright and cheery, beyond even many yet in the bloom of youth and unacquainted with sorrow, that we never called her old. . . . . And yet, although we saw not the usual appearance of it, we rejoice in the fact that she did live to be old ; that she came to her grave in a full age as a shock of corn cometh in in its season ! We are glad because she lifted up her face without spot ; because she was steadfast and did not fear ; because her age was clearer than the noonday ; because she shined forth and was ever as the morning. And though she scarcely wore the hoary head,[1] yet how perfectly was she entitled to its honors as a crown of glory when it is found (as in her case it could never have otherwise been) in the way of righteousness."

Having now traced the history of the First Church, from 1645 to the present time, we return to take up that of the Second, or South Church at the point to which we have carried it, the beginning of the present century.

The third minister of the South Parish, the REV. JUSTIN EDWARDS, was a strictly Calvinistic preacher. His theological belief was the result of the teaching of Andover Theological Seminary in its early days. He had been reared among the traditions and influences set in motion by the eminent divine of Northampton, and derived his early religious impressions from persons who had listened to the living words of the Rev. Jonathan Edwards. In regard to his settlement over the South Church, his biographer[2] says : " The church in Andover, to which the venerable Rev. Samuel Phillips had ministered almost sixty years from its formation, in 1711, and then the Rev. Jonathan French almost thirty-seven years, had now been nearly three years' destitute of a pastor. . . . . A somewhat serious division was existing in the congregation, turning on the vital points of evangelical truth. Mr. Abbot[3] and others were alarmed for the interests of the congregation, and after becoming satisfied of the qualifications of Mr. Edwards (then a student in the Seminary), the wish was expressed to him that he should leave the Semi-

---

[1] Miss Osgood, in the later years of her life, was almost totally deaf. With her lived her sister, seventy-four years old, totally blind. The death of the younger followed that of the elder within a few months.

These two sisters, daughters of Capt. Timothy Osgood, were the last of the many generations of the name who have lived on the ancient homestead.

[2] *Memoir* by Rev. William A. Halleck.

[3] Samuel Abbot, Esq., one of the founders of the Theological Seminary.

nary, though scarcely half through the regular course, assume the charge of a congregation of not far from two thousand souls scattered over a large territory, attempt to heal their divisions, and all with the expectation that his revered instructors and his fellow students would be among his constant hearers."

After considerable hesitation he accepted the proposal, although he at first declined on the ground that he was as yet "a mere child in theology."

He entered on a most laborious course of pastoral duty, often visiting ten or fifteen families in a day, reading the Bible and conducting family prayer, and taking the names of all the children, so that he might supply them with religious books and tracts. He also formed a society (1814) called the "Andover South Parish Society for the Reformation of Morals." This had in view the prevention of profanity, Sabbath breaking, and intemperance. Of the latter evil in the town of Andover Dr. Edwards's report of the year's work gives a graphic description : —

"As to intemperance, although some individuals are still reeling to and fro, and some families clothed in woe by this iniquity, yet the evil has been greatly lessened. A few years ago $15,000 were expended in this town for ardent spirits in a year, $8,000 more than was paid for the support of the gospel, and of all the schools, highways, State and county taxes, and all other town expenses. The people the last year did not probably expend one third of that sum. Ardent spirits, in the respectable part of the community, are becoming unfashionable, and dispensed with in social visits. Many workmen are employed on condition of refraining from ardent spirits, and it is found that better men are secured, and that they do more business, and in a better manner than before. The practice of taking wine at funerals is almost abolished, and it begins to be understood that ardent spirits, except in special cases, as a medicine, are not only entirely useless, but ruinous to the bodies and the souls of men."

Besides his efforts for the reformation of the adults of the parish, Dr. Edwards took systematic measures for the religious training of the children. He established a sort of circulating library of "small books" (as they are called in his record) in each of the district schools of the South Parish, giving books as rewards to the children who learned the largest number of Scripture texts and answers in the Catechism. The account of the method pursued in the distribution of these books, which were all of such religious and doctrinal teaching as Dr. Edwards believed correct, shows how truly parochial the public schools of the South Parish then were, according to the theory and practice of Dr. Edwards. No parish priest of the old country was more completely guardian and director of the day-schools than was the pastor of the South Church of Andover fifty years ago.

Besides these labors, Dr. Edwards was active in philanthropic work extending far beyond the bounds of his parish, embracing in its scope the world. He undertook, in 1821, the office of Corresponding Secretary of the New England Tract Society, with which three members of his parish were connected, Mr. Blanchard as treasurer, and Messrs. Flagg and Gould, printers and business agents. He was also connected with other missionary societies during his pastorate. He continued in charge of the South Church till 1827. Then, after a brief pastorate over the Salem Street Church in Boston, he engaged in active labors as General Agent and Secretary of the American Temperance Society. He visited prisons, hospitals, and private houses, exhorting and helping the unhappy inebriates. Six years of such self-denying labors he spent, an exile from his home and family, and a wanderer from place to place.

In 1836 Dr. Edwards was elected president of the Theological Seminary, in which office he continued six years. He was in this office the same indefatigable worker that he had been as a pastor, especially in the direction of promoting missionary organizations.

In 1842 he resigned his connection with the Seminary and undertook missionary labor, as agent of the American and Foreign Christian Union. In this he continued seven years. His latest years were devoted to writing a commentary on the Bible. His published works were numerous, chiefly tracts and sermons. His arduous labors undermined his constitution, and at sixty-six years of age, July 23, 1853, he died of inflammation of the brain. He was travelling in Virginia at the time of his death, with his daughter. The mournful journey home was accomplished August 1st, and on the following day the tired body was laid to rest in the burying ground of the Theological Seminary.

Dr. Edwards married, September 17, 1817, Miss Lydia Bigelow, daughter of Asa Bigelow, Esq., of Colchester, Conn. They had six children. The second son, Rev. Jonathan Edwards, was ordained minister of Woburn, September 7, 1848. The youngest daughter was married to the Rev. Thomas H. Haskell.

West Parish.

We now turn to the contemporary ministers of the Third Parish of Andover, which was created in 1826. In 1771, when there was talk of building a new meeting-house in the South Parish, some members were desirous to be set off to form a new parish. They represented that they were five or six miles from the meeting-house, and were unwilling to be taxed to pay for the building of a new house of worship, unless it could be located so as to accommodate them better. This division, at a time when a new minister (the Rev. Mr. French) was about to be settled, would be very inopportune. Accordingly, the idea of a new house was abandoned, and, to preserve harmony, it was agreed to defer it for ten years. When the subject came up again it was attended with great discussion and division of feeling. The inhabitants of the west part of the town were persistent to have the meeting-house placed more conveniently for them, or else to be set off. Mr. Isaac Osgood and others of the west part of the town, in 1788, petitioned the General Court for a division of the parish, and the setting off of a certain part, under the name of the Third Parish in Andover. The parish chose a committee, Mr. Samuel Phillips and others, to go before the General Court to oppose the granting of the petition. The committee's report, in the Parish Records, is that "the House had concurred with the Senate in allowing Isaac Osgood and others to withdraw their petition."

The parish afterward voted, in order to satisfy the disaffected and preserve the harmony as well as the unity of the parish, to discharge them from all obligations and taxes for the building of the new meeting-house, and yet to allow them the privilege of seats, provided they shall "surcease all opposition to the measures of the Parish for building the meeting House, and shall continue their union and harmony with the Parish, as it subsisted before the measures taken by them for building a meeting-house."

At last, in 1826, a division was peaceably effected and the parish lines defined and marked off. The West Parish included[1] 158 families: adults 544; children 326; inhabitants 870. The church was organized in November, 1826. A meeting-house of granite was built, — the "Stone Meeting-House." It is the oldest house of worship now standing in the limits of ancient Andover (North and South), except the chapel of the Theological Seminary, and is a substantial and really beautiful edifice for a country parish. It was dedicated and a sermon preached by Dr. Edwards, December 26, 1826.

The first pastor of the West Parish, the REV. SAMUEL C. JACKSON, D. D., was ordained June 6, 1827, being then twenty-five years old. He resigned his charge September 25, 1850, on account of infirm health, which made pastoral duties too onerous. He then became Assistant Secretary of the Massachusetts Board of Education and acting State Librarian. Before his formal dismissal from his parish he had entered (1849) on the duties of these offices of the Commonwealth. He discharged them with marked ability until within a short time before his death. This occurred July 26, 1878. He was seventy-six years old, having been born March 13, 1802. He was a native of Dorset, Vt., a graduate of Middlebury College and of Andover Theological Seminary. He received the degree of Doctor of Divinity from Middlebury College. He had been invited (1839) to accept the presidency of the college. Before Dr. Jackson decided to make the ministry his profession, he had spent two years in the study of law. This legal study gave him a wider range of interest and knowledge than is usually enjoyed by the strictly and technically instructed clergyman. In regard to this, says Professor

[1] *Historical Discourse*, 1827, by Rev. Samuel C. Jackson.

Park, in a Memorial of Dr. Jackson: "These two years of legal study and office-work had a visible effect on his subsequent life. They gave a kind of manliness to his methods of discourse. Some of his speeches in the town meetings of Andover, and before committees of the legislature at Boston, elicited a common remark that he was born to be a lawyer. His counsels on civil affairs, given at Andover and at the State House in Boston, have produced a visible effect, the value of which will not soon be forgotten."

Respecting Dr. Jackson's official labors in Boston the then Secretary of the Board of Education, Rev. Barnas Sears, LL. D., writes : " Few men in the State House were more consulted or more trusted than he. His personal influence was felt far beyond the line of his official duties. Men coming to Boston in the interest of colleges and other institutions, or of humane and Christian enterprises, would rarely fail to consult with him. His sound judgment, strict integrity, and interest in everything pertaining to the public welfare, gave him, in a high degree, the confidence of wise and good men."

During his life Dr. Jackson retained his residence in Andover. The services which he rendered to the town during the half-century that he was a citizen, are as inestimable as they were unostentatious. In his own parish his work was faithfully and well done. He built up a church on solid foundations and trained a community of exceptional sobriety and good sense. While he never lost relish for or influence in scholarly circles of theologic culture, he adapted himself with ease to the wants and peculiarities of a country parish, moulding and shaping it as few men have the skill to do, and keeping it alike from harmful conservatism and the dangers of instability and love of change.

Dr. Jackson was deeply interested in the educational institutions of Andover. He gave his time freely, while he was a pastor, to visiting the district schools. He was thirty years a trustee of the Theological Seminary and Phillips Academy, and fifty years trustee of Abbot Academy.

In his social and domestic life he was cheerful and genial as well as sincere and true. He had a playful humor and keen wit, but in indulging them never overstepped the bounds of ministerial dignity and decorum.

Dr. Jackson married (1829) Miss Caroline True, of Boston, a lady of fine culture and remarkable intellectual strength, peculiarly qualified to preside as the "minister's wife" in the parish of their common interest and charge. They had five children, two sons and three daughters.

The younger son, Mr. William Jackson, is in mercantile business in Boston.

The elder son, Samuel Charles Jackson, a young man of great promise and fine culture, died in 1869, at the age of twenty-eight. A memorial of his life (published for private distribution) was written by his sister, Susanna E. Jackson. Dr. Jackson's eldest daughter, Caroline R. Jackson, assisted him in the State Library. and during his failing health, and after his death, took a very prominent and responsible charge.

Miss Susanna E. Jackson was formerly teacher and sometime acting principal of Abbot Academy; also, preceptress in the Providence High School.

Miss Mary A. Jackson is married to the Rev. William H. Warren, Springfield, Ohio.

Among the more influential members of the West Church, in its early days, were the brothers Messrs. John and Peter Smith, and their partner in business, Mr. John Dove. Mr. Peter Smith is still [1] one of the deacons, having held the office forty-eight years. Deacon Solomon Holt has been in office forty-nine years, having succeeded his father, Deacon Solomon Holt, who died after three years' service. Deacon Jacob Dascomb was in office nearly forty-two years. Deacon Nathan Mooar has served twenty-nine years.

The Rev. George Mooar, D. D., pastor of the South Church, was reared under the ministry of Dr. Jackson, and was for a time an inmate of his household.

In the later years of his life, after his resignation of his parish, Dr. Jackson was a resident of the South Parish and a member of the Chapel Church. His grave[2] is in the burying ground of the Theological Seminary.

---

[1] Died July 6, 1880.
[2] A monument has been erected by the bequest of the late Mr. Hiram French, a former parishioner and member of the West Church.

The successor of Dr. Jackson, the second minister of the West Parish, was REV. CHARLES H. PEIRCE, a graduate of the Theological Seminary, 1850. He was ordained soon after his graduation. His ministry continued five years. He left many friends, when he resigned to go to a western State. He died, 1865, in Milbury, Mass., being then pastor of a church in that town.

The West Church is noticeable as still retaining the good old custom of long pastorates. Dr. Jackson was pastor twenty-three years (and except for infirm health his connection with the parish would not then have terminated), and the present [1] minister, the REV. JAMES H. MERRILL, has been also twenty-three years in office. There is something, in these days of change, peculiarly pleasant in such country parishes, where the minister grows old with his people, honored and beloved, known in every house of his parish by years of attendance on occasions of joy or sorrow (marriage, birth, and death), the counsellor of the young, the friend of those in middle life, and the consoler of the aged and feeble; his children growing up, going out from and coming back to the places of their early associations, welcome guests and happy visitors.

The three sons of Mr. Merrill received their preparatory education in the schools of Andover, and graduated at Amherst College.

Rev. James G. Merrill is pastor of a Congregational church at Davenport, Iowa.

Mr. William F. Merrill is Superintendent of the Toledo, Peoria, & Warsaw Railway.

Mr. George C. Merrill is Instructor in Natural Sciences, Phillips Academy, Andover.

[1] During the writing of the above the Rev. Mr. Merrill resigned his charge (December 1, 1879), on account of feeble health and the burden of so large a parish. The parish, in accepting his resignation, expressed deep regret at its necessity. Although Mr. Merrill has been forty years in the ministry, he is only sixty-five years old; after temporary rest it is hoped he will be able to resume in a measure pastoral labors. His loss will be deeply felt not only by his parish, but in the educational institutions of the town, especially in the Board of Trustees of the Punchard School. He has been longer in office than any other clergyman of the Board.

REV. AUSTIN H. BURR was installed April 29, 1880.

Miss Sarah E. Merrill, formerly a teacher in the Punchard High School, was married November, 1879, to the Rev. Joseph D. Wilson, Rector of St. John's Reformed Episcopal Church, Chicago.

Miss Lucia G. Merrill is a teacher in Straight University, New Orleans.

The Rev. Mr. Merrill married, 1839, Miss Lucia W. Griswold, daughter of Dr. Oliver Griswold, Fryeburg, Me. This lady's influence and her helpfulness in the social life of the parish were invaluable.

Having thus traced the history of the origin and progress of the West (or Third) Parish, of Andover, we now return to the point whence we digressed, — the South Church, in 1826, at the time of the creation of the new parish, and the close of Dr. Edwards's pastorate.

The successor of Dr. Edwards was the Rev. MILTON BADGER, D. D. He was ordained January 3, 1828. He was a native of Coventry, Conn. (the parish now called Andover), and was born May 6, 1800. He was the youngest of twelve children of Enoch and Mary Badger. He graduated at Yale College, 1823, studied at Andover Theological Seminary and at Yale Divinity School, while also performing the duties of tutor. Immediately upon his completing the course of study, he received the call to the vacant pulpit at Andover. Ordained January 3, 1828, he continued his pastorate until, in 1835, he accepted the office of Associate Secretary of the American Home Missionary Society. He was reluctant to resign his pastoral office, but was strongly urged to do so by the friends of the Missionary Society, who regarded him as remarkably fitted for this work. His success in this field of labor justified the expectations formed. A sketch [1] of his life and labors, published soon after his death, gives a graphic account of the changes which were wrought during the years of his missionary labor, 1835 to 1869, in the churches of the Western States and Territories, and his unremitting labors in his office. The sketch also quotes letters from several

[1] Sketch of Rev. Milton Badger, D. D., by Rev. David B. Coe, D. D., Congregational Quarterly, January, 1875.

eminent men, acquaintances of Mr. Badger, while he was pastor at Andover. Rev. Asa D. Smith, D. D., says: —

"Dr. Badger's name awakens in me a host of touching recollections. When I entered Andover Theological Seminary he was pastor of the old church in what was then the South Parish. I soon became intimately acquainted with him, and I noted with deep interest the singleness of purpose, directness, and earnestness with which he gave himself to his work. That was a time of remarkable revivals in religion, and he entered into them with all his heart. Protracted meetings, as they were called, were held in many places. I recall one held in his parish, the remembrance of which I shall carry to my grave — I trust, to heaven."

Rev. Leverett Griggs, D. D., says : —

"There was never greater prosperity in the Old South Church than when Milton Badger was its pastor. Students at Andover in 1831 will never forget the protracted meeting at which Beecher and Wisner preached, and the 'Judgment Anthem' was sung. It was in Dr. Badger's pulpit that Charles G. Finney was introduced to New England."

The Rev. George Mooar says in the "South Church Manual," that this ministry was a continuous revival; during the seven and a half years of its continuance, three hundred and thirty persons were added to the church, nearly all of whom joined by profession. "The memories of the pastor under whom these results were reached are still fresh and very precious in many families."

Dr. Badger died in Madison, Conn., March 1, 1873.

The wife of Dr. Badger, Mrs. Clarissa Munger Badger, of Madison, is still living, and is an occasional visitor to the place of her husband's only pastorate. Besides her labors as a minister's wife, Mrs. Badger did much in Andover to awaken and cultivate æsthetic and literary taste among the young people. She painted with much feeling and delicacy the wild flowers which are so abundant in Andover, and arranged her paintings in a volume, with appropriate poetical selections. Some of her books, given as souvenirs, are among the most highly prized volumes in the parish. At the age of seventy-five she still continues this pleasant employment.

Of Dr. Badger's five children only two lived to manhood.

These were sons, both of whom entered the medical profession, — Dr. George Badger died at Panama; Dr. William Badger lives at Flushing, Long Island.

The fifth minister of the South Church, Rev. LORENZO L. LANGSTROTH, was ordained May 11, 1836. After three years' service, finding his health insufficient for the discharge of parochial duties, he resigned and severed his connection with the church March 30, 1839.

He was born in Philadelphia, December 25, 1810, graduated at Yale College, 1831, studied theology at New Haven. After his dismission from the South Church, he was Principal, for a year, of Abbot Academy. He then removed from Andover. He now lives in Oxford, Ohio, where he has been engaged in raising bees. He has written some treatises on this branch of industry.

The sixth pastor of the South Church, Rev. JOHN L. TAYLOR, D. D., was installed July 18, 1839. He has been a resident of Andover forty years, having, since his resignation of his charge of the church, 1852, been connected with the Theological Seminary, first as treasurer of the Board of Trustees, and, since 1868,[1] Smith Professor and Lecturer on Pastoral Theology.

Dr. Taylor has taken a deep interest in the educational institutions of Andover, and made some valuable contributions to their history. He prepared the "Memorial of the Semi-Centennial Celebration of the Founding of the Theological Seminary" (1858), also delivered a "Memorial Discourse at the last Sabbath Afternoon Service in Bartlet Chapel," October 1, 1876, which was published by request of the Board of Trustees. But the work by which he is most widely known, and which takes rank among the standard works of American biography, is the " Life of Judge Phillips," or " A Memoir of his Honor Samuel Phillips, LL. D."

Dr. Taylor married Miss Caroline Lord Phelps, daughter of Col. Epaphras Lord Phelps, of East Windsor, Conn. She died April 3, 1868.

Mrs. Taylor's cordial interest and helpful service to the

[1] On account of feeble health, Dr. Taylor recently resigned his active connection with the Seminary, but is still retained as Professor Emeritus.

members of the parish were continued after the official connection of Dr. Taylor as pastor had ceased, and many mourned at her death the loss of a true friend and counsellor.

Three of the five children of Dr. and Mrs. Taylor died in childhood. The youngest son, Frederic H. Taylor, died at twenty-one. He had graduated at Phillips Academy and entered into mercantile business, having become a partner in the firm of Maxwell, Pratt & Co., New York, before he was twenty years of age. He left his entire property to the Theological Seminary toward the founding of a professorship, which is to bear his name. Dr. Taylor's eldest son, the Rev. John Phelps Taylor, is pastor of the Second Congregational Church in New London, Conn.

The seventh pastor of the South Church, REV. CHARLES SMITH, was installed October 26, 1852.

After a year's service he accepted a call to the Shawmut Church, in Boston, but, in 1861, returned to Andover, and was again installed as pastor of the South Church. He continued his second pastorate for fifteen years with acceptance, until impaired health compelled him to relinquish pastoral labor and seek recuperation in a European tour. He now resides in Andover. He was a native of Hatfield, Mass., graduate of Amherst College, 1842, of Andover Theological Seminary, 1845. His first ordination was at Warren, October 12, 1847.

Mr. Smith married Miss Caroline L. Sprague, daughter of Mr. Joseph E. Sprague, of Salem (High Sheriff of Essex County).

Their eldest son, Edwin Bartlett Smith, is in mercantile business in Boston.

The second son, Charles Sprague Smith, is pursuing a course of study in one of the universities of Germany.

The REV. GEORGE MOOAR, D. D., pastor of the South Church six years only, and then obliged to seek a more favorable climate, ought, nevertheless, to be named among the ministers of long residence, for there is probably none whose interests and sympathies are more completely identified with those of Andover. He was a native of the West Parish of Andover, trained under the ministry of its first pastor, Rev.

Dr. Jackson, who discovered and encouraged his taste for study, and gave him advice and aid in obtaining a liberal education and fitting for the gospel ministry.

Appreciating the honor of being called to the largest church in the town of his nativity (the second instance of such a call in the town in two hundred years), and inspired by the historic associations of the ancient parish, Mr. Mooar undertook, in addition to his onerous pastoral duties, the task of preparing a manual of the church, which should gather together and preserve the valuable information, fast sinking into oblivion on decaying gravestones, in musty manuscripts, and in the failing memories and traditions of members of the parish. This manual contains a history of the parish and of the church, lists of officers and members, more than two thousand names, with the dates of their reception and dismission, — the whole forming a lasting memorial of the church, and of the pastor who performed this labor of love.

Dr. Mooar was ordained October 10, 1855, dismissed March 27, 1861. He was fitted for college at Phillips Academy; graduated at Williams College, 1851; at Andover Theological Seminary, 1855. He is now pastor of the Congregational Church, Oakland, Cal., and Professor in the Pacific Theological Seminary.

During Dr. Mooar's pastorate of the South Church, and largely owing to his unremitting exertions, a new meeting-house was built (1860), the one now in use. It is one hundred and nine feet long, seventy-one feet wide; has pews in the body of the house for seven hundred persons, in the gallery for two hundred persons. The cost was about $20,000.

The pastorate of Mr. Mooar intervened between the two pastorates of the Rev. Mr. Smith, which have been already sketched.

The successor of Mr. Smith, the present pastor, REV. JAMES H. LAIRD, was ordained May 10, 1877. He is a native of Milton, Penn. He graduated, 1860, at Oberlin College, where he also studied theology.

The deacons of the South Church, during the one hundred and fifteen years in which it was the only church in the south part of the town (except that of the Theological Seminary), were John Abbot (elected 1711), William Lovejoy (1711), Nehemiah Abbot (1720), John Abbot, Jr. (1720), Isaac Abbot (1744), Joseph Abbot, Jr. (1744), John Dane, Jr. (1755), Hezekiah Ballard (1755), Joshua Holt (1766), Zebadiah Abbot (1785), Daniel Poor (1794), Isaac Abbot (1794), Nathan Abbot (1794), Abiel Pearson (1801), Mark Newman (1811), Zebadiah Abbot, Jr. (1813), Amos Blanchard (1825). Deacon Amos Abbot (1826), and Deacon Paschal Abbot (1827), were elected to take the place of those set off to the West Parish.

The historical sketches of the three territorial parishes of Andover are now completed. We have seen that the limits of the First Parish were coextensive with those of the town, that the town was taxed for the support of "The Church of Christ," until 1709, when two precincts were formed by topographical boundaries, and then each precinct or parish held its meetings and assessed its taxes for the support of its church. From 1710 to 1826 there were but two parish churches (North and South), and, in 1826, the West Parish was set off from the South Parish by topographical bounds. Also, some of the residents of the east part of Andover were, in 1740, by vote of the North Parish, and act of the General Court, "set off to the North Parish in Boxford, to all intents and purposes," paying their parish charges in that town, and relinquishing their rights and privileges in the North Parish of Andover.

The inhabitants of the town of Andover, as thus marked off, must attend divine worship at their respective meeting-houses; and if, as in time was allowed, any chose to go elsewhere "to meeting," they must still be assessed for the support of the Congregational church in the parish where they lived. This state of things was, as every reader of the church history of New England knows, far from satisfactory to many. Petition after petition was presented to the General Court and to the National Congress, by persons and religious bodies who were not in favor of such an established church; but although at times temporary relief was afforded, there was no real liberty, until, in 1833, the third article in the Bill of Rights was so amended that church and state were separated.

Since that time a great change has taken place. Parishes are no longer defined by surveyors with rod and chain. General Courts give themselves no concern who shall be assessed with the North, or who with the South Parish. Constables no longer carry men and women to jail for declining to pay their rates in support of the parish church, and holding worship in their own houses under the ministrations of a Separatist preacher. The lines of demarcation are now purely social and sectarian, and "Societies" have taken the place of "parishes."

The first intruder upon the charmed circle of the Andover parishes (after the Theological Seminary Church), was the Methodist Episcopal Church and Society, 1829. A meeting-house was built in the South Parish, and worship sustained for about ten years. The church was supplied with preachers by the New England Conference ; not having, during a large part of the time, a resident pastor. It had a feeble and struggling existence, and about 1840 was disbanded. The list of ministers is given in the tabular statement at the close of this chapter.

The next religious society was of the Baptist denomination. During the ministry of the first pastor of the South Parish, a citizen had made a vain attempt to secure exemption from taxation, in order to attend a Baptist meeting in a neighboring town, but without success. It was chiefly owing to the persistency of the Baptists, upheld first by the Episcopalians, and afterward by the Unitarian Congregationalists, that full liberty of conscience and worship had been secured, and the Bill of Rights had been amended so as to remove taxation, except voluntary, for the support of religious teachers and churches. The Baptists, therefore, made haste to avail themselves of their privileges, and to establish their houses of worship in the very centres of the Congregational Parishes, sometimes when their small numbers and limited means made the support of a minister difficult.

The Baptists at Andover formed a church in 1832, and, aided by their brethren elsewhere, built a meeting-house, the same now standing. They continued to sustain pastors and regular worship for about fifteen years. There was then only interrupted and infrequent service until 1857. At that time the scattered church members gathered together and united with the Baptist Church in Lawrence, under the charge of the Rev. Frank Remington, who held a series of revival meetings at Andover, and largely added to the membership of the church. In July, 1858, the church was reorganized, and the Rev. William S. McKenzie was installed as pastor. Since the resignation of this pastor there have been various supplies, and some settled pastors. The last pastor resident in Andover was Rev. H. R. Wilbur, 1876. A list of the pastors is given in the tabular statement at the end of this chapter.

The "Evangelical Church of North Andover," 1834, was the next religious organization made in the town. The establishment of the Theological Seminary had tended to bring questions of creed more prominently before the churches, and to emphasize the importance of doctrinal distinctions. The churches and individuals more and more came to consider it a duty to define their position, and to range themselves conspicuously on one side or the other of the denominational lines which, about the beginning of the present century, began to be sharply drawn. The questions which finally ended in the division of the Congregational body into Unitarian and Trinitarian were discussed with more and more earnestness and acrimony. The North Church, from the beginning, had been more Arminian than Calvinistic in tendency, although its pastors had associated in cordial fellowship with their brother clergy of Calvinistic creed, and even in the later time the names of Dr. Symmes and Mr. Loring were on the "Andover Association" (now of the Calvinistic and Trinitarian Congregational order). But a strong feeling had grown up in the town, that the First Church was not of the true faith, or supporting an Evangelical ministry, and that another church ought to be organized in the North Parish for the accommodation of individuals of the First Church who were not in sympathy with its prevailing tone, and for persons of Calvinistic faith who had become residents of the parish but had not removed their connection from the churches in the respective towns of their former residence.

The South and West churches, and the church of the Theological Seminary favored this movement, and aid was pledged by the Home Missionary Society. Subscriptions were obtained among the churches of the county, and a meeting-house was erected at North Andover, a little east of the North Meeting-house. This house of worship was dedicated September 3, 1834, and on the same day the "Evangelical Church" was organized. It consisted of thirty-one members. Seven (one male and six females) members were from the First Church, fourteen from the South Parish; the others were from churches in various towns, but probably nearly all residents of North Andover. The names of the male members were: Jedidiah Farnham (deacon of the First Church), Jesse Pierce, Joseph Cummings, Aaron Henry, Albert Hervey, David Gray, Jr., Timothy Stacy.

The church was supplied with preachers for some months by the neighboring churches. In 1835, September 9th, the first minister was installed, — the Rev. Jesse Page.[1] For several years the church received aid from the Home Missionary Society. Deacon Farnham was also a generous contributor, and about 1840 his son-in-law, Mr. George H. Gilbert, who had begun the manufacturing of machinery on the Cochichawick, afforded material aid to the Society. Subsequently, the Hon. George L. Davis, and successive members of the firm of Gilbert, Gleason & Davis, and Davis, Wiley & Stone, became liberal supporters of the church.

In 1865, the original house of worship at the centre of the town was abandoned, and a new and commodious church edifice was built in the machine-shop village. To this, Mr. George L. Davis contributed $10,000, Mr. John A. Wiley $5,000, and Mr. Joseph M. Stone, $5,000.

The Evangelical Church has had six pastors, all of whom have been able and godly ministers, influential not only in their own church and society, but an acquisition to the community.

The names of the ministers are as follows: Rev. Jesse Page, graduate of Dartmouth College, 1831, of Andover Theological Seminary, 1835, ordained at North Andover September 9,

---

[1] Now living in Atkinson, N. H.

1835; Rev. William T. Briggs, graduate of Oberlin Institute, 1844, ordained at North Andover November 4, 1846; Rev. Levi H. Cobb, graduate of Dartmouth College, 1854, Andover Theological Seminary, 1857, ordained at North Andover October 28, 1857; Rev. Benjamin F. Hamilton, graduate of Amherst College, 1861, Andover Theological Seminary, 1864, ordained at North Andover June 28, 1865; Rev. Rufus C. Flagg, graduate of Middlebury College, Vt., installed at North Andover September 26, 1872; Rev. George Pierce, graduate of Dartmouth College, 1863, installed at North Andover October 16, 1878.

In the year 1835, a new ecclesiastical element was introduced into Andover South Parish, and the anomaly of a "parish" within a parish created. This was the establishment of the Protestant Episcopal Church, and the formation of Christ Church and Parish. The name "Parish," borrowed from the English Church, where the parish system was like that which the New England Puritans adopted, had in this instance no significance of topographical bounds. The advent of the Methodists and the Baptists into the community where for nearly two hundred years the Congregational had been the sole church, had made some stir; but these bodies were small and of little influence compared with the other religious societies. The occasion was, however, one of considerable interest and importance when, on a Sunday in 1835, the Right Reverend B. B. Smith, of the Diocese of Kentucky, conducted a liturgical service in Andover. The establishment of this church was due to the efforts of Mr. Abraham Marland, the founder of the Marland Manufacturing Company. He was a native of Ashton Parish, Lancashire, England, and a zealous and conscientious adherent of the established church. In his youth, he had risked the disapproval of his employers and the opposition of his comrades, who were of a dissenting congregation, in order to obey his conviction of the duty of confirmation. After he was settled in business at Andover, he resolved, as he said, that there should be an Episcopal church in this village, "even if the whole cost of it were borne by himself alone."

In August, 1835, in compliance with a petition of twenty-three persons, a warrant was issued by a Justice for calling a Parish Meeting of the Protestant Episcopal Society of Andover. Subsequently, stock was subscribed to the amount of $6,000, in sixty shares.

Abraham Marland and Benjamin H. Punchard subscribed each ten shares.

Hobart Clark, John Marland, William S. Marland, and John Derby, each five shares.

Samuel S. Valpey, G. K. W. Gallishan, three shares.

John Flint, Samuel Gray, Nathan Frye, William P. Millett, Garret Wilson, were other subscribers at Andover. There were also some from Boston and vicinity.

Messrs. Abraham Marland, Samuel Merrill, Esq., and Samuel Gray, were chosen a committee to make arrangements for public worship, which was held in the Bank Hall, until the church was built. The church was consecrated October 31, 1837, and the first rector of the parish, Rev. Samuel Fuller, D. D., was instituted November 1, 1837. At the services were present not only the clergy of the Episcopal Church, but those of the town generally, and the professors in the Theological Seminary, among them the venerable Dr. Woods. President Justin Edwards, being detained at home by illness, wrote to the rector a letter[1] of regret, closing with the following expression of Christian sympathy:—

"Hoping that the Lord will be with you and grant you his presence, that he will fill your House with his Glory, and the hearts of all who worship in it with his love, I am truly yours."

Dr. Fuller resigned his charge in June, 1843, to accept a professorship in the Theological Seminary of the diocese of Ohio. In July, 1849, he was again invited to resume his charge. He remained rector of the parish till October, 1859, a total of sixteen years. He was one of the first trustees of the Punchard Free School, which was founded by the liberality of a member of his parish.

The church was supplied for a time by the Rev. George Packard, D. D., subsequently rector of Grace Church, Lawrence. In 1845 Rev. Henry Waterman, D. D., entered on

[1] See *A Historical Sketch of Christ Church*, by the Rev. Samuel Fuller, D. D.

the office of rector, and continued till 1849. The successor of the Rev. Dr. Fuller, in his second rectorship, was Rev. Benjamin N. Babbit (1860), followed by Rev. James Thompson (1869). The present rector, Rev. Malcolm Douglass, D. D., has served since April, 1875.

All the rectors of Christ Church have been gentlemen of scholarly culture and marked ability; and this church and parish has included some of the most honored and influential names of Andover,— citizens who have not only contributed to build up their own religious society, but have made large donations to the institutions of the town, as well as taken a prominent part in its business enterprises and among its professional men.

Mr. Abraham Marland, who has been called the father of this church, died February 20, 1849, aged seventy-seven years. The funeral services took place on the following Friday in the presence of a large congregation. The rector delivered a memorial address, which was subsequently printed. The particulars of Mr. Marland's business career will be noted in a future chapter. Respecting his Christian character and the termination of his long and useful life, his rector said, " It is quite unnecessary to make his Christian virtues, or his Christian deeds, the theme of a lengthened public eulogy. Our aged friend died where he had long lived and labored, and where his social and moral excellences had long commanded the respect and good will of all around him, ... and when the hour of his dissolution drew on, it was an hour of sweet, tranquil, childlike waiting for the summons to go. After a very gradual and lingering decay he sank gently and serenely to his final rest."

The Christ Church parsonage lot, and the rectory and the burial-ground, were the gifts of Mr. Marland and his son, Mr. John Marland.

Mr. Benjamin H. Punchard, son-in-law of Mr. Marland, was a liberal giver to Christ Church,[1] and left a testamentary bequest of seven thousand dollars. He also bestowed on missionary and benevolent societies an amount not less than

[1] During this writing the death of one of the oldest and most honored officers of Christ Church has occurred, the Hon. Francis Cogswell, warden for twenty years.

ten thousand dollars, besides making a bequest of seventy thousand dollars to found the Free School in Andover, which bears his name.

In 1837 a Universalist Society was established in the South Parish of Andover. Forty-six men, "friends of Christianity and believers in the final holiness and happiness of all mankind, through our Lord and Saviour Jesus Christ" (as is stated in the Society's records), subscribed the Constitution, which was adopted November 5, 1837. The committee who drafted this were John Foster, 3d, Seth Chase, Alonzo Smith.

The object of the Society was declared to be "the promotion of truth and morality among its members, and also the world at large, and as the gospel of the Lord Jesus Christ is calculated above all truth to inspire the heart with the emotions of benevolence and virtue, this Society shall deem it one of its main objects to support the preaching of this gospel, according to the Society's ability, and to aid in spreading a knowledge of it among men."

The Society records state that the committee had received "*no answer*" to their application to the bank directors for the use of the Masonic Hall, as a place for public worship, and that "*appearances indicate they would not.*" They, therefore, voted to build a house of worship at a cost of not more than $2,500. This meeting-house stood at the present corner of Main Street and Punchard Avenue, and has been latterly used as a school-house, and is now removed and sold to private parties.

The Universalist Society sustained worship with considerable regularity for about twenty-five years. Its Ladies' Aid Society continues to exist, but otherwise the Society is extinct.[1] The list of ministers is given at the end of this chapter, in the tabular statement. The first was Rev. Joseph Grammar, ordained October 3, 1838. The last, the Rev. Hiram A. Philbrook, installed 1868. The minister longest in office, also town clerk in 1855, and who has returned to live

[1] Services have been recently held, conducted by the Rev. Varnum Lincoln, and a large attendance indicates the revival of the society.

in Andover, is Rev. Varnum Lincoln. He resigned, 1856. The second pastor, Rev. S. P. Landers, published a tract on some doctrines of Universalism in reply to Professor Stuart.

Since 1840 the following churches have been organized in Andover (North and South Parishes): Methodist Episcopal Church, North Andover (1845); Free Christian Church, Andover (1846); Protestant Episcopal Church, Ballardvale (1850); Methodist Episcopal, Ballardvale (1850); Union Congregational, Ballardvale (1850); Roman Catholic Church, Andover[1] (1852); Roman Catholic Church, North Andover[1] (1868).

The many ministers of the Methodist Church and their short stay make it impossible to particularize in regard to them. Their names are given in the tabular statement. The Methodist denomination has steadily gained ground, and in numbers and influence is an acknowledged power in the community.

The Free Christian Church, organized 1846, received its name from various circumstances of its origin; it took an active stand in favor of freedom in the anti-slavery movement; some of its members were by early association attached to the Free Church of Scotland, and liked the old name; the seats in the meeting-house were free to all; and finally, the church itself was at the outset independent of other organizations, and not in ecclesiastical association with the Congregational churches. Nearly half its members were from the former Methodist Society in Andover, and the church edifice was the Methodist Meeting-house, removed and remodelled.

The prominent movers in the organization of this church, and zealous pioneers in the anti-slavery cause, were the partners, Messrs. John Smith[2] and John Dove. To the labors of the last named, and his eminent virtues, an appropriate tribute was paid by his pastor, Rev. G. F. Wright, in a memorial discourse, November 26, 1870. Although a notice of his life is

---

[1] The town being divided 1855, the South and West Parishes constitute "Andover."

[2] Mr. Smith is still actively connected with the church, and, therefore, no mention need be made of his many benefactions.

given in connection with the manufactures of Andover, the following extract from this memorial may here be made: —

"When now, at the close of his earthly career, we are led to consider the large space he occupied in the business enterprises of Andover, and the extent to which he has aided the religious and educational institutions of the place, and when we remember how much the honor of our town has been enhanced by his charities abroad, we cannot avoid admiring the providence of God which brought him here and prepared the way for his success."

After detailing the history of Mr. Dove's life, and the remarkable chain of circumstances — "providences" — which led him to Andover, and resulted in his successful business career, his pastor speaks of his moral and religious character, and especially of one characteristic, his ready sympathy and generous sensibilities, leading him sometimes to an extreme of benevolence: —

"He was naturally disposed to trust his fellow-men. He counted in business on the triumph of the better qualities of human nature. Indeed, his generosity of disposition was such, that he was no doubt sometimes imposed upon by beggars. On one occasion, when wishing to go out upon the street, he found himself without an overcoat fit for the occasion; for, as he came in at the door, he had slipped his best one on to the back of a shivering tramp who appealed for his aid. At another time, and for a similar reason, he found himself with nothing but his broadcloth suit when business called for a coat of gray."

Mr. Dove was a constant and generous contributor to the Temperance Society of the State, and to those societies which furnish the rudiments of education to the freedmen of the South; but his largest gifts were to schools of a higher grade, and to the libraries of his own town. He gave largely to help establish a school in his native town in Scotland. A gift of seven thousand dollars attested his interest in those who read the books in the Memorial Hall Library, in Andover. But the work of the ministry, and of higher theological education, was most prized and assisted by him. . . . . He gave several thousand dollars to the Chicago Theological Seminary, and smaller gifts to Oberlin College, and thirty thousand dollars to the Library of the Andover Theological Seminary.

Among the other principal original members and supporters of this church were Dea. James Smith, Dea. Joshua Blanchard, Dea. Ammon Russell, Dea. Thomas Clark, Mr. William G. Donald, Dea. George Foster.

The church has had eight pastors, whose names are given in the tabular statement. The one longest in office, the present pastor, Mr. George Frederick Wright, was installed 1872. Mr. Wright has, in addition to his ministerial labors, made a series of geological explorations in Andover and vicinity, which have added materially to scientific knowledge. The results of these he has embodied in papers published by the Boston Society of Natural History, "Remarkable Gravel Ridges of the Merrimack Valley," and "The Kames and Moraines of New England;" also, recently published, a valuable book, entitled "The Logic of Christian Evidences."

The next religious organization was in the Ballardvale district, — the Protestant Episcopal Church, organized 1846. This was continued only a few months, and as there were not persons enough in the village to support an Episcopal Church, a Union Church of the various denominations was formed. Finally, in 1850, two societies were organized, the Union Congregational and the Methodist Episcopal.

The pastor of the Union Church (ultimately Congregational), from the first was the Rev. Henry S. Greene. He has been nearly forty years in office. He was born 1807, graduated at Amherst College, 1834, and at Andover Theological Seminary, 1837, was thirteen years' minister in Lynnfield, having been forty-two years a preacher of the gospel.

He married, 1840, Miss Mary P. Abbot, daughter of Capt. Stephen Abbot, of Andover, who died 1878, aged seventy-one. All their children are dead. The eldest, Henry M. Greene, died within a little over a year after his graduation at Amherst College. The aged minister [1] is thus, to use his own words, "left all alone — yet not alone."

The Methodist Episcopal Church of Ballardvale has been supplied in part by preachers from other towns, and has had some resident pastors.

[1] Rev. Mr. Greene died June 11, 1880.

The Roman Catholic faith was brought to Andover in 1755 (if not before), by the French Acadians, but it did not then obtain any hold, the Puritan prejudice against it being very strong.

In 1852 the Church of St. Augustine was established at Andover, the Fathers of the Order of Saint Augustine, at Lawrence, conducting services. About 1862 there were resident pastors. The present pastor is the Rev. Father Maurice J. Murphy. This society are building a new church to be completed in the summer of 1881.

In 1868 the Church of St. Michael was established at North Andover. The ministers are the Fathers of the O. S. A., Lawrence.

In the later period, the number of students for the ministry has increased with the population. Following are the names which have been collected, though probably these do not include all who have been residents, or natives of the two towns of Andover and North Andover: —

REV. JOSHUA CHANDLER (son of Abiel Chandler), graduate of Harvard College, 1807; ordained at Swanzey, N. H.; pastor at Bedford and Pembroke; died, 1854.

REV. JACOB HOLT (son of Dane Holt), graduate of Dartmouth College, 1813; pastor at Brookline, N. H.; died at Ipswich.

REV. PETER OSGOOD (son of Peter Osgood, Esq.), graduate of Harvard College, 1814; was ordained minister of Sterling, N. H., 1819; resigned charge on account of failing health, 1839; resident at North Andover; died, 1865, aged seventy-two.

PROF. SAMUEL PHILLIPS NEWMAN (a son of Dea. Mark Newman), was a graduate of Harvard College, 1816; student in Andover Theological Seminary; Professor in Bowdoin College, 1820–1839; died, 1842.

REV. ASA CUMMINGS, D. D. (son of Dea. Asa Cummings, North Andover), was a graduate of Harvard College, 1817; student in Andover Theological Seminary, 1820; minister of North Yarmouth, 1821; editor of the "Christian Mirror," Portland, Me. 1826–1855; died on a sea voyage, 1856, aged sixty-six.

REV. JOHN R. ADAMS, D. D. (son of Mr. John Adams, Principal of Phillips Academy), graduate of Yale College, 1821; Andover Theological Seminary, 1826; ordained, 1831, Presbyterian Church, Londonderry, N. H.; minister at Great Falls, Brighton, and Gorham, Me.; chaplain of Fifth Maine Regiment and One Hundred and Twenty-first New York Regiment, 1861–1865; died at Northampton, Mass., 1866, aged sixty-four.

CHURCHES AND MINISTERS, ETC.   497

PROF. STEPHEN FOSTER (son of John Foster, North Andover) graduated at Dartmouth College, 1821; Andover Theological Seminary, 1824; ordained, 1824; home missionary in Texas, Professor of Latin and Greek, and President of East Tennessee College; died at Knoxville, in 1835, aged thirty-seven.

REV. NATHANIEL GAGE (son of Nathaniel Gage, North Andover) was a graduate of Harvard College, 1822; tutor in the college; ordained minister of Unitarian Church, Nashua, N. H., 1827; preached in Haverhill, Mass., Petersham, Westborough, and Ashby; died at Cambridge, 1861.

REV. AMOS BLANCHARD, D. D. (son of Dea. Amos Blanchard), was a graduate of Yale College, 1826; student of theology at Yale Theological School and at Andover Theological Seminary, 1829; ordained minister of First Church, Lowell, 1829; of Kirk Street Church, Lowell, 1845-1870; died, 1870, aged sixty-three.

REV. WILLIAM ADAMS, D. D., LL. D. (son of Mr. John Adams, Principal of Phillips Academy), born 1807; fitted at Phillips Academy; graduated at Yale College, 1827; Andover Theological Seminary, 1830; ordained, 1831, Brighton, Mass.; pastor of Madison Square Presbyterian Church, New York, from 1834 till his death, August 31, 1880

REV. LEONARD WOODS, D. D. (son of Professor Woods), fitted at Phillips Academy; graduate of Union College, 1827; Andover Theological Seminary, 1830; instructor in Hebrew, Andover, 1830; Professor of Sacred Literature, Bangor Theological Seminary, 1835-1839; President of Bowdoin College, 1839-1866; died in Boston, December 24, 1878, aged seventy-one years, six months.

ISAAC FOSTER (son of John Foster, North Andover) was a graduate of Dartmouth College, 1828; student two years in Andover Theological Seminary; teacher, Portland, Me., Exeter, N. H., Kingston, R. I., 1830-1839; not ordained; resident of North Andover.

REV. JOSHUA EMERY (son of Joshua Emery), graduate of Amherst College, 1831; Andover Theological Seminary, 1834; ordained minister at Fitchburg; pastor at North Weymouth.

ANDREW PETERS (son of John Peters, of North Andover) was a student of Harvard College in the class which graduated 1832. He was studying with a view to fitting for the Unitarian Ministry, but died in 1831 of a fever brought on by a pedestrian tour of the White Mountains.

REV. DANIEL BATES WOODS (son of Professor Woods) was a graduate of Union College, 1833; of Andover Theological Seminary, 1837; ordained, 1839; pastor of Presbyterian Church, Springwater, N. Y.; pastor in Virginia, 1845; teacher in Pennsylvania, Ohio, and Missouri.

REV. SERENO T. ABBOT (son of Asa Abbot), graduate of Amherst College, 1833; Andover Theological Seminary, 1836; ordained, 1837, minister of Seabrook, N. H.; died, 1855, aged forty-nine.

REV. SAMUEL H. EMERY (son of Joshua Emery) was a graduate of Amherst College, 1834; Andover Theological Seminary, 1837; ordained, 1837, at Taunton, Mass. ; pastor at Bedford, Taunton, Quincy, Ill., Providence, R. I., 1869.

EDWARD BLANCHARD (son of Dea. Amos Blanchard) was a student in Yale College, 1834, intending to fit for the ministry; died, 1834, aged twenty.

REV. WILLIAM JOHN NEWMAN (son of Dea. Mark Newman) was a student of Yale College and Bangor Theological Seminary, 1834; ordained at Stratham, N. H., 1836; pastor in York, Me. ; died, 1850.

REV. WILSON INGALLS (son of Ezra Ingalls) graduated at Union College, 1836; was tutor in the college one year; pastor of Dutch Reformed Church in the State of New York, at Glenville, N. Y., 1854.

REV. HENRY CALLAHAN (son of Robert Callahan), born at North Andover, graduate of Union College, 1836; Andover Theological Seminary, 1840 ; pastor of Presbyterian Church, Niagara Falls, N. Y., 1845-1849 ; Oxford, N. Y., 1851-1861.

REV. CHARLES S. PUTNAM (son of Mr. Simeon Putnam, Principal of Franklin Academy, North Andover) graduated at Union College, 1838; studied divinity at Episcopal Seminary, Virginia, and Andover Theological Seminary, 1846 ; rector at Woodbury, Derby, Warehouse Point, and Wallingford, Conn.; Church of the Redeemer, Brooklyn, N. Y.; died at Hanover, N. H., 1860, aged forty-two.

REV. DANIEL EMERSON (son of Professor Emerson), graduate of Western Reserve College, 1839 ; Andover Theological Seminary, 1842; ordained, 1844; missionary and teacher in the West, 1845-1855.

REV. THOMAS E. FOSTER (son of Capt. Thomas Foster) graduated at Yale College, 1840 ; was teacher in Phillips Academy ; graduate of Andover Theological Seminary, 1848 ; preached in various places ; not ordained ; died at Andover, 1851, aged thirty.

REV. JOSEPH W. BURTT studied privately ; was ordained in State of New York, 1843 ; pastor of Baptist Church, North Chelmsford.

REV. JONATHAN EDWARDS (son of President Justin Edwards) graduated at Yale College, 1840; Andover Theological Seminary, 1847; was ordained minister of Woburn, 1848 ; pastor in Rochester, N. Y., Dedham, Mass., Grantville, 1879.

PROF. JOSEPH EMERSON (son of Professor Emerson) graduated at Yale College, 1841 ; studied in Andover Theological Seminary, 1845 ; was Professor of Ancient Languages in Beloit College, 1848, to the present time.

REV. EDWARD F. ABBOT (son of Dea. Zebadiah Abbot) studied theology at Gilmanton, N. H.; was ordained minister of church in Milton, N. H., 1846, at Dublin, N. H., 1855, at Ipswich, Mass., 1855.

REV. JOHN N. PUTNAM (son of Mr. Simeon Putnam, Principal of Franklin Academy, North Andover), graduate of Dartmouth College, 1843; of Andover Theological Seminary, 1849; Professor of Greek, Dartmouth College ; ordained, 1852 ; died on a sea voyage, 1863, aged forty-one.

REV. CHARLES A. AIKEN, D. D. (son of Mr. John Aiken), graduate of Dartmouth College, 1846; teacher in Phillips Academy (1848-49); graduate of Andover Theological Seminary, 1853; studied in the Universities of Berlin and Halle; was ordained, 1854, at Yarmouth, Me.; Professor in Dartmouth College and New Jersey College, 1859-1869; President of Union College; now Professor in Princeton Theological Seminary.

REV. DANIEL T. NOYES, graduate of Yale College, 1847; Andover Theological Seminary, 1851; ordained at Dorchester, 1853; pastor in Wisconsin; Lieutenant Sixth Wisconsin Battery; killed in action at Corinth, Miss., October 4, 1862, aged thirty-eight.

REV. SAMUEL EMERSON (son of Professor Emerson), graduate of Yale College, 1848; of Andover Theological Seminary, 1851; preached at Enfield, N. H.; was a teacher and missionary in Virginia, 1856-1858; resident in various places.

REV. GEORGE MOOAR, D. D. (son of Benjamin Mooar), was a graduate of Williams College, 1851; Andover Theological Seminary, 1855; pastor of South Church, Andover; pastor at Oakland, Cal., 1861; Professor of Theology in the Pacific Theological Seminary.

PETER SMITH BYERS (son of James Byers) was confirmed in Christ Church, 1843; graduated at Harvard College, 1851; was teacher of the classics in Phillips Academy, 1851, Principal of Abbot Academy, 1853, and Principal elect of the Punchard Free School. He died March, 1856, aged twenty-nine.

MR. OSGOOD JOHNSON (son of Mr. Osgood Johnson, Principal of Phillips Academy) graduated at Dartmouth College, 1852; studied in Andover Theological Seminary two years; was Principal of High Schools at Worcester and at Cambridge; died 14th April, 1857, aged twenty-five.

JOHN FRYE (son of Mr. Enoch Frye, of North Andover), a student in Phillips Academy; died July 18, 1853, aged twenty years.

REV. STEPHEN BARKER (son of Henry Barker, of North Andover) was a graduate of Harvard Divinity School, 1856; ordained at Leominster, 1857; chaplain of a Massachusetts regiment three years; one year agent of the Sanitary Commission; has relinquished the ministry.

REV. JOHN F. AIKEN (son of Mr. John Aiken), graduate of Dartmouth College, 1858; teacher in Phillips Academy; counsellor-at-law in New York; studied for the ministry in Andover Theological Seminary; preached at Pawlet, Vt., and Chichester; recently deceased.

REV. SIMON G. FULLER (son of Rev. Dr. Fuller), graduate of Harvard College, 1858; of Trinity College, 1864; rector at Syracuse, N. Y.; died, 1872.

REV. EDWIN S. BEARD (son of Rev. Mr. Beard, resident at Andover) graduated at Yale College, 1859; Andover Theological Seminary, 1862; was ordained, 1863; pastor of the Second Presbyterian Church, Easthampton, L. I.; now, 1879, Brooklyn, Conn.

REV. THADDEUS H. BROWN (resident with relatives at Andover) graduated at Yale College, 1860; Andover Theological Seminary, 1864; was ordained, 1866, North Woodstock, Conn.; died, 1868, aged thirty.

REV. WILLIAM EDWARDS PARK (son of Professor Park) graduated at Yale College, 1861; Andover Theological Seminary, 1867; ordained pastor of the Central Church, Lawrence, 1867; now pastor in Gloversville, N. Y.

REV. ALLEN C. BARROWS (son of Professor Barrows), graduate of Western Reserve College, 1861; served in the Eighteenth United States Infantry, 1861-1864; teacher at Phillips Academy, 1864-1866; Professor in Western Reserve College, 1866-1871; ordained pastor of church, Kent, Ohio, 1871; still in office.

REV. JOHN PHELPS TAYLOR (son of Professor Taylor) graduated at Yale College, 1862; Andover Theological Seminary, 1868; ordained pastor of the South Church in Middletown, Conn., 1868; now pastor in New London, Conn.

REV. WILLIAM H. BEARD (son of Rev. Mr. Beard), student at Union Theological Seminary; resident licentiate of Andover Theological Seminary, 1866; pastor South Killingly, Conn.

REV. JAMES G. MERRILL (son of the Rev. James H. Merrill, of the West Church) graduated at Amherst College, 1863; at Andover Theological Seminary, 1866; ordained pastor of church in Mound City, Kansas, 1867; now pastor in Davenport, Iowa.

REV. JOHN H. MANNING (son of Thomas Manning), graduate of Andover Theological Seminary, 1864; home missionary, Tennessee, 1865; pastor at Brookline, N. H., 1867; died August 19, 1868, aged forty-four.

REV. DAVID MCGREGOR MEANS (son of Rev. James Means), graduate of Yale College, 1868; student of Andover Theological Seminary; Professor of Logic and Philosophy in Middlebury College.

REV. DAVID S. MORGAN, student in Andover Theological Seminary, 1866; ordained at Worthington, Mass., 1867; preached in Wisconsin and Iowa; recently deceased.

MR. WILLIAM W. EATON (son of Mr. James Eaton, principal of the English Department of Phillips Academy), a graduate of Amherst College, 1868; student of Andover Theological Seminary, 1869; temporary instructor in the Classics, Phillips Academy; student three years in Germany; assistant to the Associate Professor of Sacred Literature in the Theological Seminary.

REV. D. J. STONE (son of Nahum Stone), ordained at Quincy Point, May, 1868; died May 18, 1871, aged thirty-one; a member of the Baptist Church, Andover.

REV. MOSES STUART PHELPS (son of Professor Phelps), a graduate of Yale College, 1869; of Andover Theological Seminary, 1872; Acting Professor of Philosophy, Smith College, 1879.

REV. LAWRENCE PHELPS (son of Professor Phelps) studied with private instruction, and in part at Andover Theological Seminary; ordained pastor in Barton, Vt., 1878.

REV. E. WINCHESTER DONALD (son of William C. Donald), graduate of Amherst College, 1869; of Union Theological Seminary, 1874; rector of the Church of the Intercession, Washington Heights, N. Y.

REV. CHARLES H. ABBOT (son of Henry W. Abbott), graduate of the Punchard High School and Chicago Theological Seminary, 1875; ordained in Huntley, Ill., 1876; now in West Springfield, Mass.

REV. GEORGE H. GUTTERSON (son of George Gutterson), graduate of Andover Theological Seminary, 1878; missionary of the American Board in India.

REV. FATHER DANIEL D. REGAN (son of John Regan) graduated at the Punchard High School; studied at Villanova College and Seminary, 1870; is in charge of the Catholic Church of Waterford, N. Y.

TABULAR STATEMENT OF PASTORS AND CHURCHES.

North Parish, First Church organized October 24, 1645.

Names of Pastors.	Date of Installation.	Close of Pastoral Relation.
Rev. John Woodbridge	October 24, 1645	1647.
Rev. Francis Dane	1648	February 17, 1697.
Rev. Thomas Barnard	February, 1682	October 13, 1718.
Rev. John Barnard	April 8, 1719	June 14, 1757.
Rev. William Symmes, D. D.	November 1, 1758	May 3, 1807.
Rev. Bailey Loring	September 19, 1810	February 22, 1850.
Rev. Francis C. Williams	February 22, 1850	May 27, 1856.
Rev. Charles C. Vinal	May 6, 1857	April 15, 1870.
Rev. John H. Clifford	August 29, 1871	

South Parish, Church organized October 17, 1711.

Names of Pastors.	Date of Installation.	Close of Pastoral Relation.
Rev. Samuel Phillips	October 17, 1711	June 5, 1771.
Rev. Jonathan French	September 23, 1772	July 28, 1809.
Rev. Justin Edwards, D. D.	December 2, 1812	October 1, 1827.
Rev. Milton Badger, D. D.	January 3, 1828	October 4, 1835.
Rev. Lorenzo L. Langstroth	May 11, 1836	March 30, 1839.
Rev. John L. Taylor, D. D.	July 18, 1839	July 19, 1852.
Rev. Charles Smith	October 28, 1852	November 28, 1853.
Rev. George Mooar	October 10, 1855	March 27, 1861.
Rev. Charles Smith	December 18, 1861	April 20, 1876.
Rev. James H. Laird	May 10, 1877	

Church of the Theological Seminary.

Organized in the autumn of 1816. Reorganized (a second church in place of the first) November 1, 1865.

Pastors, the Professors in the Seminary.

West Parish, Church organized December 5, 1826.

Names of Pastors.	Date of Installation.	Close of Pastoral Relation.
Rev. Samuel C. Jackson, D. D.	June 6, 1827	September 25, 1850.
Rev. Charles H. Peirce	October 9, 1850	January 1, 1855.
Rev. James H. Merrill	April 30, 1856	December 1, 1879.
Rev. Austin H. Burr	April 29, 1880	

Methodist Episcopal Church (Andover), organized 1829.

Rev. W. Emerson, } 1829.
Rev. Nathan R. Spaulding,
Rev. Selah Stocking, 1830.
Rev. R. Spaulding, } 1831.
Rev. Mark Staple,
Rev. Le Roy Sunderland, } 1832.
Rev. C. S. M. Reading,
Rev. P. Crandall, } 1833.
Rev. R. D. Easterbrook,
Rev. S. W. Wilson, } 1834.
Rev. D. Culver,
Rev. S. W. Wilson, } 1835.
Rev. E. H. Downing,
Rev. A. Kent, 1836.
Rev. Abraham D. Merrill, 1837.
Rev. Amos Binney, 1838.
Various preachers, 1839.
Rev. Zechariah A. Mudge, 1840–1841.

Baptist Church, organized October 3, 1832.

Names of Pastors.	Date of Installation.	Close of Pastoral Relation.
Rev. James Huckins	August 28, 1834	October 25, 1835.
Rev. George J. Carleton	June 15, 1836	October 5, 1838.
Rev. Nathaniel Hervey	August 11, 1839	1841.
Rev. Benjamin S. Cobbett	February 8, 1842	October 5, 1847.
Rev. Silas B. Randall	October 1, 1848	October, 1849.
Rev. William S. McKenzie	July 28, 1858	December, 1860.
Rev. Charles K. Colver	August, 1861	November, 1863.
Rev. Daniel C. Litchfield	February, 1864	May, 1868.
Rev. H. R. Wilbur	April, 1872	October, 1876.
Various preachers	1876	1879.

Evangelical Church of North Andover, organized September 3, 1834.

Names of Pastors.	Date of Installation.	Close of Pastoral Relation.
Rev. Jesse Page	September 9, 1835	June 7, 1843.
Rev. William T. Briggs	November 4, 1846	May 1, 1855.
Rev. Levi H. Cobb	October 28, 1857	October 3, 1864.
Rev. Benjamin F. Hamilton	June 28, 1865	September 13, 1871.
Rev. Rufus C. Flagg	September 26, 1872	October 31, 1877.
Rev. George Pierce	October 16, 1878	

Protestant Episcopal (Christ) Church, organized August 6, 1835.

Names of Pastors.	Date of Installation.	Close of Pastoral Relation.
Rev. Samuel Fuller, D. D.	October 1, 1837	August, 1843.
Rev. George Packard, D. D. (Minister)	September 1, 1843	1845.
Rev. Henry Waterman	November, 1845	July 31, 1849.
Rev. Samuel Fuller, D. D.	October 1, 1849	October 1, 1859.
Rev. Benjamin B. Babbit	April 1, 1860	October 26, 1868.
Rev. James Thompson	November 10, 1869	July 27, 1874.
Rev. Malcolm Douglass, D. D.	April, 1875	

Universalist Society, organized November 15, 1837.

Names of Pastors.	Date of Installation.	Close of Pastoral Relation.
Rev. Joseph Grammar	October 3, 1838	July 14, 1839.
Rev. S. P. Landers	September 15, 1839	November 29, 1840.
Rev. William H. Griswold	April 1, 1841	1842.
Rev. Lyman W. Dagget	April 1, 1843	1845.

Names of Pastors.	Date of Installation.	Close of Pastoral Relation
Rev. H. C. Hodgdon (Supply)		
Rev. Varnum Lincoln	July, 1851	May, 1856.
Rev. Hiram Philbrook (Supply)	April, 1858	April, 1859.
Various supplies	1860	1865.
Rev. Varnum Lincoln (Supply)	1879.	

Methodist Episcopal Church (North Andover), organized 1845.

Rev. Stephen G. Hiler, 1845–1846.	Rev. William M. Hubbard, 1862–1863.
Rev. James Dean, 1846–1847.	Rev. John Middleton, 1863–1864.
Rev. William Pentecost, 1849–50.	Rev. George E. Chapman, 1864–1866.
Rev. S. S. Cook, 1850–1851.	Rev. Nathaniel Bemis, 1866–1868.
Rev. Ichabod Marcy, 1851–1853.	Rev. John T. Day, 1868–1871.
Rev. John C. Smith, 1853–1855.	Rev. Linus Fish, 1871–1873.
Rev. William F. Lacount, 1855–1857.	Rev. Joseph W. Lewis, 1873–1875.
Rev. Nathan A. Soul, 1857–1858.	Rev. Burtes Judd, 1875–1876.
Rev. Rodney Gage, 1858–1860.	Rev. William P. Blackmer, 1876–1879.
Rev. George Sutherland, 1860–1862.	Rev. Joseph Candlin, 1879.

Ballardvale. Protestant Episcopal Emanuel Church, organized August 7, 1846.

Names of Pastors.	Date of Installation.	Close of Pastoral Relation.
Rev. W. H. Moore	November 9, 1848	August, 1849.

Ballardvale. Union Congregational Church. Society organized 1850; Church, December 31, 1854.

Names of Pastors.	Date of Installation.	Close of Pastoral Relation.
Rev. Henry S. Greene	April 1, 1855	June 11, 1880.

Ballardvale. Methodist Episcopal Church, organized February, 1850.

Rev. S. G. Hiler.	Rev. John Mansfield.	Rev. A. M. Osgood.
Rev. S. S. Cook.	Rev. A. O. Hamilton.	Rev. G. Osgood.
Rev. A. F. Bailey.	Rev. Edward B. Otheman.	Rev. T. Parkinson.
Rev. John B. Foot.	Rev. G. Ellis.	Rev. E. Leesman.
Rev. O. S. Horne.	Rev. W. F. Lacount.	Rev. W. Buzzell.
Rev. Pliny Wood.	Rev. John S. Day.	Rev. W. Wignall.
Rev. M. F. Warren.	Rev. H. D. Weston.	Rev. W. Wilkie.
Rev. Joseph Scott.	Rev. J. Short.	

Free Christian Church, organized May 7, 1846.

Names of Pastors.	Date of Installation.	Close of Pastoral Relation
Rev. Elijah C. Winchester	February 1, 1846	September 10, 1848.
Rev. Sherlock Bristol	October 16, 1848	October 24, 1849.
Rev. William B. Brown	August 31, 1850	April 1, 1855.
Rev. Caleb E. Fisher	June 1, 1855	May 4, 1859.
Rev. Stephen C. Leonard	August 16, 1859	November 5, 1865.
Rev. James P. Lane	April 4, 1866	March 30, 1870.
Rev. Edwin S. Williams	September 1, 1870	April 4, 1872.
Rev. George Frederick Wright	June 10, 1872.	

504   HISTORICAL SKETCHES OF ANDOVER.

Roman Catholic Church, St. Augustine's (Andover), erected 1852.

Names of Pastors.	Date of Installation.	Close of Pastoral Relation.
Rev. Michael Gallagher	1862	August, 1869.
Rev. Ambrose A. Mullen	1869	July, 1876.
Rev. Maurice J. Murphy	1876.	

Roman Catholic Church, St. Michael's (North Andover), erected 1868.

Names of Pastors.	Date of Installation.	
Rev. M. J. Doherty	1868	Temporary supply.
Rev. William Orr	1869	Temporary supply.
Rev. James Murphy	1872.	

Names of Divinity Students in Chronological Order.

Graduation.	Name.	Place of Settlement.
1660. H. U.	Simon Bradstreet [1]	New London, Conn.
1693. H. U.	Simon Bradstreet [1]	Charlestown.
1703. H. U.	Joseph Stevens [1]	Charlestown.
1709. H. U.	John Barnard [1]	First (North) Church.
1723. H. U.	Andrew Peters [1]	Middleton.
1723. H. U.	Jonathan Frye [1]	Died of Wounds received in Battle.
1727. H. U.	John Blunt	Newcastle, N. H.
1732. H. U.	Thomas Barnard [1]	Newbury.
1734. H. U.	Phineas Stevens [1]	Boscawen.
1735. H. U.	Samuel Chandler	York, Me.
1735. H. U.	John Phillips	Exeter, N. H.
1737. H. U.	Abiel Abbot	Not ordained; died 1737.
1743. H. U.	Edward Barnard [1]	Haverhill.
1747. H. U.	Abiel Foster	Canterbury, N. H.
1757. H. U.	Nathan Holt	Danvers.
1761. H. U.	Jacob Emery	Pembroke, N. H.
1767. H. U.	Moses Holt	Preached for a short time only.
1769. H. U.	Stephen Peabody [1]	Atkinson, N. H.
1771. H. U.	David Osgood, D. D.	Medford.
1784. H. U.	John Abbot	Professor in Bowdoin College.
1786. H. U.	Robert Gray	Dover, N. H.
1789. H. U.	Jonathan Osgood [1]	Gardner.
1790. H. U.	Peter Holt	Epping, N. H.
1792. H. U.	Abiel Abbott, D. D.	Haverhill.
1798. H. U.	Jonathan French, D. D.	North Hampton, N. H.
1800. D. C.	John Dane	Newfield, Me.
1801. D. C.	Thomas Abbot Merrill	Middlebury, Vt.
1805. H. U.	John Lovejoy Abbot	Boston, First Church.
1807. H. U.	Joshua Chandler	Swanzey, N. H.
1813. D. C.	Jacob Holt	Brookline, N. H.
1814. H. U.	Peter Osgood [1]	Sterling, Mass.
1816. H. U.	Samuel Phillips Newman	Professor Bowdoin College

[1] Residents of North Andover.

CHURCHES AND MINISTERS, ETC. 505

Graduation.	Name.	Place of Settlement.
1817. H. U.	Asa Cummings, D. D.[1]	North Yarmouth, Me.
1821. D. C.	Stephen Foster[1]	Greenville, Tenn.
1821. Y. C.	John R. Adams, D. D.	Londonderry, N. H.
1822. H. U.	Nathaniel Gage[1]	Nashua, N. H.
1826. Y. C.	Amos Blanchard, D. D.	Lowell.
1827. Y. C.	William Adams, D. D.	Brighton.
1827. U. C.	Leonard Woods, D. D.	Professor Bangor Theological Seminary.
1828. D. C.	Isaac Foster[1]	Not ordained.
1831. A. C.	Joshua Emery	Fitchburg.
1831. H. U.	Andrew Peters[1]	Died while a student.
1833. U. C.	Daniel Bates Woods	Springfield, N. Y.
1833. A. C.	Sereno T. Abbot	Seabrook, N. H.
1834. A. C.	Samuel Hopkins Emery	Taunton.
1834. Y. C.	Edward Blanchard	Died while in College.
1834. Y. C.	William John Newman	Stratham, N. H.
1835. Y. C.	Joseph W. Faulkner	Not ordained.
1836. U. C.	Henry H. Callahan	Oxford, N. Y.
1836. U. C.	Wilson Ingalls	Glenville, N. Y.
1838. U. C.	Charles S. Putnam	Woodbury, Conn.
1839. W. R. C.	Daniel Emerson	Home Missionary.
1840. Y. C.	Thomas E. Foster	Not ordained.
	Joseph W. Burtt	North Chelmsford.
1840.	Edward Abbot	Milton, N. H.
1840. Y. C.	Jonathan Edwards	Woburn.
1841. Y. C.	Joseph Emerson	Professor in Beloit College.
1843. D. C.	John N. Putnam	Professor in Dartmouth College.
1847. Y. C.	Daniel T. Noyes	Dorchester.
1848. Y. C.	Samuel Emerson	Enfield, N. H. (Supply).
1851. W. C.	George Mooar, D. D.	Andover, South Church.
1851. H. U.	Peter Smith Byers	Not ordained.
1852. D. C.	Osgood Johnson	Teacher Cambridge High School.
	John Frye[1]	Died while a student in Phillips Academy, 1853.
1856. Harvard Divinity School	Stephen Barker[1]	Leominster (now in business).
1858. D. C.	John F. Aiken	Pawlet, Vt.
1858. H. U.	Simon Greenleaf Fuller	Syracuse, N. Y.
1859. Y. C.	Edwin S. Beard	Easthampton, L. I.
1860. Y. C.	Thaddeus H. Brown	North Woodstock, Conn.
1861. W. R. C.	Allen C. Barrows	Kent, Ohio.
1861. Y. C.	William Edwards Park	Lawrence.
1862. Y. C.	John P. Taylor	Middletown, Conn.
1863. A. C.	James G. Merrill	Mound City, Kansas.
1864. A. T. Sem.	John H. Manning	Brookline, N. H.
1865. A. T. Sem.	William H. Beard	South Killingly, Conn.

[1] Residents of North Andover.

Graduation.	Name.	Place of Settlement.
	D. J. Stone	Quincy Point.
1866. A. T. Sem.	David S. Morgan	Worthington.
1868. Y. C.	David McGregor Means.	Professor Middlebury College.
1868. A. C.	William W. Eaton	Instructor in Andover Theo. Sem.
1869. Y. C.	Moses Stuart Phelps	Professor in Smith College.
1869. A. C.	E. Winchester Donald	Washington Heights, N. Y.
1875. Chicago Theo. Sem.	Charles H. Abbot	Huntley, Ill.
1878. A. T. Sem.	George H. Gutterson	Missionary in India.
1878. Private instruction and A. T. S.	Lawrence Phelps	Barton, Vt.
1870. Villanova College.	Daniel D. Regan	Waterford, N. Y.

William Regan, Timothy Regan, and John O'Brien are studying for the ministry in Villanova College. John Cronley is in Montreal Seminary.

Charles R. Pollard is studying for the ministry in Wilbraham Seminary, 1880.

BURYING-GROUNDS AND CEMETERIES.

The first settlers made their burying-ground close by the meeting-house, as it was the custom to have the churchyards in England. Allusion to this burying-place has been made in the chapter on the "Memorials of the Early Settlers," and in various other parts of this history. It is one of the spots most suggestive of historic memories of all in Old Andover. Here, if anywhere, we can hold converse with the fathers, and feel that the names which we read were borne by men and women who were alive in our town when its inhabitants numbered but a score, and when the first grave was made of the thousands that have received the successive generations of citizens.

There are now only two stones remaining with legible inscriptions, bearing date prior to 1700. One of these is in memory of John Stevens, who died April 11, 1662; the other, in memory of Timothy Swan,[1] who died 1692, February 16, in the thirtieth year of his age. The gravestone does not tell the tale that he was supposed to have been brought to his grave by the malice and wickedness of witchcraft. About two hundred and fifty stones are of date between 1700 and 1800; some eighty between 1800 and 1825; four or five between 1825 and 1855, one erected since 1855. About 330 inscriptions are legible.

[1] See Chapter III.

Three pastors of the First Church are buried here, whose gravestones remain, — the Rev. Thomas Barnard, the Rev. John Barnard, Rev. William Symmes. The grave of the Rev. Francis Dane, which was probably in this burial-ground, is now unmarked.

In this burying-ground was doubtless buried the soldier, young Joseph Abbot (son of George Abbot, Sen.), who on the 18th of April, 1676, fell defending his brother and himself from the savages, — the first soldier who was buried in Andover.

Here lies the dust of the two North Andover Colonels [1] in the Revolutionary service, James Frye and Samuel Johnson, whose gravestones are standing. Here are the gravestones of Dr. John Kittredge, Dr. Ward Noyes, and others of honorable name and service, officers in the Old French Wars and the Revolution ; and the tomb of the Hon. Samuel Phillips, — a stately monumental pile.

One of the curiosities is the gravestone of "Primus a faithful servant of Mr. Benjamin Stevens who died July 25 1792, aged 72 years 5 months 16 days."

The stones from 1700 to 1750 are all characterized by a severe simplicity. Merely the names of the dead, with the date of their birth and death or their age. The use of the prefix "Mr." is noticeable, as much a title of distinction or rank as "Colonel" or "Rev." is now. The few emblems and symbols used were of three principal patterns, the most common a cherub's head with wings. The skull and crossbones appear but seldom.

The burying-ground was not adorned or beautified, and hardly guarded from desecration short of actual destruction. As late as 1830, sheep were allowed to feed there : —

"*Voted*, that the burying ground shall be fed with no other creature than sheep.

"*Voted*, that the parish committee agree with a sexton, and Dispose of the Apples and Feed in the burying-ground to the best advantage."

The following order for gravestones for the old burying-

[1] See Chapter V.

ground is found among some ancient manuscripts preserved in the family of the persons who ordered them: —

"Mr. Robert mulican of Bradford: Ser pray make: for me Two Grave Stones: one for David Foster jeuner of Andover: who Died the 22: day of December: in the year of our Lord: 1736, in the 20th year of his age: the son of David and Lidea Foster of Andover.

"And one for Lidea Foster the daughter of David and Lidea foster of Andover: who died in the 17th year of her age in the year of our Lord 1736, and when they are made: send me word: and I will come and pay you for them.   DAVID FOSTER.

"And one for Isaac Foster: the son of Joshua and Mary Foster of Andover who died in the third 3: year of her age in the year 1738. Pray send me word when it is made: and I will satisfye you for it.   JOSHUA FOSTER.

"Let them all be made: before you send us word the 3 day of April 1739."

The orders were executed, and the gravestones are standing now, and show how well Mr. Robert Mullican executed the work which was left to his direction. He substituted the more high-sounding phrase, "Departed this life" for the simple "Died."

This burying-ground was increased in extent from time to time, by grants from the proprietors of additional land. It continued to be used occasionally down to about 1845.

The customs or fashions of funeral services, when this burial-ground was principally in use, were very unlike those now in the town, although in some places the ancient usages are again coming into vogue. The pall-bearers received presents of gloves, rings, and scarfs from the friends of the deceased. The bier was carried from the house to the grave by the bearers, who often walked for miles.

In 1703, it was voted by the town, that " a hansom piece of Black broadcloth be bought for a funerall cloath for the Towne use and that payment be made for it out of the Towne Treasury."

There was no hearse in town till 1797. Then it was voted to have one built (at Salem).[1]

[1] Abbot's *History of Andover*.

Prayers were made at the grave. After the burial service, invited guests returned to the house and partook of refreshments.

According to the custom of the time, wines and strong liquors were provided. The free use of strong liquors at funerals was rebuked by the Rev. Mr. Phillips in a sermon, 1720. This custom of eating and drinking after funerals is often misunderstood and misrepresented. It was an absolute necessity for the bearers, after a walk of many miles, and often exposure to severe weather, to be at once refreshed with food and drink. The kind and quantity provided accorded with the fashion of the day, which was to use liquors on all occasions of dining and supping where friends met together. The increase of burial-grounds, and the consequent diminution of the distance of walking, was a reason for less abundant provision, and the gradual doing away with a fashion which (whatever else in the way of rings and gloves may be done) it cannot be desirable to revive.

The second burying-ground of the North Parish (one was laid out in the South Parish on the division of the precincts) was laid out in 1817, on land bought of Mr. Jonathan Stevens, lying in the rear of Franklin Academy, near the meeting-house.

The third burial-place of North Andover was laid out in 1850. It consisted of eleven acres, which, by subsequent additions, has been increased to about twenty-five acres. It lies about a half mile southeast of the North Meeting-house, on the Marble Ridge Road. The original name, Andover Cemetery, was changed in 1875 to Ridgewood Cemetery.

The cemetery was consecrated October 10, 1850. An address was made by the Rev. William T. Briggs, reviewing the history of burial-places. The occasion was an impressive one. It was the afternoon of a mild autumn day; the trees were beginning to fade from their brilliant hues into the sere and yellow tints that remind of the decay of the year and of mortal life. The large assembly, listening to the voice of prayer and the consecration (a service scarcely till then known in the town) of this peaceful spot where, ere many years, nearly all would lie down in their last rest, were hushed into solemnity. The hymn sung was written for the occasion by Mrs. A. D. T. Whitney, who is connected with North Andover families, and a frequent visitor to the town : —

HYMN.

"We come to consecrate to-day,
  With spirits hushed and words of prayer,
A sweet, still spot, that we may lay
  In days to come our loved ones there.

"But yesterday 't was common ground ;
  Henceforth not even a flower shall spring
Out from its bosom but shall be
  Unto our hearts a holy thing.

"We stand among our future graves,
  Around us lies the unbroken sod,
And who shall first be slumbering here
  None knoweth save the Omniscient God.

"When grief shall darken in the soul,
  And dust to dust with many a tear
Be given, O Father, then let love
  Come down to meet the mourner here.

"In beauty we would clothe the spot,
  And O may strength and grace be given,
To robe our lives in beauty, too,
  And make our resting-place in heaven."

The first grave of an adult here made was that of Capt. Francis Ingals, in November, 1850.

Here was buried the Rev. Bailey Loring, also the Rev. Peter Osgood, ministers who participated in the exercises of consecration. Here one and another of the active business men of North Andover have rested from their labors, — manufacturers, merchants, farmers, whose enterprise and sagacity have built up the town's industries, extended its fame, and endowed its institutions of learning and religion, until, beneath the sod, which thirty years ago was unbroken, there are now more than five hundred graves.

All the original trustees of the cemetery have gone to their final rest, — Rev. Peter Osgood, Hon. George Hodges, Dea. Otis Bailey, Mr. Edmund Davis, Dr. Samuel Johnson; the first treasurer also, Mr. Henry Osgood, and the second treasurer, Mr. Horace N. Stevens, and the later trustees, Mr. Francis Hodges, William Johnson, Esq., and James Johnson, Esq., all repose in this spot, which they had spent so much time and thought to adorn and make attractive. The following is from a report of the Trustees of the Cemetery Association, a tribute to the memory of Mr. James Johnson, of Boston, who, by his request, was buried here in his native town: —

"The trustees, in presenting their report, would notice the death of one of their number, which occurred at Boston, April 26, 1855. No one has taken a deeper interest in our cemetery, nor contributed so liberally to its funds, as James Johnson, Esq., and we would bear testimony to his untiring zeal, his wise counsels, and his faithful services as a trustee. Born in this town, he always retained a love for the place of his nativity, and was desirous that his remains might repose in this beautiful city of the dead. As a merchant, he had been successful in business, and had accumulated a large property; and through all the changes of a long life maintained the reputation of an honest man, — 'that noblest work of God.' He was ready to encourage merit, and many a young man has been indebted for his success in life to his timely assistance. We would cherish the memory of his virtues; and hold up for the imitation of our young men his example of perseverance and honesty, which secured to him not only wealth but the respect and esteem of the community in which he lived and all who knew him."

The old sexton, who has done melancholy service for townsmen in the three burying-grounds of North Andover (having digged the first of the many graves of his making in 1825, in the first burying-ground), still walks about the places of his long employment and views the ground where he must shortly lie. The aged man[1] leaning on his staff at the cemetery gate, often watches (listening, for he can hardly see), as if with envy, his successor in the mournful seat of dignity on the slow-moving hearse.

[1] John Frye, sexton and grave-digger, 1825 to 1854.

South Parish Burying-yard.

The South Parish "Burying-yard," as it is named in the earliest parish records, was laid out about the time of the organization of the church. The first person buried here was Robert Russell, who died December, 1710. The oldest inscription is on the gravestone in memory of Mrs. Ann Blanchard, wife of Mr. Jonathan Blanchard, who died February 29, 1723.

The parish took great care in regard to the burying-yard to keep it well fenced, a committee being yearly elected to look after the repairs of the meeting-house, the parsonage, and the "Burying yard Fence." It was voted, 1714, to "buy a burying cloth, always when used to be left at Decon Abbots'." In 1757 it was again voted to "buy a burying cloth for the use of the Inhabitants." In 1798 it was voted "to procure a hearse," and soon after to build a hearse house.

The first two pastors of the church, Rev. Mr. Phillips and Rev. Mr. French, were buried here. The tombstone originally erected to the memory of Mr. Phillips is changed or replaced by a modern monument in memory of the Phillips family, many of whom repose here.

This burying-ground is not in any respect essentially different from the earlier one in the North Parish. The ancient gravestones are much the same in style, with merely change of names. There are few of the quaint and incongruous epitaphs, which are so often found in ancient burial grounds, among the inscriptions of the tombstones in the old Andover burying-grounds. Good sense and good taste characterize most of the epitaphs.

The South Parish Burying-yard has been, from 1710, and still is, one of the principal burial places of the town, especially of the families connected with the South Church. It has been enlarged many times, and is now laid out with lots and modern improvements. It contains some elegant and costly monuments to the memory of eminent citizens of Andover.

This burying ground has probably been the scene of more funeral pomp and parade than any other in the town. The burial of the first minister of the South Church, the Rev. Mr. Phillips, was attended, as has been previously noted, with considerable ceremony, six ministers officiating as pall-bearers, all having rings and gloves presented by the parish.

The funeral of Lieutenant-governor Phillips was attended with great pomp. The long procession, including the Governor and Councillors, the President of the Senate, and other civil officers, with the dignitaries of the literary and religious institutions of Andover, and the long train of citizens and students, wound down the hill from the mansion-house (while the bell tolled solemnly), and entering the gateway stood in reverent awe while the last rites were paid to the distinguished citizen who had done so much for the town of his nativity.

Again, in 1809, was a scarcely less impressive scene at the burial of the Rev. Jonathan French. Here, also, since then have been many impressive funeral tributes to the memory of the eminent members of the South Parish of Andover, names than which few are more honorable.

West Parish Burying-ground.

As early as 1692 "those men on ye west side of Shawshin river" were granted "ye libertie of a buring-place by ye wayside, near ye head of a place called Rowell's Folly, provided they fence it handsomely against swine and other creatures within a year from date."

This condition they do not seem to have fulfilled, or to have taken up the land, for in 1748 the same place is again spoken of as offered: —

"Then measured and bounded out one acre of land for a buring place for ye town's use, lying on ye southerly side of ye way that Leads from Mr. William Foster's to Ensign John Foster's, near ye Head of Rowell's Folly brook."

Finally, in 1751, the ground was accepted.

"*June*, 1751. A parcel of Land Bounded out for a Buring place on ye southerly side of ye way over Shashin river, near ye Head of Rowell's Folly, accepted to be laid out."

But no action in regard to laying it out is found in the proceedings of the South Parish, or anything to indicate that before 1791 there was more than one burying ground in the parish. At that time it was voted "to erect a sutable fence around the piece of land laid out for a burying place near Paul Hunt's house." Whether this was the same land referred to in the former votes of the town has not been ascertained. But, from this time, whenever repairs are annually provided for it is for the fences of the burying *yards* (not, as formerly, *yard*, in the singular number), showing that, notwithstanding the acceptance of the lot, in 1751, a second grave-yard was not laid out till twenty years later. The earliest stones are about 1790 to 1795.

The number of graves of soldiers (who died in the late civil war) in this burying ground is remarkable, considering the remoteness of the parish from the centres of business and the excitements of crowds. From the various knolls and rising grounds, as one looks off over the cemetery, are seen everywhere fluttering in the breeze the little flags, the stars and stripes, that are the patriot's memorial. From one point of view thirty were counted, and there were many besides not visible from this point, and some graves or headstones without the colors. This large number shows that a deep, earnest spirit of patriotism must have pervaded this rural parish, the same spirit that inspired the men of '75, Ames, Furbush, Boynton, Holt, and others, who were officers or soldiers at Lexington and Bunker Hill and Stillwater, and were of the stock that General Burgoyne pronounced invincible, — the yeomanry of New England.

The three burial places of the three parishes were the only ones in the town till the present century, except some private and family lots on homesteads.

In 1810 the burying ground of the Theological Seminary was added to the number. This is in some respects one of the most noteworthy cemeteries in Andover. It is on the Institution Hill, to the eastward of the buildings. Elevated, and commanding an extensive prospect, it is yet shut in from view and is a quiet secluded spot, pleasant and soothing to linger in. Here repose the remains of the fathers of the Seminary, — Woods, Stuart, Porter, the two Edwardses, and many other scholars and divines who have made their home at Andover, besides the teachers in the academies, and students who have died far from home. Here, also, among the stately marbles and sonorous inscriptions and titles are little graves of many households. One marble cross attracts notice, — the only monument of this form in the burying ground. It is in memory of the son of Professor and Mrs. Harriet Beecher Stowe, a youth of nineteen, who was drowned in the Connecticut River, while he was a member of Dartmouth College. It was in reference to this bereavement that the mother wrote the touching little poem "Only a Year."

Here are monuments to benefactors and trustees of the Seminary and Academy, among them Samuel Farrar, Esq., Mr. Jonathan Taylor, Mr. John Aiken, and Mr. John Dove. The mausoleum of the latter, a stately pile of Scotch granite inscribed with gilded letters, and reached by an ascent of granite stairs, is an affecting reminder of the contrasts in the life of the man who entered Andover a penniless youth, and in the town of his adoption acquired the fortune which his munificence made a blessing to its seats of learning.

In this cemetery also humble merit has its memorial from grateful patrons. Beside the monument of Professor Porter, is a plain stone whose inscription states that Almira Quacumbush was for thirty years a faithful domestic in the family of Dr. Porter, and died in full Christian hope. This was the woman whose name has a place in the Semi-centennial address of Dr. Nehemiah Adams. Alluding to the custom of the students to do the mowing in Professor Porter's grounds, he says: "Then came Myra from the front door, — Myra Quacumbush, black but comely; and, like Evangeline bringing 'drink for the reapers,' she served us, overseers and laborers, without distinction, with sweetened water."

In 1840 Christ Churchyard was given to the parish by Mr. Abraham Marland. The honored dead of many members of this parish repose here.

The Roman Catholic Cemetery was occupied about 1855. Its consecration has not yet been made.

Spring Grove Cemetery was laid out in 1871 as a burial place for the town of Andover.

Mr. William G. Means was one of the first movers in regard to this cemetery, and selected the site and gave the granite gate-posts at the entrance.

The main avenue is the old railroad track. A clear spring of water bursting from the sides of the embankment, gives the name to the cemetery. The grounds cover about forty acres. The cemetery was consecrated October 15, 1871. Rev. William E. Park delivered the address of consecration. Mr. William G. Means made a statement of the history of the cemetery. The hymn of consecration was the same written for the North Andover Cemetery.

The first superintendent was Mr. Samuel Raymond, who did much toward the tasteful laying out of the grounds, and the arrangement of the lots. Here he erected a monument to the memory of his brave son, Walter Landor Raymond, who at the age of sixteen enlisted in the Forty-fourth Massachusetts Regiment of Volunteers, August 15, 1862, and died in Salisbury prison December 25, 1864, and was buried in the trenches.

Spring Grove Cemetery is in some parts thickly wooded, and it demands a large appropriation of money to improve it properly for the purposes of a cemetery. But its location and its natural beauties are unsurpassed, and it will, no doubt, eventually become one of the most beautiful burial places in the county.

A cemetery for the city of Lawrence is contemplated to be located in the vicinity of Den Rock.

In closing this chapter the writer recalls vividly the address of consecration of the North Andover Cemetery, heard thirty years ago, but much more distinctly remembered than many "greater" discourses heard since. It reviewed the history of burying-places in all ages, taking either for a text or a prominent thought the words of Scripture, which may not inappropriately close this chapter: —

"*And Abraham stood up from before his dead, and spake unto the sons of Heth, saying, I am a stranger and a sojourner with you; give me a possession of a burying place with you that I may bury my dead out of my sight . . . . and the field of Ephron, which was in Machpelah, which was before Mamre, ... the field and the cave which was therein, and all the trees that were in the field were made sure unto Abraham for a possession of a burying place.*" — Gen. xxiii. 3, 17, 20.

CHAPTER VII.

PUBLIC SCHOOLS AND PUBLIC LIBRARIES.

The Classical Grammar School.

EARLY in its history Andover was favored with excellent school advantages, in the instruction of Mr. Woodbridge and Mr. Dane, the ministers, both of whom kept a private school. The town also took special interest in Harvard College, from the fact that Mr. Bradstreet's sons were students there, and that Mr. Benjamin Woodbridge, the first graduate of the college, had come to make his residence in Andover. In 1678 a contribution or assessment, the "complement for ye new building of ye college," was sent to Cambridge: this consisted of twelve bushels of corn.

In the year 1700 Andover first took measures to fulfil the law requiring every town of one hundred families to make provision for preparing boys for college, by "setting up a Grammar School." The instruction in these schools was required to fit the student who wished to enter college to "read any classical author into English, and readily speak and make true Latin, and write it in verse as well as prose, and perfectly decline the paradigms of nouns and verbs in the Greek tongue."

It was not expected that the master of the Grammar School would teach all his pupils the classics, but such as wished to be prepared for college were to have the privilege. The school was probably in the main composed of all the children in the town, when it was first established, and before other schools were added in the outskirts, as there were after fifty years. Besides the Grammar School, and before its day, there were small schools kept by school dames, as is hereafter described. The first town action relating to the Grammar School is the following : —

"*Feb.* 3, 1789. *Voted and passed*, that a conveniant school-house be erected at y* parting of y* ways, by Joseph Wilson's, to be twenty foot long and sixteen foot wide."

It was not easy to find a master, there being few educated young men ready, but in 1703 the town selectmen were empowered to engage a schoolmaster, and in 1704 Mr. Dudley Bradstreet was agreed with. He is the first of whom record is found. He was succeeded by Mr. Henry Rust. The salary paid was about forty pounds a year.

Mr. John Barnard taught in 1709, and afterward went to teach in Boston.

After Mr. Barnard left the town for Boston, it seems to have been difficult to find a schoolmaster and keep up the school. The difficulties which the selectmen experienced are thus graphically detailed [1]: —

To Ensign Samuel Frye. These present Pray Favor our Town so far as may be.

Andover, *March:* y* 16th, 1712-13.

This may certifye eny to whom it may consern : That y* Selectmen of said Town have taken all the care and pains : they could for to procuer a schoolmaster for our Towne for y* year Last past : but could not obtaine one : First we Agreed with Mr. Obadiah Ayers, of havrell, for half a year, only he expected Liberty if he had a better call or offer : which we thought would be only to the work of y* ministry : but however he was pleased to take it otherwise and so Left us : whereupon we fourthwith aplyed ourselves to the collidge : To the president for advice : and he could tell us of none, only advised us to the Fellows to ask them : and they advised to Mr. Rogers, of Ipswich : for they could tell us of no other : and we applyed ourselves to him and got him to Andover. But by Reason our reverand Mr. barnard could not dieat [2] him he would not stay with us : and since we have sent to Newbury and : Salsbury and to Mistick : for to hier one and cannot git one : and we doe take the best care we can for to bring up our children to Reeding by school Dames : and we have no Gramer Schoole in our Town as we know of : and we are now taking the best care we can for to obtaine one, therefore pray that we may be Favoured : so fare as may be : for we cannot compell gentellmen to come to

[1] *Essex Court Files*, from a paper read before the Essex Institute, by H. M. Brooks, 1854.
[2] "Board."

us; and we do suppose they are Something afraid by y' Reason we Doe Ly so exposed to our Indyen Enemys: pray consider our great extremitie in that Regard, and we shall doe our uttermost to answer the tru intent of the Law in that behalf. So we Rest your humble petitioners:

GEORGE ABBOT,
JOHN ASLEBE,   } *Selectmen*
EPHRAIM FOSTER,   *of*
NEHEMIAH ABBOT, } *Andover.*"

The next record found is an engagement with Mr. Joseph Dorr, and the next year Mr. William Cooke, who, after a short time, was succeeded by Mr. Thomas Paine, and next is a record, "Mr. Withum, com to keep school in our Towne the 2nd of Sept. 1718."

After the division of the town into Precincts, a Grammar School-house was built by the South Parish. It took three years of voting before the building was accomplished.

"1714, *Mar.* 29. *Voted*, that the Precinct will build a school-house, that it shall be twenty-two feet by sixteen feet wide and six foot stud."

"1717, *Feb. Voted and passed*, that Dea. Lovejoy, Timothy Abbot, Samuel Preston, jr., be and is a committee for to build and finish our School-house."

"1718. That the Committee will set up the school-house upon the Hill on the South-west of the Meeting-House, That it be forthwith built and finished."

The next schoolmaster was obliged to teach alternately in the two Parishes.

"ANDOVER, *the 12th of January,* 1719 | 20.

"This day mutually agreed with and Between the Selectmen of Andover and Mr. James Bailey to keep a gramer School for one year following for forty-four pounds, and he is to teach children to Read and elder persons to wright and Sifer as far as they are capable for the Time being, according to the Regular methods of such a school, and to keep the School in each precinct for the s^d Term of Time, and to begin the schoole about three quarters of an hour after seven a'clock and to keep it according to the accustomed manner in the Sheer Towne. Witness our hands," etc.

Mr. Bailey kept the school two years, and then, after one other teacher from abroad, a resident of the town was hired.

"*September* 2nd, 1723. The selectmen of Andover from the day of the date hereof agreed with Mr. Andrew Peeters that he should keepe a Grammer School a twelve month In the said Towne, allso that he wold Teach boys to Read, Rite, and Cypher, and that he wold teach and keep schoole in each precinct according to each Precinct's Pay, for which Service the Selectmen of s^d Town promised to Give the s^d Andrew Peeters forty-four pounds."

After a time, the remote districts beginning to become more thickly settled and populous, demanded to have a school kept in their neighborhood, and so the master became, as it were, peripatetic. The itineratings of one teacher are thus set forth in the records:—

"*Sept.* ye 1, 1729. Philemon Robbins came first to keep a school in Andover, and began his school in ye south end of ye Town and continued there 3 months, and then went behind the pond in ye first day of December and continued there until the 25th day of said December, and then Returned to the middle of the Town and was sent to the south end of the towne and continued there until the Last of January, and then was sent and continued in the middle of the town into ye Last of February next, and then was sent behind the pond in ye 3^d day of March and to continue there fourteen nights and then ye 16th March was returned to ye middle of ye towne, and continued there nine weeks."

It is interesting to find, on comparison of dates, that this schoolmaster was the Rev. Philemon Robbins, known for his spirited resistance to ecclesiastical tyranny. His memoir, written by his grandson, Rev. Thomas Robbins, D. D., is included in "Sprague's Annals of the American Pulpit." The writer evidently did not know of his ancestor's residence at Andover. He says: "My impression is that he taught school for some time after his graduation." The town records show that he began the school the year of his graduation, 1729. His vicissitudes of school-keeping foreshadowed others more disagreeable. Says the writer of the memoir, after recording his ordination at Branford, Conn., 7th February, 1732: "Here he continued experiencing more than the ordinary vicissitudes of clerical life to the end of his days." He technically violated the law forbidding one minister to preach in another minister's parish without invitation and by mutual exchange. He was deposed, but afterward tacitly reinstated.

About 1755 regular schools were established in the outskirts. It was voted that these "outskirt schools may be within a mile and a half of the Centre School."

Whether the Centre School, often referred to, was identical with the Grammar School, seems difficult to determine. So far as can be judged from the records it appears that the intention was to have, in the original Grammar School-houses, a school kept by a college graduate, where all those students who wished to take a classical course of study should go to school, that this school should be kept up throughout the year, and that there should be outskirt schools a part of the year. It would sometimes happen, doubtless, that there would be no students to fit for college, and no absolute necessity for a college graduate in the Centre School. But of forty-five names of masters of the Grammar School, before 1792, all but five are found on the lists of Harvard graduates.

In 1758 and 1759, Mr. Joshua Holt, Jr., and Mr. Theodore Carlton kept the school, neither being a college graduate. Possibly this may have had something to do with the difficulty in respect to two scholars who wished to study Latin.

"*May*, 1758. It was voted to see if the Town will take under consideration the Afair of Two Lating Scholars sent into Town and Boarded by Mr. William Foster and sent to our Gramer School, and it *Passed in the Afirmative*.

"It was voted to see if the Two Latin Scholars Taken into Town and Boarded by Mr. William Foster should be taught or Instructed by our Gramer School Master in our school houses, and it *Passed in the negative*."

The establishment of Phillips Academy, in 1778, made a Grammar School in the South Parish no longer a necessity; but the town in 1779 appropriated two hundred pounds for a Grammar School, and two hundred for reading, writing, and ciphering schools, as before. This burden was not, however, cheerfully borne by all the tax-payers, and, for a time, the Grammar School had a precarious existence, and was only sustained in the North Parish. At length the North Parish began to agitate the question of an Academy, or, as it was called, "Free School," similar to the Phillips Academy; and when, in 1799, the Franklin Academy was built, the Classical Grammar School ceased to exist.

Following is a list of such names of schoolmasters as have been found in the records.[1]

1704.[2]	Dudley Bradstreet.	1753.	Benjamin Butler.
1707.	Henry Rust.	1755.	Abiel Foster.
1709.	John Barnard.	1758.	Joshua Holt, Jr.
1712.	Obadiah Ayers.	1759.	Theodore Carlton.
1712.	Mr. Rogers.	1760.	John Farnum.
1714.	Joseph Dorr.	1764.	Edward Wigglesworth.
1716.	William Cooke.	1766.	Israel Perley.
1717.	Thomas Paine.	1767.	Stephen Peabody.
1718.	Daniel Witham.	1768.	Nathaniel Lovejoy (5 years).
1720.	James Bailey.	1773.	Samuel Tenney.
1722.	Moses Hale.	1774.	Eliphalet Pearson.
1723.	Andrew Peters.	1775.	Oliver Peabody.
1728.	Isaac Abbot.	1775.	Thomas Whiting.
1728.	Timothy Walker.	1776.	John Rice.
1729.	Philemon Robbins.	1777.	Abraham Cummings.
1732.	Thomas Skinner.	1778.	Isaac Bridges.
1734.	Samuel Phillips.	1779.	Timothy Trumbull.
1737.	John Phillips.	1780.	William Symmes, Jr.
1739.	Edward Barnard.	1790.	Samuel Holyoke.
1740.	Joseph Holt (10 years).	1791.	Nathan Lakeman.
1752.	Thomas Hibbard.	1791.	Daniel Gould.

There were thirty-four college graduates from Andover before the establishment of Phillips Academy in 1778. These included, besides the ministers already mentioned, the following: —

Samuel Bradstreet (1653), physician in Boston.

Isaac Abbot (1723), trader, of Andover; died 1754.

Hon. Samuel Phillips (1734), trader, of North Andover; representative; councillor; founder of Phillips Academy; died 1790.

John Phillips, LL. D. (1735), founder of Phillips Academy, Exeter.

Joseph Osgood, M. D. (1737), physician, of North Andover.

Joseph Holt (1739), master of Grammar School; resident of Wilton, N. H.

---

[1] These are scattered and confused, — the reckonings with the masters being jotted down wherever there was a blank space. The alphabets are lost, and the writing often is illegible.

[2] The dates indicate the first record found.

Hon. Jedediah Foster (1744). Brookfield. Counsellor at law; Justice of Superior Court 1776.

Col. Peter Frye (1744). Salem. Justice of Court of Common Pleas; tory and refugee.

Isaac Osgood (1744), trader of Haverhill.

John Farnum (1761), master of Grammar School; member of Convention for framing State Constitution.

Nathaniel Lovejoy (1766), trader; Brigadier-general of militia.

Hon. Samuel Osgood (1770), member of Provincial Congress; of Continental Congress; Postmaster-general.

Lieut.-gov. Samuel Phillips (1771), Justice of Court of Common Pleas.

THE DISTRICT AND GRADED SCHOOLS. — The schools which in early time bore a resemblance to the common or district school, were called "reading, writing, and ciphering" schools. These, from being but one, became numerous with the growth of the town, and were variously called at different periods, "outskirt schools," "squadron schools," as, for example, in the town records, "the school in Blanchard's Squadron," or "Barker's Squadron," etc. These schools were kept by male teachers (but not generally by college graduates), up to at least the present century. In the very earliest period of the town history there were schools kept by school-dames where young children were taught the rudiments of knowledge. These schools were often kept by some goodwife who had not a large household to look after, in a room of her own dwelling. Here she divided her time between teaching the children and doing her household duties, like the schoolmistress of Old England, immortalized by Shenstone.

The district school as it was, has been so often described as to need no description here. The location was usually in the exact territorial centre of the district, however unsuitable the spot might be. The floor of the room sloped up to the back seat; a wood fire blazed at one end of the room; a ferule on the master's desk served the double purpose, to punish idlers and to rap on the window-sash to call scholars into the school. A pile of wood at the door was heaped up for the large boys to saw at odd times.

Flagellations were a regular part of the school exercises.

The mending of pens also was an important office of the master, who might often be seen with three or four quills stuck behind his ears, and a group of urchins, with inky hands and faces, waiting around, nudging and jostling one another, or watching curiously while the master brought the blunt nib of the pens to a fine point with the sharp knife.

The outskirt or district schools began to be kept in addition to the Central Grammar Schools, about 1750. They were under the charge of masters chiefly, until near the beginning of the present century.

Judge Phillips's influence did much to secure the permanency of these schools through the year, and the employment of female teachers. He gave money for the better education and qualification of women for teachers.

The schools were visited by the ministers, and it was expected that they would attend to the moral and religious instruction of the children. The Rev. Dr. Justin Edwards introduced a system of catechising with great thoroughness in the doctrines of the Assembly's Catechism, which, before his time, was always more or less a part of the school instruction.

The pupils of the district schools were at first of all ages, from the child of four years to the young man arrived at his majority. The increase of population led to the grading of the schools in the villages into primary, intermediate, and grammar grades preparatory to the High School.

In 1879 the town of Andover had one grammar school and twelve district schools, four of which were graded, making twenty-one schools. Connected with these were thirty teachers. In 1879 the town of North Andover had six district schools, two of which were graded, making in all thirteen schools, including the grammar schools. In these were fourteen teachers.

During the past year some changes have been made in the graded schools, and the system revised.

The oldest living master of a district school in the towns of Andover and North Andover is supposed to be Mr. Farnham Spofford,[1] now eighty-two years old. He was educated

[1] Deceased October 17, 1879, in Washington, D. C. His body is buried in the North Andover Cemetery.

at Franklin Academy. From 1818 to 1827 he taught in the district schools of the town of Andover (North and South). In 1827 he removed to Nantucket, and there, till 1841, was principal of the South Grammar School. In 1841 he returned to North Andover, and resided here with his family, teaching occasionally in the winter schools until 1850.

A relic of the pedagogical labors of one ancient district schoolmaster is at hand, — a speech prepared by him " to the Honorable Inspectors of the School." It is inscribed "School Finishing at Pilfershire."[1] The writer was Master John Ingalls, probably about 1790-1800.

The diary of Ruby Foster,[2] published by her pastor, Rev. Dr. Eaton, of Boxford, gives the first record of the life of any woman teacher of the district schools. She writes (1810) : —

"I have left our dear habitation and begun keeping school. Many were the tender emotions excited in my breast, and an undertaking so important and so new to me could not fail of engaging my solicitude and anxiety. God bless me in my School. Give my scholars hearts to obey and improve, and myself redoubled activity, strength, and wisdom."

The district schools of the South Parish have for nearly eighty years received a small sum annually from the Free School Fund, created by the sale of the proprietors' lands in 1801.

Writing Schools, kept in the evening, were a part of the old-fashioned educational privileges. Each pupil provided his lamp or candle (set sometimes in a turnip hollowed out for a candlestick), and prepared himself with quills and writing-paper. The master set the copies, or brought them on slips of paper. To make flourishes with the pen was accounted a triumph of chirographical skill. The succession of writing-masters is lost in oblivion.

Singing Schools were more regularly kept, as a preparation for divine worship. In 1771, Mr. Nathan Barker and Mr. John Pearson were famous singers of the North Parish. In the South Parish Mr. Eliphalet Pearson, Principal of Phillips

[1] " Pilfershire," a name applied to a part of North Andover.
[2] *Miscellaneous Writings of Ruby Foster, who died in Andover, Mass., Aug. 5th, 1812, in the 21st year of her age*, etc.

Academy, kept a singing school. Other singing-masters it is unnecessary to record here.

The singing school was often kept in the school-house, or in the meeting-house, although the latter place was not readily granted:—

"*South Parish*, 1782. Put to vote to see if the Parish will assign the three hindmost of the Body Seats in the Meeting-house for the Singing School to set in, and it Past in the Negative."

"1788. Being put to vote to see if the Parish will appropriate any seats in the meeting-house for the accommodation of those who have taken pains to improve themselves in the art of Singing, and it passed in the Negative."

In 1809 a Musical Society was flourishing in the parish, and asked pecuniary aid, which was rendered by the parish on certain conditions, in order, as they say in their report, to encourage that "deliteful and important part of public worship."

There are few persons who have reached middle life and lived in a rural district who do not remember the old-fashioned singing-school in winter, the merry sleigh-loads jingling up to the meeting-house, the frolicsome unpacking from the capacious pung, or the family sleigh, the groping up-stairs in the dim light to the singing-seats, the scampering and fun of the younger folks at recess, behind the high-backed pews, the awed look now and then down into the dark shadows of the pews below stairs, and at the great pulpit shrouded in ghostly white canopy; the scraping of the master's violin and the call to order, the tuning of bass-viol by some stalwart rustic musician, the pitching the tune and the starting off on the notes *do-re-mi*, then a stamp of the master's foot, another start off, and so on, winding up with "Coronation" and "Old Hundred."

The *Dancing school* was, though in some neighborhoods under protest, a not unknown institution. Spangled slippers and high-backed combs are still shown, that figured at dancing schools fifty years ago, and traditions are told of mischief-loving boys, who vexed their elder brothers and sisters in the hall of the country inn by shooting off peas from pop-guns, across the floor on which the dancers were practising minuets and cotillons. Some colored fiddler usually made music for the dancers. Cato, of North Andover, was famous.

The oldest relic found of any dancing "School" is a card of Mr. Ansart's School Ball, at Isaac Parker's Hall, April 11, 1808. "Dancing to commence precisely at four o'clock, P. M."

Punchard Free (High) School, Andover.[1]

On the 4th of April, 1850, Mr. Benjamin Hanover Punchard, of Andover, dying, left a bequest of fifty thousand dollars, with a reversion (to be paid on the death of his widow) of twenty thousand dollars, for the purpose of founding a free School.

This munificent donor to his adopted town was a native of Salem, to which town his ancestors came, as early as 1680, from the island of Jersey. Until about his tenth year, when his father died, he was sent to public and private schools kept by eminent teachers, where he laid the foundation of a good education. But being compelled to labor for his own support he was unable to continue study in school, and sought employment, first as a copyist and afterward as a clerk in a West India store, in Boston. By unremitting diligence and conscientious fidelity he gained the confidence of his employers, and at twenty became a partner in the firm. But his hard labors during the period of youth broke down his constitution, and, shattered in health at twenty-eight, he gave up business and removed to Andover, with the view of recruiting his exhausted energies. He had at this time already acquired a considerable fortune. In 1828 he became a stockholder in the Andover bank, and in 1829, in partnership with his brother-in-law, Mr. John Derby, opened a store in Andover. In 1834 he entered into the Marland Manufacturing Company with Mr. Abraham Marland, whose daughter he had married.

His infirm health compelled him to seek frequent change of scene and climate, and he travelled extensively in the Southern States and in the British Isles. The great and time-honored seats of learning, the universities and schools

[1] Some other temporary "high schools" have been kept, but without a special school building, and only of brief duration.

of England, particularly impressed his mind and appealed to his imagination and sympathies, and, doubtless, from these he was led to the thought of founding a school in Andover.

He provided that the school should be under the direction of eight trustees, of whom the rector of Christ Church should be one, also the ministers of the South and West Parish Congregational Societies should be members, the other five to be chosen by the inhabitants of Andover in town meeting. The school was to be free, and no sectarian influence to be used, the Bible to be in daily use and the Lord's Prayer, in which the pupils are to join audibly with the teacher in the morning at the opening.

The town [1] chose a committee, of which N. W. Hazen, Esq., was chairman, to draft resolutions expressive of appreciative acceptance of this donation. Among these resolutions was the following : —

"That we will cherish the memory of his many virtues ; that we recognize the obligations conferred upon us by his enterprise and success in adding to the wealth and increasing the prosperity of the town ; and that we recommend to the trustees under his will, to whom he has so largely confided the superstructure of the school, to adopt the most effectual means to associate his name and memory with the institution which he has founded and so munificently endowed."

A school building was erected of brick, with stone basement, with trimmings of freestone. It was seventy-five feet long, forty-five wide, two stories high. It was dedicated September 2, 1856. This building was destroyed by fire December 15, 1868. Another school-house of somewhat similar construction was erected at the expense of the town, to serve for a High School, Andover being relieved by act of the Legislature from the support of any other High School.

The first principal elect of the Punchard Free School was Peter Smith Byers, A. M., of Andover. He never filled the chair of instruction, being in infirm health at the time of his election, March 13, 1854. He resigned the position April 7, 1855, and died March 19, 1856.

The first principal of the Punchard School was a gentleman of rare scholarship, and surpassing excellence and beauty

[1] *Biographical Memoir of Mr. Punchard.*

MEMORIAL HALL

PUNCHARD FREE SCHOOL

of character. The memory of such a man is a legacy to any institution with which his name stands associated.

Peter Smith Byers was born in Brechin, Scotland, September 12, 1827. He was the eldest son of James Byers and Mary Smith Byers (a sister of Messrs. James, John, and Peter Smith, of Brechin and Andover). In his ninth year he came with his parents to Andover. At sixteen he was confirmed in Christ Church, and began to study with a view of entering the ministry. He was fitted for college at Phillips Academy, and graduated at Harvard, 1851, the third in rank in a class of sixty-three members. He was for two years instructor in Latin and Greek in Phillips Academy, and in 1853 elected Principal of Abbot Academy, whence he was called to the principalship of the Providence High School. Soon after, the trustees of the Punchard School elected him to the office of Principal, and, that his failing health might be restored by rest from care and labor, offered him a salary without service, while the school building should be erecting.

The death of Mr. Byers was a loss deeply felt in the community, especially in the educational circles of Andover. His gentleness and his goodness had endeared him to all who knew him, and his scholarship and dignity of character commanded respect. The memorial discourse of his rector at his funeral was published by his college classmates, one of whom writes in regard to him: "In his threefold character as a scholar, a gentleman, and a Christian he had the entire respect and confidence of all our class. If I were to single out any one who had a more uniform and high respect from all, and who had a higher influence than any other upon the class, I should certainly single him. Until the grave shall have closed over the last of his friends and classmates, the direct influence of his Christian example will live upon earth."

The second Principal was Nathan M. Belden, A. M., of Wilton, Conn., graduate of Trinity College, elected January 1, 1856; resigned February 27, 1857.

The third Principal was Rev. Charles H. Seymour, of

Haverhill, elected February 27, 1857; resigned October, 1858.

The fourth Principal was Mr. William G. Goldsmith, of Andover, graduate of Harvard College, elected November, 1858; resigned April, 1870; reëlected 1871; now in office.[1]

Johnson High School, North Andover.

By the joint donation of Col. Theron Johnson, $10,000, and the Hon. Moses T. Stevens, $5,000, with addition of other money from the town, and the gift of the tower clock by Gen. Eben Sutton, North Andover was provided with a handsome brick building for a High School and Town Hall (Johnson High School and Stevens Hall).

The building was dedicated May 21, 1867. An address was made by the Hon. George B. Loring. The names of the principals, with the time when they began to teach, are as follows : —

SAMUEL C. SMITH, Rutland, Mass., graduate of Amherst College, 1867.

LEMUEL S. HASTINGS, St. Johnsbury, Vt., Dartmouth College, 1870.

PERCIVAL G. PARRIS, Paris, Me., Union College, 1872.

ANNIE HOWE, Marlborough, Mass., Wellesley College, 1875.

GEORGE N. CROSS, Methuen, Mass., Amherst College, 1876.

Public Libraries.

The Public or Town Library is now recognized as an adjunct and supplement to the school system, at least in theory, the object of the towns in appropriating money for the support of a free library being the enlightenment of the people.

The forerunner of the public library was called the "Social Library." In enumerating the social libraries of America, the report of the National Bureau of Education, 1875, says, "The chief means of literary culture open to Americans a hundred years ago were (in Massachusetts) at Salem a social library, one at Leominster, one at Hingham." To this should be

---

[1] During the interim Mr. Goldsmith was instructor in Phillips Academy, the town of Andover meanwhile supporting a High School temporarily until the completion of the Punchard School Building.

added "one at North Andover," for in 1770 a social library was in existence here which continued to distribute books and receive new shareholders for at least seventy years. The books were finally sold at auction, and almost every old family now has books with the label "Andover Social Library." Three catalogues of this library are in existence, one a manuscript, date 1770, one printed 1823, one 1837.

One of the rules and regulations of the Catalogue of 1770 is that, "For the futer no person shall be admitted a member whose place of residence from the north Meeting-House in Andover exceeds ten miles. Each member shall pay not less than four dollars in cash."

The reason for naming this among the public libraries is that practically it was so. The subscribers gave as a motive for founding it that they were "sensible of the Public advantage of a well-chosen library." The members were allowed to " make over " their interest for any length of time to any person approved by the library committee, and thus the reading public could be supplied with books. The books in this library were chiefly "divinity, phylosophy, physick, history, and poetry." Under "miscellaneous" were two or three works of fiction.

This library was kept in the store of Mr. Phillips. After his death, the books were given out by Miss Abbot, the housekeeper and gardener. The library was kept also at the store of Nathan H. Frost; Capt. Phineas Stevens also had charge of it.

Other local library associations have had existence, one in the Frye village, under the patronage of Messrs. Smith, Dove & Co. A social book-club — private — has been in existence at North Andover for about thirty years.

The first public or free town library, "Memorial Hall," Andover, owes its existence to the thoughtfulness and munificence of Messrs. John and Peter Smith and Mr. John Dove, supplemented by the contributions of other citizens of Andover. In 1870, Mr. John Smith, visiting the public library in Dresden, was impressed with the value of such an institution as a means of education for the people, and he conceived the plan of founding a library in the town of Andover, which should be at the same time (as he expressed the thought in a letter on the subject), "a Memorial Hall, to commemorate and keep in remembrance the names of those who gave their lives in defending our national flag and saving my adopted country to God and liberty." This letter, addressed to his son, Mr. Joseph W. Smith, authorized him to pledge to the town the sum of twenty-five thousand dollars, on condition that an equal sum should be subscribed by others, for the erection of a building and providing for a library. To this pledge Mr. Peter Smith and Mr. John Dove added twelve thousand dollars; Mr. John Byers made a donation of three thousand dollars as a memorial of his brother, Peter Smith Byers, first principal of the Punchard School; Mr. Joseph W. Smith added one thousand dollars; the town voted an appropriation of $4,500, formerly made for a soldiers' monument; Mr. John Smith added five thousand more, and again three thousand; and individual contributions varying from hundreds of dollars, subscribed by prominent citizens, to the child's gift of a few cents, swelled the sum devoted to patriotism and free education till it reached a total of $62,949.70.

The Memorial Hall was built by Messrs. Abbot and Jenkins, and cost, including the grading and ornamenting the grounds, about $40,000. The building was dedicated, with appropriate exercises, on Memorial Day, May 30, 1873. The Memorial Room has marble tablets, in memory of fifty-two soldiers of Andover. The library contains about seven thousand volumes. The librarian is Mr. Ballard Holt.

A public library was established at North Andover in 1875 by a donation of Gen. Eben Sutton. It has received aid from Messrs. Davis and Stone, and Hon. Willard P. Phillips, and also is supported in part by the town. It contains about four thousand volumes. The librarian is Mr. Alfred L. Smith. It is kept at the manufacturing village, Merrimack District.

A library for the free use of the residents of Ballardvale was opened 1878, the proprietor of the mill, Mr. J. Putnam Bradlee, furnishing about one thousand books (of which he is the owner) for circulation. The favor was appreciated by the public, and the books are well read and carefully used.

CHAPTER VIII.

ACADEMIES.

Phillips Academy.

PHILLIPS ACADEMY (or Free School, as it was first called) owes its foundation to the plans and suggestions of Samuel Phillips, Jr., Esq., Judge Phillips, or Lieutenant-governor Phillips, as he is variously styled. He was fitted for college at Dummer Academy, graduated at Harvard College, 1771, and in 1775 set in operation plans for the establishment of the Academy. He enlisted the interest of his father and his uncles, and induced them to make the donations which were the foundation of the Academy. The names of the Phillips family who in the early years of the Academy were its chief founders and upholders, are Hon. Samuel Phillips, North Andover; Hon. John Phillips, Exeter; Hon. William Phillips, Boston; Lieutenant-governor Samuel Phillips, son of Hon. Samuel Phillips; Lieutenant-governor William Phillips, son of Hon. William Phillips.

The constitution and deeds of trust were signed April 21, 1778.

The preamble declares the end of the school to be "the instructing youth not only in English and Latin grammar, writing, arithmetic, and those sciences wherein they are commonly taught, but more especially to learn them the great end and real business of living."

The constitution provides that "no person shall be chosen as a principal instructor unless a professor of the Christian religion, of exemplary manners, of good natural abilities and literary acquirements, of a good acquaintance with human nature, of a natural aptitude for instruction and government."

It was also declared to be "the duty of the master, as the age and capacities of the scholars will admit, not only to instruct and establish them in the truth of Christianity, but also early and diligently to inculcate upon them the great and important Scripture doctrines of the existence of one true God, the Father, Son, and Holy Ghost, of the fall of man, the depravity of human nature, the necessity of an atonement and of our being renewed in the spirit of our minds, the doctrine of repentance toward God and of faith toward our Lord Jesus Christ, of sanctification by the Holy Spirit and of justification by the free grace of God, through the redemption that is in Jesus Christ, in opposition to the erroneous and dangerous doctrine of justification by our own merit or a dependence on self-righteousness, together with the other important doctrines of our holy Christian religion."

The twelve original trustees were: Samuel Phillips, John Phillips, William Phillips, Oliver Wendell, John Lowell, Josiah Stearns, William Symmes, Elias Smith, Jonathan French, Samuel Phillips, Jr., Eliphalet Pearson, Nehemiah Abbot.

The original plan was to locate the school in the North Parish, on the land formerly the Old Training Field on the hill east of Deacon Phillips's house, but the owner was unwilling to sell the land. Therefore, lands (principally an estate of Solomon Wardwell and an estate of George Abbot) were bought on the hill in the South Parish, and, soon after, Judge Phillips removed his residence to that part of the town.[1]

---

[1] Judge Phillips occupied for a few years the old dwelling-house on the Abbot estate. This has been called the "birth-place of the Academy;" for here the first meetings of the trustees were held. It was also the residence of the first three preceptors of the Academy. In later times Dr. Leonard Woods lived here, and delivered his first course of lectures in theology in the west room, which is now used as a dining-room by the Academy Club. An attic window, which commands a pleasant sunset view, is shown as the spot where, during the dark hours of the Revolution, Madam Phillips, in her husband's absence from home, used to seek refuge from care and communion with Heaven.

Judge Phillips, in order to give a convenient dwelling-house to the preceptors of the Academy, removed from this house to another temporary abode (the red house on the Woburn road, near Main Street), and finally, in the winter of 1782, he occupied his permanent home, the mansion-house.

This was the largest and most elegant house which had ever been built in the town. Its raising was an occasion of universal interest. The whole town were gathered together on the hill, watching with mingled anxiety and delight as sec-

PHILLIPS ACADEMY.
[*The "Classic Hall."*]

PHILLIPS ACADEMY.
[*The New Building.*]

The First Academy was fitted up from a joiner's shop on the estate of Solomon Wardwell. This was removed to the north corner of the present Main and Phillips Streets. It was thirty-five by twenty feet, and had seats for about forty students.

In 1785, a new academy was built west of the present site of Brechin Hall. This was destroyed by fire in January,' 1818.

The third academy was built 1818, south of the Seminary Buildings, the present gymnasium. Its school-room Dr. Holmes describes : —

> "The morning came ; I reached the classic hall ;
> A clock-face eyed me, staring from the wall ;
> Beneath its hands a printed line I read :
> YOUTH IS LIFE'S SEED-TIME; so the clock-face said :
> Some took its counsel, as the sequel showed, —
> Sowed — their wild oats, and reaped as they had sowed.
> How all comes back ! the upward slanting floor, —
> The masters' thrones that flank the central door, —
> The long, outstretching alleys that divide
> The rows of desks that stand on either side, —
> The staring boys, a face to every desk,
> Bright, dull, pale, blooming, common, picturesque."

The Divinity College, or Theological Seminary, was added to the Academy 1808, and later a Teachers' Seminary, or Normal School, subsequently changed to the English Department. This occupied the Stone Academy, afterward used as a general school building, on the east side of Main Street nearly opposite the present Phillips Academy. It was destroyed by fire December 21, 1864. The present Academy was erected in 1865.

tion after section of the heavy frame was raised. The Rev. Mr. French made a fervent prayer for its successful accomplishment, and, when all was finished without accident, thanks and festivity followed.

Judge Phillips kept open house, and entertained guests of high and of low degree with dignified courtesy and generous hospitality. Many were the illustrious visitors at the mansion-house. Here, in the southeast parlor, General Washington was received by Madam Phillips and her friends, during his Presidential tour. The chair in which he sat was adorned by Madam Phillips with a ribbon: this, on the day when she heard the news of his death, she took off and put in its stead a mourning badge of crape.

After the death of Judge Phillips his mansion-house was purchased by the trustees, and Madam Phillips removed her residence to the house of Samuel Farrar, Esq.

The Academy was incorporated October 4, 1780, under the name of Phillips Academy, being the first incorporated Academy in the State.

The donations of the Phillips family to the Academy before 1830, besides the original donation of lands by the founders, amounted to over seventy-five thousand dollars. Gifts to the Academy from other sources have been considerable. Samuel Farrar, Esq., the Treasurer of the Board of Trustees, gave his salary for many years, which, with the income added to it by investment, made a total of about fifteen thousand dollars. He also gave his law library, and made a testamentary bequest of his whole estate, some ten thousand dollars. Three of the present chairs of the Faculty are endowed : —

The Principal's, on the Peter Smith Byers foundation, about forty thousand dollars, — a memorial gift, 1878, twenty thousand dollars contributed by Mr. Peter Smith, ten thousand dollars by Mr. John Smith, ten thousand dollars by Mr. John Byers.

The chair of Natural Sciences is on the George Peabody [1] Foundation, — a donation of twenty-five thousand dollars from the noted banker.

The chair of Latin is on the John C. Phillips [2] Foundation, — a gift of twenty-five thousand dollars by the gentleman whose name it bears.

The school was opened for instruction April 30, 1778. The influence of Judge Phillips brought students from all parts of the country. The two nephews of General Washington, and the sons of Richard Henry Lee, were among the members of the school.

The Hon. Josiah Quincy, a boy of six years, was taken from his mother's tender care and sent to the new boarding-school, where he had a hard time, and would have suffered even more if good Parson French had not been a father to him. He says his mother yielded to what she believed to be "duty" to send her son to school. In regard to his sorrows and troubles he writes : —

[1] Mr. Peabody's father was born in North Andover.
[2] A nephew of Mr. Wendell Phillips, and a descendant from Mr. John Phillips, of Boston, brother of Rev. Samuel Phillips, of Andover.

"Child as I was my mind was abroad with my bats and my marbles. It delighted in the play of the imagination. The abstract and the abstruse were my utter detestation. The consequences were that I often came home to Mr. French in tears, having been either censured or punished. I found in his bosom a neverfailing place of rest for my sorrow and suffering."

The Principals of the Academy for a hundred years [1] have been : —

1778–1786	ELIPHALET PEARSON, LL. D.
1786–1793	EBENEZER PEMBERTON, LL. D.
1795–1809	MARK NEWMAN, A. M.
1810–1833	JOHN ADAMS, LL. D.
1833–1837	OSGOOD JOHNSON, A. M.
1837–1871	SAMUEL H. TAYLOR, LL. D.
1871–1873	FREDERIC W. TILTON, A. M.
1873	CECIL F. P. BANCROFT, Ph. D.

ELIPHALET PEARSON (1778–1786) was born in Byfield, Newbury, 1752, son of a farmer, Daniel Pearson; graduated at Harvard College 1773, and in 1774 taught the Andover Grammar School. He had an original and inventive genius, besides being a classical scholar, and was a teacher of singing, a helper in the manufacture of gunpowder, a practical landscape gardener, laying out the college grounds. In 1786 he was elected Professor of Hebrew in Harvard College. In 1806 he resigned the office, and returning to Andover was active in founding the Theological Seminary, of which he was elected Associate Professor of Sacred Literature. He resigned office after a year, and, in 1820, removed to Harvard, Mass., and engaged in agriculture. He died at Greenland, N. H., September 12, 1826, aged 74 years. He married Priscilla Holyoke, daughter of President Holyoke, of Harvard College. Their daughter, Mary Pearson, was married to the Rev. Ephraim Abbot, of Greenland, N. H. Dr. Pearson married again, 1785, Sarah Bromfield, daughter of Edward Bromfield, Esq. Their son, Henry Bromfield Pearson, graduated at Harvard College, 1816; was an attorney at law in Philadel-

[1] The Academy celebrated its centennial, which was a memorable occasion, June 5 and 6, 1878. Many liberal gifts were then made for the school's re-endowment.

phia. Edward Pearson was a resident of Harvard, Mass. Margaret Pearson was married to the Rev. I. H. T. Blanchard, pastor of the Unitarian Church, Harvard.

EBENEZER PEMBERTON, LL. D. (1786-1793), was born in Boston, 1747. He was grandson of Mr. Ebenezer Pemberton, minister of the Old South Church, and brought up by his uncle, the Rev. Dr. Ebenezer Pemberton. He was a graduate of Princeton College, 1765; studied theology, also law; was principal of Plainfield Academy, Conn., before he came to Andover. He was beloved by the students of the Academy, and governed it with ease. After resigning his position, he removed to Billerica, where he had a school; also, he taught in Boston. He acquired no property, and was in his old age paid an annuity by his former pupils as a testimony of their gratitude. He died 1835, June 25, aged eighty-nine. He married Miss Elizabeth Whitewell, of Salem, and had a son and two daughters.[1]

MARK NEWMAN, M. A. (1795-1809), was born at Ipswich, September 7, 1772, fitted for college at Phillips Academy, Exeter. He was an inmate of the family of Dr. John Phillips who, from interest in his talents and character, gave him the privilege of the Academy, he being unable to pay the tuition fees. He graduated at Dartmouth College 1793, and became Assistant Principal of Phillips Academy 1794, and Principal in 1795. He was eminently respected in the fifteen years of his office as Preceptor, and the forty years in which he was connected with the Board of Trustees. He was licensed to preach, and supplied the church in West Newbury; was a prominent member of the South Church for fifty-seven years, and deacon from 1811 to 1845. After resigning his office in the Academy, he was for many years a bookseller and publisher of religious books. He died[2] June 15, 1859, aged almost eighty-seven years.

Mr. Newman married, 1795, Miss Sally Phillips. She died 1811. Their children were: Prof. Samuel P. Newman; Mr. Mark H. Newman, of Andover; Rev. William John New-

---

[1] So far as I have been able to learn, the family name is extinct.
[2] At his death a memorial sermon was preached by his pastor, the Rev. Mr. Monar, with the title *The Enduring and Varying Beauty of a Good Man's Life*.

man; Margaret Newman; Sarah Phillips Newman; Hannah H. Newman, married to Rev. S. A. Fay.

Mr. Newman married a second wife, — Mrs. Abigail Dodge, of Salem. Their daughter, Anna Dodge Newman, died at the age of twenty-two.

JOHN ADAMS, LL. D. (1810–1833), was born at Canterbury, Conn., September 18, 1772, graduated at Yale College, 1795. He was a teacher in Plainfield and Colchester previous to his connection with Phillips Academy. He was an able and efficient instructor and principal, — after the fashion of the time severe, yet kindly, and a friend to all good students.

> "Supreme he sits, — before the awful frown
> That bends his brows, the boldest eye goes down."

The later years of Dr. Adams's life were spent in Illinois in labor for Sunday-schools, in which he was eminently useful.

Dr. Adams married, 1798, Miss Elizabeth Ripley, of Colchester, Conn. They had eleven children, two of whom died in infancy. In 1829, Mrs. Adams died. In 1831, Dr. Adams married Miss Mabel Burrit, of Troy, N. Y.

Of the sons the eldest was the late Rev. William Adams, D. D., LL. D., of New York.

Mr. Ripley Adams, a graduate of Yale College, and Principal of Academies in Georgia and South Carolina, died 1870. Rev. John R. Adams, D. D., died 1866, and was buried in the Chapel Cemetery, at Andover.

Of Dr. Adams's daughters, four were married to ministers, — Mary[1] to Rev. Daniel Hemenway; Elizabeth R. to Rev. George Cowles (both drowned in the wreck of *The Home*, 1837); Harriet H.[1] to Rev. John Q. A. Edgell; Abby A. to Rev. Albert M. Egerton, also to Richard McAllister, of Milledgeville, Ga.; Emily J. to Mr. J. H. Bancroft, of Jacksonville, Ill.; Phebe P.[1] to Mr. William H. Campbell.

OSGOOD JOHNSON, M. A. (1833–1837), son of Mr. Osgood Johnson, was born at Andover September 9, 1803; graduated at Dartmouth College 1828; was teacher in Phillips Academy from 1828 until he became Principal. He was uni-

---

[1] Deceased.

versally beloved and respected ; a man of rare qualities. He died at the age of thirty-four, deeply lamented.

> "A loving soul to every task he brought,
> That sweetly mingled with the lore he taught." [1]

Mr. Johnson married Miss Lucretia Bly, of Hanover, N. H. Their children were : Mr. Osgood Johnson, who studied for the ministry, became Principal of the Cambridge High School, and died 1837, at the age of twenty-five ; Lieutenant A. O. Johnson, who was mortally wounded at the battle of Missionary Ridge, Tenn., November 25, 1863, and died at the age of twenty-seven ; Lucretia O. Johnson, married to Rev. William B. Wright ; Frances Johnson, who died at the age of fifteen.

SAMUEL H. TAYLOR, LL. D. (1837-1871), was born in Londonderry, N. H., October 3, 1807, graduated at Dartmouth College 1832. He did not enter college till he was eighteen, having been then for some years in active labor and supervision of a farm. He studied for a time in Andover Theological Seminary, and was meanwhile tutor in Dartmouth College. Continuing his studies in theology, he graduated from the Seminary 1837, when he accepted the Principalship of Phillips Academy, which he held till his death. As an instructor of youth, Dr. Taylor was second in reputation to none. His methods of teaching and government, although such as would, perhaps, not now be satisfactory, kept the standard of Phillips Academy so high that few schools equalled, and scarcely one surpassed it. He was not only a disciplinarian and teacher but a scholar, the author and editor of some of the most valuable classical text-books, and a gentleman of dignified, almost courtly manners. He was an indefatigable worker, and died at his post. On Sunday, January 29, 1871, although suffering from indisposition, he walked through a severe snow-storm to the Academy to meet his Bible-class. As he entered the vestibule, surrounded by the students, he fell in a sudden fit of fainting, or exhaustion, and, in ten minutes after, he was dead.

The funeral services were held in the Academy Hall, Feb-

[1] *The School-Boy*, by Dr. O. W. Holmes.

ruary 2, 1871. From a "Memorial," by Professor Park, is quoted the following extract, in regard to Dr. Taylor's rigid exaction of obedience: "He had a stern conscience, a keen sense of duty, a deep regard for obligation. He deemed it his duty to insist on strict regularity in his school. The future usefulness of his pupils required it. He believed that one of the dangers to which this democratic land lies exposed is a disrespect of law; he, therefore, believed that he was performing an act of kindness to his pupils when he accustomed them to obey."

Dr. Taylor married a daughter of Rev. Dr. Parker, of Londonderry, N. H. Her death, which occurred some years after that of Dr. Taylor, was like his, on the Sabbath, and almost instantaneous.

Two of Dr. Taylor's sons are teachers: Mr. George H. Taylor, formerly Instructor in Phillips Academy, now Principal of Kinderhook Academy, N. Y.; Mr. Arthur F. Taylor, Assistant Instructor in Physics in the University of Pennsylvania. The eldest son, Mr. James Taylor, is connected with the Fairbanks Scale Works, St. Johnsbury, Vt.

FREDERICK W. TILTON A. M. (1871-1873), graduate of Harvard College, 1862, Superintendent of Schools, Newport, R. I., is now Principal of the Rogers High School, Newport.

CECIL F. P. BANCROFT, Ph. D. (1873-   ), graduate of Dartmouth College, 1860, Principal of Appleton Academy, Mount Vernon, N. H. (1860-1864), graduate of Andover Theological Seminary, 1867, Principal Lookout Mountain Educational Institutions, Tenn., 1867-1872, is the present Principal of Phillips Academy, 1880.

Among the instructors in the English Department, some of whom were widely known, was Mr. James Eaton, author of the series of arithmetics which bears his name. He was eighteen years a teacher in the Academy, and died in the service, 1865. His son, Mr. William W. Eaton, is an Instructor in the Theological Seminary.

Mr. William H. Wells, author of a text-book on English Grammar, which was long used in our schools, preceded Mr. Eaton in office. He was afterward Principal of the Putnam

Free School at Newburyport. He now lives in Chicago, where he was for many years President of the Board of Education.

The private boarding-school of Master William Foster was opened some years after Phillips Academy, and was chiefly intended for boys who did not wish to take a classical course. Mr. Foster lived on his father's estate, the home of his boyhood. He made additions to the house to adapt it to the wants of his large household, which numbered sometimes more than twenty-five. The ancient house, as he remodelled it, still stands, — a long, rambling building, nestled under the hill, a little off Central Street, a half-mile west from the South Church. Near the street was a school-house, now removed.

The old family manse has names of boys carved on its walls, and many nicks of their penknives in its wainscotings. A large part of the furniture and books of Master Foster are stored in the garret, queer chests of drawers, strong desks, and toilet sets at which, no doubt, reluctant lads made themselves presentable at early morning hours. Some aged persons now remember having seen the boys at table, seated on long benches, and each with a bowl of milk or chocolate, and the fresh loaf, baked on the great brick oven's bottom, nicely swept clean of the live coals. The boys had ovens in the sand-hill near the house, where at night, when they were supposed to be safe in bed, they roasted unlucky chickens, which disappeared mysteriously from the roost.

Mr. Foster's mother presided over the household, — a gentle, placid lady of the old school, a sister of Samuel Abbot, Esq., the founder of the Theological Seminary. She died in 1820, aged eighty-seven. The school was continued till within a few years of her death.

Mr. Foster married, late in life, Miss Sally Kimball, of Plaistow, N. H. He had one son, the late Mr. William Phillips Foster.

Franklin Academy — Male Department.

The establishment of Phillips Academy in the South Parish, diminished the interest of a part of the town in the support of a classical grammar school, and reduced the advantages of the residents of the North Parish who were remote from the new academy. This parish, therefore, soon began to contemplate establishing a free school, or academy. In 1787, the subject came up for discussion, and Mr. Frederick Frye offered to give a piece of land for the site. But the location was not acceptable. In 1799, Mr. Jonathan Stevens gave land on the hill north of the meeting-house. Subscriptions were made by some of the principal citizens. The academy also received a fund of a little more than eight hundred and seventy-five dollars from the division of the proprietors' money. The academy was built in 1799. It had been provided that the school should be for both sexes, and it was the first incorporated academy in the State where girls were admitted. The academy was built with two rooms of equal size, — the north room for the male department, the south room for the female department. A preceptor and preceptress had charge respectively of the two departments. The school was incorporated in 1801 as the North Parish Free School, and in 1803, by act of the General Court, the name was changed to Franklin Academy. This school, though now discontinued, had a flourishing life of more than fifty years, and numbered among its members students from more than a hundred different towns, a dozen States, and several foreign countries. No history of it has been written, no catalogue issued, no records kept of the names of the instructors. Two manuscript records have been found, one containing the names of the male students from 1800 to 1802, and from 1811 to 1834, the other the names of the female students from 1801 to 1821. The names of the preceptors are nowhere found recorded, and the recollections of the pupils and residents of the town in regard to them are indistinct and often conflicting. The following are such facts as the means of information supply.

The first Preceptor was Mr. [presumably the Rev. Micah] Stone, of Reading, a graduate of Harvard College 1790, tutor 1796, student of theology with Rev. Jonathan French, Andover, settled 1801 at Brookfield.

Mr. James Flint (Rev. Dr. Flint, of Salem) was Preceptor, 1800-1801.

Mr. Nathaniel Peabody was Preceptor from 1801 to 1804, during which time the name of the school was changed to Franklin Academy. Mr. Peabody was a graduate of Dartmouth College, 1800. He went from the Franklin Academy to Billerica, where he was also engaged in teaching, and where he studied medicine. After an extended course of study in other places, he settled in Salem, and continued to practice his profession during the greater part of his life. As a Preceptor of Franklin Academy, he was respected and beloved. A memento of his friendly relations with his pupils, and of their proficiency in composition, he kept through life, and it was found among his private papers after his death. It is an elaborate oration, with the heading: —

"*A Voluntary Address of Students of Franklin Academy, April 3, 1804. — Written by Dale, pronounced by Farnum.*"

After Mr. Peabody there was a Preceptor for a short time, supposed to have been Mr. Joseph Hovey,[1] a graduate of Harvard College, 1804.

Mr. Samuel L. Knapp was Preceptor in 1805 and 1806. He was a graduate of Harvard College, 1804. He afterward practised law in Newburyport, was editor of the "Boston Gazette" and "Boston Monthly," author of "Sketches of Distinguished Americans," and a book on American literature. He was a man of marked peculiarities, and was regarded as a sort of odd genius by the people of North Andover, although all recognized that he was a man of uncommon ability. He was a favorite with the young folks. One instance of his eccentricity was his buying a load of wood for a poor family, to prevent the town officers from chopping the limbs off the elm-tree planted by Chaplain Frye. The story has been told that he bought and took a deed of the land around the tree, but this is contradicted, and the statement made that he bought a lot to be buried in, on the road or lane, commonly called Judy Wood's lane.

Mr. Knapp subjected the pupils to few rules. The students from out of town lived as sons and daughters with families of culture (boys and girls in one household), and re-

[1] Not sufficiently ascertained.

ceived parental care. One of the principal homes was that of Mr. Peter Osgood (the father of the Rev. Peter Osgood).

The reminiscences of the few who yet remain of the early students of Franklin Academy, are of delightful days. The notions of propriety in the North Parish were then much relaxed from the rigidity of Puritan customs, and many social recreations were permitted to the young folks. These festivities the elders directed and shared. The following is a copy of a card, a relic of the good times of the Franklin Academy students. It will be noted that the name of the Preceptor heads the list of managers.

ANDOVER BALL.

The company of Mr. W. Johnson is requested at Mr. Parker's Hall on Tuesday Evening at 6 o'clock, August 19, 1806.

S. KNAPP,
J. KITTREDGE,
D. BERRY,
B. W. HILDRETH,
} *Managers.*

Another card of later date fixes the time at five o'clock. It is elaborate in finish, adorned with musical deities and instruments, and printed in the best style of art. The managers, E. Dale, S. Osgood, D. Robinson. The card of latest date has gone back still another hour of the day, a presage of the time when there would be no more school balls for Franklin Academy students : —

MR. ANSART'S
SCHOOL BALL,
At Isaac Parker's Hall, Andover,
On *Monday, April* 11, 1808.
Dancing to commence precisely at
4 o'clock P. M.

After Mr. Knapp, Mr. Samuel M. Burnside was the Preceptor. He was a graduate of Dartmouth College 1805. He studied law with the Hon. Artemas Ward, and settled in Worcester.

Mr. James Cushing Merrill, graduate of Harvard College 1807, was Preceptor about 1810. Under his tuition three North Andover "boys" were fitted for college : Rev. Peter Osgood, Dr. Samuel Johnson, and Dr. John I. Carlton, who graduated 1814.

Mr. Timothy Hilliard, graduate of Harvard College 1809, was Preceptor about that time. He was afterward minister in Sudbury ; in 1814 he became a physician and practised at Nashua, N. H. The only memory of him found in North Andover is, to use the phrase of the narrator, "his chasing white-faced bumble-bees on his way to school."

Other early Preceptors were Mr. David Damon, a graduate of Harvard College 1811, subsequently a minister at West Cambridge ; Mr. Page (possibly the Rev. Robert Page, a graduate of Bowdoin College) ; Mr. John Cleaveland, of Topsfield, a graduate of Bowdoin College 1821, counsellor at law, New York. Two Preceptors of the year 1825 are now living. One, the Rev. Seth Waldo, taught a few months in the summer of that year. He has been during most of the time since, more or less engaged in teaching, either in charge of academies or private pupils. He is a graduate of Amherst College and Andover Theological Seminary, 1834 ; was Principal of Oberlin College Institute, and has been a preacher in various places in the West, as a Home Missionary, and Principal of a select school in Geneseo, Ill. He married Miss Abiah Spofford, of North Andover.

Mr. Stephen Coburn, of Ipswich, was preceptor of Franklin Academy, from September, 1825, to May, 1826. He was a graduate of Andover Theological Seminary, not ordained ; a teacher in Ipswich after he left North Andover ; postmaster of Ipswich in 1832. He held the latter office more than a quarter of a century. He is now in his eighty-third year.

But in the school traditions one name has overshadowed all other names. The terrors of Master Simeon Putnam's discipline have been so faithfully handed down by the students who experienced them, that it has come to be a current belief in the neighborhood that his day dates back to the early period of the school. "Old Put," he is most often called, although he was only forty-seven years old when he died. The anachronisms and the legends on this subject are amusing, and illustrate the saying, "The evil that men do lives after them, the good is oft interred with their bones."

Mr. Putnam was from Rutland, Mass., a graduate of Harvard College, 1811. He studied divinity, but from overwork broke down and was unable to preach. He took his second degree in 1817, and about that time came to take charge of Franklin Academy. He married Miss Abigail B. Fay, of Concord, Mass., a lady of great excellence and a friend to many a school-boy, who, but for her tenderness, would have felt himself friendless under the master's stern discipline.

Mrs. Putnam outlived her husband by nearly twelve years, residing in the house which he had built at Andover. Mr. Putnam carried on the academy till shortly before his death, May 19, 1833, with an interval of a little over a year, 1825-1827, when the Trustees, becoming dissatisfied with the terms of their agreement with him, and his large receipt of profits, took the school into their own hands. He at once erected a building for his use on the hill near his house (the Bradstreet house), north of the burying-ground, and there continued his "classical school." Franklin Academy could not compete with Mr. Putnam's private school, and in 1827 new terms of agreement with him were entered into. He and his partner, and associate principal, the Rev. Cyrus Pierce, leased the Franklin Academy from the Trustees, agreeing to "receive all the children of inhabitants of the North Parish, at a tuition of twenty-five dollars for forty-five weeks, or in that proportion for a term, and to allow the Trustees the use of his school-house for their Female School thereon, such portions of the year as they may require."

The state of the school is thus described, 1829:[1] "It is constantly and deservedly rising in reputation for thorough instruction and moral discipline. . . . . Its reputation is inferior to none, and it has never been more flourishing than at the present time."

[1] Abbot's *History*.

Mr. Putnam was, there can be no question, often unjust, though probably not intentionally so, always harsh, and sometimes cruel to the idle and disobedient. He had many bad boys to manage; some of whom were, no doubt, made worse by his severity. Many of them lived with him in his house, and by their perpetual misdoing and perverseness rasped his nerves and exasperated his temper. He was in ill health, a sufferer most of the time with acute neuralgia, and the constant strain broke him down in the prime of manhood. It has been common to hear little that was kindly about Master Putnam in the place of his residence. It was, however, with the conviction that he must have had some strong and good points of character, that this attempt to write a brief biography was undertaken, for no man without ability, and some proper discharge of a preceptor's duty could, for nearly fifteen years, have kept such a school as the Franklin Academy was under Mr. Putnam; its ranks constantly filled by students from all parts of the country, and that while within two miles was Phillips Academy with the advantages of endowment and the reputation of almost a half-century. This belief has been confirmed by the testimony of one of the most eminent of Mr. Putnam's pupils. Prof. Cornelius C. Felton, in giving some facts in regard to his own education, to the biographer of Harvard Graduates (Dr. John L. Sibley), paid a tribute to Master Putnam's instruction. The statement, as taken down from Professor Felton's lips, is kindly allowed to be here used:—

"Early in the summer of 1822, his (Prof. Felton's) father sent him to Mr. Simeon Putnam's private academy at North Andover, and there he stayed a year and three months. When he went there, the intention was that he should stay only one term (on account of his father's straitened circumstances). Mr. Putnam was an enthusiastic scholar, a great lover of the classics and of Edmund Burke, a man very austere in his manners, but gentle and kind to all who wanted to study, and who awakened extravagant enthusiasm in all his pupils. After some time, Mr. Putnam, knowing his father's circumstances, called him up one day and told him he wanted him to go to college, and that he would trust him for his tuition bill until he was able to pay him. This was in the summer of 1822.

He came to college in 1823. In this year and a quarter, while at Franklin Academy, he read 'Sallust' four times, 'Cicero's Orations' four times, 'Virgil' six times, 'Græca Minora' five or six times, and the poetry of it, till he could repeat nearly all of it by memory; the 'Annals and Histories of Tacitus,' 'Justin,' 'Cornelius Nepos,' the 'Anabasis of Xenophon,' four books of 'Robinson's Selections from the Iliad,' Greek Testament four times, besides writing a translation of one of the Gospels and a translation of 'Grotius de Veritate,' which he brought in the manuscript to college. He also wrote a volume of about two hundred pages of Latin exercises, and one of about one hundred pages of Greek exercises, and studied carefully all the mathematics and geography requisite to enter college."

After such students, it is no wonder Mr. Putnam had small patience with dunces, or even with the ordinary commonplace boys, more fond of frolic than of Burke and the classics.

The sons of Mr. Putnam were Rev. Charles S. Putnam, rector in the Church of the Redeemer, Brooklyn, N. Y., who died at forty-two, 1860; Prof. John N. Putnam, of Dartmouth College, who died at the age of forty-one, 1863. Both were graduates of Andover Theological Seminary.

Other Preceptors were Rev. Cyrus Pierce, 1833; Benjamin E. Cotting, M. D., 1833; John A. Richardson, A. M., 1833-1836; John White Brown, Esq., and Dr. Charles Allen, 1839-1840; Hon. George B. Loring, 1841. Dr. Loring was the first Preceptor, native of the town. He was a student of Franklin Academy, graduate of Harvard College, 1838, and Medical School, 1842. He is a resident of Salem. He was elected representative to Congress, 1876 and 1878, and is at present a member. Mr. Hiram Berry, Preceptor, 1845-1847, is a resident of North Andover. He was representative to the Legislature in 1873.

The succeeding teachers were Mr. Isaac T. Case and Mr. Spencer Wells, graduates of Bowdoin College. The school was given up about 1853.

Franklin Academy. — Female Department.

While the advantages of classical education were provided for boys as early as 1647 in the colony, it was not thought necessary or suitable for girls (except in families of wealth and leisure), to devote much time to study. The wives and daughters of some of the principal citizens of Andover, in the first half century, did not write their names : Sarah Osgood, wife of the first representative to the General Court; Hannah, wife of the representative Thomas Chandler; Hannah, relict of George Abbot and Rev. Francis Dane (but possibly because of the infirmity of age when she signed the paper found); Margery, mother of Thomas Osgood; Mary, wife of Daniel Poor; Rachel, wife of Richard Sutton; Sarah, wife of Joseph Wilson; Mary, wife of Andrew Foster; Mary, wife of Job Tyler; Rebecca, wife of Robert Eames; Rebecca Marble; Elizabeth, wife of Dea. John Abbot, and mother of the Harvard graduate, 1737. Abiel Abbot; several daughters of Henry Gray; Sarah, wife of Samuel Phelps; Ruth, wife of Edward Phelps; Sarah, relict of Samuel Preston,—and many other women of good social standing, made their mark on the papers and legal documents to which their assent was required. Nor was Andover an exceptional town in this respect. This inability of women to write appears in all the towns in the colony, and was also common in the old country. One of the daughters of the poet Milton, who read Latin by rote to her blind father, could not write her name. It is true that many men of ancient Andover could not write; but, as a rule, the women were less instructed than the men. Gradually, however, studies, as accomplishments, became fashionable, especially for the daughters of the wealthy. The first record of the education of an Andover young lady we have from a French gentleman, the Marquis de Chastellux, who in 1782-83 made a tour of the United States, and visited our town : —

"Nous nous arretames a South Andover, cinq milles au dela de Bilerika, dans une mauvaise auberge tenue par un nommé Foster. Sa femme avait des enfants charmans, mais elle me parut extravagante, et je crois qu'elle etait un peu ivrée. Elle me montra avec beaucoup d'importance un livre dans lequel lisait sa fille ainee & je fus surpris de trouver que c'etait un livre de prière en langue italienne. Cette meme fille qui etait agée a peu pres de dix-sept ans me recita aussi une prière en langue indienne. Elle n'y comprenait rien et l'avait apprisé par hazard d'un domestique indien.

Mais sa mere trouvait tout cela admirable. Nous nous contentames de faire repaitre nos chevaux dans ce mauvais cabaret & nous en partimes a une heure & demie." [1]

Some interesting glimpses of the social life of the young ladies, and also of their attainments in composition, are obtained from letters of correspondence (1787 and 1795) between the daughters of Dr. Thomas Kittredge and their friends. These letters, simple and unstudied, are bright and vivacious, and present a favorable idea of the young ladies' epistolary training.

One addressed to Miss Patty Kittredge describes the musical efforts of the writer:—

"Dec. 18, 1795.

"Thank you, my dear girl, for your friendly letter; also for the song. It is a pretty little thing, but I shall not dare to sing it with you, and if I can make music enough to get Abbot to sleep I shall be glad. You would laugh to see what a scampering there is when I attempt to sing. Sir gives a look of disapprobation, jumps up, shrugs his shoulders, and retires. The deacon,[2] with a sagacious stare, comes up with his usual vivacity, and asks the favor of a song. To gratify the good old Bachelor, I begin to tune up; then down comes the Almanack and he is mighty busy; not to see when the moon fulls, but merely to pass away time; indeed, every part of the family is affected in some way or other. Spring lays by the fire motionless, the cats are all up dancing cotillons; they make quite a burlesque appearance, and all at my expense, too. Is it not abominable?"

Another correspondent, Miss Lucy Foster, then visiting at Canterbury, N. H., speaks of the loneliness, and contrasts it with the gayeties of Andover:—

---

[1] "We stopped at South Andover, five miles below Billerica, in a wretched inn kept by a man named Foster. His wife had some charming children; but she appeared to me extravagant (in her boasting), and I think she was a little intoxicated. [The excitement of talking face to face with a Marquis might readily make the simple woman of Andover seem *ivrée*.] She showed me with much importance a book in which her eldest daughter read, and I was surprised to find it was a prayer-book in the Italian tongue. This same daughter, who was about sixteen years of age, recited to me also a prayer in the Indian language. She understood nothing of it, having learned it by chance of an Indian domestic. But her mother found all this admirable. We contented ourselves with having our horses fed in this wretched tavern, and took our departure from it at half-past one."

[2] The deacons at this time were Isaac Abbot, Nathan Abbot, Daniel Poor.

"I hear oftener than I wish to of your dances and other amusements, not, my dear girl, that I wish you to be deprived of them; far from it, altho' I am not altogether happy, I wish my friends all the happiness they can enjoy, but at the same time it wounds my feelings to think of those diversions which you know I am so fond of, and can't partake of them."

. Andover seems to have been a remarkably social town, for another correspondent from Salem writes to Miss Kittredge: —

"Tell Susan she must hasten her visit, for all the girls are impatient to see her; but I suppose she is loth to part with all her amusements in Andover to come to poor dull Salem, for I assure you, Patty, that it is quite as dull as ever. I was in company with Polly Orne the other afternoon. She said that she wished to see you very much, for she had often heard you spoken of as being very handsome."

Miss Lucy Foster writes again in regard to a "young minister." She says: "he is in pursuit of a wife, and wants one that is *young, handsome, and gay*. I know of none that will answer his purpose. I suppose it will avail nothing if I send him," etc.

And so on. The letters show what these young ladies were doing. One is full of good advice, not to read too many novels, but when deeply interested to stop reading and "take up your stocking," referring to the knitting which every young woman was supposed to have begun, ready to "take up" when not otherwise occupied.

These letters make no allusions to school or study; but undoubtedly these girls were sent out of town to some private school for a part of their schooling.

The establishment of Franklin Academy in 1799-1800 made provisions for the education of girls. In respect to this educational movement the town of North Andover may claim distinction, for this Academy was the first incorporated institution in Massachusetts to which young ladies were admitted, and it also made provision for them at the outset.

The names of the preceptresses of the Academy have been even more difficult to find than those of the preceptors. The first seems to have been Miss Stone, who merely taught needle-work.

The first preceptress who gave instruction in the studies of the school was a lady of rare gifts and attainments, and the story of her life and her preparation for the position of a teacher is instructive.

Elizabeth Palmer was born in 1777, at Watertown, Mass. Her father had been in affluent circumstances in business with her grandfather, Gen. Joseph Palmer. But reverses came; his estate was sold under a mortgage to Governor Hancock. He went to live on a farm at Framingham, fell into despondency, and was of little assistance to his family during the few remaining years of his life. He died suddenly by an accidental fall, while he was living away from his family as tutor to some pupils.

During this trying period Elizabeth, then a mere child, was almost her mother's sole dependence, performing household labor, spinning, and making clothing, and even doing out-of-door labor. Yet through all, she had, as she writes in her journal, an unconquerable desire for literary improvement, and when the day's labors were over she found solace and rest in reading over and over again their small library of standard English authors. After some time she obtained the assistance of her great aunt, Madam Cranch, the sister of Mrs. Abigail Adams. The sister of these two ladies was married to Rev. Stephen Peabody, of Atkinson, N. H., a former resident of North Andover. She invited Miss Palmer to become a member of her household and take the place of a daughter, her own daughter having lately died. In her adopted home Miss Palmer felt it a duty to make herself useful, and as she was excessively sensitive lest she should be dependent, and there was much work to be performed, her labors were hard and perplexing. She not only rendered aid in domestic duties, but also was often called upon by the students in the Atkinson Academy who were members of the minister's family, for assistance in their studies. She also found time occasionally to indulge her literary tastes, and wrote poetry, which was published in the Haverhill "Gazette." She made the acquaintance of Mr. Nathaniel Peabody, a student of Dartmouth College, while at Atkinson, and became engaged to be married. When he was Preceptor of Franklin Academy she accepted the position of Assistant or Preceptress, although she was very distrustful of her qualification for the situation. She was, however, remarkably successful, stimulating the pupils under her charge to the same love of learning which she had, and inspiring them with respect and affection. In 1802 she was married to Mr. Peabody. In 1804 they removed to Billerica, where she continued to teach. In Salem, where they subsequently lived, she, with her sister, had charge of a young ladies' school, and continued to the latest years of her life an ardent enthusiasm for learning and teaching.

She was the mother of Miss Elizabeth Peabody, Mrs. Nathaniel Hawthorne, and Mrs. Horace Mann.

Mrs. Peabody's successor as Preceptress was a lady who had received all advantages of education and culture, — Miss Abby Dowse, of Cambridge, Mass. She had attended the ladies' academy in Cambridge and the private school of the Misses Cushing at Hingham, who were among the most accomplished teachers of the day. She is described by her contemporaries as a lady of rare personal beauty, of great dignity and grace of manner, of a sweet disposition, and clear and cultivated mind. She was beloved by her pupils and by all who knew her. She was married in 1808 to Peter Gilman Robbins, M. D., who had been a student of medicine under Dr. Thomas Kittredge, and who died at the early age of twenty-six, leaving two sons, the Rev. Chandler Robbins, D. D., and the Rev. Samuel D. Robbins.

Some of the other preceptresses were: Miss Susan Bulfinch, of Lynn, who, in 1815, was married to the Rev. Daniel Poor, D. D., one of the first missionaries to Ceylon; Miss Mansfield, of Salem; Miss Charlotte Verstille, of East Windsor, Conn.; Miss Bancroft, daughter of Dr. Bancroft, of Worcester; Miss Joanna Prince, of Beverly; Miss Bradford, of Boston; Miss Nancy Denney; Miss Adeline Abbot and Miss Susan Abbot, daughters of Rev. Dr. Abiel Abbot, of Beverly; Miss Hannah Osgood, of North Andover (also a preceptress in Hampton Academy), now living, in her eighty-sixth year, of clear and strong mind and ready memory; Miss Martha Lincoln, married to Mr. John White Brown; Miss Mary Kendall. Miss Lucy Jane Hamlen was the last preceptress who taught in the Academy, a private school. She was married to the Rev. Hollis Russell, of Schoolcraft, Mich.

Abbot Academy.

In the growth of the town of Andover the centre of population gradually changed from the original site of the first meeting-house, in the north part of the town, to the neighborhood of the Phillips Academy and the Theological Seminary, in the South Parish, these educational institutions of themselves creating almost a village for their residences and accommodations. The West Parish also formed another centre around its meeting-house. These parishes were not accommodated by the location of the Franklin Academy. Parents could not conveniently send daughters daily to the school, and were not inclined to have them board in the North Parish. Thus for fifty years after the establishment of Phillips Academy the young ladies in the South and West Parishes, who did not avail themselves of the Franklin Academy, had no advantages in the town except those of small private schools, or home instruction. Some of these advantages were superior, and the women educated by them, though without diploma or certificate of graduation, have proved their excellence. Professor Stuart and other professors supported a select school for their daughters, and also many young ladies went out of town to the academies or family schools, where young ladies were taught.

The residents of Andover in process of time came more and more to feel the importance of having an academy for young women, on the same religious and denominational bases as the institutions for young men. In the movement to establish such an academy, the Rev. Dr. Jackson, pastor of the West Church, and the Rev. Mr. Badger, of the South Church, and Dea. Mark Newman, were prominently influential. Samuel Farrar, Esq., also took an active part, advising and directing the beneficence of the founder, Mrs. Sarah Abbot. This lady, a widow (wife of Nehemiah Abbot), and childless, made the trustees of the Academy residuary legatees of her estate of ten thousand dollars, and gave one thousand dollars toward the erection of an academy building. On her security, Mr. Farrar advanced the sum necessary to complete the building. Mrs. Abbot, although she had not herself enjoyed the advantages of early education, appreciated their value, and in her relations with the students of Phillips Academy (her husband had been steward of the Commons) had made many a poor boy presents of books, and otherwise rendered aid to indigent students. It therefore afforded her satisfaction to connect her name with an institution which promised to provide educational advantages for her own sex.

Besides the bequest of Mrs. Abbot, the Academy has received large gifts from other residents of Andover:[1] about seven thousand dollars from the Hon. George L. Davis, of North Andover, and four thousand dollars from each of the brothers, Mr. John Smith and Mr. Peter Smith. Mr. Mark Newman gave an acre of ground for the site of the Academy building. It now has twenty-three acres of grounds tastefully laid out.

The school opened May 6, 1829, with seventy pupils. There have been about three thousand different members in fifty years.

Abbot Academy, the first academy incorporated in the State for the education of girls solely, started with a standard of education as high as any which exists for women to-day, including in its course of study the Latin and Greek languages.

It is doubtful if the school ever in its early years fully realized in its practical workings the plans of its founders for classical study. It gradually conformed to the popular sentiment in favor of a modified course of instruction for young ladies. But the fact that such high ground was taken at the outset by men of the sagacity and practical wisdom of Dr. Jackson, Samuel Farrar, and the others, is an interesting and significant fact. Dr. Jackson lived to see his theories of women's education carried into practice in the establishment of colleges for women.

The Abbot Academy celebrated its fiftieth anniversary June 11 and 12, 1879. The gathering of alumni, and the

[1] The late Mr. Hiram French left a considerable testamentary bequest. Mr. Warren F. Draper has made several donations.

reminiscences and recognitions in the changes of time, were of deep and tender interest to many hearts.[1]

The principals of the Academy in the fifty years have been the following: —

Charles Goddard, A. B.	1829-1831
Samuel Lamson, A. M. [Rev.].	1832-1835
Samuel G. Brown, A. M. [Rev. LL. D.]	1835-1838
Rev. Lorenzo L. Langstroth	1838-1839
Timothy D. P. Stone, A. M. [Rev.]	1839-1842
Asa Farwell, A. M. [Rev.]	1842-1852 [2]
Peter Smith Byers	1853-1853
Miss Nancy J. Hasseltine	1854-1856
Miss Maria J. B. Browne	1856-1857
Miss Emma L. Taylor	1857-1859
Miss Philena McKeen	1859-

A history of the Academy has been recently published, written by Miss Philena McKeen, and her sister, Miss Phebe McKeen. This was the last literary work of the gifted lady, Miss Phebe McKeen, and published after her death.

[1] The names of the trustees for fifty years, as given in the semi-centennial catalogue, are as follows: —

Mark Newman, M. A., elected 1828; Rev. Milton Badger, D. D., 1828; Rev. Samuel C. Jackson, D. D., 1828; Samuel Farrar, Esq., 1828; Hon. Hobart Clark, 1828; Hon. Amos Abbott, 1828; Amos Blanchard, 1828; Rev. Aaron Green, 1829; Rev. Horatio Bardwell, D. D., 1834; Rev. Lorenzo L. Langstroth, 1836; Rev. Samuel Fuller, D. D., 1838; Rev. Lyman Coleman, D. D., 1838; Rev. John L. Taylor, D. D., 1840; Prof. Bela B. Edwards, D. D., 1843; Rev. Amos Blanchard, D. D., 1843; Hon. Alpheus Hardy, 1845; Rev. Henry B. Holmes, 1848; Prof. Simon Greenleaf, LL. D., 1849; Peter Smith, 1849; Prof. Edwards A. Park, D. D., 1851; Rev. Miner G. Pratt, 1851; Rev. William B. Brown, D. D., 1851; Nathaniel Swift, 1851; Edward Buck, Esq., 1854; Samuel Gray, 1855; Rev. Caleb E. Fisher, 1855; Edward Taylor, 1859; Hon. George L. Davis, 1859; Peter Smith, 1870; Warren F. Draper, 1868; George Ripley, 1870; George W. Coburn, 1870; Prof. Egbert C. Smyth, D. D., 1870; Hon. Rufus S. Frost, 1870; Hiram W. French, 1873; Rev. Francis H. Johnson, 1876; Rev. Edward G. Porter, 1878.

[2] Rev. J. B. Bittinger, Acting Principal, 1849-1850.

CHAPTER IX.

THEOLOGICAL SEMINARY.

THE Andover Theological Seminary was dedicated September 28, 1808. The establishment of a school of divinity was a part of the original plan of the founders of Phillips Academy, although not to make it a distinct institution. But the growing numbers of candidates for the ministry, who usually went to finish their studies with the pastors, burdened the latter with a great care, and led to the plan of a school for their training. The Rev. Mr. French is said to have originated the idea of a seminary at Andover, and he was aided in carrying it out by Dr. Eliphalet Pearson.

The first donors of money, the founders and associate founders, were: Madam Phebe Foxcroft Phillips, Andover (South Parish); Hon. John Phillips, Andover (North Parish); Samuel Abbot, Esq., Andover; Hon. William Bartlet, Newburyport; Moses Brown, Esq., Newburyport; Hon. John Norris, Salem.

The name of Madam Phillips heads the list by reason of the priority of her donation;[1] but in every respect there was a propriety in giving to her this place of honor. She was the beloved wife of the projector of the Academy (which contained the plan of the Divinity School), and had shared and stimulated his benevolent undertakings. She was the daughter of one of the eminent men of Cambridge, Hon. Francis Foxcroft, and had received every social and educational advantage which intercourse with the learned and cultivated could confer. Her beauty of person was remarkable; her sweetness and grace of manner charmed all who met her; her conversational powers were so extraordinary that it was said by a contemporary, that "her style of conversation sur-

[1] Mr. Bartlet gave money earlier, but to found a seminary at Newbury.

HON. JOHN PHILLIPS, LL.D.
[1719-1795.]

HON. WILLIAM PHILLIPS.
[1722-1804.]

HON. SAMUEL PHILLIPS.
[1715-1790.]

REV. SAMUEL PHILLIPS.
[1690-1771.]

HON. JOHN PHILLIPS
[1776-1820.]

HIS HONOR SAMUEL PHILLIPS, LL.D.
[1752-1802.]

MADAM PHOEBE PHILLIPS.
[1741-1812.]

THE PHILLIPS FAMILY, OF ANDOVER
Founders and Benefactors of Institutions of Learning and Religion

passed that of any one, male or female, in this country." She was, moreover, a writer of considerable ability, as appears in her long letters to her husband, her sons, and the youth who, in the course of their studies at Andover, came under her influence. Nor were her gifts and graces merely those which adorn and make attractive and lend a charm to social intercourse. To these she added a strength and self-reliance rare among ladies of her social standing. These were, no doubt, largely called forth by the circumstances of her position as the wife of a public servant almost constantly absent from home; she being left to preside over a large household and to look after many dependents.

Such a woman's name, therefore, does not misbecome the high place assigned it in the rolls of the Andover Theological Seminary. In her life and character she has left to it a legacy which multiplies an hundred fold the value of her donations. Mrs. Phillips was a deeply religious woman. Underlying all her courtesies and kindnesses, and directing her intellectual energies and aspirations, was a profound sense of accountability to God. During her whole life this had been the mainspring of her activities, and to inspire in other hearts the same sentiments of piety which she herself cherished, became with her advancing age more and more the object of her supreme desire. She was past threescore years when she made the donation for the Theological Seminary. She had outlived her husband who was her junior in age by nine years; she had laid in the grave one of her sons in the flower of his youth, and though, on the whole, her life had been as abundant in earthly blessing as usually falls to the lot of mortals, she had had enough of vicissitude, and seen enough of the instability of worldly hopes to incline her to leave behind some lasting memorial which might emphasize to her generation and to future generations her conviction of the supreme importance of the things that are unseen and eternal. To look forward in imagination to the long flow of beneficent influences which her gift was to set in motion, filled her heart with pious rapture; and if she could have foreseen how the number of students (thirty-six), with which the Seminary opened, as was then thought, auspiciously, would increase until it amounted in a half-century to more than two thousand, she would have felt even greater satisfaction in the decision which she made to devote this offering to heaven.

Hon. John Phillips, who joined with his mother in this donation, was a merchant of the North Parish. He was a graduate of Harvard College (1795), and had studied for the legal profession, but on account of his health did not pursue it. He was an influential citizen, and his early death, at the age of forty-four, was widely mourned. In his grandsons, four brothers of one household,[1] clergymen, of whom the eldest is the Rev. Phillips Brooks, D. D., is continued the succession in the gospel ministry of the descendants from the Rev. George Phillips, the first minister of Watertown, 1630.

The third named of the founders of the Seminary, Samuel Abbot, Esq., merchant of Andover, endowed the Abbot professorship and made bequests which amounted to the large sum of one hundred and ten thousand dollars. Having no children he lavished all his affection on the Theological Institution. His belief in its claims upon him was strong and undoubting. He felt himself directly called of God to make the donation. In regard to the spirit in which he made his bequest, the Rev. Dr. Woods said in a funeral sermon: —

"Religious beneficence had become his grand object. To this he had consecrated much of the wealth which God had given him. . . . . This Institution was his favorite object, and its prosperity constituted much of his comfort in the concluding years of his life. . . . . He connected with it his most solemn devotions, his purest pleasures, his best hopes of the church's prosperity. . . . . He felt more and more satisfied that in his religious charity he had been directed by the spirit of God, and had done what he should rejoice in forever."

While the Andover lovers of learning were revolving the project of a school of theology, the same subject had been under consideration in another part of Essex County. The Rev. Dr. Spring, of Newburyport, and Dr. Hopkins, of Salem, had almost simultaneously formed a plan for a theological seminary, and had enlisted in the enterprise three rich mer-

[1] Rev. Frederick Brooks, deceased, Rev. Arthur Brooks, Rev. John Brooks.

chants of their respective parishes, — the associate founders before named. When the plans of the two parties became known to each other, it was, after long and anxious discussions, and many delays and doubts, decided to unite their contributions of money and influence for the upholding of one institution, rather than to attempt the maintenance of two similar and rival schools. In order, however, to come to this conclusion, much concession and compromise were required, not only of sectional feeling but of theological dogma. The Hopkinsian and the Calvinistic doctrines, and the many shades of them which were variously visible to the theologians of the time, according to their respective points of view, had to be adjusted and provided for in the foundation of a seminary for mutual coöperation, and it was a work not easily accomplished. The compromise which resulted in a school of theology, on a broad foundation, and the establishment of this institution at Andover, were due largely to the persistent efforts of Dr. Pearson. "He spent," says Professor Park, "nine months in his efforts to effect a union between the two seminaries. During these nine months his plan had been often well-nigh defeated, and the blame of starting it had been laid at his door. During these nine months he had journeyed alone in his chaise (a distance of twenty miles), thirty-six times from this hill to Newburyport, and there reasoned with the keen dialecticians who opposed the Seminary at Andover. During the same nine months he had also taken frequent solitary rides from this hill to Boston, and there confronted the men who opposed the Seminary at Andover, and also that at Newbury. He had spent three weary months in controversy with one class of men who were inimical to his plans and to him also." But he succeeded at last. Hopkinsian and Calvinist joined hands.

"The Hopkinsians (to finish the above quotation) nominated Pearson as the Calvinistic Professor, the Calvinists nominated Woods as the Hopkinsian Professor; the Hopkinsians praised the vigilance of Pearson, the Calvinists praised the diplomacy of Woods, and by such interchange of courtesy the present institution was formed."

One of the associate founders of the Seminary, the Hon.

John Norris, of Salem, was also, in a sense, an Andover citizen. He owned and occupied, for a time, as his summer residence, the Bradstreet house, and was an attendant of the South Church. He made his donation to the seminary in a truly devout spirit. It is said that, when he took the money from the bank in specie, he set it apart by special prayer as to a sacred service. His intention was to give five thousand dollars, but by the influence of Mrs. Norris, his wife, he was induced to double the sum. So great was this lady's interest in the Seminary that, when smitten with sudden and mortal illness, she rallied her strength to sign, in dying, a will,[1] adding to the former donation thirty thousand dollars.

Mr. Moses Brown made his donation, said Dr. Woods, "with readiness, simplicity, and generous kindness." He gave at first ten thousand dollars, and afterward endowed a professorship with the sum of twenty-five thousand dollars.

Mr. William Bartlet made the largest donation, giving twenty thousand dollars to the associate fund, fifteen thousand for the endowment of a professorship, seventy-five thousand for the chapel and professors' houses; and he left a legacy of fifty thousand, — a total of one hundred and sixty thousand dollars. Of this munificent giver, Dr. Leonard Bacon said: "I count it among the privileges of my life to have had even so slight an acquaintance with a man who knew so well what his great wealth could do for his felicity."

In regard to these benefactors of Andover Theological Seminary, a speaker at the semi-centennial celebration, 1858, exclaimed: "They are dead; but is their spirit dead? Are there no more such benefactors? I tremble for the precious treasure in the house now over our heads, lest the want of some fire-proof building should consign the wisdom of ages to an incendiary ruin!"

Brechin Hall, the new Library Building erected in 1865, was the noble response to this appeal. The three donors, their joint donation amounting to sixty thousand dollars, were the three partners in the manufacturing firm of Smith, Dove, & Company, adopted citizens of Andover, natives of Scotland.

[1] This was contested, but pronounced to be valid.

The library building was named for their native town of Brechin. One of the donors, Mr. John Dove, has passed to his reward, leaving a good man's fragrant memory. His last will added to his former donations a bequest of ten thousand dollars. The brothers, Mr. John Smith and Mr. Peter Smith, are still [1] with us (the elder over eighty years of age), their benefactions too frequent in the town for any figures long correctly to record their total.

The various professorships are named from the donors whose gifts constitute their foundation, the Abbot, Bartlet, and Brown Professorships being named from the three founders of the Seminary. The Hitchcock Professorship is named for Mr. Samuel A. Hitchcock, of Brimfield, who gave nearly one hundred and fifty thousand dollars to the Seminary in the course of twenty years. The Jones Professorship is named for Mr. Frederick Jones, of Boston, who, about 1867, gave fifteen thousand dollars to the Seminary. The Stone Professorship is named for Mrs. Valeria G. Stone, of Malden, who made a gift of one hundred and fifty thousand dollars as a memorial of her husband, the late Mr. Daniel P. Stone.

Respecting the early professors, the Fathers of the Seminary, a few brief sketches may here be added.

The life of Dr. Pearson has already been alluded to, — his connection with the Andover Grammar School, his principalship of Phillips Academy, and his agency in establishing the Theological Seminary. His influence was chiefly in the direction of literary and æsthetic culture rather than in favor of precise doctrinal distinctions and technicalities of creeds. It has been intimated that he sometimes regretted his labors to effect a compromise of the conflicting elements, seeing how difficult it is to make such compromises permanent. He resigned his connection with the Seminary after one year, but continued through life to cherish an interest in its welfare.

The name which represents Andover theology for the first

---

[1] Since the above was written, they have given $30,000 to the Phillips Academy. Mr. Peter Smith died July 6, 1880, while this work was in press. He left a bequest of $10,000 to be added to the Smith and Dove Fund for the Brechin Hall Library.

forty years is Leonard Woods. Dr. Woods was clear, strong, and unwavering in his doctrinal opinions, and was well fitted to build up and defend a system of theology, and to create in other minds the conviction which was in his own mind of its impregnability. It is said that a young minister, under examination, becoming confused by the catechisings of some of the clergy, themselves somewhat befogged in clouds of their own raising, apologized : " If Dr. Woods would ask me one or two questions, the whole thing would be cleared up." In regard to Dr. Woods's system, and his faith in it, his biographer and son-in-law, Rev. Edward A. Lawrence, D. D., says : " He claimed to be in the line of theological succession from Christ through Edwards, Calvin, Augustine, and the Apostles. This creed was his Christianity. It was old, but he believed not worn out, nor the less true for its age. He could no more change it than the facts of his religious history. 'No change,' said he, in his last sickness, to one who questioned him on this point."

It is related that when Dr. Woods entered on his first pastorate he drew up a series of articles of his belief and requested to have it read before the church. His pastor, the Rev. David Osgood, D. D., minister of the church of Medford, of which Mr. Woods was then a member, heard the statement. He himself was opposed to creeds, and becoming impatient under the repetition of the young minister's frequent "I believe," exclaimed : " You believe ten times as much now as you will when you are as old as I am ! " But the good pastor was mistaken. Age only deepened and strengthened the beliefs of Dr. Leonard Woods, and, however men may differ from him in their estimate of the value of creeds, or disagree with him in doctrine, none can fail to respect his sincerity and admire his fearless adherence to what he believed to be true.

Next in order of time of election stands the name of Rev. Edward Dorr Griffin, D. D., the first professor of Sacred Rhetoric, whose impassioned yet classic eloquence, cutting like a two-edged sword and scathing like the fire of heaven, drew from Daniel Webster the remark to a critic of Dr. Griffin : " If you are going the same way with the lightning it won't hurt you ; if not, you had better keep out of its way."

The successors of Dr. Griffin in the same chair were Prof. Ebenezer Porter, D. D., and Prof. James Murdock, D. D., the one a majestic preacher and Christian gentleman, whose memory is embalmed, or rather perennially alive, in the Porter Rhetorical Society; the other described by Professor Stowe as "a little dry man with a large elastic brain and nerves like cat-gut, who never took hold of a subject that he did not hold it till he had got all out of it that there was in it."

Among the earliest names, and one latest to be forgotten, is Moses Stuart. Of him said Dr. Wayland: "When the history of Biblical learning in this country shall be written, and the names of those who have done worthily shall shine in letters of light, who can doubt the first place in that roll will, by universal consent, be inscribed with the name of Moses Stuart?"

To Professor Stuart's private character, Professor Park, in a memorial address, paid the following tribute: "It is no common virtue which is honored in every farmer's cottage of the town where he has lived for two and forty years, and which is venerated by missionaries of the cross in Lebanon and at Damascus. I have heard him praised by Tholuck and Neander, and Henderson and Chalmers, and by an Irish laborer and a servant boy, and by the families before whose windows he has taken his daily walk for almost half a century."

Of the later professors it is beyond our limits to speak. Their very names awaken tender recollections in the hearts of Andover graduates and affectionate gratitude in many homes of Andover which their ministrations have blessed.

Names of the Professors in the Order of their Inauguration.

	Elected.	Dismissed.
Rev. Eliphalet Pearson, D. D.	1808	1809
Rev. Leonard Woods, D. D.[1]	1808	1846
Rev. Edward Dorr Griffin, D. D.	1809	1811
Rev. Moses Stuart, M. A.	1810	1848
Rev. Ebenezer Porter, D. D.	1812	1834
Rev. James Murdock, D. D.	1819	1828
Rev. Ralph Emerson, D. D.	1829	1853
Rev. Edward Robinson, D. D., LL. D.	1830	1833
Rev. Thomas Harvey Skinner, D. D., LL. D.	1833	1835
Pres. Justin Edwards, D. D.	1836	1842
Rev. Edwards Amasa Park,[1] D. D.	1836	–
Rev. Bela Bates Edwards, D. D.	1837	1852
Rev. Austin Phelps,[2] D. D.	1848	–
Rev. Calvin Ellis Stowe, D. D.	1852	1864
Rev. Elijah Porter Barrows, D. D.	1853	1866
Rev. William Greenough Thayer Shedd, D. D.	1853	1862
Rev. Egbert Coffin Smyth, D. D.	1863	–
Rev. Joseph Henry Thayer, M. A.	1864	–
Rev. Charles Marsh Mead, Ph. D.	1866	–
Rev. John Lord Taylor, D. D.[2]	1868	–
Rev. John Wesley Churchill	1868	–
Rev. John P. Gulliver	1879	–
Rev. William J. Tucker	1880	–
LIBRARIANS.		
Samuel Farrar, M. A.	1808	1844
Rensellaer David Chanceford Robbins, M. A.	1844	1848
Rev. Edward Robie, M. A.	1848	1851
Samuel Harvey Taylor, LL. D.	1851	1866
Rev. William Ladd Ropes, M. A.	1866	–
TREASURERS.		
Samuel Farrar, M. A.	1807	1840
Samuel Fletcher, M. A.	1841	1850
Daniel Noyes, M. A.	1850	1852
Rev. John Lord Taylor, D. D.	1852	1868
Edward Taylor, Esq.	1868	–

[1] Theology.   [2] Resigned, 1879. Professor Emeritus.

Faculty as now Constituted.[1]

REV. EDWARDS A. PARK, *Abbot Professor of Christian Theology.*
REV. JOHN L. TAYLOR, *Professor Emeritus of Theology and Homiletics in the Special Course.*
REV. AUSTIN PHELPS, *Professor Emeritus of Sacred Rhetoric.*
REV. JOHN P. GULLIVER, *Stone Professor of the Relations of Christianity to Science.*
REV. EGBERT C. SMYTH, *Brown Professor of Ecclesiastical History.*
REV. J. HENRY THAYER, *Associate Professor of Sacred Literature.*
REV. CHARLES M. MEAD, *Hitchcock Professor of the Hebrew Language and Literature.*
REV. WILLIAM J. TUCKER, *Bartlet Professor of Sacred Rhetoric and Lecturer on Pastoral Theology.*
REV. J. WESLEY CHURCHILL, *Jones Professor of Elocution.*
—— ——,[2] *Smith Professor of Theology and Homiletics in the Special Course.*

The trustees of the Seminary include those of the Phillips Academy. Besides the twelve original members before mentioned in the sketch of the Academy, there are on the Triennial Catalogue (1870), fifty-two names, which include some of the most influential clergymen and laymen of the Trinitarian Congregational Church. Of the pastors of Andover, three have been trustees: Rev. Justin Edwards, D. D., Rev. Samuel C. Jackson, D. D., Rev. John L. Taylor, D. D. The names of the laymen, of Andover, are Hon. John Aiken, M. A., 1844 to 1867, Edward Taylor, Esq., 1867 to the present time. Mr. Aiken died in 1867. Respecting his services as a trustee, his memorialist[3] says: " For every important discussion in the sessions of the Board he was prepared as but few of its members could be, so that for many years no man can be said to have done so much as he toward determining its whole policy and action, yet in all that period no member of the Board seemed less than he to be aspiring to lead it, or more willing than he to be influenced by the judgment of others in it, rather than tenacious of his own."

---

[1] Catalogue of 1879–1880.
[2] Prof. John L. Taylor resigned.
[3] "Memoir of John Aiken," by Rev. John L. Taylor, *The Congregational Quarterly*, July, 1867.

Mr. Aiken was a resident of Andover from 1850 till his death, in 1867, during which time he was agent for a manufacturing company of Lawrence, in active business, and conducting, with executive ability, large and important enterprises. But while engaged in practical affairs he kept up the scholarly tastes and the religious associations which he had formed before his removal to Andover. Born at Londonderry, N. H., 1797, he graduated at Dartmouth College, 1819; was tutor in the college, studied law, and after a time entered into business in connection with one of the mills at Lowell. While there, in 1844, he became a trustee[1] of Andover Seminary.

Mr. Aiken's eldest son, Rev. Charles A. Aiken, D. D., is professor in Princeton Theological Seminary.

Another son was the late Rev. John F. Aiken.

The Library of the Seminary, in Brechin Hall, contains about thirty-seven thousand volumes, besides the religious reviews and periodicals. It has in its collection some rare manuscripts, and also a museum of curiosities from foreign lands whither missionaries have gone, — idols and gods of wood and stone, and emblems of the religious worship of various heathen nations, — all of which make it a place of interest even to a casual visitor. The walls are hung with portraits of the founders and benefactors of the Andover institutions of learning, and busts of the professors adorn the room, so that here is, as it were before one's eyes, the history of Andover Theological Seminary, and we seem to stand in

---

[1] The late Dea. Peter Smith was elected a trustee in 1870. Not only his large donations to the Seminary, but also his personal character and influence gave him a claim to this place of honor. Though of modest, unassuming manners, a plain business man, he yet had the dignity of conscious rectitude and the firmness of simple truth. Though not technically a scholar, he was the friend of scholars. Interested in great educational and philanthropic enterprises, his mind was expanded to embrace the world in plans of beneficence, and yet without losing sympathy for the humblest charity at home. He inspired the confidence and respect and won the affection of the men of learning who were his associates, as he inspired the confidence and respect and won the affection of the most unlettered operative, employé in his mill, or of the little child in the Sunday-school. But to recount his virtues or write his biography is beyond our limits. His name receives frequent mention in other parts of these sketches. His death occurring after the main body of the text is in type, there is only room for this brief tribute to his memory.

THE THEOLOGICAL SEMINARY

BRECHIN HALL

the very presence of the men whose names are familiar on the printed page.

The Seminary printing-press, as it might not improperly be called, may here be mentioned, for although in some of its aspects it was an industrial enterprise, it was also, especially at first, largely an educational and religious force, under the supervision of the officers of the Institution. Theologians have been actually type-setters in the Andover printing-office. When Professor Stuart made his Hebrew Grammar he was in daily supervision of the compositors. Through his influence and assistance the printing of Oriental languages, then new in America, was begun; and there were at Andover types for eleven Eastern languages. In 1821, Dr. Codman made a donation to the Seminary for the purchase of Greek and Hebrew types. This was called for him the Codman Press.

In the printers themselves, the Seminary had able and willing assistants. Messrs. Timothy Flagg and Abraham J. Gould were in hearty sympathy with the aims of the religious and theological institutions which their work was to serve, and it was through their unremitting efforts and their cordial coöperation with the Faculty of the Seminary that the Andover press at that time acquired so high a reputation in the educational and religious world. Both these partners were members of the South Church (Mr. Gould was deacon for twenty-three years), and they regarded their printing press as a trust, to be used for the service of their religious and theological faith.

It is estimated that the publications at Andover of the professors have had a circulation of about four hundred thousand copies.[1] Here the "Bibliotheca Sacra" (now edited by Professor Park) has reached its thirty-seventh volume; here the American Tract Society printed its first tracts. Here was started the first temperance newspaper, the "Journal

[1] "There have been," said a speaker in making this statement at the Centennial celebration, "forty professors, but their wives and daughters, six women, have published books which have had a circulation of at least a million copies." The women referred to were, probably, the following: Mrs. Margaret Woods Lawrence, Mrs. Harriet Woods Baker, Mrs. Elizabeth Stuart Phelps, Mrs. Sarah Stuart Robbins, Mrs. Harriet Beecher Stowe, Miss Elizabeth Stuart Phelps.

of Humanity," 1829. Here the "Biblical Repository" was printed for a time.

It is not in place now to give the history of the several business firms in charge of this press. In 1833 Mr. Flagg died, and was succeeded in the firm by Mr. Mark H. Newman, a graduate of Bowdoin College, whose influence was still further in the direction of educational culture. The press, in 1841, passed from the original proprietors to Messrs. Allen, Morrill, and Wardwell, afterward to Mr. John D. Flagg, and in 1854 it came into the hands of the present proprietor, Mr. Warren F. Draper, who is largely engaged in the publication of theological and educational works.

Following are some biographical memoranda of the professors who have been longest connected with the Seminary and chiefly identified with Andover: —

A Summary of Biographical Memoranda of Professors of the Theological Seminary, long[1] Residents of Andover.

PROF. LEONARD WOODS, D. D., was born at Princeton, Mass., June 19, 1774. He graduated at Harvard College 1796; taught school at Medford; united with the church there; studied for the ministry with Dr. Backus, of Somers, Conn.; was ordained 1798 pastor of church at West Newbury, Mass.; inaugurated professor in Andover Theological Seminary September 28, 1808; resigned 1846; died August 24, 1854. Dr. Woods married Abigail Wheeler, daughter of Joseph Wheeler, Judge of Probate for Worcester. They had ten children, four sons and six daughters.

The sons were: Mr. Samuel Woods, merchant, resident in Pittsford, Vt., about eighty years old in 1878, the oldest alumnus of Phillips Academy present at the Centennial celebration; Mr. Joseph Woods, who died at the age of twenty-five, while studying for the ministry; Pres. Leonard Woods, D. D., LL. D., Professor in Bangor Theological Seminary, President of Bowdoin College, who died 1878; Rev. Daniel Woods, a graduate of Andover Theological Seminary, a teacher in Pennsylvania and Ohio.

The daughters of Professor Woods were: Mary Woods, married to Prof. Thomas Mather Smith, D. D., of Kenyon College, and mother of Rev. John Cotton Smith; Abby Woods, married to Richard Salter, M. D.; Margaret Woods, married to Rev. E. A. Lawrence, D. D.; she wrote "Light on the Dark River;" Harriet

[1] Twenty years or more; also those who died in office.

Woods, married to Rev. Abijah R. Baker, D. D.; she is the author of nearly two hundred Sunday-school books; Sarah Woods; Sophia Woods, married to the Rev. William B. Hayden.

PROF. MOSES STUART was born at Wilton, Conn., March 26, 1780; graduated at Yale College 1797; studied law; read theology with Rev. Dr. Dwight; was ordained pastor of church in New Haven 1806; inaugurated professor at Andover February 28, 1810; resigned 1848; died January 4, 1852. Professor Stuart married Abigail Clark, daughter of James Clark, of Danbury, Conn. They had four sons and five daughters. One of the sons died at an early age.

The three sons who lived to manhood were: Prof. Isaac Stuart, graduate of Yale College, Professor of Ancient Languages in College of South Carolina, author of many books; James C. Stuart, M. D., of Syracuse, N. Y.; Moses Stuart, graduate of Yale College, who died soon after graduation, while studying law.

The daughters who lived to womanhood were: Elizabeth Stuart ("H. Trusta"), married to Prof. Austin Phelps, D. D.; Sarah Stuart (author of the "Win and Wear" Series, and contributions to the "Congregationalist," "Reminiscences of Old Andover Days"), married to Prof. R. D. C. Robbins; Mary Stuart, married to Prof. Austin Phelps; Abby Stuart, married to Rev. George H. Anthony.

PROF. EBENEZER PORTER, D. D., son of Captain Thomas Porter, was born at Cornwall, Conn., October 5, 1772; graduated at Dartmouth College 1792; valedictorian; taught school in Washington, Conn.; was called to the charge of the church in that town; ordained September 6, 1796; elected to the chair of Sacred Rhetoric in Andover Seminary 1811; was President temporarily. He was almost the entire time of his professorship in infirm health. He died April 8, 1834. Dr. Porter married Lucy P. Merwin, the daughter of Rev. Noah Merwin, of Washington, Conn.

PROF. RALPH EMERSON, D. D., was born at Hollis, N. H., August 18, 1787. His father was deacon of the First Church, his grandfather pastor. He graduated at Yale College 1811; was tutor 1814 to 1816; ordained, 1816, pastor of a church in Norfolk, Conn.; inaugurated professor in Andover Theological Seminary 1829; resigned 1853; went to live in Newburyport; subsequently removed to the West; died at Rockford, Ill., May 20, 1863, aged 76. He had six sons and three daughters.

The sons: Rev. Daniel Emerson, Prof. Joseph Emerson, Rockwell Emerson, Esq., counsellor, New York, Rev. Samuel Emerson, Mr. Porter Emerson, Mr. Ralph Emerson (Rockford, Ill.).

The daughters: Mary Emerson, married to Prof. Joseph Haven, D. D.; Elizabeth Emerson, married to Rev. Simon J. Humphrey; Charlotte Emerson, teacher in Rockford Seminary, Ill.

PROF. BELA BATES EDWARDS, D. D., was born at Southampton, Mass., 1802; graduated at Amherst College 1824; was tutor in the college, Assistant Secretary of the American Education Society, and editor of "American Quarterly and Bibliotheca Sacra;" was elected Professor of Hebrew in Andover Seminary in 1837, of Biblical Literature 1848; died at Athens, Ga., April 20, 1852. His body was buried in the chapel cemetery at Andover. Professor Edwards married Jerusha W. Billings, daughter of Charles E. Billings, of Conway, Mass. Their two sons died, one in childhood, one in early manhood, while a student at Yale College. Both bore the same name, George Edwards. The daughter, Sarah B. Edwards, was married to Rev. William Edwards Park. Mrs. Edwards, after the death of Professor Edwards, resided in Andover, taking charge of a small family school for young ladies, with a view of aiding her son in obtaining his education.

PROF. EDWARDS A. PARK, son of Prof. Calvin A. Park, was born at Providence, R. I. He graduated at Brown University 1826; at Andover Theological Seminary 1831; was ordained pastor of a church at Braintree, Mass., December, 1831; elected to the chair of Sacred Rhetoric in Andover Theological Seminary 1836; to the chair of Christian Theology 1847. Professor Park married Anne Maria Edwards, born at Northampton, daughter of Mr. William Edwards, great-granddaughter of Pres. Jonathan Edwards.

Their children: one son and two daughters; one daughter died in infancy; the other resides with her parents. Professor Park's son, Rev. William Edwards Park, is pastor of a church at Gloversville, N. Y.

PROF. AUSTIN PHELPS, D. D., was born at West Brookfield, Mass.; graduated at the University of Pennsylvania 1837; at the Theological Seminary of Yale College 1839; was resident student in Andover Theological Seminary 1842; elected Professor of Sacred Rhetoric 1848; resigned 1879. Professor Phelps married Elizabeth Stuart, who died 1852, Mary Stuart, who died 1856 (both were daughters of Professor Stuart), Mary Johnson, daughter of Mr. Samuel Johnson, of Boston, sister of Rev. Francis H. Johnson, of Andover.

The eldest son is the Rev. Moses Stuart Phelps, Professor of Philosophy in Smith College. The second son, Rev. Lawrence Phelps, pastor in Barton, Vt.

The only daughter is Elizabeth Stuart Phelps, author of "Gates Ajar," "Hedged in," and other works.

The younger sons are: Francis Johnson Phelps, a student in Yale College. Edward Phelps, a student in Phillips Academy.

PROF. ELIJAH PORTER BARROWS was not a resident of Andover for the length of time which has been selected to define the word "long" in these notes, but his family associations were largely with the town. All his five sons but one were students of Phillips Academy, and three daughters were members of Abbot Academy.

Nathan Barrows, M. D., graduate of Cleveland Medical School 1855, was a teacher in Phillips Academy. Prof. Allen C. Barrows fitted for college at Phillips Academy; graduated at Western Reserve College 1861; served in the Eighteenth United States Infantry, 1861 to 1864, as a soldier from Andover; was teacher of Latin and Greek at Phillips Academy 1864 to 1866; has been professor in Western Reserve College; and is pastor in Kent, O. Elijah P. Barrows died at Andover, 1864. Mr. William E. Barrows and Franklin Barrows are in mercantile business.

Of five daughters three are married: Fanny L. Barrows, married to Rev. Thomas Dagget; Martha P. Barrows, to Prof. C. H. Hitchcock, of Dartmouth College; Sarah M. Barrows, to Edward Dummer, Esq., of Boston.

CHAPTER X.

MILLS AND MANUFACTURES.

The mill is the first industrial enterprise of which there is any record. Before mention is made of planting corn, improving land, or any industry whatever, the saw-mill is spoken of. This was a necessity preparatory to the building of dwellings, and also an important source of income, the settlers in the inland plantations sometimes doing a considerable business in the sale of lumber, which was floated down the rivers and exported to the Barbadoes, in exchange for cargoes of West India goods. There are records which show that Mr. Simon Bradstreet carried on trade of this sort, buying lumber for export in various places. He is said, by some writers, to have built the first saw-mill at North Andover, on the Cochichawick, in 1644. But of this I find no record. The first mill mentioned in the town records, 1661, is spoken of as having been built by the town, the "first comers of inhabitants" who were at the charges of purchasing the plantation and building the minister's house, the mill, and the meeting-house."

The first mill-owner, of whom mention has been found in written records, is Joseph Parker. He died in 1678, leaving his "corne-mill on the Cochichawick," valued at twenty pounds, to his son Joseph.

Stephen Johnson owned a saw-mill. He was granted by the town in 1671 "so much old seader timber as would make twentie thousand of shingles, and, in 1672, timber to make ten thousand shingles of cedar already cut down."

It is believed that Joseph Parker's mill-privilege was at or above the present site of the Stevens mills. In 1684, this mill was appraised at one hundred pounds. In 1699, it is referred to in the records as "y^e *old* mill which was formerly Joseph Parker's."

In 1695, liberty was granted "to set up a saw-mill on Cochichawick river, about three or four rods above y° lower ford, on condition that this do not stop the passage of the fish called alewives."

The owners of this mill-privilege were Corp^l. Samuel Osgood, John Abbot, Jr., Thomas Abbot, Senr., Joseph Chandler, and Henry Chandler. The grants, in various places, of lands and timber for the encouragement of men to build saw-mills and grist-mills were numerous for more than fifty years from the settlement of the town. Hardly a stream or brook of any size that was not put in requisition by the settlers as water-power for grinding or sawing. To trace all these and their various owners would be a long and profitless task for general information, although it is a matter of interest sometimes for individuals to know the history of the water-power in their vicinity or on their estates. Sawing wood for shingles was a profitable business, and there was such a demand for them in the town that the inhabitants were forbidden to sell them out of town without special permission.

"No man shall cut any shingles to sell out of town till they have liberty of the selectmen," was a vote in 1670. But the same year the town voted "to grant Mr. Walker and John Hazelton (of Bradford) to get 15 or 16 thousand of seader shingles, or so many as will cover their meeting-house, provided they cut down no trees, but take such as are cut down already."

And again, "Granted to Mr. John Rogers, minister of Ipswich, to get so many seder shingles as will repair his house, provided he cut down no trees."

In 1686, Henry Ingals, Jr., was granted "liberty to set up a saw-mill on Musketo Brook, below Boston meadow-way, and Henry Holt to sett up a saw-mill on Ladle-Meadow Brook."

In 1715, Henry Gray had a mill for grinding scythes on or "near Scoonk river," and other mills for grist and timber were in operation. In the year 1753, Humphrey Holt sold to Asa Abbot "one half of a saw-mill erected on Shashin river, so called, and near the Pine Plaine, called Preston's Plain, with the Intrest and Privilidge of one quarter part of the Dam built across said river for the use of s[d] mill and the Grist-mill adjoyning thereto, with Liberty to lay Timber and Boards on the Land (of William Chandler, late of Andover, deceased) adjoyning to said mill, and also to carie Timber and Boards to and from s[d] Mill across said Land, as there shall be Necessary Ocation in the use and Improvement of said Mill and dam as there shall be ocation forever, which s[d] Mill & Privileges thereoff [he] did purchase of s[d] William Chandler, Dec[d]."

In 1764, Asa Abbot sold this interest in the saw-mill to Nathan Abbot.

In 1786, Asa Abbot, Jr., conveyed a part of the same property to Nehemiah Abbot, — one fourth "part of the saw-mill that stands on Shawshin river, near Timothy Ballard's Dwelling-house."

In 1794, Timothy Ballard owned a mill-privilege, probably the same. This was the early "improvement" of the water-power at Ballardvale.

An interesting relic of a grist-mill, of considerable importance to Andover people who lived in the west part of the town, and of profit to its owner, is a petition (dated May 27, 1752) of James Kittredge, of Tewksbury, to the General Court, in which he shows that about twenty-seven years before he "erected a Grist-mill and built a Dam across Shawshin River," in the part of Billerica afterward Tewksbury. He says that the people of the neighboring towns, Wilmington and Andover, had "great dependence" on his mill. He states that he has been sued for damage in flowing land, and relates in full his grievances, which, however, are of no special interest at the present time. The petition is signed by citizens of several towns interested in the mill. In Andover were: Samuel Bailey, Samuel Bailey, Jr., Joseph Blanchard, Obadiah Johnson, Thomas Hagget, residents of the West Parish.

Most of the ancient saw and grist mills have disappeared from the town. They are, however, of sufficiently recent operation for every country-bred reader of these sketches, who is of adult age, to recall some one or more: the unpainted, weather-beaten building on the bank of the mill-stream; piles of cedar wood, or pine slabs blockading the door; rafts of logs darkening the mill-pond; the dash of waters on the incessant wheel; the harsh grind of the saw deeper and deeper into the heart of the monarchs of the forest; the meal-bags standing on end, or piled sidewise, their distended bellies a temptation to nibbling mice; the dusty miller, lord of the noisy domain, gossiping with the farmers, or lifting up their youngsters to look into the corn-hopper; the pleasant rustic scenes about the mill; the woods of pine, hemlock, spruce, and birch, or the sturdier oak, cedar, and maple; the coves in the stream covered with lily-leaves, pickerel-weed, and arrowhead, or fringed with cardinal flowers and dodder, where, in the shade, the perch and bass, or the speckled trout lie, and the angler practises his "noble art," while sleepy turtles sun themselves in rows on some log, rabbit and squirrel scampering in the leaves on the shore, partridge drumming in the wood, and pigeon and quail whirring through the bushes,—all these associations are familiar to the lover of country-life who has ever carried grist to mill.

Early in the town's history, at the same time with and often a part of the saw-mill and grist-mill, was the fulling-mill, where the cloth, home-spun and woven, was finished and pressed. Spinning was an important branch of labor. At one time, the towns were obliged by law to have a certain amount of spinning done, according to the number of inhabitants. The women and children were much employed in this work. In 1731, spinning-schools were established in Boston, and, after the Revolution, when imported goods were prohibited by the patriotic sentiment, the art of spinning revived. The town of Andover, in 1787, made an appeal "to the good sense and virtuous dispositions of the female sex, to the younger as well as the elder, that they would, by their engaging example, economy, and simplicity in dress, giving preference to that clothing which is produced from our flocks and from our own fields encourage home industries."

A relic of the spinning-wheel (about the Revolutionary period) is the following:—

"*Mrs. Holt's Receipt for Spinning and Weaving.*

"Mrs. Abbot. ——   The spinning of seventy-two skeins £   s.   d.
    comes to 0. 18.   0
The weaving of nineteen yards comes to 0.   7. 11
    The whole 1.   5. 11
Rec'd the contents of the above in full.   AMY HOLT."

Many such a "spinster"[1] had preceded Amy Holt in Andover, and if some of the ancient spinning-wheels which, in the revival of old fashions, have lately been brought out of the dust of garrets, could be understood in their humming, they would perhaps tell such tales of the Amys and Dorcases of our town as that told by the poet of the Puritan maiden at her wheel : —

> "Then as he opened the door, he beheld the form of the maiden
> Seated beside her wheel, and the carded wool like a snow-drift
> Piled at her knee, her white hands feeding the ravenous spindle,
> While with her foot on the treadle she guided the wheel in its motion.
> . . . .
> She rose as he entered and gave him her hand in signal of welcome
> Saying, I knew it was you, when I heard your step in the passage,
> For I was thinking of you as I sat there singing and spinning."

In a paper labelled a "*Perticular Account of the Things that Phebe Has Received att & since her Going away,*" Andover, July 2, 1765, are mentioned : "One Linning Wheel, One Wooling Wheel, Fine cloth, 16 yd of Diripee, 48 yd of Toe Cloth, 26 yd of Cotton & Linning, 20 yd of Linning, 24 yd of Bed-ticken."

The business of weaving was also carried on, not only in a domestic way, but as a trade by many skilled workmen, who took orders for much cloth which was carried to be finished at the fulling-mills. Such skilled weavers, familiar with the operations of cloth manufacture in the old country, were the men who first put in operation the fulling-mills and clothing-mills in the colony, and were the pioneers in the manufacturing industries of the country, — some of them becoming owners, and others managers of the mills for men who furnished the capital. The first of these weavers, of whom men-

[1] Spinster, a woman who spins. — *Webster*.

tion is found in Andover, was Richard Sutton. He was only a short time resident in the town, removing before there was any action taken to give encouragement for a fulling-mill. It is not improbable that if he had remained he would have undertaken this industry, as he was not without means to do so. It is an interesting coincidence, already noted, that his descendants, after the lapse of two hundred years, not knowing of this brief residence of their ancestor, should have established the name in the town, and the business of manufacturing, which, in its simpler forms, was not unlikely to have been begun by him had he remained a resident.

In 1673, Walter Wright and Edward Whittington, weavers, were granted encouragement for setting up a fulling-mill.

"Granted to Edward Whittington and Walter Wright the abovesaid land (by William Ballard's), with more adjoining thereto, for the encouragement of erecting a fulling-mill, which they promise to set about in ye spring."

Edward Whittington was drafted for service in the Indian war with the Narragansets, in 1675, and it is not unlikely that the building of the mill was postponed or abandoned for that reason. It took a good deal of time and much encouragement to get such an enterprise started. The town, however, seemed determined to have a fulling-mill:—

"1682. Granted libertie to any man y^t ye towne or committee they shall chose to sett up a saw-mill, fulling-mill, and grist-mill upon Shawshin river near Roger's Brooke, to take up twenty acres of land adjoining to ye sd place, and to enjoye it ye same forever, with ye privileges of a townsman. Capt. Dudley Bradstreet, Left. Jno Osgood, Ensign Thomas Chandler, Dea. John ffrie, Sen., John Stevens are chosen a committee to act in this affair to make articles with such person or persons as they shall judge fitt."

So far as the writer can make out from the records, it seems that the persons who did actually set up and put in operation the long talked-of fulling-mill were Joseph and John Ballard. Their names have not been found mentioned as weavers, and it may be that they furnished the capital for Walter Wright, who was a permanent resident of the town and is always designated as "weaver."

"1689. *Voted*, that ye twenty acres of Land granted to a mill on Shawshin River shall be enjoyed by Joseph and John Ballard and their heirs soe long as they shall keep up a grist and fulling-mill for ye good and benefit of the Town, and in case by ye providence of god, s^d mills or dam should come to such casualtie as to be wholly spoyled, and they repair it not within three years after such casualty, then s^d land to Revert to the Towne."

In 1718, Samuel Frye built a saw and grist-mill on the Shawshin, at the place called from him and his descendants Frye village. His son added to this a fulling-mill. During the Revolutionary period, Mr. Theophilus Frye was a miller and clothier at this place.

As early as 1689 encouragement was given for the erection of "Iron-works."

"*Voted*, that ye town will allowe such incouragement, both of woodland and mine, toward ye setting up of iron-works as may be most convenient to ye towne, and not damnifye ye mill upon Shawshin river."

Thomas Chandler owned iron-works, and the Lovejoys had iron-works on the Shawshin River, supposed to have been near the site of the present Marland Mills.

Such, in brief, is an outline of the beginnings of the manufacturing operations which have, in a modified, or, rather, amplified form, continued until the present time; the fulling-mill being the parent of the clothing-mill and the manufactory; the iron-works of the foundry and machine-shop.

The first mill which was a manufactory proper, and which gave a name abroad to Andover as a manufacturing town, was the powder-mill of Mr. Samuel Phillips, built in the winter of 1775-6. Its history has been traced in connection with the Revolutionary War. It was in operation in March, 1775, and turning out gunpowder for the use of the Continental army before any other mill in the State was ready for work. This mill stood north of the present Marland Mills, on the same side of the Shawshin River. It was continued for twenty years with profit to the owners; but the dangers and risks were great, and the local unpopularity of the manufacture, after the death of several persons by repeated explosions, led to its discontinuance, — the immediate necessity and profit of it having passed away with the return of peace. The manufacture of paper was gradually substituted for that of gunpowder, the operations beginning in 1789, in the powder-mill, during a temporary suspension of the powder-making. Mr. Phillips began this manufacture, having, as a superintendent of the paper-works, Mr. Thomas Houghton, who had been a paper manufacturer in England. He having been involved in a lawsuit in regard to what he regarded as an unjust tax on his paper had become embarrassed, and had finally failed in his business and quitted the country. After looking about some time in the United States, he came to Andover and entered into an engagement with Judge Phillips. Interesting letters which he wrote home have been preserved, from which extracts have been made in a former chapter. It may not be out of place to quote here briefly from these papers to show the courage and fortitude and faith of this man who had been broken down in his fortunes, exiled from his country, and separated from all his kindred. His example might be a lesson and a help to many, who, in the vicissitudes of business fortunes, find themselves at middle or advanced life without business or capital, and almost without credit, and with a family to provide for. Thomas Houghton's letters to his wife and his sons are full of patience and resignation, while at the same time they bear witness to his diligent endeavors to retrieve his fortunes. To his wife he writes : —

"Do, my dear Life, endeavor to reconcile thyself to the dispensation of Providence, for we are told 'that a sparrow does not fall without the special permission of our heavenly Father, and the very hairs of our head are numbered.' Consequently, not any event happens to the children of men, but what he permits, and all for their final good; for one of the greatest poets says: 'Whatever is, is best.' Therefore I trust it will be for our final good that we have been afflicted, and may truly say, —

"Father, I bless thy chastening hand,
How kind was thy chastising rod."

But his trust in a Supreme Ruler of events did not prevent him from active exertions to better his condition and to build up a successful business at Andover. In regard to the hopes which inspired him, of the ultimate success of the enterprise of paper-making, he writes: —

"Mr. Phillips has so much interest in the State and is a man of such consequence in it that I flatter myself we shall have advantages that other paper-makers cannot enjoy. The State printers have promised Mr. Phillips their custom. I am informed they will take at least to the amount of £1200 a year of us. He has also great interest, both in Boston, Cambridge, and Salem, and many other places."

The paper-making operations, as has been said, were first begun in the powder-mill, there being no work going on at the time. Mr. Houghton understood that he was to have full possession of the powder-mill until the paper-mill should be ready for running; but while he was getting things ready for work, an order for powder was received. Whereupon, the foreman of the powder-mill came in and ordered Mr. Houghton to take away his engines and apparatus, and leave the room for the gunpowder-making. This interference, which threatened to ruin his undertakings, Mr. Houghton greatly resented. He wrote a letter to Mr. Phillips, threatening to dissolve partnership and quit the paper-works. Mr. Phillips, however, settled the difficulty, and the work of building the paper-mill, which had been under way for three months, was hastened. This was June, 1789. Mr. Houghton, in April, 1789, had written respecting the mill and his connection with Mr. Phillips the following in a letter to his family: —

"The mill is planned and preparation getting forward for Building as fast as possible. She is to have two engines and two vats, one for writing and printing, the other for common paper."

.... "Mr. Phillips builds the mill and I am to manage the work. My care and management is to stand against the Rent and we are to share profits equally."

The following inventory or description of the paper-mill is among the manuscripts of Mr. Phillips. It bears no date, but was evidently written near the time of the erection of the mill: —

"A building occupied as a Paper Mill, 36 by 32 feet, with two vats upon the ground floor, which have a Cast Iron pot in each of them, sunk into Brick chimneys, for heating the vats. The first floor has two-engines for beating-stuff, a room for dressing rags, with a brick chimney and fire place, also two other rooms for rags. The second floor is occupied for a Rag ware-house.

"Another building connected to the mill by a covered passage way of 20 ft. long, used for drying and keeping paper before finished, 20 by 24 feet, at the end next the mill; a part of the drying-house is taken off for a finishing room, 27 by 24 feet, in which is a cast-iron stove used in the winter season. At one side of the finishing-room is a sizing copper set with bricks and brick chimney. Another building 35 feet from the mill, that is 24 ft. by 20, for Rags and finished paper. Another building, 131 feet from the mill, 20 by 13 ft., for Rope and other lumber. No other building near on the same side of the river. A Grist Mill upon the opposite side of the river, at about 140 feet distance."

Mr. Houghton, in one of his letters, speaks of the difficulty of obtaining competent workmen: "I wish I could have one or two good hands from England. The wages is a great inducement; for good ones, used to writing-paper in every stage, we would give 15 shillings per week and board, or 15 shillings per week and an addition equal to board." He says, also, that there is a scarcity of paper rags, but that the people have been instructed to save them. A specimen of the kind of instruction given is found in the "Massachusetts Spy," November 26, 1778, in regard to the paper-mill in Sutton. It is an interesting item in regard to the origin of the "rag-bag," that time-honored institution in the New England household:—

"It is earnestly requested that the fair daughters of Liberty in this extensive country would not neglect to serve their country by saving, for the Paper Mill in Sutton, all Linen and Cotton-and-Linen Rags, be they ever so small, as they are equally good for the purpose of making paper as those that are larger. A *bag* hung up at one corner of a room would be the means of saving many which would be otherwise lost. If the ladies should not make a fortune by that piece of economy, they will at least have the satisfaction of knowing that they are doing an essential service to the community, which, with eight pence per pound, the price now given for clean white rags, they must be sensible will be a sufficient reward."

The paper-works at Andover were not at first so profitable as had been anticipated. The difficulties in getting started were great, and other manufactories in the vicinity came into competition with the Andover paper-mill, and the modes of doing business, — the facilities for putting the paper in the market, were not such as Mr. Houghton had been used to in the old country. He writes home: —

"I had many difficulties to encounter, ... so that even now (July 24, 1791), the whole works have been but little more than a year at work; and from the credit we are forced to give, and the stock kept to supply our customers, I am still considerably indebted to my Honorable partner; for here is not Stationers, as in England, to take our paper as soon as made, but we must keep assorted stock by us. Ours at this time, in paper of different qualities, is not less than three thousand dollars. Our rags and utensils is not less than a thousand more, and I dare say we have given credit to the amount of nearly two thousand; therefore I must be at this time pretty largely indebted to the manufactory. Here is many paper-mills erected within about twenty miles to thirty miles of us, and they have since we began both advanced the price of rags and lowered the price of paper; nevertheless, I dare say that, if it please God to spare my life, and that of my Honble partner, a few years, we shall do very well, for our customers are of the best sort."

He speaks of his prudent and economical habits, and his avoidance of needless expense: —

"I keep no company, go to no neighbors' houses, except Judge Phillips's; neither do I spend sixpence on a tavern in six months, neither do I wish to do it; but I hope it will not be long before I have my share clear. I wait impatiently for that much-desired period, and hope it is not far distant."

Mr. Houghton, in his religious connection, was a Friend or Quaker. His expressions of pious feeling make a large part of his letters. His moralizings on the labors of men to heap up uncertain riches are instructive and pertinent to the present time: —

"And although it has pleased Almighty God to bring us down in this life from an envied to an humble state, yet I trust it will in the end work together for our good and his glory; for we may truly say that we have toiled and moiled, early and late, with a view to obtain a little worldly wealth to support us in our old age, and to help us place our offspring creditably in the world ; yet we have experienced what the inspired prophet says : —

> "'That if we rise before the sun,
> And work and toil when day is done,
> Careful and sparing eat our bread,
> To shun that poverty we dread,
> 'T is all in vain till God has blest ;
> He can make rich and give us rest."

After a year or two the business began to prosper, and, in 1795, Mr. Houghton became a partner. His son succeeded him. After the death of Judge Phillips, his son, Col. John Phillips, was partner. In 1811 the mill was burned, but rebuilt. In 1820 Colonel Phillips died, and the mill property passed into other hands. Paper manufacturing was carried on by Messrs. Amos Blanchard, Daniel Poor, and Abel Blanchard. The mill and privilege were ultimately purchased by the Marland Manufacturing Company for woollen manufactures, and the manufacture of paper ceased.

About 1789 the era of woollen manufactures began in New England. The Federal Government being established on a firm foundation, capitalists directed their attention to the encouragement of home manufactures, and emigrants from the old country sought in the United States an opportunity to become rich and influential, as they might be, by connecting their skilled labor with American capital. Among the emigrants were the brothers, Arthur, John, and James Scholfield. The name of Arthur Scholfield is famous in the history of woollen manufactures. He made, and in part invented, carding machines superior to any then known in the country. He constructed them from his remembrance of those in England, with the aid of some pieces which he succeeded in smuggling. He set a machine in operation in the mill at Byfield, under management of the first incorporated manufacturing company in New England. He afterward went with his patron, Mr. Samuel Slater, to Pittsfield, and there made the first fine broadcloth in the country. The Scholfields bought land at North Andover, and mill-privileges on the Cochichawick, and on the Shawshin, near its junction with the Merrimack. At the latter place, Stephen Poor had had a clothing-mill about 1800. James Scholfield set up one of the improved carding-machines made by his brother Arthur Scholfield, and carried on the business of making fine woollen goods in a small wooden building on the Cochichawick. He did a considerable business, and his mill was made use of by the country people around, to get their wool carded for domestic spinning and weaving, as well as to furnish fine goods. But he lacked the capital needed to carry on the manufacture extensively, and in 1812 he sold out his business and engaged to manage the mills erected by Mr. Nathaniel Stevens at the mill privilege further up the stream.

Messrs. Abel and Paschal Abbot, of Andover (South Parish), bought the mill privilege, land and buildings, of James and Arthur Scholfield, and, erecting a larger mill, carried on the manufacturing about a year, and then sold (1813) to Abraham Marland and Isaac Osgood, who, after a year, sold to Samuel Ayer. In 1826, the property fell, by foreclosure of a mortgage (Samuel Ayer having failed, become deeply involved in debt, and quitted the town) to Mr. William Sutton, of Danvers.

In this mill of Mr. Marland, and in other early mills of the Andovers, it was the custom for the wives and daughters of the managers and owners to work, just as it had been for them to spin or weave, or perform domestic service, in their homes.

From the foregoing, it appears that among the first woollen manufactures with the improved machinery that marked the beginning of the era of New England manufactures, was that undertaken by the inventors of the machinery at North Andover, in what is now known as the district of Sutton's Mills on the Cochichawick, near its junction with the Merrimack. The course of this manufactory to the present time we will now trace, although, meanwhile, others were started which have been more continuously in operation.

As was said, the original movers in the enterprise abandoned it. Samuel Ayer failed, and the mill did not wholly prosper until it passed into the hands of its present owners. Mr. William Sutton, being a gentleman of ample fortune, as well as of great business activity and judgment, at once revived the woollen manufactures in the mill which had fallen into his hands. He put in power-looms, which had largely supplanted the hand-looms in the progress of manufactures, and had effected a revolution in the mills throughout the country. Mr. Sutton was a resident of Danvers, president of the bank, and otherwise of large business connections, but he kept constant oversight of the mill, and by his wise management insured the success of the business. At his death, in 1832, he left this flourishing business in charge of his sons, Mr. William Sutton and Mr. Eben Sutton.

Mr. Eben Sutton died in 1864, aged sixty-one years. His death was sincerely mourned by the great company of operatives and employés, in whose welfare he had taken a cordial interest, as well as lamented by his friends, the influential citizens of Danvers, Salem, and the Andovers. In regard to his conduct of these large business operations, an obituary notice says: —

"By his sagacious management and persevering industry, he was enabled to accumulate a princely fortune, and, inheriting a handsome property from his father, he has probably left one of the largest fortunes in Massachusetts."

Gen. William Sutton, in 1865, relinquished the charge of the mills to his son, Gen. Eben Sutton, of New York, who became a resident of North Andover, first on the homestead of the Hon. Gayton P. Osgood, and afterward at North Andover Centre, on the place purchased by him from Mr. Armstrong Farnham. He is now the sole proprietor of the mills. The cordial good feeling which characterized the relations of his ancestors with the operatives continues with the present proprietor, whose hearty interest and generous donations have greatly contributed to the comfort and improvement of the tenants of the manufacturing village.

The Sutton Mill at present employs about one hundred and thirty operatives, and manufactures into flannel about 450,000 pounds of wool per annum.

Gen. Eben Sutton also now owns the mill above the first one on the stream, — that known as the North Andover Mill.

Its history to the time when Mr. Sutton took control is briefly as follows.

Soon after Mr. William Sutton began manufacturing at the lower mill privilege of the Cochichawick, Mr. George Hodges, of Salem, came to North Andover, and in 1828, with Mr. Edward Pranker, commenced the manufacture of white flannels in the old stone mill near the present brick mill. In 1839 the new mill was put in operation. It was owned by a company consisting of Mr. Eben Sutton, Dr. Joseph Kittredge, and Capt. George Hodges. After the death of Dr. Kittredge, in 1847, Mr. Sutton bought out the other owners, Captain Hodges continuing the manufacturing with his son, Mr. Frank Hodges, till 1860, when Mr. George Hodges, Jr., and Mr. Samuel L. Hodges, leased the mill, and, with Mr. Frank Hodges, formed the firm of Hodges Brothers. Owing to the death of Mr. Frank Hodges, in 1865, the company was dissolved, but the mill was run for a time by Mr. George Hodges. In 1847 he had removed to Oxford, where he carried on manufacturing, and where he now resides. Mr. Samuel L. Hodges removed to Leicester in 1849, and engaged in manufacturing, which he continued for twenty-five years.

Capt. George Hodges was one of the most honored citizens of North Andover; his name synonymous with integrity and high-mindedness. Chosen to offices of trust in the town, representative to the General Court and State Senator, he filled every office with dignity and wisdom. The following obituary notice (dated December 6, 1862) relates the particulars of his death, and shows the esteem in which he was held: —

"Hon. George Hodges, of North Andover, the well-known manufacturer, met with an accident on Wednesday last, which on Saturday closed a long, useful, and honorable life. He fell while descending a flight of stairs in a building in Andover, where he had been to attend to some business in the insurance office, breaking the bones of his left elbow in a dreadful manner. He bore up, under the operation of extracting the fractured bones and setting the arm, with cheerful courage and Christian fortitude; but being in years (almost reaching his seventy-first), and of large frame and great weight, nature could not survive the shock, and he has been gathered to his fathers, while enjoying among his family, wife, children, and grandchildren, a green old age, full of love and equal affection for all. He has served the State, this town, and his fellowmen faithfully and honestly. A man of large heart, kind to all, one of nature's noblemen in looks and in action, he leaves no ordinary void in the community in which he has so long lived."

Mr. Frank Hodges, whose untimely death, in the prime of life, caused the dissolution of the company, was a gentleman of finished manners, scholarly tastes, and high moral principle. A sufferer from chronic disease, he was disabled in a great measure for the active business of life in early manhood, although he superintended the mill until near the time of his death.

In 1867, a stock company was formed, to carry on manufacturing in the North Andover Mills. The mills are owned by Gen. Eben Sutton, who is the treasurer of the corporation. Mr. John Elliot is superintendent. They employ about one hundred operatives and manufacture into flannel 300,000 pounds of wool per annum.

The oldest manufacturing business in the Andovers, that has been carried on with uninterrupted success from its commencement to the present time, is that at the Stevens Mills, established in 1813. The founder of this flourishing manufacturing business being a native of Andover, and descended through five generations (residents of the town), from John Stevens, one of the first settlers, ought to receive special notice.

Capt. Nathaniel Stevens was the son of Mr. Jonathan Stevens, of North Andover. He was born in 1786, died 1865. He was educated at the Franklin Academy, made a sea voyage before the mast, served in the War of 1812 as a lieutenant, was a trader at North Andover. He married, 1815, Miss Harriet Hale,[1] daughter of Mr. Moses Hale, of Chelmsford.

Mr. Hale, the father-in-law of Captain Stevens, was one of the pioneer manufacturers of the State, and a man of enthusiasm in his business. Through his influence, Mr. Stevens had resolved to embark in manufacturing. In 1813 he en-

[1] She is now living in her eighty-seventh year, bright and active and of clear memory.

gaged James Scholfield to run a mill, and, entering into partnership with Dr. Joseph Kittredge and Mr. Josiah Monroe, they began to build (near the site of the first saw-mill on the Cochichawick) a wooden mill. This is the same now in use. It has been rebuilt in parts from time to time, brick walls being gradually substituted for the wooden ones.

Mr. Stevens, by perseverance and energy, soon mastered the business in all its details, and was capable of managing it without assistance. He decided to give up the manufacture of broadcloth, in which he had at first experimented and which was difficult and of precarious profit, and to confine himself to the manufacture of flannels. In 1828 and 1831 he bought out his partners and took the sole control. He had often been warned at the outset that he was engaged in an undertaking of great risk, and that he would lose his time and money in trying to carry on manufactures. Mr. Abbot Lawrence, the importer, especially warned him that he could not compete with British manufactures. "Take my advice," said he one day when Mr. Stevens had carried a load of flannels to Boston. "Sell out your mill and go into some other business." "Never," replied Mr. Stevens, "so long as I can get water to turn my mill wheel." Captain Stevens became one of the richest and most respected manufacturers of the county, carrying on the business for fifty years with prosperity. He lived to see his five sons established in the same business: the two eldest, Mr. Charles A. Stevens and Mr. Henry H. Stevens, in the western part of the State; the three youngest, the Hon. Moses T. Stevens, Mr. George Stevens, and Mr. Horace N. Stevens, at North Andover and Haverhill. His grandson, Mr. Nathaniel Stevens (son of Mr. Moses T. Stevens), has charge of the mill at Haverhill. Two of the brothers, Mr. George Stevens and Mr. Horace N. Stevens, died in the prime of manhood, leaving a memory honored for probity and beloved for all social and domestic virtues. In July, 1879, Mr. Moses T. Stevens purchased the Marland Mills at Andover. He has connected these and the Haverhill mill with the mill at North Andover by a telephone. The Stevens mills at North Andover employ about eighty-five operatives, and manufacture into flannel about 300,000 pounds of wool per annum.

The success of the Stevens mills has been of advantage to the community, both directly and indirectly. Through the liberal donation of Mr. Moses T. Stevens, the Town Hall of North Andover was built, in connection with the Johnson High School, and the First Church and Parish have been recipients of frequent generosity.

Having thus traced the origin and progress of the woollen manufactures at North Andover, on the Cochichawick, we turn now to those at Andover (South Parish) on the Shawshin.

The first of these manufactories, which has continued in operation until the present time, about seventy years (with only a brief suspension), was established by Mr. Abraham Marland from Ashton Parish, Lancashire, England. He came to Andover in 1807, and lived in the town forty-two years. He learned manufacturing in the old country, in his uncle's mills, and at Leeds and Holbeck. In 1801, he emigrated to America, and, for a few years, was in charge of manufacturing at Beverly. He there made the acquaintance of some Andover men, through whom he learned of the excellent water-power of the various streams of this vicinity, and was induced to turn his attention in this direction. He was advised by Mr. Samuel Slater not to think of making a living in America by manufacturing, but to put his money into a farm. But, believing that what his adviser seemed to have found profitable he might hope to succeed in, he persisted in his purpose. His first undertaking was to spin cotton for domestic weaving; but this he abandoned, as the working in cotton impaired his health. A relic of this cotton manufacturing is found, — an advertisement of a trader of Haverhill in a newspaper of January, 1810.

"COTTON YARN.

THOMAS R. APPLETON

Informs the public that he has been appointed Agent for *Abraham Marland's Cotton Factory*. He now offers for sale Cotton-Warp Filling, and Knitting-Yarn, of all numbers, wholesale and retail, at the manufacturers' prices. . . . . .

" N. B. *Please to call and examine the goodness of the Cotton Yarn.*"

About 1810, Mr. Marland began the manufacture of woollen cloth at Abbot Village, in a small wooden building below the present stone-arch bridge. Here, during the War of 1812, he made army blankets. He also, for a year (as has been before said), carried on a mill at North Andover. About 1821, he entered into an arrangement with Mr. Peter C. Brooks, under whose control the paper-mill property had fallen, in regard to building and operating a woollen-mill on this site, Mr. Brooks agreeing to furnish capital and erect the buildings, and Mr. Marland to carry on the manufacturing, taking a lease for twenty years, and promising to pay a liberal per cent. on the capital. A brick mill and a brick block for boarding-houses were built, and in 1821 to 1823 the machinery from the old mill transferred to this new one, and new machinery added. In 1828, Mr. Marland bought the property, including the mill privilege on both sides of the river, the paper-mill, and a gristmill and thirty acres of land. He continued to operate the mill, built a new factory, put in new machinery, and made other improvements, till, in 1834, the Marland Manufacturing Company was incorporated: Abraham Marland, Benjamin H. Punchard, and John Marland, the grantees, and with William S. Marland, the only stockholders. They began with a capital stock of $60,000. They manufactured various kinds of goods, — water-proofs, cloakings, cassimeres, whatever the changing fashions required. Mr. Abraham Marland was president of the company till his death in 1849. He not only built up a successful business, but became an influential citizen, and a benefactor to the town of his adoption. He was chiefly instrumental in establishing the Protestant Episcopal Church in Andover, and made to it generous donations. His social connections in the town were honorable, — the various members of his large family joining with the Marland name some of the most esteemed and influential names of Andover and vicinity. On the death of Mr. Marland, Mr. Nathan Frye became president of the company and continued in office for nearly thirty years, maintaining a name for probity and energy. The Hon. Francis Cogswell, son-in-law of Mr. Marland, was treasurer for many years. The treasurers of the company have been, since Mr. Cogswell, Mr. Josiah W. Chamberlin, of Boston, and Mr. Samuel Raymond, of Andover, gentlemen of ability and honor. In the recent financial crisis of the country, this manufacturing company became embarrassed, and, in July, 1879, the mills, machinery, and all the property were sold to Mr. Moses T. Stevens, of North Andover, who now carries on the manufacturing. The mills employ about one hundred and fifty operatives, and manufacture about 500,000 pounds of wool per annum.[1]

In 1836, a woollen manufacturing company was incorporated at Andover under the name of the Ballardvale Manufacturing Company. Mr. John Marland was treasurer and agent, and had the management of the mills; he and his brother, Mr. William S. Marland, withdrawing from the Marland Manufacturing Company. They bought the property and mill-privilege owned by Timothy Ballard, from whom they named the company and village. Mr. Abraham J. Gould, Mr. Mark Newman, and others, were associated in the company. They manufactured cotton and woollen goods, and also experimented in the manufacture of silk. This last, and the introduction of the silk-worm into Andover, form an interesting episode in Andover manufactures. Mulberry-trees, the food of the silk-worm, were then planted, and the raising of silk-worms was undertaken by several families.

Mr. John Marland was the moving spirit of these progressive enterprises. He was, as a well-known manufacturer remarks, "in advance of his times." For this reason he could not always realize his ideals and carry out all the plans which he projected. He was destined rather to open paths for other persons to go forward in to their advantage, than to

---

[1] Since the writing of the above has occurred the death of one of the most esteemed officers of the Marland Manufacturing Company, the Hon. Francis S. Cogswell. He was born December 31, 1800, at Atkinson, N. H., and was eighty years old when he died. He had been thirty-eight years a resident of Andover, held the offices of Cashier of the Andover Bank, President of the Boston and Maine Railroad, Director of Bank, and Treasurer of the Manufacturing Company. This latter office he held till he was seventy-two years old. He was a graduate of Dartmouth College, and had entered the legal profession, practising in Dover, N. H., before his removal to Andover. He retained through life his scholarly habits and literary tastes. He was a warden of Christ Church, and a devout adherent to its doctrines, although charitable and catholic in his sympathies.

persevere in ways of gain for himself. But he had real inventive genius and did a great work for manufactures, some of the improvements which he introduced being among the most valuable. The first piece of "fine white flannel" made in the United States is said to have been made in the mills of the Ballardvale company, the machinery for double spinning having been put in successful operation.

Also the company put in worsted machinery, in 1842 sending their agent (Mr. Charles Barnes) to England to buy the machinery. The manufacture of delaines was carried on for some years, the worsted mill being leased in 1850 to Mr. Jeremiah S. Young, brother-in-law of Mr. Marland. He, in 1853, transferred this branch of the business to the Pacific mills, at Lawrence, of which company he had become treasurer. The manufacture of fine flannel was continued till 1866, when the company, as a corporation, ceased to exist, and the Ballardvale mills became a private enterprise. The proprietor, at the time of this writing, is Mr. J. Putnam Bradlee, of Boston; Mr. James Shaw, manufacturer.

Other well-known manufacturers of Andover, 1815-1837, were the brothers Abel and Paschal Abbot. They began at North Andover, on the Cochichawick (as has been before related), but about 1814 removed their works to Abbot Village and built the wooden mill on the west side of the river, and after a time added other buildings. They did cotton and woollen spinning and made flannels and cassimeres. The country people came here from long distances to get their wool spun for domestic knitting and weaving. The manufacturers employed about twenty hand-looms before the use of the power-loom. The first foreman of the mill, Abiel Russell, is now living in his ninety-second year. In the employ of the Messrs. Abbot, in 1817, was Mr. Daniel Saunders, who for a time leased the mill and carried on the business, but in 1823 removed to Salem, N. H., and, subsequently returning, established himself at North Andover. In the financial crisis of 1837 the Abbot brothers failed, and their property passed into the hands of Messrs. Smith, Dove & Company. Another woollen mill, temporarily run, was under the management and ownership of Mr. James

Howarth and Mr. Abijah Chase, of Salem. They made flannel in the stone mill on the east side of the Shawshin, about 1824. The business was carried on by James Howarth's sons, John Howarth & Co., till 1837, and afterward by various persons, till 1843. Then, the property which had been leased for carrying on woollen manufacture, by Mr. Henry H. Stevens, passed into the hands of Messrs. Smith, Dove & Company.

The mills now in operation at the Abbot village, and at the Frye village, are used for the manufacture of flax, and are owned by the firm of Smith, Dove & Company. The senior partner of the firm is Mr. John Smith. He first started with the manufacture of cotton machinery. He came to America from Brechin, Scotland, in 1816, and obtained employment as a journeyman machinist, in Medway. There he met Joseph Faulkner and Warren Richardson, from Andover, workmen in the same shop with himself. They, about 1822, formed the plan of setting up in business for themselves; Mr. Smith taking the lead of the enterprise. Fortunately for their undertaking, they obtained an order for machinery in advance, and thus got a successful start, establishing themselves first at Plymouth. Through the influence of Mr. Faulkner's friends from Andover they were induced to transfer their business to this town. They bought the then unoccupied mill-privilege on the Shawshin, at Frye village, and in 1824 Mr. John Smith built the machine-shop now standing on the east side of the river, and they removed their works from Plymouth to Andover. Here they did an extensive business in the manufacture of cotton machinery, obtaining contracts for machinery in a cotton mill in New Market, N. H., and for other large establishments. In 1829 Mr. Richardson died, and in 1831 also Mr. Faulkner. Mr. John Smith was then assisted in charge of the machine-shop, by his younger brother, Peter Smith, who had come from Scotland in 1822, and been in the employ of the firm at Plymouth. In 1833, another employé began work, who subsequently became a member of the firm, and was the means of changing its operations, as a manufacturing company, and of introducing a new and successful enterprise.

Mr. John Smith had received a letter from Scotland recommending to his notice a young man from Brechin who had recently emigrated to America. Going to the city of New York on business, Mr. Smith found there his countryman, among strangers without satisfactory employment, and almost discouraged, but sustained in hope by the cheerfulness of his strong, sensible wife. Mr. Smith made him an offer, which he at once accepted. He came to Andover without delay, and began to work in the machine-shop. This young man was John Dove, whose inventive genius contributed so largely to the establishment and success of the manufacturing company, ultimately formed under the name of Smith, Dove & Company.

John Dove and Peter Smith had, when boys, worked together in the flax mills owned by Mr. Dove's father, in Scotland, and now, talking over old times, they formed a project to start a flax-mill at Andover. Mr. Dove had not only inventive genius, but enthusiasm. He was confident of success, if he could get the means to carry out the plan, and finally he succeeded in enlisting Mr. John Smith's interest, and by him was furnished with means to go to Scotland, to obtain further knowledge of the machinery there used, and get drawings from which to manufacture what was needed to start with.

Meanwhile, Mr. Smith built a new mill on the west side of the river, and in 1836 the business was begun, — the first manufacture of flax in America ; Mr. John Smith taking his two employés, Peter Smith and John Dove, into partnership. He, however, continued the manufacture of machinery until the flax manufacture proved successful. Then he gave up the machine-shop, and put all his capital into the flax manufactory. Flax-yarns for carpet weavers, sail-twines, shoe-threads, and other similar goods, were made, at first in small quantities, for the demand was not large, owing to the preference for British manufactures. But the prejudice gradually died out, and it was not many years before the mills were doing a large and remunerative business, the demand for their goods exceeding the supply. Accordingly, in 1843, the company purchased the water-power and buildings of the woollen mills at Abbot village, and put in flax machinery, thus greatly increasing their productions. In 1864 a joint stock company was incorporated, under the name of the Smith & Dove Manufacturing Company, of which Mr. John Smith was President, and Mr. Peter Smith Treasurer. In 1865 a brick mill was built at Abbot village. Hand and machine shoe-thread, linen yarns and twines for carpet manufacture, etc., are made ; about 2,000,000 pounds of flax and flax-tow are annually consumed. Some three hundred operatives are employed.

Mr. John Dove died in 1876. It has been said he possessed remarkable inventive genius. He was familiar with the progress of science in many departments, finding time, even in the midst of active labors, for much reading in his favorite lines of study, and never losing, to the day of his death, his ardor of mechanical invention. It was fortunate for him, and for his partners, that at the outset he met in his employer a true friend, who appreciated his rare gifts. The value to the community, both directly and indirectly, of their large and successful business can hardly be estimated.

The munificent benefactions of the three partners, to their adopted town and to their native town, have been spoken of in other chapters of these sketches. Selections from a Memorial Discourse regarding Mr. Dove, have been given ; also, the recent death of Mr. Peter Smith has been noted, and a brief tribute paid to his memory in connection with the history of the Theological Seminary, of which he was a trustee and benefactor. He was born in Brechin, Scotland, September 21, 1802, and died at Andover July 6, 1880.

The oldest of the three original partners, Mr. John Smith, in his eighty-fifth year, is thus left the last. Still young in spirit and active in body, he enjoys the fruits of a successful life, and the pleasure of witnessing the growth and usefulness of the various institutions which his liberality has contributed to found or endow.

The sons of the three original partners are connected with the manufacturing company : Mr. Joseph W. Smith, Messrs. James B., Peter D., and Benjamin F. Smith, and Mr. George W. W. Dove.

Next to the mills was, as has been said, the establishment of "Iron-Works" in ancient Andover. The first settler, Thomas Chandler, blacksmith, owned extensive iron works. Just what these ancient iron-works were does not fully appear. Probably they were for smelting and refining the ore which was found in the town, a sort of blomary. As late as 1770 Col. James Frye owned iron-works, which he then gave up, advertising to sell, "as he is done with the iron-works." He offers also for sale a strong negro boy twenty years old, who is a good farm hand, "and can *work in iron-work*, both at blowing and refining."

The first foundry in the Andovers was built to furnish castings of machinery for Messrs. Davis and Furber's manufactory at North Andover. The builder and first operator proved untrustworthy, got deeply in debt, and quitted the town. The property passed into the hands of Boston men, and in 1842 was leased from them by Mr. Edmund Davis, an iron founder from Dover, N. H. When the business began, all the work was done by Mr. Davis and his son, with the help of one man. At the end of twenty years they employed about fifty men. In 1863 they took down their building and transferred the foundry to the city of Lawrence. "E. Davis and Son" was then and is now the name of the firm. Mr. Edmund Davis, senior, ultimately removed his residence to Portsmouth, N. H., but retained more or less supervision of the foundry until his death, in 1867. His long residence in North Andover identified him prominently with its interests, both in secular affairs and in the religious society, "The Evangelical Church, of North Andover," with which he was connected. He was one of the original trustees of the Cemetery, and owned a lot, where his remains were buried. Mr. Davis was a singularly unobtrusive man, but one who commanded respect. From an obituary notice, written by a minister who knew him well, the following is an extract relative to his character:—

"None knew him who were not struck with the benignity, justness, and peace-loving nature of the man. It was in the family, however, that his worth was the most conspicuous. As a husband and a father few could be compared to him. Others may be as faithful, but few combine gentleness with dignity, reserve with ease, strictness with affectionate geniality as he did."

The business established by Mr. Davis is carried on by his son, Mr. George Edmund Davis, who resides at North Andover.

Another foundry was built at North Andover by the manufacturing company of Messrs. Davis & Furber. The manufacture of machinery, so long carried on at North Andover under this firm name, originated in 1828 at Andover (South Parish). Jonathan Sawyer, of Harvard, and Russell Phelps, of Sutton, machinists, came from a shop in Worcester, and began the manufacture of machinery, under the patronage of Mr. Abraham Marland, in the lower part of his mill. In 1832 they sold the business to three of their employés, Charles Barnes, George H. Gilbert, and Parker Richardson. The shop was removed to the paper-mill, and in 1836 transferred to North Andover, on the Cochichawick, at what is called Machine Shop Village. Mr. Barnes withdrew from the firm to enter into the employ of the Ballardvale Manufacturing Company, but in 1838 resumed his connection. Messrs. Gilbert and Richardson bought the saw and grist-mill of Mr. Isaac Osgood, and built a machine shop and carried on business till 1841, when they dissolved the partnership and sold the saw-mill to the original owner. The same year, Mr. George L. Davis, a nephew of Mr. Gilbert, who had been employed by the firm for about six years, formed a copartnership with Mr. George H. Gilbert and Benjamin W. Gleason for five years, Messrs. Davis and Gleason being the managers. They leased the machine-shop and water-power, bought the tools, and from that time to the present Mr. Davis has continued the manufacture of wool machinery.

In 1846 Mr. Gilbert[1] retired from the firm, and in 1848 Mr.

[1] Mr. George H. Gilbert, in 1841, together with Mr. Charles A. Stevens, son of Captain Nathanael Stevens, of North Andover, removed to Ware in the western part of the State, and there began woolen manufacturing, in which they were eminently successful. After about ten years, dissolving partnership, each continued business for himself and both became founders of manufacturing companies among the most successful in New England. Mr. Gilbert died in 1868. A costly monument to his memory has been erected by his son in the North Andover Cemetery, which was the burial place of his wife, a daughter of Deacon Jedidiah Farnham.

Charles Furber joined it. In 1851 Messrs. Davis and Furber bought the entire interest. In 1857, on the death of Mr. Furber, Mr. Davis was for a short time sole proprietor. In 1858 Mr. Daniel T. Gage and Mr. John A. Wiley joined the firm, but in 1860 the former withdrew. In January, 1861, Mr. Joseph M. Stone, a builder of locomotives, from Manchester, N. H., became a partner. In 1867 the sons of the partners, George G. Davis,[1] Joseph H. Stone, and James H. Davis, became members of the firm.

The buildings, from the one little room in the Marland Mill, are now grown to a group of several large factories, shop, and foundry, at North Andover. The machinery made is in operation in mills in all parts of the United States.

Hon. George L. Davis, who embarked in the enterprise at a time when it was hazardous, has stood by it in all vicissitudes, and by his perseverance and ability established a manufacture honorable to the town, as well as a source of wealth to himself. Many institutions, educational and religious, have reaped benefit from the prosperity of this business and the liberality of its founder.

Mr. Furber, whose name since his death is retained in the company, made his way up from poverty to influence and honor. He died in 1857, at the age of thirty-nine, deeply mourned by his numerous friends. He was at the time of his death a representative to the Legislature for North Andover.

Mr. Stone and Mr. Wiley are among the most influential citizens of the manufacturing village, and liberal contributors to all enterprises for its prosperity, and for the general welfare of the town.

The manufacture of machinery was attempted on a large scale at Ballardvale in 1847 by an incorporated company, of which Mr. John Marland was a principal member. They made machinery and steam-engines in the large stone manufactory built by the company, and which, after some reverses, they sold to the Whipple File Manufacturing Company.

This company was organized 1860, with a capital of $500,000.

[1] Since withdrawn to enter a firm in Boston.

They purchased the machine-shop at Ballardvale, and built other large buildings, and put in crucible and steel-smelting apparatus. In 1866 they had a capital of one million dollars. The enterprise was the largest ever entered upon in Andover, employing about six hundred operatives. But in 1869 the company failed. The stock was owned principally by parties in Boston. The works are now idle.

The above are the principal manufactures of the Andovers, which, in one form or another, trace their beginning to the ancient times. Among the modern industries or manufactures may be noted a rubber factory, also an ink factory now owned and carried on by William C. Donald & Co. It is not a part of the plan of this chapter to trace the history of any other than the mills and manufactures which originated in the beginning of the town history, and were the "improvement" of the water-power of the streams and rivers. These manufactures have been the principal source of the town's wealth and prosperity.

They resulted in the establishment of the bank, railroad, and other commercial facilities. To the great importance of the manufactures of Andover, witness is incidentally borne in a petition, 1825, for the establishment of a bank: —

"The trading and manufacturing capital of the town has very much increased within a few years past by the erection of several establishments for the manufacturing of cotton and woollen cloths and for other purposes. . . . Your petitioners are confident that the amount of mercantile and manufacturing business done among them, ... and which is manifestly increasing, and the amount of money transactions growing out of that business, are sufficiently large to render a banking institution a great convenience," etc.

Any sketch of the rise and growth of Andover manufactures should also include mention of the origin of the manufacturing city of Lawrence, which in 1847 was set off from Methuen and Andover, and incorporated as a city in 1853. This city not only occupies some twenty-five hundred acres of Old Andover territory, but also owes its existence chiefly to the sagacity and perseverance of an Andover citizen.

Daniel Saunders learned the business of cloth-dressing and wool-carding in his native town, Salem, N. H. He came to

Andover in 1817 to seek employment, and, after working on a farm, entered the mill of Messrs. Abel and Paschal Abbot, in Andover, where he ultimately obtained an interest in the business, taking a lease of and managing the mill. Being solicited by his former employers to return to his native town and start a woollen mill there, he did so, and remained for a time, but, about 1825, removed to Andover, and settled in the North Parish, for a time leasing the stone mill erected by Dr. Kittredge, and afterward building a mill on a small stream which flows into the Cochichawick. Here he carried on the business of cloth-dressing and wool-carding for some years. In 1839 or 1840 he purchased a mill in Concord, N. H., and carried on manufacturing there, but retained his home at North Andover. About 1842 he gave up the woollen mill at North Andover, sold his house to Mr. Sutton, and removed to what is now South Lawrence, Andover West Parish, south of the Merrimack River, near the old "Shawsheen House." The tract of country in this vicinity was flat and sandy, covered principally with a growth of pine trees. It went by the name of Moose Country. At the point near Mr. Saunders' house, which was a more improved and attractive locality, were two taverns, the Shawsheen House and the Essex House. These were relics of the palmy days of the old stage routes and turnpikes and the Andover tollbridge, which, erected in 1793 at a great cost, was the wonder of the country people and the sorrow of the stockholders for many years. This "Moose Country" was the ancient "Shawshin Fields," where, during the Indian wars, blockhouses were built, to protect the Andover farmers in their ploughing and planting and harvesting. The neighborhood of the taverns was, during the provincial period and the Revolution, and even down to the present century, a considerable business centre. The taverns, long owned by the Poor family, had store of legend and tradition connected with them. The bridge was also freighted with memories and anecdotes, which old settlers handed down to the younger generation. Even in Mr. Saunders' day, the glory had not all passed away. Here was the grand gathering to welcome General Lafayette, when in 1825 he made his tour from Boston to Concord, N. H.; and here glittered resplendent the cavalcade of Andover troops which escorted the hero on his journey. But with the decline of the turnpike and the stage lines, and the advent of the railway, the prosperity of Moose Country waned; the taverns became silent, the bridge comparatively deserted, and the river Merrimack flowed amid scenes almost as solitary as when the Indian paddled his canoe, and was the sole tenant of the forests. But to the seemingly practical man of business, who had taken up his abode in these solitudes, they were suggestive of schemes and plans of activities which to the ordinary observer seemed as visionary as any ever cherished by the writers of romance. The former glory of Moose Country was nothing in comparison with the brighter days which he foresaw.

From a careful study of the river, he came to the belief, not till then entertained, that there was a fall in its course below the city of Lowell sufficient to furnish great waterpower. He became so confident of this, and of the ultimate improvement of this water-power, that he proceeded to buy lands along the river which secured to him the control of flowage. This he did without communicating his plans to any of the citizens. Having made all things ready, he secured the coöperation of capitalists, to whom he unfolded his project. The Merrimack Water Power Association was formed, of which Mr. Saunders and his son, Mr. Daniel Saunders, Jr., then a law student in Lowell, became members. Mr. Samuel Lawrence, of Lowell, being Chairman, and Mr. John Nesmith, Treasurer. Mr. Nathaniel Stevens, and other citizens of Andover, also joined the association. When the scheme began to be talked of, it created a great sensation among the farmers who owned most of the land along the river. Their ancestral acres assumed a sudden importance in their eyes. They had to decide whether they would sell for double the money which ever had been offered for the lands, or whether they would hold the property in hope of greater gain.

The company could not at first decide at what point to construct the dam, whether at its present site, Bodwell's Falls, or farther up the river, near Peters's Falls. They, therefore, bonded the land along the river. This, however, it was difficult in some cases to do, and some parties of Andover refused entirely to sell, so that the new city was built up at first mainly on the Methuen or north side of the river. In March, 1845, the Legislature granted to Samuel Lawrence, John Nesmith, Daniel Saunders, and Edward Bartlett, their associates and successors, the charter of the Essex Company, authorizing, among other things, the construction of a dam across Merrimack River either at Bodwell's Falls or Deer Jump Falls, or at some point between the two falls. The dam was begun in 1845, and was three years in building. The completion of it made a fall almost like a second Niagara in breadth and volume of water. The unbroken sheet of water was 900 feet wide, the masonry 1,629 feet in length, and rising in some parts over forty feet in height. The thunder of the cataract, when the dam was first built, could be heard for two or three miles. The old Andover farmers "could not sleep o' nights," as they said, for thinking what might happen in the spring freshets, and the jarring of the ground was so great near the river bank as to rattle doors and shake down dishes in the cupboards, and seriously disturb the equanimity of orderly housewives. It would be a long task to recount all the predictions, fulfilled and unfulfilled, made by the wiseacres, from the day when "Saunders's folly" was their theme, to the day when, his visions and plans more than realized, he saw a city of thirty thousand inhabitants, and manufactories larger than any in the world. Mr. Saunders died in 1872, aged seventy-six years. He married a daughter of Mr. Caleb Abbot, of Andover. Two of his sons are residents of Lawrence, — Daniel Saunders, Esq., and Caleb Saunders, counsellors at law. The former was born in Andover, graduated at Harvard College, 1844. He has been mayor of Lawrence and representative to the Legislature. The latter was born at North Andover, graduated at Bowdoin College, 1859. He was mayor of Lawrence, 1877.

The agricultural industry of the town of Andover was a principal part of its prosperity from the first; but, in selecting the order of the topics to be considered, the plan of these sketches accords with the order which appears in the town records; the meeting-house, the school, and the mill being the principal subjects of general interest and legislation.

To cover the entire history of the town in all its departments of enterprise, there should be added an account of the agricultural and general industries, and trade; stores, banks, post-offices, stage-routes, bridges, railways; of the professional men, physicians, lawyers, authors, editors, artists; and the town history and action under the Federal Constitution, including the War of 1812, the Civil War, and other important crises in the history of the nation and the commonwealth, as well as biographical sketches of all the eminent citizens, and the natives of the Andovers who have become eminent in other communities.

Few towns offer wider field for historical research or a more honorable record than Old Andover, the present towns of North Andover and Andover.

APPENDIX.

ADDITIONS AND CORRECTIONS.

PAGE

3   The term city, as applied to Boston, is here used in the general sense, according to the definition: "A large town, a large number of inhabitants in one place." The incorporation with a city government was not made until 1822, although as early as 1650 it was petitioned for, on the ground that the town was "so populous and that such a concourse of people being here from all parts, a form of government was needed by which to administer 'speedy justice.'"

10 Mrs. Bradstreet's name is written "Ann," in the copy of the deed. In the only full autograph (a facsimile is given in the New England Historical and Genealogical Register for July 1859,) she herself spells it "Anne."

17 The will of John Osgood is incorrectly transcribed in several particulars.
Read: "July [not June] 23. In the name off God, amen." etc. Insert: "I bequeath and give my soule into the hand of God my heavenly ffather, through the medyation of Jesus Christ my Blessed Saviour and Redeemer, my body to the earth from whence it was taken, my Good and Chattels as foloweth." . . . .
Read: "To my sonn Stephen Osgood, at 21 years [not 18 years.]
Read, in items, bequests to *three* daughters, Mary, Elizabeth, and Hannah, each "25 pounds to be paid at 18 years of age."
Read: "*It*. I do give to my daughter S[or M]arah Clements 20s. — *It*. I do give to her daughter Bakah 20 shillings to be payd when she is 7 years of age, but if she dy before that time to be null."

20 In the inventories and wills which follow, the intention of the writer was not to give all the items as an exact and complete transcript of each paper, but simply selections, showing

the customs and style of living of the time. The omissions have not, however, in all cases been indicated. The following is, therefore, added. *Inventory of Mr. John Osgood's Estate.* Additional items: "Purse and apparel (£16); a flock bed and furniture, foure augers, a gouge, two hammers and a broad chisel, slay (£8), cart and wheeles, another cart and wheeles, a cart rope, five yoke and the hookes, three chayers, ploughs and irons, a harrow, five sives, a spade and crow, three sithes, five sickles, one mat hook, pitchforks and a grindstone, nayles, foure sacks, cheese."

Read, probably [nearly erased]: "eighteen [not eight] swine."

Read: "carsai" [not "carsamere"]; for "canvace, 15s" [not 9s].

It is not deemed necessary to specify the price named for each item.

23 Read: "Isaac F. Osgood, postmaster."

24 Read: *Inventory of John Stevens's estate:* "pronges" [not "ploughs"] after "sawes, axes etc." Insert, after horses: "Three sheep," also "debts" (£2).

The full inventory has a "sequel" as it is called, specifying what he had given to his eldest son John, and also the signature of this son to the following: "These testifye y' I John Stevens doe accept of the above specified estate appointed mee of my father before his death in full satisfaction for my portion amounting to seventy-foure pounds, provided the honored Court at Salem shall see good to confirme it." The statement is also made that the widow Elizabeth Stevens came into Court and gave oath to the truth of the inventory to the best of her knowledge." The "sequel," or bequest to the son, consisted of the following items: "*Imp.* a house, orchard and land. — *It.* one cowe, two steeres of two yeare old and a yearling, two swine and two sheep. — *It.* all y⁵ rights and privileges that is to be granted by y⁵ towne by virtue of twenty-five acres of ground granted to mee, John Steevens. — *It.* three acres of home meadow."

32 In the list of proprietors who were householders, read: "John Aslebe" [not "John Abbot"]. Insert: "Stephen Johnson, Thomas Poor."

35 A "Complaint of Christopher Osgood," in the County Court Records 1662, illustrates still more fully the rude state of the primitive society. He had had arrested and brought to trial,

Thomas Johnson with whom he had quarrelled about the ownership of a hoe which Johnson demanded. The two men had come to blows, and a violent struggle, in which Osgood complained that Johnson was near killing him. The mother of Christopher Osgood, interfering in her son's behalf, told Thomas Johnson that a curse was pronounced in Scripture against him for "Ronging the widow and y* fatherless and that *God* would plead their cause." The offender's answer was not according to Puritan standards: "He replied in a scofing and in a sneering way and sayd: 'Aye: doe: doe: trust to him, trust to him, he will help you, no question.'" A few years after this, Thomas Johnson was constable; possibly he was at this time, as he claimed that he was about his proper business.

49   Foot-note 2. The second figure 2 after the name of Andover should be transferred to the name Merrimack.

72   Foot-note 1. Read: "pages 689 [not 681] and 715."

84   Foot-note 2. Read: "p. 441 [not 44]."

89   Read: "Mr. Nathan Frye, President" [not Treasurer].

93   *Inventory of Daniel Poor.* Read: "matts [not malts] after "cords" etc. Read: "more pewter, brass and iron forgott," after "iron potts" etc. Read "seven score [not "about one hundred"] acres of land and more plough land and meadow." Read: "Wade's [not Woodchuck] meadow."

107   *List of persons who took oath of allegiance 1678.* Omit from the list the name of John Abbot junior; omit "junior" after John Poor. Add to the list the following names:—

      Abraham Foster,   Stephen Parker,   Samuel Phelps,
      Timothy Johnson,   Edward Phelps, Senr., Joseph Stevens.

Read in the list "104 years" [not 101 years], for the age of Andrew Foster. This does not agree with the statement in the town records, that Andrew Foster died aged 106 years in the year 1685. The list states that Robert Gray and Henry Salter are "not inhabitants" but "y* present." This is explained in regard to the former by the fact that he was a "mariner."

117   Read: "Rev. Francis H. Johnson."

119   The will of Rev. John Wilson of Boston makes no mention of a son Joseph. It therefore seems improbable that the Andover settler was his son. [See "N. E. Hist. and Gen. Register," vol. xvii.]

120 *List of Taxpayers of Minister's Rates.* "*North End of the Town.*" Read: "John Abbot junr. [not George Abbot Senr.] John [not Job] Cromwell." Insert: "Richard Barker junr., William Barker, John Farnum, senr., Sergt. Ephraim Stevens."

"*South End of the Town.*" Read: "Ephraim Davis [1] [not William Dane], Ebenezer [1] [not Hananiah] Barker." Insert: "John Ballard, John Chandler, James Johnson, Lef't. Thomas Johnson, Thomas Osgood, John Russ, Thomas Russell."

131 *Bradstreet House.* The following should be inserted in the history:—

"After the death of Col. Dudley Bradstreet, his house was purchased for a residence by the Rev. Thomas Barnard, the parsonage having been destroyed by fire in 1707. Rev. John Barnard also lived here, and here probably were born his sons, the Rev. Edward Barnard and the Rev. Thomas Barnard."

148 Read: "Haverhill" [not Haverill].

155 Read: "Windham" [not Wenham.] Insert "LL.D." after the name of Hon. John Phillips (of Exeter).

157 Read: "Hon. Willard P. Phillips."

161 Read: "1827" [not 1822] for the date of installation of the Rev. Nathaniel Gage. He graduated at Harvard College 1822.

163 Cutshamache or Cutshamakin was the sachem in whose wigwam the apostle Eliot held his religious meetings for the Indians.

178 Classification of the Indian Wars. The treaty of peace at the conclusion of the French and Indian war was not ratified till 1763, although the conquest of Canada by the English put an end to the fighting in New England.

180 Lovewell's Fight took place May 8, 1725.

200 Read: "Sarah Hawkes" [not Fawkes]. Insert: "Mary Marston, wife of John Marston."

231 Read: "Jona. Elatson" [not Elarson].

245 Read: "Took no part in [not of] the fighting."

262 Lieutenant-colonel [afterward Colonel] John Osgood lived at North Andover, in the house still standing on the old homestead to the northeast of the house which was the home of the Hon. Samuel Osgood, and to the southeast of the mansion built by Isaac Osgood, Esq., and near the Timothy Johnson homestead. This Osgood house is evidently of most ancient date. In general style of construction it is similar to and is of about the same size as the Bradstreet house. The addition

---

[1] This appears by comparison with other lists written by different clerks.

of luthern windows in the front roof gives it a somewhat imposing appearance. The house was, doubtless in its day, a fine mansion. Tradition says that a provincial governor was entertained here. There can be little doubt that in Colonel Osgood's time many a military hero tarried here and talked over his exploits with his brother officer in the king's service. Indeed, it is not unlikely that the house dates back to the earlier colonial days, and it is not impossible that here Mistress Mary Osgood was arrested for witchcraft. But the actors and the sufferers of the Osgood name, in the drama of the centuries are gone from their old abode; and the house, though still owned by their descendants, is tenanted by modern emigrants from the Old Country, who know or care little about those of two hundred years gone.

Mr. Moody Bridges, who was active in the military service of the Old French War and in the civil service of the Revolutionary time, lived at North Andover, in the house now owned by Oliver Stevens, Esq. This was purchased, after the death of Mr. Bridges, from his son, Henry G. Bridges, mariner, by Mr. Isaac Stevens. It was the birth-place of Mr. Stevens's illustrious son, Major-general Isaac I. Stevens, who was killed in the battle of Chantilly, Va., September 1, 1862, while, rallying his troops to victory, he held the colors in his hand. The house, which, judging from its construction, must have been quite ancient, has been tastefully remodelled for a summer residence by its present owner. In a deed of partition, in 1810, the house is designated as the "Mansion house of the late Mr. Moody Bridges, Gentleman."

270   Foot-note 1. — Since the writing of the text, I have learned that Paul Mascarene, the royal governor, removed to Boston and made his residence there. In the State Archives is a petition of John Mascarene of Boston (dated September 24, 1778), which states that the petitioner's son, Paul Mascarene, has lately returned from his "education in the country" (doubtless at Andover), and being "destitute of business" is desirous to be allowed to go to Jamaica with Henry Shirley. It would seem that the Mascarenes were not in full sympathy with the Revolution, for the petitioner says he has been "wholly deprived of his income" by reason of the "unhappy dispute," yet he claims to be a "well-wisher to the country."

293   Read: "Lord North [not North's] Parliament."

319   "Jeremiah Blanchard of Andover" is one of the names of

prisoners in the Old Mill Prison in England, taken on board the brig *Hasket and John*, May 3, 1781.

331 The statement that Dr. Abiel Abbot lived during the Revolution is an error. He died at the age of twenty-eight, in the year 1764. His widow lived till 1815, to the age of seventy-seven.

343 The powder-mill at Stoughton was bought from the State (Mr. Samuel Phillips being one of the agents in the sale) by Major Samuel Osgood in April, 1779. In October of the same year it was blown to atoms. The remains of it passed into the hands of Mr. Phillips, who in 1792 sold it to some iron-mongers.

375 Read: " de Riedesel " [not de Reidesel].

377 A contributor to the " New England Historical and Genealogical Register " [vol. xxvi.], Rev. B. F. de Costa, adduces what he regards as evidence that the expedition of Colonels Brown and Johnson to Ticonderoga was a failure and did not, as the great historians have thought it did, hasten the surrender of General Burgoyne. Original letters of Colonel Brown are quoted to show that his repulse at Diamond Island more than counterbalanced any former gain, and that the British lines of communication were left unbroken. But we may venture to suggest that though this may have been a partial defeat, it was a defeat which like that of Bunker Hill taught the British what a foe they had to deal with. Whether this expedition of Colonels Brown and Johnson cut the communications of Burgoyne or not, it showed him that the New England yeomanry would not cease their " private expeditions " or leave him a way of retreat.

421 Read: " and is [not in] ye kingdom of our Lord and Saviour."

425 Mrs. Anne Bradstreet was not at first pleased with the New England churches. She says : " I found a new world and new manners, at which my heart rose, but after I was convinced it was ye way of God, I submitted to it and joined to ye c^h at Boston."

427 Insert " D. D." after " Rev. Benjamin Stevens."

428 The act of incorporation of the South Precinct was not till May, 1709, although in November, 1708, the General Court ordered that the town "be forthwith divided into two distinct Precincts," and appointed a committee "to perform the division *within the space of two months.*" The committee ran the

boundary line and reported to the court in April, 1709. The first parish meeting was held June 20, 1709.

441 Insert "Rev." before the names of Nathan Holt and Jacob Emery.

444 Read "October 17" [not 7], date of the ordination of Rev. Samuel Phillips.

448 Read: "He (Rev. William Symmes) was ordained [not married] 1758, November 1." The relationship between him and the Rev. Thomas Symmes of Boxford was, according to the best authorities (the genealogists differ in their statements), that of second cousins; their fathers, Rev. Zechariah Symmes of Bradford and Mr. William Symmes of Charlestown and of Medford, being cousins.

454 Read: "either" [not eitehr].

476 The corner-stone of the West Parish Meeting House was laid June 15, 1826. The members to form the West Parish and church were dismissed from the South Church, November 28, 1826, organized as a church December 5, 1826, met for worship in their meeting-house, December 31, 1826, but the act of incorporation of the Parish was not passed till March 3, 1827. The meeting-house was built by individuals who were indemnified from loss by the sale of the pews.

483 Read "October 28" [not 26], for the date of installation of Rev. Charles Smith.

493 Read "1876" [not 1870], the year of the "Memorial Discourse" for Mr. John Dove.

504 The names of Rev. John Woodbridge and Rev. Benjamin Stevens, D. D., are not included in this list (although previously mentioned), because it is not ascertained with certainty that they can be claimed, strictly speaking, as of Andover. [see pages 425 and 427]. The following names should be included in the list: Rev. Dudley Bradstreet of Groton [page 427], Rev. James Chandler of Rowley [page 440], Rev. John Chandler of Billerica [page 441], Prof. Charles A. Aiken [page 496]. Some names are in this list, of which it was not thought necessary to give biographical memoranda in previous pages. But the name of Rev. Jonathan Osgood of Gardner is specially noteworthy. During nearly all his ministry (1791 to 1822), he was a practising physician, a member of the Massachusetts Medical Society. He also for a part of the time was a school-master.

Read "1756" [not 1747], for the date of graduation of Abiel Foster [see page 441].

509   Read : " Prayers were *not* made (by the Puritans) at the grave." Refer to page 20 for the same statement.

547   Read : " To allow .... for their Female School therein " [not thereon].

555   Read : " religious and denominational basis " [not bases].

556   Read : " alumnæ " [not alumni] of Abbot Academy.

580   Read : " It (the powder mill) was in operation March, 1776 " [not 1775].

The statement (page 460) in regard to the residence of Rev. Abiel Abbot, D. D., author of the "History of Andover," should be somewhat modified. He was a visitor rather than a resident on the old Abbot homestead, which was the birthplace of his wife, Elizabeth Abbot, daughter of Capt. John Abbot. When he came to make his home at Andover he bought the ancient Poor estate on the Shawshin, at North Andover, which from him was for some time called "The Priest Abbot Place."

CONTRIBUTORS AND SUBSCRIBERS[1] FOR THE PUBLICATION AND ILLUSTRATION OF THIS VOLUME.

Mr. John Abbot	Andover.
Rev. Phillips Brooks, D. D.	Boston.
Mr. John Byers	New York.
Gen. William J. Dale	North Andover.
Hon. George L. Davis	North Andover.
Mr. George W. W. Dove	Andover.
Misses Dove	Andover.
Moses Foster, Esq.	Andover.
Mr. J. D W. French	North Andover.
Rev. Francis H. Johnson	Andover.
Rev. Samuel Johnson	North Andover.
Col. Theron Johnson	North Andover.
Misses Kittredge	North Andover.
Hon. Amos A. Lawrence	Boston.
Hon. George B. Loring	Salem.
Mr. William G. Means	Andover.
Mr. John C. Phillips	Boston.
Trustees of Phillips Academy	Andover.
Trustees of Punchard Free School	Andover.
Hon. William A. Russell	Lawrence.
Mr. Charles W. Shattuck	Lawrence.
Mr. Edward Shattuck	Boston.
George O. Shattuck, Esq.	Boston.
Mr. Joseph Shattuck	Lawrence.
Mr. John Smith	Andover.
Mr. Joseph W. Smith	Andover.
Mr. Peter Smith	Andover.
Hon. Moses T. Stevens	North Andover.
Mrs. Nathaniel Stevens	North Andover.
Oliver Stevens, Esq.	Boston.
Mr. Joseph M. Stone	North Andover.
Gen. Eben Sutton	North Andover.
Mr. William H. Wardwell	Boston.
Mr. John A. Wiley	North Andover.

[1] All the above-named persons pledged subscriptions for copies to the amount of at least twenty-five dollars, and most of the number contributed from twenty-five to fifty dollars for two to four copies. Mr. John C. Phillips, of Boston, subscribed one hundred dollars for illustration of the institutions of learning and their founders. Rev. Chandler Robbins, D. D., paid for the use of the steel-plate for the engraved portrait of Mr. Simon Bradstreet. Mr. Joseph W. Smith, in addition to his subscription, assumed a large part of the risk of publication.

INDEX.[1]

A.

Abbot, 83-88, 108-110.
Abbot, Abel, 84. 586, 594, 602.
Abbot, Mr. Abiel, 83, 439, 441, 504.
Abbot, Abiel, M. D., 83, 248, 272, 331 [see 611].
Abbot, Abiel, D. D., 83. 459, 460, 504, 613.
Abbot, Adeline, 554.
Abbot, Albert, 109.
Abbot, Alfred A., 109.
Abbot, Hon. Amos, 109, 401, 485.
Abbot, Asa, 88, 294, 295, 356, 576.
Abbot, Barachias, 294, 295.
Abbot, Benjamin, 85, 107, 120, 203, 205.
Abbot, Benjamin, LL. D., 83.
Abbot, Charles H., 501.
Abbot, David, 294.
Abbot, Edward F., 498, 505.
Abbot, Ephraim, 52, 63.
Abbot, George, Sen., 9, 11, 12, 13, 31, 32, 64, 65, 74, 83, 84, 85, 86, 107, 120 [see 609], 173, 174.
Abbot, George ("of Rowley"), 9, 31, 32, 107, 108, 109, 120, 411, 412.
Abbot, George, 242, 288, 294, 295, 335, 444, 534.
Abbot, Hannah, 83, 84, 85, 86.
Abbot, Henry, 83, 279, 294, 301, 302, 388, 391, 409.
Abbot, Isaac, 83, 154, 248, 297, 323, 401, 405, 485, 522.
Abbot, John, 32 [see 607], 40, 69, 72, 83, 85, 86, 107 [see 608], 120 [see 609], 137, 151, 152, 242, 261, 268, 294, 295, 340, 352, 359, 373, 386, 387, 391, 412, 441, 444, 485, 575.
Abbot, Prof. John, 83, 387, 389, 459, 504.
Abbot, John Lovejoy, 84, 335, 461, 504.
Abbot, Jonathan, 248, 249, 392.

Abbot, Joseph, 85, 170, 173, 259, 294, 295, 485, 507.
Abbot, Moses, 392.
Abbot, Nathaniel, 85, 120.
Abbot, Nehemiah, 65, 109, 120, 137, 157, 294, 295, 356, 391, 392, 409, 444, 485, 534.
Abbot, Paschal, 84, 485, 586, 594, 602.
Abbot, Priscilla, 87.
Abbot, Samuel, 84, 456, 558, 560.
Abbot, Sarah, 87, 531, 555.
Abbot, Sereno T., 497, 505.
Abbot, Stephen, 83, 362, 386, 391, 495.
Abbot, Susan, 554.
Abbot, Timothy, 88, 120, 174, 175, 176, 386.
Abbot, William, 107, 120, 140, 152, 295.
Abbot, Thomas, 34, 107, 120, 143, 239, 259, 575.
Abbot, Zebadiah, 345, 356, 408, 485.
Acadians, 238, 244, 245, 246, 248, 249.
Academies, 533-558.
Academy, Abbot, 555-558.
Academy, Franklin, 542-555.
Academy, Phillips, 533-542.
Adams, Isaac, 242, 246.
Adams, Israel, 159, 252.
Adams, Capt. John, 160, 301, 303, 309, 373, 391, 469.
Adams, John, LL. D., 537, 539.
Adams, Rev. John R., 496, 505, 539.
Adams, Col. Joseph, 160, 246.
Adams, William, 383, 497, 505, 539.
Adventure, Bark, 58.
Agawam, 2, 3, 163.
Agriculture, 11, 154, 175.
Aiken, 498, 499, 505, 515, 567, 568, 612.
Albany, 154, 169.
Alden, Timothy, 465.
Allen, 11, 32, 77, 105, 106, 107, 120, 200, 202, 466, 549.
Allyn, Peter, 144.
Almipagon, Lake, 258.
Ames [Eimes], 104, 126, 406.

[1] For names of Revolutionary soldiers and others not indexed, refer to "List," page 611.

616 INDEX.

Ames, Capt. Benjamin, 126, 297, 298, 301, 317, 318, 319, 350, 391.
Ames [Eimes], Robert, 120, 126.
Amesbury, 168, 180.
Amherst, N. H., 170.
Ammunition, 185, 292, 317.
Andover, description of, 10, 402, 403.
Andover, England, 11, 294.
Andros, Sir Edmund, 134.
Andrew, Joseph, 120.
Animals, 19, 33, 34, 36, 37, 143, 155.
Appleton, 136, 332, 333, 591.
Apprentices, 46-53, 285.
Armitage, Joseph, 73.
Aslebe, John, 32 [see 607], 64, 72, 120, 121, 137, 168, 185, 435.
Ashton, 591.
Aslet, John, 11, 62, 106, 107.
Atkinson, 457, 593.
Austin, 120.
Ayer, Samuel, 586.
Ayers, Obadiah, 522.

B.

Babbit, Rev. Benjamin B., 491, 502.
Badger, Rev. Milton, 461, 480, 501.
Bailey, 65, 155, 270, 271, 324, 325, 519, 522, 576.
Balden, 107, 109.
Ballard, 11, 32, 36, 69, 102, 107, 120 [see 609], 170, 197, 198, 203, 221, 406, 485, 576, 579, 580, 593.
Ballard's Pond, 36.
Ballardvale, 493, 495, 503, 574, 593.
Ballardvale Manufacturing Company, 593, 594, 599.
Bancroft, Cecil F. P., Ph. D., 537, 541.
Bank, 601.
Baptists, 462, 486, 487, 502.
Barbadoes, 73, 146.
Barker, 7, 8, 11, 18, 30, 32, 56, 62, 85, 90, 106, 107, 109, 120, 137, 138, 148, 168, 170, 210, 212, 221, 226, 232, 233, 239, 252, 294, 291, 337, 416, 435, 466, 469, 499.
Barnard, 11, 32, 45, 104, 107, 120, 148, 416.
Barnard, Rev. Edward, 131 [see 609], 438, 441, 504, 522.
Barnard, Rev. John, 39, 131 [see 609], 150, 427, 432-439, 501, 504, 518, 522.
Barnard, Rev. Thomas, 39, 131 [see 609], 182, 198, 228, 300, 422, 427-432, 438, 440, 501, 507.
Barnes, Charles, 594, 599.
Barrows, 500, 505, 566, 573.
Bartlet, Edward, 604.
Bartlet, William, 463, 558, 562.

Bean, Samuel, 407.
Bear, Jockey, 246.
Beard, 499, 500.
Belden, Nathan M., 529.
Bennington, 362, 367, 374.
Berry, 155, 242, 545, 549.
Beverly, 591.
Beverly, John, 274, 275.
Bibliotheca Sacra, 569.
Billerica, 8, 51, 52, 60, 61, 62, 67, 165, 172, 201, 202, 276, 303, 307, 308, 309, 401, 441, 550, 576.
Bixby, 107, 109, 110, 120, 153.
Blake, 11, 106, 416.
Blanchard, 32, 64, 69, 120, 121, 124, 294, 295, 304, 382, 485, 497, 505, 512, 585, 610.
Blanchard's Pond, 121, 124.
Blockhouses, 184.
Blumpy, 246.
Blunt, 65, 107, 110, 120, 274, 406, 440.
Bodwell, 120, 122, 242.
Bodwell's Falls, 603, 604.
Boscawen, 25.
Boundaries, 61, 62, 63.
Boston, 3 [see 606], 27, 29, 30, 46, 54, 66, 98, 119, 135, 160, 171, 181, 228, 246, 260, 289, 305, 327, 333, 335, 393, 417.
Boxford, 51, 52, 101, 178, 196, 211, 254, 298, 301, 338, 438.
Boynton, 308, 321, 322.
Bradford, 53, 134, 148, 149, 168, 179, 185, 187, 298, 448, 575.
Bradlee, J. P., 532, 594.
Bradstreet, Anne, 10, 12, 14, 77, 78, 127, 128, 420, 606, 611.
Bradstreet, Dorothy, 14, 76.
Bradstreet, Col. Dudley, 14, 69, 72, 75, 107, 110, 120, 130, 131, 134, 136, 137-143, 151, 168, 182, 183, 224, 226, 228, 235, 412, 413, 609.
Bradstreet, Rev. Dudley, 14, 427, 518, 522, 612.
Bradstreet, John, 13, 14, 45.
Bradstreet, Mercy, 14, 76.
Bradstreet, Samuel, 14, 136, 522.
Bradstreet, Sarah, 14.
Bradstreet, Mr. Simon, 8, 9, 10, 11, 12, 14, 33, 34, 46, 47, 73, 77, 78, 127-130, 134, 137, 138, 151, 173, 229, 233, 414, 415, 574.
Bradstreet, Rev. Simon, 14, 420, 425, 504.
Bradstreet House, 126-131 [see 609] 132.
Bragg, 391.
Brattle, Rev. Mr., 228.
Brechin, 595, 596, 597.
Brechin Hall, 562.
Breton, Cape, 238, 240, 241, 273.

INDEX. 617

Brewer, Thomas, 107.
Bridges, 40, 50, 107, 111, 120, 137, 200, 222, 226, 262, 277, 290, 292, 293, 295, 356, 391, 392, 413, 522, 610.
Briggs, Rev. William T., 489, 502, 509.
Brookfield, 100.
Brooks, Rev. Phillips, D. D. 156, 560.
Brown, Colonel, 374, 376, 377.
Brown, John White, 549.
Browne, M. J. B., 557.
Brown, Moses, 558, 562.
Browne, Rev. Samuel G., 557.
Brown, Rev. Thaddeus H., 499, 505.
Bunker Hill, 238, 317, 318, 321-327.
Burgoyne, 368, 369, 377, 383.
Burnside, Samuel M., 545.
Burnum, Jeremiah, 282.
Burroughs, Rev. George, 208, 214.
Burying-ground, North Parish, 506-512.
Burying-ground, South Parish, 512-513.
Burying-ground, West Parish, 513-514.
Burying-ground, Theological Seminary, 514-515.
Burying-ground, Christ Church, 515.
Burying-ground (Ridgewood Cemetery), 509-512.
Burying-ground, Roman Catholic, 515.
Burying ground (Spring Grove Cemetery), 515, 516.
Burying-ground (Den Rock Cemetery), 516.
Burtt, Rev. Joseph W., 498, 505.
Bussell, 120.
Butler, Benjamin, 522.
Byers, John, 532, 536.
Byers, Peter S., 477, 528, 529, 532, 536, 557.

C.

Callahan, 498, 505.
Cambridge, 7, 61, 128, 289, 302, 303, 304, 305, 306, 313, 321, 332, 339, 388, 389, 517.
Carrier, 106, 120, 199, 200, 201-210, 219, 232.
Carlton, 107, 112, 120, 239, 522.
Cary, Arthur, 51, 52.
Case, Isaac T., 549.
Chandler, 96-98.
Chandler, David, 297.
Chandler, James, 98, 440, 612.
Chandler, John, 96, 97, 98, 107, 120 (see 603), 137, 149, 153, 168, 185, 441 (69).
Chandler, Joseph, 98, 239, 575.
Chandler, Joshua, 98, 344, 496.
Chandler, Lieut. Nathan, 242, 277, 294, 295.

Chandler, Phebe, 205, 208.
Chandler, Philemon, 98, 356.
Chandler, Rev. Samuel, 98, 239, 253, 440, 504.
Chandler, Thomas, 11, 13, 32, 47, 48, 49, 50, 85, 96, 97, 107, 120, 136, 137, 168, 172, 179, 211, 444, 580, 598.
Chandler, William, 10, 32, 34, 66, 67, 69, 70, 71, 85, 96, 97, 137, 138, 576.
Channing, William E., D. D., 15, 130.
Chase, Abijah, 595.
Chegnecto, 250.
Chelmsford, 77, 165, 171, 177, 179, 246, 383.
Chickering, 155, 392.
Chubb, 82, 120, 122, 181, 182, 183.
Church (First), North, 410-441, 447-452, 461, 464-472, 501.
Church, South, 441-447, 452-457, 461, 472-475, 480-485, 501.
Church, Theological Seminary, 462-464, 501.
Church, West, 475-480, 501.
Church, Methodist Episcopal (Andover), 486, 502.
Church, Baptist, 486, 502.
Church, Evangelical (North Andover), 487-489, 502.
Church, Christ, Protestant Episcopal (Andover), 489-492, 502.
Church, Universalist, 492, 502.
Church, Methodist Episcopal (North Andover), 493, 503.
Church, Free Christian, 493-495, 503.
Church, Protestant Episcopal (Ballardvale), 495, 504.
Church, Union Congregational (Ballardvale), 495, 503.
Church, Methodist Episcopal (Ballardvale), 495, 503.
Church, St. Augustine's, Roman Catholic (Andover), 246, 248, 249, 493, 496, 504.
Church, St. Michael's, Roman Catholic (North Andover), 493, 496, 504.
Churches and Pastors, Tabular Statement, 501, 502, 503, 504.
Churchill, Prof. J. W., 566, 567.
Civil Officers, 136, 137, 278, 279, 391.
Clark, 155, 157, 490, 557.
Clay-ground, 30.
Cleaveland, John, 546.
Clements, 17, 21, 76, 606.
Clifford, Rev. John H., 469, 470, 501.
Cobb, Rev. L. H., 489, 502.
Coburn, Stephen, 546.
Cochichawick, 2, 5, 7, 8, 27, 574, 575, 586, 590.
Cogswell, Francis, 491, 592, 593.
Cooke, William, 522.
Commissions, 242, 256, 331, 386.

Common Lands, 29, 30, 32, 104.
Concord, 82, 148, 177, 188, 246, 307, 308, 309, 602, 603.
Constitution, State, 355, 356, 357.
Constitution, Federal, 131, 396, 399, 404.
Coroner's Jury, 144.
Cornwallis, 388.
Cotting, Benjamin E., M. D., 549.
Cotton, Seaborn, 76.
Cromwell, John, 120 [see 609].
Cross, George N., 530.
Crown Point, 244, 251, 252, 254, 256, 259, 260, 262, 263.
Cummings, 155, 488, 496, 522.
Cutshamache, 26, 27, 163, 166, 609.

D.

Dale, 117, 160, 544, 545.
Dam, 604, 576, 580.
Damon, David, 546.
Dana, Richard H., 15, 130.
Dane, 32, 46, 82, 85, 107, 112, 120 [see 609], 140, 199, 200, 221, 226, 228, 233, 294, 304, 444, 485, 501, 517.
Dane, Rev. Francis, 32, 85, 86, 107, 112, 196, 199, 218, 224, 228, 232, 235, 421, 424, 501, 517.
Danvers, 196, 300, 441.
Dark Day, 387.
Davis, 121 [see 609], 188, 488, 556, 557, 598, 600.
Davis, Edmund, 511, 598.
Davis, George Edmund, 162, 599.
Davis, George L., 488, 556, 557, 599, 600.
Dearborn, General, 327, 330.
Declaration of Independence, 354.
Deeds, 8, 9, 12, 27, 85, 94.
Deer Jump, 184, 604.
Delaines, 594.
Dennison, Daniel, 167, 169, 173.
Den Rock, 313, 516.
Description of Andover, 10, 401, 402.
Detroit, 258.
Devil's Baptism, 198, 212, 219, 222.
Devil's Covenant, 206, 211, 212, 220, 221.
Diamond Island, 377, 611.
Donald, 495, 501, 506, 601.
Dorchester, 26, 163, 357.
Dorr, Joseph, 522.
Douglass, Rev. Malcolm, D. D., 491, 502.
Dove, George W. W., 507.
Dove, John, 493 [see 612], 494, 531, 532, 563, 595, 597.
Dover, 15, 398.
Dowse, Abby, 554.

Dracut, 74.
Draper, 200, 557, 570.
Dudley, Joseph, 134.
Dudley, Thomas, 167, 418, 420.
Dunbar, Major, 305.
Dunstable, 40, 179, 188.
Dupee, 249.

E.

Early Settlers, 1–163, 11, 32, 107, 120, 155.
Eaton, 500, 506, 541.
Edward, Fort, 354, 362, 363, 364, 367.
Edwards, Prof. Bela B., 566, 572.
Edwards, Jonathan, 472, 498, 505.
Edwards, Justin, 461, 472, 473, 474, 475, 490, 501, 524, 566.
Elliot, John, 589.
Eliot, the Apostle, 165, 609.
Eimes [see Ames].
Eirres, 107, 120.
Emerson, 498, 499, 505, 566, 571.
Emerson, Mr. John, 222, 223.
Emery, 120, 123, 441, 497, 505.
Emigration, 147, 148.
Esbert, 246, 248, 249.
Essex County, 167, 168, 172, 178, 179, 242, 296, 300, 351, 352, 380.
Essex Gazette, 275, 295, 296, 327.
Exeter, 14, 83, 147, 155, 177.

F.

Farnham or Farnum, 32, 85, 92, 107, 113, 120 [see 609], 137–140, 204, 239, 444.
Farnham, Armstrong, 113, 587.
Farnum, Capt. Benjamin, 294, 296, 304, 307, 317, 320, 321, 323, 327, 341, 351, 361, 362, 363, 364, 365, 368, 371, 372, 391, 409, 469.
Farnham, Jedidiah, 469, 488, 599.
Farnum, John, 242, 269, 277, 293, 295, 356, 523.
Farrar, Samuel, 457, 515, 536, 555, 556, 566.
Farrington, 30, 120, 123, 200, 252, 270, 277, 278, 297, 335.
Farwell, Asa, 557.
Fashions and Social Customs, 16, 25, 35, 76, 77, 78, 79, 86, 113, 114, 283, 284, 285, 288, 402, 403, 404, 508, 509, 607.
Faulkner, 82, 83, 109, 120, 151, 170, 505, 595.
Faulkner, Abigail, 199, 200, 216, 217, 218.
Faulkner, Edmond, 11, 32, 65, 72, 74, 82, 107, 138, 167, 174, 180, 416.

INDEX. 619

Felton, Cornelius C., 548.
Ferries, 59, 60.
First Resident on Record, 7, 8.
Fisheries, 152, 153, 165, 575.
Five-mile Pond, 56, 198, 222, 237.
Flagg, Rev. Rufus C., 489, 502, 569.
Flint, James, 543.
Foster, 99–102.
Foster, Abraham, 99, 107 [see 608], 120.
Foster, Abiel, 101, 441, 504 [see 612], 522.
Foster, Ann, 99, 200, 207, 213, 214.
Foster, Andrew, 11, 32, 99, 107 [see 608], 121, 153, 205.
Foster, Asa, 101, 268, 277, 288, 294, 295, 406.
Foster, David, 101, 508.
Foster, Dwight, 100.
Foster, Ephraim, 69, 100, 101, 107, 120, 142, 211, 438.
Foster, George, 102.
Foster, Isaac, 101, 258, 259, 497, 508.
Foster, Jedediah, 100, 291, 523.
Foster, John, 101, 242, 259, 277, 288, 513.
Foster, Joshua, 508.
Foster, Lucy, 551.
Foster, Moses, 101.
Foster, Ruby, 525.
Foster, Simon, 101.
Foster, Stephen, 101, 497, 505.
Foster, E. Thomas, 102, 498, 505.
Foster, William, 101, 104, 294, 444, 513, 521, 542.
Foster's Pond, 99.
Foundry, Davis & Furber, 599.
Foundry, E. Davis & Son, 598.
Fouquett, 347.
Francis, Colonel, 362, 366.
French, J. D. W., 116.
French, Jonathan, 279, 328, 329, 356, 384, 387, 409, 452–457, 459, 501.
French and Indian War, 238–286.
French War, Officers, 277 [see 253].
Frye, 88, 89, 107, 120, 121, 168, 239, 251.
Frye, Abiel, 251, 277.
Frye, Eunice, 199, 222, 228, 230, 233.
Fryeburg, 190, 316, 317, 332.
Frye, James, 69, 88, 137, 143, 148, 170, 238, 241, 242, 252, 253, 258, 270, 277, 288, 293, 295, 297, 301, 317, 322, 323, 339, 350, 391, 507, 598.
Frye, John, 11, 30, 32, 69, 88, 107, 121, 135, 137, 138, 139, 200, 226, 416, 469, 499.
Frye, Jonathan, 88, 186, 188, 190, 440.
Frye, Gen. Joseph, 88, 239, 244, 245, 249, 250, 257, 260, 261, 262, 263, 264, 265, 272, 277, 278, 279, 316, 317, 331, 391.
Frye, Nathan, 89 [see 608], 490.

Frye, Nathaniel, 137, 168, 238, 278, 435.
Frye, Peter, 88, 446, 523.
Frye, Samuel, 107, 120, 139, 148, 168, 221, 294, 295, 518, 580.
Frye, Theophilus, 580.
Fuller, 490, 499, 502, 505.
Funerals, 20, 408, 409, 438, 508, 509 [see 613].
Furbush, Charles, 65, 155, 255, 307, 317, 319, 320, 324, 339, 391.
Fyrmin, Giles, 4, 7.

G.

Gage, 33, 161 [see 609], 497, 505, 600.
Gaming, 69, 71.
Garrison, 172, 177.
Gates, General, 367.
George, Lake, 244, 251, 252, 253, 255, 258.
Gilbert, 488, 599.
Gleason, B. W., 599.
Gloucester, 7, 171, 441.
Goddard, Charles, 557.
Godfrey, John, 53, 54, 196.
Goldsmith, William G., 530.
Gould, 155, 522, 569, 593.
Grammar, Rev. Joseph, 492, 502.
Grand Pré, 245.
Granger, 92, 120, 244.
Grants of land, 63, 65, 147, 575.
Graves, Mark, 32, 85, 120, 123, 152.
Gravestones, 23, 43, 84, 110, 111, 112, 233, 237, 349, 350, 438, 445, 447, 448, 449, 507, 508, 513, 514, 516.
Gray, 85, 107, 113, 114, 460, 504, 575.
Greene, 495, 503.
Griffin, Prof. E. D., 564, 566.
Groton, 14, 123, 126, 179, 383, 427, 612.
Gulliver, Prof. J. P., 566, 567.
Gunpowder, 185, 316, 317, 342–349, 580 [see 613].
Gutterson, 107, 114, 121, 501.

H.

Hadley, 422.
Hagget, 65, 121, 123, 124, 176, 304, 326, 365, 576.
Haines, Jonathan, 183.
Hale, 522, 589.
Hall, 333, 349.
Halifax, 244.
Hancock, 290, 397.
Hamilton, Rev. B. F., 489, 502.
Hardy, 155, 341, 353.
Harvard College, 89, 288, 334, 417, 427, 517.
Hasseltine, N. J., 557.

620 INDEX.

Hastings, Lemuel S., 530.
Haverhill, 7, 53, 55, 56, 59, 147, 148, 149, 177, 180, 183, 185, 196, 298, 407, 416, 441.
Hawkes, Sarah, 116, 200 [see 609].
Hawthorne, 188, 554.
Hazen, Nathan W., 396, 528.
Heath, General, 346.
Hibbard, Thomas, 522.
Highways, 64.
Hilliard, Timothy, 546.
Hitchcock, 563.
Hodges, 588.
Holmes, Oliver Wendell, 14, 130, 406, 535, 540.
Holt, 11, 21, 32, 55, 56, 62, 69, 76, 94, 95, 96, 107, 120, 139, 140, 141, 148, 202, 205, 253, 255, 273, 277, 294, 295, 304, 416, 441, 460, 496, 504, 522.
Holt, Rev. Jacob, 496.
Holt, Capt. Joshua, 95, 288, 294, 295, 301, 303, 356, 391, 392, 393.
Holt, Moses, 441.
Holt, Nathan, 441.
Holt, Rev. Peter, 460.
Holyoke, Samuel, 522.
Hooper, Thomas, 121.
Houghton, 400, 401, 402, 581, 582, 583.
House-lots, 29, 31, 33.
Houses, Ancient and Historic, 18, 24, 82, 86, 88, 95, 116, 125, 127, 155, 157, 158, 161, 190, 312, 389, 401, 443, 534, 542, 609, 610.
How, 155, 157, 331.
Howarth, 595.
Howe, Annie, 530.
Hoyt, John, 180.
Hubbardton, 375.
Hugh (Murderer), 80, 81.
Hunting, 37, 38.
Hutchinson, 74, 107, 114, 120, 181, 268.

I.

Incorporation of Town of Andover, 11.
Incorporation of South Parish, 611.
Incorporation of West Parish, 612.
Independence, Mt., 374, 375, 376, 377, 378.
Indians, 2, 26, 27, 57, 66, 71, 163-194, 238, 258, 262.
Indians, Hostile, at Andover, 169, 170, 173-176, 180-183.
Indians, "Praying," 165, 166.
Indian, Assacumbuit, 181.
Indian, Cutshamache, 27, 163, 166.
Indian, Numphow, 165.
Indian, Passaconaway, 26, 150, 163.
Indian, Roger, 27, 164.
Ingalls, 30, 32, 75, 76, 102, 107, 109, 114, 115, 120, 137, 138, 142, 144, 151, 168, 253, 254, 277, 294, 295, 392, 498, 525, 575.
Ink Factory, 601.
Inns and Innholders, 65-75, 279, 280, 385, 401, 406.
Insurrection, Shays's, 392, 393, 394, 395.
Intemperance, 66, 68, 69, 81, 384, 436, 473.
Inventories, 20 [see 606], 21, 24 [see 607], 79, 93 [see 608], 283.
Ipswich, 2, 3, 4, 7, 12, 43, 55, 71, 73, 76, 136, 169, 173, 220, 282, 421.
Iron Works, 152, 580, 598.

J.

Jackson, Rev. Samuel C., 461, 476, 477, 478, 501.
Jacques, Henry, 11, 32, 106.
Johnson, 116, 117.
Johnson, Abigail, 200.
Johnson, Andrew, 239, 254.
Johnson, Elizabeth, 200, 218, 219.
Johnson, Francis, 120, 200, 218.
Johnson, Rev. Francis H., 117, 557, 572.
Johnson, Hannah, 230, 254.
Johnson, James, 121 [see 609].
Johnson, James, Esq., 117, 511.
Johnson, John, 32, 107, 121, 142, 144, 152.
Johnson, Osgood, 117, 499, 505, 537, 539.
Johnson, Rebecca, 200, 225, 412.
Johnson, Returne, 107.
Johnson, Col. Samuel, 116, 242, 293, 294, 295, 296, 298, 350, 352, 355, 358, 372, 374, 375, 376, 377, 378, 380, 391, 392.
Johnson, Capt. Samuel, 116, 294, 320, 352, 353, 374, 376, 377, 381, 391, 409.
Johnson, Rev. Samuel, 116.
Johnson, Stephen, 32 [see 607], 107, 138, 148, 200, 574.
Johnson, Theron, 117, 530.
Johnson, Thomas, 32, 62, 64, 68, 73, 76, 107, 116, 121 [see 609], 137, 138, 142, 148, 151, 153, 168, 228, 608.
Johnson, Timothy, 107 [see 608], 116, 137, 142, 144, 148, 168, 183, 238, 240, 435, 609.
Johnson, William, 68, 107, 121, 140, 444.
Johnson, Lieut. William, 373, 386, 387.
Johnson, William, Esq., 117, 468.
Johnson High School, 117, 530.
Jones, Frederick, 563.
Jones, Lieutenant, 363, 364.

K.

Kempe, 107, 117.
Kennebec River, 177, 243.
Kimball, 155.
Kittery, 25.
Kittredge, 155, 157, 159.
Kittredge, James, 280, 576.
Kittredge, Dr. John, 157, 158, 159, 271, 280, 281, 507.
Kittredge, Dr. Joseph, 159, 588, 590, 602.
Kittredge, Mrs. Hannah, 159, 470.
Kittredge, Patty, 551.
Kittredge, Dr. Thomas, 158, 329, 330, 391, 396, 409, 551.
Knapp, Samuel L., 190, 544.

L.

Lacey, 107, 117, 120, 200, 207, 216, 219.
Ladle Meadow Brook, 575.
Lakeman, Nathan, 522.
Lamson, Samuel, 557.
Lancaster, 179, 337.
Landers, Rev. S. P., 493, 502.
Langstroth, Rev. L. L., 461, 482, 501.
Laundré, 248, 249.
Lawrence, 109, 132, 166, 590, 594, 601, 603, 604.
Lexington, 297, 301, 305, 307, 308, 309, 313.
Library, Ballardvale, 532.
Library, Harvard College, 334, 335.
Library, Memorial Hall, 531, 532.
Library, North Andover, 532.
Library, Social, 530.
Library, Theological Seminary, 568.
Lincoln, Rev. Varnum, 493.
List of Freeholders, 11.
List of Proprietors, Householders, 32 [see 607].
List of Men to Work on Road, 64.
List of Early Innholders, 72.
List of Early Records of Marriages, 75.
List of Persons who took Oath of Allegiance (1678), 107 [see 608].
List of Tax-payers for Minister's Rate (1692), 120, 121 [see 609].
List of Early Town Officers, 137-142.
List of Representatives and other Civil Officers, 136, 137, 278, 279, 391.
List of Early Officers of Militia, 168, 169, 242.
List of Occupations, 151.
List of Family Names (1746), 155.
List of Soldiers in Narraganset Expedition, 170.
List of Towns garrisoned, 177.
List of Persons slain by Indians, 177, 179, 180, 183.
List of Persons accused of Witchcraft, 199, 200, 201 [see, also, page 221].
List of Deaths in the King's Service (1745), 239.
List of Acadians, 249.
List of Deaths at Lake George, 251.
List of Officers in French War, 277 [see, also, page 253].
List of Revolutionary Committees, 288, 293, 294, 295, 356, 392, 396, 409.
List of Revolutionary Soldiers [see Revolutionary Rolls].
List of Revolutionary Officers, 391.
List of Divinity Students, 425, 426, 427, 440, 441, 457, 458, 459, 460, 461, 496-501, 504-506 [see 612].
List of Churches and Ministers, 501-504.
List of Masters of the Ancient Grammar School, 522.
List of Principals of Punchard Free School, 529.
List of Principals of Johnson High School, 530.
List of Trustees of Phillips Academy, 534.
List of Principals of Phillips Academy, 537.
List of Preceptors of Franklin Academy, 545, 546, 549.
List of Preceptresses of Franklin Academy, 552-555.
List of Principals of Abbot Academy, 557.
List of Trustees of Abbot Academy, 557.
List of Professors of Theological Seminary, 566, 567.
List of Treasurers and Librarians, 566, 567.
Littleton, 337.
Little Hope Brook, 13.
Local Names, 38.
Londonderry, 149, 407.
Loring, 39, 132, 461, 465, 468, 501, 510, 530, 549.
Louisburg, 238, 239, 323.
Lovejoy, 11, 32, 43, 62, 64, 69, 75, 99, 120, 121, 137, 145, 170, 253, 301, 303, 352, 357, 383, 391, 409, 522, 523, 580.
Lovewell's Fight, 187, 609.
Lowell, 165.
Lynn, 3, 7, 16, 73, 171.

M.

Machine Shops, Ballardvale, 600, 601.
Machine Shop, Davis & Furber's, 599.

Machine Shop, Smith, Faulkner, & Richardson, 595.
Manning, John II., 505.
Marble, 107, 117, 141, 148, 151, 231, 239, 320, 352.
Marblehead, 170, 345.
March, Col. John, 58, 59, 184.
Market, Clerk of, 140, 141, 153.
Market Town, 57. 153.
Marland, 489, 490, 491, 527, 585, 586, 590, 592, 593. 599.
Marlborough. 179.
Marriages, 75, 76, 81, 424, 450, 454.
Marston, 30, 65, 107, 117, 120, 139, 170, 221, 226.
Martin, 32, 45, 107, 138, 148, 151, 240.
Mascarene, 270 [see 610].
Mather, 79, 80, 89, 135, 174, 182, 206, 222, 417, 419.
McKeen, Misses, 557.
McKenzie, Rev. William S., 487.
McRea, Jane, 363. 364.
Mead, Prof. C. M., 566, 567.
Means, Rev. D. McGregor, 500, 506.
Means, William G., 516.
Medfield. 177.
Medford, 14, 22, 458.
Meeting-house, 28, 134, 198, 241, 410, 411. 428, 430, 432, 434, 442, 451, 455, 466, 476, 486, 488.
Memorial Hall, 531, 532.
Menotomy, 307, 314, 335.
Merrill, 460, 479, 500, 501, 546.
Merrimack, 49 [see 608].
Merrimack River, 2, 147, 150, 152, 153, 165, 172, 184. 301, 586, 602, 603.
Methuen, 60, 266, 267, 271, 298, 301, 312, 378, 379, 434, 601, 604.
Middleton, 163, 440.
Military Organization, 166, 167, 168, 169, 400.
Mill, Cotton, Marland, 591.
Mills, Flax, Smith, Dove & Company, 595. 596, 597.
Mills, Fulling and Clothing, 578, 579, 580, 586.
Mill, Paper, 581-585.
Mill, Powder, 342-349, 580, 581, 613.
Mills, Saw and Grist, 152, 574. 575, 576, 577, 579, 580, 599.
Mill, Scythe-grinding, 114, 575.
Mills, Woollen, Abbot's, 586.
Mills, Woollen, Ayer's, 586.
Mills, Woollen, Ballardvale, 593, 594.
Mills, Woollen, Howarth & Chase, 595.
Mills, Woollen, Marland, 586, 591, 592.
Mills, Woollen, North Andover, 588, 589.
Mills, Woollen, Saunders, 602.
Mills, Woollen, Scholfield's, 585.
Mills, Woollen, Stevens's, 589, 590.
Mills, Woollen, Sutton's, 587, 588.
Ministers, 3, 5, 7, 89, 131, 216, 226, 410-506.
Montreal, 258, 273, 274.
Mooar, or More, 64, 121, 124, 243, 304, 478, 483, 484, 499, 501.
Morgan, Rev. D. S., 500.
Moose Country, 603.
Murder, 43, 79, 80.
Murdock, Prof. James, 565, 566.
Murphy, Rev. Maurice J., 496, 504.
Musketo Brook, 575.

N.

Narraganset, 170, 579.
Negroes, 39-43, 71, 177, 323, 324, 450, 598.
Nesmith, John, 603.
Newbury, 3, 5, 6, 7, 18, 23, 55, 58, 168, 186, 219, 306, 419.
New Castle, 440.
New London, 14.
Newman, 409, 485, 496, 498, 537, 538, 539, 555, 556, 593.
Newport, 381, 382.
Nichols, 107, 120.
Nod, Land of, 63, 99.
Norris, 131, 558, 562.
Noyes, 155, 157, 253, 255, 256, 276, 331, 448, 499.
Numphow, 165.
Nutfield, 148.

O

Occupations, 151.
Ordinaries, 16, 70.
Osgood, 15-23.
Osgood, Christopher, 69, 93, 96, 107, 136, 137, 138-142, 151, 168, 177, 184, 185, 226, 231, 444, 607, 608.
Osgood, David, 22, 65, 288, 328, 329, 389, 458, 504, 564.
Osgood, Gayton P., 22, 587.
Osgood, Dr. George, 331, 373, 469.
Osgood, Hannah, 22, 554.
Osgood, Henry, 22.
Osgood, Hooker, 121, 142, 169.
Osgood, Isaac, 22, 23, 277, 294, 468, 475, 523, 586, 599, 609.
Osgood, Isaac F., 23 [see 607].
Osgood, John, 11, 15, 17 [see 606], 20, [see 607], 32, 57, 62, 64, 66, 72, 76, 107, 134, 135, 136, 137, 138-142, 151, 152, 167, 168, 171, 175, 178, 179, 185, 226, 230, 241, 261, 279, 416, 469, 600.
Osgood, Rev. Jonathan, 504 [see 612].

INDEX.   623

Osgood, Dr. Joseph, 22, 294, 331, 336, 469, 522.
Osgood, Mary, 75, 76, 199, 201, 222, 223, 228, 230, 233, 606, 610.
Osgood, Peter, 22, 288, 295, 356, 391, 392, 394. 396, 496 [see 504].
Osgood, Samuel, 22, 293, 304, 306, 315, 335, 356, 391, 399, 465, 523, 609.
Osgood, Sarah, 21.
Osgood, Susan, 471, 472.
Osgood, Stephen, 46, 107, 138, 139, 148, 606.
Osgood, Thomas, 69, 107, 121 [see 609], 153, 413.
Osgood, Timothy, 22, 107, 120, 137, 142, 435.
Otis, James, 278, 389, 390.
Oxford, 246.

P.

Packard, Rev. George, D. D., 490, 502.
Page, 488, 502, 546.
Paine, Thomas, 522.
Paper Mill, 581-584, 599.
Park, 477, 500, 503, 561, 565, 566, 567, 572.
Parker, 11, 18, 32 [see 608], 47, 72, 74, 102, 103, 104, 107, 120, 137, 144, 148, 151, 170, 177, 201, 210, 244, 255, 206, 267, 273, 277, 378, 416, 418, 419, 574.
Parks, 132.
Parris, Percival G., 530.
Pawlet, 377.
Peabody, 155, 160, 161, 162, 277, 284, 301, 342, 352, 356, 391, 392, 457, 504, 522, 536, 544, 553.
Peabody, Nathaniel, 544.
Peabody, Elizabeth P., 553
Pearson, 242, 344, 485, 522, 523, 534, 537, 558, 561, 563, 566.
Peekskill, 382, 383.
Peirce, Rev. Charles H., 479, 501.
Pemaquid, 180, 181.
Pemberton, Ebenezer, 537, 538.
Pennacook, 148, 149, 150, 151.
Pequauket, 180, 263.
Perley, Israel, 522.
Peters, 70, 72, 110, 121, 124, 142, 143, 153, 179, 180, 309, 411, 410-419, 520, 522.
Peters's Falls, 603.
Peters's "Wading Place," 184.
Petitions of Early Settlement, 4, 5, 18, 57, 61, 66, 67, 68, 69, 147.
Petitions of Early Indian Wars, 167, 171, 172, 173, 178, 181.
Petitions of Witchcraft, 213, 217, 218, 220, 223, 229, 230, 231, 233, 235.

Petitions of French and Indian War, 240, 243, 244, 247, 250, 251, 252, 253, 254, 255, 256, 258, 259, 260, 262, 263, 264, 265, 266, 268, 270, 271, 272, 273, 274, 280, 281, 282.
Petitions of Revolution, 324, 325, 345, 378.
Phelps, 32 [see 608], 107, 118, 121, 152, 170, 509.
Phelps, Prof. Austin, 500, 566, 572.
Phelps, Elizabeth Stuart, 500, 501.
Phelps, Rev. Lawrence, 500, 506.
Phelps, Prof. Moses Stuart, 500, 506.
Phillips, Rev. George, 155.
Phillips, 155-157.
Phillips, Hon. John, LL. D., 155, 440, 447, 522, 553, 554.
Phillips, Hon. "Col." John, 156, 403, 558, 560, 583.
Phillips, Mr. John C., 536.
Phillips, Madam, 156, 306, 395, 446, 539.
Phillips, Rev. Samuel, 149, 154, 155, 429, 430, 432, 439, 441, 443, 444, 445, 446, 147, 507.
Phillips, Hon. Samuel, 154, 155, 238, 271, 286, 288, 289, 290, 293, 295, 356, 391, 431, 447, 522, 553, 554.
Phillips, Lieut.-gov. "Judge" Samuel, 156, 288, 293, 315, 316, 334, 342, 343, 356, 391, 395, 409, 436, 582.
Phillips, Wendell, 14, 130, 536.
Phillips, Hon. William, 155, 291, 332, 433, 447, 553, 554.
Phillips, Hon. Willard P., 157 [see 609], 552.
Phillips Academy, 333-542.
Phillips Manse at North Andover, 155, 156, 157.
Phillips Mansion House, Andover, 534
Physicians, 4, 14, 157, 158, 159, 160, 197, 213, 248, 255, 256, 271, 329, 330, 331, [see 611], 336, 612.
Pickering, 500.
Pierce, etc., 158, 502, 547.
Pike, Maj. Robert, 169, 170.
Plaisted, Colonel, at Andover, 253.
Plantation, 4, 5, 6, 117.
Poor, 11, 32 [see 9-?], 62, 72, 73, 91, 92, 93 [see 608], 94, 107, 128, 137, 138, 150, 151, 221, 244, 258, 271, 294, 311 [see 611], 321, 323, 324, 395, 466, 479, 488.
Poor, Col. Thomas, 247, 248, 301, 310, 311, 353, 380, 391.
Poor, Gen. Enoch, 328, 380, 381.
"Popgun," 214, 216.
Porter, 413, 504, 550, 571.
Post 120, 221.
Post Rider, 407.

Powder Mill, 342-349, 580 [see 613], 611.
Preston, 49 [see 608], 107, 118, 120, 148, 152, 170, 208, 519, 575.
Proprietors, 28, 32 [see 607], 525, 543.
Provincial Congress, 292, 305, 315, 316.
Public Libraries, 530-533.
Public Schools, 517-530.
Punchard, Benjamin H., 491, 527, 592.
Punchard Free School, 527-530.
Purchase of Plantation, 26.
Putnam, 330, 498, 505, 546-549.
Putnam, Ann, 197, 219, 236.

Q.

Quakers, 414, 415, 584.
Quichichwick, 2, 5.
Quincy, Josiah, 443, 454, 536.

R.

Raymond, Samuel, 516, 593.
Reading, 8, 10, 62, 63, 99.
Regan, Rev. Daniel D., 501, 506.
Remington, Rev. Frank, 487.
Representatives to General Court, 136, 137, 278, 279.
Revolution (1689), 135, 136.
Revolution (1775), 286-410.
Revolutionary Battles, 300, 301, 305, 308, 309, 317, 318, 322, 330, 332, 336, 365, 367, 368, 369, 378, 380.
Revolutionary Camp life, 335, 336, 337, 370.
Revolutionary Captains and Companies:—
 Abbot, Capt. Henry, 302.
 Abbot, Capt. John, 340, 359, 373, 386.
 Abbot, Capt. Stephen, 362, 386.
 Adams, Capt. John, 373.
 Ames, Capt. Benjamin, 298, 319.
 Farnum, Capt. Benjamin, 320, 341, 362, 371.
 Furbush, Capt. Charles, 319.
 Holt, Capt. Joshua, 303, 358.
 Johnson, Capt. Samuel, 353, 359, 374, 381.
 Lovejoy, Capt. Nathaniel, 303, 358, 359.
 Peabody, Capt. John, 342.
 Poor, Captain (acting), Peter, 302.
 Poor, Capt. Thomas, 297.
Revolutionary Committees, 288, 293, 294, 295, 356, 392, 396, 409.
Revolutionary Deserters, 370, 371.
Revolutionary Diaries and Letters, 296, 299, 305, 306, 307, 308, 309, 310, 311, 312, 314, 322, 327, 328, 330, 332, 333,
334, 335, 336, 337, 343, 346, 347, 354, 362, 365, 366, 367, 368, 369, 379, 371, 375, 377, 384, 388, 389, 395, 399, 400, 401, 402, 403, 404, 407, 408.
Revolutionary Minute-men, 296, 297, 298, 305, 307, 309.
Revolutionary Officers, 391.
Revolutionary Petitions, Speeches, etc., 290, 294, 299, 304, 315, 318, 320, 324, 325, 345, 350, 355, 378, 379, 380, 383, 384, 392, 393, 394.
Revolutionary Refugees (patriot), 313, 314, 332, 333.
Revolutionary Rolls, 297, 298, 302, 303, 311, 319, 320, 340, 341, 342, 352, 353, 358, 359, 360, 361, 362, 371, 373, 374, 381, 382, 386.
Revolutionary Song, 312.
Rice, John, 522.
Richardson, 77, 105, 549, 595, 599.
Ridge, Great, or Indian, 99.
Riedesel, 366, 375.
Roads, 55, 56, 57, 64.
Robbins, Rev. Chandler, 132, 554.
Robbins, Philemon, 520, 522.
Robinson, 69, 75, 107, 118, 120, 438.
Robinson, Rev. Edward, D. D., 566.
Roger, 27.
Rogers, 6, 7, 44, 129, 191, 518, 522.
Ropes, Rev. William L., 566.
Rose Meadow Brook, 30.
Rowell, 32, 69, 513.
Rowell's Folly Brook, 513.
Rowley, 5, 7, 24, 43, 44, 55, 168, 440, 471.
Roxbury, 47, 55.
Rubber Factory, 601.
Russ, 11, 32, 45, 121 [see 609], 144, 148, 277.
Russell, 32, 101, 107, 119, 121 [see 609], 144, 148, 512, 594.
Rust, Henry, 522.

S.

Salem, 3, 7, 56, 57, 63, 170, 196, 198, 203, 210, 225, 237, 300, 594.
Salter, 107 [See 608].
Saltonstall, 168, 251.
Saratoga, 354, 367.
Saunders, 594, 601, 602, 603, 634.
Sawyer, 301, 599.
Scarborough, 177.
Scholfield, 585, 586.
Schools, Academies, 533-558.
Schools, Dancing, 526.
Schools, District, 523-525.
Schools, Grammar (Ancient), 516-523.
Schools, Grammar (Modern), 524.
Schools, High, 527-530.

School, Master Foster's, 542.
School, Singing, 525.
Schools, Spinning, 577.
Schools, Theological Seminary, 558-574.
Schools, Writing, 525.
Schoolmasters [see Principals and Preceptors], 522, 524, 525.
Servants, 39-51, 324, 388, 450.
Sessions, 50, 107.
Sewall, Judge, 134, 182, 433.
Sextons, 412, 511.
Seymour, Rev. Charles H., 529.
Shattuck, 155, 364, 365, 367, 369.
Shawshin, 2, 9, 10, 13, 144, 152, 198, 212, 575, 579, 580, 595, 602.
Shays, 392, 393, 395.
Shedd, Prof. W. G. T., 566.
Silk, 593.
Sheep Pasture, 36.
Sibson, Capt. Joseph, 142, 238.
Sign of the Horse Shoe, 70.
Singletary, 76, 120.
Skinner, 522, 566.
Slater, 585, 591.
Small-pox, 202, 252, 282, 371.
Smith, Rev. Charles, 483 [see 612], 484, 501.
Smith, Dove & Company, 594, 595, 596, 597.
Smith, John, 478, 529, 531, 532, 536, 556, 563, 595, 596, 597.
Smith, Lydia, 333.
Smith, Joseph W., 532.
Smith, Peter, 478, 529, 531, 536, 556, 557, 563, 568, 595, 596, 597.
Smith, Samuel C., 530.
Smyth, Prof. Egbert C., 566, 567.
Snow-shoe Men, 184, 186.
Sorcery, 229.
Spofford, 324, 546.
Sprague, Martha, 211.
Spring, 132, 560.
Stages, 405, 406.
Stamp Act, 286, 287.
Stevens, 23-26.
Stevens, Abiel, 145.
Stevens, Asa, 242, 251.
Stevens, Benjamin, 25, 30, 40, 120, 137, 150, 168, 184, 186, 187, 427, 507, 612.
Stevens, Bimsley, 304, 305, 391, 406.
Stevens, Charles A., 26, 590, 599.
Stevens, Ephraim, 85, 107, 120 [see 608], 140, 141, 142, 144, 148, 173, 185.
Stevens, Horace N., 469.
Stevens, Henry H., 590, 595.
Stevens, Isaac I., Gen., 26, 610.
Stevens, James, 25, 26, 112, 238, 241, 254, 191, 310, 311, 335, 337.
Stevens, John, 11, 23, 24 [see 627], 25, 32, 62, 64, 107, 121, 138, 151, 167, 179, 429.
Stevens, Jonathan, 377.
Stevens, Joseph, 25, 107 [see 608], 425, 469.
Stevens, Moses T., 26, 530, 590, 591, 593.
Stevens, Nathan, 32, 85, 107, 120, 137, 140, 141, 148, 170.
Stevens, Nathaniel, 25, 586, 589, 599, 603.
Stevens, Oliver, 26, 610.
Stevens, Phineas, 25, 26, 440.
Stevens, Timothy, 32, 46.
Stevens, William, 26.
Stevens Hall, 530.
Still-house, 72.
Stillwater, 367, 368, 378, 380.
Stone, 107, 120, 121, 500.
Stone, Joseph M., 488, 600.
Stone, Rev. T. D. P., 557.
Stone, Valeria G., 563.
Stoughton, 342, 343, 611.
Stores, 154, 408.
Stoves, 455.
Stowe, 515, 565, 566.
Stuart, 565, 566, 571.
Suicide, 445.
Sutton, S., 9, 13, 33, 34, 62, 137, 530, 579, 583, 586, 588, 589.
Swan, 30, 59, 120, 125, 144, 210, 214, 237, 242, 506.
Symmes, 131, 186, 187, 356, 396, 397, 398, 409, 432, 447, 448, 449, 450, 464, 501, 522, 534, 612.

T.

Taverns [see Inns], 149, 280, 405, 406, 602.
Taxation, 120, 133, 134, 135, 146, 277, 286, 287, 336, 392.
Taylor, Edward, 566.
Taylor, Emma L., 537.
Taylor, John L., Prof., 202, 316, 401, 461, 482, 483, 501, 566, 567.
Taylor, John P., Rev., 483, 505.
Taylor, Samuel H., LL. D., 537, 540.
Tenney, Samuel, 522.
Tewksbury, 280, 281, 307, 308.
Thayer, Prof. J. H., 566, 567.
Theological Seminary, 558-574.
Theological Seminary Library, 568.
Theological Seminary Printing Press, 570.
Ticonderoga, 268, 353, 354, 361, 362, 363, 366, 367, 372, 374, 375, 376, 377.
Tilton, 537, 541.
Toothaker, 120, 125, 202.
Topsfield, 8, 14, 168, 170.

INDEX.

Town Clerks (early), 138.
Town Meetings, 32, 33, 133, 134, 135, 136, 141, 145, 287, 292, 293, 294, 296, 385, 392, 393, 410, 411.
Town Officers (early), 137-142.
Town Records, 137, 145, 183.
Town Standard of Weights and Measures, 144, 145.
Town Treasurers (early), 141, 142.
Traders (early), 154, 280, 295, 408.
Travelling, 3, 15, 28, 49, 56, 57, 58, 65, 67, 69, 73, 74, 222, 278, 280, 284, 285, 338, 401, 405, 407.
Trumbull, Timothy, 522.
Tucker, Prof. William J., 566, 567.
Tumbrils, 46.
Tyler, 32, 46, 47, 48, 54, 120, 125, 196, 201, 217, 222, 226, 251, 254, 282.
Tything-men, 140, 413.

U.

Upton, John, 73.

V.

Varnum, 74, 397.
Valley Forge, 370, 371, 372.
Vessels, 58, 59.
Vinal, Rev. Charles C., 468, 501.
Vincent, 246.
Vintners, 65, 72.

W.

Wade, 14, 76, 92, 182, 281, 608.
Waldo, Seth, 546.
Walker, Timothy, 149, 439, 522.
Waltham, 246.
Wamesit, 165, 177, 180.
Ward, 3, 4, 7, 77, 304, 417.
Wardwell, 107, 119, 121, 201, 210-213, 220, 221, 534, 374, 742, 326, 251, 319.
Wardwell, Samuel, 201, 210-213, 220, 221.
Ware, 599.
Washington, 333, 336, 339, 346, 369, 401, 408.
Weddings, 74, 75, 76, 77, 79, 450.
Wells, 541, 549.
Wendell, 332, 534.
Wenham, 3, 7, 10, 155 [see 609].
West Point, 383, 386.

White, 120, 153, 446.
Whitefield, 434.
Whiting, Thomas, 522.
Whittington, 107, 148, 170, 579.
Wigglesworth, Edward, 522.
Wilbur, Rev. H. R., 487, 502.
Wiley, 155, 488, 600.
William, Castle, 279.
William Henry, Fort, 258, 262, 264, 265, 266, 376.
Williams, Rev. Francis C., 468, 501.
Wilmington, 62.
Wills, 17, 84, 86, 91, 102, 103, 104, 106, 108, 114, 121, 284, 606.
Wilson, 107, 119, 151, 226, 233, 469, 518, 608.
Winnipiseogee, 186.
Winslow, 243, 244.
Winthrop, 3, 5, 313, 314, 344.
Witchcraft, 194-238.
Witchcraft, Mr Brattle's Account, 228.
Witchcraft, Mr. Dane's Account, 231.
Witchcraft, Accusations, 195, 196, 198, 199, 200, 204.
Witchcraft, Condemnations, 199, 200, 201, 207-209, 210, 214, 216, 218, 219, 220.
Witchcraft, Confessions, 201, 206, 207, 212, 213, 219, 221-223, 224, 227, 229, 232, 233, 234, 235.
Witchcraft, Petitions, 215, 217, 218, 220, 224, 225, 226, 230, 231, 233, 235.
Witchcraft, Relic, 237.
Witham, Daniel, 519, 522.
Wolf Hooks, 37.
Woburn, 10, 60, 97, 149, 171, 306.
Woodbridge, Benjamin, 11, 32, 89, 517.
Woodbridge, John, 5, 6, 26, 27, 89, 163, 416, 417-420, 425, 501, 612.
Woods, 497, 561, 564, 566, 570.
Worcester, 246, 337.
Wright, 34, 35, 107, 110, 140, 144, 152, 153, 255, 277, 579.
Wright, Rev. G. F., 493, 495, 503.
Writing, 13, 550.

Y.

York, 240, 241.
Young, 415, 594.
Young Folks, 36, 41, 45, 46, 47, 53, 68, 69, 76, 78, 84, 104, 196, 206, 217, 219, 220, 228, 229, 232, 236, 237, 413, 473, 481, 518, 536, 537, 542, 545, 548, 551, 577.

www.ingramcontent.com/pod-product-compliance
Lightning Source LLC
Chambersburg PA
CBHW021220300426
44111CB00007B/373